Renault 15 & 17 Owners Workshop Manual

GW00496874

Peter G Strasman and John H Haynes Member of the Guild of Motoring Writers

Models covered
UK:
    Renault 15 and 17 TS, TL, GTL and Gordini
    1289 cc, 1565 cc, 1605 cc and 1647 cc
USA:
    Renault 15 and 17 Coupe, Sport Coupe, GTL and Gordini
    95.5 cu in (1.56 liter), 100.5 cu in (1.65 liter)

ISBN 0 85696 763 7 (Hardback)
ISBN 0 85696 768 8 (Paperback)

ABCDE
FGHIJ
KLMNO
PQRST

Printed in England

THE
BOOK

AUTOMOTIVE
PARTS &
ACCESSORIES
ASSOCIATION MEMBER

HAYNES PUBLISHING GROUP
SPARKFORD YEOVIL SOMERSET BA22 7JJ ENGLAND
distributed in the USA by
HAYNES PUBLICATIONS INC
861 LAWRENCE DRIVE
NEWBURY PARK
CALIFORNIA 91320
USA

Acknowledgements

Thanks are due to Regie Renault for the supply of technical information and certain illustrations, to Castrol Limited who supplied lubrication data, and to the Champion Sparking Plug Company who supplied the illustrations showing the various spark plug conditions.

The bodywork repair photographs used in this manual were provided by Holt Lloyd Ltd who supply 'Turtle Wax', 'Dupli-color Holts' and other Holts range products. Sykes Pickavant Limited provided some of the workshop tools.

About this manual

Its aim

The aim of this manual is to help you get the best value from your vehicle. It can do so in several ways. It can help you decide what work must be done (even should you choose to get it done by a garage), provide information on routine maintenance and servicing, and give a logical course of action and diagnosis when random faults occur. However, it is hoped that you will use the manual by tackling the work yourself. On simpler jobs it may even be quicker than booking the car into a garage and going there twice, to leave and collect it. Perhaps most important, a lot of money can be saved by avoiding the costs a garage must charge to cover its labour and overheads.

The manual has drawings and descriptions to show the function of the various components so that their layout can be understood. Then the tasks are described and photographed in a step-by-step sequence so that even a novice can do the work.

Its arrangement

The manual is divided into 12 Chapters, each covering a logical sub-division of the vehicle. The Chapters are each divided into Sections, numbered with single figures, eg 5; and the Sections into paragraphs (or sub-sections), with decimal numbers following on from the Section they are in, eg 5.1, 5.2, 5.3 etc.

It is freely illustrated, especially in those parts where there is a detailed sequence of operations to be carried out. There are two forms of illustration: figures and photographs. The figures are numbered in sequence with decimal numbers, according to their position in the Chapter – eg Fig. 6.4 is the fourth drawing/illustration in Chapter 6. Photographs carry the same number (either individually or in related groups) as the Section or sub-section to which they relate.

There is an alphabetical index at the back of the manual as well as a contents list at the front. Each Chapter is also preceded by its own individual contents list.

References to the 'left' or 'right' of the vehicle are in the sense of a person in the driver's seat facing forwards.

Unless otherwise stated, nuts and bolts are removed by turning anti-clockwise, and tightened by turning clockwise.

Vehicle manufacturers continually make changes to specifications and recommendations, and these, when notified, are incorporated into our manuals at the earliest opportunity.

Whilst every care is taken to ensure that the information in this manual is correct, no liability can be accepted by the authors or publishers for loss, damage or injury caused by any errors in, or omissions from, the information given.

Introduction to the Renault 15 and 17

The Renault 15 and 17 have one basic body style, a three-door Coupe. An electrically-operated sun roof model is available. This has a rollback type roof panel to give it a semi-convertible appearance.

The car was manufactured in a wide range of mechanical and body trim specifications giving variations in engine style and transmission type, plus the options of power-assisted steering and fuel injection. These models are well equipped and apart from one or two assemblies, maintenance and overhaul operations are generally simple and easy to perform. Some checking and adjustment work must be left to the Renault dealer as specialised equipment is necessary. The work concerned, however, will not be required frequently.

The Renault 15 and 17 range is of more conventional design than many models produced by the company and should present little difficulty as a subject for the DIY mechanic.

Contents

	Page
Acknowledgements	2
About this manual	2
Introduction to the Renault 15 and 17	2
General dimensions, weights and capacities	6
Use of English	7
Buying spare parts and vehicle identification numbers	8
Tools and working facilities	9
Jacking and towing	11
Recommended lubricants and fluids	13
Safety first!	14
Routine maintenance	15
Fault diagnosis	17
Chapter 1 Engine	21
Chapter 2 Cooling, heating and air conditioning systems	71
Chapter 3 Fuel and emission control systems	85
Chapter 4 Ignition system	121
Chapter 5 Clutch	137
Chapter 6 Manual transmission	143
Chapter 7 Automatic transmission	179
Chapter 8 Driveshafts	189
Chapter 9 Braking system	196
Chapter 10 Electrical system	217
Chapter 11 Suspension and steering	294
Chapter 12 Bodywork and underframe	312
Conversion factors	334
Index	335

Renault 15GTL

Renault 17TS

5

Renault 17 Sports Coupe (1973 US model)

Renault 15 Sports Coupe (1973 US model)

General dimensions weights and capacities

General dimensions

Overall length
To 1976 .... 4.26 m (13.97 ft)
1976 on .... 4.37 m (14.3 ft)

Overall width .... 1.63 m (5.35 ft)

Overall height .... 1.31 m (4.30 ft)

Ground clearance (unladen)
R1300 .... 111.1 mm (4.375 in)
R1313, R1323, R1317, R1327 .... 130.2 mm (5.125 in)
R1302, R1312, R1322, R1318, R1328 .... 120.1 mm (4.750 in)

Wheelbase .... 2.44 m (8.0 ft)

Track (front)
R1300 .... 1309.6 mm (51.56 in) other models 1339.8 mm (52.75 in)

Track (rear)
R1313, R1323, R1317, R1327 .... 1339.8 mm (52.75 in)
R1300, R1302, R1312, R1322, R1318, R1328 ... 1309.6 mm (51.56 in)

Weights (kerb)
R1300 .... 965 kg (2128 lb)
R1301 .... 985 kg (2172 lb)
R1302 .... 1005 kg (2216 lb)
R1304 .... 1005 kg (2216 lb)
R1308 .... 1005 kg (2216 lb)
R1312 .... 1015 kg (2238 lb)
R1313 .... 1055 kg (2326 lb)
R1314 .... 1040 kg (2293 lb)
R1316 .... 1040 kg (2293 lb)
R1317 .... 1050 kg (2315 lb)
R1318 .... 1040 kg (2293 lb)
R1322 .... 1035 kg (2282 lb)
R1323 .... 1075 kg (2370 lb)
R1324 .... 1075 kg (2370 lb)
R1326 .... 1135 kg (2503 lb)
R1327 .... 1160 kg (2558 lb)
R1328 .... 1080 kg (2381 lb)

For vehicles with automatic transmission add 25 kg
For vehicles with air conditioning add 25 kg

Capacities
Fuel tank .... 12.0 Imp gal (14.5 US gal 55.0 l)

Cooling system
Type 810 engine (1289 cc) .... 8.8 Imp pts (5.3 US qts 5.0 l)
Type 807, 843, 844 engines (1565 cc, 1647 cc, 1605 cc) .... 9.7 Imp pts (5.8 US qts 5.5 l)
Type 821, 841 engines (1565 cc, 1647 cc) .... 11.5 Imp pts (7.0 US qts 6.6 l)

Engine
Type 810 (with filter change) .... 6.0 Imp pts (3.13 US qts 3.25 l)
Types 807, 821, 841, 843, 844 (with filter change) .... 7.5 Imp pts (4.25 US qts 4.25 l)

Manual transmission .... 3.5 Imp pts (2.1 US qts 2.0 l)

Automatic transmission
From dry .... 10.5 Imp pts (6.5 US qts 6.0 l)
At routine fluid change .... 5.0 to 6.50 Imp pts (3.0 to 3.90 US qts 3.0 to 4.0 l)

Power assisted steering .... 1.2 Imp pt (0.7 US qt 0.675 l)

Braking system .... 0.7 Imp pt (0.42 US qt 0.4 l)

Steering rack .... 1.25 oz 23.0 cc (grease)

Use of English

As this book has been written in England, it uses the appropriate English component names, phrases, and spelling. Some of these differ from those used in America. Normally, these cause no difficulty, but to make sure, a glossary is printed below. In ordering spare parts remember the parts list may use some of these words:

English	American	English	American
Aerial	Antenna	Motorway	Freeway, turnpike etc
Accelerator	Gas pedal	Number plate	License plate
Anti-roll bar	Stabiliser or sway bar	Paraffin	Kerosene
Bonnet (engine cover)	Hood	Petrol	Gasoline (gas)
Boot (luggage compartment)	Trunk	Petrol tank	Gas tank
Bulkhead	Firewall	'Pinking'	'Pinging'
Cam follower or tappet	Valve lifter or tappet	Propeller shaft	Driveshaft
Carburettor	Carburetor	Quarter light	Quarter window
Catch	Latch	Retread	Recap
Choke/venturi	Barrel	Reverse	Back-up
Circlip	Snap-ring	Rocker cover	Valve cover
Clearance	Lash	Saloon	Sedan
Crownwheel	Ring gear (of differential)	Seized	Frozen
Disc (brake)	Rotor/disk	Side indicator lights	Side marker lights
Drop arm	Pitman arm	Side light	Parking light
Drop head coupe	Convertible	Silencer	Nuffler
Dynamo	Generator (DC)	Spanner	Wrench
Earth (electrical)	Ground	Sill panel (beneath doors)	Rocker panel
Engineer's blue	Prussian blue	Split cotter)for valve spring cap)	Lock (for valve spring retainer)
Estate car	Station wagon	Split pin	Cotter pin
Exhaust manifold	Header	Steering arm	Spindle arm
Fault finding/diagnosis	Trouble shooting	Sump	Oil pan
Float chamber	Float bowl	Tab washer	Tang; lock
Free-play	Lash	Tappet	Valve lifter
Freewheel	Coast	Thrust bearing	Throw-out bearing
Gudgeon pin	Piston pin or wrist pin	Top gear	High
Gearchange	Shift	Trackrod (of steering)	Tie-rod (or connecting rod)
Gearbox	Transmission	Trailing shoe (of brake)	Secondary shoe
Halfshaft	Axleshaft	Transmission	Whole drive line
Handbrake	Parking brake	Tyre	Tire
Hood	Soft top	Van	Panel wagon/van
Hot spot	Heat riser	Vice	Vise
Indicator	Turn signal	Wheel nut	Lug nut
Interior light	Dome lamp	Windscreen	Windshield
Layshaft (of gearbox)	Countershaft	Wing/mudguard	Fender
Leading shoe (of brake)	Primary shoe		
Locks	Latches		

Miscellaneous points

An 'oil seal', is also fitted to components lubricated by grease!

A 'damper' is a 'shock absorber', it damps out bouncing, and absorbs shocks of bump impact. Both names are correct, and both are used haphazardly.

Note that British drum brakes are different from the Bendix type that is common in America, so different descriptive names result. The shoe end furthest from the hydraulic wheel cylinder is on a pivot; interconnection between the shoes as on Bendix brakes is most uncommon. Therefore the phrase 'Primary' or 'Secondary' shoe does not apply. A shoe is said to be 'Leading' or 'Trailing'. A 'Leading' shoe is one on which a point on the drum, as it rotates forward, reaches the shoe at the end worked by the hydraulic cylinder before the anchor end. The opposite is a 'Trailing' shoe and this one has no self servo from the wrapping effect of the rotating drum.

Buying spare parts and vehicle identification numbers

Buying spare parts

Spare parts are available from many sources, for example: Renault dealers, other garages and accessory shops, and motor factors. Our advice regarding spare part sources is as follows:

Officially appointed Renault garages – This is the best source of parts which are peculiar to your car and are otherwise not generally available (eg complete cylinder heads, internal gearbox components, badges, interior trim etc). It is also the only place at which you should have repairs carried out if your car is still under warranty – non-Renault components may invalidate the warranty. To be sure of obtaining the correct parts it will always be necessary to give the storeman your car's vehicle identification number, and if possible, to take the old part along for positive identification. It obviously makes good sense to go straight to the specialists on your car for this type of part for they are best equipped to supply you.

Other garages and accessory shops: These are often very good places to buy materials and components needed for the maintenance of your car (eg spark plugs, bulbs, fan belts, oils and greases, filler paste etc). They also sell general accessories, usually have convenient opening hours, charge lower prices and can often be found not far from home.

Motor factors: Good factors will stock all of the more important components which wear out relatively quickly (eg clutch components, pistons, valves, exhaust systems, brake cylinders/pipes/hoses/- seals/shoes and pads etc). Motor factors will often provide new or reconditioned components on a part exchange basis – this can save a considerable amount of money.

Vehicle identification numbers

Modifications are a continuous and unpublicised process carried out by the vehicle manufacturers, so accept the advice of the parts storeman when purchasing a component. Spare lists and manuals are compiled upon a numerical basis and individual vehicle numbers are essential to the supply of the correct component. Two vehicle identification plates are located within the engine compartment on the right-hand wing valance.

Diamond shaped plate
A   Vehicle type number
B   Chassis number
C   Last two figures of year of production

Oval shaped plate
1   Vehicle type
2   Manual or automatic
3   LH or RH steering and duty
4   Optional equipment fitted in production
5   Fabrication number
6   Year of production

Paint code
This is stencilled on the left-hand wing valance.

Vehicle designations
1289 cc	R1300
1565 cc	R1301, R1302, R1304, R1308, R1312, R1313 R1322, R1323, R1324
1605 cc	R1317, R1327
1647 cc	R1308, R1314, R1316, R1318, R1326, R1328

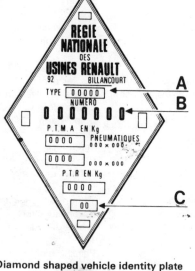

Diamond shaped vehicle identity plate

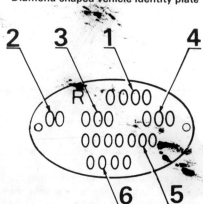

Oval shaped vehicle identity plate

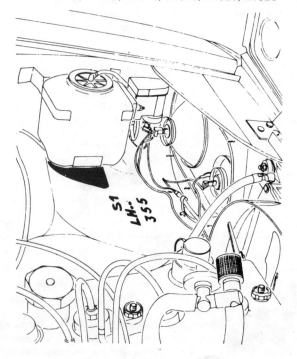

Paint code

Tools and working facilities

Introduction

A selection of good tools is a fundamental requirement for anyone contemplating the maintenance and repair of a motor vehicle. For the owner who does not possess any, their purchase will prove a considerable expense, offsetting some of the savings made by doing-it-yourself. However, provided that the tools purchased are of good quality, they will last for many years and prove an extremely worthwhile investment.

To help the average owner to decide which tools are needed to carry out the various tasks detailed in this manual, we have compiled three lists of tools under the following headings: *Maintenance and minor repair, Repair and overhaul,* and *Special*. The newcomer to practical mechanics should start off with the *Maintenance and minor repair* tool kit and confine himself to the simpler jobs around the vehicle. Then, as his confidence and experience grow, he can undertake more difficult tasks, buying extra tools as, and when, they are needed. In this way, a *Maintenance and minor repair* tool kit can be built-up into a *Repair and overhaul* tool kit over a considerable period of time without any major cash outlays. The experienced do-it-yourselfer will have a tool kit good enough for most repair and overhaul procedures and will add tools from the *Special* category when he feels the expense is justified by the amount of use to which these tools will be put.

It is obviously not possible to cover the subject of tools fully here. For those who wish to learn more about tools and their use there is a book entitled *How to Choose and Use Car Tools* available from the publishers of this manual.

Maintenance and minor repair tool kit

The tools given in this list should be considered as a minimum requirement if routine maintenance, servicing and minor repair operations are to be undertaken. We recommend the purchase of combination spanners (ring one end, open-ended the other); although more expensive than open-ended ones, they do give the advantages of both types of spanner. All fixings on the Renault 15/17 are to metric standards

Combination spanners - 10, 11, 12, 13, 14 & 17 mm
Adjustable spanner - 9 inch
Engine sump/gearbox/drain plug key
Spark plug spanner (with rubber insert)
Spark plug gap adjustment tool
Set of feeler gauges
Brake adjuster spanner
Brake bleed nipple spanner
Screwdriver - 4 in long x $\frac{1}{4}$ in dia (flat blade)
Screwdriver - 4 in long x $\frac{1}{4}$ in dia (cross blade)
Combination pliers - 6 inch
Hacksaw (junior)
Tyre pump
Tyre pressure gauge
Oil can
Fine emery cloth (1 sheet)
Wire brush (small)
Funnel (medium size)

Repair and overhaul tool kit

These tools are virtually essential for anyone undertaking any major repairs to a motor vehicle, and are additional to those given in the *Maintenance and minor repair* list. Included in this list is a comprehensive set of sockets. Although these are expensive they will be found invaluable as they are so versatile - particularly if various drives are included in the set. We recommend the $\frac{1}{2}$ in square-drive type, as this can be used with most proprietary torque wrenches. If you

cannot afford a socket set, even bought piecemeal, then inexpensive tubular box spanners are a useful alternative.

The tools in this list will occasionally need to be supplemented by tools from the *Special* list.

Sockets (or box spanners) to cover range in previous list
Reversible ratchet drive (for use with sockets)
Extension piece, 10 inch (for use with sockets)
Universal joint (for use with sockets)
Torque wrench (for use with sockets)
'Mole' wrench - 8 inch
Ball pein hammer
Soft-faced hammer, plastic or rubber
Screwdriver - 6 in long x $\frac{5}{16}$ in dia (flat blade)
Screwdriver - 2 in long x $\frac{5}{16}$ in square (flat blade)
Screwdriver - 1$\frac{1}{2}$ in long x $\frac{1}{4}$ in dia (cross blade)
Screwdriver - 3 in long x $\frac{1}{8}$ in dia (electricians)
Torx screw bits or wrenches
Pliers - electricians side cutters
Pliers - needle nosed
Pliers - circlip (internal and external)
Cold chisel - $\frac{1}{2}$ inch
Scriber
Scraper
Centre punch
Pin punch
Hacksaw
Valve grinding tool
Steel rule/straight-edge
Allen keys (metric)
Selection of files
Wire brush (large)
Axle-stands
Jack (strong scissor or hydraulic type)

Special tools

The tools in this list are those which are not used regularly, are expensive to buy, or which need to be used in accordance with their manufacturers' instructions. Unless relatively difficult mechanical jobs are undertaken frequently, it will not be economic to buy many of these tools. Where this is the case, you could consider clubbing together with friends (or joining a motorists' club) to make a joint purchase, or borrowing the tools against a deposit from a local garage or tool hire specialist.

The following list contains only those tools and instruments freely available to the public, and not those special tools produced by the vehicle manufacturer specifically for its dealer network. You will find occasional references to these manufacturers' special tools in the text of this manual. Generally, an alternative method of doing the job without the vehicle manufacturer's special tool is given. However, sometimes, there is no alternative to using them. Where this is the case and the relevant tool cannot be bought or borrowed, you will have to entrust the work to a franchised garage.

Valve spring compressor (where applicable)
Piston ring compressor
Balljoint separator
Universal hub/bearing puller
Impact screwdriver
Micrometer and/or vernier gauge
Dial gauge
Stroboscopic timing light

Dwell angle meter/tachometer
Universal electrical multi-meter
Cylinder compression gauge
Lifting tackle (photo)
Trolley jack
Light with extension lead

Buying tools

For practically all tools, a tool factor is the best source since he will have a very comprehensive range compared with the average garage or accessory shop. Having said that, accessory shops often offer excellent quality tools at discount prices, so it pays to shop around.

Remember, you don't have to buy the most expensive items on the shelf, but it is always advisable to steer clear of the very cheap tools. There are plenty of good tools around at reasonable prices, so ask the proprietor or manager of the shop for advice before making a purchase.

Care and maintenance of tools

Having purchased a reasonable tool kit, it is necessary to keep the tools in a clean serviceable condition. After use, always wipe off any dirt, grease and metal particles using a clean, dry cloth, before putting the tools away. Never leave them lying around after they have been used. A simple tool rack on the garage or workshop wall, for items such as screwdrivers and pliers is a good idea. Store all normal wrenches and sockets in a metal box. Any measuring instruments, gauges, meters, etc, must be carefully stored where they cannot be damaged or become rusty.

Take a little care when tools are used. Hammer heads inevitably become marked and screwdrivers lose the keen edge on their blades from time to time. A little timely attention with emery cloth or a file will soon restore items like this to a good serviceable finish.

Working facilities

Not to be forgotten when discussing tools, is the workshop itself. If anything more than routine maintenance is to be carried out, some form of suitable working area becomes essential.

It is appreciated that many an owner mechanic is forced by circumstances to remove an engine or similar item, without the benefit of a garage or workshop. Having done this, any repairs should always be done under the cover of a roof.

Wherever possible, any dismantling should be done on a clean, flat workbench or table at a suitable working height.

Any workbench needs a vice: one with a jaw opening of 4 in (100 mm) is suitable for most jobs. As mentioned previously, some clean dry storage space is also required for tools, as well as for lubricants, cleaning fluids, touch-up paints and so on, which become necessary.

Another item which may be required, and which has a much more general usage, is an electric drill with a chuck capacity of at least $\frac{5}{16}$ in (8 mm). This, together with a good range of twist drills, is virtually essential for fitting accessories such as mirrors and reversing lights.

Last, but not least, always keep a supply of old newspapers and clean, lint-free rags available, and try to keep any working area as clean as possible.

Spanner jaw gap comparison table

Jaw gap (in)	Spanner size
0.250	$\frac{1}{4}$ in AF
0.276	7 mm
0.313	$\frac{5}{16}$ in AF
0.315	8 mm
0.344	$\frac{11}{32}$ in AF; $\frac{1}{8}$ in Whitworth
0.354	9 mm
0.375	$\frac{3}{8}$ in AF
0.394	10 mm
0.433	11 mm
0.438	$\frac{7}{16}$ in AF
0.445	$\frac{3}{16}$ in Whitworth; $\frac{1}{4}$ in BSF
0.472	12 mm
0.500	$\frac{1}{2}$ in AF
0.512	13 mm
0.525	$\frac{1}{4}$ in Whitworth; $\frac{5}{16}$ in BSF
0.551	14 mm
0.563	$\frac{9}{16}$ in AF
0.591	15 mm
0.600	$\frac{5}{16}$ in Whitworth; $\frac{3}{8}$ in BSF
0.625	$\frac{5}{8}$ in AF
0.630	16 mm
0.669	17 mm
0.686	$\frac{11}{16}$ in AF
0.709	18 mm
0.710	$\frac{3}{8}$ in Whitworth; $\frac{7}{16}$ in BSF
0.748	19 mm
0.750	$\frac{3}{4}$ in AF
0.813	$\frac{13}{16}$ in AF
0.820	$\frac{7}{16}$ in Whitworth; $\frac{1}{2}$ in BSF
0.866	22 mm
0.875	$\frac{7}{8}$ in AF
0.920	$\frac{1}{2}$ in Whitworth; $\frac{9}{16}$ in BSF
0.938	$\frac{15}{16}$ in AF
0.945	24 mm
1.000	1 in AF
1.010	$\frac{9}{16}$ in Whitworth; $\frac{5}{8}$ in BSF
1.024	26 mm
1.063	$1\frac{1}{16}$ in AF; 27 mm
1.100	$\frac{5}{8}$ in Whitworth; $\frac{11}{16}$ in BSF
1.125	$1\frac{1}{8}$ in AF
1.181	30 mm
1.200	$\frac{11}{16}$ in Whitworth; $\frac{3}{4}$ in BSF
1.250	$1\frac{1}{4}$ in AF
1.260	32 mm
1.300	$\frac{3}{4}$ in Whitworth; $\frac{7}{8}$ in BSF
1.313	$1\frac{5}{16}$ in AF
1.390	$\frac{13}{16}$ in Whitworth; $\frac{15}{16}$ in BSF
1.417	36 mm
1.438	$1\frac{7}{16}$ in AF
1.480	$\frac{7}{8}$ in Whitworth; 1 in BSF
1.500	$1\frac{1}{2}$ in AF
1.575	40 mm; $\frac{15}{16}$ in Whitworth
1.614	41 mm
1.625	$1\frac{5}{8}$ in AF
1.670	1 in Whitworth; $1\frac{1}{8}$ in BSF
1.688	$1\frac{11}{16}$ in AF
1.811	46 mm
1.813	$1\frac{13}{16}$ in AF
1.860	$1\frac{1}{8}$ in Whitworth; $1\frac{1}{4}$ in BSF
1.875	$1\frac{7}{8}$ in AF
1.969	50 mm
2.000	2 in AF
2.050	$1\frac{1}{4}$ in Whitworth; $1\frac{3}{8}$ in BSF
2.165	55 mm
2.362	60 mm

A Haltrac hoist and gantry in use during a typical engine removal sequence

Jacking and Towing

Jacking

In order to avoid repetition, the procedure for raising the car to carry out work underneath it is not included before each relevant operation described in this Manual.

It is to be preferred and is certainly recommended that the car is positioned over an inspection pit or raised on a lift. As these facilities are seldom available to the home mechanic, use ramps or jack up the car strictly in accordance with the following guide and observe the requirement for axle safety stands.

The jack supplied with the car should only be used for wheel changing. The jack and its wheelbrace handle are located in the luggage compartment (photo). Insert the jack in one of the lifting points located under the sill. Use the one nearest to the roadwheel being removed (photo). Do not raise the car until the hub trim has been removed and the wheel nuts released, but not unscrewed more than a turn or two. Raise the car, remove the wheel nuts and take off the roadwheel.

Refit by reversing the removal operation, but only tighten the nuts fully when the weight of the car is again on the wheels.

When raising the car in order to carry out repair or overhaul operations, preferably use a trolley jack, a hydraulic bottle jack or a screw type jack.

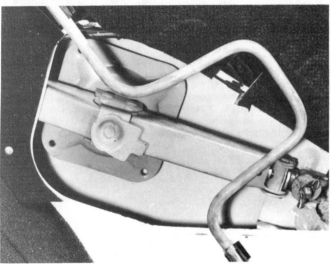

Car jack and wheelbrace

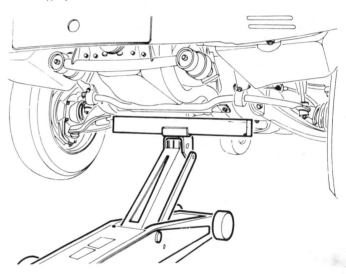

Raising front end

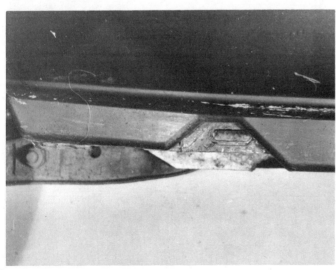

Sill jacking point

Towing hook

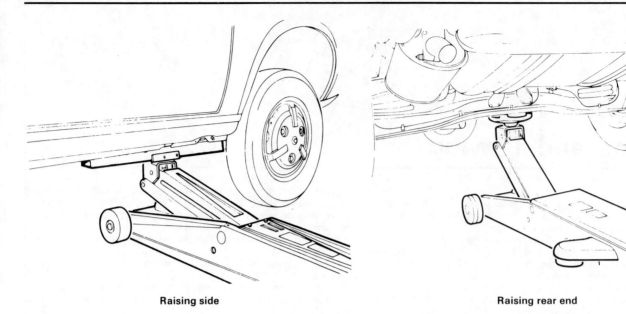

| Raising side | Raising rear end |

Lift the front end by placing a strong block between the side members in line with the suspension arms.

Lift the side by taking the load on a strong block located to the rear of the front jacking point on the sill.

Lift the rear end by positioning the jack under the centre of the rear axle beam.

Never get under the car until the jacks have been supplemented with axle stands placed under strong underframe members.

Towing

Towing hooks are provided front and rear and although primarily intended for lashing down the vehicle during transportation, tow ropes can be attached to them for emergency towing of another vehicle or to be towed.

If the car is equipped with automatic transmission then it must only be towed if the front wheels are raised off the ground. This is because the transmission oil pump is only operational when the engine is running and the transmission would be damaged by lack of lubrication without the engine operational.

In extreme urgency the car can be towed by another vehicle provided the following conditions are observed. The towing speed should be restricted to 30 kmh (18 mph) and to a distance of 50 km (30 miles). An additional 4.0 Imp pts (2.4 US qts 2.0 l) of fluid must be poured into the transmission before towing commences.

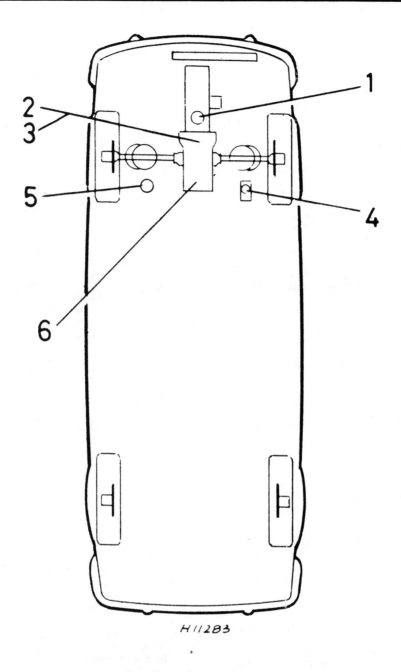

H11283

Recommended lubricants and fluids

Component or system	Lubricant type or specification	Castrol product
1 Engine	20W/50 multigrade	GTX
2 Manual transmission	SAE 80W hypoid gear oil to API GL4 or AP1 GL5	Hypoy light
3 Automatic transmission	Automatic transmission fiuid (Dexron type)	TQ Dexron®
4 Brake fluid reservoir	SAE J1703 hydraulic fluid	Castrol Girling Universal Brake and Clutch Fluid
5 Power assisted steering	Automatic transmission fluid (Dexron type)	TQ Dexron®

Safety first!

Professional motor mechanics are trained in safe working procedures. However enthusiastic you may be about getting on with the job in hand, do take the time to ensure that your safety is not put at risk. A moment's lack of attention can result in an accident, as can failure to observe certain elementary precautions.

There will always be new ways of having accidents, and the following points do not pretend to be a comprehensive list of all dangers; they are intended rather to make you aware of the risks and to encourage a safety-conscious approach to all work you carry out on your vehicle.

Essential DOs and DON'Ts

DON'T rely on a single jack when working underneath the vehicle. Always use reliable additional means of support, such as axle stands, securely placed under a part of the vehicle that you know will not give way.

DON'T attempt to loosen or tighten high-torque nuts (e.g. wheel hub nuts) while the vehicle is on a jack; it may be pulled off.

DON'T start the engine without first ascertaining that the transmission is in neutral (or 'Park' where applicable) and the parking brake applied.

DON'T suddenly remove the filler cap from a hot cooling system — cover it with a cloth and release the pressure gradually first, or you may get scalded by escaping coolant.

DON'T attempt to drain oil until you are sure it has cooled sufficiently to avoid scalding you.

DON'T grasp any part of the engine, exhaust or catalytic converter without first ascertaining that it is sufficiently cool to avoid burning you.

DON'T syphon toxic liquids such as fuel, brake fluid or antifreeze by mouth, or allow them to remain on your skin.

DON'T inhale brake lining dust — it is injurious to health.

DON'T allow any spilt oil or grease to remain on the floor — wipe it up straight away, before someone slips on it.

DON'T use ill-fitting spanners or other tools which may slip and cause injury.

DON'T attempt to lift a heavy component which may be beyond your capability — get assistance.

DON'T rush to finish a job, or take unverified short cuts.

DON'T allow children or animals in or around an unattended vehicle.

DO wear eye protection when using power tools such as drill, sander, bench grinder etc, and when working under the vehicle.

DO use a barrier cream on your hands prior to undertaking dirty jobs — it will protect your skin from infection as well as making the dirt easier to remove afterwards; but make sure your hands aren't left slippery.

DO keep loose clothing (cuffs, tie etc) and long hair well out of the way of moving mechanical parts.

DO remove rings, wristwatch etc, before working on the vehicle — especially the electrical system.

DO ensure that any lifting tackle used has a safe working load rating adequate for the job.

DO keep your work area tidy — it is only too easy to fall over articles left lying around.

DO get someone to check periodically that all is well, when working alone on the vehicle.

DO carry out work in a logical sequence and check that everything is correctly assembled and tightened afterwards.

DO remember that your vehicle's safety affects that of yourself and others. If in doubt on any point, get specialist advice.

IF, in spite of following these precautions, you are unfortunate enough to injure yourself, seek medical attention as soon as possible.

Fire

Remember at all times that petrol (gasoline) is highly flammable. Never smoke, or have any kind of naked flame around, when working on the vehicle. But the risk does not end there — a spark caused by an electrical short-circuit, by two metal surfaces contacting each other, or even by static electricity built up in your body under certain conditions, can ignite petrol vapour, which in a confined space is highly explosive.

Always disconnect the battery earth (ground) terminal before working on any part of the fuel system, and never risk spilling fuel on to a hot engine or exhaust.

It is recommended that a fire extinguisher of a type suitable for fuel and electrical fires is kept handy in the garage or workplace at all times. Never try to extinguish a fuel or electrical fire with water.

Fumes

Certain fumes are highly toxic and can quickly cause unconsciousness and even death if inhaled to any extent. Petrol (gasoline) vapour comes into this category, as do the vapours from certain solvents such as trichloroethylene. Any draining or pouring of such volatile fluids should be done in a well ventilated area.

When using cleaning fluids and solvents, read the instructions carefully. Never use materials from unmarked containers — they may give off poisonous vapours.

Never run the engine of a motor vehicle in an enclosed space such as a garage. Exhaust fumes contain carbon monoxide which is extremely poisonous; if you need to run the engine, always do so in the open air or at least have the rear of the vehicle outside the workplace.

If you are fortunate enough to have the use of an inspection pit, never drain or pour petrol, and never run the engine, while the vehicle is standing over it; the fumes, being heavier than air, will concentrate in the pit with possibly lethal results.

The battery

Never cause a spark, or allow a naked light, near the vehicle's battery. It will normally be giving off a certain amount of hydrogen gas, which is highly explosive.

Always disconnect the battery earth (ground) terminal before working on the fuel or electrical systems.

If possible, loosen the filler plugs or cover when charging the battery from an external source. Do not charge at an excessive rate or the battery may burst.

Take care when topping up and when carrying the battery. The acid electrolyte, even when diluted, is very corrosive and should not be allowed to contact the eyes or skin.

If you ever need to prepare electrolyte yourself, always add the acid slowly to the water, and never the other way round. Protect against splashes by wearing rubber gloves and goggles.

Mains electricity

When using an electric power tool, inspection light etc, which works from the mains, always ensure that the appliance is correctly connected to its plug and that, where necessary, it is properly earthed (grounded). Do not use such appliances in damp conditions and, again, beware of creating a spark or applying excessive heat in the vicinity of fuel or fuel vapour.

Ignition HT voltage

A severe electric shock can result from touching certain parts of the ignition system, such as the HT leads, when the engine is running or being cranked, particularly if components are damp or the insulation is defective. Where an electronic ignition system is fitted, the HT voltage is much higher and could prove fatal.

Routine maintenance

Maintenance is essential for ensuring safety and desirable for the purpose of getting the best in terms of performance and economy from your vehicle. Over the years the need for periodic lubrication – oiling, greasing and so on – has been drastically reduced, if not totally eliminated. This has unfortunately tended to lead some owners to think that because no such action is required the items either no longer exist or will last for ever. This is a serious delusion. It follows therefore that the largest initial element of maintenance is visual examination. This may lead to repairs or renewals.

The summary below gives a schedule of routine maintenance operations. More detailed information on the respective items is given in the Chapter concerned. Before starting on any maintenance procedures, make a list and obtain any items or parts that may be required. Make sure you have the necessary tools to complete the servicing requirements.

At weekly intervals

Check engine oil level and top up if necessary (photos)
Check coolant level
Check battery electrolyte level
Check brake fluid reservoir level
Check windscreen washer fluid level (photo)
Check operation of all lights and electrical equipment
Check tyre pressures (COLD) including spare wheel

Every 3000 miles (4800 km)

Clean spark plugs and re-gap
Check manual gearbox oil level and top up if necessary (photo)
Check automatic transmission fluid level
Check power-assisted fluid level
Check contact points dwell angle

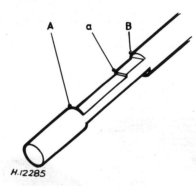

H.12285

Engine oil dipstick (Renault 15)

A   Minimum   B   Maximum   (a) Factory filled oil level

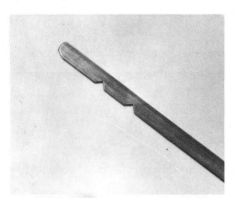

Engine oil dipstick markings (Renault 17)

Topping up with engine oil

Typical washer fluid reservoir

Topping up manual gearbox

Engine sump drain plug

Manual gearbox drain plug

Every 6000 miles (9600 km)

Renew engine oil and filter
Renew manual gearbox oil
Check disc pad wear
Adjust rear brake shoes (where appropriate)
Check rear shoe linings for wear
Check brake flexible hoses for condition
Check clutch adjustment
Check and adjust valve clearances
Check front wheel alignment
Check condition of exhaust system
Check tyres for wear and sidewall damage
Clean crankcase ventilation system hoses and flame trap
Check manifold nuts for tightness
Check condition and tension of all drivebelts
Check condition of cooling hoses
Renew contact breaker points and adjust dwell angle and ignition timing
Check idle speed and mixture (CO)

Every 12 000 miles (19 000 km)

Renew spark plugs

Every 18 000 miles (28 000 km)

Drain and refill automatic transmission
Renew brake servo air filter

Every 24 000 miles (38 000 km)

Clean EGR system (N. America)
Renew spark delay valve (N. America)

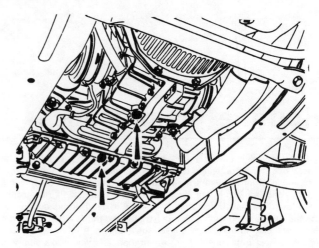

Automatic transmission drain plugs

Renew idle delay valve (N. America)
Renew evaporative control system charcoal canister (N. America)
Inspect all emission control hoses for condition and secure connections

Every 12 months (autumn)

Renew anti-freeze mixture

Every 2 years

Renew brake hydraulic system fluid by bleeding

Fault diagnosis

Introduction

The vehicle owner who does his or her own maintenance according to the recommended schedules should not have to use this section of the manual very often. Modern component reliability is such that, provided those items subject to wear or deterioration are inspected or renewed at the specified intervals, sudden failure is comparatively rare. Faults do not usually just happen as a result of sudden failure, but develop over a period of time. Major mechanical failures in particular are usually preceded by characteristic symptoms over hundreds or even thousands of miles. Those components which do occasionally fail without warning are often small and easily carried in the vehicle.

With any fault finding, the first step is to decide where to begin investigations. Sometimes this is obvious, but on other occasions a little detective work will be necessary. The owner who makes half a dozen haphazard adjustments or replacements may be successful in curing a fault (or its symptoms), but he will be none the wiser if the fault recurs and he may well have spent more time and money than was necessary. A calm and logical approach will be found to be more satisfactory in the long run. Always take into account any warning signs or abnormalities that may have been noticed in the period preceding the fault – power loss, high or low gauge readings, unusual noises or smells, etc – and remember that failure of components such as fuses or spark plugs may only be pointers to some underlying fault.

The pages which follow here are intended to help in cases of failure to start or breakdown on the road. There is also a Fault Diagnosis Section at the end of each Chapter which should be consulted if the preliminary checks prove unfruitful. Whatever the fault, certain basic principles apply. These are as follows:

Verify the fault. This is simply a matter of being sure that you know what the symptoms are before starting work. This is particularly important if you are investigating a fault for someone else who may not have described it very accurately.

Don't overlook the obvious. For example, if the vehicle won't start, is there petrol in the tank? (Don't take anyone else's word on this particular point, and don't trust the fuel gauge either!) If an electrical fault is indicated, look for loose or broken wires before digging out the test gear.

Cure the disease, not the symptom. Substituting a flat battery with a fully charged one will get you off the hard shoulder, but if the underlying cause is not attended to, the new battery will go the same way. Similarly, changing oil-fouled spark plugs for a new set will get you moving again, but remember that the reason for the fouling (if it wasn't simply an incorrect grade of plug) will have to be established and corrected.

Don't take anything for granted. Particularly, don't forget that a 'new' component may itself be defective (especially if it's been rattling round in the boot for months), and don't leave components out of a fault diagnosis sequence just because they are new or recently fitted. When you do finally diagnose a difficult fault, you'll probably realise that all the evidence was there from the start.

Electrical faults

Electrical faults can be more puzzling than straightforward mechanical failures, but they are no less susceptible to logical analysis if the basic principles of operation are understood. Vehicle electrical wiring exists in extremely unfavourable conditions – heat, vibration and chemical attack – and the first things to look for are loose or corroded connections and broken or chafed wires, especially where the wires pass through holes in the bodywork or are subject to vibration.

All metal-bodied vehicles in current production have one pole of the battery 'earthed', ie connected to the vehicle bodywork, and in nearly all modern vehicles it is the negative (–) terminal. The various electrical components – motors, bulb holders etc – are also connected to earth, either by means of a lead or directly by their mountings. Electric current flows through the component and then back to the battery via the bodywork. If the component mounting is loose or corroded, or if a good path back to the battery is not available, the circuit will be incomplete and malfunction will result. The engine and/or gearbox are also earthed by means of flexible metal straps to the body or subframe; if these straps are loose or missing, starter motor, generator and ignition trouble may result.

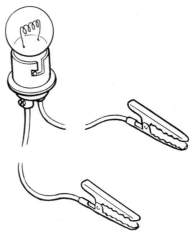

A simple test lamp is useful for tracing electrical faults

Assuming the earth return to be satisfactory, electrical faults will be due either to component malfunction or to defects in the current supply. Individual components are dealt with in Chapter 10. If supply wires are broken or cracked internally this results in an open-circuit, and the easiest way to check for this is to bypass the suspect wire temporarily with a length of wire having a crocodile clip or suitable connector at each end. Alternatively, a 12V test lamp can be used to verify the presence of supply voltage at various points along the wire and the break can be thus isolated.

If a bare portion of a live wire touches the bodywork or other earthed metal part, the electricity will take the low-resistance path thus formed back to the battery: this is known as a short-circuit. Hopefully a short-circuit will blow a fuse, but otherwise it may cause burning of the insulation (and possibly further short-circuits) or even a fire. This is why it is inadvisable to bypass persistently blowing fuses with silver foil or wire.

Spares and tool kit

Most vehicles are supplied only with sufficient tools for wheel changing; the *Maintenance and minor repair* tool kit detailed in *Tools and working facilities,* with the addition of a hammer, is probably sufficient for those repairs that most motorists would consider attempting at the roadside. In addition a few items which can be fitted without too much trouble in the event of a breakdown should be carried. Experience and available space will modify the list below, but the following may save having to call on professional assistance:

Spark plugs, clean and correctly gapped
HT lead and plug cap – long enough to reach the plug furthest from the distributor
Distributor rotor, condenser and contact breaker points
Drivebelt(s) – emergency type may suffice
Spare fuses
Set of principal light bulbs
Tin of radiator sealer and hose bandage
Exhaust bandage
Roll of insulating tape
Length of soft iron wire
Length of electrical flex
Torch or inspection lamp (can double as test lamp)
Battery jump leads
Tow-rope
Ignition waterproofing aerosol
Litre of engine oil
Sealed can of hydraulic fluid
Emergency windscreen
'Jubilee' clips
Tube of filler paste

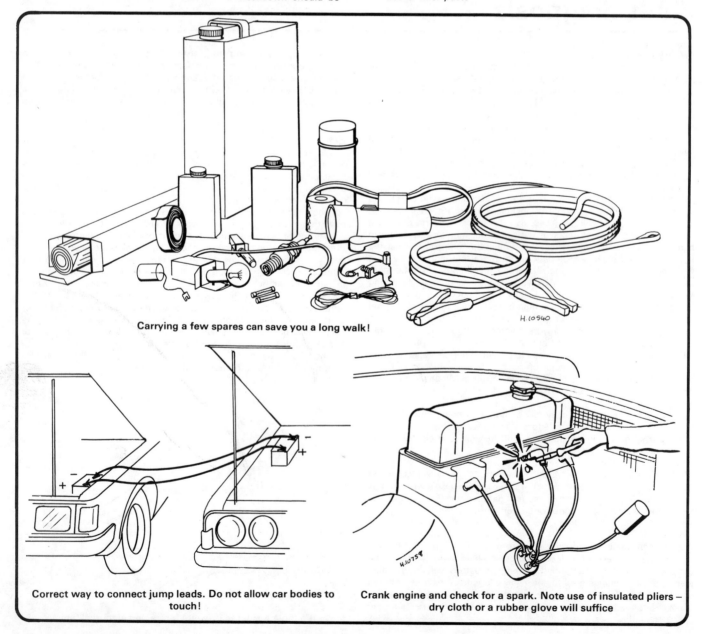

Carrying a few spares can save you a long walk!

H.10540

Correct way to connect jump leads. Do not allow car bodies to touch!

Crank engine and check for a spark. Note use of insulated pliers – dry cloth or a rubber glove will suffice

If spare fuel is carried, a can designed for the purpose should be used to minimise risks of leakage and collision damage. A first aid kit and a warning triangle, whilst not at present compulsory in the UK, are obviously sensible items to carry in addition to the above.

When touring abroad it may be advisable to carry additional spares which, even if you cannot fit them yourself, could save having to wait while parts are obtained. The items below may be worth considering:

Clutch and throttle cables
Cylinder head gasket
Alternator brushes
Fuel pump repair kit
Tyre valve core

One of the motoring organisations will be able to advise on availability of fuel etc in foreign countries.

Engine will not start

Engine fails to turn when starter operated
Flat battery (recharge, use jump leads, or push start)
Battery terminals loose or corroded
Battery earth to body defective
Engine earth strap loose or broken
Starter motor (or solenoid) wiring loose or broken
Automatic transmission selector in wrong position, or inhibitor switch faulty
Ignition/starter switch faulty
Major mechanical failure (seizure)
Starter or solenoid internal fault (see Chapter 10)

Starter motor turns engine slowly
Partially discharged battery (recharge, use jump leads, or push start)
Battery terminals loose or corroded
Battery earth to body defective
Engine earth strap loose
Starter motor (or solenoid) wiring loose
Starter motor internal fault (see Chapter 10)

Starter motor spins without turning engine
Flat battery
Starter motor pinion sticking on sleeve
Flywheel gear teeth damaged or worn
Starter motor mounting bolts loose

Engine turns normally but fails to start
Damp or dirty HT leads and distributor cap (crank engine and check for spark)
Dirty or incorrectly gapped distributor points (if applicable)
No fuel in tank (check for delivery at carburettor)
Excessive choke (hot engine) or insufficient choke (cold engine)
Fouled or incorrectly gapped spark plugs (remove, clean and regap)
Other ignition system fault (see Chapter 4)
Other fuel system fault (see Chapter 3)
Poor compression (see Chapter 1)
Major mechanical failure (eg camshaft drive)

Engine fires but will not run
Insufficient choke (cold engine)
Air leaks at carburettor or inlet manifold
Fuel starvation (see Chapter 3)
Ballast resistor defective, or other ignition fault (see Chapter 4)

Engine cuts out and will not restart

Engine cuts out suddenly – ignition fault
Loose or disconnected LT wires
Wet HT leads or distributor cap (after traversing water splash)
Coil or condenser failure (check for spark)
Other ignition fault (see Chapter 4)

Engine misfires before cutting out – fuel fault
Fuel tank empty
Fuel pump defective or filter blocked (check for delivery)
Fuel tank filler vent blocked (suction will be evident on releasing cap)
Carburettor needle valve sticking
Carburettor jets blocked (fuel contaminated)
Other fuel system fault (see Chapter 3)

Engine cuts out – other causes
Serious overheating
Major mechanical failure (eg camshaft drive)

Engine overheats

Ignition (no-charge) warning light illuminated
Slack or broken drivebelt – retension or renew (Chapter 2)

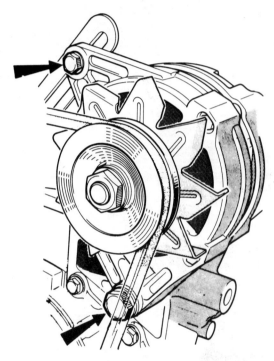

A slack drivebelt may cause overheating and battery charge problems. Slacken bolts (arrowed) to adjust

Ignition warning light not illuminated
Coolant loss due to internal or external leakage (see Chapter 2)
Thermostat defective
Low oil level
Brakes binding
Radiator clogged externally or internally
Electric cooling fan not operating correctly
Engine waterways clogged
Ignition timing incorrect or automatic advance malfunctioning
Mixture too weak

Note: *Do not add cold water to an overheated engine or damage may result*

Low engine oil pressure

Gauge reads low or warning light illuminated with engine running
Oil level low or incorrect grade
Defective gauge or sender unit
Wire to sender unit earthed

Engine overheating
Oil filter clogged or bypass valve defective
Oil pressure relief valve defective
Oil pick-up strainer clogged
Oil pump worn or mountings loose
Worn main or big-end bearings

Note: *Low oil pressure in a high-mileage engine at tickover is not necessarily a cause for concern. Sudden pressure loss at speed is far more significant. In any event, check the gauge or warning light sender before condemning the engine.*

Engine noises

Pre-ignition (pinking) on acceleration

Incorrect grade of fuel
Ignition timing incorrect
Distributor faulty or worn
Worn or maladjusted carburettor
Excessive carbon build-up in engine

Whistling or wheezing noises

Leaking vacuum hose
Leaking carburettor or manifold gasket
Blowing head gasket

Tapping or rattling

Incorrect valve clearances
Worn valve gear
Worn timing chain
Broken piston ring (ticking noise)

Knocking or thumping

Unintentional mechanical contact (eg fan blades)
Worn drivebelt
Peripheral component fault (generator, water pump etc)
Worn big-end bearings (regular heavy knocking, perhaps less under load)
Worn main bearings (rumbling and knocking, perhaps worsening under load)
Piston slap (most noticeable when cold)

Chapter 1 Engine

Contents

Part 1 General
Engine – removal methods 4
Engine oil and filter 2
General description 1
Major operations possible – engine in car 3

Part 2 1289 cc (Type 810) engine
Connecting rod/piston/liner assemblies – removal and
refitting 8
Crankcase ventilation system 21
Cylinder head – dismantling, decarbonising and reassembly 19
Cylinder head – removal and refitting (engine in car) 5
Engine – complete dismantling (engine removed) 17
Engine – examination, renovation and dismantling of major
assemblies 18
Engine – initial start up after major overhaul 24
Engine – reassembly 22
Engine ancillaries – removal 16
Engine dismantling – general 15
Engine (leaving automatic transmission in car) – removal
and refitting 12
Engine (leaving manual transmission in car) – removal and
refitting 9
Engine/manual transmission – separation and reconnection 11
Engine (with automatic transmission) – removal and refitting 13
Engine (with manual transmission) – removal and refitting 10
Lubrication system 20

Oil pump – removal and refitting (engine in car) 7
Sump pan – removal and refitting (engine in car) 6
Valve clearances – adjustment 23

*Part 3 1565 cc, 1605 cc, 1647 cc (Type 807, 821, 841,
843, 844) engines*
Connecting rod/piston/liner assemblies – removal and
refitting (engine in car) 28
Crankcase ventilation system 37
Cylinder head – dismantling, decarbonising and reassembly 35
Cylinder head – removal and refitting (engine in car) 25
Engine – complete dismantling (engine removed) 33
Engine – examination, renovation and dismantling of major
assemblies 34
Engine – initial start up after major overhaul 41
Engine – reassembly 39
Engine ancillaries – removal 32
Engine dismantling – general 31
Engine reassembly – general 38
Engine or engine/transmission – removal and refitting 30
Fault diagnosis – all engines 42
Lubrication system 36
Oil pump – removal and refitting (engine in car) 27
Sump pan – removal and refitting (engine in car) 26
Timing cover oil seal – renewal 29
Valve clearances – adjustment 40

Specifications

Engine type	810 – 05
	810 – 06
	810 – E-7 – 05
	810 – 10
Application	Model R 1300
Displacement	1289 cc (78.6 cu in)
Bore	73.0 mm (2.87 in)
Stroke	77.0 mm (3.03 in)
Compression ratio	9.5 : 1

Maximum power (DIN) .... 60 bhp at 5500 rev/min

Maximum torque (DIN) .... 67.3 lbf ft at 3500 rev/min

Firing order .... 1-3-4-2 (No. 1 at flywheel end)

Crankshaft
Number of bearings .... 5 (No. 1 nearest flywheel)
Bearing material .... White metal
Endplay .... 0.05 to 0.23 mm (0.002 to 0.009 in)
Thrust washer thicknesses .... 2.28 – 2.38 and 2.43 mm (0.090 – 0.094 – 0.096 in)
Crankpins .... Roll hardened
Nominal diameter .... 43.96 mm (1.7307 in)
Regrind size .... 43.71 mm (1.7209 in)
Main bearing journals .... Roll hardened
Nominal diameter .... 46 mm (1.811 in)
Regrind size for repair size bearing shells .... 45.75 mm (1.801 in)

Liners
Bore .... 73 mm (2.874 in)
Diameter of bottom centering location .... 78.5 mm (3.091 in)
Liner protrusion .... 0.04 to 0.11 mm (0.002 to 0.0045 in)
Box seal thicknesses available:
Blue mark .... 0.08 mm (0.003 in)
Red mark .... 0.10 mm (0.004 in)
Green mark .... 0.12 mm (0.0047 in)

Connecting rods
Bearing material .... White metal

Pistons
Gudgeon pin fitting .... Interference fit in the small end free turning in the piston
Direction of fitting .... Arrow towards the flywheel end
Gudgeon pin length .... 62 mm (2.7/16 in)
Gudgeon pin diameter .... 20 mm (0.787 in)
Piston fitting direction .... Arrow to flywheel

Piston rings
Number 3

Cylinder head
Cylinder head depth:
Nominal .... 72.0 mm (2.834 in)
Minimum repair size .... 71.5 mm (2.815 in)
Maximum bow of gasket face .... 0.05 mm (0.002 in)

Valve guides
Internal diameter .... 7 mm (0.276 in)
External diameter:
Nominal .... 11 mm (0.433 in)
Repair sizes:
With 1 groove .... 11.10 mm (0.437 in)
With 2 grooves .... 11.25 mm (0.443 in)

Valve seats
Seat widths:
Inlet .... 1.1 to 1.4 mm (0.043 to 0.055 in)
Exhaust .... 1.4 to 1.7 mm (0.055 to 0.067 in)

Valves
Head diameter:
Inlet .... 33.5 mm (1.319 in)
Exhaust .... 30.3 mm (1.193 in)
Stem diameter .... 7 mm (0.276 in)
Angle .... 90° (included)

Valve springs
Free length (approx) .... 42 mm (1.65 in)

Valve timing
Inlet valve opens .... 22° BTDC
Inlet valve closes .... 62° ABDC
Exhaust valve opens .... 65° BBDC
Exhaust valve closes .... 25° ATDC

Valve clearances
Cold:
    Inlet .... 0.15 mm (0.006 in)
    Exhaust .... 0.20 mm (0.008 in)
Hot:
    Inlet .... 0.18 mm (0.007 in)
    Exhaust .... 0.25 mm (0.010 in)

Tappets
External diameter:
    Nominal .... 19 mm (0.748 in)
    Repair size .... 19.2 mm (0.756 in)

Pushrods
Length .... 173.0 mm (6.881 in)
Diameter .... 6.0 mm (0.236 in)

Oil pump
Oil pressure:
    At 600 rev/min .... 0.7 bar (10 psi)
    At 4000 rev/min .... 3.5 to 4 bars (50 to 55 psi)

Oil capacity .... 6.0 Imp pts, 3.60 US qts, 3.41 l

Engine type .... **807-10 manual, 807-11 auto, 807-12 fuel injection, 821-15 manual, 821-16 auto**

Application .... Models   R1301
    R1302
    R1312
    R1313
    R1322
    R1323

Displacement .... 1565 cc (95.4 cu in)
    Bore .... 77.0 mm (3.03 in)
    Stroke .... 84.0 mm (3.30 in)

Compression ratio
    (807) .... 9.25 : 1 or 10.25 : 1 (fuel injection)
    (821) .... 8.6 : 1

Maximum power (SAE) .... 102 bhp at 5800 rev/min

Maximum torque (SAE) .... 95.5 lbf ft at 3000 rev/min

Firing order 1-3-4-2

Crankshaft
Number of main bearings 5
Endfloat .... 0.05 to 0.23 mm (0.002 to 0.009 in)
Thrust washer availability .... 2.80 mm (0.110 in)
    2.90 mm (0.114 in)
    2.95 mm (0.116 in)
Main bearing journal diameter .... 54.8 mm (2.158 in)
Regrind diameter for oversize shell bearings
Roll hardened crankshaft .... 54.55 mm (2.148 in)
Regrind tolerances .... 0.013/0.001 mm (0.0005/0.00004 in)
Crankpin diameter .... 48.0 mm (1.890 in)
Regrind diameter for oversize shell bearings
Roll hardened crankshaft .... 47.75 mm (1.880 in)
Regrind tolerances .... 0.018/0.002 mm (0.0007/0.0001 in)

Connecting rods
Bearing shells .... Aluminium/tin

Big-end side play .... 0.31 to 0.57 mm (0.012 to 0.022 in)

Liners
Bore .... 77.0 mm (3.032 in)
Base locating diameter .... 82.5 mm (3.248 in)
Liner protrusion .... 0.15 to 0.20 mm (0.006 to 0.008 in)

Base seal thicknesses:
Blue .... 0.08 mm (0.003 in)
Red .... 0.10 mm (0.004 in)
Green .... 0.12 mm (0.0047 in)

Pistons
Type .... Alloy
Gudgeon pin length .... 68.0 mm (2.677 in)
Fuel injection .... 66.4 mm (2.614 in)
Gudgeon pin diameter:
External .... 20.0 mm (0.787 in)
Fuel injection .... 21.0 mm (0.827 in)
Internal .... 13.0 mm (0.512 in)
Fuel injection .... 13.0 mm (0.512 in)
Piston fitting direction .... Arrow to flywheel
Piston rings .... 2 compression, 1 oil control
Top .... 1.75 mm (0.069 in) thick
Second .... 2.0 mm (0.079 in) thick
Oil control .... 4.0 mm (0.158 in) thick

Cylinder head
Depth (807) nominal .... 93.5 mm (3.681 in)
(821) .... 81.45 mm (3.207 in)
(807) minimum repair size .... 93.0 mm (3.661 in)
(821) .... 80.95 mm (3.187 in)

Valve guides
Internal diameter .... 8.0 mm (0.315 in)
External diameter .... 13.0 mm (0.511 in)
Repair sizes:
With one groove .... 13.10 mm (0.516 in)
With two grooves .... 13.25 mm (0.521 in)

Valve seats
Seat widths:
Inlet .... 1.5 to 1.8 mm (0.059 to 0.070 in)
Inlet (Fuel injection) .... 1.3 to 1.6 mm (0.051 to 0.063 in)
Exhaust .... 1.7 to 2.0 mm (0.067 to 0.079 in)

Valves
Head diameter:
Inlet (807) .... 40.0 mm (1.575 in)
(821) .... 37.0 mm (1.457 in)
Fuel injection (807) .... 42.1 mm (1.657 in)
Exhaust (807) .... 35.35 mm (1.391 in)
(821) .... 33.0 mm (1.299 in)
Stem diameter .... 8.0 mm (0.315 in)
Angle .... 90° (included)

Valve springs (free length)
Outer (807) .... 54.3 mm (2.138 in)
(821) .... 48.4 mm (1.91 in)
Fuel injection (807) .... 43.7 mm (1.720 in)
Inner (807) .... 46.8 mm (1.842 in)
(821) .... 38.4 mm (1.50 in)
Fuel injection (807) .... 41.50 mm (1.634 in)

Valve timing

Engines with carburettor	Type 807	Type 821
Inlet valve opens	24° BTDC	10° BTDC
Inlet valve closes	68° ABDC	42° ABDC
Exhaust valve opens	68° BBDC	46° BBDC
Exhaust valve closes	24° ATDC	10° ATDC

Engines with fuel injection		
Inlet valve opens	40° BTDC	
Inlet valve closes	72° ABDC	
Exhaust valve opens	72° BBDC	
Exhaust valve closes	24° ATDC	

Valve clearances
Hot or Cold:
Inlet .... 0.20 mm (0.008 in)

Inlet (Fuel injection)	0.25 mm (0.10 in)
Exhaust	0.25 mm (0.10 in)
Exhaust (Fuel injection)	0.30 mm (0.12 in)

Tappets
External diameter	12.0 mm (0.472 in)
Repair size	12.20 (0.480 in)

Pushrods
Length:	
Inlet (807)	78.0 mm (7.0 in)
(821)	88.0 mm (3.5 in)
Exhaust (807)	110.0 mm (4.3 in)
(821)	88.0 mm (3.5 in)
Diameter	6.0 mm (0.236 in)

Oil pump
Oil pressure (80°C – 176°F):	
At idle	2 bar (30 lbf/in²)
At 4000 rev/min	4 bar (60 lbf/in²)

Oil capacity
....	7.5 Imp pts, 4.5 US qts, 4.25 l

Engine type
....	**844 – 12 fuel injection**

Application
....	Model R 1317, R 1327

Displacement
....	1605 cc (98 cu in)
Bore	78.0 mm (3.07 in)
Stroke	84.0 mm (3.30 in)

Compression ratio
....	10.25 : 1

Maximum power (DIN)
....	110 bhp at 6000 rev/min

Maximum torque (DIN)
....	98 bhp at 4500 rev/min

Firing order
....	1-3-4-2

Crankshaft
Number of main bearings	5
Main bearing shell material	Aluminium/tin
Crankshaft endfloat	0.045 to 0.23 mm (0.002 to 0.009 in)
Thrust washer thicknesses available	2.80 mm (0.110 in)
	2.85 mm (0.112 in)
	2.90 mm (0.114 in)
	2.95 mm (0.116 in)
Main bearing journal diameter	54.80 mm (2.158 in)
Regrind diameter	54.55 mm (2.148 in)
Crankpin diameter	48.0 mm (1.890 in)
Regrind diameter	47.75 mm (1.880 in)
Regrind tolerance	-0.011 to +0.013 mm (-0.0004 to + 0.0005 in)
Big-end side play	0.31 to 0.57 mm (0.012 to 0.022 in)

Liners
Bore	78.0 mm (3.071 in)
Base locating diameter	(82.5 mm (3.248 in)
Liner protrusion	0.15 to 0.020 mm (0.006 to 0.008 in)
Base seal thicknesses:	
Blue	0.08 mm (0.003 in)
Red	0.10 mm (0.004 in)
Green	0.12 mm (0.004 in)

Pistons
Type	Alloy
Gudgeon pin length	66.4 mm (2.614 in)
Gudgeon pin diameter:	
External	21.0 mm (0.827 in)
Internal	13.0 mm (0.512 in)
Piston fitting direction	Arrow to flywheel

Piston rings .... 2 compression, 1 oil control
    Top .... 1.75 mm (0.069 in) thick
    2nd (taper) .... 2.0 mm (0.079 in) thick
    Oil scraper .... 4.0 mm (0.158 in) thick

Cylinder head
Depth – nominal .... 93.5 mm (3.681 in)
    Minimum repair size .... 93.0 mm (3.661 in)

Valve guides:
    Bore (inlet and exhaust) .... 8 mm (0.315 in)
    Standard outside diameter .... 13 mm (0.512 in)
Repair sizes:
    With one groove .... 13.10 mm (0.516 in)
    With two grooves .... 13.25 mm (0.521 in)

Valve seats
Seat angle .... 90° (included)
Seat widths:
    Inlet .... 1.3 to 1.6 mm (0.051 to 0.063 in)
    Exhaust .... 1.7 to 2.0 mm (0.067 to 0.079 in)

Valves
Head diameter:
    Inlet .... 42.1 mm (1.657 in)
    Exhaust .... 35.35 mm (1.391 in)
Stem diameter .... 8.0 mm (0.315 in)
Angle .... 90° (included)

Valve springs
Free length:
    Outer .... 43.7 mm (1.720 in)
    Inner .... 41.50 mm (1.634 in)

Valve timing
Inlet valve opens .... 40° BTDC
Inlet valve closes .... 72° ABDC
Exhaust valve opens .... 72° BBDC
Exhaust valve closes .... 40° ATDC

Valve clearances
Hot or Cold:
    Inlet .... 0.25 mm (0.020 in)
    Exhaust .... 0.30 mm (0.012 in)

Tappets
External diameter .... 12.0 mm (0.472 in)
Repair size .... 12.20 mm (0.480 in)

Pushrods
Length:
    Inlet .... 78.0 mm (3.07 in)
    Exhaust .... 110.0 mm (4.3 in)
Diameter .... 6.0 mm (0.236 in)

Oil pump
Oil pressure (80°C – 176° F)
    At idle .... 2 bar (30 lbf/in²)
    At 4000 rev/min .... 4 bar (60 lbf/in²)

Oil capacity
Oil capacity .... 7.59 Imp pts, 4.5 US qts, 4.25 l

Engine type
Engine type .... **841-15 auto. (Canada), 841-16 auto (Canada), 843 E.7-05 manual, 843 F-7-06 automatic**

Application
Application .... (Type 841) R1304, 1314, (Type 843) R1318, 1328

Displacement
Displacement .... 1647 cc (100 cu in)
    Bore .... 79.0 mm (3.11 in)
    Stroke .... 84.0 mm (3.30 in)

Compression ratio
Compression ratio .... 9.3 : 1

Maximum power (DIN)	98 bhp at 5750 rev/min	
Maximum torque (DIN)	97.6 lbf ft at 3500 rev/min	
Firing order	1-3-4-2	

The specifications for this engine are as for the Type 844 engine with the exception of the following differences.

Gudgeon pin length	69.0 mm (2.7 in)	
Gudgeon pin diameter:	**Type 841**	**Type 843**
External	20.0 mm (0.787 in)	21.0 mm (0.827 in)
Internal	12.0 mm (0.472 in)	12.0 mm (0.472 in)

Valve seat width

Inlet .... 1.5 to 1.8 mm (0.059 to 0.071 in)

Valve head diameter

Inlet .... 38.7 mm (1.523 in)

Exhaust .... 34.5 mm (1.358 in)

Valve timing

Inlet valve opens .... 30° BTDC

Inlet valve closes .... 72° ABDC

Exhaust valve opens .... 72° BBDC

Exhaust valve closes .... 30° ATDC

Valve clearances

Hot or Cold:

Inlet .... 0.20 mm (0.008 in)

Exhaust .... 0.25 mm (0.010 in)

Pushrods

Length:

Inlet .... 79.0 mm (3.1 in)

Exhaust .... 110.0 mm (4.3 in)

Diameter .... 6.0 mm (0.236 in)

Torque wrench settings	**Nm**	**lbf ft**
Cylinder head bolts		
Type 810 engine (hot or cold)	56	41
All other engines:		
Stage 1 (cold)	41	30
Stage 2 (cold)	82	60
Stage 3 (engine warm)	88	65
When checking torque of bolts at service intervals:		
Stage 1 (50 mins after switching off engine)	88	65
Stage 2 (engine completely cold and each bolt unscrewed ¼ turn **one at a time**)	84	62
Manifold nuts	15	11
Main bearing cap bolts	61	45
Big-end bearing cap nuts	46	34
Flywheel bolts	50	37
Driveplate bolts (automatic) to crankshaft	68	50
Camshaft sprocket bolts	20	15
Camshaft pulley bolt	68	50
Crankshaft pulley bolt	115	85
Bellhousing bolts 8.0 mm	25	18
10.0 mm	35	26
Rocker shaft pedestal bolts (Type 810 only)	20	15
Driveplate to torque converter bolts	34	25

PART 1 GENERAL

1 General description

All engines fitted to the Renault 15 and 17 range are of four-cylinder in-line type constructed from light alloy with wet liners.

The engine is mounted in the conventional fore and aft attitude with the gearbox/final drive located behind it and transmitting power through open driveshafts to the front roadwheels.

All engines have a five bearing crankshaft.

The camshaft runs in four bearings and is driven by a chain from a sprocket on the front end of the crankshaft.

The valves are of overhead, pushrod operated type. On the 1285 cc engine, the valves are arranged in line, but on the larger capacity engines, they are arranged in Vee formation with a crossflow type cylinder head.

The oil pump and the distributor are driven by a shaft geared to the camshaft.

In the interest of simplicity of reference, this Chapter is divided into separate Sections, covering the 1285 cc engine and then as a group, the 1565 cc, 1605 cc and 1647 cc engines.

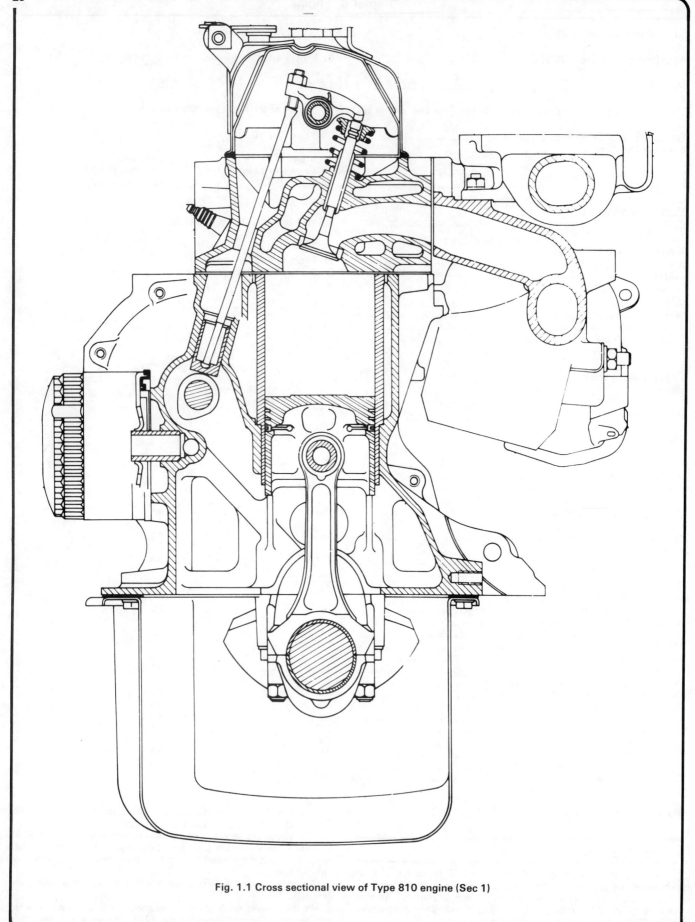

Fig. 1.1 Cross sectional view of Type 810 engine (Sec 1)

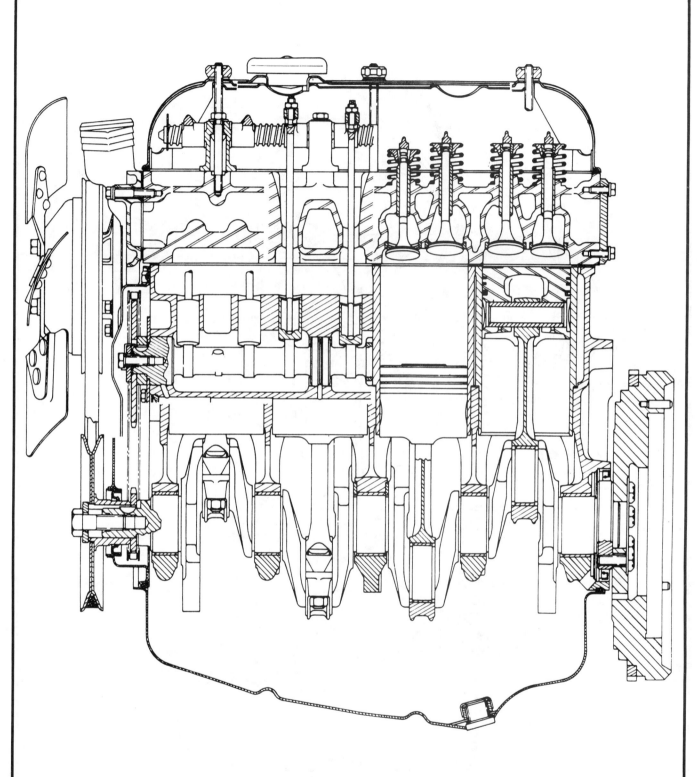

Fig. 1.2 Longitudinal sectional view of Type 810 engine (Sec 1)

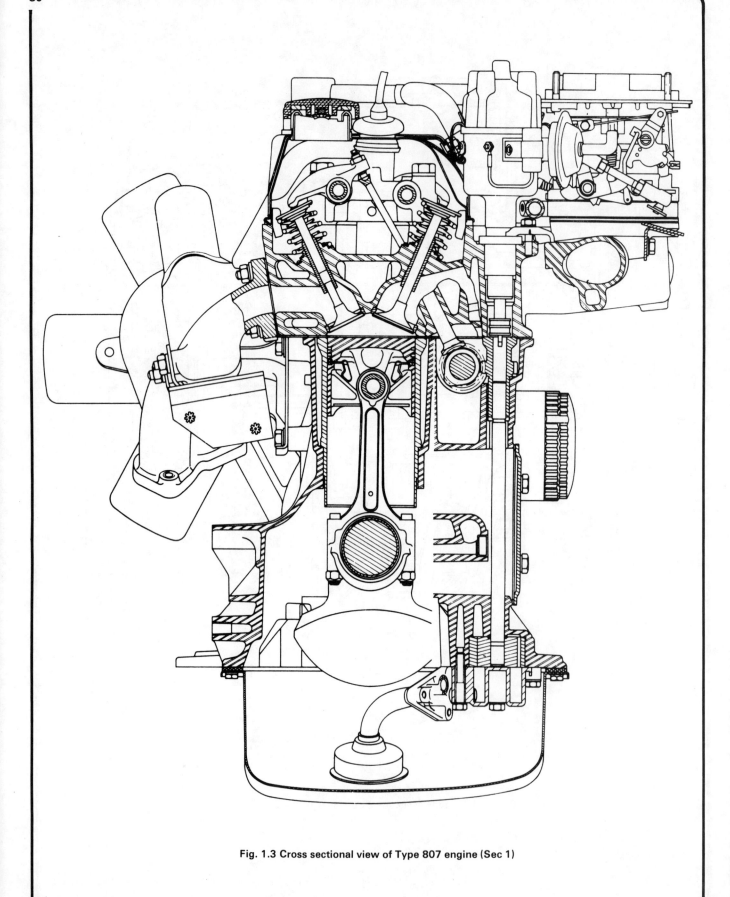

Fig. 1.3 Cross sectional view of Type 807 engine (Sec 1)

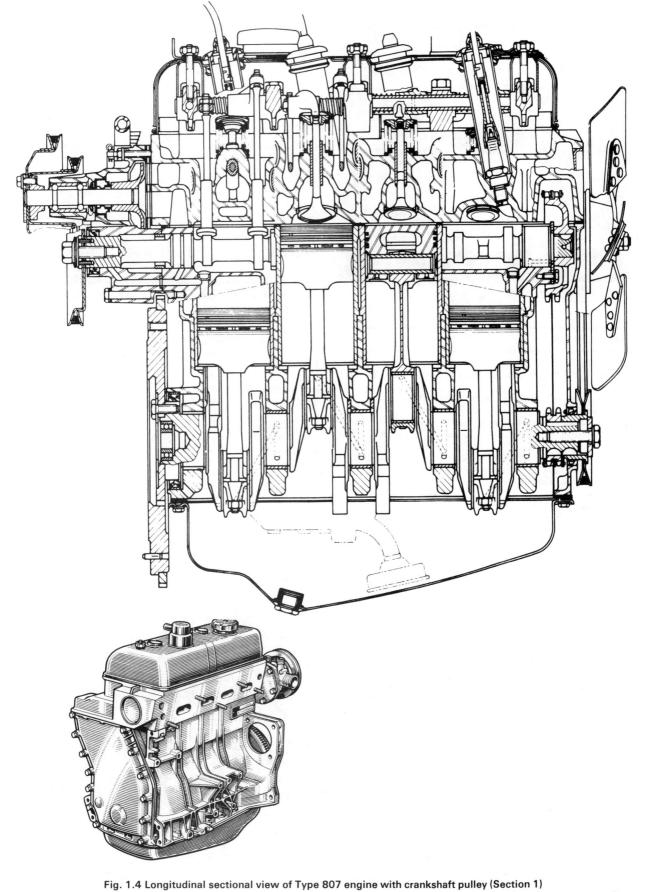

Fig. 1.4 Longitudinal sectional view of Type 807 engine with crankshaft pulley (Section 1)

Inset – engine without crankshaft pulley

2.6 Removing oil filter

2 Engine oil and filter

1   The engine oil level should be checked at the weekly inspection.
2   To do this, withdraw the dipstick, wipe it clean, re-insert it and withdraw it again.
3   The oil level should be within the MIN and MAX marks on the dipstick. If necessary, top up with the specified grade of oil. Remove the oil filler cap on the rocker cover and pour in the oil. To raise the oil level from the minimum to maximum levels requires 2 Imp pts, 1.2 US qts, 1.0 l.
4   At the intervals specified in Routine Maintenance the engine oil should be drained hot and the oil filter renewed.
5   Place a container under the engine sump and remove the drain plug.
6   While the engine oil is draining, unscrew the disposable, cartridge type oil filter. An oil filter wrench will almost certainly be required to remove the oil filter. These are obtainable at most motor accessory stores. Alternatively, the filter can be unscrewed by driving a large screwdriver right through it towards its end, and using the screwdriver as a lever (photo).
7   Smear a little grease on the rubber sealing ring of the new filter and screw it into position using hand pressure only – not a tool.
8   Refit and tighten the drain plug.
9   Pour in the correct quantity of fresh engine oil.
10 Start the engine. It will take a few seconds for the oil pressure warning lamp to go out. This is normal and the delay is caused by the empty oil filter cartridge filling up.
11 Switch off the engine, wait a few minutes and then check the oil level and top up if necessary.
12 On these engines, do not use flushing oil as it is impossible to drain it from the camshaft oil bath and severe wear is then likely to occur in the camshaft bearings if they are running in flushing oil.

3 Major operations possible – engine in car

1   The following operations can be carried out without the need to remove the engine from the car.

   Removal and refitting of:
   (a) Cylinder head
   (b) Sump
   (c) Oil pump
   (d) Connecting rod/piston/liner assemblies
   (e) Timing cover oil seal (certain Type 807 engines only)

4 Engine – removal methods

1   The engine may be removed on its own or together with the manual or automatic transmission for later separation.

Warning: Vehicles equipped with air conditioning
2   Whenever overhaul of a major nature is being carried out on the engine some components of the air conditioning system may obstruct the work. Other items of the system cannot be unbolted and moved aside sufficiently, within the limits of their flexible connecting hoses, to give good access. In these cases the system should be discharged by your dealer or a competent refrigeration engineer.
3   As the system must be completely evacuated before recharging, the necessary vacuum equipment to do this is only likely to be held by your dealer.
4   The refrigerant fluid is Freon 12 and although harmless under normal conditions, contact with eyes or skin must be avoided.
5   If Freon comes into contact with a naked flame, then a poisonous gas will be created which is injurious to health.
6   On vehicles operating in North America, additional disconnection operations will be required for the emission control systems (refer to Chapter 3).

PART 2 1289 cc (TYPE 810) ENGINE

5 Cylinder head – removal and refitting (engine in car)

1   Disconnect the battery, remove the air cleaner.
2   Drain the cooling system as described in Chapter 2.
3   Disconnect the radiator and heater connecting hoses, also those from the carburettor throttle block.
4   Disconnect the HT leads from the spark plugs and the ignition coil centre socket.
5   Disconnect the LT lead from the coil negative terminal.
6   Disconnect the coolant temperaure sender unit lead.
7   Disconnect the brake servo vacuum hose.
8   Disconnect the fuel flow and return hoses from the carburettor.
9   Disconnect and unclip the crankcase emission hoses from the rocker cover.
10 Disconnect the throttle control linkage from the carburettor.
11 Disconnect the choke control cable from the carburettor.
12 Remove the distributor (Chapter 4).
13 Remove the alternator and drivebelt (Chapter 10).
14 Remove the fan shroud (Chapter 2).
15 Remove the retaining screws and take off the rocker cover.
16 Disconnect the exhaust downpipe at the manifold connecting flange.
17 Disconnect the hot air intake for the air cleaner.
18 Release the rocker arm adjusting screws and unscrew them until by pushing the rocker arms against the tension of the coil springs, the pushrods can be withdrawn. Keep the pushrods in their originally fitted order.

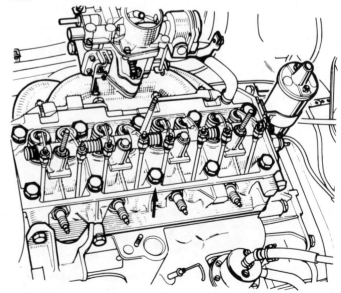

Fig. 1.5 Cylinder head bolt not to be unscrewed initially (Sec 5)

19 Unscrew each cylinder head bolt, progressively, half a turn at a time except for the one nearest the distributor mounting hole. Remove all the bolts except the one mentioned.

20 From this point onwards, follow the removal instructions precisely otherwise if any attempt is made to lift the cylinder head, the cylinder liner base seals will be broken with the result that the liners will have to be removed and new seals fitted as described later.

21 The bolt that is still in position should be released by about one turn. This bolt passes through a hollow dowel and the method of releasing the cylinder head is to get it to swivel on the dowel so avoiding disturbing the cylinder liners.

22 Strike the ends of the cylinder head in a sideways direction to release it, but use a plastic-faced hammer or a block of wood as an insulator if a club hammer is used.

23 Once released, remove the bolt, take off the cylinder head and fit liner clamps. The clamping tool (Mot 521) is designed to maintain pressure on the cylinder liner base seals while the head is off. This is particularly important if the crankshaft should be inadvertently rotated (photo).

24 If the cylinder head is to be dismantled and decarbonised, remove the manifolds. In any event it is imperative that the mating surfaces of cylinder head and block are scrupulously clean. Remove every trace of carbon or old gasket material without scratching the alloy. Do not allow dirt to drop into the oil passages and mop out any oil from the

cylinder head bolt holes in the block. Any oil left in them can generate enough hydraulic pressure to crack the block when the cylinder head bolts are screwed home.

25 Commence refitting by removing the clamping tool and placing a new cylinder head gasket on the block with the HAUT-TOP mark uppermost. Do not use any jointing compound (photo).

26 Lower the cylinder head into position and screw in the bolts finger tight (photo).

27 Tighten the bolts to specified torque in the sequence shown. Fit the manifolds using a new gasket. Tighten nuts to specified torque (photo).

28 Fit the pushrods (photo).

29 Adjust the valve clearances as described in Section 23.

30 Refit the rocker cover.

31 Reconnect all wires, control cables and hoses.

32 Reconnect the exhaust pipe.

33 Refit the distributor (Chapter 4).

34 Refit the alternator (Chapter 10).

35 Refit the fan shroud.

36 Fill and bleed the cooling system (Chapter 2).

37 Refit the air cleaner.

38 Connect the battery.

39 After 600 miles (1000 km) running, the torque of the cylinder head bolts should be checked COLD.

5.23 Cylinder liner retaining clamp

5.25 Cylinder head gasket

5.26 Fitting cylinder head

5.27 Tightening cylinder head bolts

5.28 Inserting pushrods

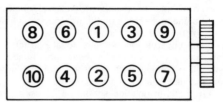

Fig. 1.6 Cylinder head bolt tightening sequence (Sec 5)

the sump downwards. If it is stuck tight, tap it off using a plastic-faced hammer.
3   Clean away all old gasket from the sump and crankcase mating faces.
4   Fit the sump side gaskets in position retaining them with the locating dowels.
5   Smear the ends of the side gaskets with jointing compound at the points where the main bearing sealing strips overlap them. New sealing strips should always be used (photos).
6   Fit the sump and tighten the bolts to the specified torque (photo).

40   To do this, remove the rocker cover and unscrew the bolt (1 in tightening sequence) through one quarter of a turn. Retighten to the specified torque.
41   Repeat the procedure on the remaining bolts in the sequence shown in the diagram. Remember that the bolts are checked one at a time, on no account unscrew all the bolts at the same time.
42   Check the valve clearances and adjust if necessary (Section 23).

7   Oil pump – removal and refitting (engine in car)

1   Remove the sump pan.
2   Unscrew and remove the oil pump mounting bolts and withdraw the pump downwards.
3   Refitting is a reversal of removal, no gasket is used at the pump mounting face. The oil pump driveshaft is splined to the distributor drivegear. The ignition timing will not be affected by removal and refitting of the oil pump (photos).

6   Sump pan – removal and refitting (engine in car)

1   Drain the engine oil as described in Section 2.
2   Unscrew and remove all the sump securing bolts and withdraw

8   Connecting rod/piston/liner assemblies – removal and refitting

1   Remove the sump pan and the cylinder head as previously described. The rod/piston/liner assemblies are removed from the top of the engine.

6.5A Sump side gasket

6.5B Sump end sealing strip (timing cover end)

6.5C Sump end sealing strip (flywheel end)

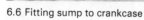
6.6 Fitting sump to crankcase

7.3A Fitting oil pump

7.3B Oil pump fitted

2 It is possible to remove the big-end bearings, pistons, connecting rods and liners from the engine with the engine still in the car, provided that the sump has been removed. Remove the cylinder head, the pistons, connecting rods and liners. With the engine removed from the car, the task is much easier and generally cleaner, but, of course, it is understood that if a quick emergency repair job is to be done and speed is of the essence, then it would be in order to do any work with the engine still in the car. The pistons, connecting rods and liners must be removed from the top of the engine once the connecting rod end caps have been removed. Remove the piston/connecting rod and liner as an assembly.

3 With the sump removed and the crankshaft exposed, each of the big-end bearing caps can be detached after removing the two nuts which hold each cap to the connecting rod stud. Rotate the engine to bring each connecting rod cap suitably into position for unscrewing the nuts.

4 With the nuts removed, each big-end bearing cap can be pulled off. It must be noted that the connecting rods and big-end caps are marked with a small punch mark on the end of the connecting rod and cap, which matches up on each one. If the same connecting rods and caps are to be re-used, they must be replaced exactly as they came out. The same applies to the big-end bearing shells which will be released as soon as the connecting rods are detached from the crankshaft. It is inadvisable to re-use these shells anyway, but if they are not renewed they must be put back in exactly the same location from which they came.

5 If any difficulty is experienced in removing the big-end bearing caps from the studs of the connecting rods, it will help if the crankshaft is revolved in order to dislodge them. If this is done, however, care must be taken to ensure that nothing gets jammed when the connecting rod comes away from the crankshaft at the top of its stroke.

6 Tap the bottom of the liners from beneath with a hard piece of wood which will not tend to split. If you hit them with steel of any kind they will crack.

7 Tap all four loose before you remove one. Lift them upwards, and note where they were fitted and which way round. Provided you have drained the cooling system well, little liquid sediment will be left although there will almost certainly be a lot of rust particles there. If the crankshaft is to remain in the block, cover it as well as you can from below with non-fluffy rag to stop the likelihood of liquid or sediment falling on the journal surfaces.

8 Carefully remove the liner base seals.

9 Once the liners have been removed from the cylinder block the piston/connecting rod can be withdrawn through the bottom of each liner. Make sure that the pistons are kept in such a way that they can be easily identified and replaced in the same liner if necessary.

10 Examination and dismantling procedure is described in Section 18.

11 If new liners are purchased wth new pistons as a set you must keep that piston with its liner. This means that if you have already fitted the pistons to the rods you must be as careful regarding the order in which the liners go back into the block, ie. that No. 1 rod with its piston still goes into its respective liner in the No. 1 position.

12 When fitting liners into the block you must first do so without the pistons fitted in the liners, but this is only a trial run. Once the liners are placed in their position you can then match the piston of the liner to the piston of the connecting rod. All liners are interchangeable in the block.

13 Check that the liners are in good, clean condition without any cracks, even hairline ones, on the outside. Make sure you have a selection of base seals of differing thicknesses. These seals are available in 0.08 mm marked with a blue spot, 0.10 mm marked with a red spot and 0.12 mm marked with a green spot. Buy the latest type. They are usually copper or aluminium coated with a plastic which softens and seals.

14 Lightly oil the holes in the block into which the liners must seat fully.

15 Hold a liner on the bench and slide the thinnest of the seals over the end. With the seal fully home place the liner carefully into the block until it sits firmly in. Do not place the seal in the block and then slide in the liner; it does not work!

16 Repeat this with the other three liners using the same thickness of seal. Tap all four liners very gently with a rubber faced hammer to make sure they are fully home.

17 Using a metric feeler gauge measure the projection of the top of each liner in turn above the surface of the block. This is done by placing the blade or blades on the block face and running your finger across (you should have clean hands anyway) from the feeler gauge to the liner top. The projection should be between 0.04 and 0.11 mm. The nearer 0.11 the better. If you are some way out remove the liners and then replace them using a different thickness of seal. Go through the permutations until you have it right. Provided you have all four liners with the same projection it matters little that one liner has used one thickness of seal and the others another.

18 Now that you have found out which seals to use, you should remove the liners, recording their order and the seals used.

19 Do not attempt to fit the pistons to the liners with the liners in the block. Remove the liners and assemble them on a bench.

20 If new piston rings, on either new pistons or the old pistons, are going into the original cylinder bores, in order to assist the bedding in, it is a good idea to remove the oil glaze which builds up on a bore as an engine becomes more used. This can be done with very fine glass paper, wrapped round a wooden plug of suitable diameter. Careful and thorough cleaning out afterwards will also be necessary, so unless you are perfectly sure that you can do this job safely, it is best not to do it at all.

21 Place the liners in their order of fitment, positioned with their flats mating with each other on the bench.

22 Oil the piston and rings liberally and fit a ring compressor. Offer the piston/rod assembly into the bottom end of the cylinder liner until the compressor is located squarely against the rim of the liner. Check that the arrow on the piston crown will be towards the flywheel when installed and the big-end numbers on the connecting rod will face away from the camshaft.

23 Fit a new shell bearing into the connecting rod half of the big end, making sure that the notch in the end of the shell lines up with the notch in the connecting rod.

24 Repeat for each piston and then place the liners and piston assemblies into the block, complete with the selected seals.

25 Lubricate the big-end journal on the crankshaft with clean engine oil and pull the connecting rod down onto the journal. Fit a new shell bearing into the cap, lining up the notch accordingly. Oil the shell and replace it onto the big-end studs. With the big-end bearing caps marked there should be no difficulty in making sure that the same cap goes onto the same connecting rod the right way round. Refit the nuts and tighten them down to the correct torque. It is a good idea to purchase a set of new big end nuts each time this job is done. These nuts do sometimes stretch and weaken. Loctite is a good additional safety measure.

26 With the pistons and liners assembled in the block recheck the liner projection with a feeler gauge as previously described. If now outside the tolerances you must disassemble and start again.

27 Do not now turn the engine over until the liner retainers are installed or the cylinder head is replaced.

9 Engine (leaving manual transmission in car) – removal and refitting

1 Disconnect and remove the battery. Remove the air cleaner.

2 With the help of an assistant, remove the bonnet as described in Chapter 12.

3 Drain the cooling system (Chapter 2).

4 Disconnect the radiator and heater hoses.

5 Disconnect the HT and negative LT leads from the ignition coil.

6 Disconnect the lead from the coolant temperature sender unit and the oil pressure switch (photo).

7 Disconnect the brake servo vacuum hose.

8 Disconnect the fuel flow and return hoses from the fuel pump and plug them.

9 Disconnect and unclip the crankcase emission hoses from the rocker cover.

10 Disconnect the throttle control linkage from the carburettor.

11 Disconnect the choke control cable from the carburettor.

12 Remove the fan shroud.

13 Disconnect the exhaust downpipe at the manifold connecting flange and gearbox crossmember.

14 Disconnect the hot air intake for the air cleaner.

15 Remove the radiator (Chapter 2).

16 Disconnect the leads from the starter motor terminals and then unbolt and remove it.

17 Unbolt the cooling fan blades and remove them.

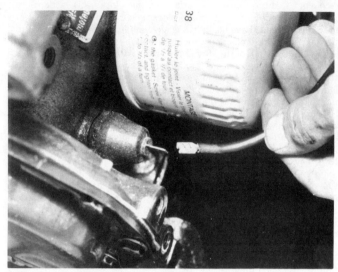

9.6 Disconnecting oil pressure switch lead

9.21 Engine front mounting

18 Unbolt and remove the cover plate from the lower front face of the clutch bellhousing.
19 Unscrew and remove the engine/gearbox connecting bolts from the upper edge of the clutch bellhousing flange.
20 Attach a suitable hoist and lifting slings to the engine and take its weight.
21 Unscrew the nut from the lower face of the right-hand engine mounting (photo).
22 Unscrew the nut from the lower face of the left-hand engine mounting.
23 Remove the bolts which secure the mounting pad to the bracket on the side of the cylinder block.
24 Carefully raise the engine until the right-hand mounting pad can be removed. **Note:** *On pre-March 1976 models, a damper may be fitted. In which case the damper front mounting will have to be removed.*
25 Raise the engine further until the top of the gearbox just makes contact with the underside of the steering box crossmember.

26 Support the gearbox in this position by placing a jack underneath it. Remove the bellhousing lower bolts.
27 Pull the engine forward until it clears the gearbox input shaft. Then lift it and remove it from the engine compartment.
28 Refitting is a reversal of removal.
29 Refill the engine with oil and coolant (Chapter 2).

10 Engine (with manual transmission) – removal and refitting

1 Refer to the preceding Section and carry out the operations described in paragraphs 1 to 15. Disconnect the starter motor leads.
2 Disconnect the clutch operating cable (see Chapter 5) and remove the cable bracket.
3 Raise the front of the car and support it securely on axle stands.
4 Using a punch, drive out the driveshaft retaining pins at the inboard ends of the shafts.
5 Using a suitable extractor, disconnect the steering tie-rod end

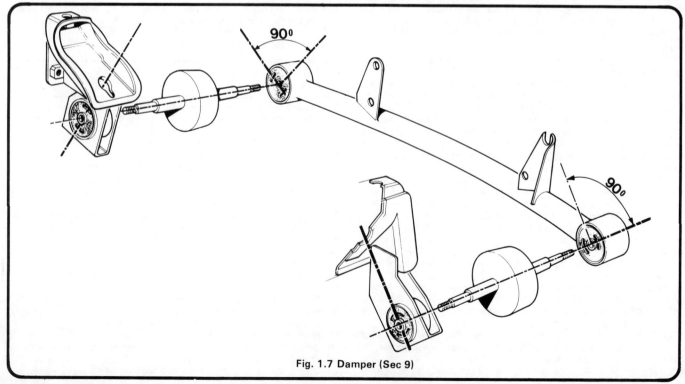

Fig. 1.7 Damper (Sec 9)

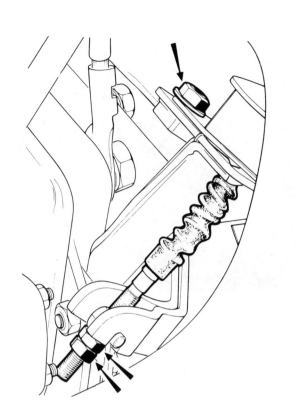

Fig. 1.8 Clutch cable adjusting nuts and bracket bolt (Sec 10)

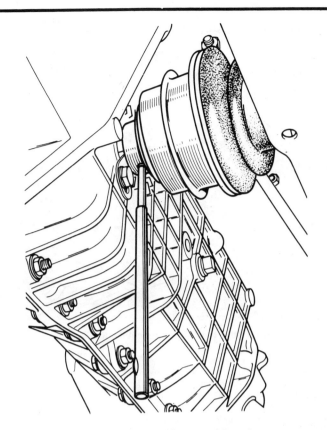

Fig. 1.9 Removing driveshaft pin (Sec 10)

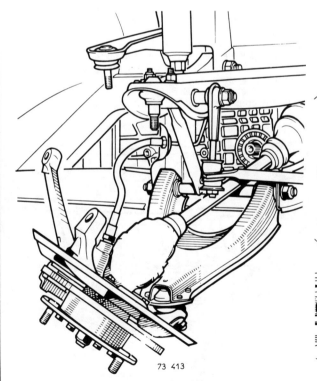

Fig. 1.10 Stub axle carrier disconnected (Sec 10)

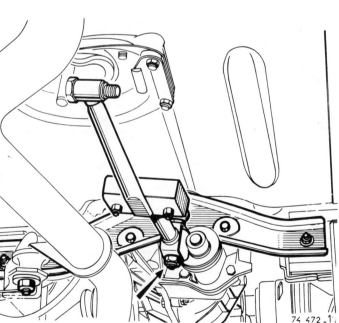

Fig. 1.11 Gearchange linkage clevis fork bolt (arrowed) (Sec 10)

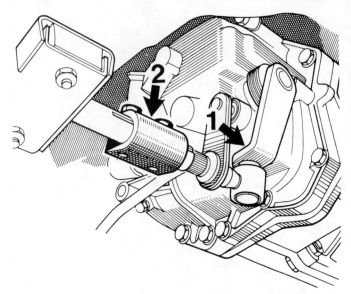

Fig. 1.12 Alternative type gearchange linkage (Sec 10)

1   Balljoint nut   *2   Damping pad*

11.4 Bellhousing to engine bolt showing special nut

balljoint and the suspension upper arm balljoint on both sides of the car. Access to the upper balljoint is very restricted for the engagement of most types of balljoint splitter tool and it is therefore recommended that the balljoint is released by unscrewing the taper pin nut except for a few threads and then driving in forked wedges.

6   Pull the tops of the stub axle carriers outwards until the inboard ends of the driveshafts are released from the transmission.

7   Unscrew the speedometer cable lock bolt at the transmission housing and disconnect the speedometer cable.

8   Disconnect the gearchange control rod by removing the clevis fork bolt at the gearbox. There is an alternative type of gearchange linkage as shown (Type 395 Transmission) and this should be disconnected in the following way: Remove the reaction arm fixing bolt from the sidemember, also the balljoint nut (1). On Type 395 arrangements, the balljoint can only be separated from the selector arm if an Allen key is used to unscrew it. Uncouple the link rod at the damping pad.

9   Disconnect the leads from the reverse lamp switch.

10 Support the rear end of the transmission on a jack. Unbolt and remove the rear mounting brackets from the bodyframe sidemembers and the supporting crossmember.

11 Remove the engine reaction rod from the steering box crossmember.

12 Attach a hoist and slings to the engine/transmission and take its weight. The shorter slings should be attached to the front of the engine so that when the weight is taken and the jack under the gearbox is removed, the engine/transmission will be inclined downward at the rear by at least 45°.

13 Disconnect the engine mountings.

14 Hoist the engine/transmission up and out of the engine compartment.

15 Refitting is a reversal of removal, adjust the clutch as described in Chapter 5 and the gear change linkage as described in Chapter 6.

16 Fill the engine with oil and coolant (Chapter 2).

11 Engine/manual transmission – separation and reconnection

1   With the combined engine/transmission removed from the car as described in the preceding Section, remove the cover plate from the lower front face of the clutch bellhousing.

2   Unscrew and remove the engine to bellhousing connecting bolts including the starter motor bolts.

3   Pull the transmission from the engine in a straight line taking care not to allow its weight to hang upon the input shaft whilst the latter is still engaged in the clutch mechanism.

4   Reconnection is a reversal of separation, but if the clutch mechanism has been disturbed, centralise the driven plate as described in Chapter 5. Note the special nuts used at the side bolt locations of the bellhousing (photo).

12 Engine (leaving automatic transmission in car) – removal and refitting

1   The operations are very similar to those described in Section 9, but the following special factors must be observed.

2   Disconnect the transmission vacuum capsule pipe from the inlet manifold.

3   Remove the grille plate from the front lower face of the torque converter housing.

4   The three bolts which connect the torque converter to the engine driveplate must now be removed. To do this, unscrew the first bolt and then turn the crankshaft to bring each succeeding bolt into view in the grille plate aperture.

5   Remove the engine to torque converter bellhousing bolts.

6   As soon as the engine is removed, retain the torque converter in its fully installed position using a clip similar to the one shown.

7   Refitting is a reversal of removal but adjust the governor control cable as described in Chapter 6, Part 2.

8   Refill the engine with oil and coolant (Chapter 2).

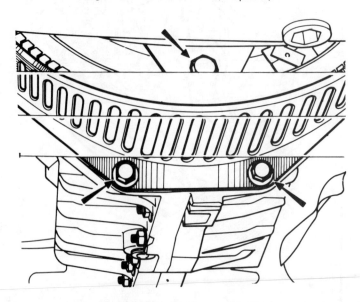

Fig. 1.13 Torque converter grille plate bolts (Sec 12)

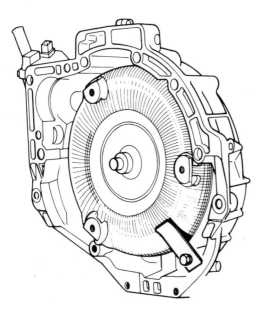

Fig. 1.14 Torque converter retaining clip (Sec 12)

13 Engine (with automatic transmission) – removal and refitting

1 Carry out the operations described in Section 9, paragraphs 1 to 15.
2 Carry out the operations described in Section 10, paragraphs 3 to 7.
3 Disconnect the speed selector control. Do this by moving the control lever to 1st gear position then disconnect the rod at the computer unit and selector lever ends (Chapter 7).
4 Remove the dipstick guide/filler tube.
5 Disconnect the governor control cable.
6 Support the rear of the automatic transmission on a jack and then unbolt and remove the crossmember.
7 Attach a hoist and slings to the engine/automatic transmission and take its weight. The shorter slings should be attached to the front of the engine so that when the weight is taken and the jack under the transmission is removed, the engine/transmission will be inclined downward at the rear by 45°.
8 Disconnect the engine mountings.
9 Hoist the engine/transmission up and out of the engine compartment.
10 Refitting is a reversal of removal, adjust the governor and selector control linkage as described in Chapter 7, Part 2.
11 Refill the engine with oil and coolant (Chapter 2).

14 Engine/automatic transmission – separation and reconnection

1 With the combined engine/transmission removed from the car as described in the preceding Section, remove the torque converter grille plate.
2 Unscrew and remove each of the three bolts which secure the torque converter to the driveplate. The crankshaft will have to be rotated to bring each bolt into view in the aperture from which the grille plate was removed.
3 Unscrew and remove the engine to torque converter bellhousing connecting bolts.
4 Remove the starter motor.
5 Withdraw the transmission from the engine taking care that the torque converter does not become displaced from its shaft.
6 Once removed, retain the torque converter using a clip as shown.
7 Reconnection is a reversal of separation, but make sure that the driveplate is mated to the torque converter so that the arm on the driveplate, which incorporates the machined angles (marked with paint), is aligned with the boss on the torque converter which is opposite to the timing dimple on the torque converter.

15 Engine dismantling – general

1 Owners who have dismantled engines will know the need for a strong work bench and many tools and pieces of equipment, which make their life much easier when going through the process of dismantling an engine. For those who are doing a dismantling job for the first time, there are a few 'musts' in the way of preparation which, if not done, will only cause frustration and long delays in the job in the long run. It is essential to have sufficient space in which to work. Dismantling and reassembly is not going to be completed all in one go and it is therefore absolutely essential that you have sufficient space to leave things as they are when necessary. A strong work bench is also necessary together with a good engineer's vice. If you have no alternative other than to work at ground level, make sure that the floor is at least level and covered with a suitable wooden or composition material on which to work. If dirt and grit are allowed to get into any of the component parts all work which you carry out may be completely wasted. Before actually placing the engine wherever it is that you may be carrying out the dismantling, make sure that the exterior is now completely and thoroughly cleaned.
2 Once dismantling begins it is advisable to clean the parts as they are removed. A small bath of paraffin is about the best thing to use for this, but do not let parts which have oilways in them become immersed in paraffin otherwise there may be a residue which could cause harmful effects later on. If paraffin does get into oilways every effort should be made to blow it out. For this it may be necessary to carry the particular part to a garage fitted with a high pressure air hose. Short oilways such as there are in the crankshaft can be cleared easily with wire.
3 Always obtain a complete set of gaskets when the engine is being dismantled – no gaskets on an engine are re-usable and any attempt to do so is quite unjustified in view of the relatively small cost involved. Before throwing any gaskets away, however, make sure that you have the replacements to hand. If, for example, a particular gasket cannot be obtained it may be necessary to make one, and the pattern of the old one is useful in such cases.
4 Generally speaking, it is best to start dismantling the engine from the top downwards. In any case, make sure it is firmly supported at all times so that it does not topple over whilst you are undoing the very tight nuts and bolts which will be encountered. Always replace nuts and bolts into their locations once the particular part has been removed, if possible. Otherwise keep them in convenient tins or pots in their groups, so that when the time comes to reassemble there is the minimum of confusion.

16 Engine ancillaries – removal

1 A word of warning at this stage is that you should always be sure that it is more economic to dismantle and overhaul a worn engine rather than simply exchange it with a Renault Factory Exchange Unit.
2 If you are intending to obtain an exchange engine complete, it will be necessary first of all to remove all those parts of the engine which are not included in the exchange. If you are stripping the engine completely yourself with the likelihood of some outside work to be done by specialists, all these items will be taken off anyway.
3 Short engines are not available from Renault Limited. It is as well to check with whoever may be supplying the replacement exchange unit what it is necessary to remove, but as a general guide the following items will have to be taken off. Reference is given to the appropriate Chapter for details of removal of each of these items.

Alternator – Chapter 10
Distributor – Chapter 4
Thermostat – Chapter 2
Carburettor – Chapter 3
Inlet/exhaust manifold – Chapter 3
Fuel pump – Chapter 3
Engine mounting brackets – Chapter 1
Distributor/oil pump drive – Chapter 1
Gearbox – Chapter 6
Clutch – Chapter 5
Dipstick – Chapter 1
Fan and its pulley – Chapter 2
Starter motor – Chapter 10
Oil filter cartridge – Chapter 1

17 Engine – complete dismantling (engine removed)

1   It is not necessary to remove the valve rocker gear from the cylinder head in order to remove the cylinder head from the engine, but where preferred, carry out the following operations.

2   Remove the rocker cover by undoing the three retaining nuts and lift off. Lift off the rocker cover gasket.

3   Breather pipes etc. will differ from model to model and should be extracted with care. All lift off easily.

4   The rocker gear is attached to the cylinder head by four fixings – two bolts and two longer studs and nuts (these longer studs act as locating points for the rocker cover). Undo the four fixings with the appropriate spanners and then lift off the rocker shaft and pedestals. Make sure that the pushrods do not 'stick' to the rocker arms.

5   Remove the cylinder head as described in Section 4. Remove the distributor drivegear. Do this by screwing a 12.0 mm bolt into the drivegear (photo).

6   With the cylinder head and the pushrods removed the tappets can be extracted (photo).

7   Each one can be removed by pushing one's index finger right into the tappet, pushing out the oil and then pulling it upwards. A technique will soon be developed to raise them up in this way.

8   Place the tappets in their correct order for inspection and correct replacement.

9   Remove the crankshaft pulley. In order to be able to unscrew the

17.5 Distributor drivegear

17.6 Tappet (cam follower)

pulley securing bolt, the flywheel starter ring gear will probably have to be jammed with a suitable tool.

10 Remove the sump and oil pump.

11 Using a socket undo and remove the timing cover fixing bolt and retrieve the washers. Now remove the timing cover and pull off the gasket.

12 Remove the chain tensioner according to type, (see next Section). The small mesh filter screen now exposed can be left in position unless it requires cleaning.

13 Unscrew and remove the camshaft sprocket retaining bolt. Withdraw the sprocket with timing chain, disengaging the chain from the crankshaft sprocket.

14 Remove the camshaft flange plate bolts and carefully withdraw the camshaft.

15 There is no need to mark the position of the flywheel in relation to the crankshaft mounting flange as the bolt holes are offset and it can only be fitted to the crankshaft flange in one position.

16 Unscrew and remove the flywheel bolts. On some models a lockplate is used under the bolt heads and the tabs will have to be flattened first.

17 It will be necessary to use a little leverage in order to draw the flywheel off and great care should be taken that it does not come off with a sudden jerk and fall down. One way of preventing this is by putting a stud, another, longer bolt with the head sawn off, into one of the bolt holes so that when the flywheel comes free, the end of the stud will support it.

18 Remove the liner/piston/rod assemblies as described in Section 8.

19 Mark the main bearing caps from 1 to 5 (No. 1 at flywheel end) also as to which way round the caps are fitted.

20 Using a good quality socket spanner remove the two bolts from each of the five main bearing caps. Then lift off each of the caps.

21 With the five main bearing caps removed the crankshaft may be carefully lifted out of the block and it should then be placed somewhere safe where it cannot fall or be damaged. The upper half main bearing shells may then be removed from the crankcase, together with the semi-circular thrust washers fitted at the centre main bearing.

22 Remove and discard the crankshaft oil seal.

23 With the engine now completely dismantled, each component should be cleaned, further dismantled (where necessary) and either renovated or renewed as described in the following Section.

18 Engine – examination, renovation and dismantling of major assemblies

Rocker gear

1   The rocker shaft can be dismantled by taking off the arms, pedestals and springs. DO NOT try to extract the two press-fit end plugs. Unclip the end retaining clips and after noting the order, slide all the parts off the shaft. Check the shaft for straightness by rolling it on the bench. It is most unlikely that it will deviate from normal, but, if it does, then no attempt must be made to straighten it, purchase a new shaft. The surface of the shaft should be free from any worn ridges caused by the rocker arms. If any wear is present, renew the shaft. Wear is only likely to have occurred if the rocker shaft oil holes have become blocked.

2   Check the rocker arms for wear of the rocker bushes, for wear of the adjusting ball ended screws. Wear in the rocker arm bush can be checked by gripping the rocker arm tip and holding the rocker arm in place on the shaft, noting if there is any lateral rocker arm shake. If

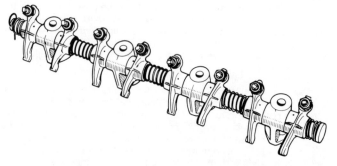

Fig. 1.15 Rocker shaft assembly (Sec 18)

shake is present, and the arm is very loose on the shaft, a new bush or rocker arm must be fitted.

3   Check the tip of the rocker arm where it bears on the valve head for cracking or serious wear on the case hardening. If none is present reuse the rocker arm. Check the lower half of the ball on the end of the rocker arm adjusting screw. On high performance engines wear on the ball and top of the pushrod is easily noted by the unworn 'pip' which fits in the small central oil hole on the ball. The larger this 'pip' the more wear has taken place to both the ball and the pushrod. Check the pushrods for straightness by rolling them on the bench. Renew any that are bent.

Cylinder head and block
4   Check for cracks. The cost of welding the alloy material must be weighed against a new casting. Threaded holes which have stripped, may have proprietary thread inserts installed to rectify.
5   For complete renovation procedure for the cylinder head, refer to Section 19.

Timing gears and chain
6   Examine the teeth on both the crankshaft gearwheel and the camshaft gearwheel for wear. Each tooth forms an inverted V with the gearwheel periphery, and if worn, the side of each tooth under tension will be slightly concave in shape when compared with the other side of the tooth, ie, one side of the inverted V will be concave when compared with the other. If any sign of wear is present the gearwheels must be renewed.
7   Examine the links of the chain for side slackness and renew the chain if any slackness is noticeable when compared with a new chain. It is a sensible precaution to renew the chain at about 30 000 miles (48 000 km) and at a lesser mileage if the engine is stripped down for a major overhaul. The actual rollers on a very badly worn chain may be slightly grooved.

Tappets (cam followers)
8   Examine the bearing surface of the tappets which lie on the camshaft. Any indentation in this surface or any cracks indicate serious wear and the tappets should be renewed. Thoroughly clean them out, removing all traces of sludge. It is most unlikely that the sides of the tappets will prove worn, but, if they are a very loose fit in their bores and can readily be rocked, they should be exchanged for new units. It is very unusual to find any wear in the tappets, and any wear is likely to occur at a very high mileage.

Camshaft
9   Inspect the camshaft bearing surfaces and the lobes for wear, scoring or pitting.
10 The camshaft runs directly in the cylinder block and any wear in the bearings is rare.

Crankshaft main and big-end bearings
11 Examine the crankpin and main journal surfaces for signs of scoring or scratches. Check the ovality of the crankpins at different positions with a micrometer. If more than 0.001 inch (0.0254 mm) out of round, the crankpins will have to be reground. It will also have to be reground if there are any scores or scratches present. Also check the journals in the same fashion. Specialist engineering firms will carry out this work and supply new shell bearings to the correct undersizes.
12 It is important to retain the roll hardening intact over a 140° sector as shown in the diagram. This is not always appreciated by the regrinder.
13 Big-end bearing failure is accompanied by a noisy knocking from the crankcase and a slight drop in oil pressure. Main bearing failure is accompanied by vibration which can be quite severe as the engine speed rises and falls, and a drop in oil pressure.
14 Bearings which have not broken up, but are badly worn, will give rise to low oil pressure and some vibration. Inspect the big-ends, main bearings, and thrust washers for signs of general wear, scoring, pitting and scratches. The bearings should be matt grey in colour. With lead indium bearings should a trace of copper colour be noticed the bearings are badly worn as the lead bearing material has worn away to expose the indium underlay. Renew the bearings if they are in this condition or if there is any sign of scoring or pitting.
15 The undersizes available are designed to correspond with the regrind sizes. The bearings are in fact slightly more than the undersize

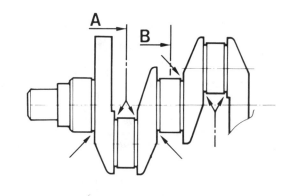

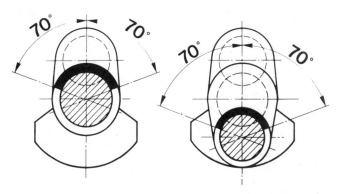

Fig. 1.16 Crankshaft regrind, roll hardening intact zones (arrowed). A and B cross sections (Sec 18)

as running clearances have been allowed for during their manufacture.
16 Never file the bearings caps to try and take up bearing wear.
17 Finally, check for wear in the clutch pilot bearing which is located in the centre of the crankshaft rear flange. The bearing may be of plain bush type or a ball-race. If wear is evident, extract the bearing using an extractor or by filling it with grease and driving in a close-fitting rod. The hydraulic pressure generated will eject the bearing. Where a plain bush is fitted, it is often possible to extract it by screwing in a thread cutting tap.

Cylinder liners
18 The cylinder bores must be examined for taper, ovality, scoring and scratches. Start by carefully examining the top of the cylinder bore. If they are at all worn a very slight ridge will be found on the thrust side. This marks the top of the piston ring travel. The owner will have a good indication of the bore wear prior to dismantling the engine, or removing the cylinder head. Excessive oil consumption accompanied by blue smoke from the exhaust is a sure sign of worn cylinder bores and piston rings.
19 Measure the bore diameter just under the ridge with a micrometer and compare it with the diameter at the bottom of the bore, which is not subject to wear. If the differences between the two measurements are more than 0.006 inch (0.1524 mm) then it will be necessary to fit new pistons and liner assemblies. If no micrometer is available remove the ring from a piston and place the piston in each bore in turn about $\frac{3}{4}$ inch below the top of the bore. If an 0.010 inch (0.254 mm) feeler gauge can be slid between the piston and the cylinder wall on the thrust side of the bore then remedial action must be taken.

Piston/connecting rod
20 A visual check only can be carried out to observe whether any movement or play can be seen when the piston is held still and the connecting rod pushed and pulled alternately.
21 If there has been evidence of small end knock with the engine at normal working temperature then the connecting rod/piston assembly

should be taken to a Renault dealer as special tools are required to dismantle and refit these components.

22 If the old pistons are to be refitted carefully remove the piston rings and then thoroughly clean them. Take particular care to clean out the piston ring grooves. At the same time do not scratch the aluminium in any way. If new rings are to be fitted to the old pistons then the top ring should be stepped so as to clear the ridge left above the previous top ring. If a normal but oversize new ring is fitted it will hit the ridge and break because the new ring will not have worn in the same way as the old, which will have worn in union with the ridge.

23 Before fitting the rings on the pistons each should be inserted approximately 3 inches (76.2 mm) down the cylinder bore and the gap measured with a feeler gauge. Remove glaze from the bores using fine glasspaper.

24 This should be between 0.015 inch (0.3810 mm) and 0.038 inch (0.9652 mm). It is essential that the gap should be measured at the bottom of the ring travel, as if it is measured at the top of a worn bore and gives a perfect fit, it could easily seize at the bottom. If the ring gap is too small rub down the ends of the ring wth a very fine file until the gap, when fitted, is correct. To keep the rings square in the bore for measurement line each up in turn by inserting an old piston in the bore upside down, and use the piston to push the ring down about 3 inches (76.2 mm). Remove the piston and measure the piston ring gap.

25 When refitting new pistons and rings to new liners the piston ring gap can be measured at the top of the bore as the bore will not now taper. It is not necessary to measure the side clearance in the piston ring grooves with the rings fitted as the groove dimensions are accurately machined during manufacture. When fitting new oil control rings to old pistons it may be necessary to have the groove in this instance widened by machining to accept the new wider rings.

26 Take great care when fitting a piston ring not to expand it too much. The safest way to fit a ring is to slide two or three feeler blades behind it at equidistant points to act as slides and to prevent the ring dropping into other grooves as it is pushed down the piston.

Flywheel and starter ring gear

27 Examine the clutch driven plate contact surface on the flywheel. If it is scored for whatever reason or tiny cracks are evident due to overheating, then it may be possible to remachine the flywheel on Type 810 engines provided the dimension C is not reduced below the specified figure shown in the diagram. Otherwise a new flywheel will have to be fitted.

28 If the teeth on the flywheel starter ring are badly worn, or if some are missing, then it will be necessary to remove the ring. This is achieved by splitting the ring with a cold chisel. The greatest care should be taken not to damage the flywheel during this process. Unless you can heat the new ring gear to an even temperature of 350°C (662°F) by flame or in an oven, leave the fitting to your dealer.

29 The ring should be tapped gently down onto its register and left to cool naturally when the shrinkage of the metal on cooling will ensure that it is a secure and permanent fit. Great care must be taken not to overheat the ring, as if this happens, the temper of the ring will be lost.

30 Note carefully that the chamfered side of the teeth on the ring must provide a lead in to the starter motor drive and must be fitted the correct way round.

31 Do not attempt to renew the starter ring gear on the torque converter fitted to an automatic gearbox. Leave it to a specialist or exchange the convertor as an assembly — see Chapter 7.

Oil pump

32 Only work on the oil pump with it scrupulously clean.

33 Unscrew the four setscrews which hold the cover face and filter to the main body.

34 Take care with the ball seating boss, the ball bearing and the pressure relief spring which will come away when the cover face is removed.

35 Take out the driven gear and then the drivegear and the shaft.

36 Clean all the parts with petrol or paraffin and check the condition of the splines on the driveshaft. They should be unchewed and straight.

37 Check the condition of the ball valve and its seating. There should be no irregularity nor ridges in either. The ball should be renewed anyway if you have reached this stage.

38 Check the spring. If possible renew it anyway at this stage. Obtain the correct replacement without fail.

39 Check the clearance between the pump gears and their body. If over 0.20 mm (0.008 in) replace the gears. Also check the cover joint face for marks and irregularities. Renew if scored.

40 It may be found that if two or more parts need replacing it is more economic and quicker to replace the whole pump. There is no exchange scheme.

Timing chain tensioner

41 One of three different types of chain tensioner may be encountered.

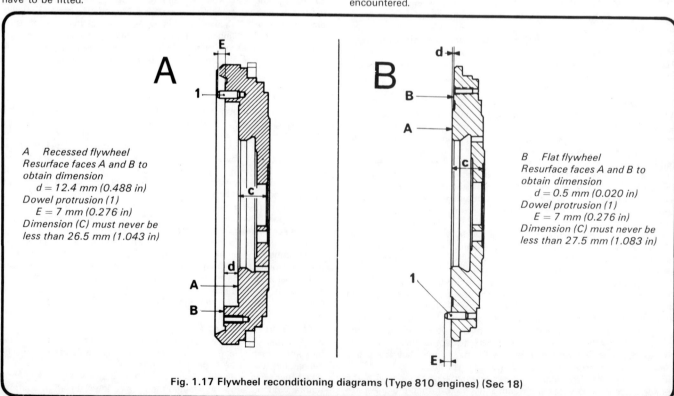

A   Recessed flywheel
Resurface faces A and B to obtain dimension
    d = 12.4 mm (0.488 in)
Dowel protrusion (1)
    E = 7 mm (0.276 in)
Dimension (C) must never be less than 26.5 mm (1.043 in)

B   Flat flywheel
Resurface faces A and B to obtain dimension
    d = 0.5 mm (0.020 in)
Dowel protrusion (1)
    E = 7 mm (0.276 in)
Dimension (C) must never be less than 27.5 mm (1.083 in)

Fig. 1.17 Flywheel reconditioning diagrams (Type 810 engines) (Sec 18)

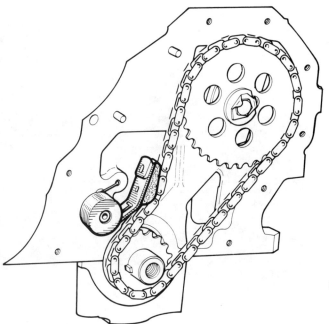

Fig. 1.18 Mechanical type chain tensioner (Sec 18)

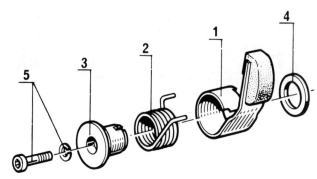

Fig. 1.19 Components of the mechanical type tensioner (Sec 18)

1   Slipper   4   Washer
2   Spring   5   Screw and self-locking washer
3   Spindle bush

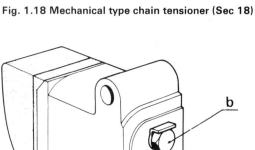

Fig. 1.20 Manual initial take-up type chain tensioner (Sec 18)

b   Plug

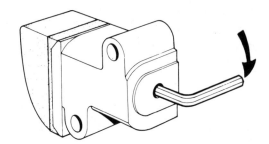

Fig. 1.21 Allen key for locking/unlocking chain tensioner (Sec 18)

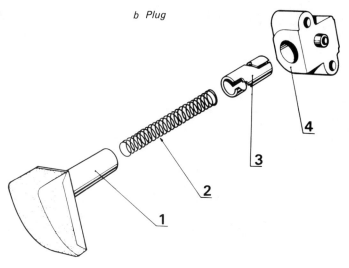

Fig. 1.22 Components of the automatic initial take-up type chain
tensioner (Sec 18)

1   Slipper   3   Piston
2   Spring   4   Tensioner body

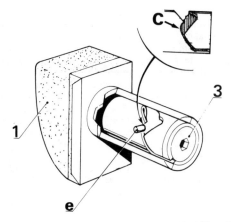

Fig. 1.23 Automatic chain tensioner assembled (Sec 18)

1   Slipper   c   Notch
3   Piston   e   Peg

18.45 Automatic timing chain tensioner components

19.3 Compressing a valve spring

42   The mechanical tension spring type should be inspected for grooving of the slipper which bears against the chain. If grooved deeply, renew it.

43   The tensioner is dismantled by prising the slipper away from the chain while the retaining screw is extracted with an Allen key.

44   **The manual initial take up type** can be unbolted and removed if the plug (b) is first removed and a 3 mm Allen key used to turn the tensioner spindle anti-clockwise.

45   **The automatic initial take up type** is removable as two separate components – the tensioner body and the piston/slipper assembly (photo).

46   The body incorporates an oil filter gauze.

19 Cylinder head – dismantling, decarbonising and reassembly

1   With the valve rocker gear removed and with the coolant pump taken off, see Chapter 2, the valves are relatively easy to remove with the cylinder head on the bench, with a proprietary spring compressor.

2   Place the cylinder head on the 'spark plug' side and fit the compressor. Work should start at one end and follow on down the head.

3   Tighten the compressor so that the 'foot' is in the centre of the valve being released. The 'claw' should sit on the top of the valve spring cap. Continue to compress the spring until the collets are loose (photo).

4   Release the pressure on the valve cap once the collets are extracted, remove the cap, the spring (single springs only are used on all valves) and the lower seat.

5   Do one combustion chamber at a time before extracting the valves themselves. Repeat the process for each chamber and record the order in which the valves are removed. Place them through a piece of cardboard in order, as you would the pushrods, for further inspection.

6   Examine the valve guides internally for wear. If the valves are a very loose fit in the guides and there is the slightest suspicion of lateral rocking using a new valve, then new guides will have to be fitted. If the valve guides have been removed compare them internally by visual inspection with a new guide as well as testing them for rocking with a new valve.

7   Valve guide renewal should be left to a Renault agent who will have the required press and mandrel. Work of this kind in a light alloy head without the correct tools can be disastrous.

8   Examine the heads of the valves for pitting and burning, especially the heads of the exhaust valves. The valve seatings should be examined at the same time. If the pitting on valve and seat is very slight the marks can be removed by grinding the seats and valves together with coarse, and then fine, valve grinding paste. Where bad pitting has occurred to the valve seats it will be necessary to recut them and fit new valves. If the valve seats are so worn that they cannot be recut, then it will be necessary to recut them and fit new

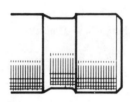

BK

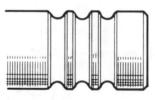

MK

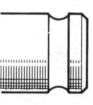

KK

Fig. 1.24 Valve collets (Sec 19)

BK Inlet   *KK Inlet and exhaust*
MK Exhaust

valves. If the valve seats are so worn that they cannot be recut, then it will be necessary to fit new valve seat inserts. These latter two jobs should be entrusted to the local Renault agent or engineering works. In practice it is very seldom that the seats are so badly worn that they require renewal. Normally, it is the exhaust valve that is too badly worn for replacement, and the owner can easily purchase a new set of valves and match them to the seats by valve grinding.

9   Valve grinding is carried out as follows. Smear a trace of coarse carborundum paste on the seat face and apply a suction grinder tool to the valve head. With a semi-rotary motion, grind the valve head to its seat, lifting the valve occasionally to redistribute the grinding paste. When a dull matt even surface finish is produced on both the valve seat and the valve, wipe off the paste and repeat the process with fine carborundum paste, lifting and turning the valve to redistribute the paste as before. A light spring placed under the valve head will greatly ease this operation. When a smooth unbroken ring of light grey matt finish is produced on both valve and valve seat faces, the grinding operation is completed.

10   Scrape away all carbon from the valve head and the valve stem. Carefully clean away every trace of grinding compound, taking great care to leave none in the ports or in the valve guides. Clean the valves and valve seats with a paraffin soaked rag then with a clean rag, and finally, if an air line is available, blow the valves, valve guides and valve ports clean.

11   Carefully remove with a wire brush and blunt scraper all traces of carbon deposits from the combustion spaces and the ports. The valve head stems and valve guides should also be freed from any carbon deposits. Wash the combustion spaces and ports down with petrol and clean the cylinder head surface free of any gasket cement or foreign matter.

12   Clean the pistons and top of the cylinder bores. If the pistons are still in the block then is it essential that great care is taken to ensure that no carbon gets into the cylinder bores as this could scratch the cylinder walls or cause damage to the piston and rings. To ensure this does not happen, first turn the crankshaft so that two of the pistons are at the top of their bores. Stuff rag into the other two bores or seal them off with paper and masking tape. The coolant passages and oilways should also be covered with small pieces of masking tape to prevent particles of carbon entering the cooling system and damaging the water pump.

13   Press a little grease into the gap between the cylinder walls and the two pistons which are to be worked on. With a blunt scraper carefully scrape away the carbon from the piston crown, taking great care not to scratch the aluminium. Also scrape away the carbon from the surrounding lip of the cylinder wall. When all carbon has been removed, scrape away the grease which will now be contaminated with carbon particles, taking care not to press any into the bores. To assist prevention of carbon build-up the piston crown can be polished with a metal polish. Remove the rags or masking tape from the other two cylinders and turn the crankshaft so that the two pistons which were at the bottom are now at the top. Place a rag or masking tape in the cylinders which have been decarbonised and proceed as just described.

14   With the head perfectly clean and having carried out all the necessary renewals and renovations as required, lightly lubricate the valve stem for the first valve to be replaced and fit it in its guide. If the same valves are being used again they should have been kept in order so that they may go back in the same place.

15   Using the same valve spring compressor that was used in disassembly, replace the valves, springs and collets in order. The closer coils of the valve springs go next to the cylinder head.

16   With the spring fully compressed pop the two collet pairs into the top of the spring seat. The collets vary in type according to date of production (see illustration). Don't attempt to engage the wrong collets with an unsuitable valve stem cut-out.

20 Lubrication system

1   Oil is drawn from the sump, pressurised by a gear type oil pump located within the sump pan and then passed through a cartridge type oil filter.

2   From the filter, oil is directed through the various passages and oilways to reach all bearings and friction surfaces.

3   An oil pressure regulating valve is incorporated in the pump.

4   The cylinder bores are splash lubricated.

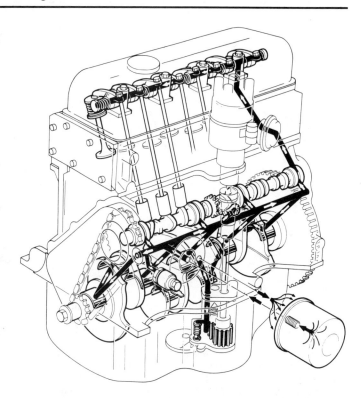

Fig. 1.25 Lubrication system (Type 810 engine) (Sec 20)

5   On later model cylinder blocks, the camshaft has an oil bath located below it. One difference that this makes is that the fuel pump is now retained to the cylinder block by two bolts and a nut.

21 Crankcase ventilation system

1   This system is designed to draw oil/combustion fumes from the engine. These fumes are created by the heating of the engine oil and by combustion gases passing the piston rings and accumulating in the crankcase.

2   The fumes are drawn out of the rocker cover by hoses connected to the inlet manifold and the carburettor air intake.

3   A calibrated jet is located inside the end of the manifold hose as an essential part of this dual ventilation circuit which varies the fume extraction between manifold and air intake according to engine vacuum conditions.

22 Engine – reassembly

Crankshaft and main bearings

1   Stand the cylinder block inverted on the bench and gather together the bearing caps, new bearing shells and have the crankshaft without the flywheel fitted alongside lined up in the way in which it will eventually be placed into the cylinder block. Make sure that the oilways in the crankshaft are all quite clear.

2   Make sure that the bearing housings in the cylinder block are perfectly clean and smooth in preparation for the fitting of the top halves of the main bearing shells. Each bearing shell has an oil hole in it, some have two, and this must line up with the corresponding hole in the cylinder block. Each shell is notched, and this notch also must line up with the corresponding notch in the cylinder block. Carefully fit each shell into its proper position, taking care not to bend, distort or scratch it in any way. When they are in position lubricate the shells with a liberal quantity of clean engine oil.

3   Making sure that the crankshaft is the right way round, next pick it up and very carefully lower it square and straight into position on the shell bearings in the crankcase.

4   Again, make sure that the bearing caps are perfectly clean and fit the shells so that the notches in their ends line up and fit snugly into the grooves in the bearing caps. There are no oilways in the bearing

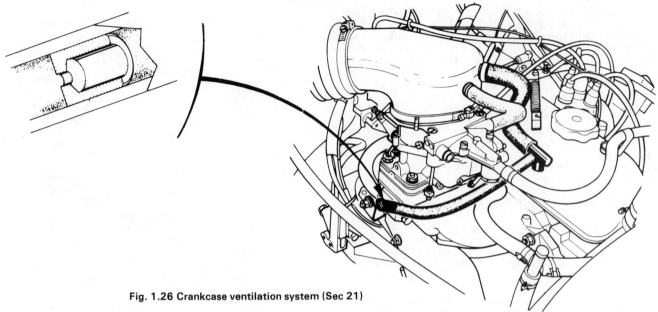

Fig. 1.26 Crankcase ventilation system (Sec 21)

caps so that the holes in the end bearing shells will not line up with anything.

5   The crankshaft endfloat is controlled by two semi-circular thrust washers which fit at the sides of the centre main bearing journal. Place these in position and slide them round into the gap between the bearing housing and the flange of the crankshaft, making sure that the white metal/grooved faces abut onto the crankshaft. Once these are in position the endfloat can be checked by pushing the crankshaft as far as it will go in one direction and measuring the gap between the face of the thrust washer and the machined surface of the flange with a feeler blade. Endfloat should be between 0.05 and 0.125 mm (0.002 and 0.009 in). (Adjusting flanges of differing size are available – the correct ones should have been supplied with the new bearing by your machinists).

6   Next arrange all the bearing caps complete with their shells so that you know precisely where each one should go. They are easily identifiable by their particular shape. As there is the possibility of a seepage of oil through the end main bearing cap mating faces it is permissible to put a very thin smear of non-setting jointing compound onto the outside edge of the vertical face where the bearing cap locates into the crankcase. Lubricate the main journals of the crankshaft liberally with clean engine oil and place all the bearing caps in position and fit the bolts. The front main bearing cap has a machined front face and this must line up with the rear surface of the cylinder block. Make sure that this is done with a straight edge before finally tightening down the bolts.

7   When all the caps are settled correctly in position, tighten the bolts down evenly, starting at No. 1, at the flywheel end and working to No. 5, using a torque spanner, to the correct torque as given under the specifications. When this has been done revolve the crankshaft to make sure that there are no intermittent tight spots. Any signs that

something is binding whilst the crankshaft is being revolved indicates that something is wrong and there may be a high spot on one of the bearings or on the crankshaft itself. This must be investigated or a damaged bearing could result.

8   Now fit the front main bearing oil seal. This is a circular oil seal, which has a very fragile inner lip. Always fit a new one. Oil it well with engine oil, and press it by hand into the correct position. Tap it gently fully home with a piece of wooden dowel until it is fully in. There should be a slight recess between it and the outer edge of the block/bearing cap.

Flywheel or driveplate

9   Locate the flywheel on the crankshaft rear flange. Make sure that the marks made before removal are in alignment (photo).

10 Screw in new bolts (do not use the original ones as they will have lost their self-locking characteristic) and tighten to specified torque (photo).

Piston/rod/liner

11 As mentioned in Section 18 the connecting rods and gudgeon pins are an interference fit requiring heat to enable them to be correctly assembled. This work should be entrusted to someone with the necessary experience and equipment. It is important that the piston and connecting rod are assembled the proper way round to ensure that the offset of the piston is on the thrust side of the cylinder.

12 To check this, make sure that the relationship of the piston crown arrow to the connecting rod big-end number is as shown (arrow towards flywheel, big-end number away from camshaft) photo.

13 Fit the piston/connecting rod/liner assemblies as described in Section 8.

22.9 Fitting flywheel

22.10 Special flywheel bolts

22.12 Piston crown directional arrow

Oil pump and sump

14 Fit the oil pump and sump as described in Sections 6 and 7.

Camshaft and tappets (cam followers)

15 Refitting the camshaft and tappets is virtually the reversal of their removal. Never refit the tappets before the camshaft. The distributor and drivegear must of course be removed.

16 Clean the timing cover end of the block.

17 Lubricate the lobes and bearing surfaces of the camshaft.

18 Insert the camshaft into the block straight and gently. You do not want to damage the lobes or bearing surfaces. With no obstructions and once fully home bolt up the flange.

19 Check the camshaft endfloat. If outside the specified tolerance, renew the flange plate.

Timing gear, chain and cover

20 Before replacing any of the timing gear check that all the cylinder block oil ducts to the timing gear are free and not covered by any dirt or old type timing cover gasket.

21 If the crankshaft has not yet had its sprocket remounted, smear the end of the shaft with oil.

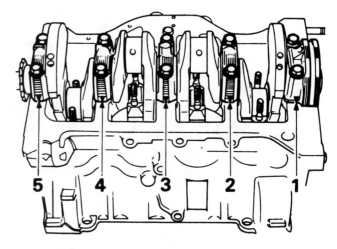

Fig. 1.27 Main bearing sequence. No. 1 at flywheel end (Sec 22)

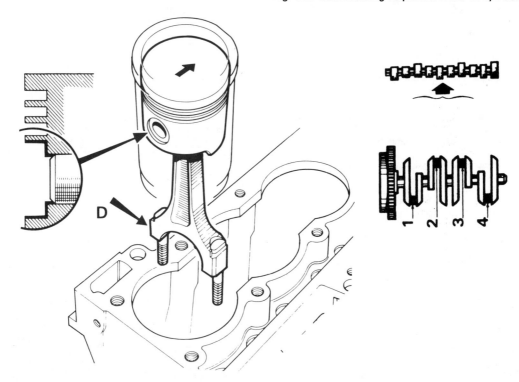

Fig. 1.28 Piston to rod alignment (Type 810) (Sec 22)

D Rod number

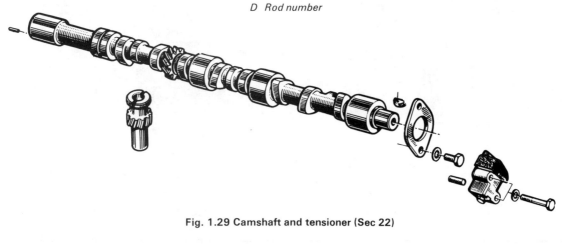

Fig. 1.29 Camshaft and tensioner (Sec 22)

23.23 Timing sprocket marks

22.30A Timing cover gasket in position

22.30B Fitting timing chain cover

22 Push in the Woodruff key and after heating the sprocket in boiling water push it onto the shaft with the timing punch mark outermost. It should slide on up to its fullest extent.

23 Place the camshaft sprocket with its arrow punched mark facing outwards just onto the camshaft. Turn the sprocket and camshaft so that the two arrow marks, on the two sprockets, camshaft and crankshaft, are nearest to each other in a straight line with the centres of the two sprockets (photo).

24 Remove the camshaft sprocket without disturbing the camshaft and fit the timing chain onto the sprocket.

25 Achieve the same positioning of the sprockets again but this time with the chain on the crankshaft sprocket as well. Press the camshaft sprocket onto the camshaft. Check the alignment again.

26 Place the flat washer, locking tab and bolt onto the camshaft sprocket and screw it in.

27 Hold the camshaft sprocket with a screwdriver through one of its centre drillings and tighten the bolt.

28 Lock the locking tab with a pair of grips.

29 Refit the chain tensioner together with its thrust plate.

30 Now set the chain tensioner according to type (see Section 18).
On manual take-up type tensioners this means turning the Allen

key clockwise until the slipper presses lightly on the timing chain.
On automatic take-up type tensioners, remove the slipper/piston and lock it in its retracted state using an Allen key. Insert the piston/slipper into the tensioner body and bolt the assembly to the crankcase. Depress the piston sharply and release it when it will tension the chain. Once the engine is started, oil, filtered through the small mesh filter will be pumped into the tensioner to maintain the correct timing chain tension hydraulically.
Where a mechanical type tensioner is fitted, engagement of the tensioner spring in the hole in the cylinder block sets the device (photos).

31 The timing cover should be replaced, as a direct reversal of the removal sequence. Inside the cover is an oil seal, similar to the main bearing oil seal on the end of the crankshaft. This should be driven out with a socket and replaced by tapping lightly. Never re-use an old seal.

Pushrods, cylinder head, valve rocker gear

32 Insert the pushrods into the cam followers.

33 Refit the cylinder head as described in Section 5 (photo).

34 Replacement of the rocker gear onto the cylinder head is again a

Fig. 1.30 Camshaft sprocket, chain and chain guides (Sec 22)

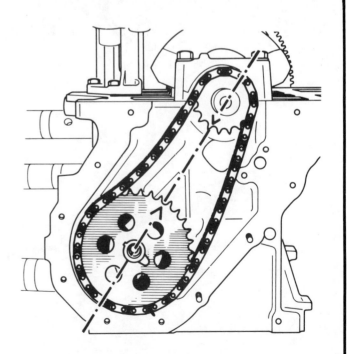
Fig. 1.31 Timing marks in alignment (Sec 22)

22.33 Fitting rocker cover

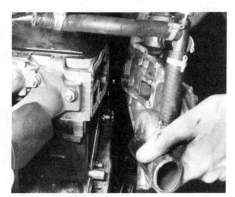

22.45 Fitting coolant pump

22.50 Fitting rocker cover

direct reversal sequence of its removal. Do not forget the washers under the two centre bolts and before tightening these two bolts and the two nuts on the outer studs, that all the ball pins are properly seated in the cups on the ends of the pushrods. Then tighten the shaft down progressively.

35 Do not fit the rocker cover until the valve clearances have been adjusted (see next Section).

36 The distributor drivegear should now be fitted. To do this, first rotate the crankshaft until No. 1 piston is at TDC. This position can be verified in one of two ways:

(a) *Mark on flywheel opposite TDC mark on scale*
(b) *Notch on crankshaft pulley opposite TDC mark on scale.*

37 Remember No. 1 cylinder is at the flywheel end of the engine and piston No. 1 must be on its firing stroke, not exhaust stroke. This can be checked by placing a finger over No. 1 spark plug hole and feeling the compression being generated or by observing that No. 4 cylinder rocker arms are in balance (rocking).

38 Screw a 12 mm diameter bolt into the distributor drivegear as a

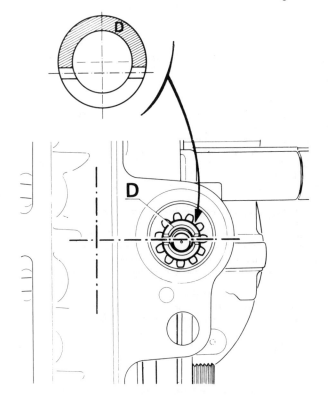

Fig. 1.32 Distributor/oil pump drivegear correctly set (Sec 22)

D Larger offset

means of holding it, while the gear is inserted into its recess. When the gear has meshed and is fully inserted, the distributor drive slot must be at right angles (90°) to the engine centre line with the larger of the offsets towards the flywheel.

39 Refit the clutch (Chapter 5) and other ancillary components which include the following items.

40 The fuel pump. Do not forget the proper gaskets which should be new ones.

41 The oil pressure sender unit. Do not forget the copper sealing ring.

42 The oil filter, cartridge type, must be fitted, replace it with a new one now. Make sure a new sealing ring is fitted and that the stud and the ring are greased, before fitment. Tighten the oil filter cartridge with hand pressure only even though a strap or chain wrench was probably required to remove the old one.

43 Fit new spark plugs. Clean their orifices with a non-fluffy rag and screw them in by hand. Do not overtighten them with a plug spanner for they may strip the thread in the aluminium head.

44 Lower the distributor into its position on the block. Make sure that the offset drive mates up with the drive pinion just placed on the block. It will mate up when it rests fully on the block.

45 Fit the distributor clamp claw and tighten. You should now time the engine correctly as described in Chapter 4 (photo).

46 Refit the water pump (if removed) and tighten the bolts. Use a new gasket. See Chapter 2.

47 Refit the coolant temperature sender unit at the front end of the cylinder head. Clean the bolt threads first.

48 Refit the generator onto the block. Make sure the spacer is fitted to the lower mounting bolt which should be pushed through from the coolant pump end. Fit the top pressed steel mounting bracket and leave the bolts loose.

49 Fit and tension the drivebelt as described in Chapter 2, Section 6.

50 Pull out the old rocker cover gasket and carefully fit in the new one. It must fit well in the groove, even if it may mean stretching it slightly to pull it over the lips (photo).

51 Place the rocker cover onto the engine.

52 Do not overtighten the three holding down nuts – just to a point where they start to push in the cover.

53 Finally make sure that the dipstick is in position in the cylinder block and that the plug leads are all connected. Make sure the firing order is correct. See Chapter 4.

23 Valve clearances – adjustment

1 The valve clearances are important as they control the amount a valve opens and when it opens and thus can affect the efficiency of the engine.

2 The clearance should be measured and set by using a feeler blade between the rocker arm and the end of each valve stem. This is done when the valve is closed and the tappet is resting on the lowest point of the cam.

3 To enable each valve to be in the correct position for checking with the minimum amount of engine turning, the procedure and order of checking should follow the sequence given in the following tables. In the table the valves are numbered 1 to 8, starting from the flywheel end of the engine. A valve is fully open when the rocker arm has pushed the valve down to its lowest point.

Exhaust valve fully open	Valves to adjust
1	6 In
	8 Ex
5	7 In
	4 Ex
8	3 In
	1 Ex
4	2 In
	5 Ex

4   Turn the crankshaft by applying a spanner to the crankshaft pulley bolt or by engaging fourth gear, jacking up a front roadwheel and turning it in its normal direction of forward travel.

5   Remember that the valve clearances differ between inlet and exhaust valves and adjustment may be made with the engine hot or cold.

6   Using two spanners, first slacken the locknut on the adjusting screw and then put the feeler of appropriate thickness, between the rocker arm and valve stem of the valve being adjusted. Slacken the adjuster if the gap is too small to accept the blade.

7   Turn the adjusting screw until the feeler blade can be felt to drag lightly when it is drawn out of the gap (photo).

8   Hold the adjuster with a screwdriver and tighten the locknut. Check the gap once more to make sure it has not altered as a result of locking the stud.

23.7 Adjusting a valve clearance

24 Engine – initial start up after major overhaul

1   The following check list should ensure that the engine starts safely and with little or no delay and that the car is ready to move:

(a)   *Fuel pipes to fuel pump and carburettor connected and tight*
(b)   *Coolant hoses to radiator and heater connected and tight*
(c)   *Radiator and block coolant drain plugs shut and tight*
(d)   *Cooling system filled and bled*
(e)   *Sump drain plug screwed and tight*
(f)   *Oil filter cartridge tight*
(g)   *Oil in sump and dipstick replaced*
(h)   *Oil in transmission unit and plugs tight*
(i)   *LT wires connected to the distributor*
(j)   *Spark plugs clean and tight*
(k)   *Valve rocker clearances set*
(l)   *HT leads all connected and secure*
(m)   *Distributor rotor arm fitted*
(n)   *Choke and accelerator cable fitted and working through their total range*
(o)   *Earthing cable from engine block to battery and battery to bodyframe secure*
(p)   *Starter motor cable to battery connected and secure*
(q)   *Generator leads connected, fan belt on*
(r)   *Oil pressure warning and coolant temperature sender unit cables connected*
(s)   *Battery charged and secure in position*
(t)   *All loose tools removed from the engine compartment*
(u)   *Clutch cable refitted and adjusted*
(v)   *Gear change linkage replaced*
(w)   *Distributor vacuum advance pipe fitted*
(x)   *Crankcase fume rebreather pipe fitted*
(y)   *Drive shafts refitted to transmission unit and roll pins, replaced and greased, and speedometer cable replaced. See Chapter 8*
(z)   *Engine mountings secure*

2   Leave the bonnet off for the initial start but replace before venturing on the road!

3   As soon as the engine starts, run it steadily at a fast tick-over for several minutes and look all round for signs of leaks and loose or unclipped pipes and wires. Watch the instruments and warning lights and stop the engine at the first indications of a fault.

4   If a number of new internal components has been fitted to the engine, restrict the speed for the first few hundred miles.

5   At the end of the first 500 miles (800 km) change the engine oil and filter, check the torque of the cylinder head bolts (Section 5) and adjust the valve clearances (Section 23).

6   If the air conditioner was disconnected, have it recharged by your dealer or a competent refrigeration engineer.

PART 3 1565 cc, 1605 cc, 1647 cc (TYPE 807, 821, 843, 844) ENGINES

25 Cylinder head, removal and refitting (engine in car)

1   On fuel injection engines, disconnect the system as described in Chapter 3, then refer to Part 2, Section 5 and carry out the operations listed in paragraphs 1 to 5 and 7 to 13. Disconnect the coolant temperature switch lead (photo).

2   Remove the coolant pump drivebelt (Chapter 2).

3   Remove the diagnostic socket and bracket.

4   Remove the distributor (Chapter 4), the fuel pump and its pushrod (Chapter 3).

5   Remove the rocker cover.

6   On cars equipped with power-assisted steering, remove the steering pump drivebelt (Chapter 11).

7   Disconnect the exhaust downpipe from the manifold. On North American models, disconnect the emission control system as described in Chapter 3 (photo).

8   Unscrew the retaining nut from the dipstick guide tube upper securing clip. The dipstick can be left in position if desired.

9   Unscrew the respective rocker arm adjustment screws sufficiently to allow each pushrod to be extracted. As the pushrods are removed, lay them out in numerical order or locate them in a piece of stiff cardboard with eight holes suitably positioned and accordingly marked.

10 Next, loosen the cylinder head bolts in the sequence shown in the Figure.

11 Extract all bolts except the two at each end and the one nearest the distributor.

12 Remove the seals and washers from the spark plug tubes.

13 Locate a large elastic band or piece of string around each of the four remaining bolts, so that when the rocker assemblies are removed, the bolts do not become dislodged from them and thus retain the assemblies as a unit. Carefully, lift the rocker shaft assemblies clear, noting which way round it was fitted.

14 Before removing the cylinder head from the block, **note the following**: *Under no circumstances lift the head vertically from the block!* The head and block both stick to the gasket, therefore a lifting action would dislodge the liners in the process and break their lower O-ring seals. If these seals are damaged or distorted in any way it is likely that coolant will leak through to the sump with dire results!

15 Pivot the cylinder head on its locating dowel (the bolt left in position near the distributor hole passes through this dowel) and catch the cam followers as they drop from the cylinder head.

16 Retain them in their originally fitted order. Now swivel the cylinder head in the opposite direction and extract the remaining cam followers.

25.1 Coolant temperature switch

25.7 Exhaust pipe to manifold connecting flange

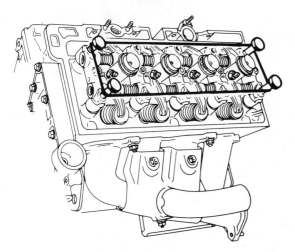

Fig. 1.33 Cylinder head/rocker bolts retained with rubber band (Sec 25)

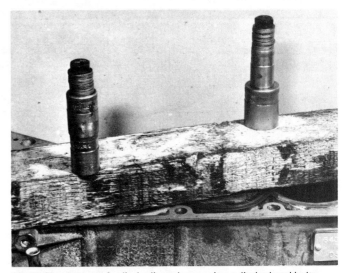

25.17 Simple type of cylinder liner clamp using cylinder head bolts, sockets and wood

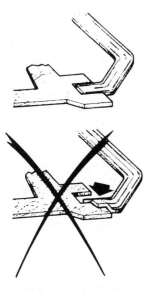

Fig. 1.34 Tappet chamber gasket seal (Sec 25)

17 The cylinder head can now be withdrawn, together with the tappet chamber seal. If the head is to be removed for any length of time, the cylinder liners must be clamped down in position to prevent them from becoming dislodged. If available, use Renault liner clamp number Mot 521. A suitable bar clamp can easily be fabricated and bolted in position if this tool is not available (photo).

18 Before fitting the cylinder head into position, make sure that all the mating surfaces are perfectly clean.

19 Insert the tappets into their original cylinder head locations and tap each one lightly to retain it in its bores when the head is being lowered. Application of some stiff grease to the tappets will assist their retention (photo).

20 Tap the cylinder head locating dowel into position in the top face of the cylinder block. Remove the liner clamps.

21 Clean out the cylinder block blind bolt holes.

22 The following operations require extreme accuracy and care, if the fitting of the cylinder head is to give a leak-free installation and the maintenance of good performance. *Do not use gasket cement.*

23 Carefully position a new gasket on the top face of the cylinder block. Check that all the bolt and water holes are clear (photo).

24 Fit the rubber seal round the edge of the tappet chamber ensuring that its ends dovetail into (not overlap) the cylinder head gasket.

25 The rocker shaft assemblies should be positioned on the cylinder

25.19 Inserting tappet (cam follower)

25.23 Cylinder head gasket and valve chamber seal in position

25.26 Distributor drive dog

25.29 Lowering cylinder head into position

25.31 Tightening a cylinder head bolt

27.2 Oil pump

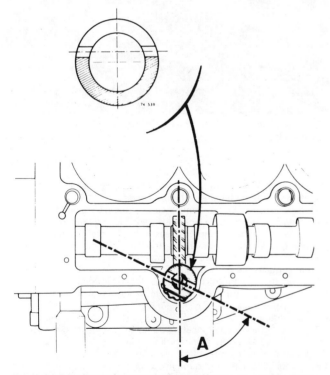
Fig. 1.35 Distributor/oil pump drivegear correctly set (Sec 25)

$A = 53°$

head before it is fitted, using the four bolts and an elastic band (as in the removal procedure).
26 Check the distributor drivegear, in case it has been disturbed. To do this, turn the crankshaft until No. 1 piston is at TDC. Check this by reference to the ignition timing marks and No. 4 cylinder valves must be rocking. Insert the drivegear so that there is an angle A of 53° between the drivegear slot and a line drawn at right angles to the camshaft with the smaller drivegear offset nearer the camshaft. This is the final position of the drivegear slot after its gear has meshed with the camshaft gear (photo).
27 Pour engine oil into the chamber under the camshaft.
28 Lower the cylinder head into position taking care not to disturb the gasket or seal.
29 Lightly lubricate the cylinder head bolts and their plain steel washers and screw them in hand tight. The two shorter bolts are at the timing cover end (photo).
30 Fit the pushrods, noting that the ones for the exhaust valves are longer than those for the inlet side.
31 Tighten the cylinder head bolts to the specified torque and in the sequence shown (photo).
32 Adjust the valve clearances as described in Section 40.
33 Reconnect all hoses, cables and leads by reversing the disconnection sequence.
34 Fit the rocker cover, fuel pump and pushrod.
35 Tension the drivebelts.
36 Fit the distributor.
37 Fill the cooling system.
38 Adjust the accelerator cable (or governor cable – automatic transmission).
39 After 600 miles (1000 km) running, the torque of the cylinder head bolts should be checked COLD as described in Section 5, paragraphs 40, 41.
40 Check the valve clearances (Section 40).

26 Sump pan – removal and refitting (engine in car)

1   Refer to Section 6, but note that the two shortest sump bolts are located at the rear edge at the rear main bearing.

27 Oil pump – removal and refitting (engine in car)

1 Remove the sump as previously described.
2 Unbolt and remove the oil pump from inside the crankcase (photo).
3 Refit by reversing the removal operations, a gasket is not used at the oil pump mounting flange.

28 Connecting rod/piston/liner assemblies – removal and refitting (engine in car)

1 These components may be removed with the engine in position in the car, if required, after removal of the cylinder head and sump.
2 It is important that where the existing cylinder liners are to be refitted, they are identified for position. Mark the top edges with quick drying paint to indicate each liner's position in the line and also its orientation so that it will be refitted exactly the same way round with the mark towards the flywheel.
3 Check the numbering of the connecting rods and the big-end caps. These should run from 1 to 4 from the clutch end of the engine and are marked on the camshaft side of the unit. In the event of these components not being marked, then dot punch them in such a way that the bearing cap will be fitted the correct way round when the mating marks are adjacent.
4 Unscrew and remove the big-end bearing cap nuts.
5 Withdraw the big-end bearing caps complete with shell bearings.
6 Withdraw each cylinder liner/piston/connecting rod assembly upwards from the cylinder block. The lower liner seals will be broken during this operation and must be cleaned from the liner and block mating faces.
7 After removal of each connecting rod, temporarily refit its matching bearing cap and shell bearing.
8 Withdraw each connecting rod/piston assembly from its cylinder liner. Do not allow the piston rings to spring outwards during removal from the liners but restrict them with the fingers to avoid breakage. If the assemblies are to be dismantled, see Section 18.
9 As explained in Section 18, on carburettor engines, the fitting of the pistons to the connecting rods will have been carried out by the Renault agent due to the difficulty of removing and inserting the gudgeon pin. Check that the pistons have been fitted correctly, however, by noting that the arrows on the piston crowns will face towards the rear (flywheel end) of the engine when the connecting rod identification markings are facing the camshaft. On fuel injection engines, fully floating gudgeon pins are used. These are easily dismantled, see Section 34.
10 If new pistons and liner assemblies have been supplied, they must be cleaned of the anti-rust coating. Soak them in a suitable solvent to remove the protective coating – do not scrape it off.
11 Keep the respective pistons and rings with their mating cylinder. They are carefully matched sets.
12 Locate the shell bearings in the connecting rod and cap big-end bearings (photo).
13 The cylinder liner protrusion must now be checked. On Type 841 and 843 engines, the base of the liner is sealed by an O-ring which acts purely as a seal not a spacer. Place each liner without its O-ring seal in the cylinder block. Measure the protrusion of the top of each

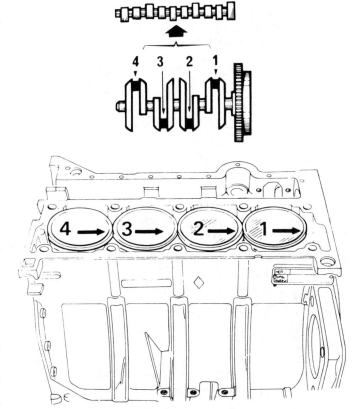

Fig. 1.36 Piston location (Sec 28)

liner above the face of the cylinder block using a dial gauge or feeler blades and a straight edge. The correct protrusion should be between 0.10 and 0.17 mm (0.004 and 0.0067 in) (photo).
14 Interchange the liners as necessary to ensure the difference in protrusion of two adjacent liners does not exceed 0.04 mm (0.0016 in) within the specified tolerance range.
15 Mark the liners for location once the ideal position has been established. Any difficulty in obtaining the correct protrusion will be due to a fault in liner or block as they are machined to a close fitted tolerance.
16 On Type 807/821 and 844 engines the liner base seals are of Excelnyl and act as both a seal and a spacer. Checking the liner protrusion is carried out in a similar way to that just described for the Type 843 engine except that seals of different thicknesses must be used to achieve the specified protrusion.
17 The correct protrusion is between 0.15 and 0.20 mm (0.006 and 0.008 in). Seals are available in three thicknesses and colour coded:

Blue	0.08 mm (0.003 in)
Red	0.10 mm (0.004 in)
Green	0.12 mm (0.0047 in)

28.12A Connecting rod big-end shell bearing

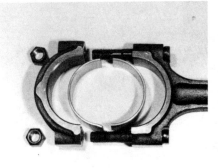

28.12B Big-end components

28.13 Checking cylinder liner projection (note engine serial number)

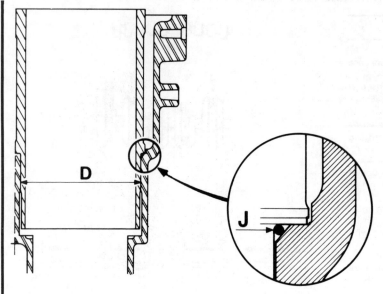

Fig. 1.37 Cylinder liner O-ring seals (Type 843 engine) (Sec 28)

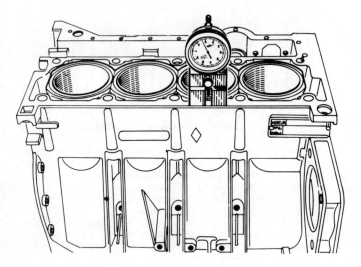

Fig. 1.38 Checking liner protrusion (Sec 28)

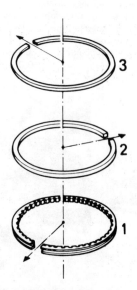

Fig. 1.39B Piston ring gap setting (Sec 28)

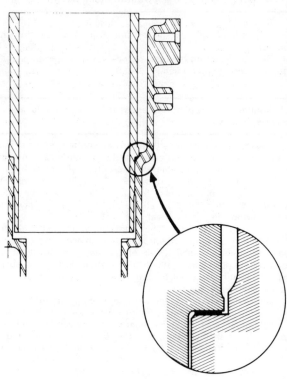

Fig. 1.39A Cylinder liner Excelnyl seals (Sec 28)

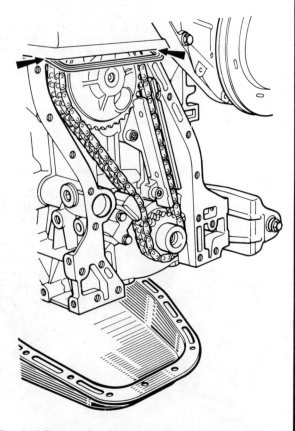

Fig. 1.40 Tappet chamber seal cutting points (Sec 28)

18 The difference in protrusion between two adjacent cylinder liners must not exceed 0.04 mm (0.0016 in) within the specified tolerance range.

19 Liberally oil the rings and ring grooves and turn the rings so that the gaps are at three different points of circle.

20 Oil the interior of the liner bore, and then using a clamp slide the piston/connecting rod assembly into the liner, fitting from the bottom of the liner upwards. The use of plenty of oil and striking blows with the hand will facilitate this operation. Ensure that fitting takes into account the liner, piston crown and connecting rod alignment marks (photos).

21 On Type 841 and 843 engines, fit an O-ring seal to the base of each cylinder liner. On type 807, 821 and 844 engines, fit the selected Excelnyl seal to the base of each liner (photo).

22 Place the liner/piston/connecting rod assembly into the cylinder block so that all the locating marks are correct.

  (a) The cylinder mark towards the flywheel
  (b) The arrow on the piston crown pointing towards the flywheel
  (c) The big-end numbers or marks on the big-ends towards the camshaft

23 Oil the crankpins and pull each connecting rod down so that its big end complete with shell bearing can be engaged on its crankpin and then the cap with shell bearing fitted (numbers or marks adjacent) and the big-end nuts tightened to the specified torque (photos).

28.20 Cylinder O-ring seal

28.21 Using piston ring clamp to install piston to liner

28.23A Fitting big-end bearing cap

28.23B Tightening big-end bearing cap nuts

28.23C Typical connecting rod and cap markings

24 Fit the remaining three piston/liner assemblies in the same way and then apply clamps to keep the liners and seals in position during the remaining engine reassembly operations.

25 Once the piston and liner assemblies are in position, the connecting rods and caps located on the crankshaft and the liners clamped in position, rotate the crankshaft to ensure that it revolves without excessive tight spots. Leave the cylinder clamps in position for subsequent operations until the cylinder head is ready to be fitted.

29 Timing cover oil seal – removal

1 This operation applies only to those Type 807 engines on Renault 15 or 17 models which have a crankshaft pulley located at the timing cover to which a belt is fitted to drive the radiator cooling fan (refer to Chapter 2).

2 Drain the engine oil, disconnect the battery.

3 Unbolt the fan shroud and push it rearward onto the fan blades.

4 Remove the air cleaner hot air pick up trunking.

5 Remove the air intake duct which runs between the air cleaner and the carburettor.

6 Remove the fan drivebelt and the cooling system expansion bottle.

7 Unbolt the radiator and move it with the expansion bottle up onto the rocker cover. There is no need to drain the cooling system, but it may improve manoeuvrability if the hose clips are released enough for the hoses to be swivelled.

8 Now remove the fan shroud and the fan assembly.

9 Unscrew the crankshaft pulley. To prevent the crankshaft from rotating, the starter motor may have to be removed and the teeth of the flywheel starter ring gear jammed with a suitable tool, but try selecting top gear with handbrake full on before going to this extra trouble.

10 Remove the engine undertray.

11 Unbolt and lower the sump pan.

12 Unbolt and remove the timing cover.

13 The old seal should be removed and the new one installed in the timing cover using a bolt, nut and washers and distance pieces. Avoid driving the seal out using a drift as this could crack the timing cover. Grease the seal lips.

14 The tappet chamber and sump seals should be cut off flush at their junction with the timing cover and new sections fitted. Apply jointing compound to the cut joints.

15 Offer the timing cover into position. If the new tappet chamber seal must be compressed before the timing cover holes will line up, use a pair of self-locking grips.

16 Fit the timing cover and sump bolts.

17 Fit the crankshaft pulley, the fan and belt. Tension the drivebelt (Chapter 2).

18 Reposition the radiator, reconnect the battery and fill the engine with oil.

19 Refit the air cleaner ducts.

30 Engine or engine/transmission – removal and refitting

1 The operations are essentially as described in Section 9 to 14 of Part 2, but if power-assisted steering is fitted, the pump drivebelt must be removed. Also move the steering pump. There is no need to disconnect the hydraulic hoses from the pump but just place the pump on the battery tray (photos).

2 On models fitted with an electric radiator cooling fan, disconnect the fan and thermostatic switch leads before removing the radiator/fan assembly.

30.1A Removing 1647cc engine (Type 843)

30.1B Engine removed

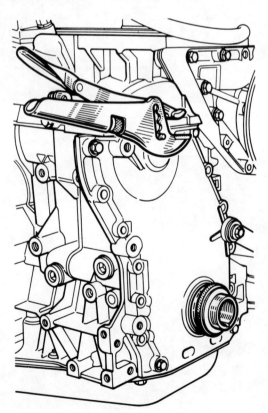

Fig. 1.41 Prising up timing cover (Sec 29)

30.4A Unscrewing camshaft pulley bolt

30.4B Removing camshaft pulley

3   Disconnect the diagnostic plug and bracket and withdraw it with its wiring harness to the side of the engine compartment.
4   Unbolt the camshaft belt pulley from the end of the camshaft. To do this, release the drivebelt idler pulley and slip off the belt. Engage a gear and apply the handbrake fully to prevent the camshaft rotating when the pulley bolt is unscrewed. Pull the pulley straight off as it is located on two roll pins (photos).

31 Engine dismantling – general

Refer to Section 15 in Part 2.

32 Engine ancillaries – removal

Refer to Section 16 in Part 2.

33 Engine – complete dismantling (engine removed)

1   Remove the cylinder head (Section 25).
2   Remove the sump pan (Section 26).
3   Remove the oil pump (Section 27).
4   Remove the piston/connecting rod/liner assemblies as described in Section 28.
5   Take out the distributor drivegear.
6   Unbolt and remove the camshaft rear bearing housing.
7   Unbolt the engine left-hand mounting bracket.
8   Unbolt and remove the timing cover. As explained in Section 29, some Type 807 engines have a crankshaft pulley which will have to be removed before the timing cover can be withdrawn. All other models have a sealed timing cover.
9   Using an Allen key as described in Section 17, release the tension of the chain tensioner by turning the key in an anti-clockwise direction and then unbolt and remove the tensioner.

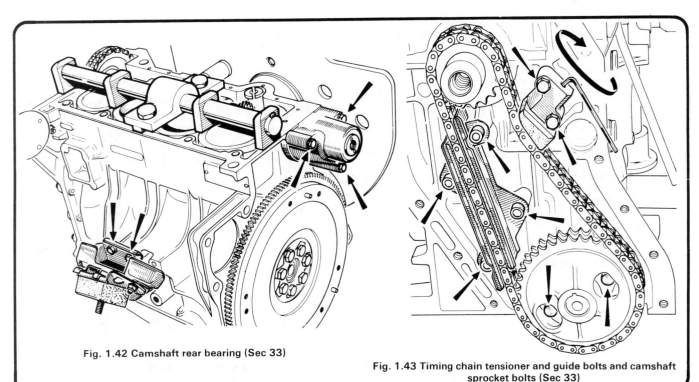

Fig. 1.42 Camshaft rear bearing (Sec 33)

Fig. 1.43 Timing chain tensioner and guide bolts and camshaft sprocket bolts (Sec 33)

33.17 Flywheel ring gear tooth lock

34.3 Rocker arms and shafts

34.14 Oil pump pressure relief valve

10 Unbolt and remove the timing chain guides.
11 Unscrew and remove the camshaft sprocket bolts.
12 Extract the crankshaft pulley Woodruff key.
13 Withdraw the camshaft and crankshaft sprockets with timing chain simultaneously. A puller may be required to withdraw the crankshaft pulley.
14 Do not attempt to remove the interference fit camshaft sprocket (see Section 34, paragraph 6).
15 Unbolt and remove the flywheel or driveplate (automatic transmission). Jam the teeth of the starter ring gear to prevent the flywheel from rotating as the bolts are unscrewed.
16 Using a centre punch, mark the main bearing caps so that they can be refitted in their original sequence and the same way round.
17 Unscrew the main bearing cap bolts, and remove all the main bearing caps except No. 1 (nearest the flywheel end of the crankshaft). Remove the bearing shells and if they are to be used again, tape them to their respective caps (photo).
18 Now remove No. 1 main bearing cap by tapping it evenly upwards at both sides. Remove the oil seal and the side seals.
19 Lift out the crankshaft and thrust washers.
20 If the bearing shells are to be used again, tape them to their respective caps.

34 Engine – examination, renovation and dismantling of major assemblies

1 The information given in Part 2, Section 18 generally applies, but observe the following additions and differences.

Rocker gear
2 To dismantle the rocker shafts, remove the roll pins and then take the components off the shaft, keeping them in their originally fitted sequence. Do not remove the blanking plugs from the ends of the shafts.
3 Reassemble by reversing the dismantling operations, but take care that the correct rocker arms are fitted to the correct shafts as their design differs between inlet and exhaust (photo).

Crankshaft
4 The clutch pilot bearing located in the centre of the crankshaft rear flange is of ball bearing type. It can be removed with a suitable extractor or by filling it with grease and then tapping in a close fitting rod. The hydraulic pressure generated will eject the bearing.

Flywheel
5 A grooved flywheel can only be rectified by renewal, no attempt must be made to re-machine it.

Camshaft
6 The camshaft sprocket and distributor drivegear are supplied as a matched pair and can only be renewed as such.
7 If a new sprocket is to be fitted to the camshaft, this is a job best

left to your dealer as the sprocket must be pressed on to provide a clearance (J) as shown in the diagram.

Piston/connecting rod
8 The piston is connected to the connecting rod on all carburettor engines, by a gudgeon pin which is an interference fit in the rod small end but floating in the piston.
9 Dismantling and reassembly of this type of piston/connecting rod should be left to your dealer as special tools are required and precise heating of the components.
10 On fuel injection engines, the gudgeon pin is fully floating in both the piston and rod. Dismantling and reassembly are therefore within the scope of the home mechanic.
11 To dismantle, extract one of the circlips from the end of the gudgeon pin. Push out the gudgeon pin with the finger and separate the components.
12 If a new small end bush is required because of wear then the oil hole in the new one must line up (when installed) with the one in the rod.
13 Connect the piston to the connecting rod by reversing the separation method, but make sure that the relationship of the arrow on the piston crown to the number on the connecting rod is as shown.

Oil pump
14 The oil pump on these larger capacity engines is of trochoid type and should be checked for wear in the following way (photo).

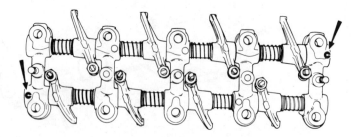
Fig. 1.44 Rocker shafts, roll pins arrowed (Sec 34)

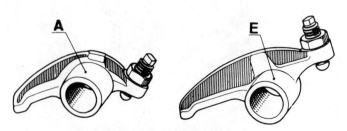
Fig. 1.45 Rocker arms (Sec 34)

A   Inlet   E   Exhaust

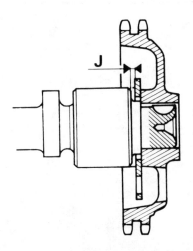

Fig. 1.46 Camshaft flange clearance (Sec 34)

J = 0.05 to 0.12 mm (0.002 to 0.0047 in)

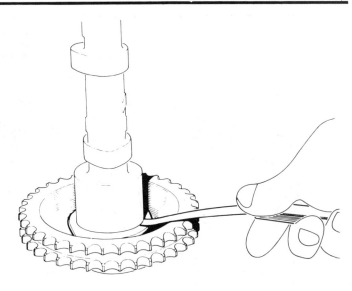

Fig. 1.47 Checking camshaft sprocket flange clearance (Sec 34)

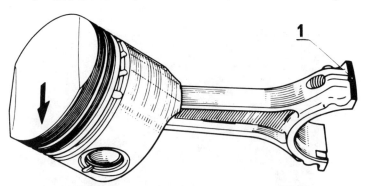

Fig. 1.48 Piston arrow to connecting rod number (1) alignment
(Type 807, 821, 841, 843, 844 engines) (Sec 34)

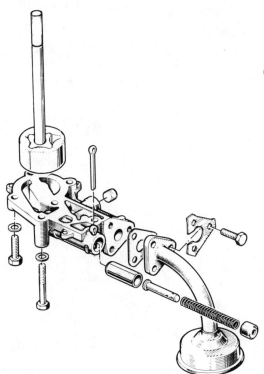

Fig. 1.50 Components of rotor type oil pump (Sec 34)

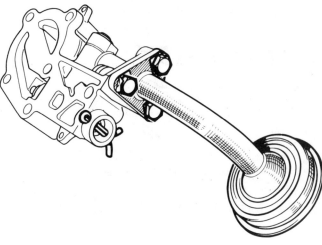

Fig. 1.49 Rotor type oil pump (Sec 34)

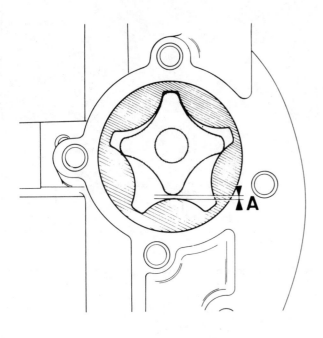

34.17A Oil pump rotors

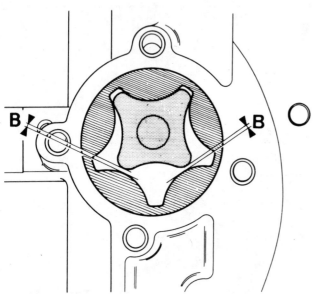

34.17B Checking oil pump rotor tip clearance

Fig. 1.51 Rotor checking diagram (Sec 34)

A   0.04 to 0.29 mm (0.002 to 0.012 in)
B   0.02 to 0.14 mm (0.001 to 0.006 in)

15 Unbolt and remove the oil pick-up pipe.
16 Extract the split pin from the pressure relief valve. Extract the cup, spring, spring guide and piston. Renew any worn or damaged components.
17 Place the rotors in their housing in the block and using feeler blades check the clearances A and B as shown. If the clearances exceed those specified, renew both rotors and driveshaft as a set (photos).
18 Reassembly and refitting are reversals of removal and dismantling. Use new gaskets.

35 Cylinder head – dismantling, decarbonising and reassembly

1 Unbolt and remove the exhaust manifold.

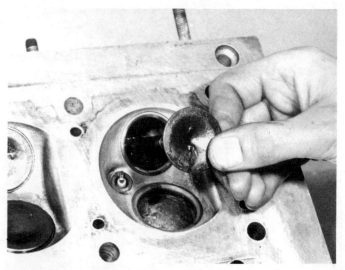

35.10A Fitting a valve

35.10B Valve spring seat

35.10C Valve spring

35.10D Valve spring cap

2 Unbolt and remove the inlet manifold complete with carburettor.
3 Remove the spark plugs.
4 Remove the coolant pump fan, pulley and pump itself.
5 Unscrew and remove the coolant temperature switch.
6 Remove the fuel pump and operating rod.
7 Remove the rear blanking plate.
8 Remove the valves as described in Section 19, paragraphs 1 to 5, but note that double valve springs are used.
9 Decarbonising and valve grinding are as described in Section 19.
10 Reassembly is a reversal of dismantling, but observe the following:

(a) *Fit the valve spring closer coils against the cylinder head*
(b) *Check that the split collets for a particular valve stem are of compatible type (photos)*

36 Lubrication system

1 The system is designed to operate in a similar way to that described in Part 2, Section 20, paragraphs 1 to 4.
2 Type 807 engines with a fuel injection system have an engine oil

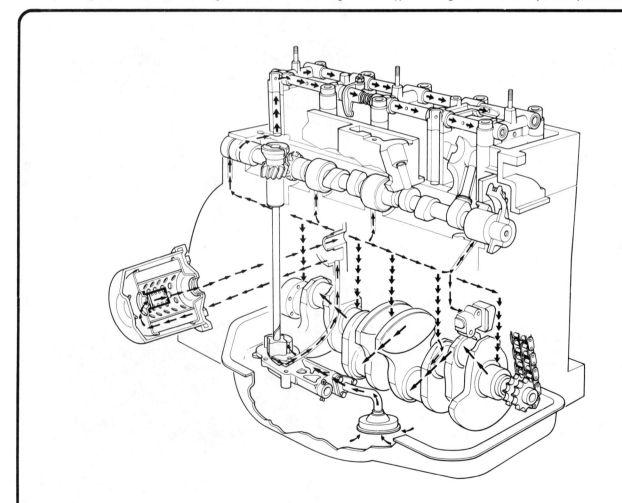

Fig. 1.52A Lubrication system (Type 807, 843, 844 engines) (Sec 36)

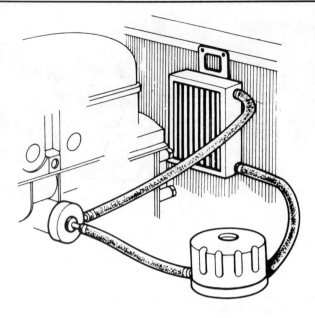

Fig. 1.52B Oil cooler on fuel injection models (Sec 36)

cooler located behind the radiator and an additional oil filter on the
right-hand side of the engine compartment.

37 Crankcase ventilation system

1   Refer to Section 21, but note that the hose routing differs on these
larger capacity engines and two calibrated jets are incorporated in the
system.

38 Engine reassembly – general

1   To ensure maximum life with minimum trouble from a rebuilt
engine, not only must everything be correctly assembled, but all the
parts must be spotlessly clean, all the oilways must be clear, locking
washers and spring washers must always be fitted where indicated
and all bearing and other working surfaces must be thoroughly
lubricated during assembly. Before assembly begins renew any bolts
or studs, the threads of which are in any way damaged, and whenever
possible use new spring washers.
2   Check the core plugs for signs of weeping and renew any that are
suspect.
3   To do this drive a punch through the centre of the core plug.
4   Using the punch as a lever lift out the old core plug.
5   Thoroughly clean the core plug orifice and using a thin headed
hammer as an expander firmly tap a new core plug in place, convex
side facing out.
6   Apart from your normal tools, a supply of clean rag, an oil can filled
with engine oil! (an empty plastic detergent bottle thoroughly cleaned
and washed out will invariably do just as well), a new supply of
assorted spring washers, a new set of gaskets and a torque spanner
should be collected together.
7   A torque wrench is essential.

39 Engine – reassembly

Crankshaft
1   Fit the upper sections of the main bearing shells into their
crankcase locations. These are the ones with oil holes and grooves.
Ensure that the locating tags engage correctly with the cut-outs in the
bearing recesses (photo).
2   Stick the two thrust washers into place, one on either side of the
centre main bearing. Use grease to hold them in position and ensure
that the white metalled sides face the crankshaft webs (photo).
3   Oil the bearings and crankshaft journals and lay the crankshaft
carefully in position in the crankcase (photo).

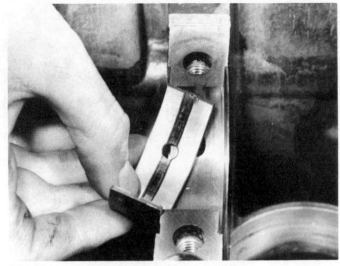

39.1 Crankcase main bearing shell

39.2 Crankshaft endfloat thrust washer

39.3 Lowering crankshaft into position

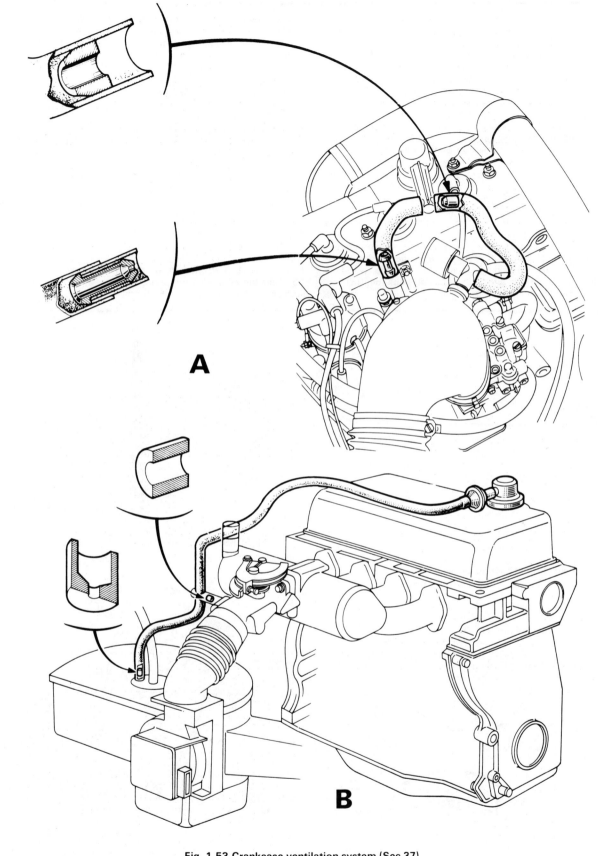

Fig. 1.53 Crankcase ventilation system (Sec 37)

A Carburettor engine
B Fuel injection engines

4   Fit the lower halves (plain) sections of the shell bearings to the main bearing caps. Oil the shells and fit them (bolts, finger tight) to main bearings 2, 3, 4 and 5, not No. 1 (photos).

5   Check the crankshaft endfloat. This may be done by using either a dial gauge or feeler gauges and prising the crankshaft first in one direction and then the other. The total permissible endfloat must be between 0.002 and 0.009 inch (0.05 and 0.23 mm) and if outside these tolerances, then the thrust washers must be changed for ones of different thicknesses as listed in Specifications (photo).

6   With its shell bearing in position, fit the No 1 main bearing cap (No. 1) and screw in the bolts, finger tight. Refer to Fig. 1.54 and measure the gap C. If the gap is less than 0.197 in (5 mm) obtain two seals 0.201 inch (5.1 mm) thick, if greater, obtain two seals 0.213 inch (5.4 mm) thick (colour identified by a white backing strip) (photo).

7   Fit the two side seals into position in the No. 1 main bearing cap. The seal groove must be to the outside and the seals projecting by approximately 0.008 inch (0.2032 mm) (photo).

8   Fitting of the No. 1 main bearing cap is critical. Obtain two studs (10 mm x 150 mm) and temporarily screw them into the crankcase. Tape the side seals to protect them during fitting and then carefully slide the bearing cap down the two studs. When the bearing cap is almost home, check that the side seals are still projecting, withdraw the protective tape and studs and fit the securing bolts (photos).

9   Tighten all main bearing cap bolts to the specified torque (photo).

10   Renew the crankshaft oil seal. Start the new seal into place using the fingers only. The seal lips are very delicate and great care must be taken to avoid damaging them. Drive it into position by using a piece of tubing of appropriate diameter (photo).

Flywheel or driveplate

11   Locate the flywheel on the crankshaft. The bolt holes are offset so it can only be fitted in one position.

12   Apply thread locking fluid to new securing bolts and tighten them to the specified torque. On some models, a lockplate is used under the bolts. Always use a new one and bend up one tab at each bolt head (photos).

13   Refitting the driveplate (automatic transmission) is similar.

Piston/connecting rod/liner assemblies

14   Refer to Section 28.

Oil pump

Refer to Section 27.

Camshaft and timing gear, tensioner and chain

16   With the engine in an upright position, oil the camshaft bearing surfaces in the crankcase. Slide the camshaft into position but

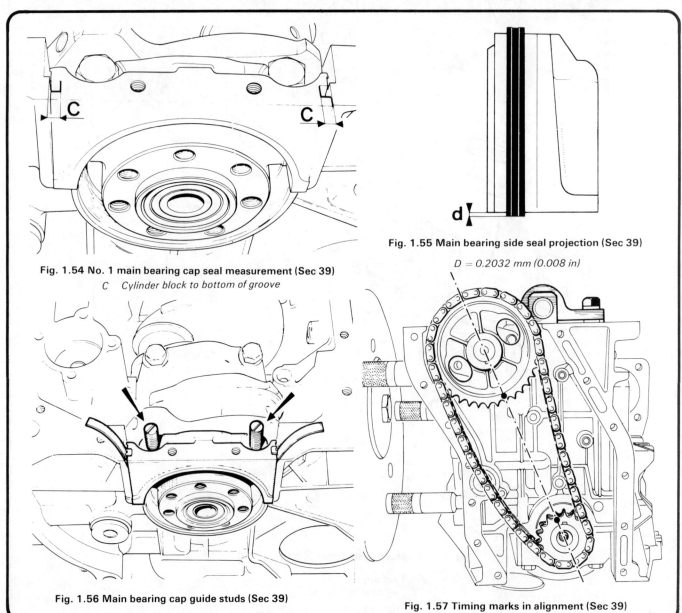

Fig. 1.54 No. 1 main bearing cap seal measurement (Sec 39)

C   Cylinder block to bottom of groove

Fig. 1.55 Main bearing side seal projection (Sec 39)

D = 0.2032 mm (0.008 in)

Fig. 1.56 Main bearing cap guide studs (Sec 39)

Fig. 1.57 Timing marks in alignment (Sec 39)

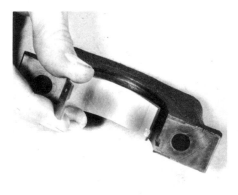

39.4A Fitting bearing shell to main bearing cap

39.4B Fitting a main bearing cap

39.5 Checking crankshaft endfloat

39.6 Measuring No. 1 main bearing cap clearance

39.7 Main bearing cap sealing strip in position

39.8A Tape to prevent damage to main bearing cap seals during fitting

39.8B Fitting No. 1 main bearing cap. Note the guide studs

39.9 Tightening main bearing cap bolts

39.10 Fitting crankshaft oil seal

39.12A Applying thread locking fluid to flywheel bolts

39.12B Tightening flywheel bolts

39.16 Installing camshaft

projecting from the face of the engine by approximately 3 inches (76.2 mm) (photo).

17 Place the chain on the camshaft sprocket.

18 Fit the crankshaft sprocket within the loop of the timing chain.

19 By turning the crankshaft and the camshaft and repositioning the crankshaft sprocket teeth in the links of the chain, a position will be reached where the crankshaft sprocket can be slid onto its key and the timing marks on both sprockets will be in exact alignment with the shaft centres (photo).

20 Heat the crankshaft sprocket to ease fitting, in boiling water.

21 Push the camshaft fully into position and screw in the camshaft retaining plate bolts. These may be fitted with lockwashers or tab type lockplates (photo).

22 The chain tensioner must now be prepared for fitting depending upon type (see Section 18). On manual take-up and automatic type tensioners fully retract the piston using an Allen key. Fit the tensioner assembly and its backing plate using the two fixing bolts (photos).

23 On manual take-up type chain tensioners, insert an Allen key and turn it until the slipper just touches the timing chain.

24 On automatic take-up type chain tensioners, depress the slipper with the finger and release it. The slipper is automatically set against the chain by this action.

25 Fit the chain anti-flail guards so that there is a parallel gap between the guard and the chain of 0.032 inch (0.8 mm) (photos).

26 Stick new timing cover gaskets into position with grease and fit the cover and securing bolts finger tight. Check that the edge of the timing cover is in alignment with the cylinder head mating surface of the crankcase before finally tightening the timing cover bolts. Cut off any excess gasket (photos).

27 On certain Type 807 engines, a crankshaft pulley is fitted. With this arrangement, make sure that a new oil seal (lips greased) is fitted to the timing cover. Fit the pulley, apply thread locking compound to the threads of its retaining bolt and tighten it to the specified torque.

Sump

28 Clean the mating flanges of the sump and crankcase thoroughly.

29 Fit a new gasket and then offer up the sump (photo).

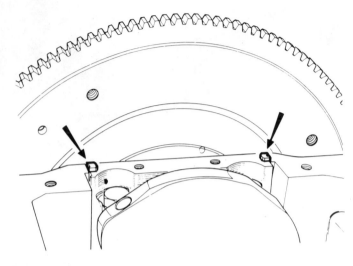

Fig. 1.58 Rear main bearing cap side seal projections (Sec 39)

30 Screw in the fixing bolts, but make sure that the two shortest bolts go into the rear main bearing cap (photo).

Camshaft bearing

31 Fit a new oil seal and O-ring to the bearing (photos).

32 Bolt the bearing into position using a new joint gasket (photo).

33 Fit the pulley roll pins so that their slots are as shown. They need not be driven right home as bolting on the pulley will seat them.

Distributor/oil pump drivegear

34 Fit the drivegear as described in Section 25.

39.19 Checking timing sprocket marks

39.21 Tightening camshaft retaining plate bolts

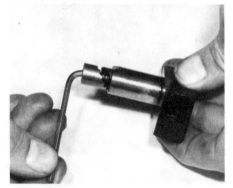

39.22A Using an Allen key to retract chain tensioner piston

39.22B Bolting chain tensioner into place

39.25A Tightening a chain guard screw

39.25B Checking chain to guard clearance

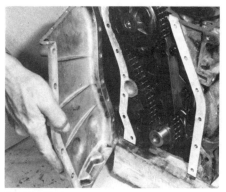
39.26A Timing cover and gasket

39.26B Cutting off surplus timing cover gasket

39.29 Sump and gasket

39.30 Tightening sump bolts

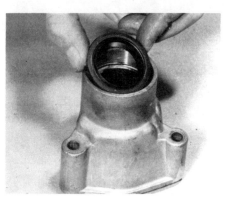
39.31A Camshaft bearing oil seal

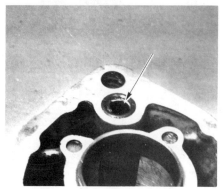
39.31B Camshaft bearing O-ring seal

Cylinder head
35 Refer to Section 25 and fit the cylinder head. Note the position of the lifting lug (photo).
36 Adjust the valve clearances as described in Section 40. Fit the rocker cover using a new gasket (photo).
37 Fit the left-hand engine mounting bracket.
38 Refit the dipstick tube and dipstick (photo).

39 Refit the alternator and bracket.
40 Fit the clutch, centralising the driveplate as described in Chapter 5.
41 Fit the fuel pump and operating rod (circlip at top end of rod) and the oil pressure switch.
42 Bolt on the inlet manifold using a new gasket, then bolt the starter motor into position. Again using a new gasket, bolt on the exhaust manifold and the heat shield for the starter motor (photos).

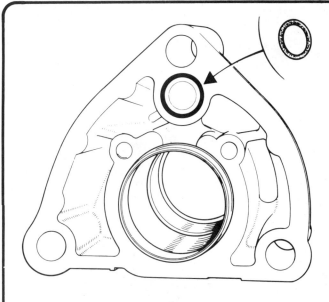
Fig. 1.59 Camshaft bearing O-ring (Sec 39)

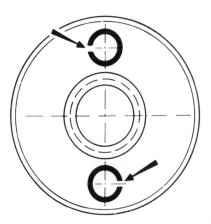
Fig. 1.60 Camshaft pulley roll pins (Sec 39)

39.32 Fitting camshaft bearing

39.35 Engine lifting lug

39.36 Fitting rocker cover

39.38 Dipstick guide tube

39.42A Offering inlet manifold into position

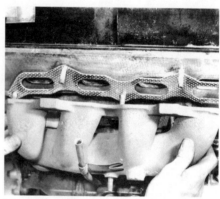
39.42B Fitting exhaust manifold

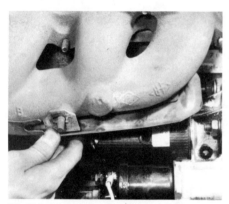
39.42C Exhaust manifold heat shield for starter

39.44 Fitting oil filter

39.45 Sparking plug leads correctly connected

39.46 Fitting coolant pump pulley

39.47 Camshaft pulley. Note groove in thrust washer

39.48 Tightening camshaft pulley bolt

43 Fit the distributor and set the approximate timing.
44 Apply oil to the sealing ring of a new oil filter cartridge and screw it on using hand pressure only (photo).
45 Fit the spark plugs and connect the leads (photo).
46 Fit the coolant pump (if removed) by reference to Chapter 2, locate the idler pulley under the two top bolts. Fit the pulley to the coolant pump (photo).
47 Do not fit the camshaft pulley and bolt until the engine is reconnected at the transmission (photo).
48 When the pulley is fitted, fit and tension the drivebelts as described in Chapter 2, Section 6 (photo).

40 Valve clearances – adjustment

1 The method of adjustment is as described in Section 23, but the table must be ignored as the valves are arranged in two lines on these larger capacity engines (photo).
2 Counting from the flywheel end of the engine the valves are as shown in the diagram.

3 Use the following table for ease of adjustment.
4 Turn the crankshaft by applying a spanner to the crankshaft pulley bolt (where fitted) or by engaging fourth gear, jacking up a front roadwheel and turning it in its normal direction of forward travel.

Valve fully open	Valves to adjust
1 Ex	3 In 4 Ex
3 Ex	4 In 2 Ex
4 Ex	2 In 1 Ex
2 Ex	1 In 3 Ex

5 Remember that the valve clearances differ between inlet and exhaust valves and adjustment may be made with the engine hot or cold.

41 Engine – initial start up after major overhaul

1 Refer to Part 2, Section 24.

40.1 Adjusting a valve clearance

Fig. 1.61 Valve location (Type 807, 843, 844 engines) (Sec 40)

'Fault diagnosis appears overleaf'

42 Fault diagnosis – all engines

Symptom	Reason(s)
Engine will not turn over when starter switch is operated	Flat battery Bad battery connections Bad connections at solenoid switch and/or starter motor Starter motor jammed Defective solenoid Starter motor defective
Engine turns over but fails to start	No spark at plugs No fuel reaching engine Too much fuel reaching the engine (flooding)
Engine starts but runs unevenly and misfires	Ignition and/or fuel system faults Incorrect valve clearances Burnt out valves Worn out piston rings
Lack of power	Ignition and/or fuel system faults Incorrect valve clearances Burnt out valves Worn out piston rings
Excessive oil consumption	Oil leaks from gaskets or seals Worn piston rings or cylinder bores resulting in oil being burnt by engine Worn valve guides
Excessive mechanical noise from engine	Wrong valve to rocker clearances Worn crankshaft bearings Worn cylinders (piston slap) Slack or worn timing chain and sprockets
Poor idling	Leak in inlet manifold gasket

Note: *When investigating starting and uneven running faults, do not be tempted into snap diagnosis. Start from the beginning of the check procedure and follow it through. It will take less time in the long run. Poor performance from an engine in terms of power and economy is not normally diagnosed quickly. In any event, the ignition and fuel systems must be checked first before assuming any further investigation needs to be made.*

Chapter 2 Cooling, heating and air conditioning systems

Contents

Air conditioning systems 13
Coolant mixtures 3
Coolant pump (Type 810 engine) – removal and refitting 8
Coolant pump (Type 807, 821, 841, 843, 844 engines) – removal
and refitting 9
Coolant system – draining, refilling and bleeding 2
Coolant temperature and electric fan switches 7
Drivebelt – removal, refitting and tensioning 6

Fault diagnosis 14
General description and maintenance 1
Heater – dismantling and reassembly 12
Heater unit – removal and refitting 11
Heating, ventilation system – description 10
Radiator – removal and refitting 5
Thermostat – removal, testing and refitting 4

Specifications

Type .... Thermo-syphon with coolant pump assistance. Pressurised with expansion bottle. Belt-driven or electric radiator cooling fan dependent upon model

Thermostat
Type .... Wax, spirit or bi-metal dependent upon territory
Temperature range .... Ten variants within the following range, rating stamped on thermostat.
    Opens .... 73 to 84°C
    Fully open .... 83 to 95°C

Coolant capacity
Type 810 engine .... 8.8 Imp pts, 5.3 US qts, 5.0 l
Type 807, 843, 844 engines .... 9.7 Imp pts, 5.8 US qts, 5.5 l
Type 821, 841 engines .... 11.5 Imp pts, 7.0 US qts, 6.6 l

1 General description and maintenace

The system is of pressurised type and sealed, but with the inclusion of an expansion bottle to accept coolant displaced from the system when hot and to return it when the system cools.

Coolant is circulated by thermosyphon action and is assisted by means of the impeller in the belt-driven water pump.

A thermostat is fitted in the outlet of the water pump. When the engine is cold, the thermostat valve remains closed so that the coolant flow which occurs at normal operating temperatures through the radiator matrix is interrupted.

As the coolant warms up, the thermostat valve starts to open and allows the coolant flow through the radiator to resume.

The engine temperature will always be maintained at a constant level (according to the thermostat rating) whatever the ambient air temperature.

The coolant circulates around the engine block and cylinder head and absorbs heat as it flows, then travels in an upward direction and out into the radiator to pass across the matrix. As the coolant flows across the radiator matrix, air flow created by the forward motion of the car cools it and it returns via the bottom of the radiator to the cylinder block. This is a continuous process, assisted by the water pump impeller.

Some models are fitted with an electric cooling fan which is actuated by the thermostat switch according to coolant temperature.

The car interior heater operates by means of water from the cooling system.

The carburettor is fitted with connections to permit coolant from the cooling system to circulate to the carburettor base, and (on some models) to the automatic choke operating mechanism.

Maintenance

Apart from renewing the coolant at the prescribed intervals, maintenance is confined to checking the coolant level in the expansion bottle. The level should be between the MIN and MAX lines. The need for persistent topping up should be investigated.

The hoses and their clamps should also be inspected regularly for security and good condition, and the drivebelt checked and adjusted or renewed as necessary.

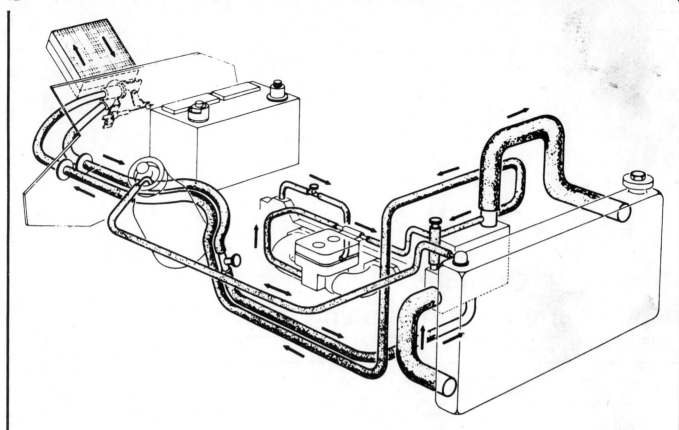

Fig. 2.1 Cooling system layout (Type 810 engine) (Sec 1)

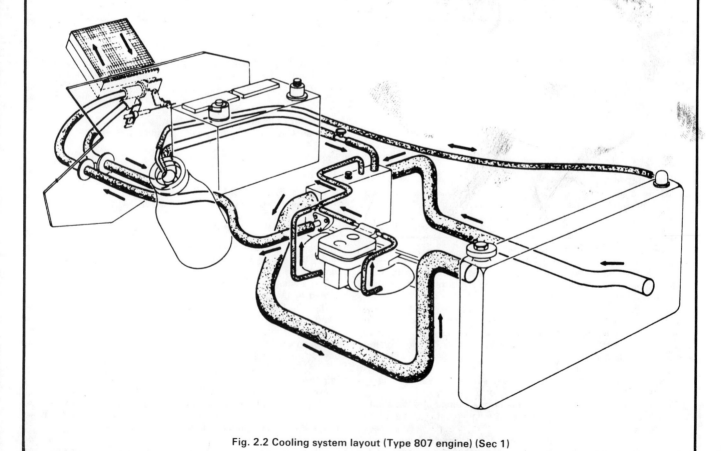

Fig. 2.2 Cooling system layout (Type 807 engine) (Sec 1)

2 Cooling system – draining, refilling and bleeding

Draining

1   If the coolant is known to be in acceptable condition for further use, have suitable containers available in which to catch it.

2   Set the heater facia control to 'Hot'.

3   Remove the expansion bottle cap. Take care to avoid scalding if the system is hot.

4   Remove the drain plug from the cylinder block. This is located adjacent to the clutch cable bracket.

5   Open the drain tap at the base of the radiator, where one is fitted. Alternatively, remove the bottom hose at the radiator stub. When the expansion bottle is empty, remove the filler plug from the radiator. Open all bleed screws.

Flushing

6   The system will only require flushing if renewal of the antifreeze or corrosion inhibitor has been neglected. In this event, flush the system through with a cold water hose until the water runs clear from the cylinder block and radiator.

7   If the radiator is badly blocked, remove it from the vehicle, and place a hose in the bottom stub, so that the water flows through it in the reverse direction to the normal cooling system flow.

8   The use of chemical descaler should only be used in a cooling system if scale and sludge formation is severe. Adhere strictly to the manufacturer's instructions.

9   Leakage of the radiator or cooling system may be temporarily stopped by the use of a proprietary sealant but in the long term, a new cylinder head or other gasket, water pump, hoses or radiator matrix must be installed. Do not attempt to solder a radiator. The amount of local heat required will almost certainly melt adjacent joints. Take it to a specialist or exchange it for a reconditioned unit.

Refilling

10   Prepare a sufficient quantity of coolant.

11   Ensure that the drain plugs and holes are tight, and in good condition.

12   Place the heater control lever to 'Hot'.

13   Open the bleed screws, removing the air filter if necessary to give access to the bleed screw on the carburettor automatic choke and coolant pump (where these screws are fitted).

14   Temporarily raise the expansion bottle as high as possible by any convenient means, leaving the tube attached.

15   Fill the radiator, and fit the cap (photo).

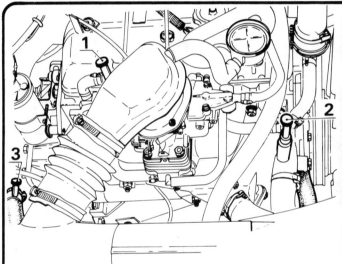

Fig. 2.3 Bleed screws on Type 810 engine (Sec 2)

2.15 Radiator cap

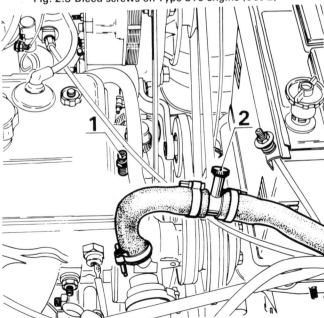

Fig. 2.4 Bleed screws on Type 807, 843, 844 engines (Sec 2)

Fig. 2.5 Expansion bottle (early type) (Sec 2)

1	Screwed ring	3	Seal
2	Valve	4	Jar

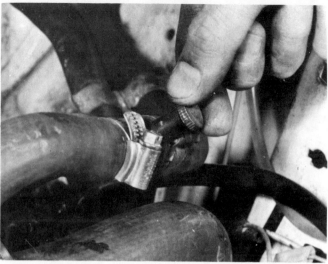

2.18A Bleed screw

2.18B Bleed screw on carburettor coolant-heated choke

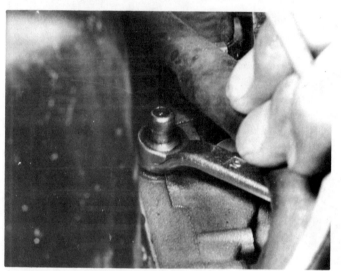

2.18C Bleed screw on coolant pump

2.21 Later type expansion bottle cap/valve

16   Complete the filling, by pouring coolant into the expansion bottle, and tighten the bleed screw as coolant starts to come from them. Top up the bottle to $2\frac{3}{4}$ in (40 mm) above the 'maximum' mark.

Bleeding
17   With the bottle cap in place, run the engine until it is warmed up, so that the thermostat is open.
18   Open the bleed screws, retightening them once a steady flow of bubble-free coolant appears. Remember the bleed screw on Weber 32 DARA carburettors (photos).
19   Refit and secure the expansion bottle.
20   When the engine has cooled, top up the coolant level in the bottle if necessary.
21   **Note:** *Should the expansion bottle be overfilled at any time and coolant be ejected through the valve in the cap then the valve must be renewed on early models or the complete plastic cap/valve assembly on later models (photo).*

3   Coolant mixtures

1   It is essential that an approved type of antifreeze is employed, in order that the necessary antifreeze and anticorrosion proportions are maintained.
2   Whilst the life of the coolant originally used in the vehicle is stated

to be 3 years or 30 000 miles (45 000 km), owners are recommended to consider removing the coolant yearly to ensure that all the essential properties of the solution are fully maintained.
3   Make up the solution, ideally using distilled water or rain water, in the proportions necessary to give protection in the prevailing climate. Percentages of antifreeze necessary are usually found on the container. Do not use too low a percentage of antifreeze, or the anti-corrosion properties will not be sufficiently effective. 30% antifreeze should be a minimum.
4   If it is suspected that the coolant strength is unsatisfactory, a check may be made using a hydrometer. Employ the instrument as instructed by the manufacturer, and using the correction tables normally supplied. If the protection is found to be insufficient, drain off some of the coolant and replace it with pure antifreeze. Recheck the coolant with the hydrometer.
5   Even in climates where antifreeze is not required, never use plain water in the system, but mix in a good quality corrosion inhibitor. This is particularly important where the light alloy content of an engine is high.

4   Thermostat – removal, testing and refitting

1   The thermostat is located in the hose attached to the water pump outlet pipe (photo).

4.1 Thermostat

4.3 Thermostat temperature marking

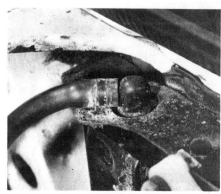
5.3 Expansion bottle hose at radiator

2   To remove the thermostat, drain sufficient coolant to allow the level to fall below the pump outlet. Remove the hose, and extract the thermostat.
3   Test the thermostat by suspending it in a pan of water, together with a thermometer. Commence warming the water, watch when the thermostat begins to open, and check the temperature. Compare the opening temperature with the temperature stamped on the thermostat (photo).
4   Transfer the thermostat to cold water, and check that it closes promptly.
5   If the thermostat does not operate as outlined, it should be renewed.
6   Refit in the reverse order to dismantling, top up the coolant, and bleed the system.
7   In an emergency it is permissible to run the car without a thermostat fitted, but this will lead to prolonged warm-up time, poor heater output and (possibly) poor fuel economy. All these drawbacks are to be preferred to overheating, however!
8   Note that the bulb end of the thermostat enters the pump.

5   Radiator – removal and refitting

1   If the car has automatic transmission and an oil cooler is fitted, unbolt the heat exchanger and place it to one side (see Chapter 7, Section 10).
2   If the car is equipped with air conditioning take care not to damage the condenser which is mounted ahead of the radiator.
3   Disconnect the battery, drain the coolant and disconnect the radiator hoses (photo).

Engine with belt-driven fan
4   Unbolt the fan shroud and push it over the fan away from the radiator.

Engines with electrically-driven fan
5   Disconnect the leads from the fan motor and from the thermostatic switch in the radiator. The fan assembly can be removed still attached to the radiator and separated later.

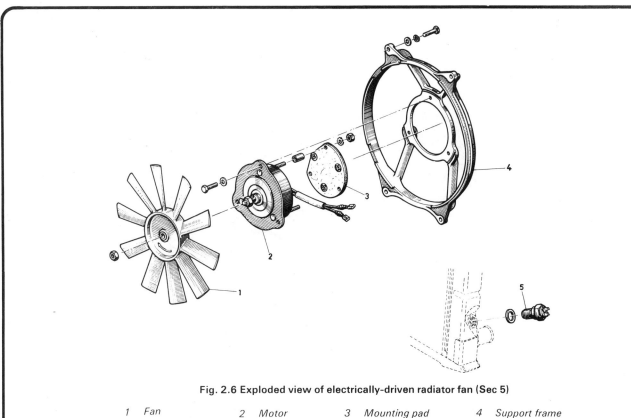

Fig. 2.6 Exploded view of electrically-driven radiator fan (Sec 5)

| 1 | Fan | 2 | Motor | 3 | Mounting pad | 4 | Support frame |
| 5 | Thermostatic switch | | | | | | |

5.6A Unscrewing radiator mounting bolt

5.6B Removing radiator with electrically-driven fan

5.6C Radiator bottom mounting lugs

All engines

6   Unbolt and remove the radiator from the car. Note the bottom mounting lugs (photos).
7   Refitting is a reversal of removal.
8   Refill the cooling system (Section 2)

6   Drivebelt — removal, refitting and tensioning

1   Various drivebelt configurations are used depending upon which accessories the belt is driving.
2   With some belt arrangements, removal and refitting of a belt is achieved by releasing the alternator mounting and adjuster link bolts and then pushing the alternator in towards the engine and slipping the belt from the pulleys.
3   If the belt is difficult to remove, turn the camshaft or crankshaft pulley (as applicable) and prise the belt to make it ride up and off the pulley rim.
4   Where a drivebelt is not being used to drive the alternator, remove the belt by slackening off the idler pulley clamp bolt.
5   Refit the new belt and then tension by prising the alternator or idler pulley as applicable.
6   Tension in accordance with the following table.
7   Additional belts with dual grooved pulleys are fitted to vehicles equipped with power steering or an air pump (emission control)

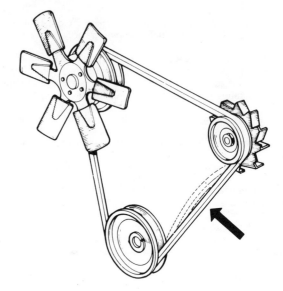

Fig. 2.7 Drivebelt (Type 810 engine) (Sec 6)

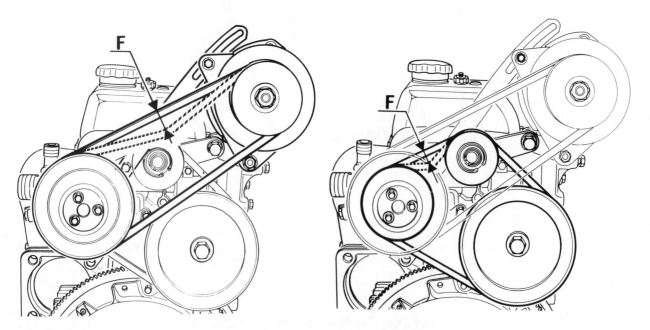

Fig. 2.8 Dual drivebelt (Type 807, 843, 844 engines) (Sec 6)

F   Deflection point

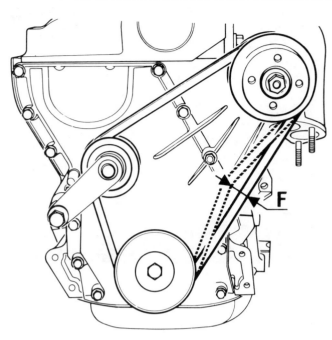

Fig. 2.9 Single drivebelt with idler pulley (Type 807, 843, 844 engines) (Sec 6)

Adjustment
Initial new belt

810 engine
4.5 to 5.5 mm (0.18 to 0.22 in)

807, 843, 844 engines
Camshaft to fan or coolant pump
1.5 to 2.5 mm (0.06 to 0.10 in)
Coolant pump to alternator
4.0 to 5.0 mm (0.16 to 0.20 in)
Power steering pump or air pump
(emission control)
4.5 to 5.5 mm (0.18 to 0.22 in)

Old belt or new belt (10 min. operation)

5.5 to 6.5 mm (0.22 to 0.26 in)

2.5 to 3.5 mm (0.10 to 0.14 in)

5.0 to 6.5 mm (0.20 to 0.26 in)

5.5 to 6.5 mm (0.22 to 0.26 in)

7 Coolant temperature and electric fan switches

1 In the event of a fault occurring in either one of these switches, first check the wiring and connections.

2 A switch can be unscrewed after first having drained the cooling system (photos).
3 The operation of the fan switch can be checked by connecting it to a battery with a test lamp in the circuit and then heating the temperature sensitive end in some water.
4 If the test lamp fails to come on by the time that the water is boiling then the switch should be renewed.
5 Testing of the coolant temperature switch cannot be done without special test instruments and the simplest way to test is by substitution of a new unit.
6 A fault in the coolant temperature gauge must be suspected if the switch is proved functional (refer to Chapter 10 for instrument removal).

8 Coolant pump (Type 810 engine) – removal and refitting

1 Disconnect the battery.
2 Drain the cooling system.
3 Disconnect the coolant hoses from the coolant pump
4 Slacken the drivebelt by moving the alternator in towards the engine.
5 Unbolt the fan shroud and rest it over the fan.
6 Remove the radiator.
7 Remove the fan shroud.
8 Unbolt the fan blades and coolant pump pulley.
9 Take off the drivebelt.
10 Unscrew and remove the coolant pump bolts.
11 Tap the pump with a plastic faced hammer to release it.
12 The coolant pump cannot be overhauled as spares are not available. A new pump complete will therefore have to be purchased.
13 Clean away all old gasket material from the cylinder head mounting face and using a new gasket, bolt the new pump into position. Tighten the pump bolts evenly.
14 Refit the hoses, pulley, fan, shroud and radiator. Tension the drivebelt (Section 6).
15 Fill and bleed the cooling system as described in Section 2.

9 Coolant pump (Type 807, 821. 841, 843, 844 engines) – removal and refitting

1 Drain the battery.
2 Drain the cooling system.
3 Disconnect the hoses from the coolant pump.
4 Slacken the drivebelt idler pulley pinch bolt.
5 Slacken the alternator mounting and adjuster link bolts.
6 Remove both drivebelts.
7 Unbolt and remove the pulley from the coolant pump and the camshaft.
8 Unscrew and remove the coolant pump bolts.
9 Tap the pump with a plastic faced hammer to release it.

7.2A Radiator fan thermostatic switch

7.2B Coolant temperature switch

10 The pump cannot be overhauled as spares are not available except to repair a leaking cover gasket. A new pump complete will therefore have to be purchased.

11 Clean away all old gasket material from the cylinder head mounting face and using a new gasket, bolt the new pump into position. Tighten the pump bolts evenly (photo).

12 Refit the hoses, pulleys and drivebelts.

13 Tension the belts as described in Section 6.

14 Fill and bleed the cooling system as described in Section 2.

10 Heating, ventilation system – description

1 The system utilises heat from the engine cooling system and the intake air is drawn from outside the car.

2 A booster fan is incorporated in the heater assembly which is located inside the car behind and below the fascia panel.

3 Temperature and air flow are fully controllable from the fascia-mounted control panel.

4 Fresh air outlets are provided above the centre console on the fascia panel.

5 The control lever arrangement differs between earlier and later models as shown.

9.11 Fitting coolant pump and gasket

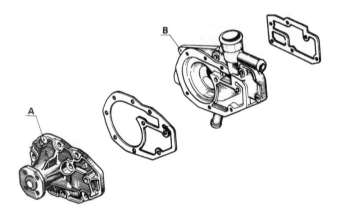

Fig. 2.10 Coolant pump components (Type 810 engine) (Sec 8)

A   Cover   B   Body

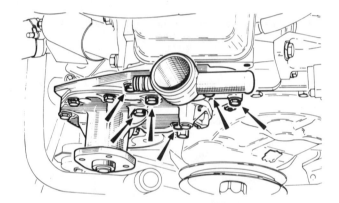

Fig. 2.11 Coolant pump mounting bolts (Type 810 engine) (Sec 8)

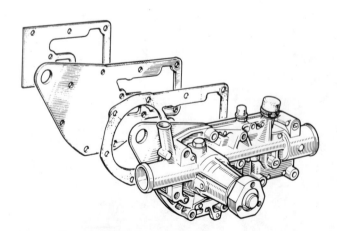

Fig. 2.12 Coolant pump components (Type 807, 843, 844 engines) (Sec 9)

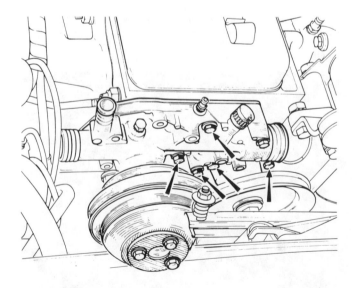

Fig. 2.13 Coolant pump mounting bolts (Type 807, 843, 844 engines) (Sec 9)

10.6 Stale air outlet slots

11.3 Heater hose connections at bulkhead

6   Stale air from the car interior is exhausted through slots at the sides of the tailgate aperture (photo).

11 Heater unit – removal and refitting

1   Working within the engine compartment, disconnect the battery.
2   The two heater hoses may now be clamped at the bulkhead provided suitable clamps are available. Failing such availability, the cooling system must be drained.
3   Disconnect the heater hoses (photo).

Pre 1976 cars
4   Working within the vehicle on cars built up until 1976, remove the radio speaker grille and the right-hand parcel shelf.
5   Extract the four screws (A) which hold the radio console (see Fig. 2.16).
6   Disconnect the leads from the windscreen washer switch.
7   Move the radio console towards the left-hand side of the fascia.
8   Extract the four screws (B) which retain the gear lever cover box and twist the cover box through one quarter turn.
9   Remove the two screws which retain the heater control panel.
10   Lower the panel behind the fascia until the heater control cables can be disconnected by prising off the retaining clips.

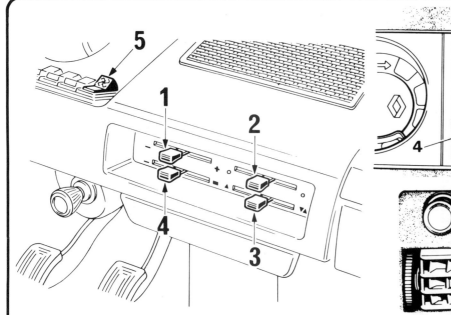

Fig. 2.14 Earlier type heater controls (Sec 10)

    1   Air intake control
    2   Temperature control (coolant valve)
    3   Hot air distribution control
    4   Vent flat control
    5   Booster switch

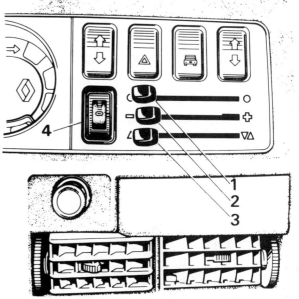

Fig. 2.15 Later type heater controls (Sec 10)

    1   Temperature control (coolant valve)
    2   Hot air control
    3   Hot air distribution control
    4   Booster switch

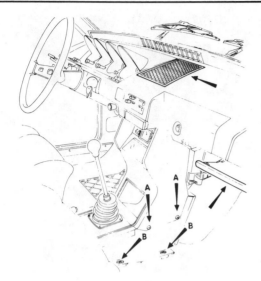

Fig. 2.16 Centre console fixing screws (Sec 11)

A   Radio console screws
B   Gear lever cover box screws

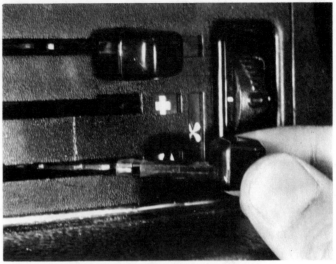

11.14 Removing heater control lever knob

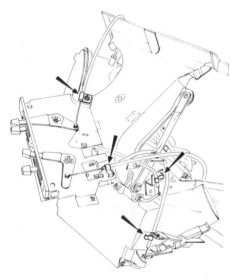

Fig. 2.17 Heater control cable clips (Sec 11)

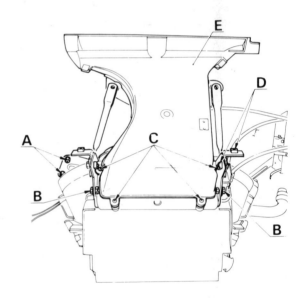

Fig. 2.18 Heater fixings (up to 1976) (Sec 11)

A   Scuttle nuts   D   Under facia bolts
B   Tie-bar bolts   E   Top cover
C   Top cover screws

11 Disconnect the cranked ends of the control cables from the lever arms on the heater.
12 Unscrew the nuts and bolts as indicated in Fig. 2.18 to release the heater assembly.
13 Withdraw the heater until the blower motor leads can be disconnected and then remove the unit from the car interior pulling the hoses through the engine compartment rear bulkhead by taking care not to spill coolant on the carpets or upholstery. The upper section (E) of the heater will be left in the car.

Post 1976 cars
14 Pull off the heater control lever knob (photo).
15 Remove the instrument panel cowl as described in Chapter 10.
16 Extract the two panel fixing screws (A) Fig. 2.19 lower the heater controls and prise off the cable clips. Disconnect the cable ends from the control arms on the heater.
17 Extract the fixing screws from the radio console and move the console to one side.
18 Extract the four screws which retain the cover box around the gear lever and turn the box through one quarter turn.

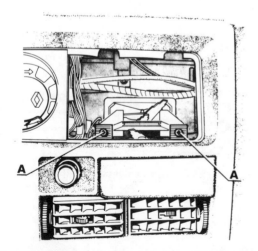

Fig. 2.19 Heater control lever panel screws (A) on later models (Sec 11)

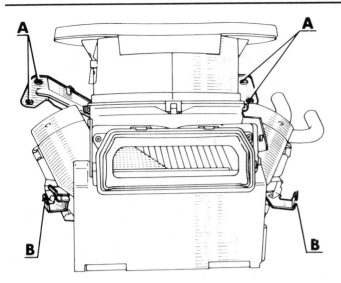

Fig. 2.20 Heater fixings (1976 on) (Sec 11)

A Scuttle nuts   B Bracket screws

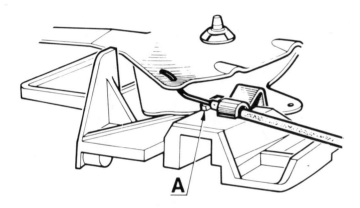

Fig. 2.21 Correct fitting of heater control cable (Sec 11)

A Control panel cable stop

19 Remove the heater securing nuts and bolts as shown in Fig. 2.20.
20 Disconnect the ducts from the heater casing.
21 Withdraw the heater until the motor leads can be disconencted, then withdraw the heater complete with hoses. Take care not to spill coolant on the carpets or upholstery.
22 Refitting is a reversal of removal, but check that the outer cable ends butt up against their stops on the control lever pivot plate before fitting the retaining clips.

12 Heater – dismantling and reassembly

1 Remove the heater as previously described.
2 Remove the heater valve (three screws).
3 Remove the heater matrix closure panel.
4 Extract the clips from the air entry shroud and remove the shroud.
5 Take out the fan/electric motor.
6 The fan can be removed from the motor spindle by extracting the socket head screw using an Allen key.

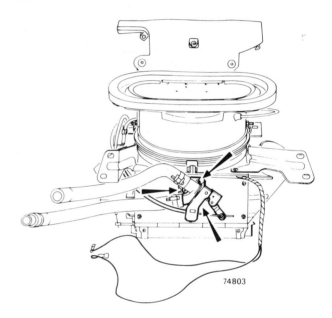

Fig. 2.22 Heater coolant valve fixing screws (arrowed) (Sec 12)

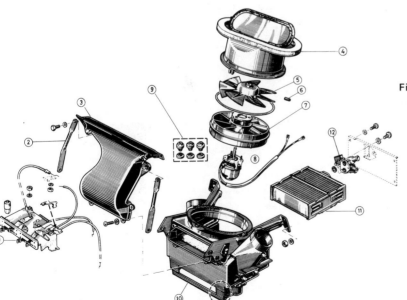

Fig. 2.23 Typical major components of heater (Sec 12)

1 Control panel
2 Tie-bar
3 Intake duct
4 Air flap assembly
5 Fan
6 Grub screw
7 Support housing
8 Fan motor
9 Motor mountings
10 Heater casing
11 Matrix
12 Coolant flow regulating valve

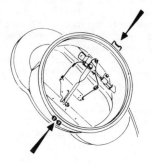

Fig. 2.24 Heater air entry shroud clips (Sec 12)

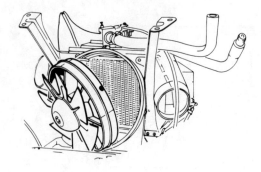

Fig. 2.25 Removing heater fan assembly (Sec 10)

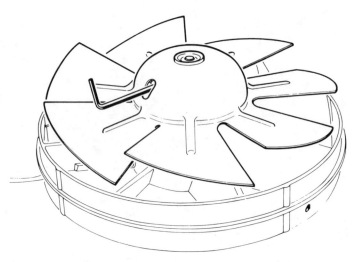

Fig. 2.26 Extracting heater fan grub screw (Sec 12)

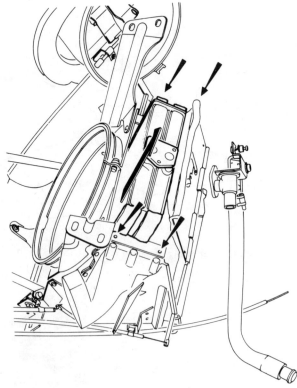

Fig. 2.27 Heater matrix removal and cover panel screws
(arrowed) (Sec 12)

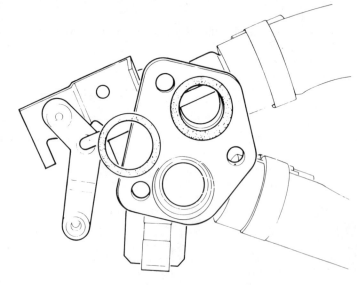

Fig. 2.28 Coolant control valve seals (Sec 12)

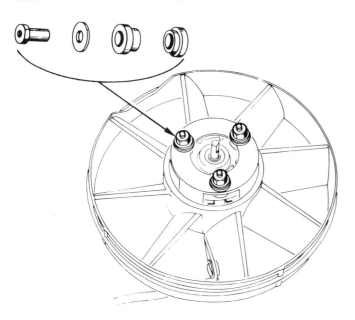

Fig. 2.29 Fitting sequence for heater fan motor mounting cushions (Sec 12)

7 Remove the three motor mounting screws and separate the motor from the supporting ring.

8 The heater matrix can be removed from the unit after first having withdrawn the valve as described in earlier paragraphs.

9 Extract the four securing panel screws and withdraw the matrix.

10 Reassembly of the components is a reversal of dismantling, but use new rubber seals in the valve and make sure that other rubber components are in good order.

11 The motor mounting cushions must be located as shown in Fig. 2.29.

13 Air conditioning system

1 Air conditioning is an option on certain models.

2 Prior to carrying out any work on the engine or fascia panel, refer to *Warning* in Chapter 1, Section 4.

3 Certain minor maintenance operations will ensure that the system functions correctly at all times.

4 During winter, run the system for a few minutes each week. This will ensure lubrication of the pump seal.

5 A reduction in efficiency may be due to the evaporator icing up when the controls are opened fully. If this happens, set knob 12 to MAX and reduce the coldness momentarily by moving knob 13 to DEFROST.

6 Occasionally check for the presence of Freon refrigerant in the sight glass on top of the dehydration tank. This check should be carried out within two minutes of switching on the system. Any replenishment must be carried out by your dealer or refrigeration engineer. The presence of air bubbles within the sight glass is indicative of a leak in the system.

7 A pool of water is often to be found under the car after it has been left standing. This is normal and is due to ice condensate melting.

8 The tension of the compressor drivebelt should be maintained to give a total deflection at the centre of the longest run of the belt of 5.0 mm (0.20 in).

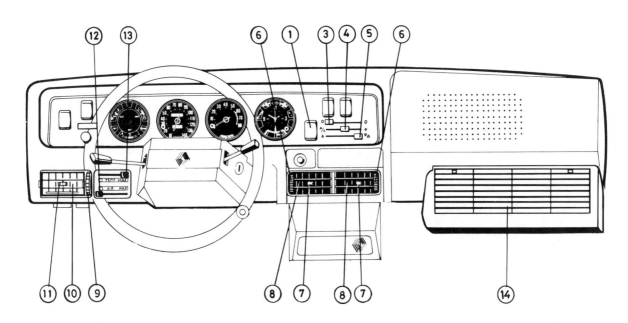

Fig. 2.30 Air conditioning system controls (Sec 13)

1   Heater fan switch
3   Air temperature control lever
4   Air flow control lever
5   Hot air directional control (demist)
6   Directional control (fresh air)
7   Directional control (fresh air)
8   Air outlet grille
9   Directional control
10 Grille
11 Directional control
12 Air flow (volume) control
13 Air temperature control lever
14 Grille

'Fault diagnosis appears overleaf'

14 Fault diagnosis – cooling system

Symptom	Reason(s)
Overheating	Coolant loss due to leakage Electric cooling fan malfunction (if applicable) Drivebelt slack or broken Thermostat jammed shut Radiator matrix clogged internally or externally Brakes binding New engine not yet run-in
Overcooling	Thermostat missing or jammed open
Coolant loss	External leakage (hose joints etc) Overheating (see above) Internal leakage (head gasket or cylinder liner) – look for water in oil and/or oil in coolant

Chapter 3 Fuel and emission control systems

Contents

Part 1 General
Air cleaner – removal and refitting 3
Air cleaner assembly and ancillary components – servicing 2
Description and maintenance 1

Part 2 Carburettor systems
Carburettor – removal and refitting 12
Carburettor overhaul – general 13
Carburettor (Solex 32/32 SEIEMA) – overhaul 14
Carburettor (Weber 32) – modifications for North American
automatic transmission vehicles 17
Carburettor (Weber 32 DARA) – overhaul 16
Carburettor (Weber 32 DIR) – overhaul 15
Carburettors – general description 10
Carburettors – idle speed and mixture adjustment 11
Fuel pump – description and cleaning 4
Fuel pump – overhaul 7
Fuel pump – removal and refitting 5
Fuel pump – testing 6
Fuel tank – removal, cleaning, repair and refitting 9
Fuel tank level transmitter – removal and refitting 8

Part 3 Fuel injection system
Accelerator cable switch – adjustment 21

Auxiliary air control valve – description, removal and
refitting 28
Control box – removal and refitting 29
Fuel filter – renewal 23
Fuel injector hoses – renewal 26
Fuel injection system – description and precautions 18
Fuel injection system – idle speed and mixture adjustment 19
Fuel injector – removal and refitting 25
Fuel pump – removal and refitting 24
Pressure regulator – adjustment 22
Pressure regulator – removal and refitting 27
Throttle switch – adjustment 20

Part 4 Emission control system, exhaust system and throttle control
Accelerator cable – renewal and adjustment 36
Air injection system – description and maintenance 32
Catalytic converter 35
EGR system maintenance indicator 34
Emission control systems – description 30
Exhaust gas recirculation system – description and
maintenance 33
Fault diagnosis – fuel and emission control systems 38
Fuel evaporative control system 31
Manifolds and exhaust system 37

Specifications

System type
All models except R1313, R1317, R1323, R1327 .... Dual barrel downdraught carburettor, rear mounted fuel tank and mechanical or electric fuel pump

R1313, R1317, R1323, R1327 .... Bosch jetronic fuel injection system

Fuel capacity .... 12.0 Imp gal (14.5 US gal/55.0 l)

Fuel grade
R15 and R17 except N. America .... 98 octane (4 star)
R17 (N. America) .... Regular low lead
Fuel injection models:
    California .... 91 octane unleaded
    Other models .... 98 octane

Carburettor – Solex 32/32 SEIEMA
Application R1301, R1304, 1972
Engine type 821, 841

Carburettor mark numbers	506	522	547
Venturi:			
Primary	23	23	23
Secondary	24	24	24
Main jet:			
Primary	117.5	155	112.5
Secondary	155	155	152.5

Air compensating jet:			
Primary	140N3	140N3	115N5
Secondary	130N3	130N3	120N5
Idle jet:			
Primary	50	52.5	50
Secondary	80	80	80
Accelerator pump jet	45	45	45
Needle valve	1.7 mm	1.7 mm	1.7 mm
Initial throttle opening	1.10 mm	1.10 mm	1.20 mm
	(0.043 in)	(0.043 in)	(0.047 in)

Idle speed:	
Manual transmission models	675 to 725 rev/min
Automatic transmission models	625 to 675 rev/min
CO level	1.5 to 2.5%
Fast idle speed (emission controlled deceleration):	
R1301	1400 to 1500 rev/min
R1304	1350 to 1450 rev/min

Carburettor – Weber 32 DIR 21

Application	All models except R1301, R1304
Engine type	810, 807, 841, 843
Carburettor mark numbers	**2300 to 2305, 4200, 4201, 32 DIR 21, 32 DIR 21 T**
Venturi:	
Primary	23
Secondary	24
Main jet:	
Primary	120
Secondary	110
Idle jet:	
Primary	70
Secondary	60
Air compensating jet:	
Primary	135
Secondary	100
Emulsifier:	
Primary	F53
Secondary	F6
Accelerator pump	50
Needle valve	1.75
Float weight	11g
Float level	7.0 mm (0.276 in)
Float stroke	8.0 mm (0.315 in)
Initial throttle opening	0.8 mm (0.035 in)
Choke part-open setting (mechanical)	5.0 mm (0.197 in)
Choke part-open setting (vacuum)	8.0 mm (0.035 in)
Idle speed:	
Manual transmission models	750 rev/min
Automatic transmission models	600 rev/min
CO level	2.5 to 3.0%

Carburettor – Weber 32 DIR 23, 32 DIR 24

Carburettor mark numbers	2702 to 2704	2600 to 2602	2603
Venturi:			
Primary	24	24	24
Secondary	24	24	24
Main jet:			
Primary	145	147	147
Secondary	150	145	150
Idle jet:			
Primary	45	52	52
Secondary	70	80	80
Air compensating jet:			
Primary	175	180	180
Secondary	180	160	160
Emulsifier:			
Primary	F9	F57	F57
Secondary	F6	F9	F9
Accelerator pump	60	60	60
Needle valve	1.75	1.75	1.75
Float weight	11g	11g	11g
Float level	5.25 mm (0.207 in)	7.0 mm (0.276 in)	7.0 mm (0.276 in)
Float stroke	8.0 mm (0.315 in)	8.0 mm (0.315 in)	8.0 mm (0.315 in)
Initial throttle opening	1.20 mm (0.047 in)	1.1 to 1.2 mm (0.043 to 0.097 in)	1.1 to 1.2 mm (0.043 to 0.097 in)

Choke part-open setting (mechanical)	6.0 to 7.0 mm (0.236 to 0.276 in)	6.0 mm (0.236 in)	6.0 mm (0.236 in)
Choke part-open setting (vacuum)	7.0 mm (0.276 in)	12.0 mm (0.472 in)	10.0 mm (0.394 in)

Idle speed:
Manual transmission models .... 750 rev/min
Automatic transmission models .... 600 rev/min in A
CO level .... 2.5 to 3.0%

Carburetor – Weber 32 DIR 32
Carburettor mark numbers   **3200 to 3203**

Venturi:
  Primary 24
  Secondary 24
Main jet:
  Primary 147
  Secondary 150
Idle jet:
  Primary 55
  Secondary 80
Air compensating jet:
  Primary 180
  Secondary 170
Emulsifier:
  Primary F57
  Secondary F9
Accelerator pump 55
Needle valve 1.75
Float weight 11g
Float level .... 7.0 mm (0.276 in)
Float stroke .... 8.0 mm (0.315 in)
Initial throttle opening .... 1.20 mm (0.047 in)
Choke part-open setting (mechanical) .... 6.0 to 7.0 mm (0.236 to 0.276 in)
Choke part-open setting (vacuum) .... 10.0 mm (0.394 in)
Idle speed:
  Manual transmission models .... 750 rev/min
  Automatic transmission models .... 600 rev/min in A
CO level .... 2.5 to 3.0%

Carburetor – Weber 32 DIR 24, 32 DIR 29, 32 DIR 39

Carburettor mark numbers	**4202, 4203**	**4500, 32 DIR 39 32 DIR 39 T 32 DIR 34 A**	**2700, 2701**
Venturi:			
Primary	23	23	24
Secondary	24	24	24
Main jet:			
Primary	120	122	140
Secondary	110	110	150
Idle jet:			
Primary	70	70	50
Secondary	60	60	70
Air compensating jet:			
Primary	135	160	175
Secondary	100	120	190
Emulsifier:			
Primary	F53	F53	F9
Secondary	F6	F6	F9
Accelerator pump	50	60	60
Needle valve	1.75	1.75	1.75
Float weight	11g	11g	11g
Float level	7.0 mm (0.276 in)	7.0 mm (0.276 in)	5.25 mm (0.207 in)
Float stroke	8.0 mm (0.315 in)	8.0 mm (0.315 in)	8.0 mm (0.315 in)
Initial throttle opening	0.8 mm (0.031 in)	1.0 mm (0.039 in)	1.20 mm (0.047 in)
Choke part-open setting (mechanical)	5.0 mm (0.197 in)	4.5 mm (0.177 in)	6.0 mm (0.236 in)
Choke part-open setting (vacuum)	8.0 mm (0.315 in)	7.0 mm (0.276 in)	7.0 mm (0.276 in)
Idle speed:			
Manual transmission models	750 rev/min		
Automatic transmission models	600 rev/min		
CO level	2.5 to 3.0%		

Carburettor – Weber 32 DIR 37

Carburettor mark numbers	4300, 4301
Venturi:	
Primary	23
Secondary	24
Main jet:	
Primary	125
Secondary	137
Idle jet:	
Primary	55
Secondary	60
Air compensating jet:	
Primary	155
Secondary	190
Accelerator pump jet	50
Needle valve	1.75
Float weight	11g
Float stroke	8.0 mm (0.315 in)
Initial throttle opening	1.2 to 1.3 mm (0.047 to 0.051 in)
Choke part-open setting (mechanical)	6.0 mm (0.24 in)
Choke part-open setting (vacuum)	9.0 mm (0.35 in)
Idle speed:	
Manual transmission models	825 to 875 rev/min
Automatic transmission models	625 to 675 rev/min in D
CO level	3.5 to 4.5%

Carburettor – Weber 32 DIR 37

Carburettor mark numbers	4303
Venturi:	
Primary	23
Secondary	24
Main jet:	
Primary	122
Secondary	137
Idle jet:	
Primary	55
Secondary	60
Air compensating jet:	
Primary	155
Secondary	190
Accelerator pump jet	50
Needle valve	1.75
Float weight	11g
Float level	7.0 mm (0.28 in)
Float stroke	8.0 mm (0.32 in)
Initial throttle opening	1.2 to 1.3 mm (0.047 to 0.051 in)
Choke part-open setting (mechanical)	6.0 mm (0.24 in)
Choke part-open setting (vacuum)	6.0 mm (0.25 in)
Idle speed:	
Manual transmission models	825 to 875 rev/min
Automatic transmission models	625 to 675 rev/min in D
CO level	3.5 to 4.5%

Carburettor – Weber 32 DIR 38

Carburettor mark numbers	4400, 4401
Venturi:	
Primary	23
Secondary	24
Main jet:	
Primary	122
Secondary	135
Idle jet:	
Primary	55
Secondary	55
Air compensating jet:	
Primary	150
Secondary	180
Accelerator pump jet	50
Needle valve	1.75
Float weight	11g
Float level	7.0 mm (0.28 in)
Float stroke	8.0 mm (0.32 in)
Initial throttle opening	1.3 to 1.4 mm (0.051 to 0.055 in)
Choke part-open setting (mechanical)	6.0 mm (0.24 in)
Choke part-open setting (vacuum)	10.0 mm (0.39 in)

Idle speed:
    Manual transmission models .... 825 to 875 rev/min
    Automatic transmission models .... 625 to 675 rev/min in D
CO level .... 3.5 to 4.5%

Carburettor – Weber 32 DIR 38

Carburettor mark numbers   4402

Venturi:
    Primary 23
    Secondary 24
Main jet:
    Primary 122
    Secondary 135
Idle jet:
    Primary 55
    Secondary 55
Air compensating jet:
    Primary 155
    Secondary 180
Accelerator pump jet 50
Needle valve 1.75
Float weight 11g
Float level .... 7.0 mm (0.276 in)
Float stroke .... 8.0 mm (0.315 in)
Initial throttle opening .... 1.3 to 1.4 mm (0.051 to 0.055 in)
Choke part-open setting (mechanical) .... 6.0 mm (0.25 in)
Choke part-open setting (vacuum) .... 10.0 mm (0.39 in)
Idle speed:
    Manual transmission models .... 825 to 875 rev/min
    Automatic transmission models .... 625 to 675 rev/min in D
CO level .... 3.5 to 4.5%

Carburettor – Weber 32 DIR 64

Carburettor mark numbers   100

Venturi:
    Primary 23
    Secondary 24
Main jet:
    Primary 122
    Secondary 140
Idle jet:
    Primary 75
    Secondary 60
Air compensating jet:
    Primary 160
    Secondary 185
Emulsifier:
    Primary F53
    Secondary F6
Accelerator pump jet 40
Needle valve 1.75
Float weight 11g
Float level .... 7 mm (0.276 in)
Float stroke .... 8 mm (0.315 in)
Initial throttle opening (extreme cold) .... 0.95 mm ± 0.05 (0.04 in ± 0.002)
Mechanical part-open setting .... 5 mm (0.2 in)
Pneumatic part-open setting .... 8 mm (0.315 in)
Idle speed .... 775 rev/min ± 25
Defuming valve .... 0.50 mm ± 0.15 (0.02 in ± 0.006)

Carburettor – Weber 32 DARA, 32 DARA 1

Application	843 engine	
Carburettor mark numbers	**5200**	**5600**
Venturi:		
Primary	23	23
Secondary	24	24
Main jet:		
Primary	122	125
Secondary	135	140
Idle jet:		
Primary	55	52
Secondary	40	40
Air compensating jet:		
Primary	170	175
Secondary	170	170

	5200	5600
Emulsifier:		
Primary	F53	F53
Secondary	F5	F5
Accelerator pump jet	50	60
Needle valve	1.75	1.75
Float weight	11g	11g
Float level	7.0 mm (0.28 in)	7.0 mm (0.28 in)
Float stroke	8.0 mm (0.32 in)	8.0 mm (0.32 in)
Initial throttle opening	1.2 to 1.3 mm (0.047 to 0.051 in)	1.4 to 1.5 mm (0.055 to 0.059 in)
Choke part-open setting (mechanical)	7.0 mm (0.28 in)	7.0 mm (0.28 in)
Choke part-open setting (vacuum)	5.0 to 7.0 mm (0.20 to 0.28 in)	5.0 to 7.0 mm (0.20 to 0.28 in)
Idle speed:		
Manual transmission models	825 to 875 rev/min	
Automatic transmission models	625 to 675 rev/min in D	
CO level	2.5 to 3.5%	

Carburettor – Weber 32 DARA 4, 4T, S, 5T

Venturi:	
Primary	24
Secondary	26
Main jet:	
Primary	132
Secondary	150
Idle jet:	
Primary	50
Secondary	45
Air compensating jet:	
Primary	180
Secondary	145
Emulsifier:	
Primary	F53
Secondary	F6
Accelerator pump	60
Needle valve	175
Float weight	11g
Float level	7.0 mm (0.28 in)
Float stroke	8.0 mm (0.32 in)
Initial throttle opening (32 DARA 4)	1.40 mm (0.055 in)
Initial throttle opening (32 DARA 5)	1.60 mm (0.063 in)
Choke part-open setting (mechanical)	7.0 mm (0.28 in)
Choke part-open setting (vacuum)	7.0 mm (0.28 in)
Idle speed:	
Manual transmission models	775 to 825 rev/min
Automatic transmission models	600 to 650 rev/min in A
CO level	2.5 to 3.0%

Carburettor – Weber 32 DARA 13

Venturi:	
Primary	23
Secondary	24
Main jet:	
Primary	125
Secondary	140
Idle jet:	
Primary	52
Secondary	40
Air compensating jet:	
Primary	185
Secondary	170
Emulsifier:	
Primary	F53
Secondary	F5
Centraliser (auxiliary venturi):	
Primary	4
Secondary	3.5
Accelerator pump jet	60
Needle valve	175
Float weight	11g
Float level	7.0 mm (0.28 in)
Float stroke	8.0 mm (0.32 in)
Initial throttle opening	1.5 mm (0.059 in)
Choke part-open setting (mechanical)	7.0 mm (0.28 in)
Choke part-open setting (vacuum)	5.0 to 7.0 mm (0.20 to 0.28 in)
Cold start electric heater coil	40W

Carburettor – Weber 32 DARA 15, 16

Carburettor mark numbers	8200	8300
Venturi:		
Primary	23	23
Secondary	24	24
Main jet:		
Primary	122	125
Secondary	135	140
Idle jet:		
Primary	55	52
Secondary	40	40
Air compensating jet:		
Primary	170	185
Secondary	170	170
Emulsifier:		
Primary	F53	F53
Secondary	F5	F5
Accelerator pump jet	50	60
Needle valve	1.75	1.75
Float weight	11g	11g
Float level	7.0 mm (0.28 in)	7.0 mm (0.28 in)
Float stroke	8.0 mm (0.32 in)	8.0 mm (0.32 in)
Choke part-open setting (mechanical)	7.0 mm (0.28 in)	7.0 mm (0.28 in)
Choke part-open setting (vacuum)	5.0 to 7.0 mm (0.20 to 0.28 in)	5.0 to 7.0 mm (0.20 to 0.28 in)
Cold start electric heater coil	40W	40W

Fuel injection system

Idle speed	1025 to 1075 rev/min
CO level	2.5 to 3.0%

PART 1 GENERAL

1 Description and maintenance

For most models, the fuel system consists of a rear mounted fuel tank, a mechanically or electrically-operated fuel pump and a dual barrel downdraught carburettor.

The exceptions to this arrangement are to be found on certain European and North American vehicles which have a fuel injection system.

All North American vehicles are equipped with an emission control system which becomes more and more sophisticated, the later the car – see Section 30.

Maintenance on all models equipped with carburettor engines normally consists of the following operations which should be carried out regularly or as specified in 'Routine Maintenance'.

(a) Renew air cleaner element
(b) Clean fuel pump
(c) Check carburettor idle and mixture adjustment
(d) Inspect all fuel hoses and unions for condition and security

For fuel injection models, refer to Part 3.

2 Air cleaner assembly and ancillary components – servicing

Carburettor models – renewal of the element

1 Open the bonnet and unscrew the wing nut from the end cover of the air cleaner casing.
2 Remove the end cover and extract the filter element.
3 Discard the element and wipe out the casing.
4 Insert the new element and refit the end cover (photos).
5 On most later models, an air intake deflector flap valve is fitted to the air cleaner. Select the WINTER or SUMMER position according to ambient temperature.
6 If the temperature is below 10° (50°F) then by selecting WINTER, warm air will be drawn from a deflector plate around the exhaust manifold (photo).
7 On later Renault 17 models, a thermostatically controlled air intake control is fitted to the air cleaner to provide an optimum air temperature all the year round at the carburettor throat.
8 On fuel injected models the air cleaner element is accessible after unclipping the casing cover.

Intake air preheating device – description

9 This unit fitted to later models is designed to prevent the carburettor from icing when the ambient air is too cold. A

2.4A Air cleaner element

2.4B Fitting air cleaner end cover

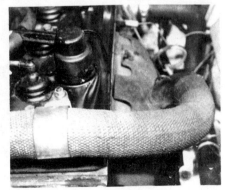
2.6 Air cleaner hot air collector hose

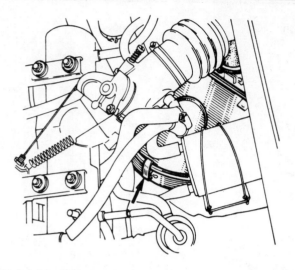

Fig. 3.1 Air cleaner casing clip on fuel injection models (Sec 2)

3.2A Air cleaner mounting

3.2B Air cleaner mounting stud and bracket

thermostatically controlled flap in the double air intake selects a combination of cold air, and warm air drawn from around the exhaust manifold. This flap is controlled by a wax thermostat element fitted to the air filter body, and is situated in the air stream.

10 When the intake air temperature drops to below 17.5°C, the element contracts and the flap pivots to shut off the cold air intake.

11 At 26°C, the element expands sufficiently to move the flap closing off the warm air intake.

12 A defuming pipe connects the carburettor and the air intake elbow on the carburettor.

Air filter capsule – functional checks

13 Remove the air filter.

14 Withdraw the filter element.

15 Place the air filter body in a saucepan of water up to the height of the filter element.

16 Using a suitable thermometer measure the water temperature. Heat the saucepan.

17 When the water is at 17.5°C, or below, the cold air intake should be shut.

18 When the water temperature rises to 26°C and above, the flap should have closed off the warm air intake.

19 If the unit is defective, replace it with a new one.

---

3   Air cleaner – removal and refitting

---

1   Open the bonnet, disconnect the air intake trunking from the cleaner casing.

2   Remove the casing mounting nuts (photos).

3   Withdraw the casing until any connecting hoses can be identified as to position and detached. Remove the casing.

4   Refitting is a reversal of removal.

PART 2 CARBURETTOR SYSTEMS

---

4   Fuel pump – description and cleaning

---

1   On Type 810 engines, the fuel pump is operated through a lever resting on a cam on the camshaft.

2   On other engine types, the fuel pump is operated by means of a pushrod again driven by a cam on the camshaft.

3   The pushrod type pump is of disposable design so that if a fault occurs, it will have to be renewed complete.

4   Cleaning either type of pump is similar. Remove the cover screws, take off the cover and extract the filter (photo).

5   Mop out fuel and sediment from the fuel pump body and clean the filter screen.

6   Refit by reversing the dismantling procedure, check that the sealing rings are in good condition and note that the projection on the filter screen of the disposable type pump must be uppermost (photo).

7   Do not overtighten the cover screws.

---

5   Fuel pump – removal and refitting

Lever-operated type (Type 810 engine)

1   Disconnect the hoses from the pump. These will include a feed and return hose to the tank and a feed hose to the carburettor. Plug the fuel inlet hose.

2   Unscrew the flange mounting nuts and withdraw the pump from the crankcase. Retain the flange gaskets and spacer (photo).

Pushrod operated type

3   Carry out the operations described in paragraph 1 (photo).

4   Unbolt and withdraw the pump from the engine cylinder head. Remove the pushrod noting that the circlip is towards the top end (photos).

Electrically-operated type

5   An electric pump is fitted instead of a mechanical unit to later model North American vehicles.

4.4 Lever type fuel pump filter

4.6 Push-rod type fuel pump filter

5.2 Removing lever type fuel pump

5.3 Hose connections to pushrod type fuel pump

5.4A Removing pushrod type fuel pump

5.4B Fuel pump push-rod with circlip at top end

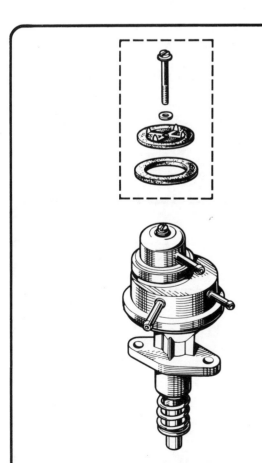

Fig. 3.2 Pushrod operated fuel pump (Sec 4)

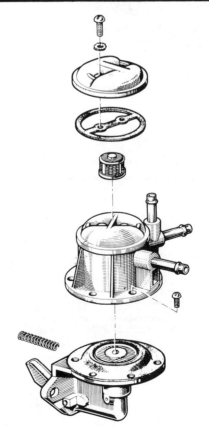

Fig. 3.3 Lever-operated fuel pump (Sec 4)

6   The pump is mounted under and towards the rear of the car.
7   To remove the pump, disconnect the battery then disconnect the leads from the pump terminals.
8   Disconnect the fuel hoses, quickly plugging the inlet one.
9   Unbolt and remove the pump.
10 Refitting is a reversal of removal.

6   Fuel pump – testing

All pumps
1   Uncouple the fuel pipe at its connection with the carburettor.
2   Spin the engine on the starter and observe if a well defined spurt of petrol is ejected from the hose. If this occurs then the fuel pump is serviceable.

Mechanically-operated pumps
3   An alternative method is to remove the pump from its location and place a thumb over the inlet port and actuate the operating lever when fitted. A substantial suction should be felt and heard if the pump is in good order.
4   Where these tests prove positive then lack of fuel at the carburettor must be due to blocked fuel lines, blocked tank vent or a sticky carburettor needle valve.

7   Fuel pump – overhaul

Lever-operated type (Type 810 engine)
1   If the pump has seen considerable service it will almost certainly be advantageous to exchange it for a factory reconditioned unit, if no obvious and easily repairable faults are apparent.
2   If it is decided to repair the pump, then before dismantling, score an alignment mark across the edges of the two mating flanges to facilitate reassembly.
3   Remove the cover and filter and the flange screws and separate the two halves of the pump body.
4   Withdraw the diaphragm by disengaging the operating rod from the pump operating lever.
5   The diaphragm and valve assemblies may be renewed if necessary as these components are available in kit form.
6   If wear has occurred in the operating lever or its spindle, then a new pump unit should be obtained.
7   Reassembly is a reversal of dismantling but ensure that the valves are correctly orientated and staked in position.

Electrically-operated pump
8   Provided that the electrical leads and hoses are secure, trouble should not occur.
9   Poor fuel delivery or slow pumping action are sometimes the result of a blocked internal filter which should be cleaned.

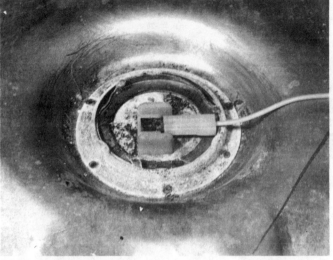

8.3 Fuel tank transmitter unit

10 Failure of the pump to operate at all may be due to incorrectly set contacts. To adjust, extract the securing screw and take off the cover. Push the lug (6) to open the contacts. The contact blade must be just touching the ridge (A). Bend the blade if necessary to achieve this.
11 If the contacts are out of alignment, unscrew the screw (V).
12 When the pump is switched off observe that the lug (6) pushes blade (7) 0.77 mm to 1.03 mm (0.030 to 0.040 in) from the ridge (A). If it does not, bend stop (D).
13 Finally check dimension X which should be between 1.67 and 1.93 mm (0.065 and 0.076 mm).
14 Refit the cover.

8   Fuel tank level transmitter – removal and refitting

All models except N. America
1   Have the fuel level in the tank fairly low. Open the tailgate and peel back the floor covering.
2   Disconnect the battery.
3   Disconnect the lead from the terminal on the transmitter unit (photo).
4   Using a suitable lever engaged with the retaining lugs on the transmitter, rotate the unit to release it.
5   Withdraw the unit carefully to avoid damaging the float or arm.
6   Refitting is a reversal of removal, but make sure that the sealing ring is in good order.

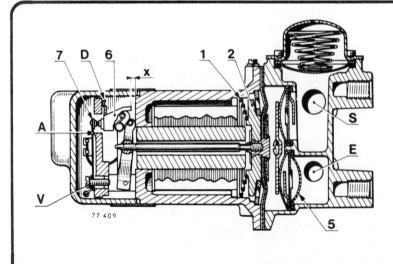

Fig. 3.4 Sectional view of electric fuel pump (Sec 7)

1	Spring
2	Core
5	Filter
6	Lug
7	Contact blade
A	Ridge
D	Stop
E	Inlet port
S	Outlet port
V	Screw
X	1.67 to 1.93 mm (0.65 to 0.75 in)

77 409

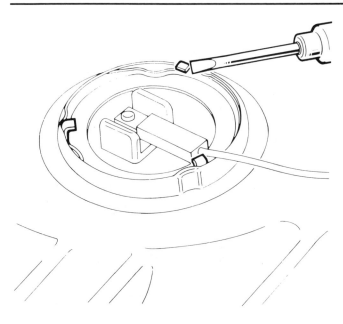

Fig. 3.5 Removing fuel tank transmitter unit (Sec 8)

N. American models
7   The operations are generally similar, but the tank should be lowered to provide access to the transmitter unit as described in the next Section.

9   Fuel tank – removal, cleaning, repair and refitting

1   Disconnect the battery.
2   On models fitted with a drain plug, unscrew it and drain the fuel into a suitable container.
3   If a drain plug is not fitted, syphon out the fuel.

All models except N. America
4   Open the tailgate and peel back the floor covering.
5   Disconnect the lead from the transmitter unit.
6   Disconnect the hose clips and then detach the vent pipe and the flexible section of the fuel filler pipe.
7   Unscrew the tank flange mounting bolts and lift the tank from its aperture.
8   The sealing mastic may need releasing with a sharp knife run round the flange if the tank refuses to move.

N. American models
9   The operations are generally similar except that the tank is bolted up from underneath the car and should be removed by lowering.

Fig. 3.6 Fuel tank transmitter (Sec 8)

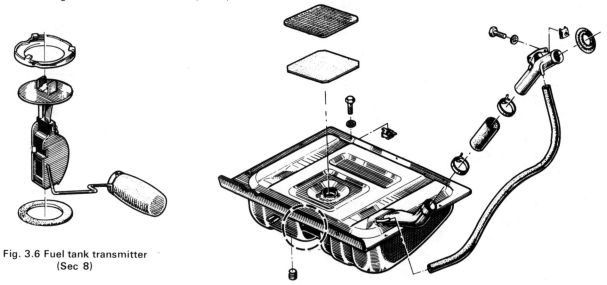

Fig. 3.7 Typical fuel tank (removable from luggage compartment) (Sec 9)

Fig. 3.8 Fuel tank (removable from beneath car) (Sec 9)

9.13 Fuel tank earth connection

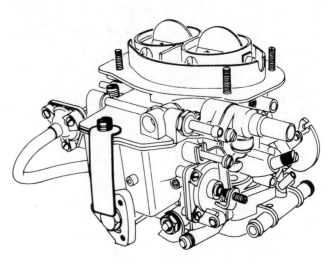

Fig. 3.9 Solex 32/32 SEIEMA carburettor (Sec 10)

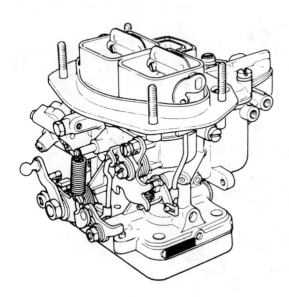

Fig. 3.10 Typical Weber 32 DIR 21 carburettor (Sec 10)

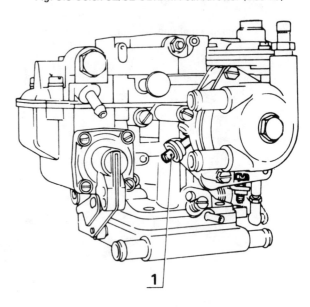

Fig. 3.11 Typical Weber 32 DARA carburettor (Sec 10)

10   If a tank has been removed to clean out sediment, remove the tank transmitter unit and then shake the tank vigorously using several changes of paraffin until the tank is clean. Leave it to drain thoroughly.
11   If the tank is leaking, a temporary repair may be made using a proprietary product made for the purpose. A permanent repair should be entrusted to experts (usually radiator repairers). On no account attempt to weld or solder a fuel tank even if it has remained empty for several days. To eliminate all danger, a fuel tank must be steamed out thoroughly.
12   With N. American vehicles, refer to Section 31 for additional disconnection operations required during fuel tank removal as a result of the fuel evaporative control system fitted.
13   Refitting on all models is a reversal of removal, note the earth wire under one of the flange bolts (photo).

10 Carburettors – general description

1   One of three types of dual barrel downdraught carburettors may be fitted depending upon engine type, model and date of production.
2   The Solex 32/32 SEIEMA and Weber 32 DIR have a manually-operated choke (cold start) system while the Weber 32 DARA has a coolant-heated automatic choke. To set this type of choke prior to starting the engine, depress the accelerator fully and release it.
3   On later model Weber 32 DARA carburettors fitted to automatic transmission North American vehicles, an extra electrically-operated choke element is fitted between the automatic choke support plate and the choke housing cover. Its purpose is to assist in rapid warm up in order to reduce exhaust emission levels at cold starting.

11 Carburettors – idle speed and mixture adjustment

Solex 32/32 SEIEMA
1   With the engine at normal working temperature, adjust the idle speed to that shown in Specifications. To do this, turn the mixture screw (B) in or out until the highest speed is obtained. If the speed is not within the range of 725 to 775 rev/min then turn the screw (A) as necessary.
2   Again turn screw (B) in or out to achieve the highest possible speed and then reduce the speed by 0 to 25 rev/min by turning screw (B) inward.
3   If the adjustment has been carefully carried out then the CO level (checked on an exhaust gas analyser) should be 2%.

4 Remember that satisfactory idling will not be achieved if the ignition system and engine are in a poor state of tune.
5 When adjusting the idle speed, make sure that all electrical equipment is off.

Fast idle (emission controlled deceleration)
6 Having adjusted the idling speed, now check and adjust the fast idle speed.
7 On cars with manual transmission, disconnect the grey (+) wire from the solenoid flap valve and insulate its end with electrical tape.

8 Connect a jump lead between the now free flap valve terminal and the (+) terminal on the ignition coil.
9 On cars with automatic transmission, disconnect the yellow wire (1) from the solenoid flap valve and connect a jump lead between the now free terminal and a good earth.
10 To adjust the fast idle turn the air screw (C) until the specified speed is obtained.
11 The CO level should now be checked and if incorrect, turn the fuel screw (D) to correct it.
12 Remove the jump leads and re-make the original connections.

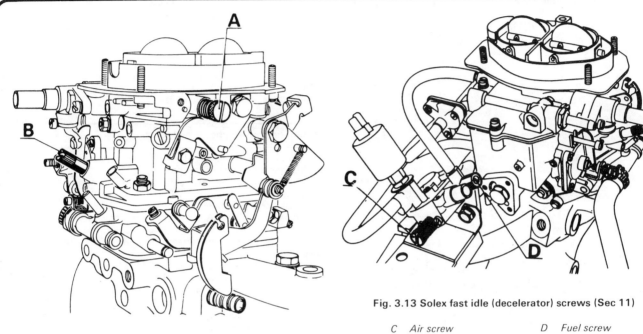

Fig. 3.12 Solex adjusting screws (idle) (Sec 11)

A Air screw   B Fuel screw

Fig. 3.13 Solex fast idle (decelerator) screws (Sec 11)

C Air screw   D Fuel screw

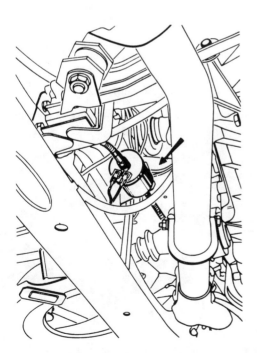

Fig. 3.14 Centrifugal speedometer cable driven switch on manual transmission cars with Solex (Sec 11)

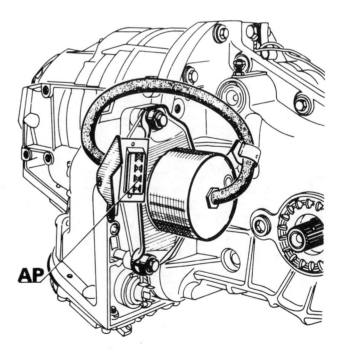

Fig. 3.15 Computer unit used for fast idle on automatic transmission cars with Solex (Sec 11)

13 It is possible to check the fast idle cut-off speed on cars with manual transmission in the following way. Cars with automatic transmission can only be checked if special equipment is available so leave this to your dealer.

14 Partially pull off the solenoid flap valve grey wire so that a test bulb can be connected between the exposed part of the terminal and earth. Do not allow the jump lead or its clip to make contact with the solenoid valve body.

15 Drive the vehicle in 2nd gear until it reaches 25 mph (40 kmh), when the test bulb should illuminate.

16 Release the accelerator and allow the car to slow down. When the road speed has decreased to 16 mph (27 kmh) the lamp should go out.

Weber 32 DIR and 32 DARA carburettors

17 With the engine at normal working temperature, turn screw (B) in or out to obtain the highest idling speed. If this speed is not within the

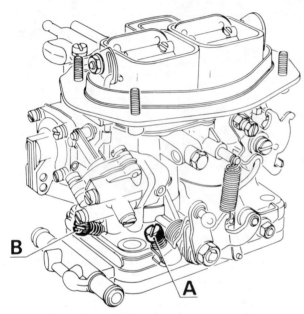

Fig. 3.16 Weber 32 DIR adjusting screws (Sec 11)

A   Throttle speed screw   B   Fuel screw

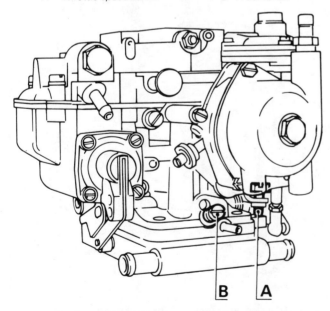

Fig. 3.17 Weber 32 DARA adjusting screws (Sec 11)

A   Throttle speed screw   B   Fuel screw

speed specified for your particular engine (see Specifications) then turn screw (A) in or out to achieve it.

18 Now turn screw (B) in to reduce the idle speed by 20 to 25 rev/min, but without making the idle rough.

19 If the adjustment has been carefully carried out, then the CO level (checked on an exhaust gas analyser) should be between 2.5% and 3.0%.

20 Refer to paragraphs 4 and 5.

Carburettors with tamperproof adjustment screws

21 Very late models are fitted with tamperproof carburettors. The idle mixture screw is set during production and sealed with a plastic cap.

22 In theory, the only adjustment required should be to the idle speed screw, but in practice, adjustment of the fuel mixture screw can become necessary after overhaul of the carburettor or because of changes in the characteristics of the engine due to carbon build up, wear and other causes.

23 To adjust, break off the plastic cap, carry out the adjustment procedure described in the preceding paragraphs and then fit a new cap if local legislation demands it.

12 Carburettor – removal and refitting

1   Remove the air cleaner, drain the cooling system.

2   Disconnect the throttle control linkage from the carburettor, also the crankcase breather hose and distributor vacuum hose.

3   On Solex and Weber 32 DIR carburettors, disconnect the choke (cold start) control cable.

4   On Weber 32 DARA carburettors, disconnect the coolant hoses from the automatic choke housing and electric choke wire (if fitted).

5   On all carburettors, disconnect the coolant hoses from the throttle valve plate block.

6   Disconnect the fuel inlet hose.

7   Unscrew and remove the four mounting nuts and lift the carburettor from the inlet manifold.

8   Refitting is a reversal of removal, but use new flange joint gaskets.

13 Carburettor overhaul – general

1   The need for complete overhaul seldom arises unless the unit is generally worn due to extended service. In this case, a new or professionally reconditioned unit is probably the most economical solution.

2   Removal and cleaning of jets will usually keep the carburettor in good working order. Repair kits are available which contain all the parts needed for minor overhaul.

3   When dismantling a carburettor, maintain strict cleanliness and use close fitting spanners and screwdrivers to remove jets and other components.

4   Never probe jets with wire to clean them, use air pressure only or

13. 4 Carburettor fuel inlet filter

in an extreme case a nylon bristle. Remember to clean the fuel inlet filter gauze which is accessible after unscrewing the union stub or the filter plug (Weber) (photo).

14 Carburettor (Solex 32/32 SEIEMA) – overhaul

1 Extract the screws which hold the top cover, disconnect link rods and springs and lift it from the main carburettor body.
2 The cover can be dismantled if necessary by removing the float, unscrewing the fuel inlet needle valve and unscrewing the fuel inlet pipe union. Inside this union a gauze type filter is located which should be cleaned.
3 The jets and other calibrated components can be removed for cleaning in a jet of compressed air.
4 Do not attempt to dismantle the valve plates or spindles for either the choke or throttle. If they are worn then it is better to obtain a new carburettor.
5 The throttle valve plate block can be detached from the main body if the securing screws are extracted.
6 Blow out all orifices with compressed air and obtain a repair kit which will contain all the necessary gaskets and other renewable items.
7 Reassembly is a reversal of dismantling but as work proceeds, carry out the following adjustments.

Initial throttle opening
8 Close the choke butterfly valve plates fully using finger pressure.
9 Using a twist drill or gauge rod of known diameter, check the gap between the edge of the primary throttle valve plate and the carburettor wall. If the gap is not as specified, bend the lug (3) on the throttle lever.

Accelerator pump travel
10 The correct adjustment of the pump can be checked in the following way.
11 Set the throttle butterfly valve plate in the idling position. This will bring the roller (4) into contact with the cam (5).
12 The adjuster screw should now be unscrewed and then screwed in again until it just makes contact with the plunger (7). Now screw the screw in between $\frac{1}{2}$ and a full turn.
13 It should be noted that the accelerator pump on these carburettors has a return outlet to relieve excess pressure. The return pipe (1) connects with the fuel pump inlet pipe (2).
14 The return pipe contains a valve (3) which if removed must always be refitted so that the two grooves and the chamfer point upwards.

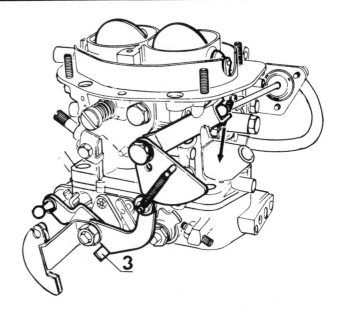

Fig. 3.19 Solex throttle lever lug (3) (Sec 14)

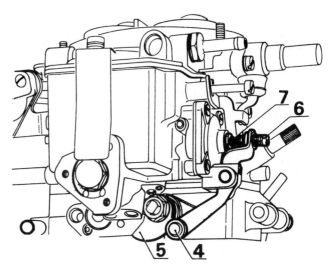

Fig. 3.20 Solex accelerator pump details (Sec 14)

4 Roller	6 Adjusting screw
5 Cam	7 Plunger

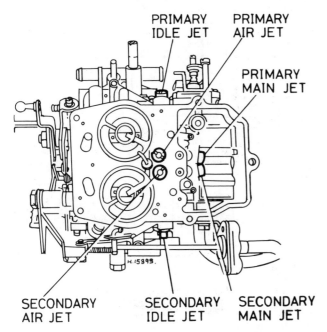

PRIMARY IDLE JET   PRIMARY AIR JET

PRIMARY MAIN JET

SECONDARY AIR JET   SECONDARY IDLE JET   SECONDARY MAIN JET

Fig. 3.18 Solex 32/32 jet locations (Sec 14)

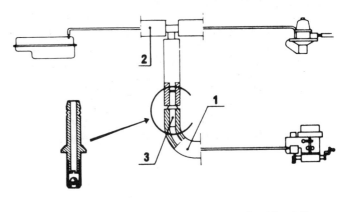

Fig. 3.21 Solex accelerator pump return line (Sec 14)

1 Return pipe	3 Valve
2 Fuel pump inlet pipe	

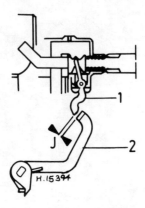

Fig. 3.22 Solex breather control valve (Sec 14)

1   Valve lever   *J   0.3 to 0.6 mm*
2   Operating lever   *(0.012 to 0.024 in)*

Carburettor breather control valve

15   At idle, the control valve shuts off the float chamber vent to atmosphere.

16   The clearance (J) between the valve lever and the operating lever (2) should be between 0.3 and 0.6 mm (0.012 and 0.024 in). Where adjustment is required bend the operating lever tip.

15 Carburettor (Weber 32 DIR) – overhaul

1   Unscrew and remove the upper body screws and withdraw the upper assembly which contains the needle valve and choke control mechanism.

2   Empty the float chamber and remove the float, taking care to retain the needle from the valve.

3   Do not dismantle the choke butterflies or spindles unless essential. Check the security of the inlet valve, but do not add or remove any of the washers located beneath it.

4   Disconnect the accelerator pump linkage from the throttle valve spindle and dismantle the pump.

5   Refer to Fig. 3.23 and remove the jets.

6   Reassembly is a reversal of dismantling, but as work progresses, carry out the following checks and adjustments.

Float level adjustment

7   Hold the float chamber cover vertically so that the float just closes the fuel inlet needle valve, but does not press the ball into the valve.

8   Check the dimension (A) measured between the face of a new gasket correctly located and the float. The dimension should be as specified for your particular carburettor at the beginning of this Chapter. If it is not, bend the tab (3). When adjustment is complete check that the float travel (stroke) is still 8.0 mm (0.315 in). If not, carefully bend tab (5).

Initial throttle opening adjustment

9   If your carburettor has a rod (1) as shown, close the choke valve plates with finger pressure and then measure the gap between the edge of the progression hole side of the primary throttle valve plate and the carburettor wall using a twist drill or similar gauge rod of known diameter. If the gap does not conform to specification, bend the link rod (1).

10   If your carburettor is not fitted with a link rod, the procedure is similar to that just described except that adjustment is carried out by releasing the locknut and turning the screw (1).

Choke valve plate part open setting (mechanical)

11   On earlier pattern carburettors, close the choke valve plates with the fingers so that the sleeve (2) comes down onto the cam (3). Using a gauge rod as previously described, measure the gap between the edge of the choke valve plates and the carburettor wall. This should be 6.0 mm (0.236 in), if it is not, bend the rod (4) to correct.

12   On later pattern carburettors, close the choke valve plates with the fingers to bring the peg (2) in contact with the lever (3). Measure the gap between the edge of the choke valve plate and the carburettor wall. This should be 6.0 mm (0.236 in). If it is not, bend rod (4) to correct.

Choke valve plate part open setting (vacuum)

13   On earlier pattern carburettors, depress the rod (5) to its stop and

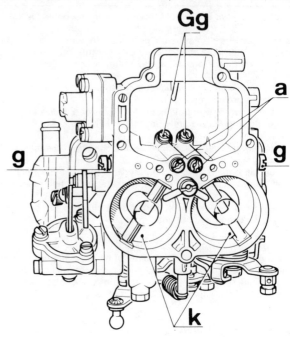

Fig. 3.23 Weber 32 DIR location of jets (Sec 15)

a   Air compensating jet   *Gg   Main jet*
g   Idling jet   *K   Venturi (choke tube)*

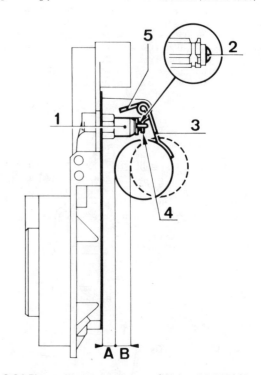

Fig. 3.24 Float adjustment diagram (Weber 32 DIR) (Sec 15)

1   Fuel inlet needle valve   *5   Stop*
2   Valve ball   *A   Level setting*
3   Float arm   *B   Float stroke*
4   Tab

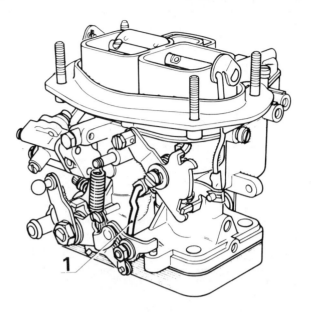

Fig. 3.25 Initial throttle opening link rod (1) (Weber 32 DIR)
(Sec 15)

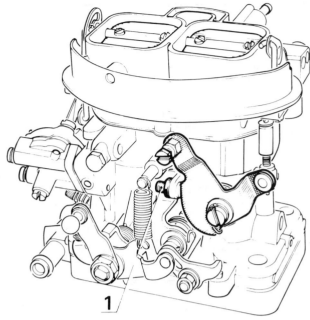

Fig. 3.26 Initial throttle opening adjuster screw and locknut
(Weber 32 DIR) (Sec 15)

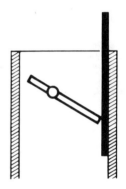

Fig. 3.27 Using a gauge rod to check valve butterfly opening
(Sec 15)

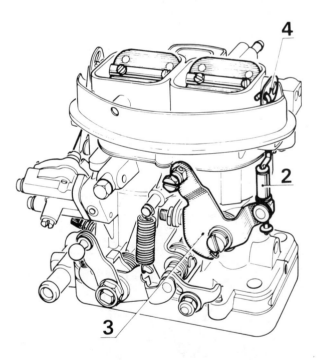

Fig. 3.28 Weber 32 DIR earlier pattern carburettor with choke
part-open setting sleeve (2), cam (3) and rod (4) (Sec 15)

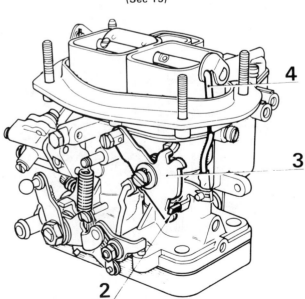

Fig. 3.29 Weber 32 DIR later pattern carburettor with choke part-
open setting peg (2), lever (3) and rod (4) (Sec 15)

then move the choke valve plates using the cam (3) until the sleeve spring (8) is slightly compressed. Measure the gap between the edge of the longer side of the choke valve plate and the carburettor wall using a gauge rod as described earlier in this Section. The gap should be as specified for your particular carburettor. If it is not, remove the plug screw (6) and turn the internal adjuster screw (7) as necessary to correct.

14 On later pattern carburettors, push the rod (5) against its stop then move the lever (3) into contact with the peg (2). Measure the gap between the choke valve plate and the carburettor wall as previously described for earlier pattern carburettors. If the gap is not as specified, adjust as for earlier pattern carburettors.

16 Carburettor (Weber 32 DARA) – overhaul

1 Unscrew and remove the upper body screws and disconnect the choke control rod. Withdraw the upper assembly which contains the needle valve choke control mechanism, and float.
2 On carburettors with later mark numbers, when removing the top

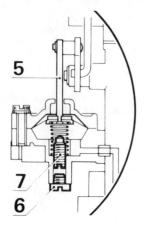

Fig. 3.30 Weber 32 DIR earlier pattern vacuum choke part-opening plug (6), adjuster screw (7) and pushrod (5) (Sec 15)

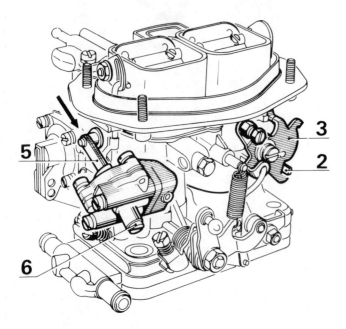

Fig. 3.31 Weber later pattern vacuum choke part-opening details (Sec 15)

section, unscrew the retaining screws and then detach the butterfly swivel rod to lever C-clip, by prising it free.
3 Loosen, but do not remove, the three screws retaining the automatic choke housing unit to the main carburettor body, enabling the choke housing to be withdrawn sufficiently to allow the top section to be detached.
4 Empty the float chamber. To remove the float, extract the hingepin, then unhook the needle valve.
5 Do not dismantle the choke butterflies or spindles unless essential. Check the security of the inlet valve, but do not add to or remove any of the washers located beneath it.
6 Remove the four screws and withdraw the accelerator pump.
7 If the automatic choke has failed, remove the complete unit and fit a new one.
8 Refer to Fig. 3.32 and remove the jets. Clean them by blowing air from a tyre pump through them, never use wire to probe them.
9 Reassembly is a reversal of dismantling, but as work proceeds, carry out the following adjustments.

Float level adjustment
10 The operations are as described for the Weber 32 DIR carburettors in Section 15.

Initial throttle opening adjustment
11 Close the choke valve plates with the fingers. Measure the gap between the edge of the primary barrel throttle valve plate and the carburettor wall. Use a twist drill or gauge rod for this purpose.
12 If the gap is not as specified at the front of this Chapter for your particular carburettor, turn the screw (1) to correct it.

Automatic choke adjustment
13 Extract the three choke housing cover screws and withdraw the cover. There is no need to disconnect the coolant hoses.
14 With the choke cover removed, close the choke vacuum plates by applying finger pressure to the spindle lever. Note the spring used as a flexible link.
15 Move the dashpot rod (7) upwards as far as it will go.
16 Hold the choke valve plate closure lever (2) against the dashpot rod (7).
17 Using gauge rods or drills, measure the part open setting of the choke flaps at the point between the long part of the flap tops and the housing wall. Check the adjustment against that given in the Specifications and, if necessary, adjust the clearance by means of the screw recessed into the top of the dashpot.

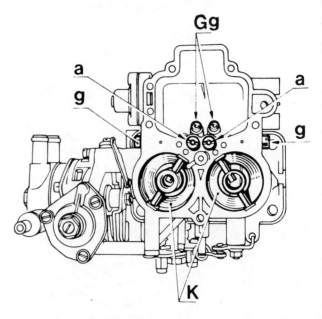

Fig. 3.32 Weber 32 DARA carburettor jet locations (Sec 16)

2	Peg	5	Pushrod
3	Lever	6	Adjuster screw plug

a	Air compensating jet	Gg	Main jet
g	Idle jet	K	Venturi (choke tube)

18 When the adjustment is completed, refit the thermostatic spring cover housing and ensure that the setting marks on the automatic choke housing and cover are in alignment.

17 Carburettor (Weber 32) – modification for North American automatic transmission vehicles

1 On these vehicles, a vacuum-operated throttle closure unit is fitted as an aid to further reducing exhaust emission levels during acceleration and deceleration.

2 Other components of the system include a centrifugal switch driven by the speedometer cable, a solenoid flap valve and throttle butterfly valve plate opener (see Fig. 3.14).

3 During acceleration, the centrifugal switch contacts close when the vehicle road speed reaches 20 mph (32 kmh). The solenoid flap valve is then energised while valve (3) remains open so connecting chamber (4) with the inlet manifold. Under these conditions, vacuum

pressure is insufficient to cause diaphragm (6) to move and it is retained by a coil spring.

4 During deceleration when the accelerator pedal is in the released position, the throttle butterflies would normally close. But due to the

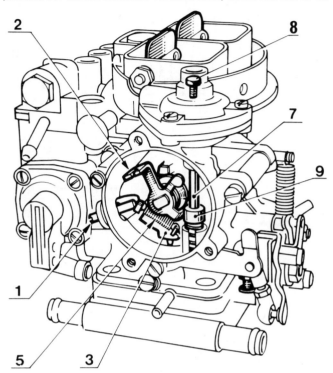

Fig. 3.34 Automatic choke (Weber 32 DARA) (Sec 16)

1 Adjuster screw (initial throttle opening)	5 Spring
2 Lever	7 Rod
3 Stepped cam	8 Adjuster screw
	9 Compensator

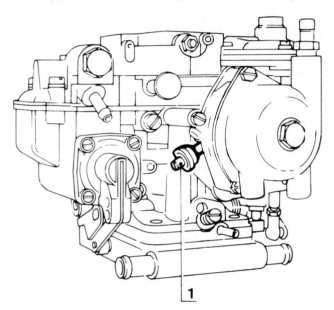

Fig. 3.33 Initial throttle opening adjuster screw (1) on Weber 32 DARA carburettor (Sec 16)

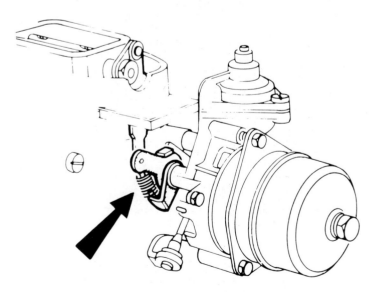

Fig. 3.35 Weber 32 DARA automatic choke flexible link (Sec 14)

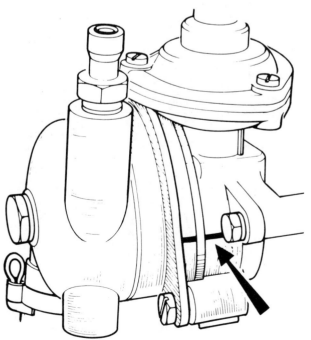

Fig. 3.36 Automatic choke housing and cover alignment (Sec 16)

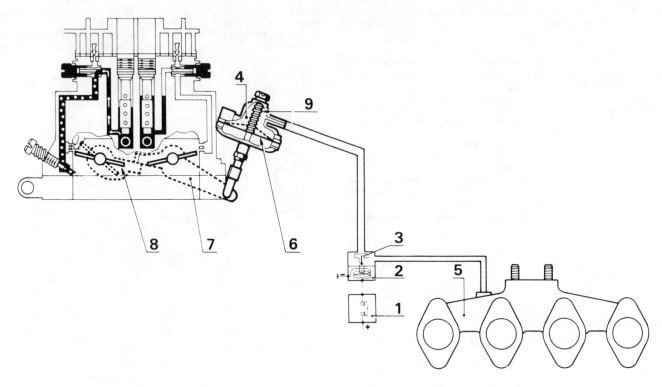

Fig. 3.37 Throttle deceleration system (Weber) (Sec 17)

1	Centrifugal switch	3	Valve	5	Inlet manifold
	(speedo cable driven)	4	Vacuum unit	6	Flexible diaphragm
2	Solenoid flap valve				

9 Spring

increased vacuum pressure created by the engine causes the diaphragm to move and through the linkage, partially opens the primary throttle valve plate to give a fast idle in the interests of reduced exhaust emissions.

5 When the road speed drops to 16 mph (kmh) the contacts in the centrifugal switch open, the solenoid flap valve is de-energized and the primary throttle closes to its normal idle position.

6 The following check and possible adjustment should be carried out in the car with the engine at normal operating temperature and idling.

7 Disconnect the vacuum pipe (which runs between the dashpot and the solenoid valve) from the solenoid valve and reconnect it to the inlet manifold (brake servo connection).

8 Rev up the engine momentarily under no load conditions to 3000 rev/min. Remove the foot from the accelerator pedal. A fast idle speed should be recorded of between 1400 and 1500 rev/min before the engine speed starts to drop to idle.

9 If the fast idle speed is not as specified, turn the vacuum unit screw (V) as necessary. If the correct speed still cannot be obtained, release the locknut (d) and disconnect the linkage from the slot in the lever. Reduce the length of the link rod by rotating it and then retighten the locknut.

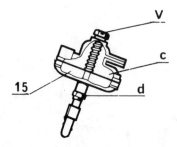

Fig. 3.38 Deceleration (fast idle) vacuum unit details

c	Vacuum chamber	v	Adjuster screw
d	Locknut	15	Vacuum unit

PART 3 FUEL INJECTION SYSTEM

18 Fuel injection system – description and precautions

1 A fuel injection system is fitted to R1313, R1317, R1323, R1327 models instead of carburettors.

2 The main purpose is for some European and North American versions to operate with lower emission levels which is a major advantage of a fuel injection system.

3 The system is Bosch electronic and consists of two main parts which are:

Fuel supply system incorporating
  Electric fuel pump
  Fuel filter
  Pressure regulator
  Fuel injectors
  Cold start injector

Control system
  Distributor
  Pressure sensor
  Auxiliary air control
  Throttle switch
  Air temperature sensor
  Coolant temperature sensor
  Temperature time switch
  Ignition/starter switch
  Control box
  Main relay
  Pump relay

4 The system operates by the electric fuel pump drawing fuel from the vehicle tank and pumping it through a filter to a ring main where it is distributed to the injectors.

5 A pressure regulator in the ring main controls the fuel pressure at 29 lbf/in^2 (2 bar).

6 The various valves monitored by the control sensors are relayed to

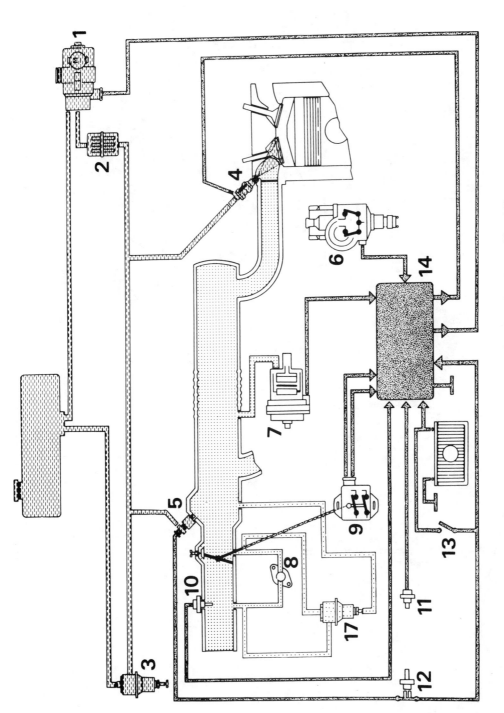

Fig. 3.39 Schematic layout of typical fuel injection system (Sec 18)

1　Electric fuel pump
2　Fuel filter
3　Pressure regulator
4　Injection

5　Cold start injector
6　Distributor
7　Pressure sensor
8　Auxiliary air control

9　Throttle switch
10　Air temperature sensor
11　Coolant temperature sensor

12　Temperature time switch
13　Ignition/starter switch
14　Control box

15　Main relay
16　Pump relay
17　Auxiliary air vacuum valve

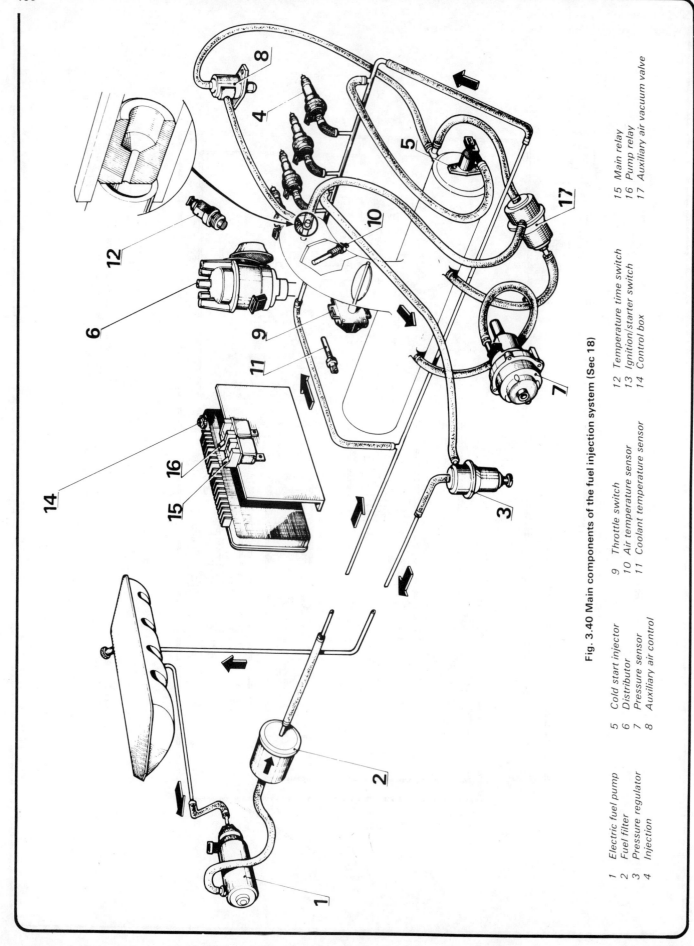

Fig. 3.40 Main components of the fuel injection system (Sec 18)

1	Electric fuel pump	5	Cold start injector	9	Throttle switch	12	Temperature time switch	15	Main relay
2	Fuel filter	6	Distributor	10	Air temperature sensor	13	Ignition/starter switch	16	Pump relay
3	Pressure regulator	7	Pressure sensor	11	Coolant temperature sensor	14	Control box	17	Auxiliary air vacuum valve
4	Injection	8	Auxiliary air control						

the control box where they are converted into electric impulses to meter the exact volume of fuel at the injectors according to prevailing engine conditions.

7   Adjustment and overhaul operations should be limited to those described in the following Sections. More complicated work should be left to your dealer or to a fuel system specialist.

8   Observe the following precautions.

(a) *Never switch on the ignition if a mains charger is connected*
(b) *Never disconnect or reconnect the computer leads if the ignition is switched on*
(c) *Never subject the computer to a temperature in excess of 80°C (176°F) by welding or paint baking at adjacent surfaces*

---

19 Fuel injection system – idle speed and mixture adjustment

Earlier models without air injection system

1   Have the engine at normal operating temperature.
2   Turn the air screw (A) right in.
3   Start the engine and unscrew the screw (B) until the engine is running at a speed of between 900 and 1000 rev/min.
4   Now unscrew the air screw (A) until the engine speed is between 1025 and 1075 rev/min.
5   The CO level can only be checked using an exhaust gas analyser. The correct percentage is between 2.5 and 3.0%. The CO level can be reduced by turning the potentiometer (1) on the control box in an anti-clockwise direction. Any adjustment will mean altering the air screw (A) afterwards to re-set the idle speed to the specified level.
6   Any failure to respond to the adjustment procedure may indicate the need for throttle switch adjustment, refer to Section 20 or 21.

Later models with air injection system

7   Clamp the air injection hose downstream of the relief valve.
8   Have the engine at normal operating temperature and idling.
9   Turn screw (A) to achieve an idle speed of 850 rev/min.
10 With an exhaust gas analyser connected in accordance with the maker's instructions, turn the screw (B) to vary the mixture until the CO level is between 1 and 3%.
11 If necessary, readjust the idle speed using screw (A).
12 Remove the hose clamps.
13 Once the hose clamps are released the engine should idle smoothly at between 850 and 950 rev/min. If outside this tolerance, turn screw (A) to correct.

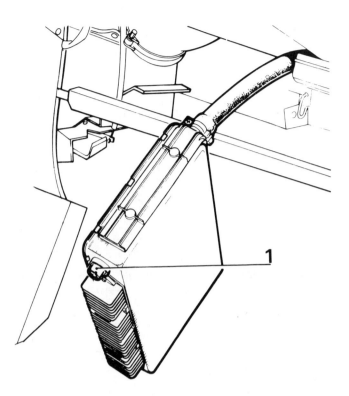

Fig. 3.42 Fuel injection system control box potentiometer (1) (Sec 19)

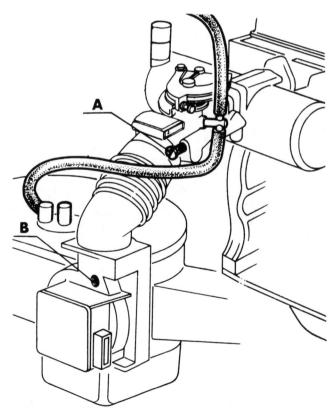

Fig. 3.43 Fuel injection adjusting screws with air inspection system (Sec 19)

A   *Throttle valve plate screw*
B   *Flowmeter bypass (mixture) screw*

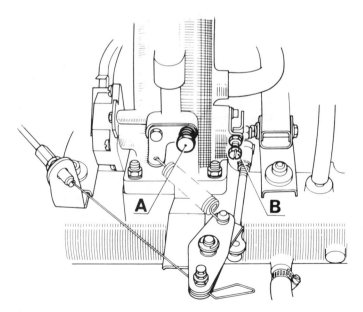

Fig. 3.41 Fuel injection system idle speed screws (Sec 19)

A   *Air screw*   B   *Throttle stop screw*

20 Throttle switch – adjustment

1   This operation may be required to position the switch so that its internal contact, which is connected to the rocket terminals for wires 17 and 14 is closed when the throttle butterfly is open by a predetermined amount. Opening of the contacts can also be checked by further movement of the switch.
2   To check the setting an ohm-meter will be required.
3   One of three different types of switch may be met with.

Early models (R1313, R1323 – 1972-73)

4   On these models, the switch is held by four screws.
5   The output terminals for the socket leading from the switch contacts for wires 17 and 14 are at the top.
6   Make sure that the idle speed is correct and then remove the plug from the switch and connect an ohm-meter across the two top switch terminals.
7   Loosen the switch screws enough to permit the switch to move stiffly.
8   Insert a feeler gauge between the throttle stop screw and the operating lever.
9   Move the switch so that the switch contacts are closed (zero resistance on ohm-meter) when a 0.15 mm (0.006 in) feeler gauge is a sliding fit between the screw and lever.
10 Move the switch again until a 0.25 mm (0.010 in) feeler blade is a sliding fit with the contacts open (00 resistance).
11 When these conditions have been met, tighten the switch screws.
12 Check the idle speed and re-adjust if necessary.

Later models (R1313, R1323)

13 The throttle switch on these models is of crimped type with the output terminals in the socket leading from the switch contacts for wires 17 and 14 located at the bottom.
14 The switch is secured by two screws.
15 To adjust, first check the idle speed and then loosen the switch screws so that it can be moved stiffly.

16 Insert a 0.70 mm (0.028 in) feeler gauge between the throttle stop screw and the operating lever.
17 Turn the switch clockwise until it is hard up against its fixing screws.
18 Now turn the switch in an anti-clockwise direction until the contacts are closed (zero resistance on ohm-meter).
19 Tighten the fixing screws.
20 Check the idle speed and adjust if necessary.

Models R1317, R1327

21 The switch on these models is also assembled by crimping. The switch is operated by a cable and the switch housing is coolant-heated.
22 Release the switch fixing screws enough to allow the switch to move stiffly.
23 Insert a 1.0 mm (0.040 in) feeler blade between the throttle stop screw and the fixed stop on the butterfly housing.
24 Turn the switch clockwise until it is hard up against its stop.
25 Now turn the switch in an anti-clockwise direction until the contacts are just closed (zero resistance on ohm-meter).
26 Tighten the switch screws and check the idle speed. Adjust to specification if necessary.

21 Accelerator cable switch – adjustment

1   Disconnect the accelerator cable from the trunnion swivel on the throttle valve assembly.
2   Adjust the pedal stop (2) to prevent the pedal stem (3) touching the bracket (4) through its sliding plate (1).
3   Insert a 3.0 mm ($\frac{1}{8}$ in) thick block between the pedal stem (3) and the stop and reconnect the throttle cable making sure that the throttle valve plate is in its idle (nearly closed) position. Remove the block.
4   Check that the coils of the compensating springs do not touch at full throttle.
5   With the accelerator pedal in the fully released position, turn in screw (5) until the switch contacts are open. Screw in a further $\frac{1}{2}$ turn to ensure a clean break.

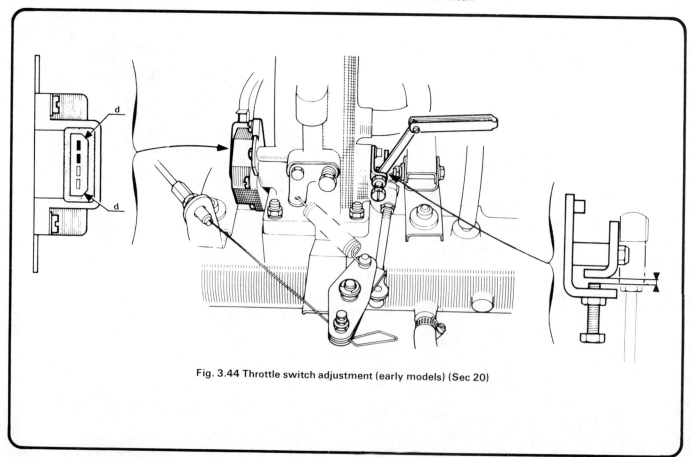

Fig. 3.44 Throttle switch adjustment (early models) (Sec 20)

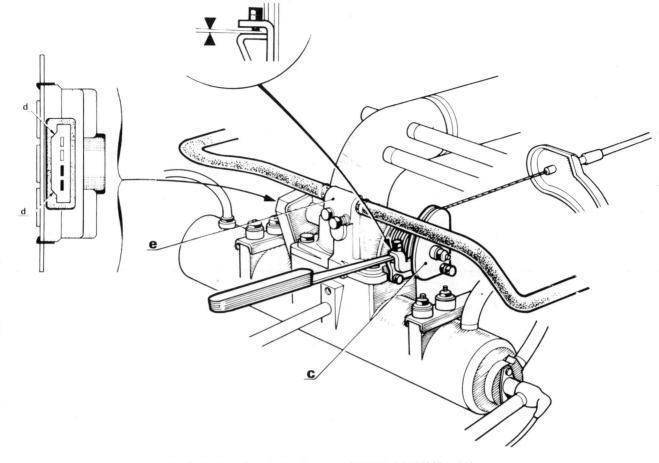

Fig. 3.45 Throttle switch adjustment (R1317, R1327) (Sec 20)

C   Cam   E   Coolant heating circuit

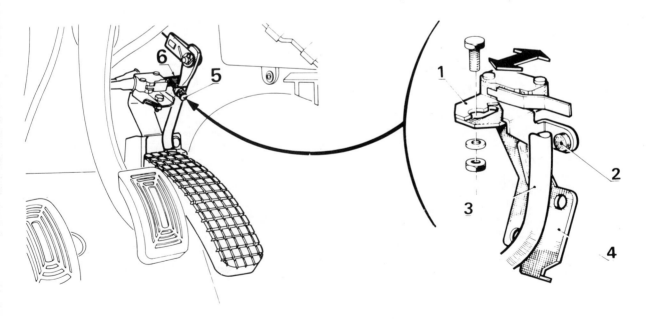

Fig. 3.46 Accelerator cable switch (Sec 21)

1   Sliding plate   3   Pedal arm   5   Screw   6   Switch arm
2   Pedal stop   4   Bracket

22 Pressure regulator – adjustment

1   A reliable pressure gauge (oil gauge is suitable) and tee piece will be required.
2   Connect the gauge using the tee piece and hose clips into the line between the injector ring main and pressure regulator.
3   Start the engine and allow it to idle.
4   The pressure shown on the gauge should be between 2 and 2.05 bar (28.5 and 29.2 lbf/in^2).
5   If it is not, release the locknut (1) and adjust using screw (2).

23 Fuel filter – renewal

1   Unbolt the fuel filter securing strap from above the fuel pump.
2   Withdraw the filter until the hoses can be disconnected from it. Be prepared for a small drainage of fuel. Discard the old filter.
3   Fit the new filter taking care to have the arrow marked on it following the direction of fuel flow.

24 Fuel pump – removal and refitting

1   Remove the pump shield.
2   Clamp the pump hoses. Self-locking grips are useful for this.
3   Unbolt the pump securing strap and withdraw the pump sufficiently far to be able to disconnect the hoses and electrical leads.
4   Refitting is a reversal of removal. Check the hose connections for leaks with the engine running.

25 Fuel injector – removal and refitting

1   Disconnect the wiring plug from the injector.
2   Release the hose clip and disconnect the fuel hose from the ring main.
3   Unscrew the fixing bolts from the injector flange. Withdraw the injector and support plate.
4   When refitting the injector clean the joint seal area thoroughly and use new seals if they are in anything but perfect condition.

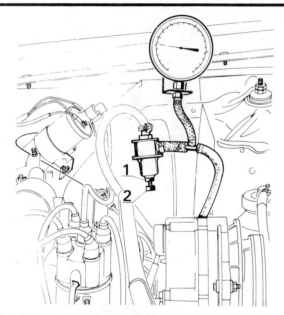

Fig. 3.47 Checking fuel injection system pressure (Sec 22)

1   *Locknut*   2   *Adjuster screw*

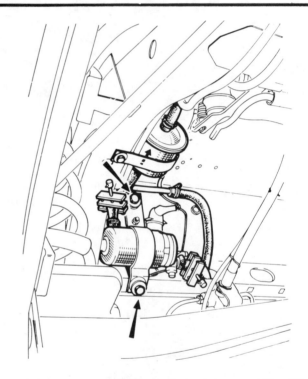

Fig. 3.48 Fuel pump and filter (fuel injection system) (Sec 24)

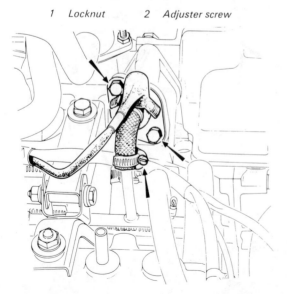

Fig. 3.49 Fuel injector flange bolts (Sec 25)

Fig. 3.50 Fuel injector and seals (Sec 25)

26 Fuel injector hoses – renewal

1 Note the alignment of the hose elbow in relation to the wiring plug socket on the injector.
2 The hoses used for original equipment are crimped in position. Carefully file or hacksaw the clips to remove them.
3 Pull off the hose but on no account attempt to grip the injector in a vice.
4 Slide on the new pipe (dry) until it contacts the shoulder on the connector nozzle.
5 Fit the clip supplied with the new hose and then set the elbow to its original angle. Tighten the hose clip until the ends of the clip are not closer than 2.0 mm (0.08 mm) together.

27 Pressure regulator – removal and refitting

1 Clamp the fuel hoses on both sides of the regulator. Self-locking grips will usually do the job.
2 Disconnect the hoses.
3 Remove the single mounting nut and withdraw the regulator.
4 Refitting is a reversal of removal, but check the pressure as described in Section 22.

28 Auxiliary air control valve – description, removal and refitting

1 This valve makes use of the vacuum pressure created in the inlet manifold during deceleration.
2 It opens a channel between that section of the fuel injection throttle housing which is above the throttle valve and the inlet manifold.
3 The increase in volume of this additional air creates a fast idle.
4 A calibrated jet is located in the hose which runs between the valve and the throttle housing.
5 To remove the valve, partially drain the cooling system.
6 Remove the air hoses and unscrew the flange bolts.
7 Refit by reversing the removal operations, but clean the mating surfaces thoroughly and use a new seal.
8 Top up the cooling system and bleed it.

29 Control box – removal and refitting

1 The control box is located under the right-hand side of the fascia panel.
2 Release the two rubber fixing bands which hold the control box to its tray.

3 Release the clip (1) and slide the cover in the direction of the arrow.
4 Unplug the wiring connector.
5 Refitting is a reversal of removal.

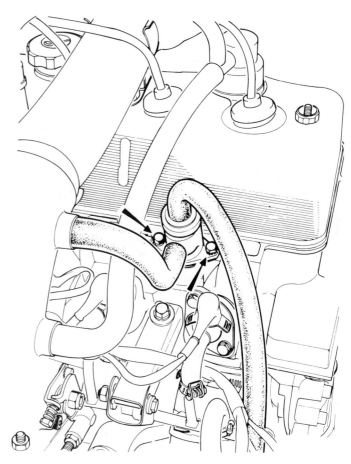

Fig. 3.52 Auxiliary air control valve fixing bolts (Sec 28)

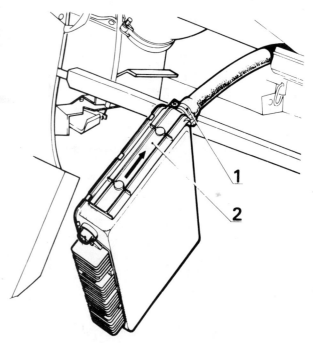

Fig. 3.53 Fuel injection system control box (Sec 29)

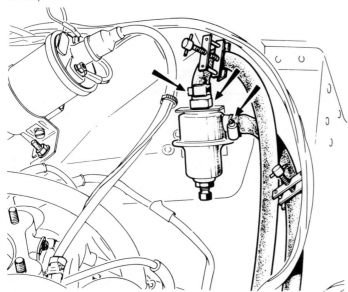

Fig. 3.51 Pressure regulator with fuel hoses clamped (Sec 27)

1 Clip   2 Slide

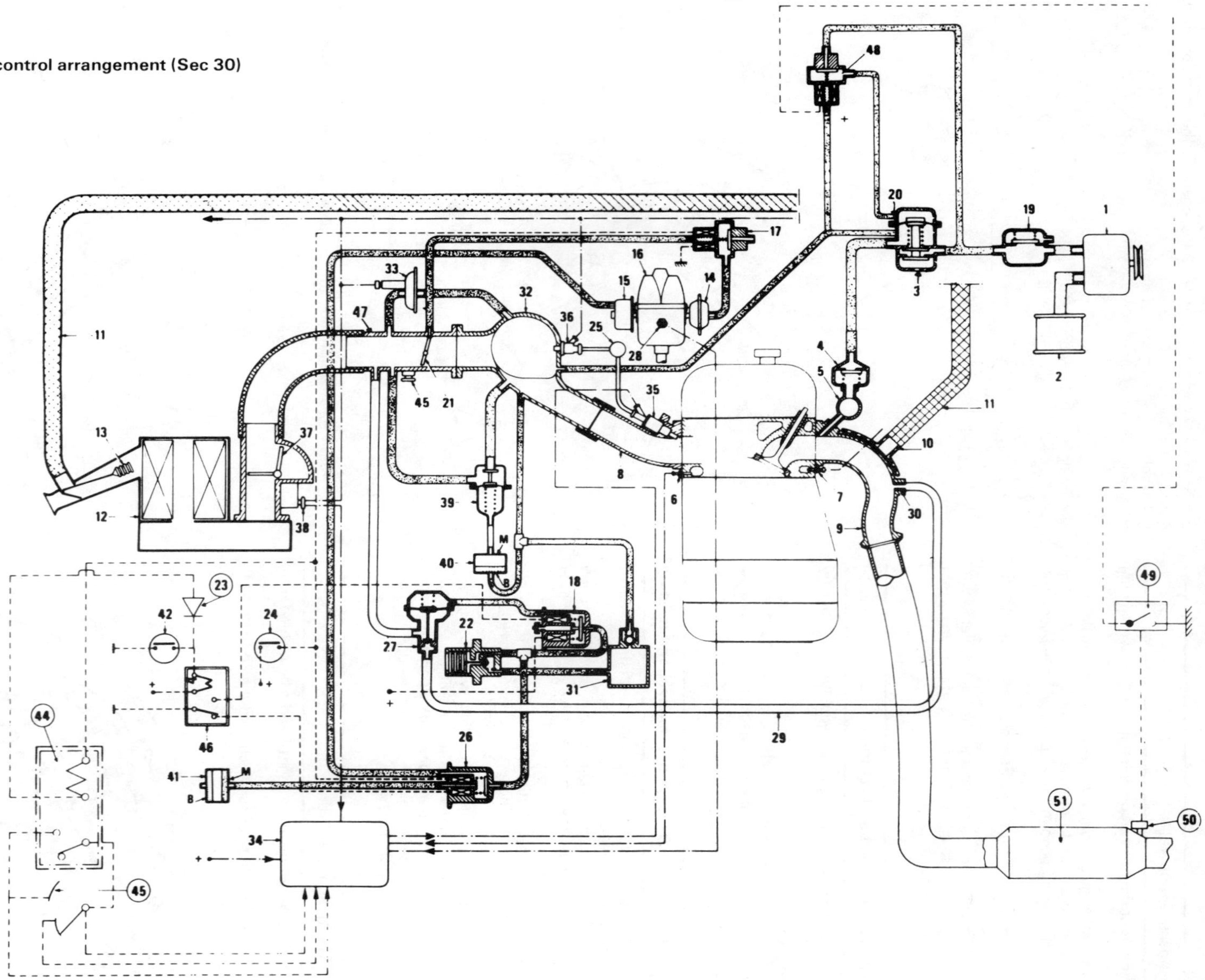

Fig. 3.54 Typical 1978 emission control arrangement (Sec 30)

1   Air pump
2   Filter
3   Diverter valve
4   Non-return valve
5   Air injection manifold
6   Coolant temperature sensor
7   Coolant temperature thermo
    time switch
8   Inlet manifold
9   Exhaust manifold
10 Pre-heater
11 Pre-heated air inlet
12 Thermostatically controlled
    air cleaner
13 Thermovalve sensor
14 Vacuum advance capsule
15 Vacuum retard capsule
16 Distributor
17 Solenoid valve advance
    capsule
18 EGR solenoid valve
19 Relief valve
20 Calibrated orifice
21 Throttle plate
22 Thermovalve
23 Diode
24 5th speed transmission
    switch
25 Fuel ring main
26 Solenoid valve
    (vacuum circuit retard)
27 EGR valve
28 Distributor terminal
29 EGR pipe
30 Calibrated orifice
31 Vacuum reservoir
32 Air manifold
33 Additional air control
    valve
34 Electronic control box
35 Fuel injector
36 Cold start fuel injector
37 Air flowmeter
38 Air flowmeter pick up
39 Deceleration valve
40 Idle delay valve
41 Spark delay valve
42 Throttle valve plate
    switch

44 Relay
45 Throttle plate position
    switch

46 Relay
47 Throttle plate housing
48 Solenoid valve

49 Relay
50 Exhaust temperature
    sensor

51 Catalytic converter
B   White
M   Brown

PART 4 EMISSION CONTROL SYSTEM, EXHAUST SYSTEM AND THROTTLE CONTROL

30 Emission control systems – description

1   All models have some sort of emission control devices. Outside North America, these devices are considered adequate if they include a crankcase breather system (see Chapter 1) an air temperature regulated air cleaner and a highly developed carburettor.
2   North American vehicles are equipped with one or more of the following systems, the later the production date of the vehicle, the more complex the arrangement.

   Fuel evaporative control system
   Air injection system (AIS)
   Exhaust gas recirculation system (EGR)
   Catalytic converter (California)
   Advance correction control system (see Chapter 4)
   Vacuum advance/retard system (fuel injection models) – see Chapter 4

31 Fuel evaporative control system

1   The system is designed to prevent vapour from the fuel tank (and carburettor) from being vented to atmosphere.
2   A sealed filler cap is fitted and vapour is stored in a charcoal filled canister when the engine is not running.
3   As soon as the engine is running, accumulations of vapour are drawn into the engine intake and burnt during the normal combustion process.
4   A check valve, expansion reservoir and pressure equalising valves are built into the circuit.
5   Normal maintenance is for a regular check on the security of connecting hoses and renewal of the charcoal canister at the specified intervals.

32 Air injection system – description and maintenance

1   A belt-driven air pump generates air pressure which is introduced into the exhaust manifold for the purpose of promoting further oxidation of the exhaust gases after they leave the combustion

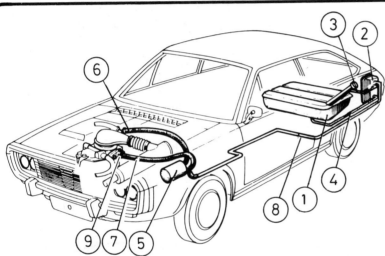

1	Fuel tank
2	Expansion reservoir
3	Pipeline
4	Pipeline
5	Canister
6	Pipeline
7	Pipeline
8	Pipeline
9	Control valve

Fig. 3.55 Typical fuel evaporative control layout (carburettor engines) (Sec 31)

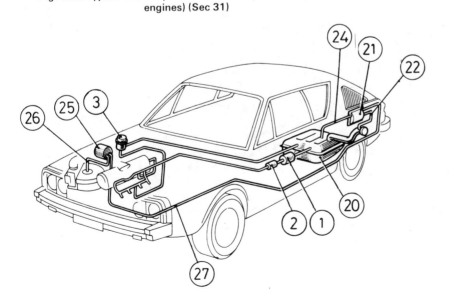

1	Electric fuel pump (FI system)
2	Filter (FI system)
3	Pressure regulator (FI system)
20	Fuel tank
21	Expansion tank
22	Pipeline
24	Pipeline
25	Charcoal canister
26	Air cleaner connecting pipe
27	Pipeline

Fig. 3.56 Typical fuel evaporative control system (Sec 31)

chambers. The noxious content is therefore reduced by converting some of the exhaust gases into carbon dioxide and water.

2   A diverter valve is incorporated in the system to cut off air injection when intake manifold vacuum is high during deceleration.

3   Normal maintenance consists of checking the hoses for condition and security.

4   Operation of the diverter valve should be checked periodically by disconnecting the hoses and blowing through it. Air should pass in one direction, but not in the other.

33 Exhaust gas recirculation system – description and maintenance

1   The EGR system is designed to re-introduce small volumes of inert exhaust gas into the combustion chamber. The effect of this is to reduce the combustion temperature and so reduce the formation of nitrogen oxide.

2   The metered amounts of exhaust gas are controlled according to engine vacuum and coolant temperature by valves and a thermoswitch.

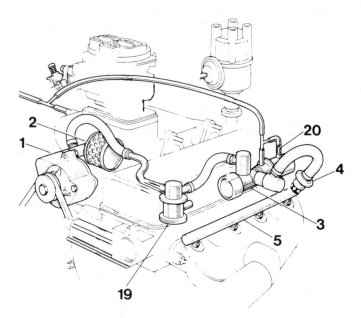

Fig. 3.57 Typical air injection system (Sec 32)

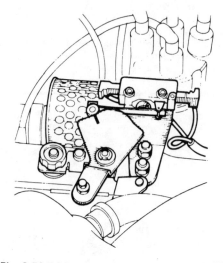

1	Air pump	5	Air injection manifold
2	Filter	19	Relief valve
3	Diverter valve	20	Calibrated orifice
4	Non-return valve		

Fig. 3.59 EGR system re-cycling valve (Sec 33)

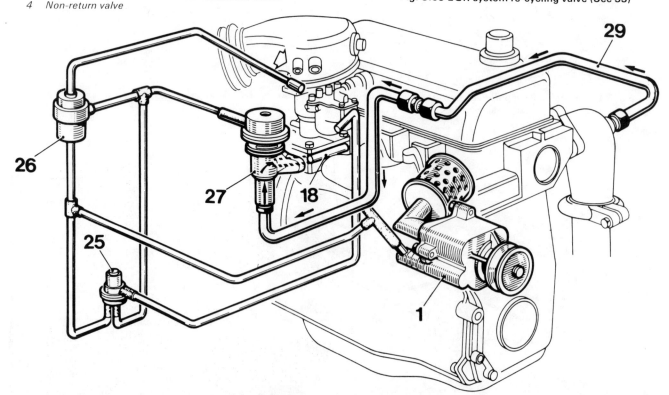

Fig. 3.58 Typical EGR system (Sec 33)

1	Air pump (AIS)	25	Valve	27	Re-cycling valve	29 Pipeline
18	Tube	26	Solenoid valve			

3   On certain models, a warning device is fitted to remind the owner to service the EGR system components (see Section 34).

4   At the specified intervals, remove the EGR valve and clean away deposits with a wire brush. Also clean carbon from the system connecting pipes, particularly the inlet manifold channel.

5   On 1974 N. American models, with automatic transmission, a switch is fitted to control the exhaust gas recycling valve. This should be checked and adjusted in the following way.

6   Place a packing piece under the throttle screw (A) and observe that the switch roller is in line with the mark on the cam. The switch is isolated in this setting. If adjustment is required release the switch screws and move as necessary.

7   Note that the thickness of the packing piece should be:

US and Canada   *2.9 mm (0.114 in)*
California   *2.6 mm (0.102 in)*

8   Check the operation by having the engine idling at normal working temperature. Move the switch roller so that it cuts off the current to the solenoid flap valve when the engine should start to idle erratically.

34 EGR system maintenance indicator

1   On these vehicles fitted with this device, it must be re-set on completion of the maintenance operation.

2   To do this, cut the sealing wires on the cover of the device which is located on the left-hand side of the engine compartment.

3   Release the clips and remove the cover.

4   Turn the knob (B) through a quarter turn in the direction of the arrow towards the O mark. This will turn off the system warning lamp and re-set the device to operate the new maintenance cycle.

5   Refit the cover.

35 Catalytic converter

1   This device is fitted into the exhaust system of California models. It is essentially a container for catalyst beads over which the exhaust gas flows and is converted to harmless water and carbon dioxide by chemical reaction.

2   An electronic sensor device is fitted to protect the catalytic converter from overheating and consists of a control box located adjacent to the fuse box, a relay and a solenoid-operated air flow valve.

3   On cars fitted with this device, avoid parking over long dry grass, extended idling and exceptionally long down gradients in low gear.

36 Accelerator cable – renewal and adjustment

With manual transmission

1   Release the cable pinch bolt in the trunnion at the engine (photo).

2   Unscrew and remove the locknut from the cable end fitting at the engine end.

3   Working at the accelerator pedal end, pull out the split pin and the clevis pin.

4   Release the cable from the engine compartment rear bulkhead by extracting the screws.

5   Withdraw the cable assembly into the engine compartment.

6   Refitting is a reversal of removal.

With automatic transmission

7   The removal operations are similar to those just described, but the cable is secured to the bulkhead by a circlip. Refit and then adjust by holding the accelerator pedal fully depressed while an assistant holds the throttle butterfly valve plate wide open. Tighten the cable pinch-bolt.

8   Tension the cable until the compensator spring at the bulkhead is compressed by about 2.0 mm (0.08 in) by turning the end fitting nuts. This in turn will ensure that the kickdown switch stop sleeve (B) has 3.0 to 4.0 mm (0.12 to 0.16 in) movement when the accelerator pedal is fully depressed.

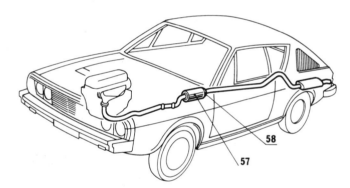

Fig. 3.62 Typical catalytic converter (57) (Sec 35)

58 Temperature sensor

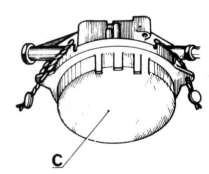

Fig. 3.60 EGR system servicing indicator (Sec 34)

C   Cover

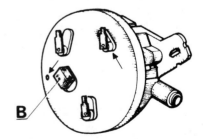

Fig. 3.61 EGR system servicing indicator resetting knob (B)
(Sec 34)

36.1 Typical throttle control bellcrank linkage

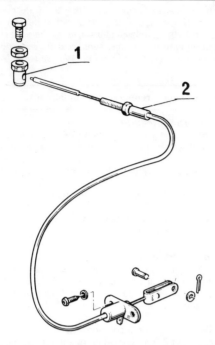

Fig. 3.63 Accelerator cable (manual transmission) (Sec 36)

1   Trunnion   2   Cable end fitting

Fig. 3.64 Accelerator cable (automatic transmission) (Sec 36)

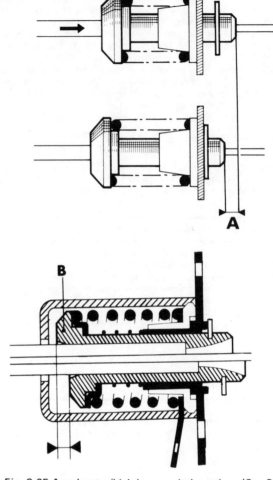

Fig. 3.65 Accelerator/kickdown switch settings (Sec 36)

A = 2.0 mm (0.08 in)   B = 3.0 to 4.0 mm (0.12 to 0.16 in)

37 Manifolds and exhaust system

1   The design of the manifolds varies according to engine type and fuel system.

2   Always use new gaskets when refitting a manifold and tighten nuts to the specified torque (see Chapter 1, Specifications).

3   The exhaust system consists of twin downpipes, an expansion box, a silencer and connecting pipes.

4   The system is suspended on flexible mountings (photos).

37.4A Exhaust flexible mounting

37.4B Exhaust flexible mounting

37.8 Exhaust front mounting nut on floor pan

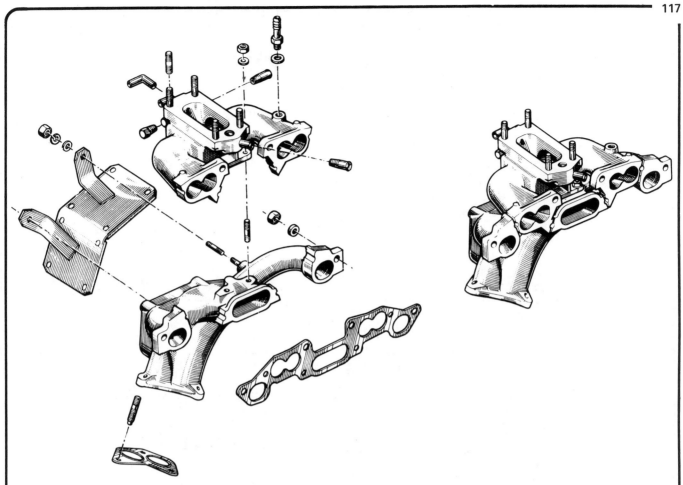

Fig. 3.66 Typical inlet manifold (carburettor engine) (Sec 37)

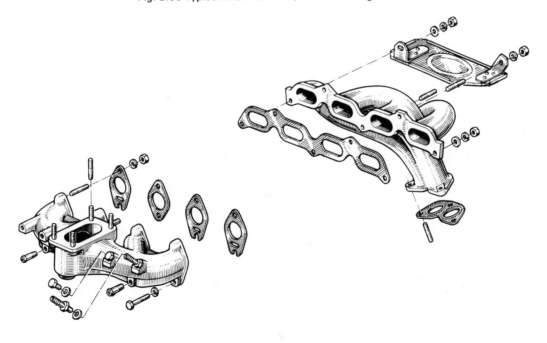

Fig. 3.67 Typical exhaust manifold (carburettor engine) (Sec 37)

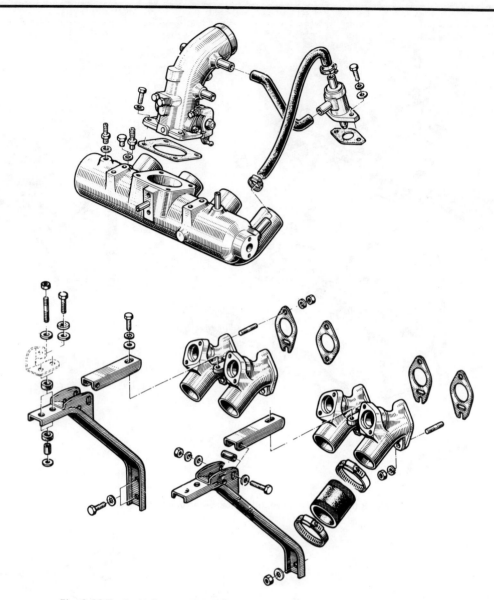

Fig. 3.68 Typical inlet manifold and air flow housing (fuel injection engines) (Sec 37)

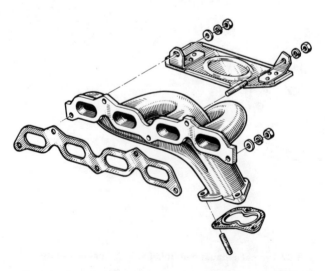

Fig. 3.69 Typical exhaust manifold (fuel injection engine) (Sec 37)

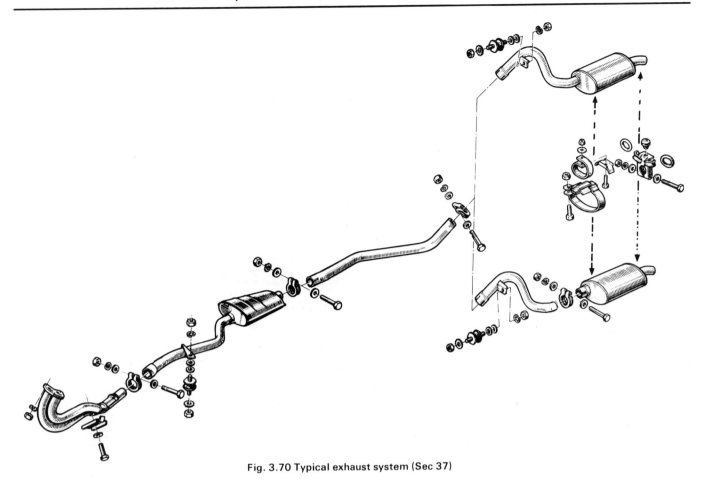

Fig. 3.70 Typical exhaust system (Sec 37)

5   Removal of the exhaust system is simply a matter of disconnecting the downpipes from the manifold and then releasing the system mountings. Withdraw the complete system from beneath the car, jacking-up, if necessary, to obtain better access.

6   It is not recommended that corroded or damaged sections of the exhaust system are removed while the system is still in position as further damage can be caused to good sections and the mountings distorted. It is better to remove the complete system where more purchase can be applied to disengage the sections.

7   Reassemble the new components but do not tighten any pipe clamps until the system has been installed on its mountings and the silencer and expansion box checked for correct alignment.

8   When removing the exhaust front mounting it may be found that due to corrosion, the flexible mounting retaining nut rotates when an attempt is made to unscrew it. Should this happen, remove the centre console inside the car (Chapter 12) and hold the mounting nut located on the floorpan (photo).

38 Fault diagnosis – fuel and emission control systems

Carburettor models

Symptom	Reason(s)
Fuel consumption excessive	Air cleaner choked giving rich mixture Leak from tank, pump or fuel lines Float chamber flooding due to incorrect level or worn needle valve Carburettor incorrectly adjusted Idling speed too high Incorrect valve clearances
Lack of power, stalling or difficult starting	Faulty fuel pump Leak on suction side of pump or in fuel line Intake manifold or carburettor flange gaskets leaking Carburettor incorrectly adjusted
Poor or erratic idling	Weak mixture Leak in intake manifold Leak in distributor vacuum pipe Leak in crankcase extractor hose Leak in brake servo hose

Fuel injection models

Symptom	Reason(s)
Engine will not start from cold but pump operates	Empty fuel tank Ignition fault Start valve faulty Fuel pump pressure too low (may be caused by corroded earth lead contact or worn pump)
Engine will not start when warm but pump operates	Empty fuel tank Start valve not cutting off Fuel pump pressure too high Fuel pump pressure too low
Fuel pump does not operate	Fuse blown Break in supply lead or corroded earth
Erratic idling	Induction housing leaking Throttle valve sticks
Idling speed too high or too low at normal operating temperature	Incorrect slow-running adjustment Incorrect ignition setting Incorrect accelerator linkage adjustment
Engine backfires on overrun	Throttle valve not returning fully
Lack of power	Fuel pump pressure too low Throttle valve not fully opening
Excessive fuel consumption	Leaky start valve

Emission control systems

Symptom	Reason(s)
Fumes emitted from engine and condensation in rocker cover	Break in crankcase ventilation system hoses Pre-heater not set to cold position in winter conditions
Fumes emitted from exhaust	Air pump drivebelt slack (if fitted) System hoses loose Incorrect ignition setting Exhaust gas recirculation pipes corroded Delay valve requires renewal Rich fuel/air mixture Worn cylinder bores or piston rings

Chapter 4 Ignition system

Contents

Transistorized ignition system – checking 11
Diagnostic socket and TDC pick-up – removal and refitting 8
Distributor – overhaul 6
Distributor – removal and refitting 5
Distributor contact breaker points – renewal and adjustment 2
Distributor variations on N. American vehicles 7
Dwell angle – checking and adjusting 3

Fault diagnosis 13
General description 1
Ignition coil and condenser 9
Ignition switch/steering column lock – removal and refitting 12
Ignition timing 4
Spark plugs and HT leads 10

Specifications

System .... 12 volt, battery, coil, mechanical contact breaker distributor. Later models equipped with transistorized, breakerless system

Firing order .... 1-3-4-2 (No. 1 at flywheel end)

Spark plugs
Renault 15
    1289 cc engine .... Champion L87Y
    1565 cc engine .... Champion N7Y
Renault 17 (1605 cc, 1647 cc)
    Carburettor engines .... Champion N9Y
    Fuel injection engines .... Champion N2G or N3
Spark plug gap .... 0.7 mm (0.028 in)

Distributor
Type .... Ducellier or Bosch mechanical breaker type. Later models equipped with breakerless distributor
Rotor rotation .... Clockwise
Contact breaker points gap (initial setting only) .... 0.4 mm (0.016 in)
Dwell angle .... 54 to 60°
Dwell percentage .... 60 to 66%
Air gap (transistorized system) .... 0.3 to 0.6 mm (0.012 to 0.024 in)

Ignition timing
Vehicle Model

Vehicle Model	Engine Type	Distributor Curve	Dynamic Timing (Stroboscopic)
R1300	810-10	R248	1° BTDC to 1° ATDC*
	810-05	R248	1° BTDC to 1° ATDC*
	810-06	R280	11° to 13° BTDC*
R1301	821-15	R246	0° to 3° ATDC*
	821-16	R258	5° to 7° BTDC*

R1302	807-10	R243	1° BTDC to 1° ATDC*
		R266	2° to 4° BTDC*
		R273	5° to 7° BTDC*
	807-11	R273	9° to 11° BTDC*
R1304	841-15	R241	(To 1973) 4° to 6° BTDC*
			(1976 on) 9° to 11° BTDC*
	841-16	R241	(To 1973) 2° to 4° BTDC*
			(1974 on) 9° to 11° BTDC*
	807-13	R272	1° BTDC to 1° ATDC at 1000 rev/min**
R1308	843-15	R243	9° to 11° BTDC*
			(1976 on) 6° to 8° BTDC at 650 rev/min*
R1312	807-10	R243	1° BTDC to 1° ATDC*
	807-10	R266	2° to 4° BTDC*
	807-10	R273	5° to 7° BTDC*
	807-11	R273	9° to 11° BTDC*
	841-15	R241	(To 1973) 4° to 6° BTDC*
			(1974 on) 6° to 8° BTDC*
	841-16	R241	(To 1973) 2° to 4° BTDC*
			(1974 on) 9° to 11° BTDC*
R1313	807-12	R278	15° to 17° BTDC at 1100 rev/min**
	807-12	R267	15° to 18° BTDC at 1100 rev/min**
	807-13	R241	1° BTDC to 1° ATDC at 1000 rev/min**
	807-15	R272	1° BTDC to 1° ATDC at 1000 rev/min**
R1314	841-15	R241	(To 1973) 4° to 6° BTDC*
			(1974 on) 9° to 11° BTDC*
	841-16	R241	(To 1973) 2° to 4° BTDC*
			(1974 on) 9° to 11° BTDC*
	807-13	R272	1° BTDC to 1° ATDC at 1000 rev/min**
R1316	843-13	R258	11° to 13° BTDC*
R1317	844-12	R278	15° to 17° BTDC at 1100 rev/min**
	844-12 (emission controlled)	R278	7° to 9° BTDC at 1000 rev/min**
R1318	843-15	R243	9° to 11° BTDC*
	843-16	R243	9° to 11° BTDC*
	843-E705 (manual)	R254	3° to 5° BTDC*
	843-E705 (manual)	R258	9° to 11° BTDC*
	843-E706 (auto.)	R258	9° to 11° BTDC**
R1322	807-10M	R273	5° to 7° BTDC*
R1323	807-11A	R273	9° to 11° BTDC*
	807-12 (emission controlled)	R278	7° to 9° BTDC*
		R267	7° to 9° BTDC*
	807-13	R241	1° BTDC to 1° ATDC at 1000 rev/min*
R1324	841-15	R241	(To 1973) 4° to 6° BTDC*
			(1974 on) 9° to 11° BTDC*
	841-16	R241	(To 1973) 2° to 4° BTDC*
			(1974 on) 9° to 11° BTDC*
	807-13	R272	0° at 1000 rev/min**
R1326	843-13	R258	11° to 13° BTDC*
	843-13	R272	12° BTDC*
R1327	844-12	R278	15° to 17° BTDC at 1100 rev/min**
	844-12 (emission controlled)	R278	1° to 3° BTDC at 1000 rev/min**
R1328	843-15	R243	9° to 11° BTDC*
	843-16	R243	(To 1977) 9° to 11° BTDC*
			(1977 on) 6° to 8° BTDC at 650 rev/min**
	843-F706 (auto.)	R258	9° to 11° BTDC**

*Distributor vacuum pipe disconnectd and plugged
**Distributor vacuum pipe disconnected

Torque wrench settings

	Nm	lbf ft
Spark plugs	31	23

1 General description

In order that the engine may run correctly it is necessary for an electrical spark to ignite the fuel/air mixture in the combustion chambers at exactly the right moment in relation to engine speed and loading. The ignition system is based on feeding low tension voltage from the battery to the coil where it is converted to high tension voltage. The high tension voltage is powerful enough to jump the gap between the electrodes of the spark plugs in the cylinders many times a second under high compression, providing that the system is in good condition and all the adjustments are correct.

Conventional ignition system

The system is divided into two circuits; the low tension and high tension.

The low tension (sometimes called primary) circuit consists of the battery, lead wire to the starter solenoid, lead from the starter solenoid to the ignition switch, lead from ignition switch to the coil low tension windings (SW or + terminal) and from the coil low tension windings (CB or − terminal) to the contact breaker points and condenser in the distributor.

The high tension circuit consists of the high tension or secondary windings in the coil, the heavily insulated lead from the coil to the distributor cap centre contact, the rotor arm, and the leads from the four distributor cap outer contacts (in turn) to the spark plugs.

Low tension voltage is stepped up by the coil windings to high tension voltage intermittently by the operation of the contact points and the condenser in the low tension circuit. High tension voltage is then fed via the centre contact in the distributor cap to the rotor arm.

The rotor arm rotates clockwise at half engine revolutions inside the distributor. Each time it comes in line with one of the outer contacts in the cap, the contact points open and the high voltage is discharged, jumping the gap from rotor arm to contact and thence along the plug lead to the centre electrode of the plug. Here it jumps the other gap — sparking in the process — to the outer plug electrode and hence to earth.

The static timing of the spark is adjusted by moving the outer body of the distributor in relation to the distributor shaft. This alters the position at which the points open in relation to the position of the crankshaft (and thus the pistons).

The timing is also altered automatically by a centrifugal device, which further alters the position of the complete points mounting assembly in relation to the shaft when engine speed increases, and by a vacuum control working from the inlet manifold which varies the timing according to the position of the throttle and consequently load on the engine. Both of these automatic alterations advance the timing of the spark at light loads and high speeds. The mechanical advance mechanism consists of two weights, which move out from the distributor shaft as engine speed rises due to centrifugal force. As they move out, so the cam rotates relative to the shaft and the contact breaker opening position is altered.

The degree to which the weights move out is controlled by springs, the tension of which significantly controls the extent of the advance to the timing.

The vacuum advance device is a diaphragm and connecting rod attached to the cam plate. When the diaphragm moves in either direction the cam plate is moved, thus altering the timing.

The diaphragm is actuated by depression (vacuum) in the inlet manifold and is connected by a small bore pipe to the carburettor body.

On all engine variants the firing order is 1-3-4-2 and the No. 1 cylinder is at the flywheel end of the engine.

A diagnostic socket is fitted to enable Renault mechanics to quickly pinpoint any problem within the ignition system and also to time it accurately. Unfortunately, without the necessary associated equipment, the diagnostic socket is of little use to the home mechanic (see Section 8).

Transistorized ignition system

Some later models are fitted with a breakerless transistorized ignition system. In place of the traditional distributor rotor, a soft iron rotor is used with one arm per cylinder. This reacts with a magnetic stator and a detecting coil. These components form a pulse generator which replaces a conventional contact breaker, but fulfils the same purpose. An advantage of this system is that it requires no routine maintenance, once correctly fitted, apart from checking the ignition timing.

Also fitted is an electronic control unit. This unit amplifies the impulses from the pulse generator, sends them to the coil and breaks this current to obtain induced HT voltage at the coil output terminal.

Special precautions with transistorized ignition system

Do not run the engine with any HT lead disconnected or damage could occur to the system. If a spark plug is removed for testing, ensure that it is properly earthed.

Avoid receiving electric shocks from the HT circuit. The voltage is higher than in conventional ignition systems and could be dangerous.

2 Distributor contact breaker points − renewal and adjustment

1 One of four types of distributor may be used depending upon model and date of production of the car.
2 At the intervals specified in 'Routine Maintenance', the contact points assembly should be renewed in one of the following ways. Do not attempt to dress the points in an effort to make them suitable for further use as this will upset the wiping action of the points faces.
3 Unclip the distributor cap and place it to one side.
4 Remove the rotor and protective cover, (Ducellier distributor).

Ducellier distributor without external adjuster

5 Pull back the retaining clip from the points pivot post and take off the insulating washer.
6 Prise the contact spring away from the terminal anchorage and slide the contact arm up and off its pivot.
7 Extract the screw which holds the fixed contact to the baseplate and remove the contact.
8 Wipe away any oil from the distributor housing and fit the new contact set, but leave the fixed contact screw loose. Apply a spot of oil to the contact arm pivot.

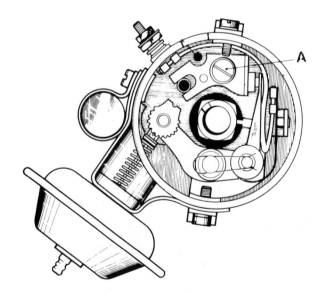

Fig. 4.1 Ducellier distributor viewed from above (Sec 2)

A   Fixed contact screw

9 Rotate the crankshaft until the heel of the spring contact arm is on a high point of the cam.
10 Set the points gap to 0.4 mm (0.016 in) using feeler blades, tighten the contact arm screw.
11 Refit the protective cover, rotor and distributor cap and check the dwell as described in the next Section.

Ducellier distributor with external adjuster

12 The operations are very similar to those described in earlier

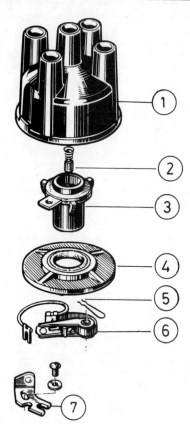

Fig. 4.2 Ducellier distributor components (Sec 2)

1 Cap
2 Carbon contact
3 Rotor
4 Protective cover

5 Spring clip
6 Contact breaker movable arm
7 Contact breaker fixed arm

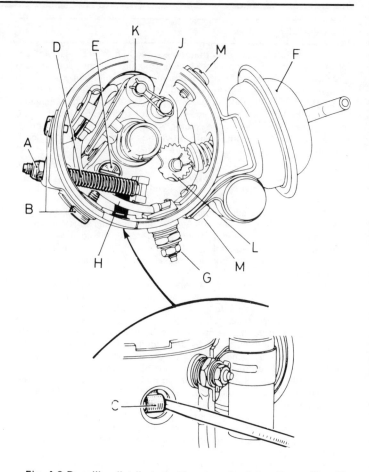

Fig. 4.3 Ducellier distributor with external points adjuster (Sec 2)

A Adjuster
B Adjuster bracket screws
C Retaining lug
D Adjuster spring and rod
E Fixed contact screw
F Vacuum capsule
G LT terminal

H LT lead
J Clip
K Spring blade
L Serrated cam
M Vacuum capsule retaining
   screws

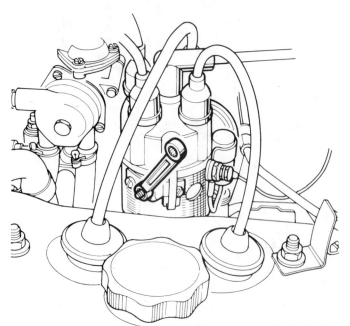

Fig. 4.4 Adjusting points gap with engine running and dwell meter connected (Sec 2)

paragraphs, but the inclusion of the external adjuster will make points renewal a little more difficult.

13 Remove the adjuster nut (A).

14 Unscrew the adjuster bracket screws (B).

15 Take out the small plug covering retaining lug (C), and use a suitable small tool to prise out the lug.

16 Remove adjustment rod and spring (D).

17 Take out screw (E) and remove the fixed contact.

18 Loosen the LT terminal (G), and detach the LT lead (H).

19 Free clip (J) from the pivot post and take off the insulating washer. Remove the moving contact whilst keeping the spring blade (K) pressed inwards, thereby releasing it from its mounting.

20 Clean the new contact faces with methylated spirit and fit them by reversing the removal operations. Apply a spot of oil to the contact arm pivot.

21 Adjust the points gap by turning the nut (A). Use feeler blades and set the gap to 0.4 mm (0.016 in) with the heel of the spring contact arm on the high point of the cam.

22 Refit the protective cover, rotor and cap and check the dwell as described in the next Section.

Bosch distributor

23 To renew the contact points on a Bosch distributor requires a

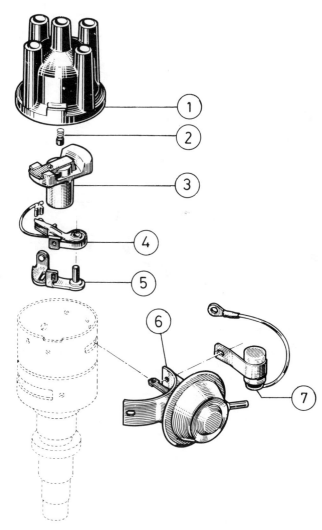

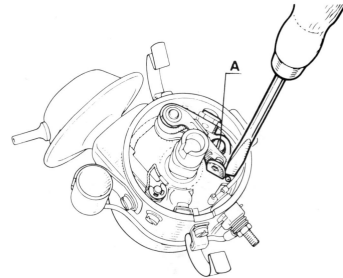

Fig. 4.6 Adjusting Bosch points gap (Sec 2)

A   Fixed contact screw

Fig. 4.5 Bosch distributor components (Sec 2)

1 Cap
2 Carbon contact
3 Rotor
4 Contact breaker movable
   arm
5 Contact breaker fixed arm
6 Vacuum advance capsule
7 Condenser

similar method to that described previously for the Ducellier unit. A
spring clip is not used, however, on the contact arm pivot post and the
points assembly should be removed as a unit after extraction of the
baseplate screw and by pressing the spring arm inwards.

Ducellier distributor with dual contact breaker

24 This type of distributor is used for certain territories in conjunction
with automatic transmission. Its purpose is to increase the ignition
advance when the choke (cold start) device is operating and the speed
selector lever is in 1, 2, A or R.
25 Adjustment of the points should be left to your dealer.

Ducellier distributor with independent solenoid operated advance/retard

26 This type of distributor is used on very late N. American models
equipped with fuel injection.

Distributor lubrication

27 Distributor lubrication should be carried out very sparingly. Apply
a smear of petroleum jelly to the distributor cam and a drop of engine
oil to the felt ring in the protective cover and to the felt pad at the top
of the distributor shaft.

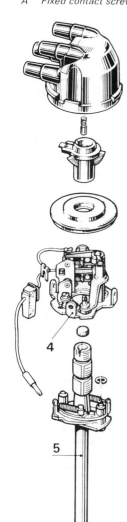

Fig. 4.7 Ducellier distributor with dual contact breaker (Sec 2)

4   Breaker assembly   5   Drive spindle

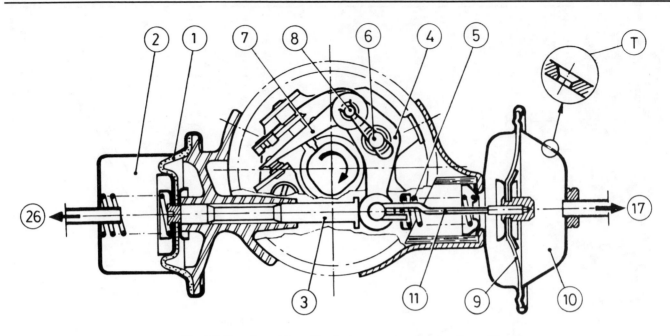

Fig. 4.8 Plan view of Ducellier dual contact breaker distributor (Sec 2)

1	Vacuum diaphragm	5	Spring	9	Diaphragm	17	Solenoid valve
2	Retard capsule	6	Pivot pin	10	Advance capsule	26	Solenoid valve
2	Spindle	7	Movable contact arm	11	Link rod	T	Vent to atmosphere
4	Lever	8	Pivot pin				

3 Dwell angle – checking and adjusting

1   Setting the contact breaker points with feeler blades must be regarded as a basic setting in order to get the engine running.
2   For optimum engine performance the dwell angle must be checked.
3   The dwell angle is the number of degrees through which the distributor cam turns during the period between the instants of closure and opening of the contact breaker points.
4   Setting the points gap by the dwell angle method not only gives a more accurate gap, but also evens out any variations in the gap which could be caused by wear in the distributor shaft or its bushes or a difference in height of any of the cam peaks.
5   The angle should be checked with a dwell meter connected in accordance with the maker's instructions. Refer to the Specifications for the correct dwell angle.
6   If the dwell angle is too large, increase the points gap, if too small, reduce it.
7   The dwell angle should always be adjusted before checking and adjusting the ignition timing. The ignition timing must always be checked after adjusting the dwell angle.

4 Ignition timing

1   Unfortunately, the ignition timing on engines fitted to this model range varies according to the vehicle type and the engine type. In addition, the design of timing marks is not consistent between engines, neither is the method used. To understand what they represent will mean referring to one of the typical illustrations.
2   The coil to distributor HT lead carries a clip which indicates the ignition timing setting for that particular engine. For example +10° indicates a dynamic timing of 10° BTDC.
3   If the HT lead clip is missing then the advance curve number must be read off from the distributor body and then checked against the table given in Specifications at the front of this Chapter.
4   You will of course know your particular model and engine number from the identification plates (refer to the Introductory Section of this Manual).
5   If the timing has been lost completely, it will be necessary to turn the engine so that the timing marks are aligned, with No 1 cylinder on

the compression stroke. (Turn the engine with a spanner on the crankshaft pulley bolt, or on manual transmission models by pushing the car with top gear engaged. Remove the spark plugs and feel for compression being generated in No 1 cylinder). Cylinder and HT lead identification is shown in Figs. 4.21 and 4.22.

Static timing – conventional ignition system
6   With the flywheel or crankshaft pulley timing marks correctly aligned as specified for your particular engine, the distributor points should just be about to open. If they are not, slacken the clamp bolt and rotate the distributor body (photo).
7   If difficulty is experienced in telling precisely when the points are open, connect a 12 volt test lamp across the points and switch on the ignition. When the points are open, the lamp will light. With the timing marks aligned, turn the distributor if necessary to the point where the test lamp is just coming on. Tighten the clamp bolt when adjustment is complete.

4.6 Typical ignition timing scale on flywheel housing

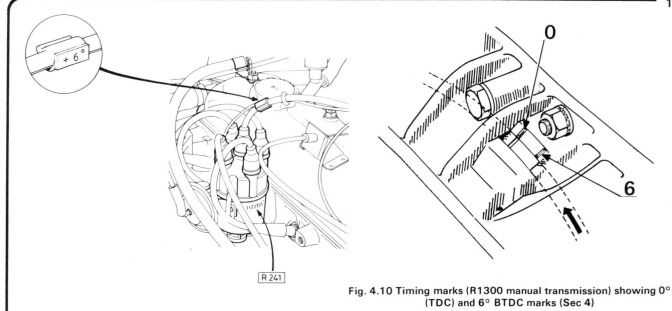

Fig. 4.9 Location of ignition timing valve and distributor curve number (Sec 4)

Fig. 4.10 Timing marks (R1300 manual transmission) showing 0° (TDC) and 6° BTDC marks (Sec 4)

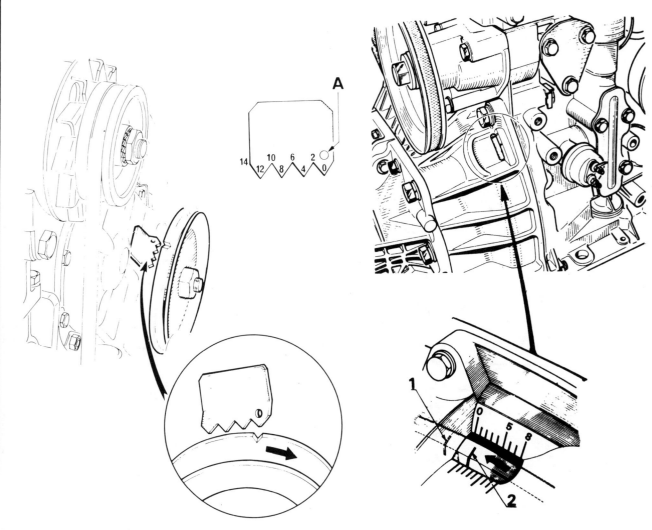

Fig. 4.11 Timing marks (R1300 automatic transmission) (Sec 4)

Fig. 4.12 Timing marks (R1301, R1304, R1313 – N. America manual transmission) (Sec 4)

A   Hole in timing plate

1   0° (TDC)   2   3° ATDC

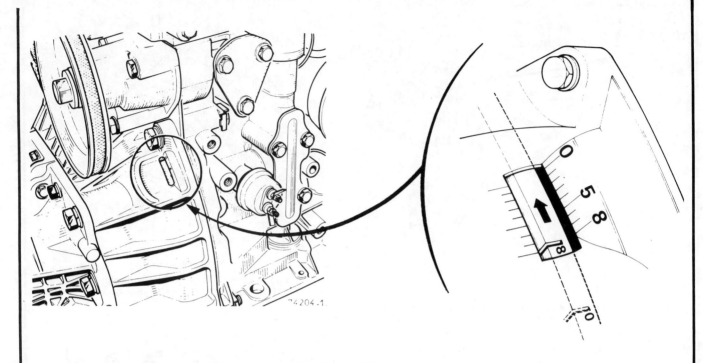

Fig. 4.13 Timing marks (R1302, R1312, R1322, R1313, R1323, R1317, R1327) (Sec 4)

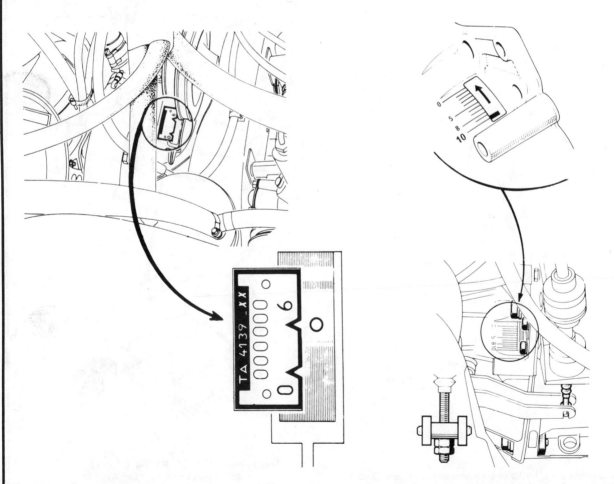

Fig. 4.14 Timing marks (R1301, R1302, R1304, R1312, R1322 automatic transmission) (Sec 4)

Fig. 4.15 Timing marks (R1318, R1328 manual transmission) (Sec 4)

10 Disconnect and plug the vacuum advance pipe at the distributor (where so specified).

11 Start the engine and shine the light onto the timing marks (depending on the strength of the timing light and the brightness of the ambient light, it may be necessary to highlight the timing marks with quick-drying white).

12 If the ignition timing is correct, the specified marks will appear stationary and in alignment.

13 If the timing marks are not aligned, slacken the distributor clamp nut and rotate the distributor slightly in the direction necessary to correct the misalignment. Tighten the clamp nut and recheck.

14 If the timing marks appear unsteady and will not stay in alignment, this may be due to wear in the distributor, or to wear in the timing gear generally.

15 Increasing the engine speed above idle should make the timing marks appear to drift apart as the centrifugal advance mechanism comes into operation.

16 Applying suction to the distributor vacuum unit should similarly cause the timing marks to move in the direction showing advance.

17 When the timing is correct, disconnect the timing light, remake the original connections and reconnect the vacuum pipe (where necessary).

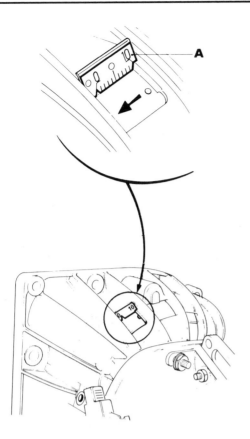

Fig. 4.16 Timing marks (R1318, R1328 automatic transmission) (Sec 4)

A   Timing fixed scale

8   The procedure above is accurate enough to enable the engine to be started. For the best results however, it is advisable to check the timing with the engine running, using a stroboscopic lamp as described below.

Dynamic timing (with stroboscope)

9   Connect a timing light (strobe) to the engine in accordance with the maker's instructions – most lights will require some connection to No 1 HT lead, and some will need to be connected to the car battery or to mains electricity as well.

5   Distributor – removal and refitting

1   All distributors have an offset drive dog, so removal is simply a matter of withdrawing the unit after first making a few simple disconnections.

2   Unclip the distributor cap and move it to one side.

3   Disconnect the LT lead from the distributor.

4   Disconnect the distributor vacuum pipe.

5   Mark the setting of the distributor body base mounting plinth to the engine and then unscrew the clamp plate nut.

6   Withdraw the distributor.

7   Refitting is a reversal of removal. Hold the distributor over its recess and gently push it downward while turning the rotor until the drive dog engages with the drivegear (photo).

8   Reconnect the LT lead and vacuum pipe and distributor cap.

9   Reset the distributor to its original setting, and tighten the clamp plate nut (photo).

10 If the distributor drivegear has been disturbed while the distributor was out of the engine then it must be re-set with the engine at TDC as described in Chapter 1, Section 22 or 25 according to engine type.

11 If a new distributor is being fitted, then its position must be set so that the contact end of the rotor will be in alignment with No.1 contact in the distributor cap when No.1 piston is at TDC on its compression stroke.

12 Unless a straightforward refitting of the original distributor has taken place, always check and adjust the ignition timing as described in Section 4.

5.7 Fitting distributor

5.9 Tightening distributor clamp plate nut

6 Distributor – overhaul

1 Before dismantling a distributor, check the availability of internal spares. If general wear has occurred, it may be more economical to obtain a new or rebuilt unit.

Ducellier type

2 Remove the contact breaker points as described in Section 2.
3 Remove the condenser.
4 Note the relationship of the serrated cam to the vacuum capsule rod. Remove the spring clip from the cam, and lift out the points pivot unit (10).
5 Remove the vacuum capsule retaining screw, followed by the capsule.
6 Remove the spring from the end of the driveshaft.
7 Mark the drive dog in relation to the cam slot in the top of the driving spindle. Tap out the pin, and remove the washers and drive dog.
8 Remove the screws which secure the baseplate, and lift the baseplate off.
9 Lift out the shaft and counterweight assembly.
10 Clean all parts, lightly lubricate as necessary, and reassemble in the reverse order to the dismantling procedure.

Bosch type

11 The operations are generally similar to those described for the Ducellier except that the advance capsule link rod is retained to the baseplate pivot with an E-clip.

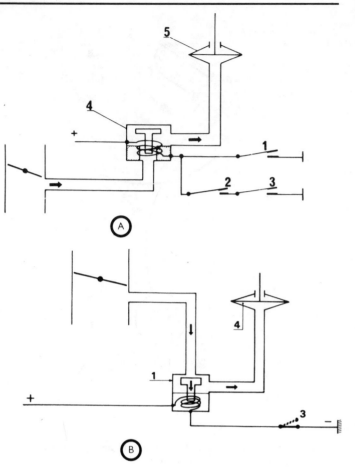

Fig. 4.18A Vacuum advance control system (R1313 N. America) (Sec 7)

A	Manual transmission	B	Automatic transmission
1	Thermal cut-out	1	Solenoid flap valve
2	Accelerator pedal switch	3	Choke control switch
3	Transmission switch	4	Vacuum capsule
4	Solenoid flap valve		
5	Vacuum advance capsule		

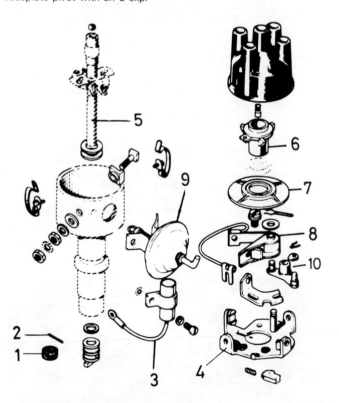

Fig. 4.17 Exploded view of Ducellier distributor (Sec 6)

1	Spring	6	Rotor
2	Retaining pin	7	Dust shield
3	Condenser	8	Moving contact
4	Baseplate	9	Advance/retard unit
5	Rotor spindle	10	Points pivot unit

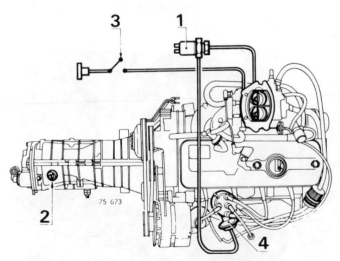

Fig. 4.18B Components of vacuum advance control system (manual transmission shown) (Sec 7)

1	Solenoid flap valve	3	Choke control switch
2	Transmission switch	4	Distributor vacuum capsule

7 Distributor variations on N. American vehicles

1 Certain modifications are incorporated in the distributors used on engines equipped with emission control systems.

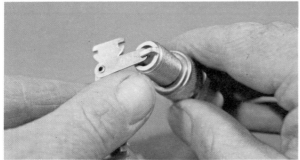

Measuring plug gap. A feeler gauge of the correct size (see ignition system specifications) should have a slight 'drag' when slid between the electrodes. Adjust gap if necessary

Adjusting plug gap. The plug gap is adjusted by bending the earth electrode inwards, or outwards, as necessary until the correct clearance is obtained. Note the use of the correct tool

Normal. Grey-brown deposits, lightly coated core nose. Gap increasing by around 0.001 in (0.025 mm) per 1000 miles (1600 km). Plugs ideally suited to engine, and engine in good condition

Carbon fouling. Dry, black, sooty deposits. Will cause weak spark and eventually misfire. Fault: over-rich fuel mixture. Check: carburettor mixture settings, float level and jet sizes; choke operation and cleanliness of air filter. Plugs can be re-used after cleaning

Oil fouling. Wet, oily deposits. Will cause weak spark and eventually misfire. Fault: worn bores/piston rings or valve guides; sometimes occurs (temporarily) during running-in period. Plugs can be re-used after thorough cleaning

Overheating. Electrodes have glazed appearance, core nose very white – few deposits. Fault: plug overheating. Check: plug value, ignition timing, fuel octane rating (too low) and fuel mixture (too weak). Discard plugs and cure fault immediately

Electrode damage. Electrodes burned away; core nose has burned, glazed appearance. Fault: pre-ignition. Check: as for 'Overheating' but may be more severe. Discard plugs and remedy fault before piston or valve damage occurs

Split core nose (may appear initially as a crack). Damage is self-evident, but cracks will only show after cleaning. Fault: pre-ignition or wrong gap-setting technique. Check: ignition timing, cooling system, fuel octane rating (too low) and fuel mixture (too weak). Discard plugs, rectify fault immediately

California, Canada
2   A vacuum advance control system is fitted to these vehicles. The
main components are:

    (a) Cylinder head thermal cut-out (1)
    (b) Accelerator pedal switch (2)
    (c) Transmission switch (3)
    (d) Distributor vacuum capsule (5)
    (e) Solenoid flap valve (4)

3   The solenoid flap valve is controlled either by the thermal cut-out,
the accelerator switch or the transmission switch according to
conditions.
4   When the coolant temperature is below 12°C (54°F) the thermal
cut-out is closed. Power is applied to the solenoid flap valve and the
vacuum advance capsule is open to atmosphere.
5   At higher coolant temperatures, the thermal cut-out is open and
the flap valve is controlled by the accelerator pedal switch and the
3rd/4th transmission switch. The accelerator pedal switch is open in
the pedal raised position. The 3rd/4th speed switch is closed during
the time when these speeds are selected.
6   It will be evident from the foregoing explanation that when 1st or
2nd speed is selected or the accelerator pedal in the raised position,
the solenoid flap valve is not energised. In this condition, the vacuum
capsule is open to atmosphere and the ignition is retarded.
7   On automatic transmission models, an advance correction control
system is also fitted.
8   The system incorporates a solenoid flap valve to apply vacuum
from the carburettor to the vacuum unit on the distributor.
9   The solenoid flap valve is actuated by a switch on the choke
control.
10   In the cold start position, switch (3) is closed. The solenoid flap
valve is supplied with power so that the advance capsule will receive
vacuum from the carburettor.

8   Diagnostic socket and TDC pick-up – removal and refitting

1   As previously mentioned, these devices are fitted to the car to
permit accurate fault diagnosis and tuning by Renault dealers having
the necessary monitoring equipment.
2   Although not of use to the home mechanic, the removal and
refitting of the devices may be a requirement during major overhaul.

Diagnostic socket
3   Disconnect the battery.
4   Remove the socket without disturbing the base (photo).
5   Refer to Fig. 4.19 and disconnect the earth wire (2), contact point
wire (3) ignition coil wire (6).

TDC pick-up
6   Extract the pick-up clamp screw and remove the pick-up from the
clutch cover plate (photos).

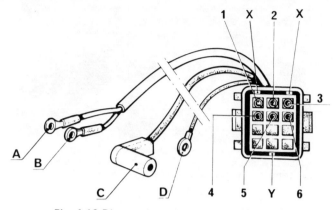

Fig. 4.19 Diagnostic socket connections (Sec 8)

1 TDC signal pick-up – Red	A To ignition coil LT output
2 Distributor earth – Yellow	– Black/Red
3 Contact points – Black	B To ignition coil + terminal
4 TDC signal pick-up – White	– Grey/Blue
5 TDC signal pick-up	C TDC pick-up to engine block
screening	D Earth – Yellow
6 Ignition coil positive – Grey	X One way locator
	Y One way locator

8.4 Diagnostic socket

8.6A TDC pick-up and clamp

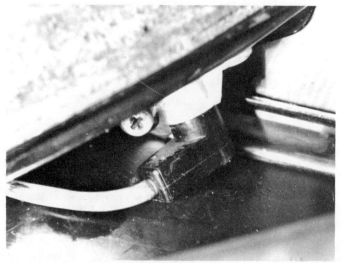

8.6B TDC pick-up located in clutch cover plate

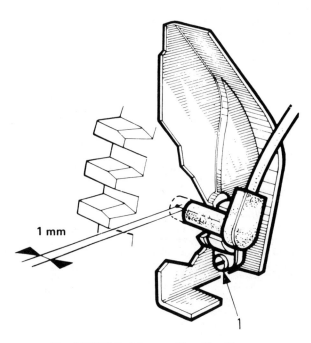

Fig. 4.20 TDC pick-up setting (Sec 8)

1 Screw for adjustment

7 Refitting and reconnection are reversals of disconnection and removal.

8 If a new pick-up is being fitted, it will automatically be in the correct position by virtue of the three pegs on it. With the pegs touching the flywheel tighten screw (1).

9 Where an old pick-up with worn pegs is being fitted, first set the pick-up to touch the flywheel, then withdraw it 0.04 in (1 mm). Tighten the clamp screw.

9 Ignition coil and condenser

1 Failure to start, misfiring, or excessive burning or pitting of the contact breaker point faces, can be caused by a failed condenser.

2 The best way to test this component is to substitute a new unit.

3 High tension current should be negative at the spark plug terminals. Check that the LT lead from the distributor connects with the negative (−) terminal on the coil.

4 Without special equipment, the best method of testing for a faulty

coil is by substitution of a new unit. Before doing this however, check the security of the connecting leads and remove any corrosion which may have built up in the coil HT sockets (photo).

10 Spark plugs and HT leads

1 The correct functioning of the spark plugs is vital for the correct running and efficiency of the engine.

2 At specified intervals the plugs should be removed, examined, cleaned, and if worn excessively, renewed. The condition of the spark plugs will also tell much about the overall condition of the engine.

3 If the insulator nose of the spark plug is clean and white, with no deposits, this is indicative of a weak mixture, or too hot a plug (a hot plug transfers heat away from the electrode slowly − a cold plug transfers it away quickly).

4 The plugs fitted as standard are as listed in Specifications at the beginning of this Chapter. If the tip and insulator nose are covered with hard black looking deposits, then this is indicative that the mixture is too rich. Should the plug be black and oily, then it is likely that the engine is fairly worn, as well as the mixture being too rich.

5 If the insulator nose is covered with light tan to greyish-brown deposits, then the mixture is correct and it is likely that the engine is in good condition.

6 If there are any traces of long brown tapering stains on the outside of the white portion of the plug, then the plug will have to be renewed, as this shows that there is a faulty joint between the plug body and the insulator, and compression is being allowed to leak away.

7 Plugs should be cleaned by a sand blasting machine which will free them from carbon more thoroughly than cleaning by hand. The machine will also test the condition of the plugs under compression. Any plug that fails to spark at the recommended pressure should be renewed.

8 The spark plug gap is of considerable importance, as, if it is too large or too small, the size of the spark and its efficiency will be seriously impaired. The spark plug gap should be set to the figure given in the Specifications at the beginning of this Chapter.

9 To set it, measure the gap with a feeler gauge, and then bend open, or close, the outer plug electrode until the correct gap is achieved. The centre electrode should never be bent as this may crack the insulation and cause plug failure if nothing worse.

10 When renewing the plugs, remember to use new plug washers, and refit the leads from the distributor in the correct firing order, which is 1-3-4-2, No.1 being at the flywheel end of the engine.

11 The plug leads require no routine attention other than being kept clean and wiped over regularly.

9.4 Ignition coil

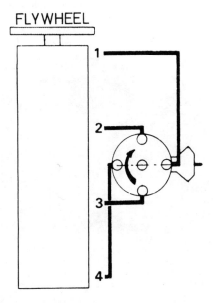

Fig. 4.21 Spark plug HT lead connections on Type 810 engine (Sec 10)

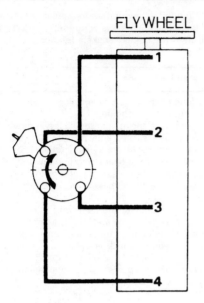

Fig. 4.22 Spark plug HT lead connections on all engines except
Type 810 (Sec 10)

12 At the specified intervals, pull the leads off the plugs and
distributor one at a time and make sure no water has found its way
onto the connections. Remove any corrosion from the end fittings,
wipe the collars on top of the distributor, and refit the leads.
13 Every 10 000 to 12 000 miles (16 000 to 19 000 km) it is
recommended that the spark plugs are renewed to maintain optimum
engine performance.
14 All engines are fitted with carbon cored HT leads. These should be
removed from the spark plugs by gripping their rubber end covers.
Provided the leads are not bent in a tight loop and compressed there
is no reason why this type of lead should fail. A legend has arisen
which blames this type of lead for all ignition faults and many owners
replace them with the older copper cored type and install separate
suppressors. In the majority of cases, it would be more profitable to
establish the real cause of the trouble before going to the expense of
new leads.
15 The spark plugs on all engines except Type 810 are located in
tubular recesses in the rocker cover. No difficulty should be
experienced in removing them with a normal plug socket or box
spanner provided the socket walls are not too thick. Make sure that the
seals at the tubular recesses are in good condition (photo).

10.15 Connecting a spark plug lead

11 Transistorized ignition system – checking

Engine will not start
1   Switch on the ignition.
2   Remove the distributor cap.
3   Remove the main HT supply lead from the distributor cap and
earth it.
4   Disconnect the other end of the HT supply lead from the coil.
Using well insulated pliers, hold this lead one eighth of an inch from
the coil centre.
5   Take a magnet and raise and lower it smartly near the distributor
winding. A spark should occur between the coil centre and the lead.
6   If no spark occurs check each component in the system.
Note: The earth point should be some distance away from the coil and
electronic control unit.

Checking the components
7   Check the security and condition of the ignition coil LT feed wire.
8   To check the detecting coil, connect an ohmmeter between the
two terminals at the detecting coil end. The needle should move. If it
remains stationary, change the coil.
9   Connect the ohmmeter between one terminal at the detecting coil
end, and the distributor earth. The needle should remain stationary. If
the needle moves, change the coil.
Note: Do not use a test bulb to check the distributor winding because
the current is too high.

Checking the ignition coil and electronic control unit
10   Switch on the ignition.
11   Connect a voltmeter between the two LT terminals on the ignition
coil.
12   Raise and lower a magnet smartly near the distributor detecting
coil.
13   If the needle moves, change the coil.
14   If the needle remains stationary, change the electronic control
unit.

Checking for a fault in the distributor
15   This requires the use of a special component called a TDC pick-up.
16   If one of these is available to you, disconnect the distributor
connector and insert two wires from the TDC pick-up into the sockets
in the connector at the electronic control unit end.
17   Move a magnet smartly towards and away from the TDC pick-up.
If a spark jumps between the ignition coil and the HT lead, the
distributor is faulty.

Ignition faulty with engine running
18   Check the security and condition of the HT leads, LT wires and
spark plugs.
19   If the poor running is still caused by the ignition system, the
electronic control unit must be suspected. The best way to test for a
faulty unit is by substitution of a new unit.

Setting the distributor air gap
20   Loosen screws 1 and 2.
21   Insert a feeler gauge of the specified thickness between the
detecting coil tip and a rotor arm.
22   Move the coil base beneath screw 1 to bring the coil tip into
contact with the feeler gauge.
23   Tighten screws 1 and 2. Recheck the air gap of each of the four
rotor arms.
Note: If the air gap is outside the tolerance range on one or more of
the arms and the correct setting is unobtainable, the distributor must
be changed.

12 Ignition switch/steering column lock – removal and refitting

1   This switch is of the Nieman type.
2   Disconnect the battery, remove the steering column shrouds and
disconnect the ignition switch wiring plug.
3   Unscrew and remove the small lock retaining bolt from the highest
point of the lock.
4   Insert the ignition key and turn it to position G.

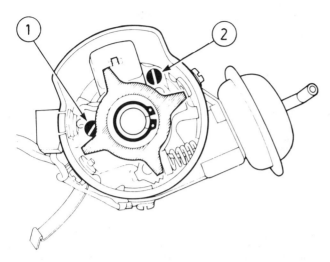

Fig. 4.23 Location of screws 1 and 2 in distributor (transistorized ignition) (Sec 11)

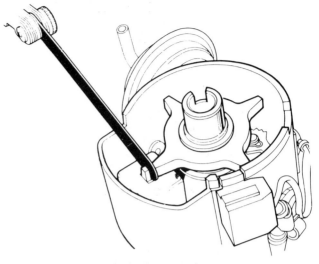

Fig. 4.24 Measuring the air gap (transistorized ignition) (Sec 11)

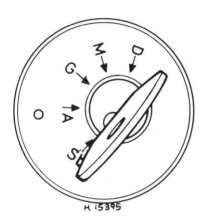

Fig. 4.25 Ignition switch positions (Sec 12)

St	Steering column locked (key withdrawn)	G	Garage – steering unlocked (key withdrawn)
A	Accessories (radio) on	M	Ignition on
		D	Starter

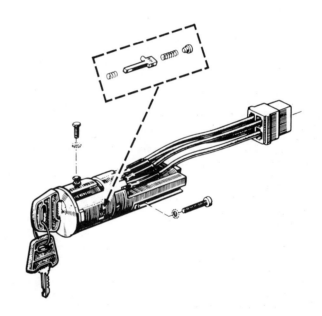

Fig. 4.26 Ignition switch/steering column lock (Sec 12)

5   Using a thin rod, depress the lock locating plunger and withdraw the assembly.

6   The ignition switch can be separated from the lock by extracting the two fixing screws.

7   Refitting is a reversal of removal.

8   It should be noted that the steering column does not lock until the key has been withdrawn and the steering wheel turned to engage the lock tongue in its cut-out.

13 Fault diagnosis – ignition system

Symptom	Reason(s)
Engine fails to start	Loose battery connections
	Discharged battery
	Disconnected wires
	Damp spark plug leads
	Damp distributor cap interior
Engine starts and runs but misfires	Faulty spark plugs
	Cracked distributor cap
	Cracked rotor
	Worn advance mechanism
	Incorrect plug gap
	Faulty coil
	Incorrect timing
	Poor earth connections
Engine overheats, lacks power	Seized centrifugal weights
	Perforated vacuum pipe
	Incorrect ignition timing
Engine 'pinks'	Timing too advanced
	Advance mechanism stuck in advanced position
	Broken centrifugal weight spring
	Fuel octane rating too low

For transistorized ignition system see Section 11

Chapter 5 Clutch

Contents

Clutch — adjustment 2
Clutch — removal, inspection and refitting 4
Clutch cable — renewal 3
Clutch pedal — removal and refitting 7

Clutch release bearing — renewal 5
Clutch release fork and shaft — removal and refitting 6
Fault diagnosis 8
General description 1

Specifications

Type	Single dry plate, diaphragm spring, torsion damped driven plate
Driven plate diameter (dependent upon model)	170.2 mm (6.7 in) 200.7 mm (7.9 in) 215.9 mm (8.5 in)
Release bearing	Sealed ball
Clutch release lever clearance	2.0 to 3.0 mm (0.079 to 0.118 in)

Torque wrench settings

	Nm	lbf ft
Clutch cover bolts	20	15
Clutch bellhousing bolts		
8.0 mm	25	18
10.0 mm	35	26

1 General description

The clutch on all models is of diaphragm spring type, operated using a cable.

Whilst the servicing operations are identical, the precise size and design of the clutch components differs according to model and date of production of the vehicle.

As there are many variations, it is imperative that the full details and identification numbers of the vehicle are given when a replacement clutch is required.

The clutch release bearing is of sealed ball type.

The clutch pedal pivots on the same shaft as the brake pedal. The release arm activates a thrust bearing (clutch release bearing) which bears on the diaphragm spring of the pressure plate. The diaphragm then releases or engages the clutch driven plate which is splined onto the gearbox primary shaft. The clutch driven plate (disc) spins in between the clutch pressure plate and the flywheel face when it is released, and is held there when engaged, to connect the drive from the engine to the transmission unit.

2 Clutch — adjustment

1 Refer to Fig. 5.3 and apply light hand pressure on the release lever (L) in the direction (A). The release bearings will be felt to make contact with the clutch diaphragm spring.

2 Release the locknut (G) and turn the adjuster nut (E) until there is a clearance (J) between the nut and lever with tension applied to the cable in a forward direction (C).

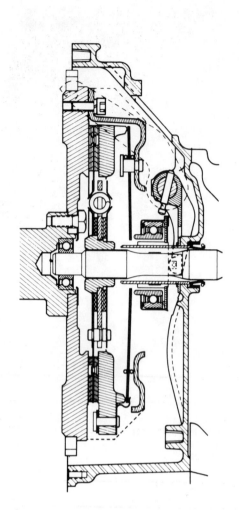

Fig. 5.1 Sectional view of clutch used on all models except R1300 (Sec 1)

Fig. 5.2 Sectional view of clutch used on Model R1300 (Sec 1)

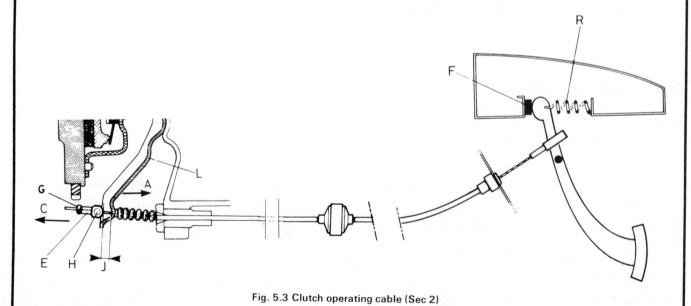

Fig. 5.3 Clutch operating cable (Sec 2)

A Rearward direction	F Stop	H Trunnion	L Release lever
C Forward direction	G Locknut	J 2.0 to 3.0 mm	R Return spring
E Adjuster nut		(0.079 to 0.118 in)	

3   The correct clearance is between 2.0 and 3.0 mm (0.079 and 0.118 in).
4   When the correct clearance is achieved, tighten the locknut while holding the adjuster nut from turning with another spanner.

3   Clutch cable – renewal

1   Remove the nuts from the cable and fitting at the transmission (photo).
2   Working inside the car, disconnect the cable from the pedal arm by extracting the lock pin and clevis pin. This job will be made easier if the circlip is removed from the end of the pedal pivot shaft and the shaft partially pushed out so that the pedal can be lowered and the pedal return spring disconnected.
3   Disconnect the cable from the stop on the pedal support bracket.
4   Withdraw the cable into the engine compartment.
5   Refitting is a reversal of removal, adjust the clearance as described in the preceding Section.

4   Clutch – removal, inspection and refitting

1   Access to the clutch is obtained by removing the transmission as described in Chapter 6.
2   Mark the position of the clutch cover in relation to the flywheel.
3   Unscrew the cover retaining bolts, one half turn at a time until the diaphragm spring pressure is released and then withdraw the cover and driven plate.
4   The reason for removal of the clutch will probably be that the clutch is slipping (see Fault Diagnosis).
5   This condition will be the result of the friction linings having worn down to the rivets or having become saturated with oil due to a leaking engine or transmission oil seal. If due to the latter, renew the crankshaft rear or clutch bellhousing oil seal at once.

3.1 Clutch cable end fitting at release lever

6   Do not atempt to re-line the clutch driven plate yourself, but obtain a new one.
7   Examine the friction surfaces of the flywheel and pressure plate. On Type 810 engines, the flywheel may be machined to remove the grooves, but only within certain conditions as described in Chapter 1, Section 18. On other engines, a grooved flywheel must be renewed.
8   Evidence of tiny cracks will indicate overheating at some stage.
9   Check segments of the pressure plate diaphragm spring for cracks and renew the assembly if apparent.

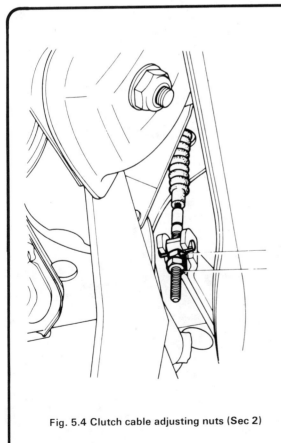

Fig. 5.4 Clutch cable adjusting nuts (Sec 2)

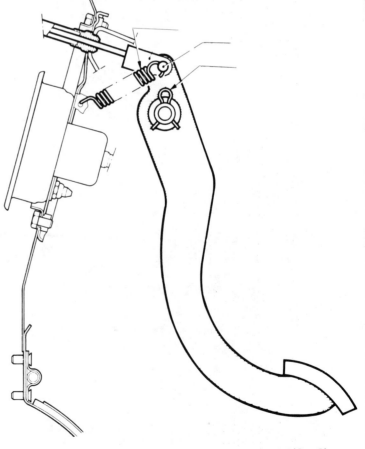

Fig. 5.5 Clutch cable attachment to pedal (Sec 3)

10 Where clutch engagement has been fierce, or clutch slip has occurred in spite of the driven plate being in good condition, renew the pressure plate assembly complete.

11 Examine the release bearing and mechanism (see Sections 5 and 6). Renew the bearing as a matter of course unless it is known to be virtually new.

12 Ensure that all frictional surfaces are clean and free from greasy deposits. Clean the contact faces of the flywheel and clutch cover using petrol.

Refitting

13 Offer up the friction plate to the flywheel, with the damper plate and springs facing towards the gearbox. The plate is marked 'Flywheel Side' (photos).

14 Offer up the cover plate assembly, lining up the marks made when dismantling. Refit the cover plate bolts, but leave them just finger tight.

15 Align the centre of the friction plate with the bearing in the end of the crankshaft. Use either a Renault or proprietary alignment tool, an old gearbox primary shaft, or failing this align the friction plate by eye by moving it about using a bar placed through the centre (photo).

16 Tighten the cover plate bolts progressively, and in a diametrically opposite sequence, to avoid distortion of the cover.

17 **Very lightly** lubricate the release bearing surface on the clutch cover spring.

18 Apply a smear of molybdenum disulphide grease to the splines of the transmission input shaft.

19 Refit the transmission. If this proves difficult, try turning the crankshaft slightly in order to align the clutch driven plate splines with those on the input shaft. Check that the transmission is being held at the same angle as the engine.

20 Once installed, adjust the clutch as described in Section 2.

5 Clutch release bearing – renewal

1 It is rare for this operation to be required other than at time of clutch driven plate renewal. However, if the bearing is heard to be noisy whenever the pedal is depressed, renew it in the following way.

2 Remove the transmission (Chapter 6).

3 Prise the legs of the spring apart and withdraw the release bearing (photo).

4 To refit, lubricate the sleeve on the gearbox shaft and the fingers of the operating fork, using molybdenum disulphide grease.

5 Place the new release bearing in position on the gearbox shaft, and refit the ends of the spring in the fork and bearing holder.

6 Refit the transmission and adjust the clutch cable.

6 Clutch release fork and shaft – removal and refitting

1 Remove the gearbox as described – Chapter 6.

2 Pull out the pins which retain the fork to the shaft. This can be

4.13A Fitting clutch components

4.13B Marking on clutch driven plate

4.15 Using clutch alignment tool

5.3 Disengaging release bearing spring leg

6.2 Clutch release fork and shaft

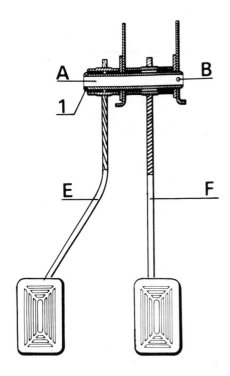

Fig. 5.7 Clutch and brake pedals (Sec 7)

A   Cross-shaft   F   Brake pedal
B   Roll pin   1   Spring retaining clip
E   Clutch pedal

together with the rubber seal.
5   Refit the pins, ensuring that dimension D in Fig. 5.6 is as indicated.
6   Refit the transmission, adjust the clutch cable as described in Section 2.

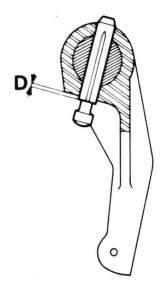

Fig. 5.6 Clutch fork retaining pin projection (Sec 6)

D   = 1.0 mm (0.040 in)

difficult without the correct tool, and if necessary a Renault agent should be consulted (photo).
3   Pull out the fork shaft, and withdraw the fork and spring.
4   To refit, lubricate the shaft with molybdenum disulphide grease or an equivalent. Place the fork and spring in position, and insert the shaft

7   Clutch pedal – removal and refitting

1   The clutch and brake pedals operate on a common cross-shaft.
2   To remove the pedals, disconnect the pedal return spring and pull the spring clip from the end of the shaft.
3   Disconnect the clutch cable and the pushrod from the pedal arms by extracting the split and clevis pins.
4   Remove one pedal from the end of the shaft.
5   Tap the shaft out of the bracket and remove the second pedal.
6   Refitting is a reversal of removal. If a new shaft is being fitted, make sure that the rollpin is fitted to it and apply some molybdenum disulphide grease to the shaft.
7   Check the clutch adjustment (Section 2).

'Fault diagnosis appears overleaf'

8   Fault diagnosis – clutch

Symptom	Reason(s)
Judder when taking up drive	Loose engine/gearbox mountings or over-flexible mountings Badly worn friction surfaces or friction plate contamination by oil leakage Worn splines in the friction plate hub or on the gearbox input shaft
Clutch spin (or failure to disengage) so that gears cannot be meshed	Clutch actuating cable clearance too great Clutch friction disc sticking because of rust on splines (usually apparent after standing idle for some length of time) Damaged or misaligned pressure plate assembly Incorrect release bearing fitted
Clutch slip – (increase in engine speed does not result in increase in car speed – especially on hills)	Clutch actuating cable clearance from fork too small resulting in partially disengaged clutch at all times Clutch friction surfaces worn out (beyond further adjustment of operating cable) or clutch surfaces oil soaked

Chapter 6 Manual transmission

Contents

Fault diagnosis 12
Gearchange linkage – removal, refitting and adjusting 3
General description 1
Lubrication 2
Transmission – removal and refitting 4
Transmission (Type 352) – dismantling 5
Transmission (Type 352) – examination and renovation 6
Transmission (Type 352) – reassembly 7
Transmission (Type 395) – dismantling 8
Transmission (Type 395) – examination and renovation 9
Transmission (Type 395) – reassembly 10
Transmission (Type 365) – dismantling and
reassembly 11

Specifications

Type 352 .... 4 forward speeds (all synchro) and reverse, incorporating differential/final drive

Application .... Renault 15/17 Models R1300, R1301, R1302, R1304, R1308, R1312, R1313, R1314, R1316, R1318, R1322, R1323, R1324, R1326

Ratios (dependent upon model and date of production)

Suffix 11, 12 or 13

1st	3.61:1
2nd	2.26:1
3rd	1.48:1
4th	1.03:1
Reverse	3.08:1

Suffix 31, 32, 33, 50, 51, 52

1st	3.46:1
2nd	2.24:1
3rd	1.48:1
4th	1.04:1
Reverse	3.08:1

Suffix 55, 56, 57, 61, 62, 63, 64, 65

1st	3.82:1
2nd	2.24:1
3rd	1.48:1
4th	1.04:1
Reverse	3.08:1

Final drive ratios

Suffix 11, 13, 31, 33, 50, 52, 55, 57, 61, 63, 64	3.55:1
Suffix 12, 32, 51, 56, 62, 65	3.77:1

Oil capacity .... $3\frac{1}{2}$ Imp pts, 2.1 US qts, 2.0 l

Crownwheel and pinion backlash ....   0.12 to 0.25 mm (0.0047 to 0.010 in)

Differential new bearing preload ....   0.9 to 3.2 kg (2 to 7 lbs)

Pinion protrusion ....   59.0 mm (2.323 in)

Type 365 ....   5 forward speeds (all synchro) and reverse, incorporating
                                                                           differential/final drive

Application ....   Renault 17 – Models R1313, R1317, R1323, R1327

Ratios (dependent upon model and date of production)
Suffix 00, 02, 03, 04, 05, 06, 07

1st	3.61:1
2nd	2.33:1
3rd	1.60:1
4th	1.21:1
5th	0.93:1
Reverse	3.08:1

Suffix 33, 34, 35

1st	3.46:1
2nd	2.24:1
3rd	1.60:1
4th	1.21:1
5th	0.93:1
Reverse	3.08:1

Final drive ratio 3.77:1

Tolerances and oil capacity as for Type 352 gearbox

Type 395 ....   5 forward speeds (all synchro) and reverse, incorporating
                                                                           differential/final drive

Application ....   Renault 17. R1313, R1316, R1318, R1323, R1326, R1328

Ratios

1st	3.82:1
2nd	2.24:1
3rd	1.48:1
4th	1.04:1
5th	0.86:1
Reverse	3.08:1

Final drive ratio 3.77:1

Tolerances and oil capacity as for Type 352 gearbox

Torque wrench settings

	Nm	lb ft
Casing half housing bolts		
7.0 mm	25	18
8.0 mm	30	22
Rear cover bolts	11	8
Bell housing bolts		
8.0 mm	25	18
10.0 mm	35	26
Reverse selector arm bolt	29	21
Crown wheel bolts	109	80
Primary shaft nut	115	85

1 General description

Three types of manual gearbox are fitted to the Renault 15/17. Type 352, 365 or 395. The first of these has four forward speeds, and the others have five speeds.

The design of all types is similar, with an aluminium gearcase in four sections, namely the clutch housing, the right- and left-hand housings (housing the main assemblies and also the differential unit), and the rear cover unit (containing the selector control shaft and selector finger). On the 365 and 395 gearbox, the rear cover also houses the fifth gear and its synchromesh assembly. All forward gears are fitted with synchromesh. Drive to the gears from the flywheel and clutch unit is via the clutch shaft, which is engaged with the primary shaft splines. The clutch shaft passes through the differential compartment. The primary shaft transmits motion via the respective gears to the pinion (secondary) shaft. The reverse idler gear is located on a separate shaft in the rear of the main casing.

Motion is transmitted when a particular gear is engaged transferring the drive from the primary to the secondary shaft, which in turn drives the differential unit and consequently the driveshafts.

The gear selector forks and shafts are located in the side of the gear casing and are actuated by the selector rod mechanism, located in the rear casing. The selector forks are in constant engagement with the synchro sliding hubs which move to and fro accordingly to engage the gear selected.

The speedometer drivegear is attached to the end of the secondary shaft, and this in turn drives the drivegear unit to which the drive cable is attached. Both the speedometer cable and driven gear unit can be removed with the gearbox in place.

On the Type 365 and 395 gearbox, work upon the 5th gear and associated parts is feasible with the unit in place in the vehicle, by first removing the rear cover. All other gear assemblies, and the differential unit, are accessible only with the unit removed from the car.

Although the transmission unit is basically simple in operation, certain dismantling, adjustment and reassembly operations require the use of specialised tools. Therefore, if you are contemplating overhauling the gearbox it is essential that you read through the relevant sections concerning your gearbox before starting any work.

Another point to consider is the availability of parts. You will not know what you require until the casing sections are separated. At this stage an assessment should be made of the work required and parts that will be needed. In some instances, certain items are only supplied as complete assemblies, and in many cases the simplest course of

1.9 Gearbox identification plate

action is to reassemble the casings and get an exchange unit – usually the most satisfactory and economical solution.

The gearbox is identified by a plate attached under one of the rear end cover bolts. The plate carries details of the type, and also the suffix and fabrication numbers (photo).

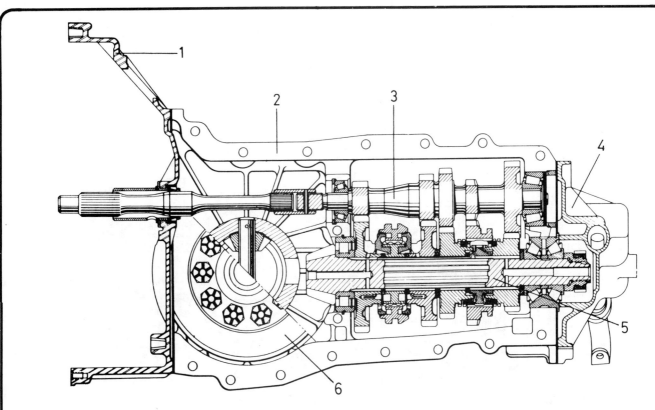

Fig. 6.1 Sectional view of Type 352 manual transmission (Sec 1)

1 Clutch bellhousing	3 Primary shaft	5 Secondary shaft
2 Casing	4 Rear cover	6 Differential/final drive

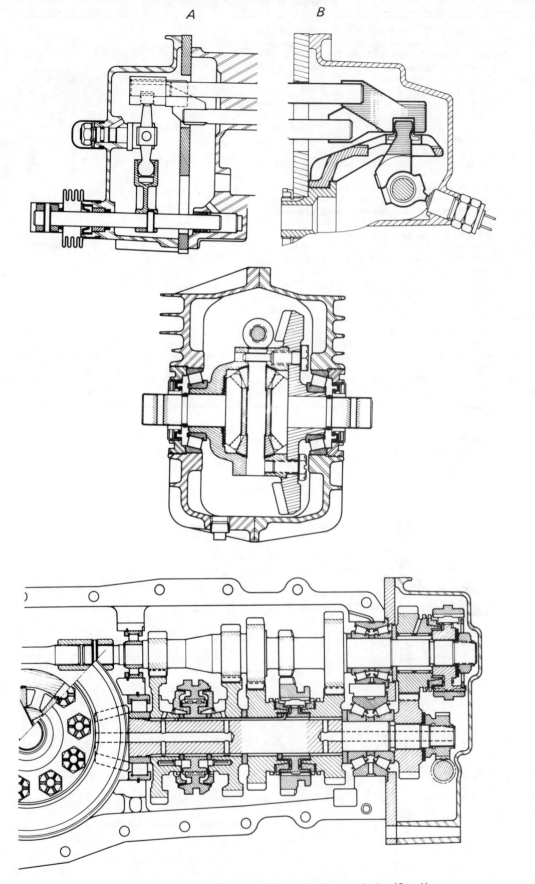

Fig. 6.2 Sectional views of Type 365/395 manual transmission (Sec 1)

A   *Early Type 365 rear cover and rocking lever*
B   *Later Type 365 and 395 rear cover and interlock*

2 Lubrication

1   At the intervals specified in 'Routine Maintenance' remove the level/filler plug from the side of the gearbox. If oil is seen to just trickle out, then the oil level is correct.

2   If topping up is required, use only oil of the specified grade. Never use additives in the gearbox, especially those claimed to have anti-friction properties as damage to the synchromesh assemblies could result.

3   Also at the specified intervals, renew the lubricant. This is best done when the oil is hot. Remove the drain and filler plugs and catch the oil in a suitable container. Refill with the specified quantity of oil.

3 Gearchange linkage – removal, refitting and adjusting

Early type (352 and early 365 transmission)

1   Working under the car, unhook the lever return spring (1).

2   Prise off the circlip (2) and slip the control rod from the spindle at the base of the gearchange control lever. Remove the control rod bolt (3).

3   Working inside the car, free the rubber bellows (3) from the floor pan.

4   Remove the bellows retainer (four screws).

5   Unscrew and remove the centre cover or console (see Chapter 12).

6   Raise the bellows and extract the three screws which secure the gearchange lever housing. Withdraw the lever assembly.

7   The gearchange lever can be dismantled into separate components if the circlip under the ball lower cup is first removed. Do not attempt to remove the gear lever knob as it is glued to the lever.

8   Reassemble using molybdenum disulphide grease.

9   Refit to the car by reversing the removal operations. Select 4th gear and allow the lever and link rod to rest under their own weight while the control lever bolt is tightened.

10   Now check the setting of reverse gear stop plate. Dimension (A) shown in the diagram should be between 5.0 to 6.0 mm (0.19 to 0.24 in). If necessary, insert washers (B) between the stop plate and the floor pan.

Later type (later 365 and all 395 transmissions)

11   Remove the reaction rod bolt on the side-member.

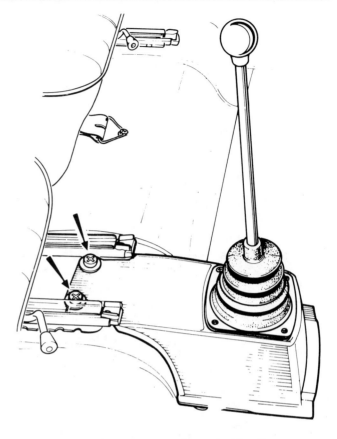

Fig. 6.4 Centre console cover bolts (Sec 3)

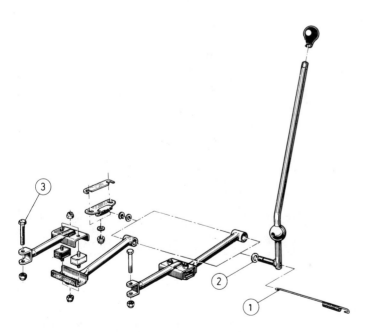

Fig. 6.3 Type 352/365 transmission gearchange linkage (Sec 3)

1   Tension spring
2   Spindle circlip
3   Control rod bolt

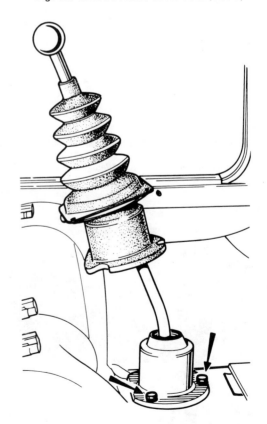

Fig. 6.5 Gearchange lever bellows and housing bolts (Sec 3)

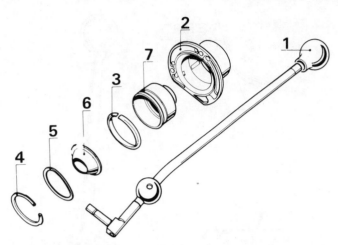

Fig. 6.6 Type 352/365 transmission gearchange lever components (Sec 3)

1	Knob	5	Wave washer
2	Housing	6	Lower cup
3	Plastic sleeve	7	Upper cup
4	Circlip		

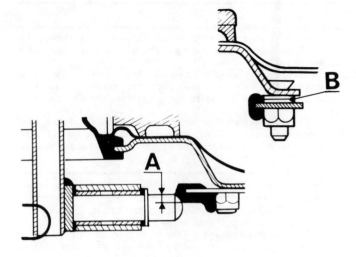

Fig. 6.7 Reverse stop plate setting diagrams (Type 352/365 transmission linkage) (Sec 3)

A   5.0 to 6.0 mm (0.197 to 0.236 in)
B   Spacer washers

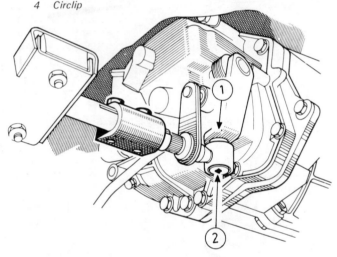

Fig. 6.8 Later Type 365 and 395 transmission linkage (Sec 3)

1   Balljoint nut   2   Allen key socket

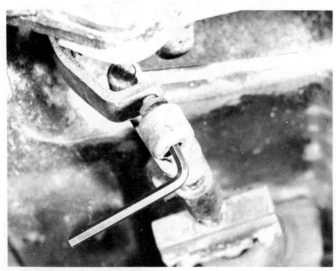

3.12 Unscrewing linkage balljoint stud

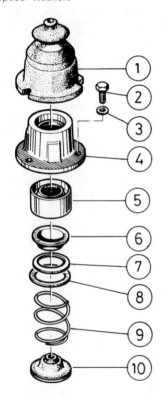

Fig. 6.9 Type 395 gearchange lever retaining components (Sec 3)

1	Bellows	6	Cup
2	Bolt	7	Washer
3	Shakeproof washer	8	Seal
4	Housing	9	Spring
5	Bush	10	Grommet

12 Remove the balljoint nut which attaches the balljoint to the selector arm. An Allen key must then be inserted into the balljoint to unscrew the ball-stud from the selector arm (photo).
13 Refitting is a reversal of removal, but carry out the following check with the gear box and linkage in neutral.
14 Dimension L – (end of lever to curved rim of casing) should be 32.0 mm (1.25 in). If necessary release the clamp pinch-bolts and

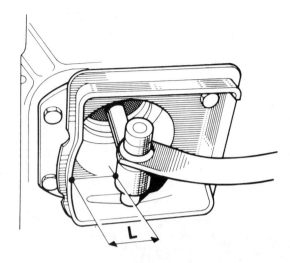

Fig. 6.10 Type 395 gearchange lever setting diagram (Sec 3)

$L = 32.0$ mm (1.25 in)

adjust the effective length of the rod. The clamp should be positioned as shown in the diagram.

4 Transmission – removal and refitting

1 The transmission can of course be removed together with the engine as described in Chapter 1. However, assuming that it is only the transmission that is to be removed, carry out the following operations.
2 Disconnect and remove the battery from the engine compartment.
3 Unbolt the starter motor flange mounting bolts also the front support bolt. Withdraw the starter motor as far as is possible.
4 Disconnect the clutch cable and its cable bracket.
5 Disconnect the exhaust downpipe from the manifold.
6 If the vehicle is powered by a Type 807 (1565 cc) engine then the camshaft and coolant pump pulleys will have to be removed, also the alternator mounting and adjuster link bolts released and the unit pushed in towards the centre of the engine.
7 Drain the transmission oil.
8 Position the car over an inspection pit or raise the vehicle on ramps or stands high enough to permit the eventual removal of the clutch bellhousing from under the car.
9 Punch out the driveshaft roll pins.
10 Using a suitable balljoint splitter, disconnect the track rod balljoints from the steering arms.

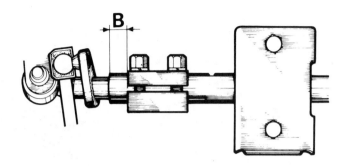

Fig. 6.11 Gearchange link rod clamp setting (Type 395) (Sec 3)

$B = 13.0$ to 15.0 mm (0.5 to 0.6 in)

11 The suspension upper balljoints should now be disconnected, but as there is insufficient access to be able to use an extractor tool, it is recommended that the balljoint is separated from the suspension upper arm by unscrewing the taper pin nut, except for a few threads and then driving in forked wedges.
12 Pull the upper end of the stub axle carrier outwards and release the inboard ends of the driveshaft from the transmission.
13 Disconnect the speedometer cable from the transmission, also the reverse lamp switch wires (photo).
14 Disconnect the gearshift linkage (Section 3).
15 Support the rear of the transmission on a jack and then disconnect the mounting crossmember (photos).
16 Remove the engine damper bracket from the steering box crossmember. This is not fitted to all models.
17 Remove the cover plate from the lower front face of the clutch bellhousing. If TDC pick-up is fitted, disconnect it (see Chapter 4).
18 Unscrew and remove the bolts from the clutch bellhousing to engine connecting flange.
19 Lower the gearbox jack until the unit can be withdrawn towards the rear of the car. Do not allow the weight of the transmission to hang upon the input shaft while the shaft is in engagement with the clutch mechanisms.
20 Refitting is a reversal of removal, but observe the following points:

(a) If the clutch has been disturbed, centralise the driven plate as described in Chapter 5.
(b) Smear the driveshaft and input shaft splines with a little molybdenum disulphide grease.
(c) Seal the driveshaft roll pin holes at both ends using silicone rubber sealant.

21 Once the transmission is installed, adjust the clutch (Chapter 5) and fill the unit with specified lubricant.
22 Adjust the gearchange linkage as described in Section 3.

4.13 Reverse lamp switch leads

4.15A Transmission mounting crossmember bolts

4.15B Transmission mounting crossmember bolts

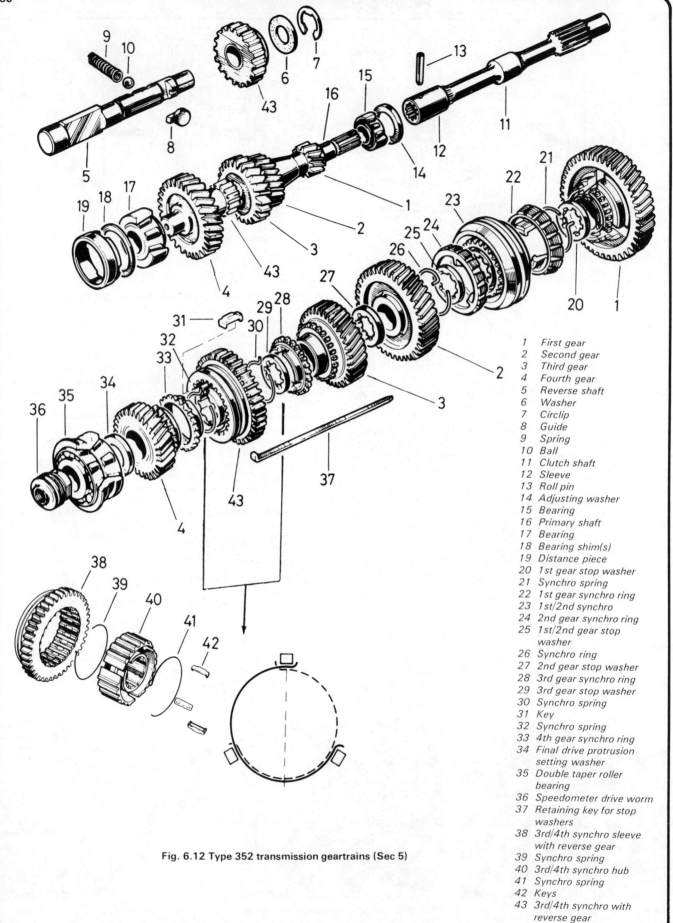

1   First gear
2   Second gear
3   Third gear
4   Fourth gear
5   Reverse shaft
6   Washer
7   Circlip
8   Guide
9   Spring
10 Ball
11 Clutch shaft
12 Sleeve
13 Roll pin
14 Adjusting washer
15 Bearing
16 Primary shaft
17 Bearing
18 Bearing shim(s)
19 Distance piece
20 1st gear stop washer
21 Synchro spring
22 1st gear synchro ring
23 1st/2nd synchro
24 2nd gear synchro ring
25 1st/2nd gear stop
    washer
26 Synchro ring
27 2nd gear stop washer
28 3rd gear synchro ring
29 3rd gear stop washer
30 Synchro spring
31 Key
32 Synchro spring
33 4th gear synchro ring
34 Final drive protrusion
    setting washer
35 Double taper roller
    bearing
36 Speedometer drive worm
37 Retaining key for stop
    washers
38 3rd/4th synchro sleeve
    with reverse gear
39 Synchro spring
40 3rd/4th synchro hub
41 Synchro spring
42 Keys
43 3rd/4th synchro with
    reverse gear

Fig. 6.12 Type 352 transmission geartrains (Sec 5)

5   Transmission (Type 352) – dismantling

General

1   Remove the reversing light switch (photo).
2   Remove the clutch release bearing (see Chapter 5).
3   Remove the clutch housing bolts, washers and spring washers, noting the correct positions for the bolts of various lengths (12 bolts).
4   Remove the clutch housing.
5   Remove the 8 bolts securing the rear cover, noting the identification tag under one bolt.
6   Remove the rear cover, then select 1st speed gear and unlock the speedometer worm gear using a thin 32.0 mm spanner.
7   Remove the primary shaft distance piece and bearing shims from under the rear cover.
8   Remove the half casing securing bolts, noting their correct positions.
9   Separate the half casings, if necessary by gentle use of a soft headed mallet.
10   Lift out the differential assembly.
11   Lift out the secondary geartrain assembly with the stop peg from the double taper roller bearing cup.
12   Lift out the primary gear shaft assembly.

5.1 Unscrewing reverse lamp switch

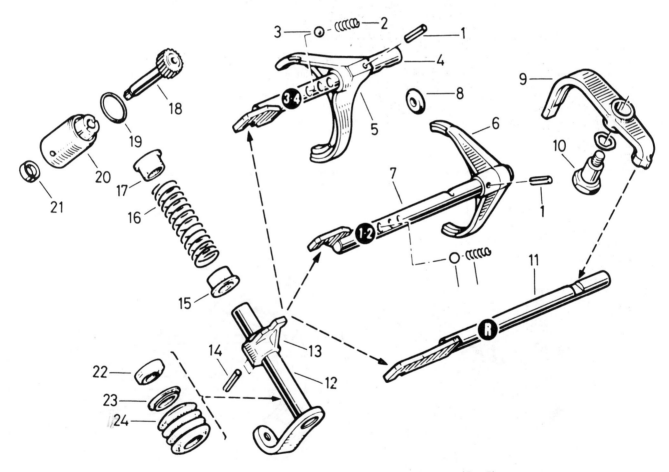

Fig. 6.13 Type 352 transmission selector components (Sec 5)

1	Roll pin	8	Locking disc	13	Selector finger	19	O-ring
2	Spring	9	Reverse selector lever	14	Roll pin	20	Bush
3	Ball	10	Reverse selector	15	Collar	21	Seal
4	3rd/4th gear selector rod		pivot	16	Spring	22	Control shaft seal
5	3rd/4th gear selector fork	11	Reverse selector	17	Collar	23	Bellows washer
6	1st/2nd gear selector fork	12	Control	18	Speedo pinion gear	24	Bellows
7	1st/2nd gear selector rod						

13 Tap the roll pin from the 3rd/4th gear selector fork, and withdraw the shaft and fork. Catch and keep the ball and spring, and remove the locking disc from between the shafts.

14 With the 1st speed selected, take the reverse selector shaft right back to the gear shift control end. Punch out the 1st/2nd selector fork roll pin, remove the shaft and fork, and retain the ball and spring.

15 Remove the pivot bolt from the reverse selector lever, remove the selector lever, and withdraw the reverse selector shaft.

16 Remove the circlip against the reverse gearwheel, and remove the shaft, gearwheel, washer and sleeve.

Primary shaft

17 Remove the bearing track rings and associated washers.

18 Support the shaft adequately, and drive out the roll pin, thereby separating the clutch shaft from the primary shaft. Note the washer inside the sleeve (photo).

19 Grip the primary shaft by its 1st speed gear in the jaws of a vice fitted with soft metal protectors and then remove the bearings from the shaft.

Secondary shaft

20 Grip the 1st speed gear of the shaft in the jaws of a vice fitted with soft metal protectors.

21 Withdraw the double taper roller bearing followed by the final drive pinion adjusting washer.

22 Remove the 4th gear and synchromesh ring.

23 Remove the 3rd/4th gear sliding synchromesh unit. Mark the relative position of the gear to the shaft and retain the hub keys.

24 A two-legged extractor will now have to be used to draw 3rd/4th synchro hub from the secondary shaft. It is inevitable that the 3rd gear will be destroyed during this operation due to the lack of space to engage the claws of the extractor.

25 Pull out the gearwheel stop washer retaining key.

26 Remove the 3rd gear stop washer, gear and synchro ring.

27 Remove the 2nd gear stop washer, gear and synchro ring.

28 Mark the position of the 1st/2nd sliding synchro sleeve in relation to the hub. Remove the gear and stop washer.

29 Remove the 1st/2nd speed synchro hub (this simply pulls from the shaft) taking care as this is done not to disturb the front roller bearing outer track.

5.18 Primary shaft to clutch shaft connection

30 Remove the 1st gear synchro ring, stop washer and gear.

31 The front roller bearing cannot be renewed independently as the inner track is bonded to the final drive pinion. To prevent the rollers and outer track becoming dislodged, fit a suitable retaining clip or clamp over the bearing as shown (photo).

Rear cover

32 Tap out the roll pins which secure the control finger, and slide out the shaft. Recover the bushes, spring, finger and bellows (photo).

33 Prise out the shaft oil seal.

34 Remove the speedo drive retaining bolt, and take out the pinion unit and seal (photo).

Differential unit

35 Major dismantling of this unit is not a task for the home mechanic,

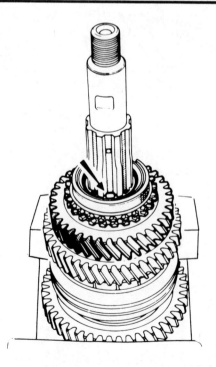

Fig. 6.14 Gear stop washer retaining key (Sec 5)

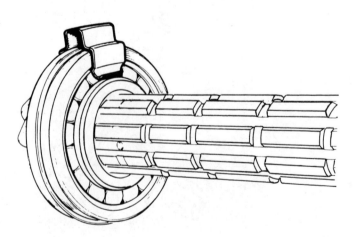

Fig. 6.15 Secondary shaft bearing retained by clip (Sec 5)

5.31 Secondary shaft stripped

5.32 Rear cover control finger and roll pins

5.34 Speedo driven (pinion) gear in rear cover

5.37A Differential bearing adjuster rings

5.37B Differential bearing oil seals

and it is recommended that the work is either entrusted to a Renault agent, or that an exchange unit be obtained.

36 Renewal of the taper roller bearings is feasible, and these should be drawn from the differential unit using a suitable puller. Hold the unit in a soft-jawed vice, and if necessary remove two diametrically opposed crownwheel holding bolts to permit the legs of the puller to be properly secured.

37 Remove the bearing outer cups from the half gearbox cases, by removing the adjuster rings, and seals (after first marking their approximate positions to aid refitting) and then pressing or driving out the cups using a suitable sized piece of tube (photos).

38 Note the O-ring seals located against the taper roller bearings.

6 Transmission (Type 352) – examination and renovation

1   Clean all parts and examine the gears for chipping and obvious wear. Check that all bearings, when cleaned and lightly oiled, are completely smooth in operation.

2   It is advised that all oil seals and gaskets be renewed as a matter of course when the unit is dismantled.

3   Obtain replacements where possible for small items such as roll pins or clips, which may have altered dimensionally when dismantled.

7   Transmission (Type 352) – reassembly

1   With all components clean, lay them out on a clean work bench.

Secondary shaft

2   Engage 1st gear synchro spring as shown making sure that it engages in the three segments (photo).

3   Slide 1st gear into position on the shaft up against the pinion bearing. Fit the stop washer and then turn it to align the keyway. Saw the hooked end from an old key and use it as a dummy key by sliding it into position down the keyway in the shaft in order to hold the stop washer during subsequent reassembly. Use one of the keyways which has an oil hole as shown in the diagram. Fit 1st gear baulk ring (photos).

4   Detach the bearing outer race temporary retaining clip.

5   Warm the 1st/2nd synchro hub in an oven or boiling water to a temperature of between 212° and 248°F (100° and 120°C). Fit the hub to the shaft with its matching mark towards 2nd gear. If a matching mark is not evident, position the hub in relation to the shaft as shown. Press the hub fully into position so that it just comes into contact with the stop washer. As the hub is pressed into position, centralise the synchro ring with the lugs below the stop washer level in order not to damage the spring. Withdraw the dummy key.

6   Next, assemble the synchro sleeve with the chamfered side facing the 2nd gear and the relative hub match markings in alignment (photo).

7   Locate the stop washer with its splines aligned with those on the shaft (photo).

8   Fit the synchro spring to the 2nd gear (in a similar fashion to that

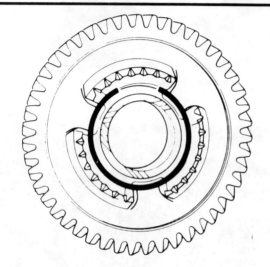

Fig. 6.16 1st gear synchro spring (Sec 7)

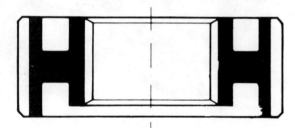

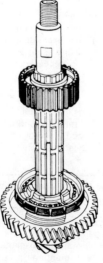

Fig. 6.18 Fitting direction of 1st/2nd synchro hub (Sec 7)

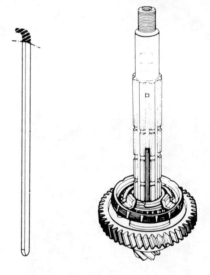

Fig. 6.17 Dummy key in position in groove with oil hole (Sec 7)

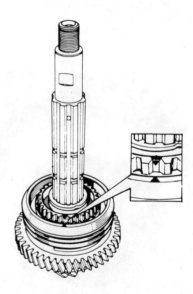

Fig. 6.19 1st/2nd synchro sleeve installed (Sec 7)

7.2 1st gear synchro spring

7.3A Fitting 1st gear to secondary shaft

7.3B 1st gear stop washer

7.3C 1st gear baulk ring

7.6 1st/2nd synchro

7.7 Synchro stop washer

7.8 Fitting 2nd gear to secondary shaft

7.9 Fitting 3rd gear to secondary shaft

7.11 Stop washer key in position

7.12A Assembled 3rd/4th synchro with reverse gear

7.12B Fitting 3rd/4th synchro with reverse to secondary shaft

7.13 Baulk ring and 4th gear fitted to secondary shaft

7.14A Pinion protrusion adjustment washer

7.14B Fitting tapered roller race

7.14C Fitting spacer

7.14D Fitting secondary tapered roller race to bearing outer track. Note large washer

7.15 Speedo worm drivegear

7.16 Secondary shaft geartrain assembled

for the 1st) and assemble the 2nd gear with synchro ring. Fit the stop washer and align the splines with those of the shaft (photo).
9   Fit 3rd gear and baulk ring to the shaft (photo).
10   Slide the stop washer into position and turn it to align the splines.
11   Remove the dummy key and slide the real stop washer alignment key down a keyway which incorporates an oil hole (photo). Assemble 3rd/4th synchro unit which incorporates reverse gear.
12   Fit 3rd/4th synchro hub to the shaft up against 3rd gear stop washer. Make sure that the groove in the synchro sleeve is nearer 4th gear when installed. The two ends of the synchro springs must engage in the same key, but they must run in opposite directions in relation to eath other when viewed from either side (photos).
13   Fit the baulk ring and 4th gear to the shaft (photo).
14   Fit the pinion protrusion adjustment washer followed by the tapered roller race, the spacer, the outer track, the large washer and then the second roller race (photos).
15   Screw on the speedometer worm gear (photo).
16   Support the shaft assembly vertically in a vice with soft jaws, fastened to the 1st gear. Select the 1st gear to lock the shaft, and tighten the speedometer worm pinion to the specified torque. When correctly tightened, do not stake it yet but wait until adjustment of the pinion protrusion has been carried out as described in later paragraphs (photo).

Primary shaft
17   Check for cleanliness of the bearings and their mounting areas on the shaft. Support the shaft and fit the bearings at each end using a press, or alternatively use a piece of tube and a hammer. Refit the clutch shaft (reverse of Section 5 paragraph 18) (photo).

Final drive pinion protrusion – adjustment
18   The correct positioning of the front face of the final drive pinion in relation to the crown wheel centre is very important and must be checked and reset as necessary if the component parts of the secondary shaft have been renewed (other than the bearings which, by virtue of the close limits to which they are manufactured, should not affect the position of the pinion by an unacceptable amount).
19   A Renault agent must be requested to carry out this check, as the home mechanic will not have access to the necessary checking tools. The dimension should be corrected, if necessary, by changing the pinion protrusion adjustment washer for another of the appropriate thickness. Refer to Section 10, paragraph 26. Stake the speedometer worm nut.

Differential bearings – fitting and adjustment
20   The bearing outer tracks should be carefully pressed or tapped into each half of the gearcase, so that they are slightly below the inner face of the casting.
21   After fitting new bearings, or refitting old ones, place the secondary shaft into the RH half gearcase, fit the differential assembly, and fit the LH half gearcase. Loosely fit the bolts. Fit the rear cover and gasket, so as to retain the rear secondary shaft bearing in the correct

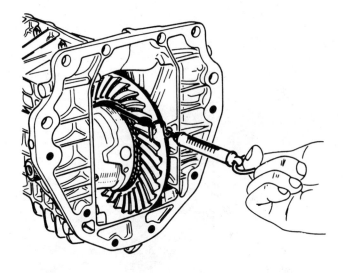

Fig. 6.20 Final drive pinion protrusion diagram (Sec 7)

A   59.0 mm (2.323 in)   1   Adjusting washer

Fig. 6.21 Checking differential bearing preload (Sec 7)

location, and tighten the half casing bolts in the correct order and to the correct torque figure.
22   Fit the differential ring nuts, but without the oil seals, as they may

7.17 Primary shaft   7.19 Worm drivegear staked to shaft

be damaged by the splines during setting-up. Screw the ring nuts home until they contact the bearing ring tracks.

23 When refitting the old bearings, the differential should be adjusted so that the assembly will revolve smoothly, but without any play. Effect the adjustment by screwing the differential ring nuts in or out as necessary, mark the final positions on the case halves and rings, and remove the rings.

24 When new bearings have been fitted, proceed basically as in paragraph 23. However, in this case a preload is necessry, and the ring nuts should be fitted so that the differential assembly is a little stiff to turn. Check the preload by wrapping a piece of cord round the differential housing, and checking with a spring balance the loading necessary to turn the differential, which should be within the specified limits.

25 If the bearings have not been removed, and providing that the differential ring nuts are marked to ensure correct refitting, then bearing adjustment should not be necessary. Refer to Section 10, paragraphs 30 to 35.

Primary shaft positioning

26 Assemble the bearing tracks and adjusting washer to the primary shaft (photo).

27 Fit the primary and secondary shafts into the RH half casing, and check the steps (R), which must be equal. Correct if necessary by changing washer (1), using a replacement of the appropriate thickness.

28 Remove the primary and secondary shaft assemblies.

Roll pin refitting

29 It should be noted that roll pins must always be fitted with the slot towards the rear cover.

Selector forks

30 Slide the reverse gear selector shaft home.

31 Position the reverse gear selector with the end in the slot in the shaft, fit the pivot bolt and tighten.

32 Position the 1st/2nd speed spring and ball in the appropriate hole (Fig. 6.23), position the selector fork, slide in the shaft, and roll pin the two together.

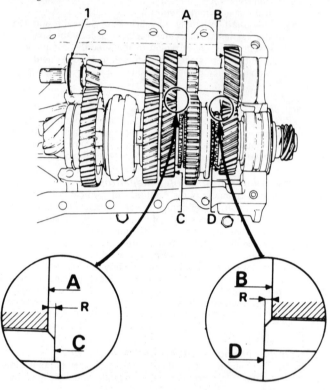

Fig. 6.22 Primary shaft positioning diagram (Sec 7)

7.26 Primary shaft bearing outer track and washer

7.33 Selector mechanism
1   Reverse 2   1st/2nd 3   3rd/4th

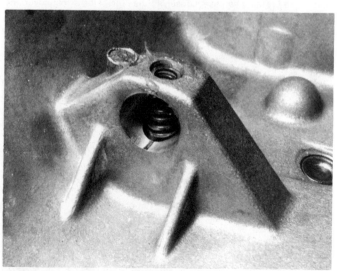

7.34A Reverse shaft detent spring

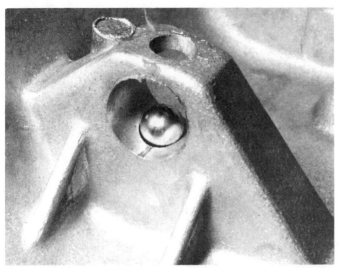

7.34B Reverse shaft detent ball

7.34C Reverse shaft key

7.34D Inserting reverse shaft with idler gear

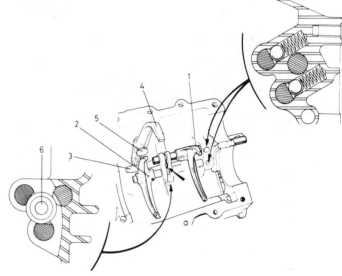

Fig. 6.23 Selector rod detent ball arrangement on Type 352 transmission (Sec 7)

1	3/4th selector shaft and fork	4	Reverse selector lever
2	1st/2nd selector shaft and fork	5	Reverse selector lever pivot
3	Reverse selector shaft	6	Locking disc

33 Position the 3rd/4th speed locking ball and spring and place the locking discs between the shafts. Position the selector fork, slide in the shaft, and roll pin the two together (photo).

Reverse gear
34 Position the spring and ball in the LH half gearcase. Start to enter the shaft, position the gearwheel and friction washer (bronze side to gearwheel), fit the guide from inside the bore, and slide the shaft home. Fit the circlip (photos).

Rear cover
35 Fit the oil seal in the cover hole, and position the collars, spring and selector finger internally (photo).
36 Fit the bellows over the shaft, insert the shaft through the case and internal components, and line up the roll pin holes in the shaft and selector finger. Fit new roll pins.

Half casings
37 Fit the primary shaft, the secondary gear train and locking peg,

7.34E Fitting reverse idler gear E clip

7.35 Rear cover oil seal

7.37A Geartrain in right-hand half casing

7.37B Installing differential/final drive

7.37C Secondary shaft lock pin (arrowed)

7.37D Gap between reverse selector arm and 1st/2nd selector fork to accept narrow diameter of primary shaft

7.38 Connecting half casings

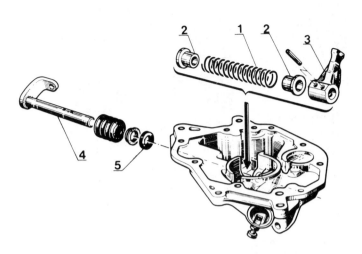

Fig. 6.24 Type 352 transmission rear cover (Sec 7)

1   Spring
2   Bush
3   Selector finger
4   Selector rod
5   Seals

also the differential assembly into the right-hand half casing. The narrow diameter of the primary shaft will pass between the 1st/2nd selector fork and the reverse selector arm (photos).

38 Smear a non-hardening jointing compound on the half gearcases, offer the LH casing up to the RH casing, and fit the half casing bolts without tightening at this stage (photo).

39 Adjust the primary shaft endplay if necessary by fitting the adjusting washers and distance washers, tapping the distance washers lightly to settle the bearings, and fitting the rear cover gasket. Place a straight-edge across the gasket, and measure the clearance between the distance washer and straight-edge (photos).

40 Change the adjusting washer if the clearance is outside the limits shown. Use as few washers as possible.

41 Smear jointing compound on the rear gasket and offer up the cover, engaging the selector finger in the selector shaft slots. Nip up the securing bolts, without tightening them (photo).

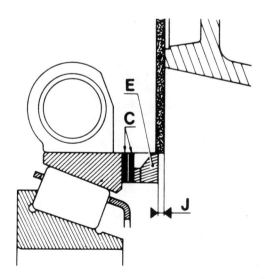

Fig. 6.25 Checking primary shaft endfloat (Sec 7)

C   Shims
E   Distance piece
J   0.02 to 0.12 mm (0.0010 to 0.0047 in)

7.39A Primary shaft endplay washer

7.39B Primary shaft endplay distance collar

7.41 Fitting rear cover

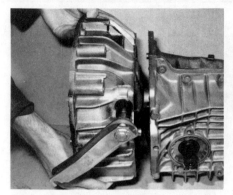
7.49 Fitting clutch bellhousing

8.4 Unbolting rear cover

8.20 Withdrawing the 5th speed selector rod and moving the rocking lever aside (arrows)

42 Tighten the half casing bolts in the correct sequence, to the correct torque setting. Tighten the end cover bolts (Fig. 6.26).
43 If the differential ring nuts are still in place, remove them, marking both nuts and gearcase if this has not already been done. Carefully remove the oil seals and fit replacements, ensuring that the seal is flush with the outer surface of the nut. Prise off the external O-ring, and fit a new one using only the fingers.
44 Wind a little plastic tape round the splines to protect the oil seal, smear a little jointing compound on the threads of the ring nuts, and screw them home until the marks are correctly aligned. Remove the plastic tape.

Crownwheel and pinion – backlash rechecking
45 Fit a dial gauge to the end of the half casing with the pointer resting on a crownwheel tooth at the extreme outer edge, but still just on the tooth flank. Check the backlash, which should be within the specified limits.
46 If backlash is excessive, loosen the ring nut on the differential side a little and screw in that on the crownwheel side by the same amount. If backlash is insufficient, reverse the procedure. Recheck and readjust as necessary.
47 Lock the rings, using the locking plates.

Clutch housing
48 Check the condition of the oil seal, and renew it if there is any doubt about its condition. Carefully drive the seal in using a suitable piece of tube.
49 Wind a little plastic tape onto the splines of the primary shaft to protect the clutch housing oil seal, smear jointing compound on the paper gasket, and fit the gasket and housing. Remove the plastic tape, and fit and tighten the housing bolts (photo).
50 Refit the clutch release bearing (see Chapter 5) and the reversing light switch.
51 Fill the unit with oil, but preferably after installation in the vehicle.

8 Transmission (Type 395) – dismantling

1 With the transmission removed and clean, unbolt and remove the clutch bellhousing.
2 Select 4th speed. Do this by turning the gearchange rod clockwise and pushing in.
3 Unscrew the 5th speed detent plug and extract the ball and spring from the rear cover.
4 Unbolt and remove the gearbox rear cover (photo). Return 4th speed selector rod to neutral.

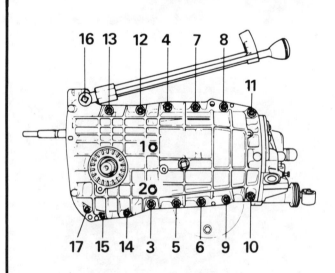
Fig. 6.26 Gearcase bolt tightening sequence (Sec 7)

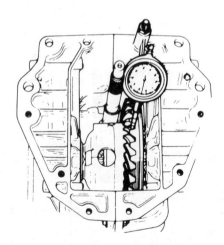
Fig. 6.27 Checking crownwheel backlash (Sec 7)

5   Lock up 5th gear and reverse gear. Do this by pushing 5th synchro sleeve in towards the gearbox and then pulling reverse selector rod out.

6   With the geartrain locked up, unscrew 5th speed synchro hub nut.

7   Using a thin (32.0 mm) open-ended spanner unscrew the speedometer worm drive gear nut.

8   Return the locked gears to neutral. This can be checked if the clutch shaft is turned, but the differential side gears can be held stationary by light finger pressure.

9   Select 4th gear by pushing in the 3rd/4th selector rod.

10 Punch out 5th speed selector fork roll pin.

11 Using quick drying paint, mark the relationship of 5th speed synchro hub and sleeve.

12 Slide off 5th speed synchro and fork.

13 Remove 5th gear.

14 Unbolt the spacer plate. A socket may have to be ground down to reach the bolt heads or alternatively use a box spanner. As the plate is removed, take care that the dowel pins are not lost.

15 If the differential is to be overhauled, then the ring nuts will have to be removed, otherwise leave them alone. Where overhaul is anticipated, carefully mark the exact position of the ring nut lock nuts and their lockplates.

16 Unscrew and remove the ring nuts using a pin wrench or similar tool.

17 Unscrew and remove the half casing connecting bolts.

18 From the right-hand half casing remove the secondary geartrain and the differential. Take out the stop peg from the double taper roller bearing outer track.

19 Also from the right-hand half casing now remove the primary shaft.

20 From the casing withdraw 5th speed selector rod. Swivel the rocking lever aside (photo).

21 Punch out the roll pin from 3rd/4th selector fork.

22 Withdraw 3rd/4th selector rod and take off the fork, but be prepared to catch the detent ball and spring which will be ejected.

23 Unbolt reverse gear selector from inside the gearcase.

24 Pull reverse selector shaft as far from the gearcase as it will come.

25 Punch out the roll pin from 1st/2nd selector fork.

26 Withdraw 1st/2nd selector rod, take off the fork and catch the detent ball and spring which will be ejected.

27 Punch out the roll pin from the reverse selector rod dog and withdraw the rod (photo).

28 Extract the circlip and remove reverse idler shaft, gear, washer and sliding key. Catch and retain the spring and ball.

Primary shaft

29 Separate the clutch (input) shaft from the primary shaft by driving out the roll pin.

30 The primary shaft bearings and adjusting spacer may be removed for renewal using a press or suitable puller.

8.27 Reverse selector rod dog

Secondary shaft

31 Secure the secondary geartrain in a vice fitted with soft metal jaw protectors. Grip the assembly by the 1st gear.

32 Remove the double taper roller bearing.

33 Remove the adjuster washer for pinion protrusion.

34 Take off 4th gear and baulk ring.

35 Mark the relationship of 3rd/4th speed synchro hub to sleeve with quick drying paint, then pull off the synchro sleeve, retain the sliding keys and springs.

36 A press or puller will now be required to remove the synchro hub from the shaft. As there is so little space between the hub and 3rd

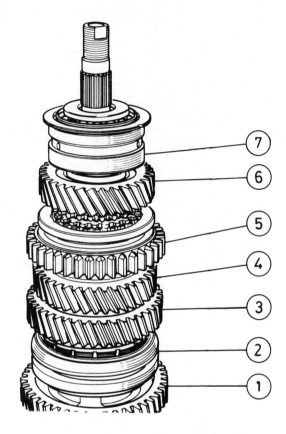

Fig. 6.28 Secondary shaft geartrain (Sec 8)

1	1st gear	5	3/4th synchro with reverse
2	1st/2nd synchro		gear
3	2nd gear	6	4th gear
4	3rd gear	7	Double tapered roller bearing

gear, the claws of the puller or press backing plate will deform the 3rd speed baulk ring so this must be renewed before reassembly.

37 Pull out the sliding key for the gearwheel stop washers.

38 Align the tabs of the 3rd gear stop washer and slide it off the shaft.

39 Remove the 3rd gear and baulk ring.

40 Slide 2nd gear stop washer off the shaft.

41 Remove 2nd gear and its baulk ring.

42 Again using quick drying paint, mark the relative position of the 1st/2nd synchro sleeve to the hub. Remove the sleeve and sliding keys.

43 Slide off the synchro hub stop washer.

44 Remove the synchro hub. This should pull off the shaft by hand pressure.

45 Take off 1st gear synchro baulk ring.

46 Remove 1st gear stop washer.

47 Remove 1st gear.

48 Fit a clip to the bearing to prevent the rollers from being displaced. This bearing cannot be renewed separately from the shaft as the inner track is bonded to the shaft.

Rear cover

49 To dismantle the rear cover, extract the two roll pins which hold the selector finger to the control shaft.

50 Expand the circlip and withdraw the shaft. Remove the interlock pivot ring nut with a 'C' spanner.

51 Renew the roll pins and the cover oil seals (photo).

Differential unit

52 The observations made in Section 5, paragraphs 35 to 37 apply. Note the planet wheel shaft is retained by a roll pin.

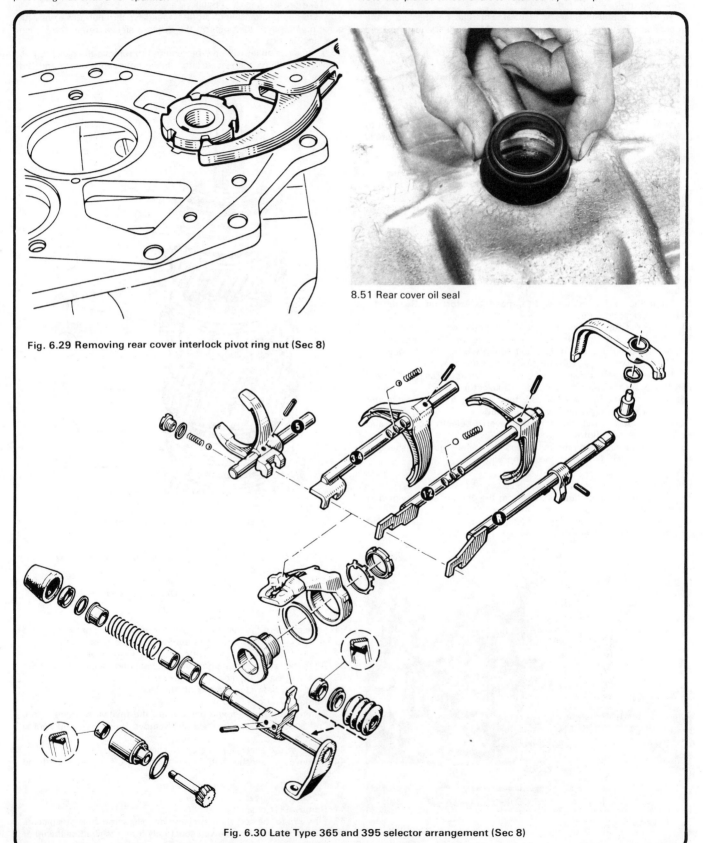

8.51 Rear cover oil seal

Fig. 6.29 Removing rear cover interlock pivot ring nut (Sec 8)

Fig. 6.30 Late Type 365 and 395 selector arrangement (Sec 8)

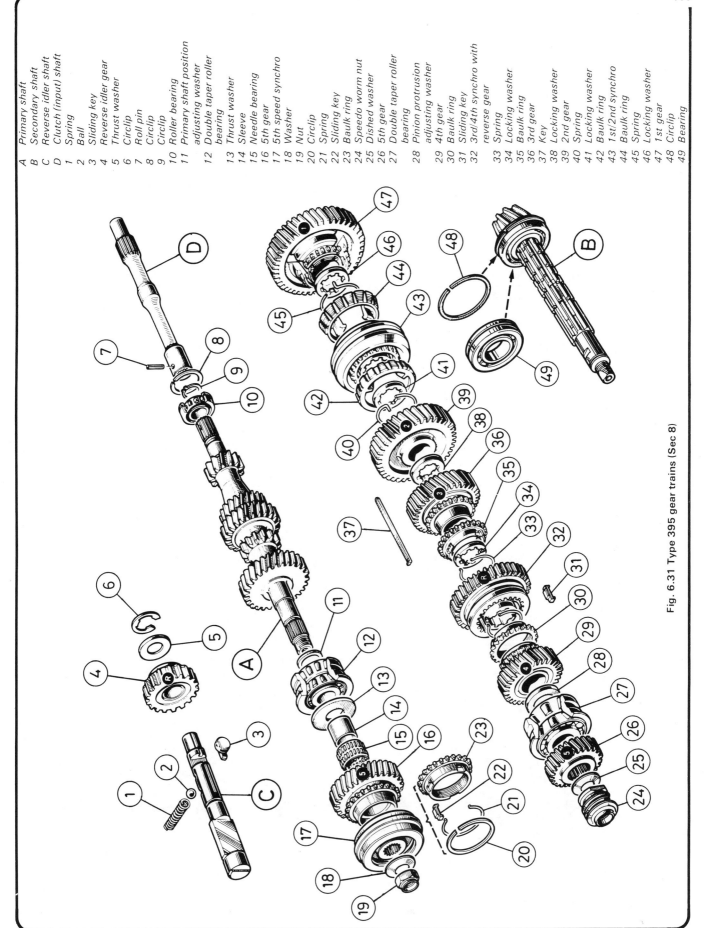

A Primary shaft
B Secondary shaft
C Reverse idler shaft
D Clutch (input) shaft
1 Spring
2 Ball
3 Sliding key
4 Reverse idler gear
5 Thrust washer
6 Circlip
7 Roll pin
8 Circlip
9 Circlip
10 Roller bearing
11 Primary shaft position
   adjusting washer
12 Double taper roller
   bearing
13 Thrust washer
14 Sleeve
15 Needle bearing
16 5th gear
17 5th speed synchro
18 Washer
19 Nut
20 Circlip
21 Spring
22 Sliding key
23 Baulk ring
24 Speedo worm nut
25 Dished washer
26 5th gear
27 Double taper roller
   bearing
28 Pinion protrusion
   adjusting washer
29 4th gear
30 Baulk ring
31 Sliding key
32 3rd/4th synchro with
   reverse gear
33 Spring
34 Locking washer
35 Baulk ring
36 3rd gear
37 Key
38 Locking washer
39 2nd gear
40 Spring
41 Locking washer
42 Baulk ring
43 1st/2nd synchro
44 Baulk ring
45 Spring
46 Locking washer
47 1st gear
48 Circlip
49 Bearing

Fig. 6.31 Type 395 gear trains (Sec 8)

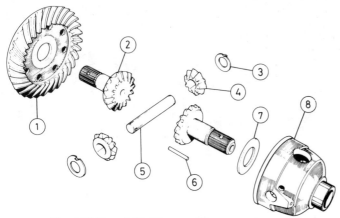

Fig. 6.32 Type 395 differential/final drive (Sec 8)

1 Crownwheel   6 Roll pin
2 Sunwheel (side gear)   7 Bakelite impregnated
3 Thrust washer   thrust washer
4 Planet gear   8 Differential case
5 Shaft

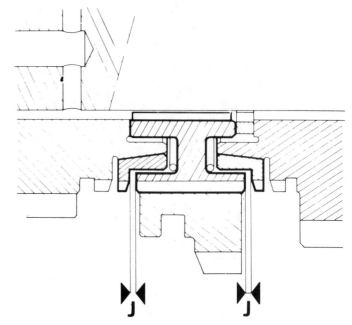

Fig. 6.33 Synchro baulk ring clearance checking diagram (Sec 8)

J = 0.20 mm (0.008 in) minimum

9 Transmission (Type 395) — examination and renovation

1   Clean all parts and examine the gears for chipping and obvious wear. Check that all bearings, when cleaned and lightly oiled, are completely smooth in operation.
2   It is advised that all oil seals and gaskets be renewed as a matter of course when the unit is dismantled.
3   Obtain replacements where possible for small items such as roll pins or clips, which may have altered dimensionally when dismantled.
4   Check for wear in the 3rd, 4th and 5th synchro baulk rings and gear cones. To do this, twist the baulk ring to make it stick to the gear cone. Using a feeler blade measure the gap between the synchro or the gear face and the baulk ring. This should not be less than 0.20 mm (0.008 in). If it is, renew the baulk ring (photo).
5   On 1st and 2nd gears, renew the baulk rings if they show evidence of wear or scoring.
6   Before separating the components of a synchro unit, mark the relative position of hub to sleeve using a spot of quick drying paint. Also note the fitted direction of both hub and sleeve when installed on the shaft.
7   When reassembling 3rd, 4th or 5th synchro, check that the ends of the springs engage in the same key, but run in opposite directions in relation to each other when viewed from either side.

10 Transmission (Type 395) — reassembly

Secondary shaft

1   Assemble the roller bearing next to the pinion gear. Retain the rollers and tracks together with a clip (photo).

2   Engage 1st gear synchro spring so that it engages with the three segments (photo).
3   Fit 1st gear (photo).
4   Fit the stop washer and 1st speed baulk ring (photo). Align the stop washer by inserting a dummy key into a keyway which incorporates oil holes. A dummy key can easily be made by cutting off the turned over end of an old key.
5   Now warm the 1st/2nd speed synchro hub in an oven or boiling water to a temperature of between 212° and 248°F (100 and 120°C).
6   Fit the synchro hub to the shaft making sure that one of its wide grooves is opposite the dummy key also that the less projecting boss is towards 1st gear (photo).
7   Withdraw the dummy key.
8   Assemble the 1st/2nd synchro sleeve.
9   Make sure that the 1st/2nd synchro sleeve has its wider chamfer facing towards 2nd gear and the alignment marks which were made before dismantling are opposite to each other (photo).
10   Fit the stop washer and align its splines (photo).
11   Fit 2nd speed baulk ring followed by 2nd gear which as with 1st gear should have its spring correctly engaged over three segments (photos).
12   Fit the stop washer and align its splines (photo).
13   Fit 3rd gear and its baulk ring (photos).
14   Fit the stop washer and align its splines (photo).
15   Fit the stop washer retaining key into one of the shaft grooves which incorporates oil holes (photo).

9.4 Checking synchro baulk ring for wear

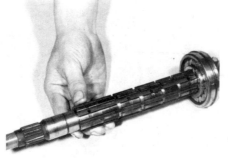

10.1 Secondary shaft with pinion bearing

10.2 1st gear synchro spring

10.3 Fitting 1st gear to secondary shaft

10.4A 1st gear stop washer

10.4B 1st gear baulk ring

10.6 1st/2nd synchro hub

10.9 1st/2nd synchro sleeve

10.10 Synchro stop washer

10.11A 2nd speed baulk ring

10.11B 2nd gear synchro spring

10.11C Fitting 2nd gear to secondary shaft

10.12 2nd gear stop washer

10.13A 3rd gear

10.13B 3rd gear baulk ring

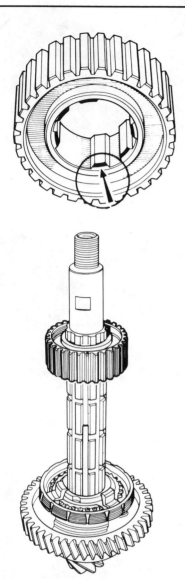

Fig. 6.34 1st/2nd synchro hub fitted direction on shaft (Sec 10)

10.14 3rd gear stop washer

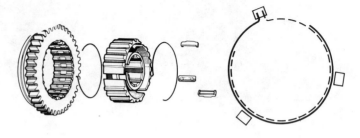

Fig. 6.35 3rd/4th synchro components and spring arrangement
(Sec 10)

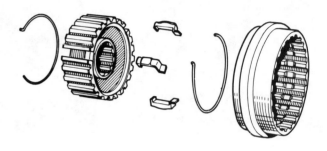

Fig. 6.36 5th speed synchro components (Sec 10)

16 Assemble the 3rd/4th synchro. Check that the marks made before
dismantling are in alignment and that the fine groove around the hub
will be nearer 4th gear when installed in the shaft also the selector fork
groove in the synchro sleeve is nearer to 4th gear. Fit the sliding keys
and make sure that the two ends of the synchro springs engage in the
same key, but run in opposite directions in relation to each when
viewed from either side. Fit the assembled synchro to the shaft,
applying pressure to the hub until it contacts 3rd gear stop washer. Do
not tap the synchro down the shaft or the synchro springs may
become disengaged from the sliding keys (photos).
17 Fit 4th speed gear baulk ring and then 4th speed gear (photos).
18 Fit the pinion protrusion adjusting washer (photo).
19 Fit one section of the double taper roller bearing (smaller diameter
towards end of shaft) (photo).
20 Fit the spacer washer (photo).
21 The secondary shaft geartrain should now be placed aside to await
reassembly of the gearbox. See paragraph 36.

Primary shaft
22 If this shaft was dismantled, refit the positioning washer, the taper
roller bearing and the spacer washer.
23 To the opposite end of the shaft fit the bearing so that its external
circlip is nearest the end of the shaft (photo).
24 Connect the clutch (input) shaft to the primary shaft using a roll
pin (photo).

Adjustments
25 Before further reassembly can continue, the following adjustments
must be carried out if new differential parts have been fitted or new
bearings or gear shafts installed.
   Pinion protrusion
   Differential bearing setting
   Primary shaft positioning

Pinion protrusion
26 The pinion protrusion can only be satisfactorily carried out by your
Renault dealer using special gauges. The need for such adjustment can
be ascertained if the secondary gear train and the differential are
placed in a half casing and measurement (A) taken. This is the distance

10.15 Stop washer retaining key

10.16A 3rd/4th synchro components

10.16B 3rd/4th synchro assembled

10.16C Synchro hub groove

10.16D Fitting 3rd/4th synchro with reverse

10.17A 3rd/4th baulk ring

10.17B 4th gear

10.18 Pinion protrusion adjusting washer

10.19 Fitting first section of tapered roller bearing to secondary shaft

10.20 Spacer washer

10.23 Primary shaft bearing and circlips

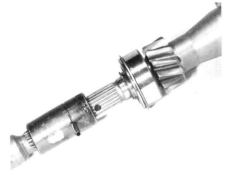

10.24 Primary shaft to clutch shaft roll pin

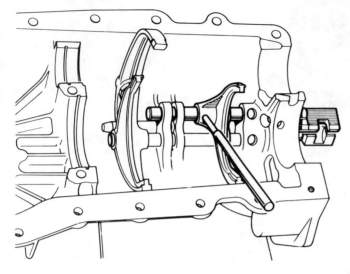

Fig. 6.37 Driving in 3rd/4th selector fork roll pin (Sec 10)

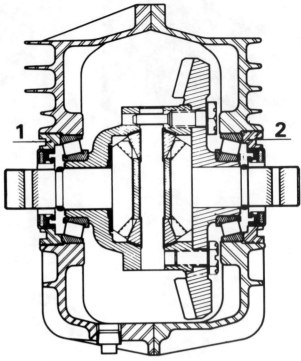

Fig. 6.38 Sectional view of differential for bearing ring nut identification (Sec 10)

1   Differential case side   2   Crownwheel side

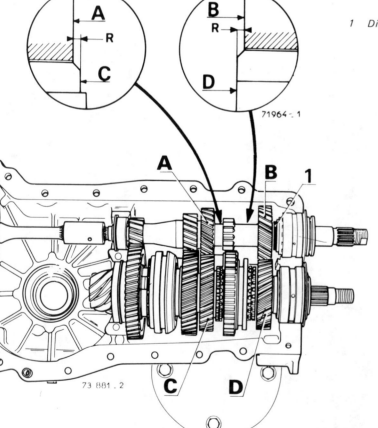

71964 - 1

73 881 . 2

Fig. 6.39 Primary shaft positioning diagram (Type 395) (Sec 10)

1   Location of adjusting washer

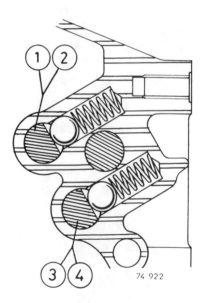

74 922

Fig. 6.40 Selector rod locations, viewed from rear cover (Sec 10)

between the centre of the crownwheel and the face of the pinion gear and it should be 59.0 mm (2.323 in). The difficulty of obtaining this measurement is of course due to the virtual impossibility of finding the centre of the crownwheel without the special Renault tools. Any adjustment is carried out by changing the washer (1).

Differential bearing preload
27 Provided the differential ring nuts and locks were marked before removal, reassembly is just a matter of returning them to their original positions. Where new or different components have been fitted then adjust in the following way. First locate the differential in the right-hand casing half section.
28 Fit the left-hand half casing and tighten the connecting bolts to the specified torque. Apply jointing compound to the ring nut threads.
29 Screw each ring nut in until they just make contact with the bearing tracks.
30 If the original bearings are being used again, check that no play is evident when the differential is turned.
31 If play is evident, continue to turn the ring nuts until play disappears. The ring nut (1) should be turned slightly more than nut (2) after reference to Fig. 6.38.
32 Mark the setting of the ring nuts and then separate the half casings and take out the differential.
33 If new differential bearings are being used, carry out the same procedure as for old bearings, but tighten the ring nuts until the differential starts to become hard to turn.
34 Check the preload by winding a cord around the differential case. Attach the end of the cord to a spring balance. The differential should turn smoothly with a pull of between 0.9 and 3.2 kg (2 and 7 lbs).
35 If the preload is insufficient, tighten the ring nut on the differential case side as necessary

Primary shaft positioning
36 Place the secondary shaft/gear assembly (less speedo worm, wave washer, 5th gear and spacer plate) in the right-hand half casing.
37 Install the primary shaft/gear assembly.
38 Gear alignment must be as shown in the diagram with the gear projections (R) of the secondary shaft gears equal. If they are not, change washer (1) for one of alternative thickness.
39 Remove the shafts.

Left-hand half casing
40 Reassembly proper may now continue. Slide in reverse gear selector rod, picking up the selector dog and roll pinning it to the rod.
41 Fit reverse gear selector arm, engaging it with the slot in the selector rod (photo).
42 Tighten the selector arm bolt to 29 Nm (21 lbf ft) (photo).
43 Fit 1st/2nd selector rod detent ball and spring. Hold them depressed while the rod is slid into position, passing it through the fingers of the reverse selector dog.
44 Engage the selector fork (so that the longer boss of the fork is furthest from the differential) with 1st/2nd selector rod and drive in the roll pin. All the selector fork roll pins should have their slots towards the rear cover when driven fully home (photo).

10.41 Reverse gear selector arm and pivot bolt

10.42 Tightening reverse gear selector arm pivot bolt

10.44 Driving in 1st/2nd selector fork roll pin

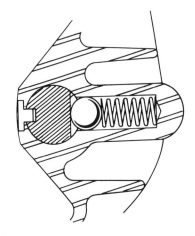
Fig. 6.41 Reverse idler shaft detent ball and spring (Sec 10)

45 Fit 3rd/4th selector rod detent ball and spring. Hold the ball depressed and slide 3rd/4th selector rod into position, picking up the selector fork. Make sure that the longer boss on the fork is towards the differential. Fix the fork with a new roll pin.

46 Select 4th gear by pushing in the 3rd/4th selector rod and keep 4th gear selected during the following reassembly operations.

47 To the right-hand half casing fit reverse idler shaft, spring and locking ball (photo).

48 Depress the ball on its spring and then slide in reverse idler shaft, picking up the reverse gear so that its projecting boss is towards the differential.

49 Fit the thrust washer (dimpled face to gearwheel) (photo).

50 Engage the sliding key as the shaft passes the cut-out and then push the shaft fully home (photo).

51 Fit the E-clip into the groove in the reverse idler shaft (photo).

52 Into the right-hand half casing fit the primary shaft with double taper roller bearing. The primary shaft will pass under the reverse selector arm at its narrowest point (photos).

53 Install the secondary shaft. Check that the stop peg for its double taper roller bearing outer track is in position (photos).

54 Lower the differential into position so that the crownwheel teeth mesh with those of the pinion gear. Note the bearing O-ring seals (photos).

55 Apply jointing compound to the mating flanges of the casing half sections (photo).

56 Fit the left-hand section to the right-hand one making sure that the reverse gear selector arm engages correctly in the cut-out in the reverse idler shaft (photo).

57 Fit the casing connecting bolts, but only tighten them finger tight.

58 Fit the spacer plate, engaging the positioning dowels and using a new gasket to which jointing compound has been applied (photos).

59 Tighten the spacer plate bolts.

60 Tighten the half casing bolts in the sequence shown and to the specified torque, noting the different torque wrench settings for the two sizes of bolts (see Specifications).

61 Fit the spacer washer to the primary shaft (photo).

62 Fit the needle roller bearing and sleeve to the primary shaft (photo).

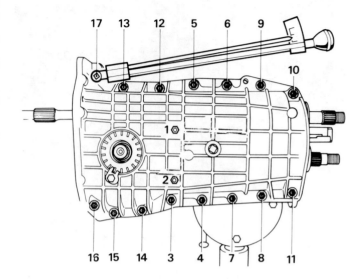

Fig. 6.42 Type 365/395 transmission bolt tightening sequence (Sec 10)

63 Fit the 5th speed idler gear to the secondary shaft (photo).

64 Fit the 5th speed synchro with selector rod and fork as an assembly to the primary shaft. Make sure that the detent notches on the rod are towards the end cover (photo).

65 Fit the dished washer to the primary shaft and screw on the nut finger tight (photo).

66 Fit the dished washer to the end of the secondary shaft and then screw on the speedo drive worm nut finger tight (photo).

10.47 Reverse idler shaft, gear and detent spring

10.49 Reverse idler shaft thrust washer

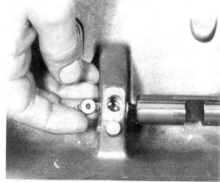

10.50A Reverse idler shaft key

10.50B Reverse idler shaft installed

10.51 Fitting reverse idler shaft E clip

10.52A Installing primary shaft

10.52B Passing primary shaft under reverse selector arm

10.53A Installing secondary shaft

10.53B Primary shaft tapered roller bearing

10.53C Secondary shaft tapered roller bearing

10.53D Secondary shaft bearing stop peg

10.54A Installing differential/final drive

10.54B Differential bearing O-ring (arrowed)

10.55 Applying jointing compound

10.56 Connecting casing sections

10.58A Fitting spacer plate

10.58B Spacer plate positioning dowels

10.61 Primary shaft spacer washer

10.62 Primary shaft needle roller bearing

10.63 5th speed idler gear

10.64 Fitting 5th speed synchro and selector rod and fork to primary shaft

10.65 Primary shaft dished washer and nut

10.66 Speedo worm gear

10.67 Driving in 5th speed selector fork roll pin

67 Push in the 3rd/4th selector rod to provide space to be able to drive in the roll pin which fixes 5th speed selector fork to its rod (photo).

68 Set the gear selector rods to the neutral mode by pulling out the 3rd/4th selector rod.

69 Now engage reverse and 5th gears simultaneously. Do this by pulling 5th speed selector rod out and pushing reverse rod in.

70 Tighten the primary shaft nut to specified torque (photo).

71 Tighten the speedometer worm drive nut as tightly as possible using a thin 32 mm spanner. The correct torque for this nut is 115 Nm (85 lbf ft).

72 Stake the shaft nuts (photo).

Rear cover

73 If the rear cover was dismantled, reassemble it by reversing the dismantling operations (see paragraphs 49-52 in Section 8) (photo).

74 Stick a new gasket in position to which jointing compound has been applied.

75 Offer up the rear cover engaging the end of the interlock lever in the cut-out in the selector rods (photo).

76 Push the cover fully home and tighten the securing bolts.

77 Fit the 5th speed selector detent ball, spring and plug, the threads of which have had jointing compound applied (photos).

78 Fit a new oil seal to the clutch bellhousing.

79 Tape the input shaft splines to prevent damage to the oil seal lips when the bellhousing is installed (photo).

80 Stick a new gasket to the gearbox front face having applied jointing compound to both sides of the gasket.

81 Bolt the bellhousing into position and remove the protective tape from the splines (photos).

82 Screw in the reverse lamp switch (photo).

83 Fit the clutch release components (if removed) as described in Chapter 5.

84 The remaining operation is to lock the differential ring nuts with the locking plates and bolts, but before doing this, check the crownwheel and pinion backlash. Where excessive, the backlash can

10.70 Tightening primary shaft nut

10.72 Staking worm gear nut

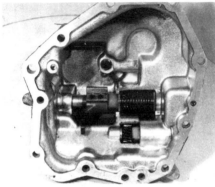
10.73 Interior of rear cover

10.75 Engaging selector rods and rocking lever as rear cover is fitted

10.77A 5th speed selector detent ball and spring in rear cover

10.77B Detent plug

10.79 Taping input (clutch) shaft splines

10.81A Connecting clutch bellhousing to gearcase

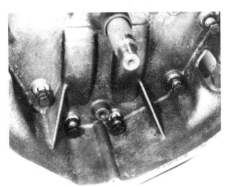
10.81B Bellhousing lower bolts

10.81C Bellhousing upper bolts

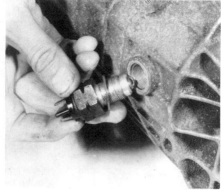

10.82 Fitting reverse lamp switch

10.86 Tightening differential bearing adjuster ring lockplate bolt

1 Planet gear
2 Thrust washer
3 Hub
4 Side gear (sunwheel)
5 Bakelite washer
6 Shaft
7 Shaft
8 Differential case
9 Tapered roller bearing
10 Crownwheel

Fig. 6.43 Type 365 transmission differential and final drive (Sec 11)

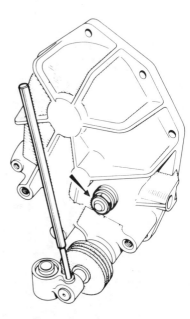

Fig. 6.44 Type 365 transmission rear cover with early type selector control (Sec 11)

1 Rocking lever pivot shaft
2 Driving out coupling roll pin

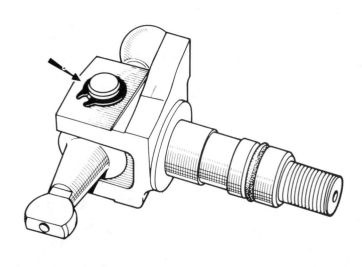

Fig. 6.45 Rocking lever pivot shaft circlip on early Type 365 transmission (Sec 11)

be detected by feel, in which case unscrew the ring nut on the differential case side and tighten the ring nut on the crownwheel side. Turn the ring nuts equally.

85 Precide backlash can only be carried out using a dial gauge with its stylus at right angles to a crownwheel tooth. The specified backlash is between 0.12 and 0.25 mm (0.0047 and 0.010 in).

86 Once the backlash is correct fit the ring nut locking plates and their bolts (photo).

87 The transmission is now ready for refitting to the car. Fill with oil after refitting.

---

11 Transmission (Type 365) – dismantling, examination and reassembly

1 Later models of the type 365 transmission are almost identical with the Type 395 except for the differential components.

2 Earlier models of the Type 365 transmission differ from later models by having the differential planet wheel shafts secured by roll pins. An interlock disc is located between the selector rods instead of the swivelling interlock lever under the rear cover as used on later Type 365 and all Type 395 transmissions.

Rear cover

3 To dismantle the rear cover on earlier Type 365 transmissions, first remove the speedometer drive gear sleeve and its O-ring seal.

4 Take out the speedometer driven gear.

5 Take off the rocking lever pivot shaft gaiter.

6 Unscrew and remove the rocking lever pivot shaft nut and washer.

7 Drive out the roll pin from the gearchange rod coupling.

8 Extract the circlip from the rocking lever pivot shaft, take off the O-ring seal.

9 Reassembly is a reversal of dismantling, but renew the O-rings and roll pin.

Selector mechanism

10 A locking ball is used on the 5th speed selector rod.

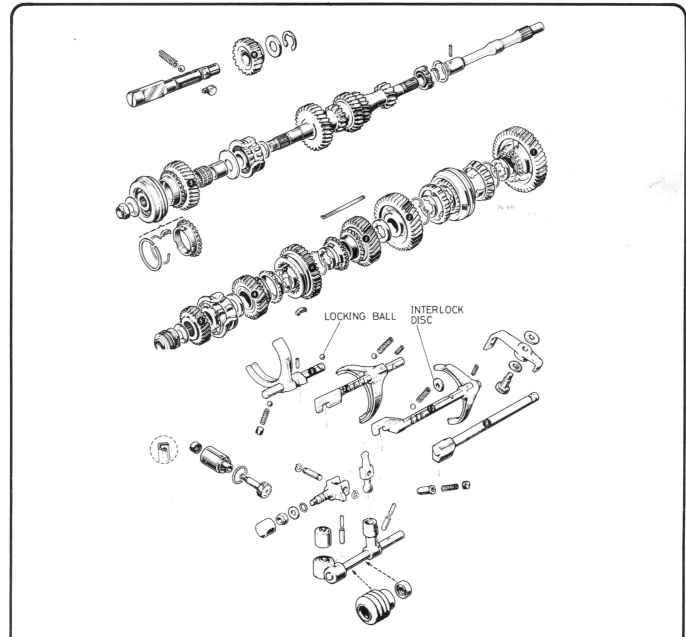

Fig. 6.46 Type 365 transmission components with early type selector control (Sec 11). Note selector rod interlock disc and 5th speed selector rod locking ball

12 Fault diagnosis – manual transmission

Symptom	Reason(s)
Weak or ineffective synchromesh	Synchronising cones worn, split or damaged.
	Baulk ring synchromesh dogs worn or damaged.
Jumps out of gear	Incorrectly assembled synchro units.
	Gearbox coupling dogs badly worn.
	Selector fork rod groove badly worn.
	Incorrect assembly of selector components.
Excessive noise	Incorrect grade of oil in gearbox or oil level too low.
	Ball or needle roller bearings worn or damaged.
	Gear teeth excessively worn or damaged.
	Incorrect crownwheel and pinion backlash.
Difficulty in engaging gear	Clutch pedal adjustment incorrect.
	Synchro units incorrectly assembled.

Chapter 7 Automatic transmission

Contents

Automatic transmission – removal and refitting 8
Automatic transmission fluid – checking,
draining and refilling 2
Driveplate – removal and refitting 9
Electronic computer – removal and refitting 7
Fault diagnosis – automatic transmission 11
General description 1
Governor – removal, refitting and adjusting 4
Kickdown switch – adjusting 6
Kickdown switch – testing 5
Oil cooler – fitting 10
Speed selector control – removal, refitting and adjusting 3

Specifications

Transmission type .... Renault TA 4139 with torque converter and epicyclic gear train. 3 forward speeds and one reverse

Ratios
1st	2.33 : 1
2nd	1.44 : 1
3rd	1.00 : 1
Reverse	2.00 : 1

Fluid capacity
From dry	5.25 Imp qts, 6.5 US qts, 6.0 l
At service fluid change	2.5 to 3.25 Imp qts 3.25 US qts 3.0 to 4.0 l

Torque wrench settings

	Nm	lbf ft
Driveplate to crankshaft flange bolts	68	50
Driveplate to torque converter bolts	34	25
Bellhousing bolts 8.0 mm	25	18
10 mm	35	26
Oil cooler valve connector to transmission casing	109	80

1 General description

The automatic transmission provides fully automatic gearchanging without the use of a clutch. An override system of manual gear selection remains available to the driver.

The transmission consists of three main assemblies, namely the torque converter, the final drive and the gearbox.

The torque converter takes the place of a conventional clutch, transmitting the engine torque smoothly and automatically to the gearbox. Increased torque is provided for starting off.

The gearbox contains an epicyclic gear train, providing three forward gear ratios and one reverse, and the mechanical, hydraulic and electrical gear train control elements.

The epicyclic gear train consists of an assembly of helical gears which provides for different ratios to be obtained, depending upon the pressure of the hydraulic feed to the receivers. The gear assembly consists of 2 sunwheels, 3 pairs of planet wheels joined by a planet wheel carrier, and an involute gear ring.

A geared oil pump located at the rear of the unit supplies oil at the required pressures to the converter, the brakes and clutches, and for gear lubrication.

The hydraulic distributor ensures the regulation of oil pressure to suit the engine load, and the pressure feed or release to the brakes and clutches. Ratio changes are effected by the operation of two solenoid ball valves, instructed by the governor and computer. Circuit pressure is controlled by the capsule and pilot valve, thus determining pressure to the receiver and controlling gear changing quality.

A freewheel transmits torque in the same direction as the roadwheels, but does not permit engine braking in first gear when D (A early models) or 2 are selected. The clutches and brakes lock or release the gear train components in various ways depending upon hydraulic feed pressure and thereby provide the different ratios.

Gearchange instruction is given by the governor and computer unit, exact moment of change varying according to vehicle speed and engine torque.

The governor is in fact an alternator, and provides power to the computer, the amount being dependent upon vehicle speed and engine loading.

The computer supplies electrical pulses to the solenoid ball valves, depending upon the position of the selector lever and upon the current received from the governor.

The kickdown switch earths one of the computer circuits, causing instant selection of a lower gear in some circumstances. The switch is operated by the throttle pedal at the extreme of travel.

The solenoid ball valves open or close hydraulic passages, to permit gear changing.

The selector lever, centrally placed inside the car, has 6 positions as follows:

P (or park): Transmission in neutral, and the driving wheels mechanically locked.

R (or reverse): Reverse gear position. When the ignition switch is on, the reversing lights will automatically illuminate.

N (or neutral): Transmission in neutral.

A or D (or drive): Gears engage automatically.

2: Second gear hold.

1: First gear hold.

Note that whenever the selector lever is moved between D, P and R, the vehicle must be stationary, the footbrake applied, and the accelerator pedal raised. The mechanism must also be unlocked, by squeezing together the top of the selector lever.

To start the engine, the selector lever must be in either the P or N positions, for safety reasons. The starter will not function in other positions.

To move away, place the selector lever in the D position and drive away on the accelerator pedal.

In special circumstances, such as on very hilly and twisting roads, the selection of 2 will prevent frequent gear changing, and will provide engine braking when moving downhill, whilst retaining automatic changing between 1 and 2. Similarly, if 1 is selected, second and third gears are not obtainable.

When the vehicle is parked, P should be selected as an additional safeguard to the handbrake.

On normal roads, the most economical use is provided by driving with the selector lever at D, and with light accelerator pressure to give gearchanges at low engine speeds. Do not use positions 1 or 2.

When driving fast, gearchanging will take place at higher speeds. To obtain snap acceleration, such as when overtaking, smartly press the throttle pedal to the floor. This will cause the kickdown switch to operate, and give an immediate change down to a lower gear.

In cold weather, wait for between $\frac{1}{2}$ and 2 minutes, depending upon the temperature, before moving the selector lever. This will prevent stalling of the engine.

The complexity of the automatic transmission unit makes it largely unsuitable for working upon by the home mechanic, and any problems arising should be discussed with a Renault agent. Trouble-free running and long life will only be obtained if the unit is serviced correctly, and is not abused.

Limit operations to those described in this Chapter.

If it is intended to tow a trailer using a car equipped with automatic transmission, refer to Section 10.

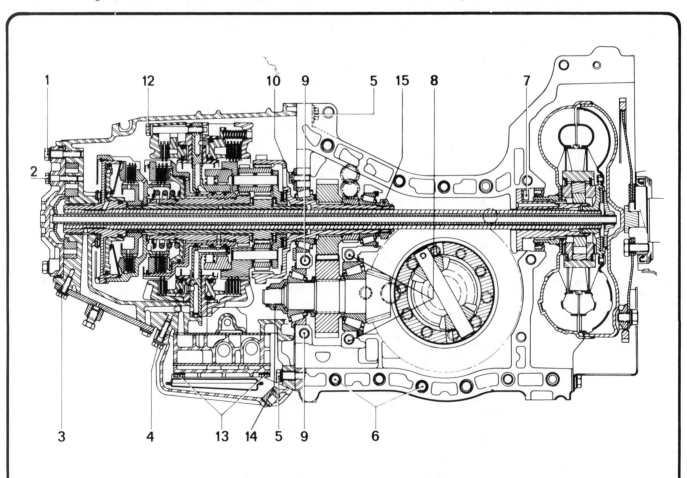

Fig. 7.1 Sectional view of automatic transmission/final drive unit (Sec 1)

1 Oil pump cover bolt	5 Casing connecting bolts	9 Half casing bolts	12 Freewheel support bolts
2 Oil pump cover bolt	6 Half casing bolts	10 Output shaft bearing	13 Hydraulic distributor
3 Lower cover plate	7 Stator bolts	thrust plate bolts	14 Final drive pinion nut
4 Sump pan	8 Half casing bolts	11 Freewheel support bolts	15 Output shaft nut

2   Automatic transmission fluid – checking, draining and refilling

Checking

1   With the vehicle on level ground, and the selector lever in P, start the engine and wait for approximately two minutes. This ensures that the converter is filled.
2   If the fluid level is now checked COLD, withdraw the dipstick, wipe it clean, re-insert it and withdraw it again. The level should be between the 1 and 2 marks.
3   The fluid will only become thoroughly hot after at least 30 minutes driving. If the fluid level is checked HOT, the level should be between marks 2 and 3.
4   Never overfill, or overheating or leakage may occur. Top up via the dipstick tube, using a clean funnel.
5   When wiping the dipstick, always use a non-fluffy rag.

Draining

6   Always drain when the transmission is hot, to ensure that the impurities held in suspension in the hot oil are disposed of.
7   Remove the dipstick.
8   Remove the drain plugs and allow the oil to drain for as long as possible.
9   Refit the drain plugs.

Refilling

10   Refill via a funnel, using one that has a filter to trap any impurities in the oil.
11   With the funnel in the dipstick tube, pour in the specified quantity of the recommended automatic transmission fluid.
12   Start up, check the level and top up as required.

3   Speed selector control – removal, refitting and adjusting

1   Set the hand control lever to position 1.
2   Working under the car, extract the split pin from the computer control arm.
3   Unscrew the nuts on the end of the control rod and from the bracket. Then remove the control arm.
4   Working inside the car, remove the control lever centre casing. Pull the casing far enough away to be able to disconnect the switch wires.
5   Remove the control lever bracket fixing bolts and withdraw the complete bracket/selector lever assembly.
6   Refitting is a reversal of removal but make sure that the selector lever and computer are in position 1.
7   The assembly must now be adjusted. To do this , first set the hand

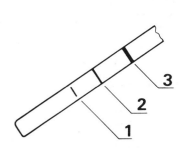

Fig. 7.2 Fluid dipstick marking (Sec 2)

1 and 2 Min and Max – COLD
2 and 3 Min and Max – HOT

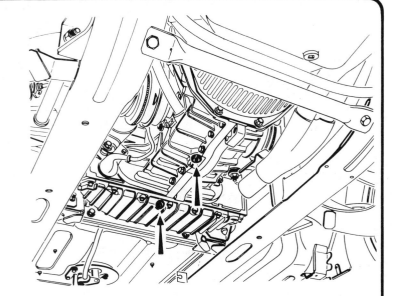

Fig. 7.3 Automatic transmission drain plugs (Sec 2)

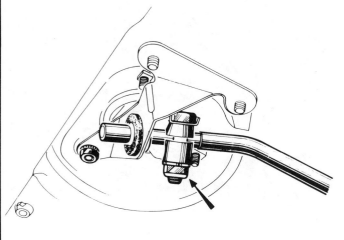

Fig. 7.4 Speed selector control rod clamp (Sec 3)

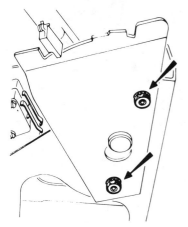

Fig. 7.5 Speed selector control rod quadrant bolts (Sec 3)

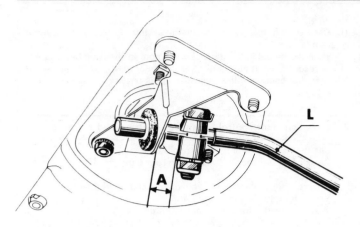

Fig. 7.6 Control rod clamp setting (Sec 3)

L Rod
A 16.0 to 18.0 mm (0.63 to 0.71 in)

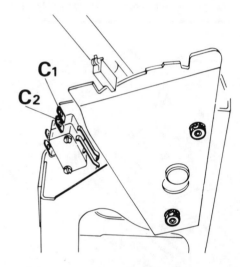

Fig. 7.7 Starter inhibitor/reverse lamp switch (Sec 3)

C1 Starter inhibitor terminal   C2 Reverse lamp

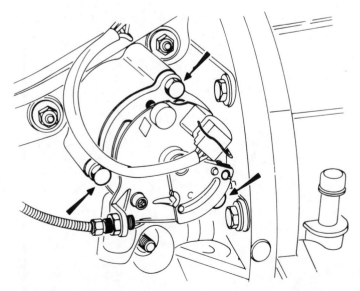

Fig. 7.8 Governor fixing screws (Sec 4)

control lever in (P). The lever must be vertical, if it is not, release the two quandrant bolts and move as necessary.
8   Set the control lever in position 1.
9   Working under the car, set the computer input shaft to position 1.
10   Now move the coupling to provide dimension (A) as shown in the diagram. Tighten the clamp.
11   Note the starter inhibitor/reverse lamp switch location. Provided the selector mechanism has been correctly adjusted, the switches should operate correctly.

4   Governor – removal, refitting and adjusting

1   Disconnect the governor control cable.
2   Disconnect the leads from the governor.
3   Disconnect the battery and its tray.
4   Extract the now accessible governor top screw and then the two lower screws.
5   Withdraw the governor.
6   Refit, using a new gasket with jointing compound applied. If any difficulty is experienced in pushing the governor home, disconnect the speedometer drive cable and turn the drivegear.
7   Once installed, adjust the governor control cable in the following way.
8   Release the cable and fitting locknut (E) and turn the end fitting (G) until the thread length is equal on both sides of the bracket.
9   Check that the cable is in its slot in the quandrant (S) and at the carburettor end attached to the cam.
10   Have an assistant depress the accelerator pedal fully then tension the cable by turning the end stop (C) at the carburettor end. The cable is correctly tensioned when the clearance (J) between the cable nipple (I) and the end of the quandrant slot is between 0.2 mm (0.008 in) and 0.7 mm (0.028 in).
11   Tighten locknuts (E) on completion.

5   Kickdown switch – testing

1   Satisfactory operation of the kickdown switch may be checked by connecting a test lamp between the switch and the battery + terminal. The lamp should illuminate when the accelerator pedal is fully depressed.
2   If it does not, renew the accelerator cable/switch as an assembly by referring to Chapter 3, Section 36.

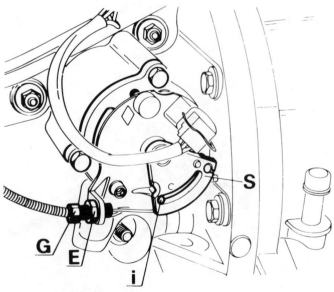

Fig. 7.9 Governor adjustment points (Sec 4)

E Locknut   i Index pin
G Threaded adjuster   S Control quadrant at transmission

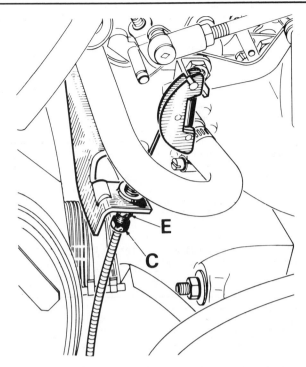

Fig. 7.10 Governor cable attachment at carburettor (Sec 4)

C   Threaded adjuster   *E   Locknut*

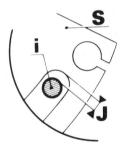

Fig. 7.11 Transmission governor quadrant correctly set (Sec 4)

i   Index pin   J   0.2 to 0.7 mm (0.008 to 0.28 in)   S   Quadrant

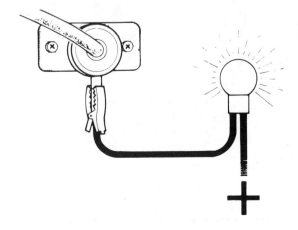

Fig. 7.12 Kickdown switch test lamp circuit (Sec 5)

6   Kickdown switch – adjusting

1   Switch adjustment is carried out by tensioning the accelerator cable as described in Chapter 3, Section 36. It must be appreciated that the settings of the accelerator pedal, accelerator cable and governor cable are all inter-related and must therefore be carried out at the same time.

7   Electronic computer – removal and refitting

1   Disconnect the cables and connector support bracket.
2   Extract the two computer fixing screws, remove the computer.
3   Refit in the following way. Turn the central shaft as far as it will go to correspond with 1st speed hold position.
4   Set the lever (L) on the side of the transmission in 1st speed hold position.
5   Offer up the computer which must be fitted with new spacers. Insert the fixing screws finger tight only.
6   Check that the central shaft and transmission lever are still in 1st speed hold and then turn the shaft and the computer unit as an assembly in the direction of the arrow. Use gentle hand pressure only, no force.
7   Tighten the computer fixing screws without squashing the plastic distance pieces.
8   Remake all connections.

8   Automatic transmission – removal and refitting

1   Disconnect the battery.
2   Unbolt the starter motor and pull it from the torque converter housing.
3   Disconnect the transmission vacuum pipe from the inlet manifold.
4   Refer to Chapter 1 and remove the camshaft pulley.
5   Disconnect the computer electrical leads and bracket.
6   Drain the transmission fluid (see Section 2).
7   The car must now be placed over an inspection pit or raised sufficiently high on ramps to provide adequate clearance to be able to remove the transmission from under it.
8   Remove the driveshaft roll pins (see Chapter 8).

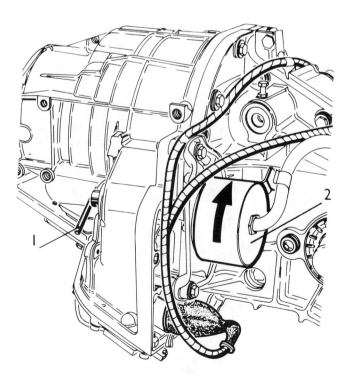

Fig. 7.13 Electronic computer (1) and speed selector lever (2) on automatic transmission (Sec 7)

9   Using a suitable balljoint splitter, disconnect the tie-rod end balljoints and the front suspension upper balljoints (see Chapter 11, Section 5).

10 Pull the upper ends of the stub axle carriers outwards and disconnect the driveshaft inboard ends from the transmission after driving out the roll pins (see Chapter 8).

11 Disconnect the speed selector control rod. Do this by moving the lever to 1st speed hold and then disconnecting at the clamp (see Section 3) and at the computer end.

12 Remove the dipstick guide/filler tube from the transmission.

13 Unbolt and remove the grille from the converter housing.

14 Release the exhaust pipe from the transmission.

15 Support the rear of the transmission on a jack preferably of trolley type.

16 Remove the transmission rear mounting crossmember.

17 Lower the jack until the speedometer and governor cables can be disconnected.

18 Unscrew and remove the bolts which connect the torque converter housing to the engine.

19 The three bolts which connect the driveplate to the torque converter must now be unscrewed. To do this, unscrew and remove the first bolt and then turn the crankshaft/driveplate to bring each succeeding bolt into view in the grille plate aperture.

20 Withdraw the engine from under and towards the rear of the car.

21 During removal, keep the torque converter fully engaged with the splines of the oil pump and retain it by using a small plate bolted to the torque converter housing.

22 Refitting is a reversal of removal, but observe the following points.

23 When connecting the driveplate and torque converter, fit the boss on the converter (which is opposite the timing hole) onto the sharply angled machined arm (marked with paint dab) of the driveplate.

24 Align the driveshaft roll pin holes with those in the differential side gears.

25 Tighten all nuts and bolts to the specified torque.

26 Adjust the governor and kickdown cables and selector control.

27 Fill the transmission with the correct grade and quantity of oil.

28 Recheck the oil level when normal road operating temperature has been reached.

9 Driveplate – removal and refitting

1   The driveplate can only be removed after the engine or transmission have been withdrawn.

2   Unscrew and remove the seven bolts which hold it to the crankshaft flange. To protect the driveplate from turning, do not jam the starter ring gear teeth with a screwdriver blade, but jam the teeth with a short piece of old ring gear. This will avoid distortion of the plate, particularly if it is to be used again.

3   A circular plate is fitted under the bolt heads.

4   If the starter drivegear is worn, renew the complete driveplate.

5   Refitting is a reversal of removal, tighten the fixing bolts to the specified torque.

10 Oil cooler – fitting

R1302, R1312, R1318, R1322, R1328 models

1   A transmission oil cooler must be fitted if it is intended to tow a trailer or caravan.

2   The cooler is supplied as a kit and consists of a supplementary transmission heat exchanger together with the necessary pipelines and connectors.

3   As the heat exchanger is to be mounted ahead of the cooling

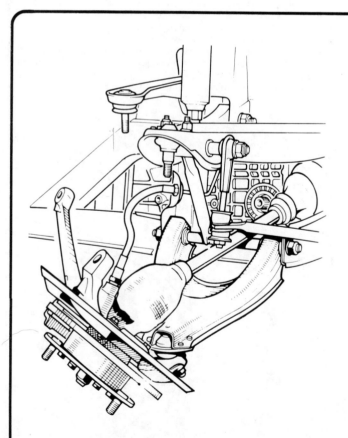

Fig. 7.14 Disconnecting driveshafts from automatic transmission (Sec 8)

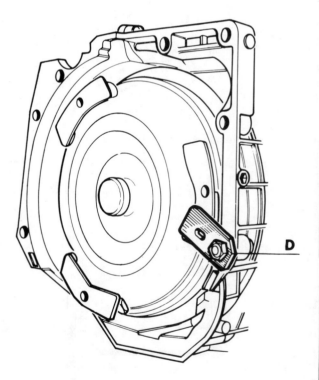

Fig. 7.15 Torque converter retaining plate (Sec 8)

system radiator, installation of such an oil cooler is not suitable for cars equipped with air conditioning where a condenser is mounted in front of the radiator.

4   To fit the oil cooler, remove the anti-roll bar (Chapter 11), the tubular crossmember, the exhaust downpipe and where fitted the damper support – refer to Chapter 1, Section 9.

5   Remove the two plugs from the side of the automatic transmission casing.

6   Smear the threads of the valve connector (C) supplied in the fitting kit with the sealing compound and screw it into the upper hole on the side of the transmission casing. Tighten to the specified torque.

7   Screw the two unions (2) into the valve just fitted and to the lower hole.

8   Unscrew the starter upper mounting bolt, locate the clip and refit the bolt.

9   Attach the shorter cranked metal pipe to the upper union and the pipe with the longer cranked length to the lower union. Secure the pipes with the clip.

10   Drain the cooling system and remove the radiator (Chapter 2).

11   Drill two 6.0 mm (0.24 in) holes in the flange at the top of the radiator in accordance with the diagram. Locate the sliding nuts and screw the oil cooler heat exchanger to the cooling system radiator.

12   Cut the flexible oil hoses to length; top hose 970.0 mm (38.2 in); bottom hose 890.0 mm (35.1 in) and secure them to the heat exchanger with clips.

13   Refit the combined radiator/oil cooler assembly.

14   Fit the supplementary clip to the wing valance and then connect the flexible hoses to the rigid cranked pipes at the transmission.

15   Reconnect all disconnected components and then fill and bleed the cooling system.

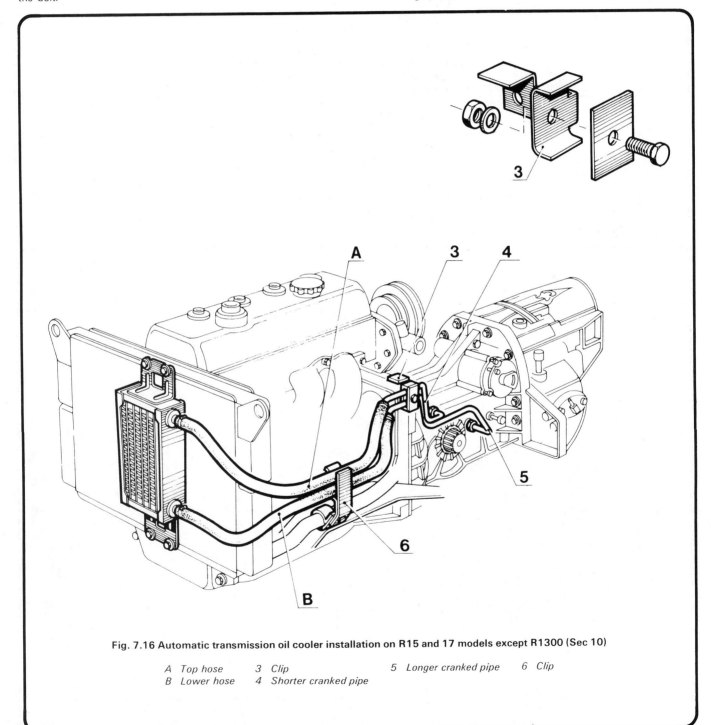

Fig. 7.16 Automatic transmission oil cooler installation on R15 and 17 models except R1300 (Sec 10)

A Top hose	3 Clip	5 Longer cranked pipe 6 Clip
B Lower hose	4 Shorter cranked pipe	

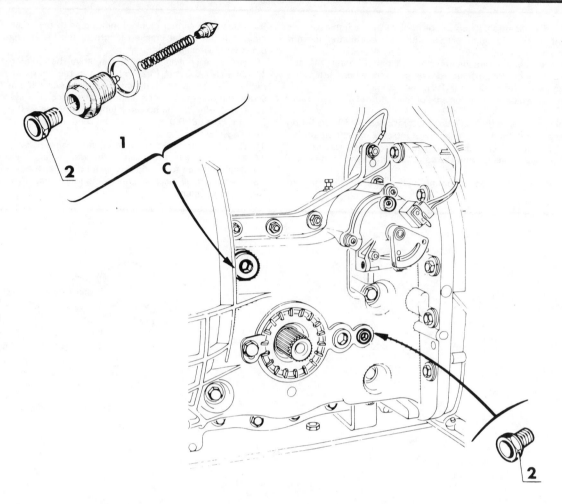

Fig. 7.17 Cooler pipe connections at transmission casing (Type R1302, R1312, R1322, R1318, R1328) (Sec 10)

C *Valve threaded connector*   1 *Valve body*   2 *Unions*

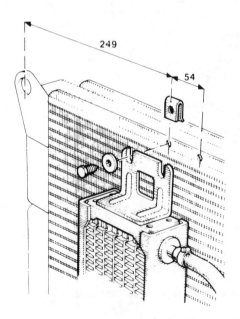

Fig. 7.18 Heat exchanger mounting to front face of radiator (dimensions in mm) (Sec 10)

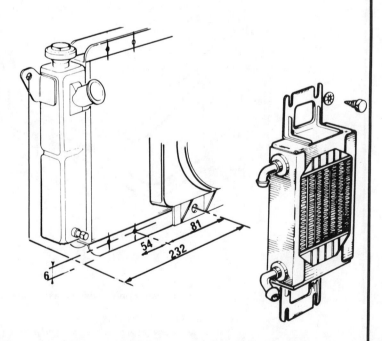

Fig. 7.19 Heat exchanger mounting to rear face of radiator (Sec 10)

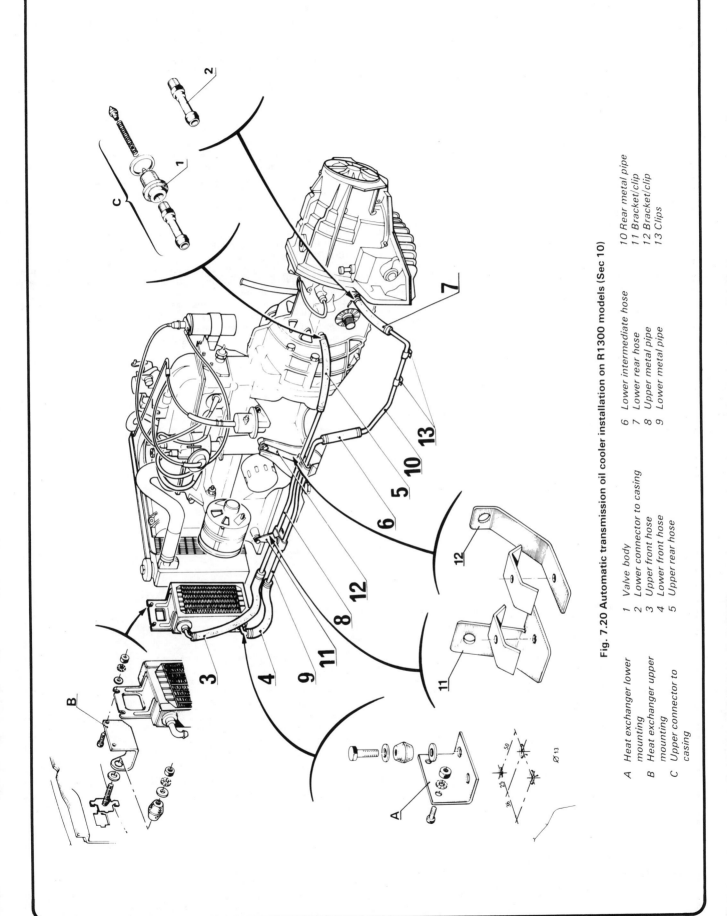

Fig. 7.20 Automatic transmission oil cooler installation on R1300 models (Sec 10)

A Heat exchanger lower
   mounting
B Heat exchanger upper
   mounting
C Upper connector to
   casing

1 Valve body
2 Lower connector to casing
3 Upper front hose
4 Lower front hose
5 Upper rear hose

6 Lower intermediate hose
7 Lower rear hose
8 Upper metal pipe
9 Lower metal pipe

10 Rear metal pipe
11 Bracket/clip
12 Bracket/clip
13 Clips

16 Top up the transmission fluid, the total capacity will now have increased by $\frac{1}{3}$ Imp pt (0.2 l).

R1300 (15TL) models

17 Fitting an oil cooler is similar to that described in earlier paragraphs, except that the heat exchanger is mounted on the crossmembers and is located at the side of the cooling system radiator on cars which have a 400 mm radiator or on the rear face of the radiator on cars with a 480 mm radiator.

18 The different hose and pipeline arrangement should be noted, cutting the hoses to length in accordance with the following dimensions.

400 mm radiator

Hose
3   420.0 mm (16.5 in)
4   240.0 mm (10.0 in)
5   240.0 mm (10.0 in)
6   180.0 mm (7.0 in)
7   160.0 mm (6.5 in)

480 mm radiator

Hose
3   360.0 mm (14.25 in)
4   160.0 mm (6.5 in)
5   240.0 mm (10.0 in)
6   180.0 mm (7.0 in)
7   160.0 mm (6.5 in)

19 As an added safeguard against overheating, a transmission oil temperature gauge may be fitted which again is available from your Renault dealer in kit form. To fit the switch, the transmission sump pan will have to be renewed and the new cover fitted which is tapped to receive the temperature switch.

20 Route the wiring to the instrument panel and connect it to the gauge which should be located in a convenient position.

11 Fault diagnosis – automatic transmission

1   Most faults in the automatic transmission can be traced to incorrect adjustment of the cables or selector linkage, or to an incorrect fluid level.

2   Diagnosis of faults other than those described in paragraph 1 requires specialised knowledge and equipment, and should be referred to a Renault agent.

3   Non-functioning of the starter motor is frequently traceable to a defect in the wiring or earthing to the transmission, or to incorrect selector lever adjustment.

4   If a serious fault in the transmission is suspected, on no account remove the transmission before the fault has been professionally diagnosed. The diagnostic equipment used by Renault dealers is designed for use with the transmission in the vehicle.

Chapter 8 Driveshafts

Contents

Description and maintenance 1
Driveshaft – removal and refitting 2
Driveshaft coupling (Bendix ball type) – bellows renewal 5
Driveshaft coupling (Type G1 62) – overhaul 4
Driveshaft coupling (Type GE 86) – bellows renewal 3
Fault diagnosis 6

Specifications

Driveshaft type .... Open, tubular, with CV joints at each end

Application

R1300 .... GE 86 coupling at roadwheel end
                                                      GI 62 coupling at transmission end

All other models .... GE 86 coupling at roadwheel end
                                                      Bendix 4 ball coupling at transmission end

Torque wrench settings

	Nm	lbf ft
Stub axle nut	163	120
Suspension upper balljoint nut	54	40
Steering arm balljoint nut	35	26
Roadwheel nuts	71	52

1 Description and maintenance

The shafts transmit the drive from the transmission unit to the front roadwheels. Each shaft has joints at the ends to allow for the relative motion between the transmission unit and the suspension.

Shaft location is by splines at each end. Roll pins retain the shaft at the transmission end, and a nut and washer at the wheel end.

A rubber bellows protects the shaft driving joints from water and dirt.

More than one type of shaft is in use, depending upon the vehicle model. When ordering a new shaft, always take the old one and

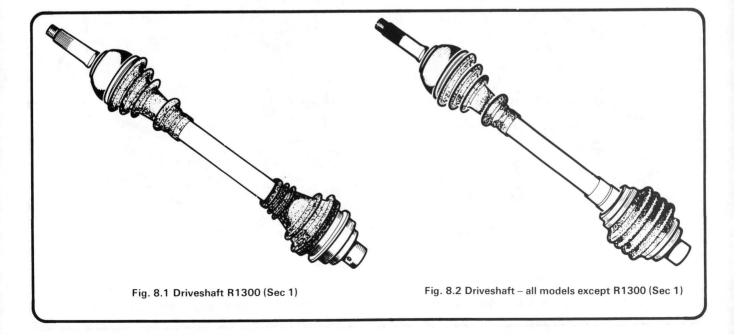

Fig. 8.1 Driveshaft R1300 (Sec 1)   Fig. 8.2 Driveshaft – all models except R1300 (Sec 1)

2.9 Removing driveshaft from stub axle carrier

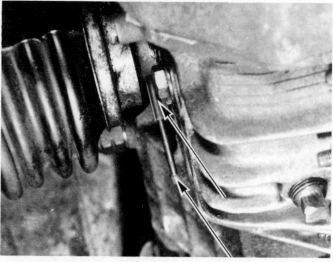

2.10 Driveshaft double roll pins

compare them to ensure correct replacement parts are supplied.

Very little work is possible upon the driveshaft assemblies by the home mechanic. Signs of wear or damage are vibration, clunking and ticking sounds, especially when cornering. A close eye should be kept on the rubber bellows, since a split here can swiftly lead to the ruin of the joint assembly.

2 Driveshaft – removal and refitting

1   Raise the front of the car on stands placed under the bodyframe side members.
2   Place a jack or stand under the front suspension lower wishbone and compress the suspension slightly.
3   Remove the roadwheel.
4   Unscrew the retaining nut and then using a suitable balljoint splitter, disconnect the tie-rod from the steering arm.

5   Disconnect the suspension upper balljoint from the stub axle carrier. Access to this balljoint is very restricted for fitting most types of splitting tool although forked wedges are suitable. If the balljoint has previously been renewed, then the balljoint fixing bolts can be undone to separate the components (see Chapter 11, Section 8).
6   Working under the car, drive out the roll pins from the inboard ends of the driveshaft.
7   Unscrew the hub nut from the outboard end of the driveshaft. To prevent the hub from rotating while this is being done, have an assistant apply the footbrake or use a long lever between two of the roadwheel studs, but protect the stud threads from damage.
8   Carefully pull the top of the stub axle outwards taking care not to strain the brake flexible hose until the driveshaft can be released from the transmission.
9   Support the stub axle carrier and push the driveshaft from the hub. If it is tight use a two or three legged extractor to remove it (photo).
10 Refitting is a reversal of removal, but align the roll pin holes at the

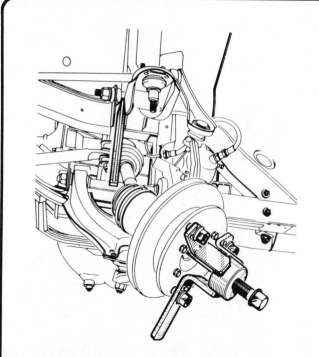

Fig. 8.3 Pressing driveshaft from hub (Sec 2)

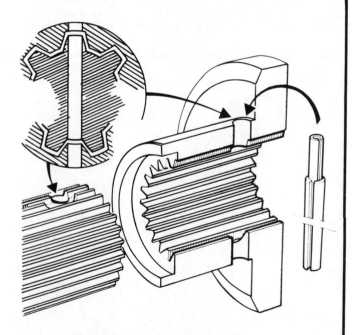

Fig. 8.4 Driveshaft roll pins and alignment (Sec 2)

3.4 Prising up end of star plate

3.5A Removing thrust button

inner ends before driving in the new roll pins. Double roll pins are used (photo).
11 Once the roll pins are fitted, seal their ends with a dab of silicone gasket compound.
12 Tighten the hub and balljoint nuts to the specified torque.

3 Driveshaft coupling (Type GE 86) – bellows renewal

1 This type of coupling is fitted at the outboard end of all driveshafts. Renewal of the bellows is the only operation which can be carried out, wear in the joint can only be rectified by renewal of the complete shaft.
2 With the driveshaft removed and clean externally, cut the bellows securing band and the bellows themselves along their complete length.
3 Remove the bellows and wipe away as much grease as possible.
4 Release the bell shaped section of the driveshaft by prising up the ends of the star plate (photo).
5 Separate the components and extract the thrust button and spring (photos).
6 A special conical expander must be used to fit the new bellows. If

3.5B Removing thrust spring

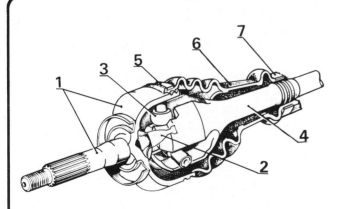

Fig. 8.5 GE 86 driveshaft coupling (Sec 3)

1	Stub axle section	5	Bellows retaining collar
2	Star plate	6	Bellows
3	Spider	7	Bellows clip
4	Shaft yoke		

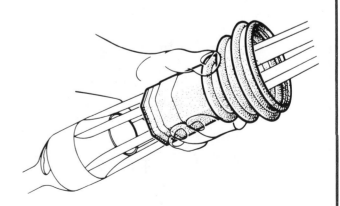

Fig. 8.6 Sliding bellows onto guide tool (Sec 3)

3.9 Using tool to fit bellows

3.13 Star plate tab in notch

3.14 Applying special grease

3.15 Engaging bellows lip with shaft groove

3.17A Bellows clips correctly fitted

3.17B Bellows retaining collar at narrow end

the official tool (T. Av 537-01) cannot be borrowed it may be possible to make up a suitable substitute.

7   Grip the driveshaft in a vice fitted with soft metal jaw protectors.

8   Fit a new bellows clip and the bellows to the expander tool. Lubricate the inside of the bellows with oil, then clean the hands thoroughly.

9   Hold the bellows with both hands and pull them smoothly down the taper of the tool until it is positioned on the circular end of the tool (photo).

10   Fit the spring and thrust button and move the roller cages towards the centre.

11   Position the star plate equidistant between the rollers as shown.

12   Connect the driveshaft yoke to the bell shaped section.

13   Engage the star plate ends in their notches (photo).

14   Spread a pack of special grease (280g of ELF S747) equally between coupling and bellows (photo).

15   Locate the lips of the bellows in the shaft retaining grooves (photo).

16   Insert a piece of rod between the bellows and shaft to equalise the air pressure within them.

17   Carefully pull the securing clip and collar into position on the bellows (photos).

4   Driveshaft coupling (Type GI 62) – overhaul

1   This type of coupling is used at the inboard end of the driveshaft on R1300 models.

2   Prise back the retaining clip from the larger diameter of the bellows.

3   Cut the bellows along their full length, remove them and wipe away as much grease as possible.

4   Using a pair of pliers, prise up the ends of the anti-separation plate.

5   Remove the yoke, taking care not to dismantle the roller cages which are matched components. Tape them if necessary to prevent separation.

6   Extract the circlip and then press the driveshaft out of the coupling spider.

7   Commence reassembly by lubricating the driveshaft and sliding a new clip and bellows into position.

8   Fit the spider to the shaft. New spiders are supplied with a plastic roller cage retainer which must be removed as work progresses.

9   Fit the spider circlip.

10   Spread a pack of special grease (140g ELF 5747) equally between bellows and yoke.

11   A wedge should now be made up in accordance with the diagram.

12   Insert the wedge between the yoke and the anti-separation plate.

13   Tap the anti-separation plate into its original position and then remove the temporary wedge.

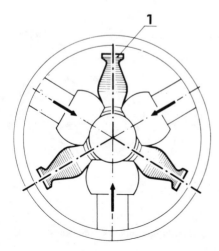

Fig. 8.7 Star plate (1) correctly located (Sec 3)

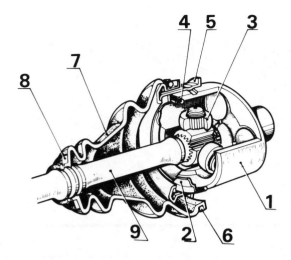

Fig. 8.8 GI 62 driveshaft coupling (Sec 4)

1 Yoke
2 Anti-separation plate
3 Spider
4 Seal
5 Cover
6 Retaining spring
7 Bellows
8 Clip
9 Driveshaft

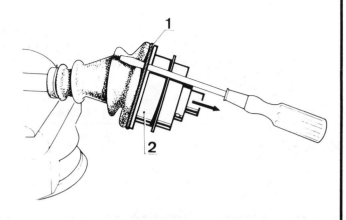

Fig. 8.9 Removing bellows retaining spring (Sec 4)

1 Spring   2 Yoke

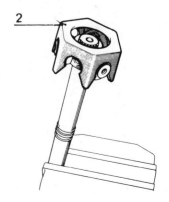

Fig. 8.10 Prising up ends of anti-separation plate (1) (Sec 4)

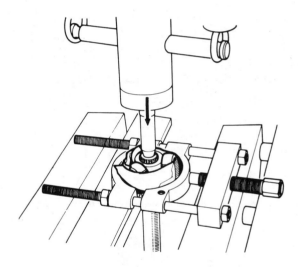

Fig. 8.11 Pressing shaft from spider (Sec 4)

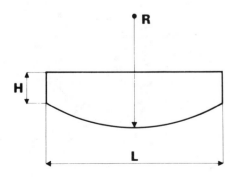

Fig. 8.12 Roller cage retainer (2) (Sec 4)

Fig. 8.13 Anti-separation plate wedge (Sec 4)

H 6.0 mm (0.025 in)
L 40.0 mm (1.57 in)
R 45.0 mm (1.77 in)

14 Engage the lips of the bellows in the grooves of the driveshaft and cover.
15 Insert a piece of rod between the lip of the bellows and shaft to equalise the air pressure.
16 Adjust the length of coupling/bellows to conform with the diagram.
17 Withdraw the temporary rod and fit the clip and spring band to the bellows.

5 Driveshaft coupling (Bendix ball type) – bellows renewal

1 This type of coupling is fitted to the inboard end of all driveshafts except those used on R1300 models. Renewal of the bellows is the only operation which can be carried out, wear in the joint can only be rectified by renewal of the complete shaft.
2 With the shaft removed from the car and cleaned externally, remove the two crimped bands from the bellows.

3 Using a centre punch, mark the position of the jaws in relation to each other.
4 Cut away and remove the bellows.
5 Separate the coupling components, clean the jaws and balls, but take care to identify the balls in relation to their original seats.
6 Commence reassembly by gripping the driveshaft in the jaws of a vice fitted with soft metal protectors.
7 Place a length of rubber tubing, 12.5 mm (-0.5 in) in diameter, across the jaws as shown.
8 Arrange the four balls opposite their tracks.
9 Offer up the opposite jaw, apply pressure and withdraw rubber tubing. The balls will seat.
10 A cone shaped guide tool will now be required to fit the bellows as described in Section 3. Unfortunately this is of different diameter (Tool No. T. AV 51) from the one used for GE 86 couplings.
11 Fit the guide tool fully over the driveshaft coupling.
12 Lubricate the inside of the bellows and slide them onto the tool.
13 Grip the larger diameter of the bellows and pull the tool out.

Fig. 8.14 Anti-separation plate wedge (1) in position (Sec 4)

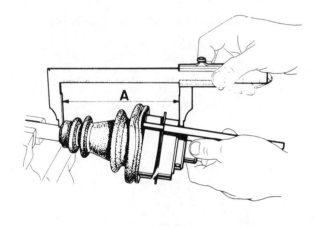

Fig. 8.15 Coupling/bellows adjustment (Sec 4)

A   152.5 to 153.5 mm (6.01 to 6.05 in)

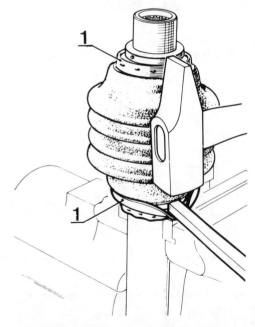

Fig. 8.16 Removing bellows bands (Sec 5)

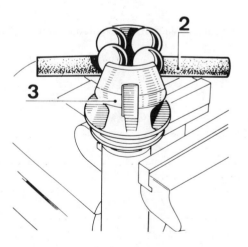

Fig. 8.17 Balls assembled (Sec 5)

2   Rubber tubing   3   Coupling jaws

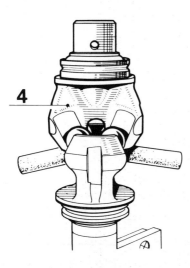

Fig. 8.18 Coupling jaws ready for connection (Sec 5)

14 Locate the bellows lip in its groove and tighten the bottom clip.
15 Pump 210g of special SJW oil into the bellows by inserting an oil gun under the bellows top lip.
16 Insert a piece of rod under the bellows top lip and the shaft to equalise the air pressure.
17 Set the coupling dimension (between machined faces) as shown in the diagram.
18 Fit the remaining bellows clip and then fit retaining clips (L) which are supplied with new shafts to prevent the coupling separating during installation of the driveshaft. Substitute clips can be easily made up using hose clips and pieces of rod.

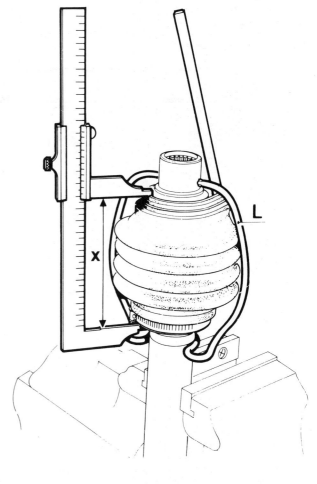

Fig. 8.20 Ball type coupling setting diagram (Sec 5)

L   Retaining clip   X   113.0 mm (4.45 in)

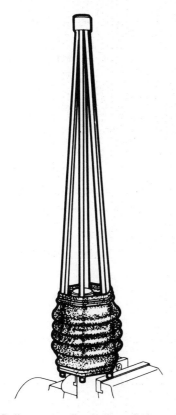

Fig. 8.19 Ball type coupling bellows fitting tool (Sec 5)

6 Fault diagnosis – driveshaft

Symptom	Reason(s)
Vibration	Bent shaft. Out of balance driveshaft couplings due to interchange of components. Out of balance roadwheels
'Clunk' during moving off	Worn shaft splines. Worn couplings
Ticking on turns	Worn couplings

Chapter 9 Braking system

Contents

Brake discs – removal and refitting 8
Brake drum – renovation or renewal 14
Brake pedal – removal and refitting 28
Brake shoes (Bendix self-adjusting) – renewal 12
Brake shoes (Girling self-adjusting) – renewal 13
Brake shoes (manual adjusters) – renewal 11
Brake switches 29
Braking system – bleeding 20
Caliper mounting bracket – removal and refitting 7
Description and maintenance 1
Fault diagnosis – braking system 30
Front disc caliper – removal, overhaul and refitting 4
Front disc pads – inspection and renewal 2
Handbrake cable – adjustment 25
Handbrake cables – renewal 27
Handbrake control lever – removal and refitting 26

Hydraulic pipes and hoses – general 21
Master cylinder – overhaul 16
Master cylinder – removal and refitting 15
Pressure drop indicator – description, removal and
refitting 19
Pressure limiting valve – removal, refitting and adjustment 18
Rear disc caliper – mechanical overhaul 6
Rear disc caliper – removal, seal renewal and refitting 5
Rear disc pads (Gordini) – inspection and renewal 3
Rear drum brakes – adjustment 9
Rear shoe linings – checking for wear 10
Rear wheel cylinder – removal, overhaul and refitting 17
Servo (Master-Vac) unit – description and testing 22
Servo (Master-Vac) – servicing 23
Servo unit – removal and refitting 24

Specifications

System type ....

Four wheel hydraulic with servo assistance. Discs front, drums rear except Gordini which has rear discs. Handbrake mechanical to rear wheels.

Front disc brakes

Disc diameter	228.0 mm (8.98 in)
Disc thickness	
R1300 (non-ventilated)	10.0 mm (0.394 in)
Other models (ventilated)	20.0 mm (0.788 in)
Disc thickness (minimum refinishing)	
R1300	9.0 mm (0.355 in)
Other models	19.0 mm (0.749 in)
Pad wear limit (includes backing plate)	7.0 mm (0.276 in)

Rear disc brakes (Gordini)

Disc diameter	228.0 mm (8.98 in)
Disc thickness	10.0 mm (0.394 in)
Disc thickness (minimum refinishing)	9.0 mm (0.355 in)
Pad wear limit (includes backplate)	7.0 mm (0.276 in)

Rear drum brakes

Drum internal diameter	
R1300	180.0 mm (7.1 in)
Other models	228.5 mm (9.00 in)
Maximum internal diameter after refinishing	
R1300	181.25 mm (7.14 in)
Other models	229.5 mm (9.04 in)

Vacuum servo unit

Diameter	
R1313, R1323, R1317, R1327	Double 160 mm (6.3 in)
Other models	152.0 mm (5.99 in)

Brake fluid ....

To SAE J1703

Torque wrench settings

	Nm	lbf/ft
Caliper bracket bolts	67	49
Disc to hub bolts	26	19
Stub axle nut	163	120
Roadwheel nut	71	52
Flexible hose to caliper	20	15
Bleed screw	8	6

1 Description and maintenance

The braking system is of four wheel hydraulic type.

On most models except Gordini (R1313, R1323, R1317 and R1327) the front brakes are of disc type with drums on the rear. On Gordini models, the rear brakes are of disc type.

The hydraulic circuit is of dual type and incorporates a pressure limiting valve to limit pressure to the rear wheels during heavy brake application which could cause rear wheel locking.

A pressure drop indicator unit is also fitted to indicate, by means of a warning lamp, any pressure drop in either circuit caused by a leak of hydraulic fluid. On some models, the pressure drop indicator incorporates a bypass to increase rear brake pressure should a leak occur in the front wheel circuit.

Vacuum servo assistance is provided.

The handbrake is floor-mounted and acts on the rear wheels only.

Regularly check the fluid level in the master cylinder unit by

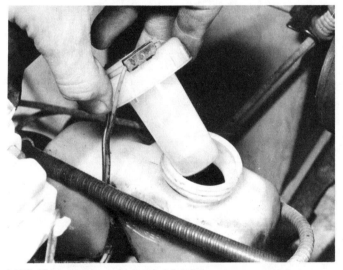

1.7 Fluid reservoir cap with low level switch

reference to the warning lamp (if fitted) or by checking the reservoir fluid level (photo).

Check the disc pad wear and the shoe lining wear at the intervals specified in Routine Maintenance. On some models, the disc pads incorporate wear indicators connected to a warning lamp.

Also at the specified intervals, renew the hydraulic fluid by bleeding.

Brake adjustment is only required on those models fitted with manually-adjusted rear shoes.

2 Front disc pads – inspection and renewal

1 The disc pads must be renewed when the thickness of the pad (friction material plus backplate) is 7.0 mm (0.28 in) or less.
2 Use a rule held at right angles on the disc to measure this.
3 Always renew the pads as an axle set (4 pads).
4 To renew the pads, raise the front of the car and remove the roadwheels.
5 Pull out the two clips which retain the sliding keys (photo).
6 Tap out the sliding keys using a punch (photo).
7 Slide out the second key.
8 Remove the caliper and disconnect the pad wear indicator lamp wires (if fitted).
9 Remove the disc pads. On some models, blade type anti-chatter springs are used, on others, wedge type wire springs are fitted.
10 Brush away all dust from the caliper jaws taking care not to inhale it. The pad retaining clips may be removed if required.
11 Push the piston fully back into its cylinder using a flat blade. This is necessary to accommodate the new thicker pads and may cause the level to rise in the master cylinder reservoir. Anticipate this by syphoning out some fluid with an old, but clean battery hydrometer or similar.
12 Fit the pad anti-chatter springs.
13 Fit the friction pads checking that they slide freely and that the stop button on genuine Renault pads is at the top of the caliper bracket (photos).
14 Slip one end of the caliper between the pad retaining spring and the key location on the caliper bracket.
15 Engage the opposite end of the caliper by compressing both pad retaining springs.
16 Slide in the first key.
17 Tap in the second key.

2.5 Removing caliper key clip

2.6 Driving out a caliper sliding key

2.13A Fitting inboard brake pad

2.13B Fitting outboard brake pad (LH roadwheel). Stop button arrowed

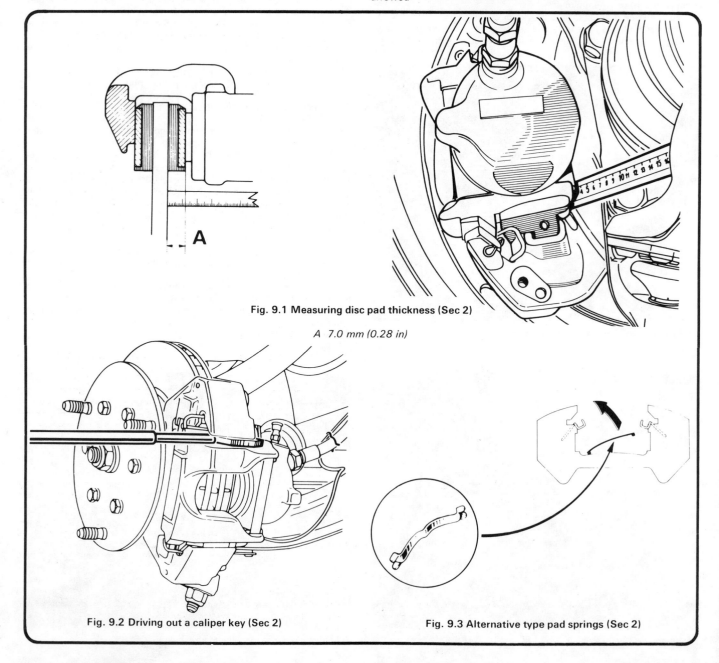

Fig. 9.1 Measuring disc pad thickness (Sec 2)

A 7.0 mm (0.28 in)

Fig. 9.2 Driving out a caliper key (Sec 2)

Fig. 9.3 Alternative type pad springs (Sec 2)

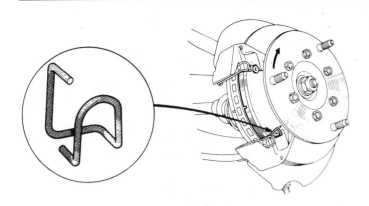

Fig. 9.4 Wedge type spring fitted to bottom pad (Sec 2)

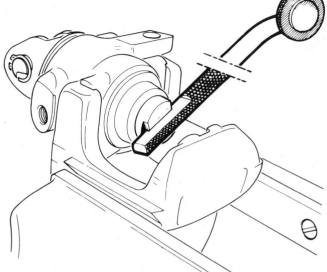

Fig. 9.7 Turning a rear caliper piston (Sec 3)

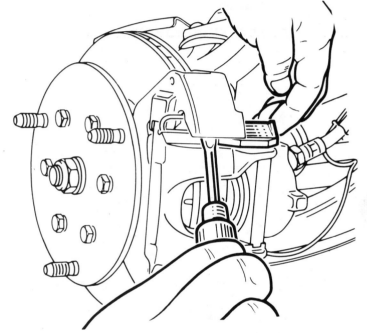

Fig. 9.5 Fitting caliper sliding key (Sec 2)

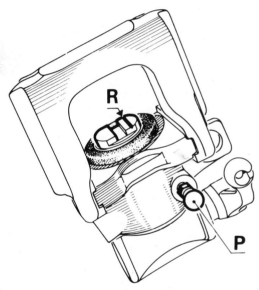

Fig. 9.8 Rear caliper piston groove (R) to bleed screw (P) alignment (Sec 3)

3 Rear disc pads (Gordini) – inspection and renewal

1   Check for wear in the pads as described for the front pads in the preceding Section.
2   If worn beyond their specified limit, renew them as an axle set (four pads).
3   Raise the rear of the car and remove the roadwheels.
4   Disconnect the handbrake cables from the caliper levers. To do this, unscrew the adjusting nuts at the junction of the primary and secondary cables until the cable end fittings can be slipped out of their seats in the levers.
5   Remove the pads as described for the front pads in the preceding Section.
6   Brush away all dust from the caliper jaws taking care not to inhale it.
7   Using a suitable tool, turn the piston until it is screwed in as far as it will go and further rotation will not make it enter any deeper. This operation will cause the fluid level in the master cylinder reservoir to rise. Anticipate this by syphoning out some fluid.
8   Align the caliper piston so that the line on the piston thrust face is towards the bleed screw.

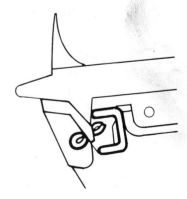

Fig. 9.6 Caliper key retaining clip (Sec 2)

18 Fit two new key retaining clips.
19 Depress the brake pedal several times to position the pads against the disc.
20 Refit the roadwheels, lower the car and top up the master cylinder fluid reservoir.

9   Refit the pads as described for the front disc brakes in the preceding Section.
10 Reconnect the handbrake cables.
11 Apply the foot brake several times to bring the pads against the disc.
12 Adjust the handbrake (see Section 25).
13 Refit the roadwheel and lower the car.

4   Front disc caliper – removal, overhaul and refitting

1   Raise the front of the car and remove the roadwheel.
2   Using two open-ended spanners, uncouple the hydraulic flexible hose from the rigid pipeline at the support bracket. Quickly cap the end of the pipeline. A bleed nipple dust cap is useful for this.
3   Remove the caliper sliding key clips and tap out the first key with a pin punch. Remove the second key.
4   Release the retaining clip on the hose support bracket and remove the caliper.
5   Unscrew the brake hose from the caliper and drain hydraulic fluid from the unit. Remove the pads (see Section 2) (photo).
6   Clean external dirt from the caliper and pull off the piston dust excluder.
7   The piston must now be ejected. To do this, apply air pressure to the hose port. Relatively low air pressure is required for this such as obtained from a tyre pump.
8   Check the piston and cylinder bore surfaces for scoring or metal to metal rubbed areas. If evident, renew the caliper piston/cylinder assembly as follows:
9   To renew the caliper cylinder it must be separated from the caliper carrier.
10 The carrier legs will have to be spread using a wedge made up to the dimensions shown in the diagram.
11 Tap the wedge into position and then depress the spring-loaded retaining plunger using a thin rod inserted into the hole in the carrier leg.
12 Slide the cylinder out of the carrier.
13 Refit the new cylinder and finally remove the temporary wedge (photos).
14 If the piston and cylinder are in good condition, extract the piston seal from its groove. Use a sharp pointed instrument for this job taking care not to scratch the cylinder bore.
15 Discard the old seal and dust excluder and obtain a repair kit which will contain all the renewable items.
16 Wash the cylinder and piston using only clean hydraulic fluid or methylated spirit. Fit the new seal into its groove using the fingers only to manipulate it into position.
17 Lubricate the piston and bore with clean hydraulic fluid and push the piston squarely into the cylinder.
18 Reconnect the flexible hose to the caliper using a new copper washer.

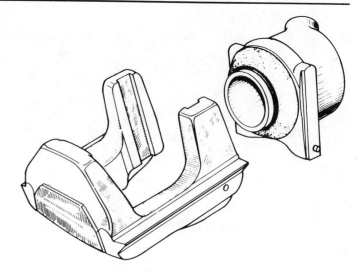

Fig. 9.9 Caliper piston and carrier (Sec 4)

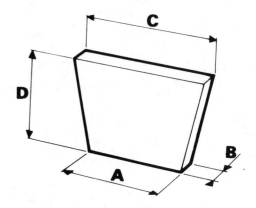

Fig. 9.10 Front caliper leg spreading wedge (Sec 4)

A   43.0 mm (1.69 in)   C   50.0 mm (1.97 in)
B   8.0 mm (0.32 in)   D   35.0 mm (1.38 in)

4.5 Brake hose detached from caliper

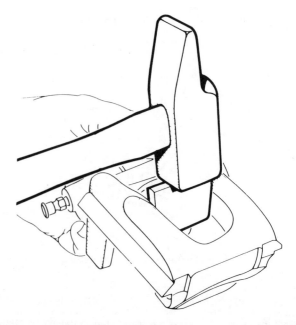

Fig. 9.11 Spreading caliper legs with wedge (Sec 4)

4.13A Refitting caliper cylinder to carrier

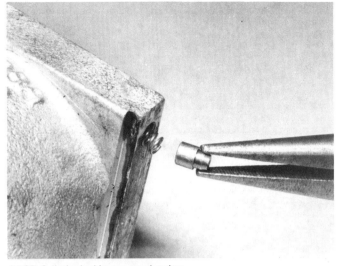

4.13B Cylinder locking peg and spring

19 Refit the caliper and pads as described in Section 2.
20 Reconnect the flexible hose to the rigid pipeline.
21 Fit the roadwheel, lower the car.
22 Bleed the brakes as described in Section 20.

5 Rear disc caliper – removal, seal renewal and refitting

1   Raise the rear of the car and remove the roadwheel.
2   Disconnect the handbrake cable (see Section 27).
3   Use a clamp on the flexible hose and then remove its banjo type union bolt and disconnect it from the caliper.
4   Refer to Section 3 and remove the caliper and disc pads.

5   Clean away external dirt and then grip the caliper in a vice fitted with soft metal protectors.
6   Pull off the piston dust excluder.
7   Using a suitable tool, unscrew the piston (see Section 3). While the piston is being rotated, apply air pressure from a tyre pump to the hose port of the caliper to eject the piston.
8   Examine the piston and cylinder bore for scoring or metal to metal rubbed areas. If evident, then the piston/cylinder must be renewed as an assembly. This will necessitate separating the cylinder from its carrier just as described for the front caliper in Section 4, paragraphs 9 to 13 except that the dimensions of the temporary wedge are different.
9   If however the piston and cylinder are in good condition, pick the

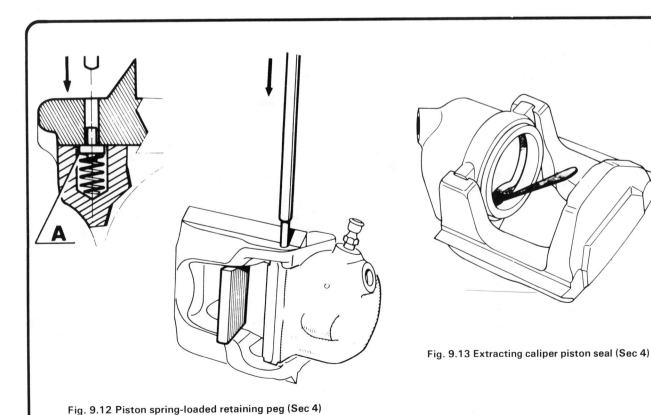

Fig. 9.12 Piston spring-loaded retaining peg (Sec 4)

Fig. 9.13 Extracting caliper piston seal (Sec 4)

piston seal from its groove using a sharp pointed tool taking care not to scratch the cylinder bore.

10 Obtain a repair kit which will contain all the renewable items.

11 Clean all components using only hydraulic fluid or methylated spirit.

12 Fit the new piston seal, manipulating it into its groove using the fingers only.

13 Apply clean hydraulic fluid to the piston and cylinder bore and insert the piston squarely using hand pressure.

14 Using a lever in the piston groove turn the piston until it is screwed in as far as it will go and further rotation will not make it enter any deeper.

15 Align the caliper piston so that the line on the piston thrust face is towards the bleed screw. Fit the new dust excluder.

16 Refit the caliper and pads.

17 Reconnect the hydraulic hose and handbrake cable.

18 Adjust the handbrake cable (Section 25).

19 Refit the roadwheel and lower the car.

20 Bleed the braking system (Section 20).

6 Rear disc caliper – mechanical overhaul

1 The normal reason for rear caliper overhaul is to renew a worn piston seal.

2 After a high mileage however, some of the mechanical components may have worn in which case the following operations should be carried out in conjunction with renewal of the piston seal which is described in the preceding Section.

3 With the caliper removed from the car and gripped in the jaws of a vice, pull off the dust excluder and unscrew and remove the piston.

4 Remove the dust cover from the handbrake end of the assembly.

5 Extract the circlip.

6 Using a suitable tool, compress the spring washers to release the operating shaft which should be pulled out.

7 Remove the pluger, the spring and dismantle the adjusting screw.

8 Carefully remove the O-ring from the adjusting screw.

9 Clean all components in methylated spirit and renew any worn components.

10 Reassembly is a reversal of dismantling but make sure that the spring washers on the adjusting screw are arranged as shown.

7 Caliper mounting bracket – removal and refitting

1 Raise the car and remove the roadwheel.

All models except R1300

2 Refer to Section 2 or 3 and remove the caliper and pads and tie them up out of the way. There is no need to disconnect the hydraulic hose.

3 Unscrew and remove the caliper bracket mounting bolts and withdraw the bracket.

R1300 models

4 The operations are similar to those described in earlier paragraphs except that a shim is located between the bracket and stub axle carrier.

5 Refitting is a reversal of removal on all except R1300 models. Tighten the bracket bolts to the specified torque.

6 On R1300 models fit the original shim unless a new disc or bracket is being fitted in which case the bracket to disc clearance must be adjusted in the following way.

7 Fit a shim 0.6 mm (0.024 in) thick between the caliper bracket and stub axle carrier. Check clearance (A) disc to bracket.

8 Refer to the table and depending upon the clearance measured, substitute a shim of suitable thickness.

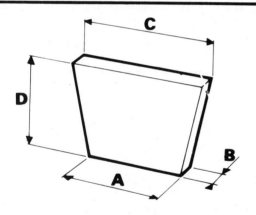

Fig. 9.14 Rear caliper leg spreading wedge (Sec 5)

A 51.5 mm (2.03 in)   C 56.0 mm (2.21 in)
B 8.0 mm (0.31 in)   D 35.0 mm (1.38 in)

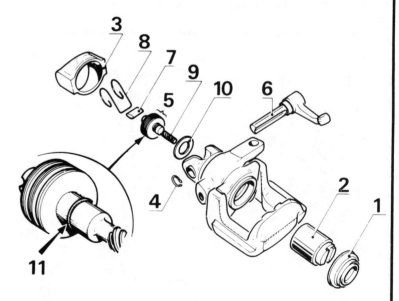

Fig. 9.15 Exploded view of rear brake caliper (Sec 6)

1 Dust excluder   7 Plunger
2 Piston   8 Spring
3 Dust cover   9 Adjusting screw
4 Circlip   10 Washer
5 Spring washers   11 O-ring
6 Handbrake operating shaft

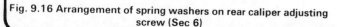

Fig. 9.16 Arrangement of spring washers on rear caliper adjusting screw (Sec 6)

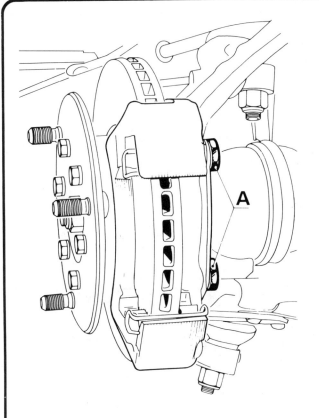
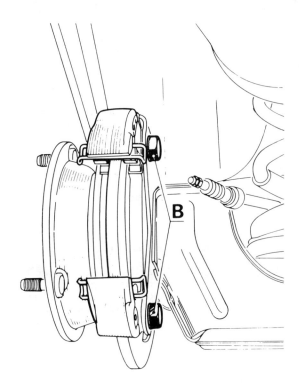

Fig. 9.17 Caliper bracket mounting bolts (all models except R1300) (Sec 7)

A   Front caliper   B   Rear caliper (Gordini)

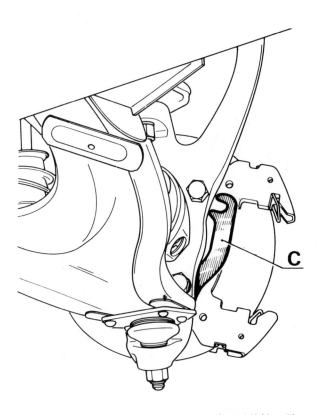
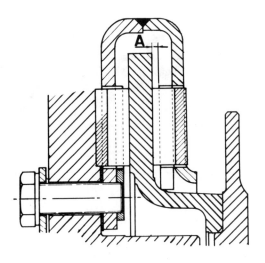

Fig. 9.19 Disc to bracket clearance (R1300) (Sec 7)

A   For values see text

Fig. 9.18 Caliper bracket mounting bolt (R1300) (Sec 7)

C   Shim

Clearance (A)	Shim thickness required
0.91 to 1.55 mm (0.036 to 0.061 in)	1.2 mm (0.047 in)
1.56 to 1.78 mm (0.062 to 0.070 in)	1.1 mm (0.039 in)
1.79 to 2.06 mm (0.071 to 0.081 in)	0.8 mm (0.032 in)
2.07 to 2.58 mm (0.082 to 0.101 in)	0.6 mm (0.024 in)
2.59 to 3.59 mm (0.102 to 0.136 in)	no shim required

8   Brake discs – removal and refitting

1   A deeply scored or unevenly worn disc must not be surface ground if its thickness will be reduced below the minimum specified (see Specifications). Fit a new disc under these circumstances.

Front disc
2   Raise the car, remove the roadwheel.
3   Remove the caliper and tie it up out of the way.
4   Unbolt the caliper bracket as described in the preceding Section.
5   Unscrew the stub axle nut. A lever located between two roadwheel studs will be required to prevent the hub from rotating, but take precautions to prevent damage to the stud threads.
6   Using a slide hammer attached to the roadwheel studs, pull the hub/disc off the driveshaft splines and out of the stub axle carrier. The hub outer bearing will come out attached to the hub (refer to Chapter 11, Section 10).
7   Unbolt and separate the hub from the brake disc.

Rear disc
8   Raise the car and remove the roadwheel.
9   Remove the caliper and tie it up out of the way. There is no need to disconnect the hydraulic hose.

10   Unbolt and remove the caliper bracket.
11   Remove the grease cap from the hub. This can be difficult, but the use of a sharp chisel or self-locking grips usually solves the problem although it is wise to have a spare cap available in case the original is damaged.
12   With the cap removed, extract the split pin, take off the nut retainer, unscrew the nut and remove the thrust washer.
13   Use a suitable three-legged extractor, to draw the hub/disc from the stub axle if it is tight.
14   Unbolt and separate the hub and disc.
15   Refitting the front disc is a reversal of removal, tighten all bolts to the specified torque. On R1300 models check the disc to bracket clearance as described in Section 7.
16   When refitting the rear hub, pack grease into the bearing and inside of the hub. Then refit the thrust washer and screw on the nut finger tight. Adjust the bearing preload in the following way.
17   Tighten the axle nut to a torque of 22 lbf ft (30 Nm) whilst turning the hub. Unscrew the nut and retighten it with the fingers until any end

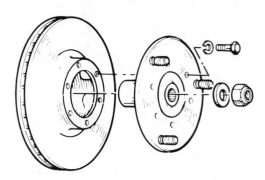

Fig. 9.20 Front hub/disc components (Sec 8)

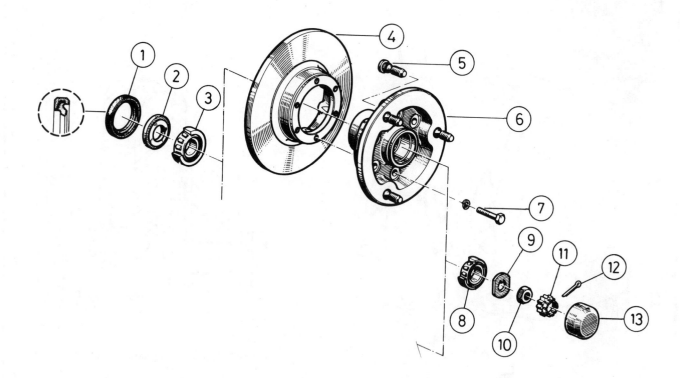

Fig. 9.21 Rear hub/disc components (Sec 8)

1 Oil seal	5 Roadwheel stud	8 Bearing	11 Nut retainer
2 Thrust ring	6 Hub	9 Thrust washer	12 Split pin
3 Bearing	7 Disc/hub connecting bolt	10 Nut	13 Grease cap
4 Disc			

play almost disappears. If a dial gauge is available, use this to achieve an endfloat of between 0.01 and 0.05 mm (0.001 and 0.002 in).

18 Fit the nut retainer and insert a new split pin.

19 Fill the grease cap half full with grease and tap it squarely into position.

20 On completion of refitting either a front or rear disc, apply the foot brake two or three times to bring the pads into contact with the discs.

21 Renewal of hub bearings is covered in Chapter 11.

9 Rear drum brakes – adjustment

1 On certain earlier models, the rear brakes are of manually adjustable type.

2 To adjust this type of brake it is recommended that a proper brake spanner is used to avoid damage to the squared adjuster.

3 Raise the roadwheels and turn either adjuster on the backplate until the wheel locks. Release the adjuster until the roadwheel is just free to turn. Repeat on the second adjuster of that wheel. Now adjust the brakes on the other rear wheel. Lower the car to the ground.

10 Rear shoe linings – checking for wear

1 Inspection of the shoe linings can only be carried out after removal of the hub/drum assembly. The drum is not separate from the hub.

2 Raise the rear of the car, remove the roadwheel.

3 Remove the grease cap, take out the split pin, remove the nut retainer, nut and thrust washer.

4 Pull the hub/drum from the stub axle. It is possible for a drum to be so badly grooved, due to not renewing the brake shoes in time, that

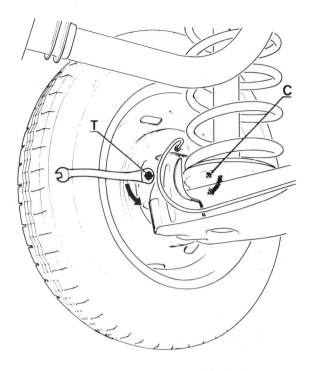

Fig. 9.22 Rear brake adjusters (C and T) (Sec 9)

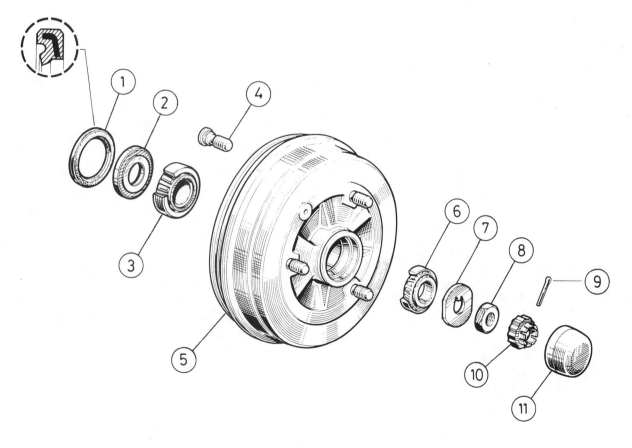

Fig. 9.23 Rear hub/drum components (Sec 10)

1 Oil seal	4 Roadwheel stud	7 Thrust washer	10 Nut retainer
2 Thrust washer	5 Brake drum	8 Nut	11 Grease cap
3 Bearing	6 Bearing	9 Split pin	

10.8A Fitting rear hub outer bearing and thrust washer (drum brake)

10.8B Fitting rear hub nut lock (drum brake)

10.8C Fitting grease cap to rear hub (drum brake)

the shoes bearing in the grooves have locked the drums to the axle and prevent their removal.

5   On manually adjusted brakes this problem can be overcome by completely slackening the adjusters.

6   On Girling and later type Bendix self-adjusting brakes, slacken the handbrake completely and prise out the blanking plug from the brake backplate.

7   Insert a screwdriver into the hole until it rests on the handbrake lever and then push the lever to free it from the stop peg on the brake shoe.

8   On earlier type Bendix self-adjusting brakes, remove the plug from the drum and insert a 5.0 mm (0.20 in) diameter rod through the hole to swivel the serrated sector from the serrated lever.

9   Brush away dust from the linings and drum interior taking care not to inhale it.

10 If the friction material has worn down to, or nearly down to, the rivet heads then the shoes must be renewed. Buy replacement shoes ready lined.

11 Renew the shoes as described in one of the following Sections according to type and as an axle set (four shoes).

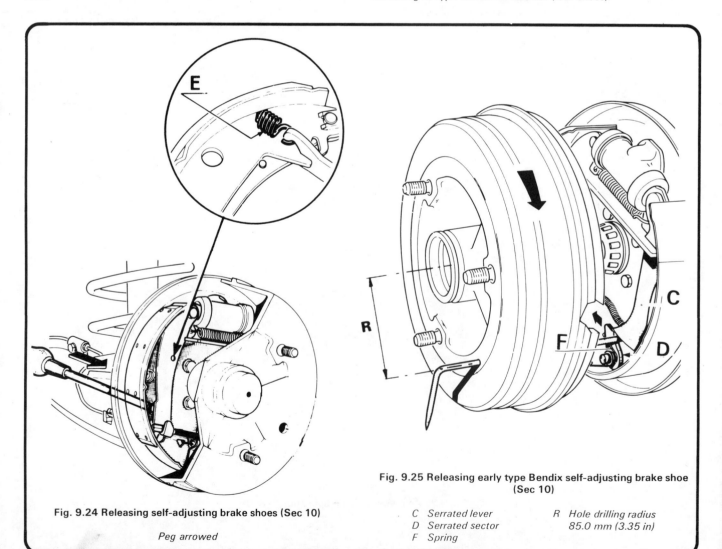

Fig. 9.24 Releasing self-adjusting brake shoes (Sec 10)

Peg arrowed

Fig. 9.25 Releasing early type Bendix self-adjusting brake shoe (Sec 10)

C   Serrated lever
D   Serrated sector
F   Spring
R   Hole drilling radius
      85.0 mm (3.35 in)

12 Refit the drum and adjust the bearing preload as described in Section 8 for disc brakes, the procedure being identical (photos).

11 Brake shoes (manual adjusters) – renewal

1   Refer to the preceding Section and remove the drum.
2   Slacken the adjusters completely and then note carefully the leading and trailing ends of the shoes (the end of the shoe not covered with friction material). Also mark the holes in the shoe webs into which the shoe return springs engage.
3   Fully slacken the handbrake cable adjuster and then disconnect the cable end fitting from the shoe lever.
4   Prise out the shoe steady clips, pull the shoes apart and take out the strut which is located between them.
5   Remove the brake shoes from the backplate together with the lower shoe return spring.
6   Reassemble the shoes so that their leading and trailing ends are as originally fitted. Reconnect the return springs, the shoe steady springs and handbrake cable.
7   Refit the drum as described in the preceding Section.
8   Repeat the operations on the opposite brake.
9   Adjust the shoes and the handbrake.

12 Brake shoes (Bendix self-adjusting) – renewal

1   Remove the brake drum as described in Section 10.
2   Note carefully the leading and trailing ends of the shoes also mark the holes in the shoe webs into which the shoe return springs engage (photo).
3   Fully slacken the handbrake cable adjuster and then disconnect the cable end fitting from the shoe lever.
4   Remove the shoe steady springs. Do this by inserting a blade of suitable width into the coil spring and turning it.
5   Disconnect the shoe upper return spring.

12.2 View of Bendix type self-adjusting rear brake

6   Pivot the serrated lever towards the stub axle and then prise the upper ends of the shoes apart. Release the strut.
7   Return the serrated sector to its original position.
8   Twist the leading brake shoe at right angles to the backplate.
9   Disconnect the end of the lower return spring with a screwdriver and withdraw both shoes.
10 Set the new shoes out in the original installed position with respect to leading and trailing ends and fit the serrated and handbrake levers to them.

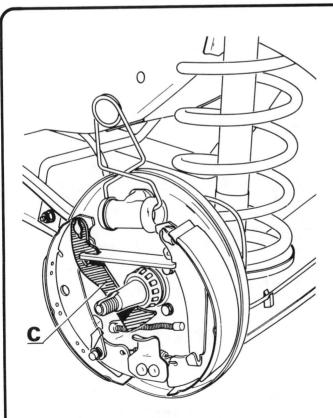

Fig. 9.26 Bendix rear brake self-adjuster serrated lever (C) (Sec 12)

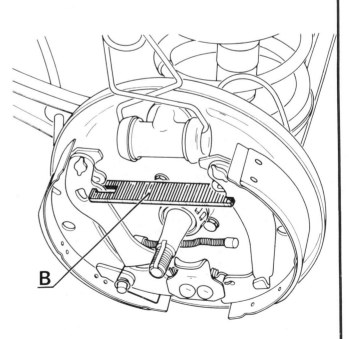

Fig. 9.27 Bendix rear shoe strut (B) (Sec 12)

11 Attach the tension spring and strut to the trailing shoe.
12 Refit the shoes, engaging the strut between them and the return springs.
13 Refit the steady springs.
14 At this stage, check the shoe strut clearance as shown in the diagram. If it is not very close to 1.0 mm (0.040 in) then the tension and return springs must be renewed.
15 Set the serrated lever and sector in such a position to give the maximum expansion to the shoes, but to allow the drum to be slid over them.
16 Refit the drum and adjust the bearings as described earlier in this Chapter.

17 Apply the foot brake several times to adjust the shoes.
18 Adjust the handbrake (Section 25).

13 Brake shoes (Girling self-adjusting) – renewal

1 Remove the drum as described in Section 10.
2 Fully release the handbrake cable and disconnect the cable from the shoe lever.
3 Note carefully the leading and trailing ends of the shoes, also mark the holes in the shoe webs into which the shoe webs engage.
4 Disconnect the shoe upper return spring and spring hook.

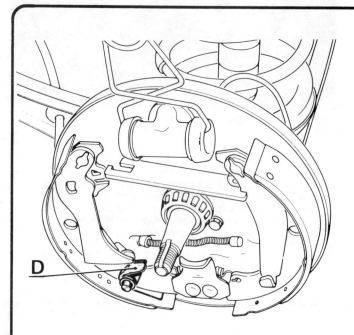

Fig. 9.28 Bendix spring-loaded serrated sector (D) (Sec 12)

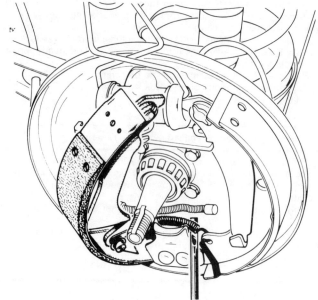

Fig. 9.29 Removing Bendix leading shoe (Sec 12)

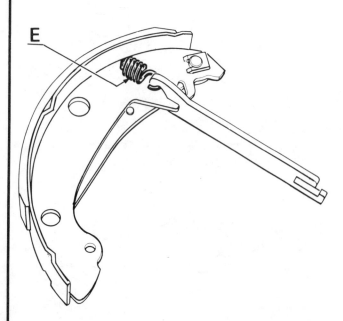

Fig. 9.30 Bendix trailing shoe and tension spring (E) (Sec 12)

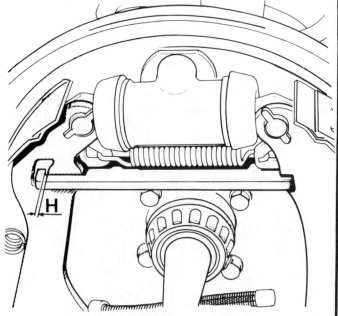

Fig. 9.31 Bendix shoe strut clearance (Sec 12)

H 1.0 mm (0.040 in)

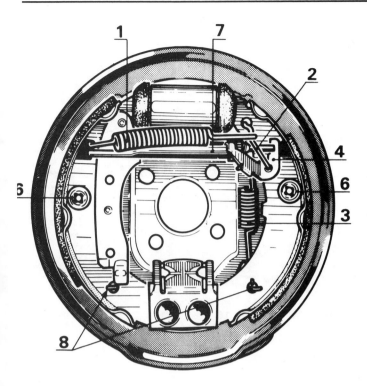

Fig. 9.32 Girling type rear brake (Sec 13)

1 Upper return spring   6 Shoe steady springs
2 Spring hook   7 Automatic adjuster strut
3 Ratchet spring   8 Shoe lower return spring
4 Ratchet

5   Unhook the ratchet spring which is connected to the self adjuster ratchet. Remove both the spring and the ratchet.
6   Remove the shoe steady springs and cups. Do this by gripping the edges of the cups with a pair of pliers, depressing them and turning them through a quarter turn before releasing them.
7   Remove the automatic adjuster strut.
8   Prise the shoes apart and remove them complete with return springs.
9   Set the new shoes out in the same installed position as the original and fit the handbrake lever to the shoe web.
10 Connect the lower return spring to the shoes and locate the spring behind the anchor plate with the shoes.
11 Fit the upper return spring and pull the shoes into position on the backplate. Remember to engage the adjuster strut between the shoes. The strut threads should be clean and greased and the strut retracted to its shortest length by rotation of the star wheel.
12 Refit the hook, self-adjuster ratchet and steady springs.
13 Connect the handbrake cable.
14 Expand the shoes by turning the star wheel until the brake drum will still just slide over them.
15 Refit the drum and adjust the bearings as described earlier in this Chapter.
16 Apply the foot brake several times to adjust the shoes.
17 Adjust the handbrake (Section 25).

14 Brake drum – renovation or renewal

1   Whenever a brake drum is removed take the opportunity to check the drum interior friction surface for deep scoring or grooving.
2   Provided the interior diameter will not be increased beyond that specified in Specifications, then the drum may be machined out.
3   If the internal diameter will be out of tolerance by such work then the drum must be renewed.
4   If a new drum is being fitted to brakes with automatic adjusters, drill a hole in accordance with the diagram so that the drum can be removed at a later date as described in Section 10.

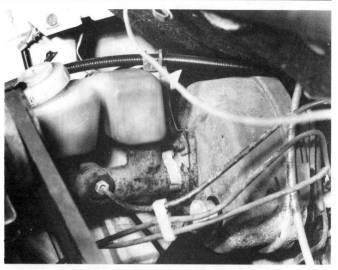

15.1 Master cylinder and servo unit

15 Master cylinder – removal and refitting

1   Using a syringe, syphon the fluid from the master cylinder reservoir (photo).
2   Remove the reservoir by pulling it upwards and rocking it from side to side until it releases from its rubber sealing collars.
3   Disconnect the electrical leads. These may be for the fluid level warning switch or the pressure differential switch or both according to model.
4   Disconnect the pipeline union nuts from the master cylinder.
5   Unbolt the master cylinder from the vacuum servo unit and remove the cylinder. If a pressure differential switch is fitted this will have to be unbolted before the master cylinder can be removed.
6   Before refitting the master cylinder, the operating clearance (X) must be checked. The clearance is measured between the end of the pushrod and the master cylinder to servo mounting face. If necessary, adjust by turning the pushrod nut (P) (Fig. 9.43).
7   Refit by reversing the removal operations.
8   Bleed the braking system on completion as described in Section 20.

16 Master cylinder – overhaul

1   On some models the master cylinder incorporates an integral pressure drop indicator warning switch. This type of cylinder cannot be overhauled, but must be renewed complete.
2   To overhaul a master cylinder without such a switch, remove it from the car and clean away external dirt.
3   Grip the cylinder carefully in the jaws of a vice.
4   Depress the pistons with a rod and unscrew and remove the stop screw.
5   Hold the pistons depressed while the circlip is extracted.
6   Release the pressure on the rod and the stop washer and primary piston will be ejected.
7   Shake out the secondary piston.
8   Examine the cylinder bore for scoring or metal to metal wear areas. If evident renew the master cylinder complete.
9   If the cylinder is in good condition wash it in methylated spirit or clean hydraulic fluid. Use nothing else.
10 The primary and secondary pistons are only supplied as complete assemblies, individual seals are not available.
11 Dip the components in clean hydraulic fluid and reassemble by reversing the dismantling operations.

17 Rear wheel cylinder – removal, overhaul and refitting

1   Remove the brake drum as described in Section 10.
2   Using pliers, disconnect the upper return spring from the shoes.

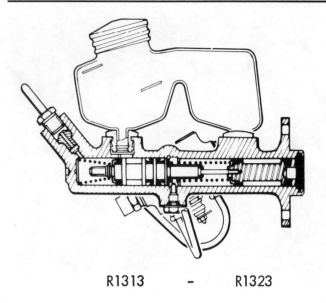
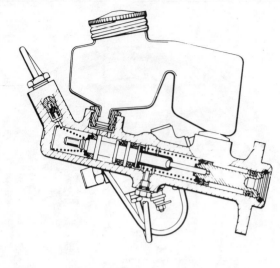

R1313   –   R1323   R1300 – R1302 – R1312 – R1322

Fig. 9.33 Sectional views of typical master cylinders (Sec 16)

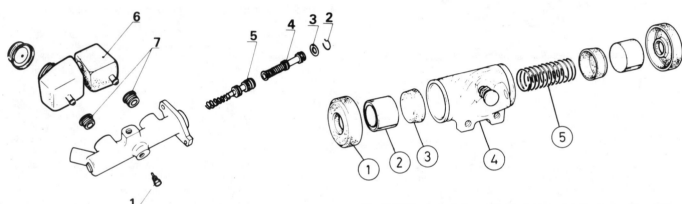

Fig. 9.34 Exploded view of brake master cylinder (Sec 16)

1	Stop screw	5	Secondary piston
2	Circlip	6	Fluid reservoir
3	Stop washer	7	Rubber seals
4	Primary piston		

Fig. 9.35 Exploded view of typical rear wheel cylinder (Sec 17)

1	Dust excluder	4	Cylinder
2	Piston	5	Return spring
3	Seal		

3   Pull the upper ends of the shoes apart.
4   Disconnect the brake pipe from the wheel cylinder and quickly cap the pipe to prevent loss of fluid.
5   Unscrew the two mounting bolts and withdraw the cylinder from the backplate.
6   Clean external dirt from the cylinder.
7   Pull off the dust excluders, withdraw the pistons, seals and springs.
8   Examine the surface of the pistons and cylinder bore. If they are scored, rusty or show metal to metal rubbed areas, renew the complete cylinder assembly.
9   If the piston and cylinder are in good condition, clean all parts in hydraulic fluid or methylated spirit – nothing else, and obtain a repair kit which will contain all the necessary renewable items. Refit the coil spring.
10 Discard the old seals and fit the new ones taking care not to cut the seal lips as they enter the cylinder.
11 Apply clean hydraulic fluid to the pistons and insert them in the cylinder bore.
12 Fit the new dust excluders.
13 Refit the wheel cylinder by reversing the removal operations.
14 Bleed the system on completion (see Section 20).

18 Pressure limiting valve – removal, refitting and adjustment

1   This valve is designed to limit hydraulic pressure to the rear wheels during heavy brake applications, in order to prevent rear wheel lock up.
2   The device is located under the floor panel towards the rear of the car and is connected through link rods to a wishbone which is sensitive to suspension height changes due to vehicle loading (photos).
3   To remove the valve, clamp the flexible hydraulic hose and disconnect it, also the rigid pipeline.
4   Disconnect the return spring.
5   Unbolt and remove the mounting bolts.
6   The valve is not repairable and if faulty must be renewed complete.
7   Refit by reversing the removal operations and then bleed the hydraulic circuit as described in Section 20.
8   The valve should now be adjusted by your dealer using a pressure gauge connected to one of the rear wheel cylinder bleed screws.
9   Temporary adjustment can be made by an on-the-road test by turning the threaded connecting link nuts up or down until there is no tendency for the rear wheels to lock under firm foot pedal applications. Shortening the effective length of the link increases the rear brake pressure, lengthening it reduces the pressure (delays rear wheel lock up).

18.2A Pressure limiting valve

18.2B Pressure limiting valve linkage

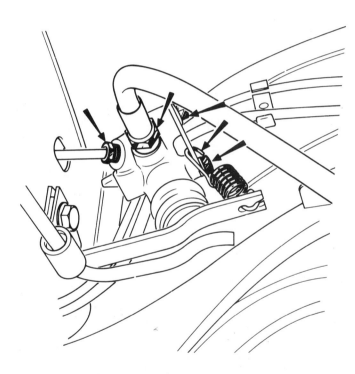

Fig. 9.36 Pressure limiting valve (Sec 18)

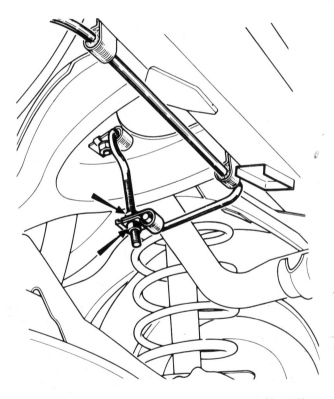

Fig. 9.37 Pressure limiting valve connecting link (Sec 18)

19 Pressure drop indicator – description, removal and refitting

1   The purpose of this device is to indicate, through a warning lamp, any drop in pressure in either one of the two brake hydraulic circuits caused by a leak.
2   A false warning may also occur if there is air in a circuit or if there is an internal fault in the master cylinder.
3   The device is basically a piston held in balance by the equal pressures of the two hydraulic circuits. Any pressure drop in one circuit will displace the piston which will close the electrical circuit and illuminate the warning lamp.
4   An alternative type of indicator switch is fitted to some models. On this switch, a bypass is incorporated to increase rear brake pressure in the event of a fluid leak in the front circuit.

5   To remove the pressure drop indicator which is located near to the master cylinder, first syphon the fluid from the master cylinder reservoir.
6   Disconnect the pipelines and the electrical load.
7   Unscrew the mounting bolt and remove the unit.
8   Refitting is a reversal of removal. Incline the unit downwards at its front end by about 30° from the master cylinder centre line.
9   Check that the pipelines are connected correctly to their original ports by reference to the diagram.
10   Bleed the complete system on completion.
11   On some later models the pressure drop indicator is integral with the master cylinder. This type of unit is not repairable, but must be renewed complete in the event of a fault developing in either the master cylinder or indicator sections.

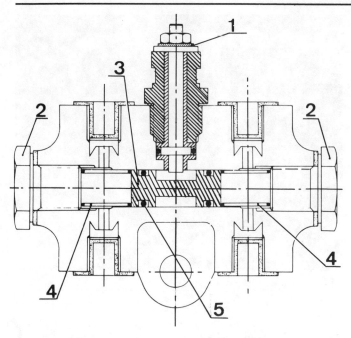

Fig. 9.38 Sectional view of pressure drop indicator without bypass
(Sec 19)

1	Electrical terminal	4	Springs
2	Sealing plugs	5	Seals
3	Piston		

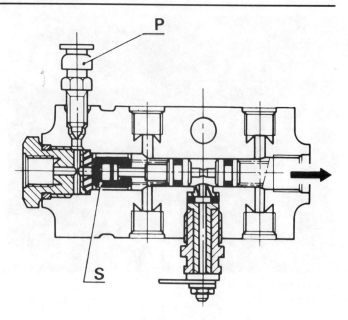

Fig. 9.39 Sectional view of pressure drop indicator with bypass
(Sec 19)

P Bleed screw   S Bypass circuit valve

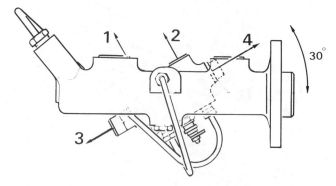

Fig. 9.41 Pressure drop indicator pipeline connections (Sec 19)

1	To RH front brake	3	To LH front brake
2	To rear brakes	4	To bypass circuit

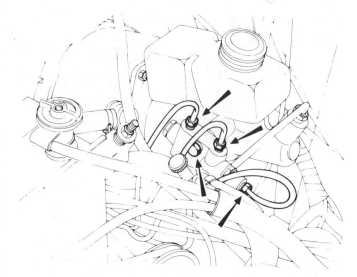

Fig. 9.40 Typical location of pressure drop indicator (Sec 19)

20 Braking system – bleeding

1   The front and rear brake hydraulic circuits are independent.
2   If the master cylinder or pressure drop indicator has been disconnected and reconnected then the complete system (both circuits) must be bled.
3   If only a component of one circuit has been disturbed then only that particular circuit must be bled.
4   If the entire system is being bled, the sequence of bleeding should be carried out by starting at the bleed screw furthest from the master cylinder and finishing at the one nearest to it. Unless the pressure bleeding method is being used, do not forget to keep the fluid level in the master cylinder reservoir topped up to prevent air from being drawn into the system which would make any work done worthless. If

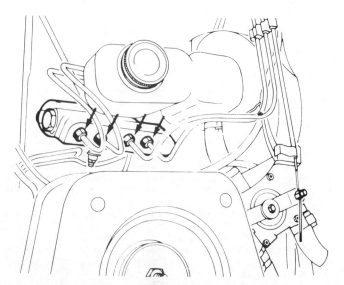

Fig. 9.42 Pressure drop indicator integral with master cylinder
(Sec 19)

a bypass tyre pressure drop indicator is fitted, the bleed screw on the indicator must be bled *after* all the other bleed screws have been bled.
5   Before commencing operations, check that all system hoses and pipes are in good condition with all unions tight and free from leaks.
6   Take great care not to allow hydraulic fluid to come into contact with the vehicle paintwork as it is an effective paint stripper. Wash off any spilled fluid immediately with cold water.
7   Destroy the servo vacuum by giving several applications of the brake pedal in quick succession.

Bleeding – two man method
8   Gather together a clean glass jar and a length of rubber or plastic tubing which will be a tight fit on the brake bleed screws.
9   Engage the help of an assistant.
10   Push one end of the bleed tube onto the first bleed screw and immerse the other end in the glass jar which should contain enough hydraulic fluid to cover the end of the tube.
11   Open the bleed screw one half a turn and have your assistant depress the brake pedal fully then slowly release it. Tighten the bleed screw at the end of each pedal downstroke to obviate any chance of air or fluid being drawn back into the system.
12   Repeat this operation until clean hydraulic fluid, free from air bubbles, can be seen coming through into the jar.
13   Tighten the bleed screw at the end of a pedal downstroke and remove the bleed tube. Bleed the remaining screws in a similar way.

Bleeding – using one-way valve kit
14   There is a number of one-man, one-way brake bleeding kits available from motor accessory shops. It is recommended that one of these kits is used wherever possible as it will greatly simplify the bleeding operation and also reduce the risk of air or fluid being drawn back into the system quite apart from being able to do the work without the help of an assistant.
15   To use the kit, connect the tube to the bleed screw and open the screw one half a turn.
16   Depress the brake pedal fully and slowly release it. The one-way valve in the kit will prevent expelled air from returning at the end of each pedal downstroke. Repeat this operation several times to be sure of ejecting all air from the system. Some kits include a translucent container which can be positioned so that the air bubbles can actually be seen being ejected from the system.
17   Tighten the bleed screw, remove the tube and repeat the operations on the remaining brakes.
18   On completion, depress the brake pedal. If it still feels spongy repeat the bleeding operation as air must still be trapped in the system.

Bleeding – using a pressure bleeding kit
19   These kits too are available from motor accessory shops and are usually operated by air pressure from the spare tyre.
20   By connecting a pressurised container to the master cylinder fluid reservoir, bleeding is then carried out by simply opening each bleed screw in turn and allowing the fluid to run out, rather like turning on a tap, until no air is visible in the expelled fluid.
21   By using this method, the large reserve of hydraulic fluid provides a safeguard against air being drawn into the master cylinder during bleeding which often occurs if the fluid level in the reservoir is not maintained.
22   Pressure bleeding is particularly effective when bleeding 'difficult' systems or when bleeding the complete system at time of routine fluid renewal.

All methods
23   When bleeding is completed, check and top up the fluid level in the master cylinder reservoir.
24   Check the feel of the brake pedal. If it feels at all spongy, air must still be present in the system and further bleeding is indicated. Failure to bleed satisfactorily after a reasonable repetition of the bleeding operations may be due to worn master cylinder seals.
25   Discard brake fluid which has been expelled. It is almost certain to be contaminated with moisture, air and dirt making it unsuitable for further use. Clean fluid should always be stored in an airtight container as it absorbs moisture readily (hygroscopic) which lowers its boiling point and could affect braking performance under severe conditions.

21 Hydraulic pipes and hoses – general

1   Hydraulic pipes and hoses should be examined periodically, the metal pipes being checked for signs of severe corrosion, and the rubber hoses for cracks. Both should be checked for any signs of chafing.
2   Renew any defective rubber hoses with new parts.
3   Metal pipes can sometimes be purchased complete and ready to fit. Alternatively, it will be necessary to have replacements made by an engineering concern who possess the necessary tools. When ordering, it is advisable to provide the manufacturer with the old pipe as a pattern.
4   Care should be taken to ensure that the correct metric pipe fittings and ends are supplied.

22 Servo (Master Vac) unit – description and testing

1   The brake servo unit operates from vacuum pressure supplied from the engine manifold. It is emphasised that it is servo assisted and

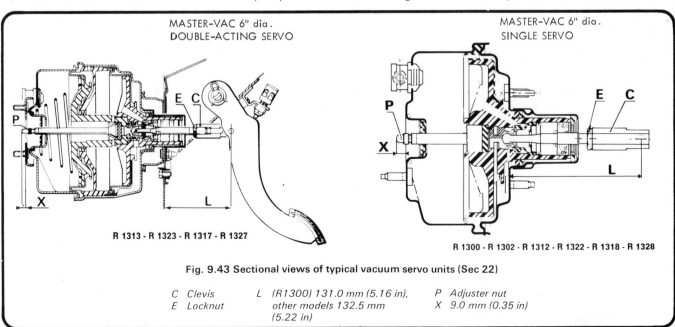

Fig. 9.43 Sectional views of typical vacuum servo units (Sec 22)

C Clevis
E Locknut
L (R1300) 131.0 mm (5.16 in), other models 132.5 mm (5.22 in)
P Adjuster nut
X 9.0 mm (0.35 in)

in the event of the unit failing then normal hydraulic braking will still be available by foot pressure.

2   Leaks in, or failure of, the servo unit may be detected by a sudden increase in the brake pedal pressure required to retard or stop the vehicle. Uneven running or stalling of the engine may also indicate leaks in the servo system.

3   Before carrying out any servicing of the unit, check for split or perished vacuum hose connections.

23 Servo (Master-Vac) – servicing

1   Servicing operations must be limited to the following components: the air filter and the non-return valve. Where failure or incorrect operation of the servo unit emanates from components other than those specified then the complete unit should be renewed on an exchange basis.

Air filter
2   At the intervals specified in Routine Maintenance, disconnect the push rod from the brake pedal, release the locknut and unscrew and remove the clevis fork.

3   Extract the spring clip which retains the air filter and pick out the filter element with a sharp pointed tool.

4   Fit the new filter by reversing the removal operations.

5   Set the dimension (L) before tightening the pushrod lock-nut.

Non-return valve
6   To renew the valve, disconnect the vacuum hose then pull and turn the valve to free it from its rubber grommet on the servo.

7   Pull out the grommet.

8   Fit a new grommet.

9   Smear a little brake fluid on the valve spigot and push it into the grommet taking care in the initial stages not to push the grommet into the servo shell.

24 Servo unit – removal and refitting

1   Disconnect the battery.

2   Syphon the hydraulic fluid from the master cylinder reservoir.

3   Disconnect the pipelines from the master cylinder.

4   Remove the pressure drop indicator mounting bolt.

5   Disconnect the vacuum hose from the servo or inlet manifold (photo).

6   Disconnect the pushrod from the brake pedal.

7   Working inside the car at the base of the steering column unscrew the two servo unit mounting nuts.

24.5 Brake servo hose connection at inlet manifold

8   Remove the servo. The master cylinder can be unbolted from it.

9   Refitting is a reversal of removal, but it is essential that dimensions L and X (Fig. 9.43) are complied with by altering the length of the pushrods.

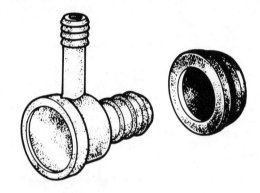
Fig. 9.45 Servo vacuum pipe connector (Sec 23)

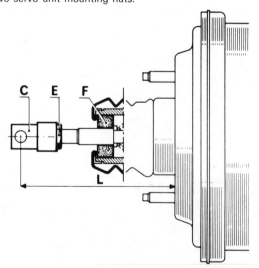
Fig. 9.44 Servo air filter fitting diagram (Sec 23)

C   Clevis
E   Locknut
F   Filter element

L   (R1300) 131.0 mm (5.16 in),
    all other models 132.5 mm
    (5.22 in)

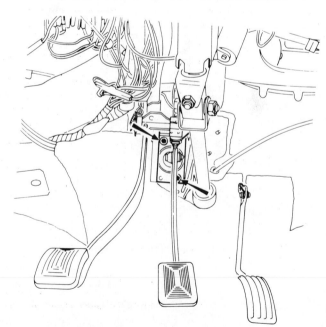
Fig. 9.46 Servo unit mounting nuts (Sec 24)

25.7 Handbrake cable equaliser

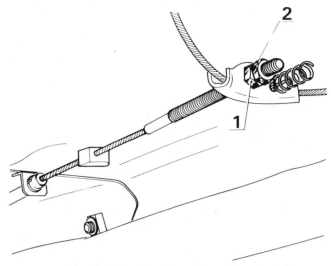

Fig. 9.47 Handbrake cable adjuster (manually adjusted rear brakes) (Sec 25)

1   Adjuster nut   2   Locknut

25 Handbrake cable – adjustment

Manually adjusted drum brakes and rear discs

1   Adjust the brake shoes (Section 9).
2   Raise the rear of the car, chock the roadwheels and release the handbrake fully.
3   Release the locknut at the equaliser, and then tighten the adjuster nut until by turning the roadwheels the linings are heard to just contact the drum.
4   The handbrake should now be fully applied after pulling it over six notches.
5   Adjust further if required and then tighten the locknut.

Automatically adjusted drum brakes

6   Have the car standing on level ground with the handbrake fully off.
7   Adjust the nut at the equaliser until there is a deflection at the centre of the secondary cable of 20.0 mm (0.79 in) under moderate hand pressure (photo).
8   The handbrake should now be fully applied after pulling it over 12 or 13 notches.

26 Handbrake control lever – removal and refitting

1   Release the handbrake fully.
2   Working inside the car unscrew the two bolts which hold the handbrake pivot bracket to the floor.
3   Withdraw the control lever sufficiently far to be able to disconnect the primary cable by pulling out the clevis pin.
4   Remove the control lever.
5   Refitting is a reversal of removal.

27 Handbrake cables – renewal

Primary cable

1   Remove the control lever as described in the preceding Section.
2   Unscrew the nuts and disconnect the primary cable from the equaliser.
3   Release the cable from its stop and remove the cable.

Secondary cable

4   Release the handbrake and unscrew the nuts at the equaliser to separate the primary cable from the equaliser.
5   On cars with drum brakes, remove the drums as previously described in this Chapter and disconnect the cable ends from the levers on the shoes.
6   On cars with rear disc brakes, slip the cable end fittings out of their seats in the caliper levers.

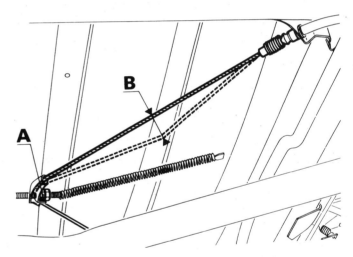

Fig. 9.48 Cable tension checking diagram (automatically adjusted rear brakes) (Sec 25)

A   Adjuster nut   B   Deflection 20.0 mm (0.79 in)

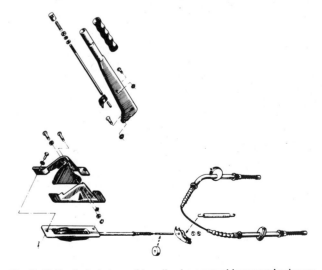

Fig. 9.49 Exploded view of handbrake control lever and primary cable (Sec 26)

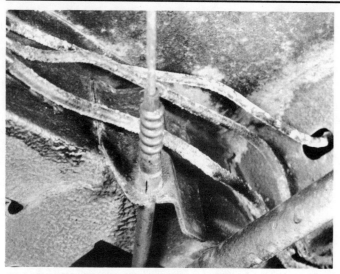

27.7 Handbrake cable support bracket

Fig. 9.50 Typical stop lamp switch (Sec 29)

7   Withdraw the cables with grommets through their body bracket apertures (photo).
8   Refitting is a reversal of removal, adjust on completion as described in Section 25.

28 Brake pedal – removal and refitting

Cars with manual transmission
1   The brake pedal operates on a common cross shaft with the clutch pedal and the removal and refitting operations are described in Chapter 5, Section 7.
2   When refitting the brake pedal, adjust the pushrod as shown in Fig. 9.43 dimension (L).

Cars with automatic transmission
3   Disconnect the pushrod from the pedal arm.
4   Extract the cross shaft clips, tap out the shaft and remove the pedal.
5   Refitting is a reversal of removal.

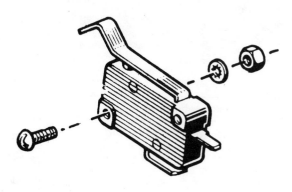

Fig. 9.51 Typical handbrake ON warning switch (Sec 29)

29 Brake switches

1   On all models a plunger type footbrake switch is used. Adjust if necessary by means of the switch fixing nuts so that the stop lamps come on when the switch plunger has emerged by 3.0 mm (0.12 in).
2   Where a handbrake ON warning switch is fitted, this is located at the base of the hand control lever. Any adjustment that may be required to the switch can be made by carefully bending the contact tab.

30 Fault diagnosis – braking system

Symptom	Reason(s)
Excessive pedal travel	Rear drum adjusters slack
	Self-adjusting mechanism to rear brakes not functioning
	Disc pads or linings badly worn
Poor braking, although pedal is firm	Disc pads or linings worn
	Disc or drums badly scored
	Seized piston in caliper or wheel cylinder
	Brake pads or linings of incorrect grade fitted
	Brake pads or linings contaminated
	Servo inoperative
Uneven braking, with vehicle swerving to one side	Seized piston in caliper or wheel cylinder
	Pads or linings contaminated
	Mixture of friction materials fitted
	Tyre pressures incorrect
Spongy brake pedal	Air in the hydraulic system
	Mounting bolts loose on one of the brake system components
	New disc pads or shoes not bedded-in
Pedal travels to floor, with minimal resistance and braking	Hydraulic system leak causing pressure loss
	Master cylinder not sustaining pressure

Chapter 10 Electrical system

Contents

Alternator – brush renewal 6	Instruments – removal and refitting 27
Alternator – description, maintenance and testing 4	Interior lamps – bulb renewal 24
Alternator – overhaul 7	Radio – fitting 37
Alternator – removal and refitting 5	Radio – interference suppression 38
Alternator diode carrier – renewal 8	Rocker switches – removal and refitting 18
Auxiliary driving lamps 39	Seat belt warning system 36
Battery – maintenance and precautions 2	Speedometer cable – renewal 28
Battery – removal and refitting 3	Starter motor – description 10
Courtesy lamp switch – removal and refitting 19	Starter motor – removal and refitting 12
Direction indicator, hazard warning unit 16	Starter motor – testing in car 11
Electric window winder – dismantling and reassembly 30	Starter motor (Ducellier) – overhaul 13
Exterior lamps – bulb renewal 23	Starter motor (Paris-Rhone) – overhaul 14
Fault diagnosis 41	Steering column switches – removal and refitting 17
Fuses and relays 15	Tailgate heated window 35
General description 1	Towing bracket wiring harness – fitting 40
Headlamp – bulb renewal 20	Voltage regulator 9
Headlamp beam – alignment 22	Windscreen washer 34
Headlamp or sealed beam unit – removal and refitting 21	Windscreen wiper blades and arms – removal and refitting 31
Horns 29	Windscreen wiper motor – overhaul 33
Instrument panel (to March 1976) – removal and refitting 25	Windscreen wiper motor and linkage – removal and refitting 32
Instrument panel (from March 1976) – removal and refitting 26	

Specifications

System type .... 12 volt negative earth, alternator, voltage regulator and pre-engaged starter

Battery .... 40 amp hour

Alternator
Type .... Paris-Rhone, Ducellier or SEV Motorola
Output .... 35, 40 or 50A at 14 volt according to model
Voltage regulator .... Remote, sealed relay type

Starter motor
Type .... Pre-engaged, Ducellier or Paris-Rhone
Output .... 740 to 1000 watts according to model
Brush length (new) .... 14.0 mm (0.55 in) or 15.0 mm (0.59 in) dependent upon model

Standard	**Minimum**
14.0 mm (0.55 in) length	8.0 mm (0.32 in)
Brush wear limit .... | 15.0 mm (0.59 in) length | 7.5 mm (0.30 in) |

Fuses
Early (typical)

Circuit No.	Circuit protected	Fuse rating (A)
A	Instrument panel, stop lamps, reversing lamps, heated tailgate window	15
B	Spare	–
C	Flasher relay	5
D	Heater booster fan	8
E	LH window winder	15
F	Right-hand window winder	15
G	Windscreen wiper	8
H	Sunroof	25
I	Electronic fuel injection system	8
J	Interior lamps, cigar lighter, clock	8

Later (typical)

1	Flasher relay, stop lamps, radio	8
2	Spare	–
3	LH headlamp (dipped)	5
4	Spare	–
5	RH headlamp (dipped)	5
6	Interior lamp, cigar lighter	8
7	LH headlamp (main) and indicator lamp	8
8	Windscreen wiper relay	16
9	RH headlamp (main)	8
10	Spare	–
11	Spare	16
12	Fuel pump relay (R.1328)	5
13	Spare	16
14	Automatic transmission or reverse lamps	5
15	Reverse lamp switch (R.1326) heated tailgate window	16
16	Instrument panel, windscreen wiper relay, wiper delay relay	5
17	Heater booster fan rheostat air conditioning	16

Bulbs (typical)

Lamp	Wattage	Type number
Headlamp	40/45	–
Quartz iodine	55	–
Sealed beam	–	4001, 4002
Parking, side marker and rear number plate	5	R19
Direction indicators	21	P25/1
Stop/tail	5/21	P25/2
Reversing lamps	21	P25/1
Car interior	5	C11 festoon
Warning, indicator instrument panel illumination	2	Wedge base

1 General description

The electrical system is a 12 volt negative earth type. The major components consist of a battery, an alternator for charging purposes, and a starter motor.

Where components are connected into the electrical system, the greatest care should be taken to see that correct polarities are observed. Failure to observe this precaution may result in irreparable damage to the items concerned.

If battery charging is to be carried out, the battery should first be disconnected. The same applies if repairs involving electric arc welding are to be carried out.

2 Battery – maintenance and precautions

1 Check the battery electrolyte level every week (photo).
2 Top up the battery as necessary, so that the plates are just

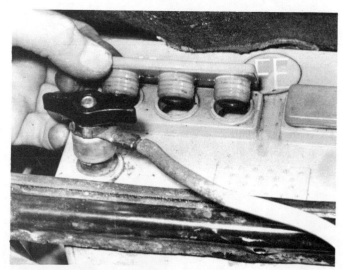

2.1 Battery vent/filler plugs (typical)

covered. Do not overfill, and use only distilled water.
3 Keep the battery top clean.
4 Keep the battery terminals and connections clean, and greased with petroleum jelly.
5 When charging the battery from an external source, do not use any naked lights in the vicinity, as the danger of an explosion caused by igniting of the battery gases is a very real one. Charging from an external source, at a low rate, can be advisable during the winter time when battery loading can be very heavy.
6 Any loss of acid can only be due to a leak in the battery casing or spillage during careless handling.
7 Leave the addition of acid or electrolyte to your service station or battery specialist.
8 An indication of battery charge can be obtained using a hydrometer and the following tables.

Table A – Specific gravity – battery fully charged

1.268 at 100°F or 38°C electrolyte temperature
1.272 at 90°F or 32°C electrolyte temperature
1.276 at 80°F or 27°C electrolyte temperature
1.280 at 70°F or 21°C electrolyte temperature
1.284 at 60°F or 16°C electrolyte temperature
1.288 at 50°F or 10°C electrolyte temperature
1.292 at 40°F or 4°C electrolyte temperature
1.296 at 30°F or −1.5°C electrolyte temperature

Table B – Specific gravity – battery fully discharged

1.098 at 100°F or 38°C electrolyte temperature
1.102 at 90°F or 32°C electrolyte temperature
1.106 at 80°F or 27°C electrolyte temperature
1.110 at 70°F or 21°C electrolyte temperature
1.114 at 60°F or 16°C electrolyte temperature
1.118 at 50°F or 10°C electrolyte temperature
1.122 at 40°F or 4°C electrolyte temperature
1.126 at 30°F or −1.5°C electrolyte temperature

3 Battery – removal and refitting

1 The battery is located in the centre of the engine compartment rear bulkhead.
2 Disconnect the negative lead and then the positive lead.

3   Release the spring-loaded nuts on the battery clamp, swivel the clamp bar upwards and remove the battery.

4   Refitting is a reversal of removal.

4   Alternator – description, maintenance and testing

1   One of three different makes of alternator may be fitted dependent upon source of supply (photo).

2   The alternator is a machine which generates alternating current, which is then rectified by diodes into direct current. Very little attention is required.

3   Certain precautions must be taken to prevent damage to the alternator system, as follows:

   (a)   *Always disconnect the battery before removing the alternator*
   (b)   *When the alternator is running, the connections must always be properly made, ie the positive terminal connected to the battery, and the alternator and battery negative terminals earthed*
   (c)   *Never disconnect the battery or the regulator when the engine is running*
   (d)   *Ensure that the regulator earth connection is always properly made*

4   To test the alternator, a voltmeter will be required, connected to the battery terminals.

5   Start the engine and allow it to idle. Switch off all electrical accessories. A reading of 14 volts should be indicated on the meter.

6   Increase the engine speed to 2000 rev/min when 15 volts should be indicated.

7   Hold the engine speed at 2000 rev/min and switch on the headlamps, heater booster fan, heated rear window and wiper motor.

4.1 Alternator mounting and adjuster link

8   The indicated voltage should be between 13 and 14 volts.

9   If the indicated voltages are not as specified, the alternator should be removed for more extensive testing by your local Renault dealer or automotive electrical engineer and subsequent overhaul.

10   If the unit has seen considerable service, consider changing it for a new or reconditioned unit.

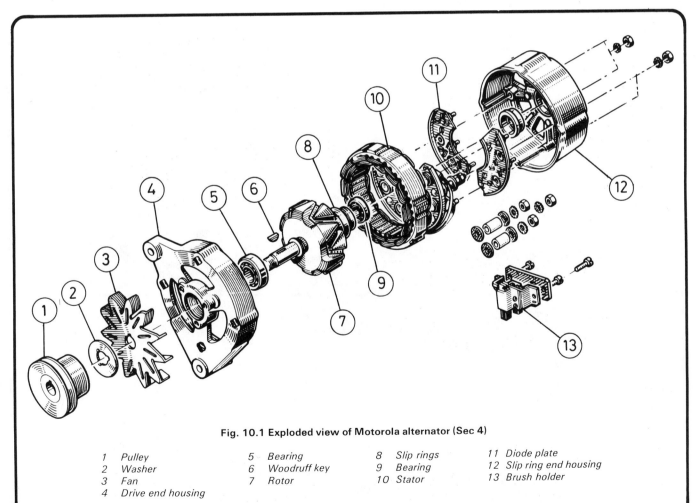

Fig. 10.1 Exploded view of Motorola alternator (Sec 4)

1 Pulley	5 Bearing	8 Slip rings	11 Diode plate
2 Washer	6 Woodruff key	9 Bearing	12 Slip ring end housing
3 Fan	7 Rotor	10 Stator	13 Brush holder
4 Drive end housing			

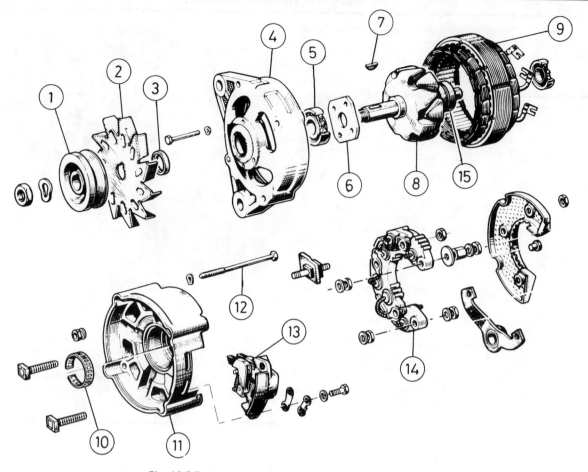

Fig. 10.2 Exploded view of Paris-Rhone alternator (Sec 4)

1	Pulley	5	Bearing	9	Stator	13	Brush holder
2	Fan	6	Retainer plate	10	Special sleeve	14	Diode carrier
3	Spacer	7	Woodruff key	11	Slip ring end housing	15	Slip rings
4	Drive end housing	8	Rotor	12	Tie bolt		

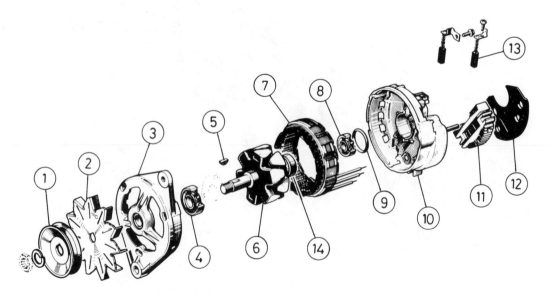

Fig. 10.3 Exploded view of Ducellier alternator (Sec 4)

1	Pulley	5	Woodruff key	9	Seal	12	End plate
2	Fan	6	Rotor	10	Slip ring end housing	13	Brushes
3	Drive end housing	7	Stator	11	Diode plate, brush holder	14	Slip rings
4	Bearing	8	Bearing				

5 Alternator – removal and refitting

1   Disconnect the battery.
2   Disconnect the leads (A) from the rear of the alternator. The leads cannot be mixed up as they have different connectors.
3   Release the bolt (B) at the adjuster link also the mounting bolt (C) and then push the alternator in towards the engine as far as possible and slip the drivebelt from the pulleys. Do not use a lever to prise the belt over the pulley rim, but rotate the pulley by means of its fixing nut and at the same time prise the belt up and over the rim with the fingers.
4   Remove the adjuster link and fixing bolts and remove the alternator from its mounting.

5   Refitting is a reversal of removal, but tension the drivebelt as described in Chapter 2, Section 6.

6 Alternator – brush renewal

1   Although the alternator need not be removed for this operation, it will certainly be made easier if it is (refer to preceding Section).

Paris-Rhone and Motorola
2   Extract the two screws which retain the brush holder. Withdraw the brush holder assembly.

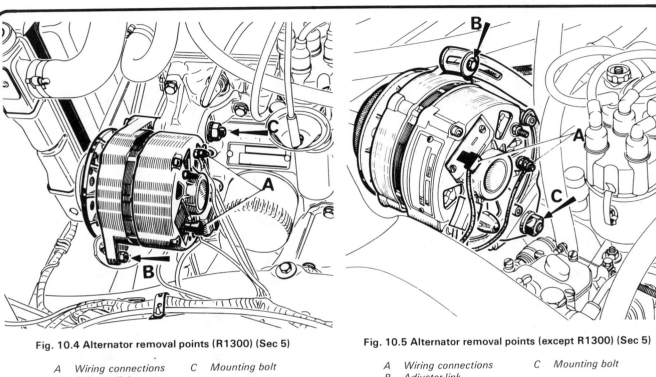

Fig. 10.4 Alternator removal points (R1300) (Sec 5)

A   *Wiring connections*   C   *Mounting bolt*
B   *Adjuster link*

Fig. 10.5 Alternator removal points (except R1300) (Sec 5)

A   *Wiring connections*   C   *Mounting bolt*
B   *Adjuster link*

SEV-MOTOROLA

PARIS-RHONE

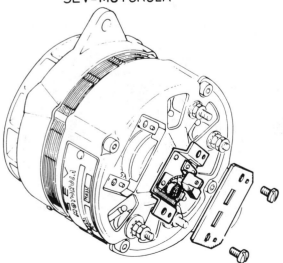

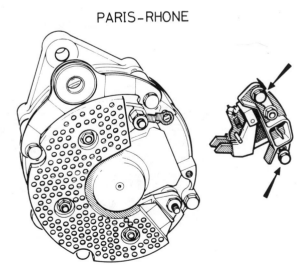

Fig. 10.6 Alternator brush holder arrangement (Sec 6)

(Motorola and Paris-Rhone)

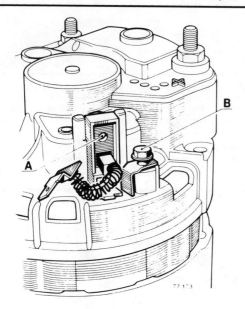

Fig. 10.7 Alternator brush holder (Ducellier) (Sec 6)

Ducellier

3   This type of alternator does not have a detachable brush holder and the brushes are retained by two screws A and B.
4   Refitting of all types is a reversal of removal.

7   Alternator – overhaul

1   The operations are similar for all makes of alternator, any detail differences will be observed from the illustrations.
2   With the unit removed from the car, clean away external dirt and grease.
3   Remove the brushes or brush holders as described in the preceding Section.
4   Unscrew the pulley nut. The safest way to do this to avoid damaging the pulley is to keep the drivebelt in the pulley groove and exert the pressure of the vice jaws on the belt. This will prevent the pulley turning as the nut is unscrewed.
5   An extractor will not normally be required to pull off the pulley, but two screwdrivers placed at opposite sides of the pulley will assist its removal.
6   Remove the nuts from the ends of the tie-rods.
7   Insert a screwdriver in the slots which are located between the

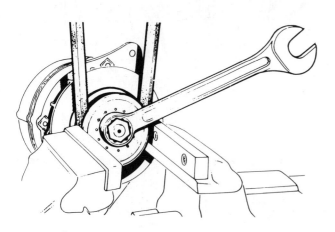

Fig. 10.8 Releasing alternator pulley nut (Sec 7)

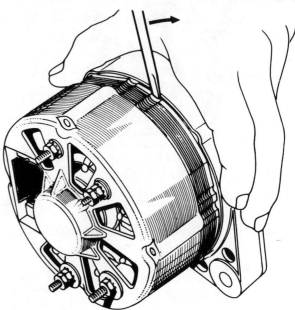

Fig. 10.9 Prising stator and drive end housing apart (Sec 7)

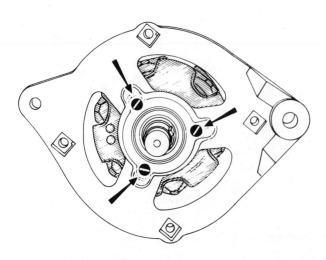

Fig. 10.10 Drive end bracket bearing retainer plate (Sec 7)

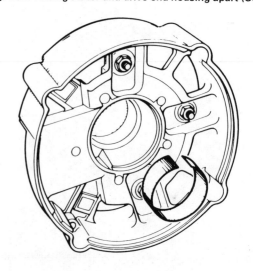

Fig. 10.11 Special sleeve being fitted to slip ring end housing (Paris-Rhone alternator) (Sec 6)

stator and the drive end bracket housing. Prise the assembly apart so that the rotor and drive end bracket come away as one. Take care not to insert the screwdriver too far or the stator windings may be damaged.

8   Extract the drive end bracket bearing retainer plate.

9   Free the rotor bearing by tapping the end of the shaft on a block of wood if it is intended to renew the bearing. The slip rings should be cleaned and if necessary polished with fine glass paper.

10 The rotor bearings may be removed using a two-legged puller. Don't forget to extract the Woodruff key before withdrawing the front bearing.

11 Press the new bearings into position using a piece of tubing applied to the bearing inner track.

12 Reassembly is a reversal of dismantling but on Paris-Rhone alternators make sure that the special sleeve is located fully at the bottom of its bore in the slip ring end housing.

8   Alternator diode carrier – renewal

Paris-Rhone
1   Remove the cover from the end of the alternator.
2   Remove the diode carrier fixing nuts and link.
3   Withdraw the diode carrier.

Motorola
4   Remove the four fixing nuts with their star washers and two insulating washers from the diode carrier.
5   Separate the stator and diode carrier from the slip ring end bearing.

Ducellier
6   On these units, the diode carrier can only be removed by unsoldering the three wires after removal of the end cover. Use a pair of long-nosed pliers as a heat sink as shown to prevent the heat travelling and damaging adjacent components.
7   Refitting is a reversal of removal, but observe the following essential points in connection with Motorola units.
8   Make sure that the insulating sleeves are correctly positioned on the positive diode carrier.
9   Space the wires which lead to the diodes neatly and check that they do not touch the rotor.

9   Voltage regulator

1   The voltage regulator is located on the left-hand wing valance within the engine compartment (photo).
2   If the battery is found to be in a continually discharged state or if

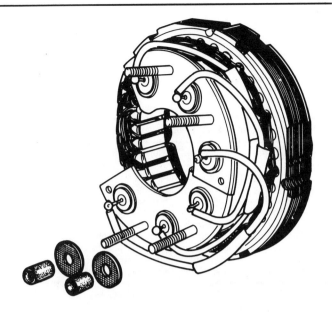
Fig. 10.13 Diode carrier (Motorola) (Sec 8)

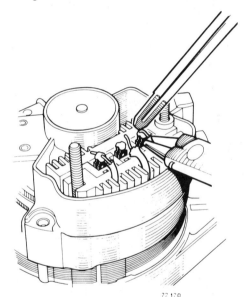
Fig. 10.14 Unsoldering diode carrier (Ducellier) (Sec 8)

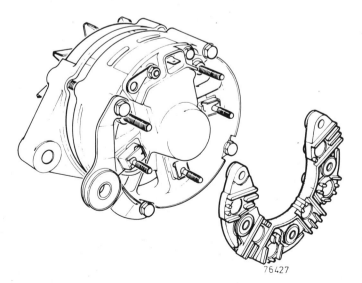
Fig. 10.12 Diode carrier and link (Paris-Rhone alternator) (Sec 8)

9.1 Voltage regulator

it is being continually overcharged and requires frequent topping up, first check the alternator (see Section 4) and if it is in order, renew the voltage regulator as a unit.

3   To remove the voltage regulator, first identify the leads on their terminals and then disconnect them.

4   Remove the securing screws.

5   Refitting is a reversal of removal.

10 Starter motor – description

1   The starter motor may be one of two makes, either Ducellier or Paris-Rhone.

2   The starter is of pre-engaged type and operates through the medium of a solenoid switch and plunger which meshes the starter drive with the ring gear on the flywheel (or torque converter – automatic transmission) fractionally in advance of the closure of the main starter motor contacts. This slight delay in energising the starter motor does much to extend the life of the starter drive and ring gear components. As soon as the engine fires and its speed of rotation exceeds that of the armature shaft of the starter motor, a built-in clutch mechanism prevents excessive rotation of the shaft and the release of the starter switch key causes the solenoid and drive engagement fork to return to their de-energised positions.

11 Starter motor – testing in car

1   If the starter motor fails to operate, check the state of charge of

the battery by testing the specific gravity with a hydrometer or switching on the headlamps. If they glow brightly for several seconds and then gradually dim, then the battery is in an uncharged state.

2   If the tests prove the battery to be fully charged, check the security of the battery leads at the battery terminals, scraping away any deposits which are preventing a good contact between the cable clamps and the terminal posts.

3   Check the battery negative lead at its body frame terminal, scraping the mating faces clean if necessary.

4   Check the security of the cables at the starter motor and solenoid switch terminals.

5   Check the wiring with a voltmeter for breaks or short circuits.

6   Check the wiring connections at the ignition/starter switch terminals.

7   If everything is in order, remove the starter motor as described in the next Section and dismantle, test and service as described later in this Chapter.

12 Starter motor – removal and refitting

Models except R1318, R1328

1   Disconnect the battery.

2   Disconnect the thick (positive) lead from the solenoid terminal also the thin solenoid feed wire.

3   Unbolt and remove the heat shield from the bottom of the exhaust manifold (photo).

4   Unscrew and remove the starter mounting flange bolts (photo).

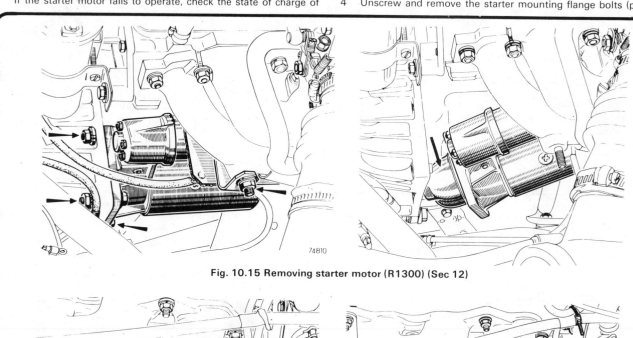

Fig. 10.15 Removing starter motor (R1300) (Sec 12)

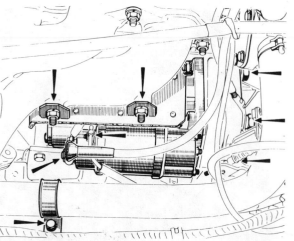
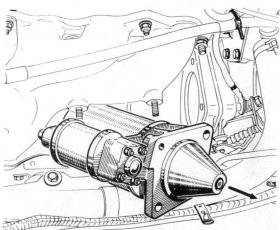

Fig. 10.16 Removing starter motor (R1302, R1312, R1313, R1317, R1323, R1327) (Sec 12)

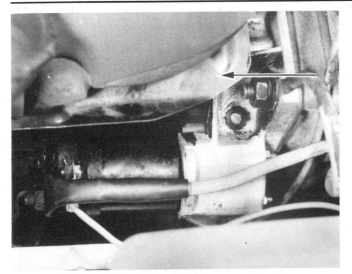

12.3 Starter motor heat shield (arrowed)

12.4 Starter motor mounting bolt

5   Partially withdraw the starter and then twist or tilt it to clear the exhaust manifold and remove it from the engine compartment.

R1318, R1328 models
6   Starter motors fitted to these models have a rear support bracket attached to the engine mounting. This must be disconnected and the bracket tilted forward otherwise the removal operations are as described in earlier paragraphs.

13 Starter motor (Ducellier) – overhaul

1   Remove the starter as previously described and clean away external dirt.
2   Extract the screws and take off the rear cover.
3   Remove the bolt which is now exposed from the centre of the armature shaft.

4   Withdraw the yoke, sliding it off the tie bolts.
5   Remove the solenoid fixing nuts.
6   Extract the wire clip and tap out the coupling fork pivot pin.
7   Remove the armature and solenoid.
8   If the commutator is dirty or burnt clean it with a fuel soaked rag and where necessary, polish it evenly with fine glasspaper. If the commutator is in really bad condition, check with your local auto electrical agent the advisability of having it skimmed.
9   The mica insulators which are located between the copper segments of the commutator must be undercut to a depth of 0.5 mm (0.020 in). Carry out this work carefully using a piece of hacksaw blade of suitable width.
10 Check the condition of the bush in the drive end housing and renew it if it is worn.
11 Check the teeth on the drive pinion for chipping also that the one-way clutch turns in one direction only.
12 The starter drive can be removed from the armature shaft if the stop ring is tapped down the shaft to expose the jump ring. Extract the

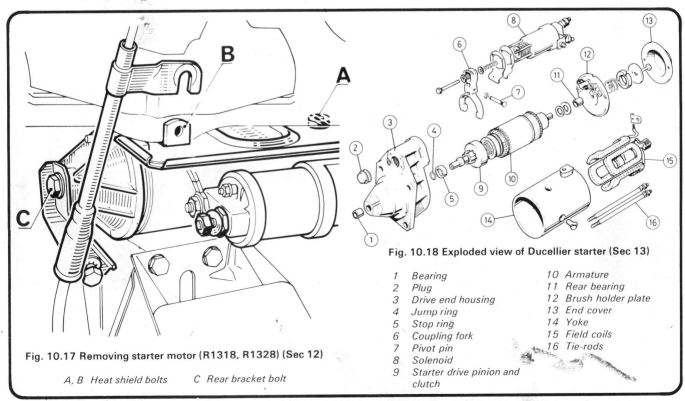

Fig. 10.17 Removing starter motor (R1318, R1328) (Sec 12)

A, B Heat shield bolts   C Rear bracket bolt

Fig. 10.18 Exploded view of Ducellier starter (Sec 13)

1 Bearing	10 Armature
2 Plug	11 Rear bearing
3 Drive end housing	12 Brush holder plate
4 Jump ring	13 End cover
5 Stop ring	14 Yoke
6 Coupling fork	15 Field coils
7 Pivot pin	16 Tie-rods
8 Solenoid	
9 Starter drive pinion and clutch	

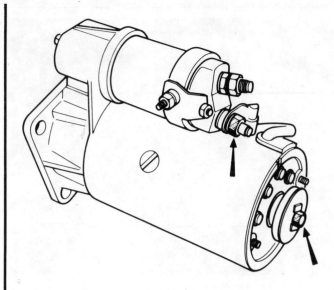

Fig. 10.19 Ducellier starter with rear cover removed (Sec 13)

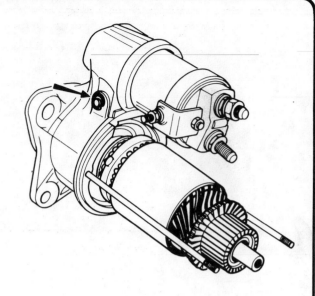

Fig. 10.20 Ducellier starter with yoke removed (Sec 13)

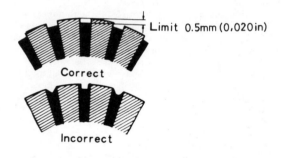

Fig. 10.21 Starter motor commutator insulator undercutting diagram (Sec 13)

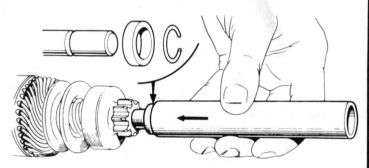

Fig. 10.22 Driving stop ring down armature shaft (Sec 13)

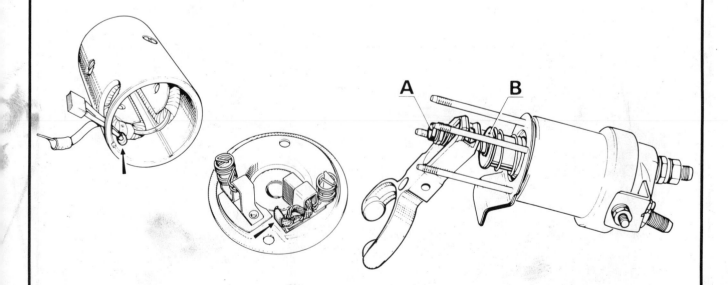

Fig. 10.23 Starter motor brush lead disconnection points (Sec 13)

Fig. 10.24 Ducellier starter solenoid and coupling fork (Sec 13)

A   Securing screw   B   Armature core

jump ring and pull off the drivegear using a small two legged extractor if necessary.

13 If the starter drive is removed from a type 6183 starter armature then when reassembling the components, align the drive with the armature so that the dogs engage correctly in their slots.

14 The brushes must be renewed if they have worn to or below their minimum specified length. To do this, the old brushes will have to be unsoldered at the points indicated by arrows in the illustration. Grip the brush lead close to the disconnection point with a pair of pliers. These will act as a heat sink and prevent heat damage to adjacent wiring. Re-solder the new brushes into position.

15 The coupling fork can be separated from the solenoid by gripping the solenoid core (B) while the screw (A) is removed.

16 Commence reassembly by lubricating the bush in the drive end housing and inserting the armature and solenoid into the housing with the coupling fork.

17 Fit the solenoid fixing nuts and then drive in the fork pivot pin and

engage its retaining spring clip.

18 Fit the fibre washer to the armature shaft followed by the plain steel washer.

19 Apply grease to the rear bush and then fit the yoke, the rear bearing, spring and washers. Check that the spring ends engage in the washer slots and ease the brushes onto the commutator by pulling them back into their holders with a piece of wire.

20 Screw in and tighten the armature shaft bolt.

21 Fit the rear cover.

22 The solenoid coupling fork must now be adjusted.

23 Prise out the plug from the front of the solenoid and check that only the smallest amount of play exists between the bolt and adjusting nut.

24 The starter drive should be resting against the armature.

25 Now press the solenoid bolt in with the finger and check that the clearance (G) is between 0.05 and 1.5 mm (0.002 and 0.059 in). Adjust the clearance as necessary by turning the adjusting nut (1).

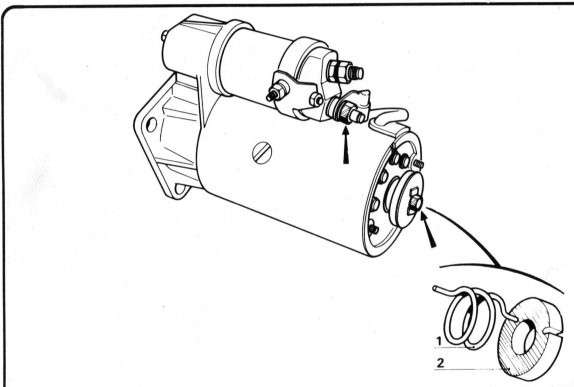

Fig. 10.25 Ducellier brush holder plate showing spring and washer arrangement (Sec 13)

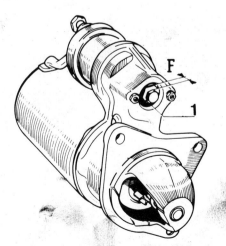

Fig. 10.26 Ducellier starter with solenoid plug removed (Sec 13)

F = Minimum clearance
1   Adjusting nut

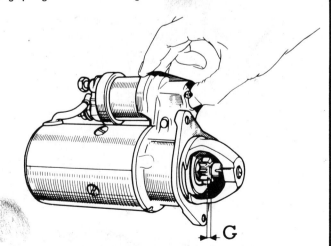

Fig. 10.27 Checking starter pinion protrusion on Ducellier starter (Sec 13)

G = 0.05 to 1.5 mm (0.002 to 0.059 in)

14 Starter motor (Paris-Rhone) – overhaul

1   Remove the starter motor as previously described and clean away external dirt.
2   Disconnect the heavy wire from the solenoid terminal.
3   Tap off the black plastic cap from the centre of the rear bearing/brush carrier plate.
4   Unscrew and remove the small bolt now exposed at the end of the armature shaft. To prevent the shaft from rotating while the bolt is unscrewed, use a screwdriver to join the pinion gear teeth in the drive end housing. Retain the bolt washers in their originally fitted sequence.
5   Unscrew and remove the tie-bolts or the nuts from the tie-rods, according to type.
6   Withdraw the rear bearing/brush carrier plate keeping the shaft washers in their originally fitted sequence.
7   Withdraw the yoke. Brush or blow out the dust, but on no account clean the field coils with solvent.
8   Extract the spring clip from the end of the coupling fork pivot pin. Tap out the pin and then unscrew the solenoid fixing nuts from the drive end housing.
9   Withdraw the armature and the solenoid from the drive end housing.
10 Inspect and renovate the commutator as described in the preceding Section.
11 Dismantle the starter drive as described for the Ducellier type starter.

12 Brush renewal is also as described in the preceding Section.
13 The coupling fork can be separated from the solenoid by screwing in the adjuster screw (A) until it frees from the nylon stop nut.
14 When reassembling the fork note that the apex (B) of its profile is away from the solenoid. Wind the adjuster screw into the stop nut. Then check that as the cut-away portions of the nylon stop nut and the nylon bush mate, they are located correctly. Continue to turn the adjuster screw until the overlap of the stop nut is about 3.0 mm (0.125 in). This setting is accurate enough for reassembly until the final adjustment is made as described in Paragraph 26.
15 Commence reassembly by applying grease to the bush in the drive end housing.
16 Fit the armature shaft into the drive end housing, positioning the thrust washers and intermediate bearing plate on Type D 8 E 71, D 8 E 118 and D 10 E 54 starters as shown in the diagram.
17 Fit the solenoid with coupling fork onto the drive end housing.
18 Tighten the solenoid fixing nuts, tap in the coupling fork pivot pin and then fit the clip to the end of the pin.
19 Fit the thrust washers against the end-face of the commutator on the armature shaft in their original sequence.
20 Slide on the yoke, aligning its locating pip in the small notch in the rim of the drive end housing, and positioning the rubber wedge correctly between the solenoid and yoke.
21 Apply grease to the bush in the rear bearing/brush holder plate and then fit the plate. This can only be achieved by inserting a thin screwdriver between the plate and yoke and pressing the brushes back into their holders in order to ease them onto the commutator. Make

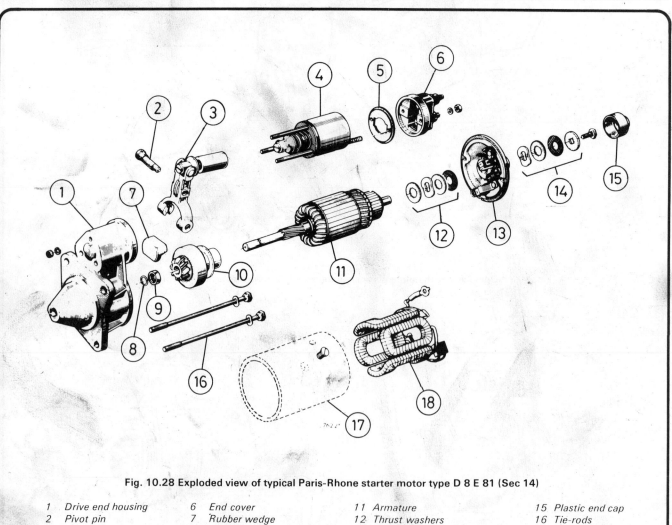

Fig. 10.28 Exploded view of typical Paris-Rhone starter motor type D 8 E 81 (Sec 14)

1 Drive end housing	6 End cover	11 Armature	15 Plastic end cap
2 Pivot pin	7 Rubber wedge	12 Thrust washers	16 Tie-rods
3 Coupling fork	8 Jump ring	13 Rear bearing/brush holder plate	17 Yoke
4 Solenoid	9 Stop ring	14 Thrust washers	18 Field coils
5 Endplate	10 Drive pinion and clutch		

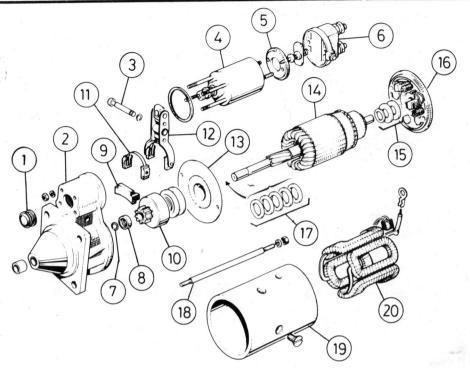

Fig. 10.29 Exploded view of Paris Rhone starter motor (Type D 8 E 71, D 10 E 54, D 8 E 118)

1	Plug	7	Jump ring	12	Coupling fork
2	Drive end housing	8	Stop ring	13	Intermediate bearing
3	Pivot pin	9	Rubber wedge	14	Armature
4	Solenoid	10	Drive pinion and clutch	15	Thrust washers
5	Plate	11	Coupling fork slides	16	Rear bearing/brush holder plate
6	End cover				

17 Thrust washers
18 Tie-rod
19 Yoke
20 Field coils

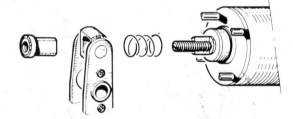

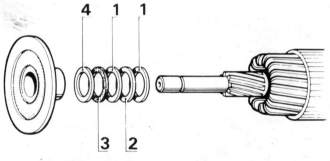

Fig. 10.31 Thrust washer arrangement on Paris-Rhone starter motor type D 8 E 71, D 10 E 54 and D 8 E 118 (Sec 14)

1 Steel washers   3 Fibre washer
2 Wave washers   4 Plain washer

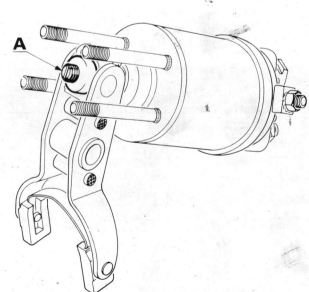

Fig. 10.30 Solenoid disconnection from coupling fork on Paris-Rhone starter motor (Sec 14)

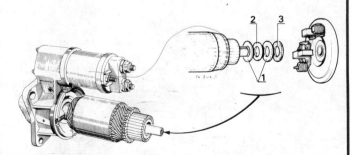

Fig. 10.32 Thrust washer arrangement on Paris-Rhone starter motor type D 8 E 81 and D 8 E 139 (Sec 14)

1 Steel washers   2 Wave washer   3 Fibre washer

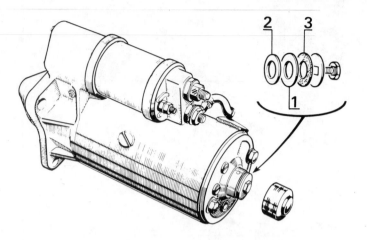

Fig. 10.33 Thrust washer arrangement on Paris-Rhone starter motors outside rear bearing plate (Sec 14)

1   *Steel washer*   2   *Wave washer*   3   *Fibre washer*

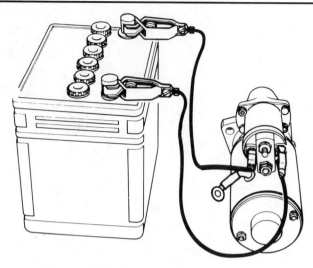

Fig. 10.34 Paris-Rhone starter solenoid pinion throw out test circuit (Sec 14)

Note disconnection of field coil wire

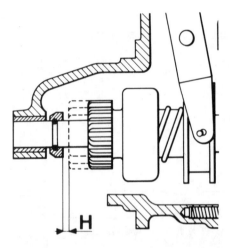

Fig. 10.35 Paris-Rhone starter drive pinion throw out setting diagram (Sec 14)

H = 1.5 mm (0.059 in)

sure that the cover notch and yoke pip are correctly aligned.
22 Screw in the tie-rods or tie-bolts.
23 Fit the thrust washers in their original sequence and then tighten the bolt. In order to prevent the armature shaft from rotating as the bolt is tightened, grip the shaft near the drive pinion, but tape the plier jaws first as the shaft must not be scored. Tap the black plastic cap into position on the rear cover.
24 Connect the field coil lead to the solenoid terminal.
25 The coupling fork must now be adjusted to ensure correct throw out of the drive pinion. To do this, first prise out the rubber plug from the front of the solenoid.
26 Connect the solenoid terminals to a battery as shown and then measure the gap H between the end-face of the pinion gear and the stop. This should be 1.5 mm (0.059 in). If it is not, turn the adjuster screw as necessary.

15 Fuses and relays

1   The fusebox is located under the instrument panel adjacent to the steering column (photo).
2   Early models have a ten position fusebox while later models have seventeen fuses.
3   In the event of failure of an electrical accessory first check the

15.1 Fuse block

15.6 Relay mounting plate

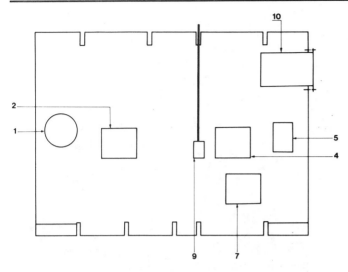

Fig. 10.36 Typical relay (accessories) plate (Sec 15)

1	Direction indicator (flasher) unit	5	Sun-roof cut-out
2	Headlamp dipped beam	7	Ignition feed relay
4	Window winder relay	9	Main feed
		10	Wiper delay relay

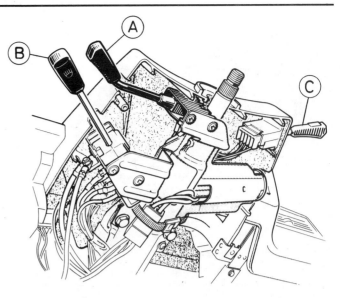

Fig. 10.37 Steering column switches (typical) (Sec 17)

A   Direction indicator   B   Lighting/horn   C   Washer/wiper

circuit fuse. If it has burned through or is broken, renew it with one of similar capacity.

4   If the fuse immediately blows again, check for damaged insulation in the wiring circuit which will probably be causing a short circuit.

5   Never try a makeshift repair on a fuse by substituting a piece of wire or a nail. Apart from damaging the component or accessory, a fire could result.

6   On later models, a relay mounting plate is also located under the instrument panel (photo).

7   To renew a relay, simply pull it from its socket and push the new one into position. On cars with an electric radiator fan the fan relay is located on the left-hand wing valance. On some models a separately mounted windscreen wiper delay relay is fitted.

8   Refer to wiring diagrams in Chapter 10 also Chapter 3 for details of relays used in the fuel injection system (R1317, R1327, R1313, R1323).

16 Direction indicator, hazard warning unit

1   This is really a relay and is located on the relay mounting panel described in the preceding Section.

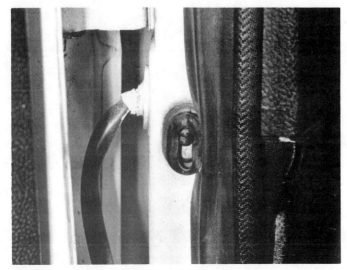

19.1 Door pillar courtesy lamp switch

17 Steering column switches – removal and refitting

1   Disconnect the battery.
2   Remove the steering column lower shroud.
3   Disconnect the wiring plug.
4   Extract the switch fixing screws and remove the switch.
5   Refitting is a reversal of removal. **Note**: *The steering wheel has been removed in the illustration in the interest of clarity only. The switches can be removed leaving the steering wheel in position.*

18 Rocker switches – removal and refitting

1   This type of switch is used on some models to control the windscreen wipers and washers also as a main lighting switch.
2   The switch is retained by small tabs.
3   To remove the switch, prise it up using a thin screwdriver until the tabs can be compressed by the end of the screwdriver.

19 Courtesy lamp switch – removal and refitting

1   These switches are located in the door pillars and are of the plunger type (photo).
2   To remove a switch, extract the retaining screw and withdraw it. Before disconnecting the leads, tape them to the pillar to prevent them from slipping into the pillar cavity.
3   Smear the switch contacts and plunger with petroleum jelly before refitting to prevent corrosion.

20 Headlamp – bulb renewal

1   Open the bonnet and pull the wiring connector plug from the rear of the headlamp.
2   Swivel the bulb retaining springs away and remove the bulb (photos).
3   If a sealing washer is used on the old bulb, transfer it to the new one.
4   If a halogen type bulb is fitted, avoid touching its glass with the fingers. If this has been done inadvertently, clean it with methylated spirit.
5   Refit by reversing the removal operations.
6   Provided the beam adjusting screws have not been touched, the headlamp beam alignment should not have changed, but even so it is recommended that the alignment is checked (see Section 22).

20.2A Headlamp bulbholder and spring

20.2B Removing headlamp bulb

21.1 Removing headlamp trim panel

21.2 Removing headlamp unit

21.3 Headlamp retaining hook

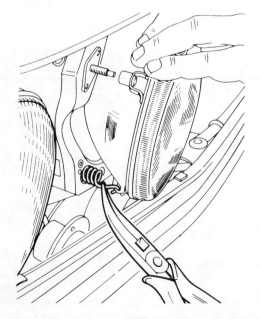

Fig. 10.38 Releasing headlamp tension spring (Sec 21)

21 Headlamp or sealed beam unit – removal and refitting

1   Extract the four screws and remove the headlamp trim panel (photo).
2   Release the small tension spring (photo).
3   Pull the lamp unit forward off its locating lugs and detach it from the spring hook on the side opposite to the tension spring.
4   Disconnect the wiring plug from the rear of the lamp and then remove the retaining ring (three screws).
5   Refit the new unit by reversing the removal operations.

22 Headlamp beam – alignment

1   This is one job best left to your dealer or service station having optical beam alignment equipment.
2   In an emergency the vertical and horizontal adjusting screws may be turned to give an acceptable non-dazzling light pattern.
3   On four-headlamp versions, the outboard headlamps are dipped and the inboard ones main beam.
4   On headlamps with front mounted beam adjusting screws, the screws are accessible without the need to remove the trim panel.

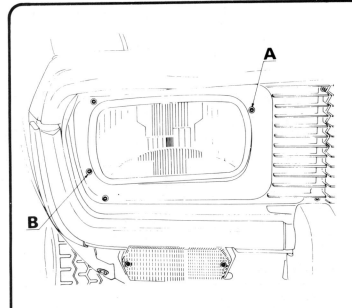

Fig. 10.39 Rectangular type headlamp beam adjusting screws (Sec 22)

A   Horizontal adjustment   B   Vertical adjustment

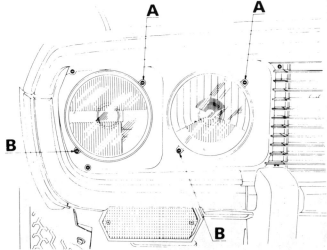

Fig. 10.40 Twin headlamp beam adjusting screws (Sec 22)

A   Horizontal adjustment   B   Vertical adjustment

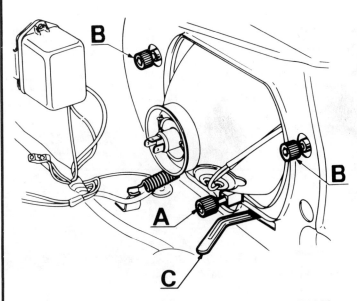

Fig. 10.41 Ride level headlamp beam control lever on later R1300 models (Sec 22)

A   Beam vertical adjustment   B   Beam horizontal adjustment
                                 C   Level control lever

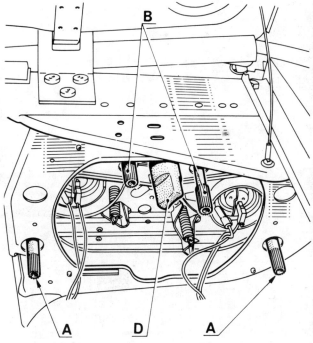

Fig. 10.42 Ride level headlamp beam control lever on R1318 and R1328 models (Sec 22)

A   Beam horizontal adjustment   B   Beam vertical adjustment
                                   D   Level control knob

5   On some models a ride level control lever or knob is fitted so that the headlamp beams may be altered to compensate for a light or heavily loaded vehicle. The knob or lever is moved fully to the left on a lightly laden car or fully to the right for a heavily laden one. On some R15 models, the lever is L shaped in which case, reverse the direction to that just described.

6   Before adjusting the headlamps, always set the ride level control to the lightly laden position.

23 Exterior lamps – bulb renewal

Front parking/direction indicator lamp
1   Depending upon model and date of production, access to the bulb is obtained by either extracting the two lamp cover screws or reaching behind the front shield and unscrewing the knurled knob which retains the bulbholder (photo).
2   Depress and then twist the bayonet fitting type bulb from its socket.

Stop, tail, rear fog, indicator and reversing lamps
3   On some models, the bulbs are accessible after having removed the lens which is held by three screws (photo).
4   On other models, access to the bulbholders is obtained after removing the lamp covers from inside the luggage compartment.

23.1 Front parking/indicator bulb

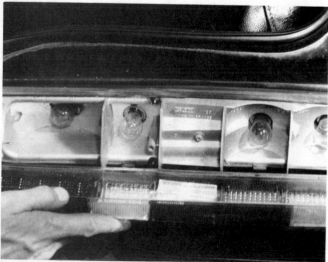
23.3 Rear lamp cluster

Rear number plate lamp
5   Remove the cover which is held by two screws.
6   Depress and twist the bulb from its socket.

Side marker lamp
7   Remove the cover which is held by two screws.
8   Depress and twist the bulb from its socket.
9   Refitting of all bulbs is a reversal of removal.

24 Interior lamps – bulb renewal

Roof lamp and luggage compartment lamp
1   On earlier models, to reach the bulb, depress and turn the lens in an anti-clockwise direction.
2   On later models carefully prise the lamp lens from the lamp base.
3   Pull the festoon type bulb from its clips.

Instrument panel light bulbs
4   Reach under the instrument panel and unscrew the two knurled knobs above the fusebox. Lower the relay bracket.
5   Reach up and pull the bulb from its contacts.

Instrument panel warning lamps
6   Some of these bulbs are accessible by reaching up behind the instrument panel. Others are obstructed and their renewal will necessitate removal of the instrument panel as described in Sections 25 or 26.
7   The bulbs are of wedge base type and can be removed after twisting and pulling the holders from their sockets (photo).

25 Instrument panel (to March 1976) – removal and refitting

1   Disconnect the battery.
2   Reach under the instrument panel and unscrew the knurled knobs on the fusebox bracket. Tilt the bracket aside.
3   On pre 1974 models, extract the screws (A) from the retaining clips. Remove the radio speaker blanking plate to reach these screws on the right-hand side. Insert a screwdriver to free the clip (B). Pull the instrument panel assembly from the upper hooks (C), disconnect the speedometer cable by unscrewing the knurled ring. Pull off the wiring plugs.
4   On later models extract the bottom left-hand clip screw and then the right-hand one which is accessible through the glovebox. Insert a screwdriver between the instrument and facia panels to release the bottom clip. Pull the panel from the top clips.
5   Pull the instrument panel gently from the facia while an assistant feeds the speedometer cable through the grommet in the engine compartment rear bulkhead.

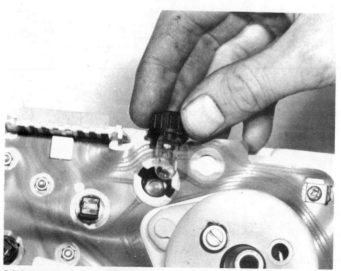
24.3 Instrument panel bulb

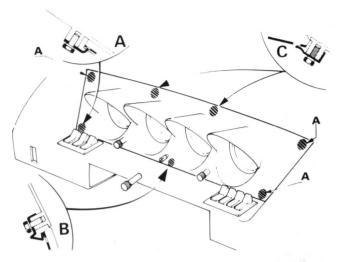

Fig. 10.43 Early type instrument panel (to 1974) (Sec 25)

A   Retaining clip screws   B   Internal clip   C   Upper fixing hooks

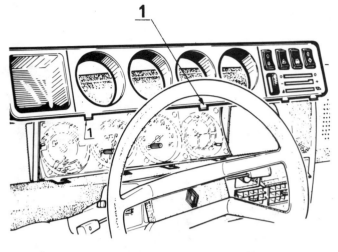

Fig. 10.44 Later type instrument panel (1976 on) (Sec 26)

1   Retaining lugs

26.5 Instrument panel wiring harness plugs

6   With the cable connection visible at the rear of the speedometer, unscrew the knurled ring with the fingers and disconnect the cable.

7   Disconnect the wiring plugs from the rear of the printed circuit. Take care not to damage the circuit board.

8   To refit the instrument panel, fit the clips, but do not tighten the screws until the panel has been manoeuvred into position with the speedometer cable reconnected also the wiring plugs.

26   Instrument panel (from March 1976) – removal and refitting

1   Disconnect the battery.

2   Pull off the heater control lever knobs.

3   Prise out the bright trim strip which runs around the instrument panel.

4   Pull the top edge of the instrument escutcheon panel towards you until the bottom lugs are released.

5   Reach behind the panel and disconnect the switch wiring plugs and the bulbholder leads. Remove the escutcheon panel (photo).

6   Reach up behind the instrument panel and disconnect the speedometer cable by squeezing the ribbed areas of the connector together.

7   Using a thin blade, release the instrument panel top clips and then push the upper edge of the panel inwards towards the front of the car. When the top of the panel has moved in far enough, the bottom retaining lugs will be released (photo).

8   Pull the instrument panel towards you far enough to be able to disconnect the wiring plugs. Withdraw the instrument panel from the facia.

9   Refitting is a reversal of removal.

27   Instruments – removal and refitting

1   The individual instruments, warning lamps and other components may be removed from the instrument panel once the panel has been withdrawn as described in earlier Sections (photo).

2   Repair of an instrument is a specialised job and it will usually be cheaper to renew it rather than have it overhauled or repaired.

28   Speedometer cable – renewal

1   Reach up behind the instrument panel and disconnect the cable from the rear of the speedometer by unscrewing the knurled ring (earlier models) or by squeezing the ribbed areas of the plastic connector (later models) (photos).

2   Working at the transmission, unscrew and remove the small locking bolt which retains the speedometer cable in the gear casing.

26.7 Instrument panel retaining lugs (arrowed)

236

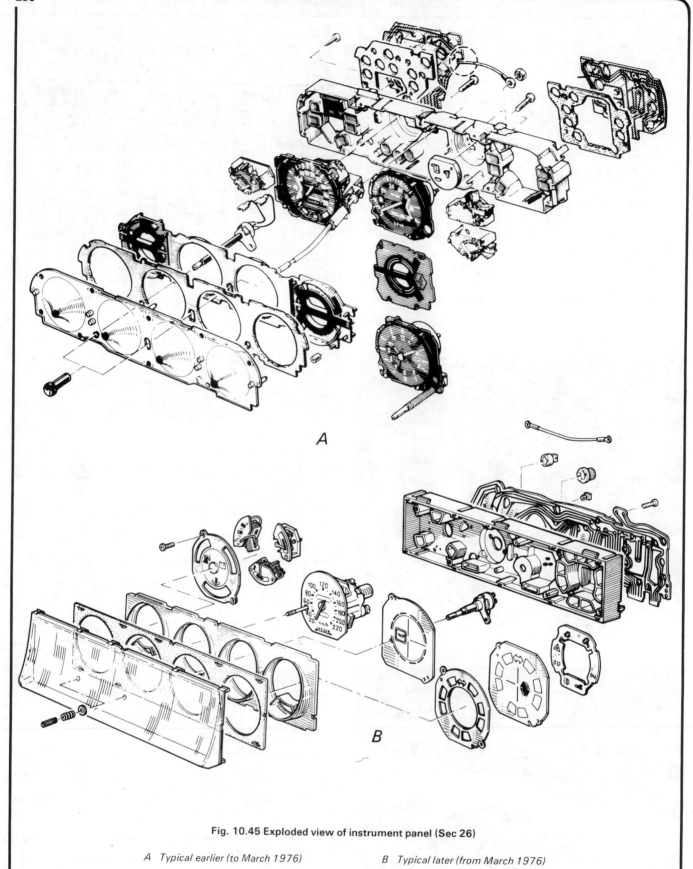

Fig. 10.45 Exploded view of instrument panel (Sec 26)

A   Typical earlier (to March 1976)   B   Typical later (from March 1976)

27.1 Rear view of instrument panel

28.1A Speedometer cable at head

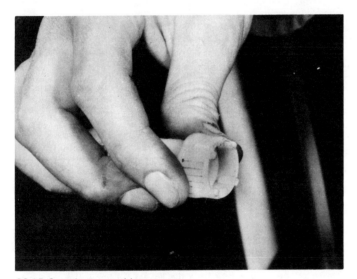

28.1B Speedometer cable connector

28.2 Speedometer cable lock bolt at transmission

Withdraw the cable from the transmission and from the engine bulkhead.
3   New cables are supplied as an inner and outer cable assembly – not as separate items.
4   Refitting is a reversal of removal.

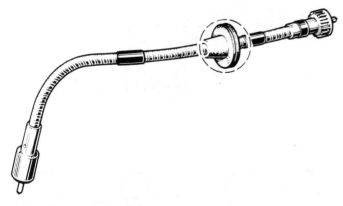

Fig. 10.46 Speedometer drive cable assembly (Sec 28)

29 Horns

1   Twin trumpet type horns are fitted which require no maintenance or adjustment apart from occasionally checking the security of the mounting bracket nuts and the connecting leads.
2   Depending upon model, the horn switch is either incorporated in the lighting switch on the steering column or in the form of buttons on either side of the steering wheel centre pad.

30 Electric window winder – dismantling and reassembly

1   Remove the mechanism from the door cavity as described in Chapter 12.
2   Unscrew the two motor mounting bolts and withdraw the motor, easing the drive spindle from the flexible coupling.
3   On cars built up until March 1976, a separate cut-out switch was fitted which is renewable. Do this by disconnecting the leads from the switch terminals, cut through the waterproof switch sealing material and extract the two mounting screws.
4   Fit the new switch and re-seal it using the sealing material supplied with the switch.
5   On later models, the cut-out switch is integral with the motor and

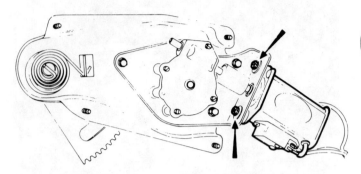

Fig. 10.47 Typical electric window winder assembly. Motor mounting bolts arrowed (Sec 30)

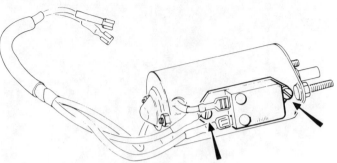

Fig. 10.48 Externally mounted cut-out switch on window winder motor (to 1976) (Sec 30)

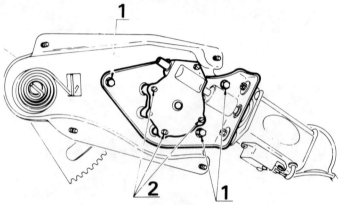

Fig. 10.49 Electric window winder mounting bracket and reduction gearcase (Sec 30)

1   Bracket screws   *2   Gearcase screws*

if switch or motor is faulty will have to be renewed as an assembly.
6   The reduction gear on all models can be removed by unscrewing bolts.
7   When refitting, make sure that the drivegear meshes correctly with the quadrant.

31 Windscreen wiper blades and arms – removal and refitting

1   One of two methods of attaching the wiper blades to their arms may be encountered. With one type, the small retaining tab is prised up with the thumb nail and the blade pulled from the arm.

2   With the other type, the wiper arm has a hook formed at its end. To disconnect the blade, pull the blade from the glass, swivel the blade and pinch the ends of the U-shaped plastic retainer together and then slide the blade out of the hook on the arm (photo).
3   Wiper blades should be renewed whenever they cease to wipe cleanly. Rubber inserts can be purchased separately and fitted to the original blades by following the individual manufacturer's instructions.
4   The wiper arms may be either a push fit onto the splined drive spindles or be bolted to the spindles according to model and date of production. With the bolt-on type, the cover cap should be raised to expose the retaining nut (photo).
5   Before removing a wiper arm, mark the position of the blades on the glass using a strip of masking tape. This will make the job of alignment, when refitting, that much easier.

32 Windscreen wiper motor and linkage – removal and refitting

1   The wiper motor and linkage should be removed as an assembly (photo).
2   Extract the screws which retain the scuttle grille panel just ahead of the windscreen (refer to Chapter 12).
3   Remove the wiper arms.
4   Release the drive spindle covers, nuts, washers and bushes.
5   Disconnect the wiring plug from the wiper motor (photo).
6   Unscrew the mounting plate screws and then withdraw the motor and linkage out in a sideways direction and remove it from the car.
7   To separate the motor from the linkage, unscrew the nut which holds the crank arm to the motor driving spindle.
8   Unscrew the three motor mounting bolts.
9   Reassembly and refitting are reversals of the removal and dismantling operations but make sure that the link and the crank arm are exactly in line when refitting the crank arm to the motor drive spindle.

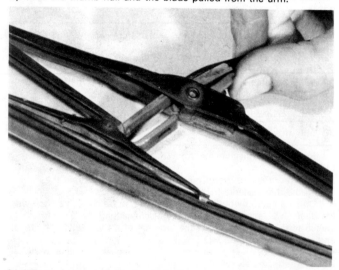

31.2 Typical wiper arm/blade connection

31.4 Splined type wiper arm spindle

32.1 Windscreen wiper motor

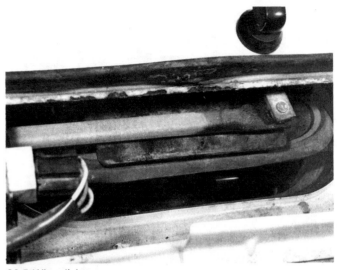

32.5 Wiper linkage

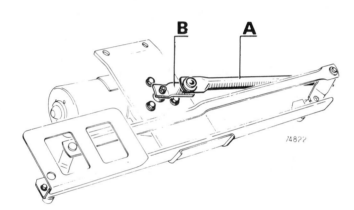

Fig. 10.50 Wiper motor crankarm and link (Sec 32)

A Link   B Crankarm

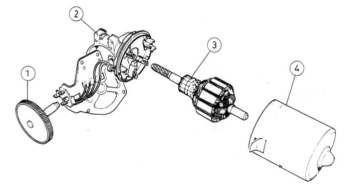

Fig. 10.51 Wiper motor components (Bosch) (Sec 33)

1 Gear   3 Armature
2 Gearcase   4 Yoke

33 Windscreen wiper motor – overhaul

1 With the motor removed from the car, clean away external dirt.

Bosch type

2 Extract the four gearcase cover screws and remove the gearcase cover. Check the gears for wear and if in good condition, wipe out the old grease and apply fresh. Refit the cover.
3 Extract the yoke fixing screws and withdraw the rear bearing housing.
4 Withdraw the armature.
5 Check the condition of the commutator and the brushes and renovate in a similar way to that described for the starter motor in Section 13.
6 Reassemble by reversing the dismantling operations, but apply grease to the armature shaft bearings.

SEV type motor

7 Remove the gearcase cover and check the gears as described in paragraph 2 for the Bosch type wiper motor.
8 Unscrew the tie-rod nuts and remove the rear bearing plate.
9 Withdraw the brush carrier and withdraw the armature.
10 Check the condition of the commutator and brushes and renovate

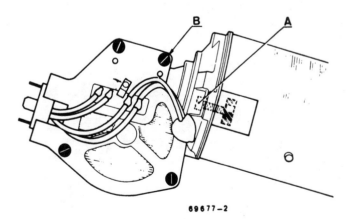

Fig. 10.52 Wiper motor screws (Sec 33)

A Yoke fixing screws   B Gearcase cover screws

in a similar way to that described for the starter motor in Section 13. Note that the brush leads are of crimped type.
11 Reassembly of the SEV type of motor is a reversal of dismantling. Apply grease to the armature shaft bearings.

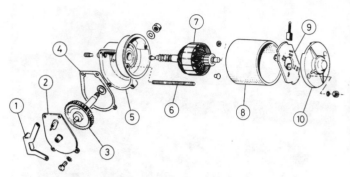

Fig. 10.53 Wiper motor components (SEV) (Sec 33)

1	Support strut	6	Tie-rod
2	Cover	7	Armature
3	Gear	8	Yoke
4	Gasket	9	Brush carrier plate
5	Gearcase	10	Rear bearing/cover

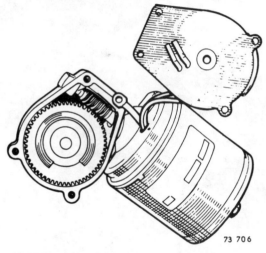

Fig. 10.54 Wiper motor with gearcase cover removed (SEV) (Sec 33)

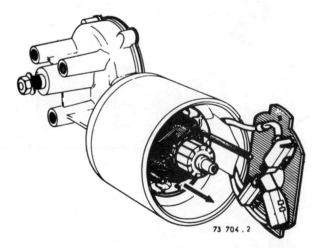

Fig. 10.55 Wiper motor brush carrier plate removed (SEV) (Sec 33)

34 Windscreen washer

1   The windscreen washer system is actuated by a switch incorporated in the wiper switch on most models although some

35.4 Tailgate contact switch

earlier Renault 15 models were fitted with a foot-operated pedal switch.
2   The washer fluid reservoir with build-in electric pump is located within the engine compartment.
3   The washer nozzles are located on the scuttle and may be adjusted by inserting a pin to give an acceptable jet pattern on the glass.
4   The jets can be removed or their feed tubes disconnected after removal of the scuttle grille panel (refer to Chapter 12).
5   In low temperature conditions, add a percentage of proprietary windscreen washer antifreeze or methylated spirit to the fluid reservoir to prevent freezing. Never use cooling system antifreeze in the washer reservoir or damage to the body paintwork may occur.

35 Tailgate heated window

1   The elements on the inside of the glass should be treated with respect. Do not allow articles of luggage to rub against them.
2   Clean the inside of the tailgate glass only with water and detergent. Wipe in the direction of the elements taking care not to scratch them with any rings on the fingers.
3   Should a break occur in the element, it can be repaired using one of the silver based paints which are readily available. Follow the manufacturer's instructions very carefully.
4   An unusual feature of the electrical circuit is the use of a contact type switch which completes the circuit only when the tailgate is firmly closed (photo).

36 Seat belt warning system

1   On North American models, a visual and audible warning system is fitted which operates for a pre-set period if the car is started or running without the front seat belts being fastened.
2   Occasionally check the security of the system connecting wires.
3   On some models an anti-theft warning system is fitted which utilises the seat belt warning system buzzer. This activates if the driver opens his door without first having removed the ignition key.

37 Radio – fitting

Radio receiver
1   If the car is not already fitted with a radio, a suitable unit can be installed in the space provided in the centre console or on late Renault 15 TL models in the facia panel.
2   Check that the radio has been set to the correct polarity (negative earth).
3   Disconnect the battery.

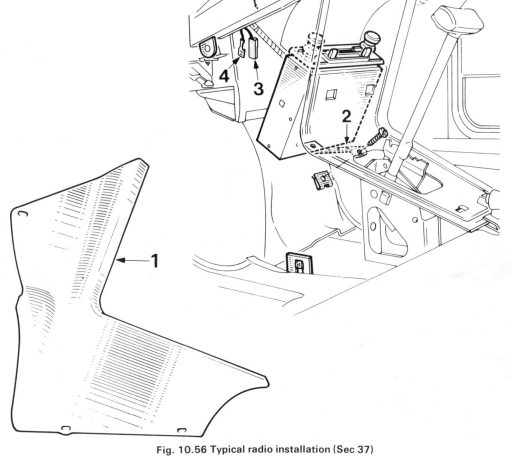

Fig. 10.56 Typical radio installation (Sec 37)

1   Console side panel   3   Power feed
2   Support strut   4   Earth

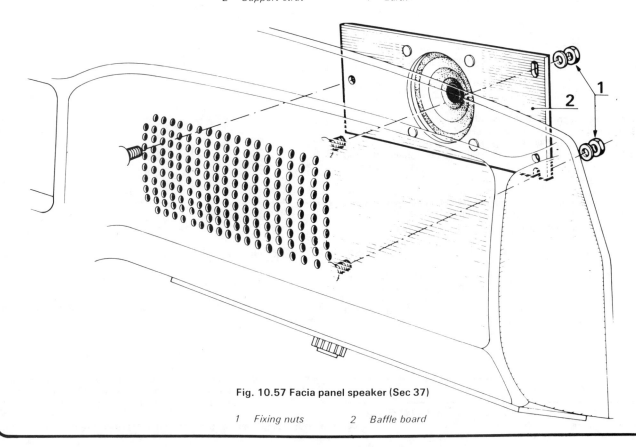

Fig. 10.57 Facia panel speaker (Sec 37)

1   Fixing nuts   2   Baffle board

4   On cars equipped with automatic transmission, remove the casing from around the speed selector lever.
5   From the centre console remove the left-hand trim panel and the radio aperture blanking plate.
6   Offer the radio into position, fit the escutcheon plate, spacers, nuts and control knobs. If necessary use the support strut supplied with some radio fitting kits.
7   Power and earth connections are provided during production of the car and can be identified by the power (spade) terminal being insulated while the earth is not. Connect the appropriate radio leads to these terminals.
8   The aerial and speaker leads must also be connected to the radio once these components have been fitted (see later paragraphs). A speaker is fitted in production on 1977 Renault 17 models equipped with air conditioning.

Single speaker
9   Offer the speaker baffle board onto the fixing studs behind the perforated grille in the facia panel on the passenger side.
10 Do not overtighten the fixing nuts.
11 Route the leads around behind the console and connect them to the radio.

Stereo speakers
12 One of three positions may be chosen for fitting twin speakers. They can be fitted to the trim panel, to the side of the front footwells, to the rear parcels shelf or into the front door trim panels.
13 Take great care cutting out the holes in the mounting panels, double check the hole diameter and position before cutting. Use the diagram if the door trim panels are to be cut.
14 If electric window winders are fitted, route the speaker leads along the winder motor wiring harness. If the car is not so equipped, holes will have to be drilled in the pillar and door edge, but make sure that the holes are fitted with grommets and the wires with a protective sleeve.
15 For other speaker installation positions, route the connecting wires under the carpets.
16 Enclose the door speakers in plastic bags to protect them from water.
17 Connect the speaker wires correctly.

Aerial
18 A wing or roof aerial may be fitted, the latter being preferred.
19 Work to the dimensions in the diagram for fitting a front wing aerial and route the cable through the blanking plugs provided into the scuttle and then into the car interior.
20 To fit a roof aerial, remove the interior rear view mirror and make a hole in the headlining to coincide with the hole in the windscreen top crossmember.
21 Drill a hole through the roof panel of suitable diameter to accept the threaded mounting base and collar of the aerial. Try a small pilot hole first to ensure that it is central within the crossmember hole.
22 Scrape the paint away from around the hole to provide a good earth bond.
23 Pass a length of cord or wire across inside the windscreen crossmember and down the right-hand windscreen pillar. If the aerial lead is taped to the end of the cord it can be drawn into position and then connected to the radio and the aerial base.
24 Set the aerial to the desired angle and lock it in position.
25 Refit the interior mirror.
26 The aerial must now be trimmed. To do this, tune into a weak station and turn up the volume. Insert a thin screwdriver into the trim screw hole in the receiver (identified in the receiver instruction book) and turn the screw in both directions until the loudest, clearest signal is received.
27 The ignition system is suppressed during production, but if interference is a problem after having installed a radio, refer to the next Section and carry out the suggested measures, in order, and checking the effect before proceeding to the next one.

38 Radio – interference suppression

1   Connect a 3µF bypass condenser in series to the (+) terminal of the voltage regulator.

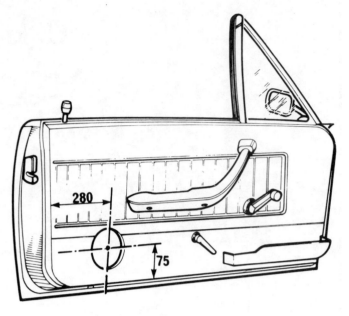

Fig. 10.58 Speaker hole cutting diagram for door panel (Sec 37)

Dimensions in mm

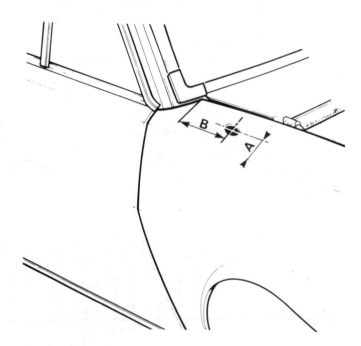

Fig. 10.59 Front wing aerial fitting diagram (Sec 37)

A   55.0 mm (2.12 in)   *B   175.0 mm (6.9 in)*

2   Fit a 1000 to 5000 ohm resistance into the input HT lead of the distributor.
3   Connect a bonding strap between the underside of the bonnet and the front body panel.
4   On Renault 17 models, particularly those with fuel injection engines, try connecting an in-line choke in series to the feed side of the windscreen wiper motor, also to the heater booster fan motor feed.
5   Substitute a screened rev-counter cable instead of the standard electric cable. Make sure that the screening is well earthed at both ends.
6   Crackling caused by static may be eliminated by connecting

bonding straps between body and anti-roll bar, the front wings and the body, the ignition coil mounting bracket and the engine.

7 Persistent clicking may be due to the ignition coil. Fit a $2.2\mu F$ condenser between the coil (+) terminal and the coil mounting bracket.

8 It is seldom that the alternator causes interference, but it can occur and may be audible as a whine, rising and falling according to engine speed.

9 Fit a condenser (2.2 or $3.3\mu F$) between one of the alternator mounting bolts and the battery (+) terminal on the alternator. If spade type terminals are used on the alternator, then a 'piggy-back' type connector will have to be used.

39 Auxiliary driving lamps

1 Fog and spot lamps are widely available for fitting to all models using the special fitting kits supplied by the lamp manufacturers.

2 Follow the instructions supplied with the lamps, but make quite sure that the following essential requirements are conformed with.

3 Bolt the lamps to a rigid mounting member where it will not vibrate, deform body components or suffer damage during bumper contact during parking manoeuvres.

4 Wire the lamps through the spare positions in the fusebox or if a spare is not available install a supplementary fuse.

5 Make sure that the lamps are positioned to conform with current regulations covering the height of lamps from the ground, otherwise the lamps can only be used in conditions of falling snow or fog in many territories.

40 Towing bracket wiring harness – fitting

1 Where a towing bracket has been fitted (see Chapter 12) then the wiring harness supplied should be connected in the following way.

2 Disconnect the battery.

3 Remove the cover from the rear lamp cluster.

4 Working within the luggage compartment drill a 14.0 mm (0.55

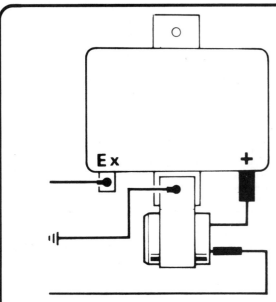

Fig. 10.60 Suppressor connection to voltage regulator (Sec 38)

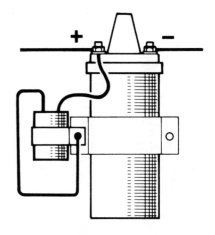

Fig. 10.61 Suppressor connection to ignition coil (Sec 38)

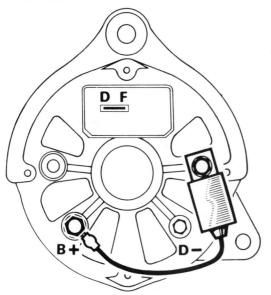

Fig. 10.62 Suppressor connection to alternator (Sec 38)

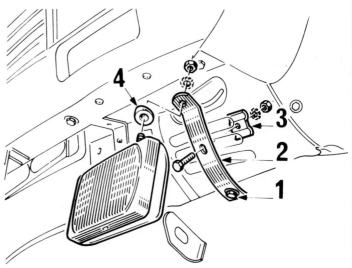

Fig. 10.63 Typical auxiliary lamp fitting kit (Sec 39)

| 1 | Screw | 3 | Backing plate |
| 2 | Bracket | 4 | Spacer |

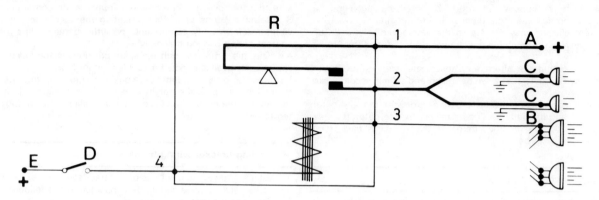

Fig. 10.64 Wiring diagram for automatically extinguishing foglamps when headlamps switched to dipped beam (Sec 39)

R Relay	*2 Connection to*	*4 Connection to instrument*	*E Connection from foglamp*
1 Connection to battery +	*foglamps (C)*	*panel switch*	*switch to main*
or starter feed	*3 Connection to dipped*		*lighting switch*
	beam wire behind LH		
	headlamp (B)		

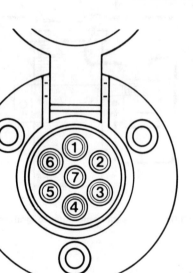

Fig. 10.65 Typical trailer wiring harness socket (Sec 40)

For key see text

in) diameter hole in the rear panel under the left-hand reversing lamp on later models or below the inboard end of the rear cluster lens on earlier models. Fit a grommet into the hole.

5   Disconnect the wiring plug from the rear lamp assembly and connect the two plugs on the towing bracket harness to the rear lamp plug and the rear lamp cluster.

6   Connect the earth wire of the towing bracket harness to the rear panel earthing screw.

7   Feed the towing bracket wiring harness through the newly fitted grommet and then through the space between the rear panel and the protective shield.

8   On the left-hand side of the rear panel trim board is an opening. In line with this hole, cut the outer insulation from the right-hand rear wiring harness so that the maroon coloured wire for the right-hand direction indicator can be cut. Using the two sleeves supplied, join these to the maroon wire in the towing bracket harness.

9   Route the red wire in the towing bracket harness under the carpet in the luggage area and then under the left-hand side passenger carpet. Remove the steering column lower shroud. Fit an in-line fuse into the red wire and then connect it to the lighting switch.

10 The rear end of the harness should be connected to a suitable socket for using a standard trailer plug.

11 Wiring colour code and standard socket connections are as follows:

Wire	Colour
Earth	Black
Stop lamps	Salmon pink
RH direction indicator lamp	Maroon
LH direction indicator lamp	Light grey
Tail lamps and number plate lamp	Yellow
Trailer interior lamp	Red

Socket number	Function
1	LH direction indicator
2	Trailer interior lamp
3	Earth
4	RH direction indicator
5	LH tail lamp and number plate
6	Stop lamps
7	LH tail lamp

41 Fault diagnosis

Symptom	Reason(s)
Starter fails to turn engine	Battery discharged
	Battery defective internally
	Battery terminal leads loose or earth lead not securely attached to body
	Loose or broken connections in starter motor circuit
	Starter motor solenoid faulty
	Starter motor pinion jammed on armature shaft
	Starter brushes badly worn, sticking, or brush wires loose
	Commutator dirty, worn or burnt
	Starter motor armature faulty

Chapter 10 Electrical system

245

Symptoms	Reason(s)
	Field coils earthed
	Gear selector lever not engaged in 'P' or 'N' (automatic transmission)
Starter turns engine very slowly	Battery in discharged condition
	Starter brushes badly worn, sticking or brush wires loose
	Loose wires in starter motor circuit
Starter spins but does not turn engine	Starter motor coupling fork sticking
	Pinion or flywheel gear teeth broken or worn
	Battery discharged
Starter motor noisy or excessively rough engagement	Pinion or flywheel gear teeth broken or worn
	Starter motor retaining bolts loose
Battery will not hold charge for more than a few days	Battery defective internally
	Electrolyte level too low or electrolyte too weak due to leakage
	Plate separators no longer fully effective
	Battery plates severely sulphated
	Drivebelt slipping
	Battery terminal connections loose or corroded
	Alternator not charging
	Short in lighting circuit causing continual battery drain
	Regulator unit not working correctly
Ignition light fails to go out, battery runs flat in a few days	Drivebelt loose and slipping or broken
	Alternator brushes worn, sticking, broken or dirty
	Alternator brush springs weak or broken
	Internal fault in alternator

Failure of individual electrical equipment to function correctly is dealt with alphabetically, item-by-item, under the headings listed below

Horn/s

Horn operates all the time	Horn push either earthed or stuck down
	Horn cable to horn push earthed
Horn fails to operate	Cable or cable connection loose, broken or disconnected
	Horn has an internal fault
Horn emits intermittent or unsatisfactory noise	Cable connections loose

Lights

Lights do not come on	If engine not running, battery discharged
	Wire connections loose, disconnected or broken
	Light switch shorting or otherwise faulty
Lights come on but fade out	If engine not running battery discharged
	Light bulb filament burnt out or bulbs broken
	Wire connections loose, disconnected or broken
	Light switch shorting or otherwise faulty
Lights work erratically – flashing on and off, especially over bumps	Battery terminals or earth connection loose
	Lights not earthing properly
	Contacts in light switch faulty

Wipers

Wiper motor fails to work	Blown fuse
	Wire connections loose, disconnected or broken
	Brushes badly worn
	Armature worn or faulty
	Fiield coils faulty
Wiper motor works very slowly and takes excessive current	Commutator dirty; greasy or burnt
	Armature bearings dirty or unaligned
	Armature badly worn or faulty
Wiper motor works slowly and takes little current	Brushes badly worn
	Commutator dirty, greasy or burnt
	Armature badly worn or faulty
Wiper motor works but wiper blades remain static	Wiper motor gearbox parts badly worn
	Faulty linkage

246

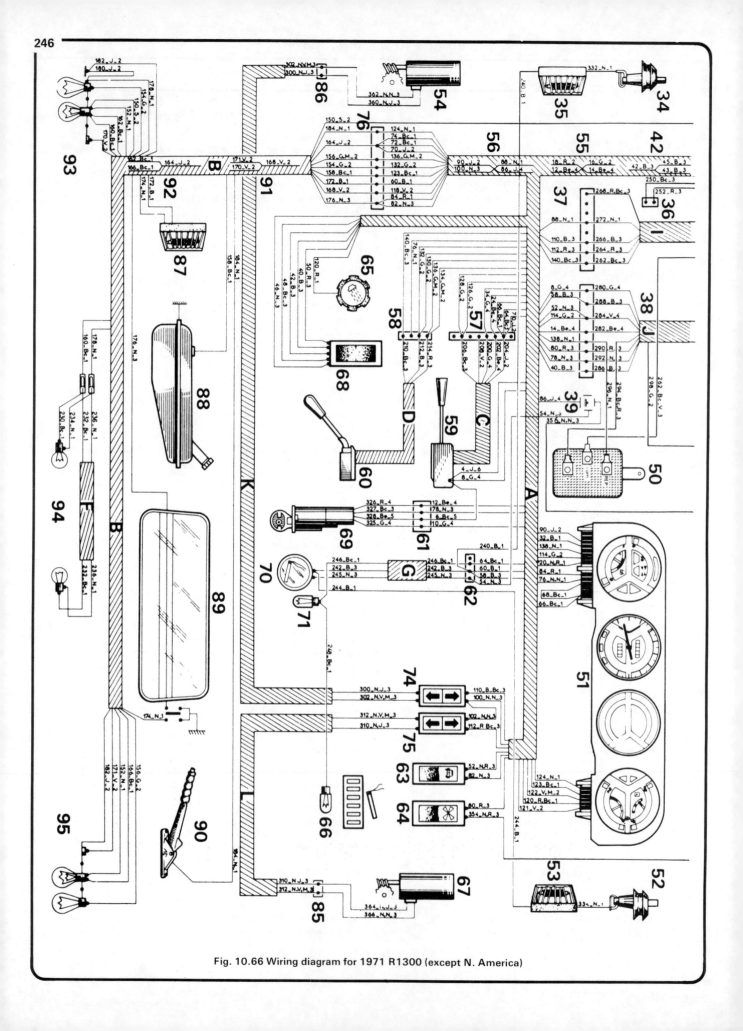

Fig. 10.66 Wiring diagram for 1971 R1300 (except N. America)

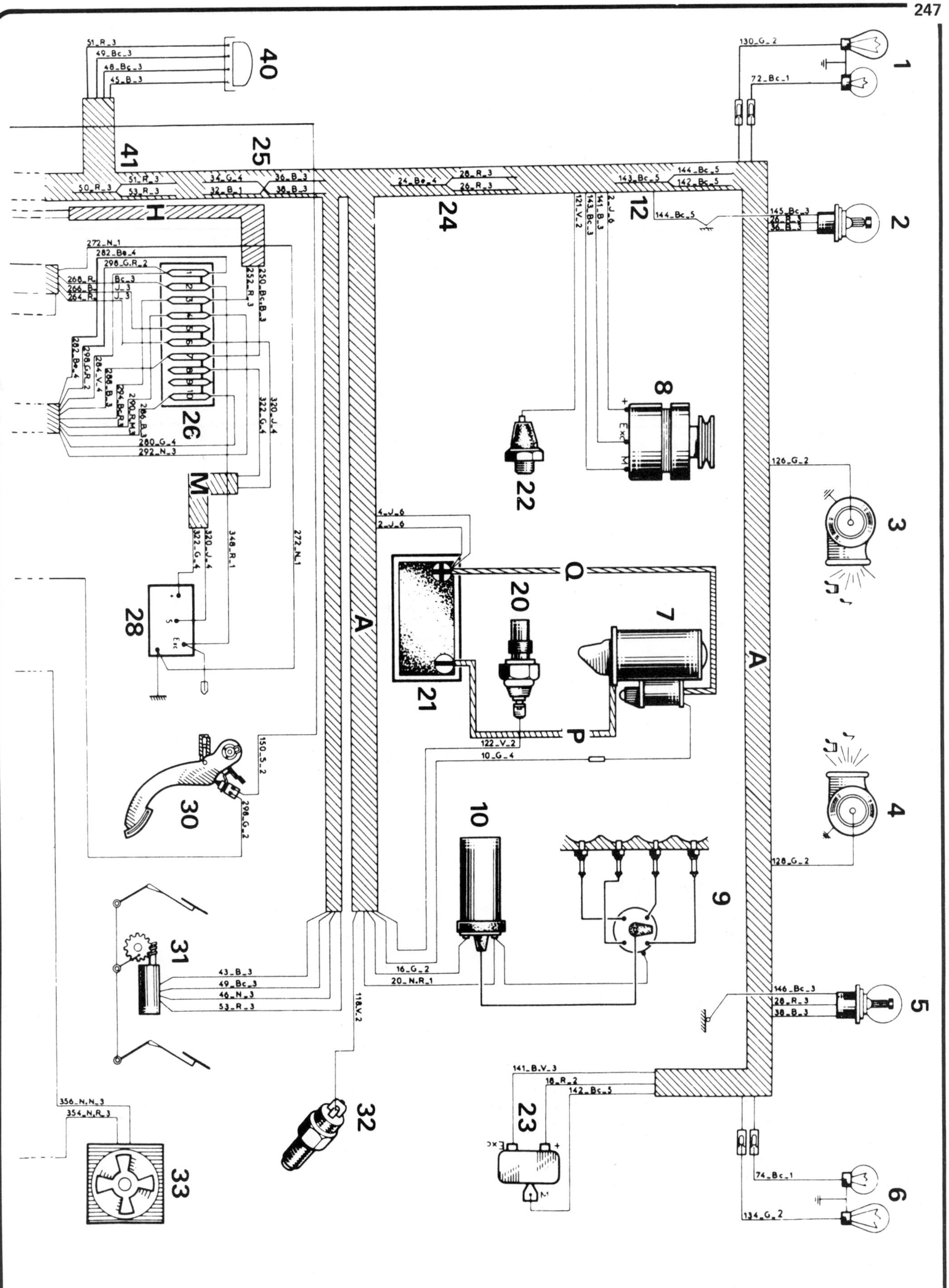

Fig. 10.66 Wiring diagram for 1971 R1300 (except N. America) (continued)

Key to wiring diagrams Figs. 10.66 and 10.67

1 LH front sidelight and direction indicator
2 LH headlights
3 LH horn
4 RH horn
5 RH headlights
6 RH front sidelight and direction indicator
7 Starter
8 Alternator
9 Distributor
10 Ignition coil
11 Electric window winder (R.1312)
12 Earth (ground) wires junction
20 Temperature sender switch
21 Battery
22 Oil pressure sender switch
23 Regulator
24 Dipped beam wire junction
25 Main beam wire junction
26 Fuses
27 Dipped beams relay (R.1312)
28 Electric window winder relay
30 Brake switch
31 Windscreen wiper
32 Reversing lights switch
33 Heating and ventilating fan
34 LH interior light earth (ground)
35 LH interior light
36 Hazard warning light system junction
37 Front harness – fuses harness junction block
38 Front harness – fuses harness junction block
39 Earth (ground) terminal
40 Electric windscreen washer pedal (R.1300)
41 Windscreen wiper wire junction (R.1300)
42 Windscreen wiper wire junction (R.1300)
50 Flasher unit
51 Instrument panel

52 RH interior light earth (ground) switch
53 RH interior light
54 LH electric window winder
55 Junction on + wires after ignition switch
56 Earth (ground) wires junction
57 Front harness – combination lighting switch junction block
58 Front harness – direction indicator switch junction block
59 Combination lighting switch
60 Direction indicator switch
61 Front harness – ignition switch wiring junction block
62 Front harness – cigar lighter wiring junction block
63 Heated rear screen switch
64 Heating – ventilating fan switch
65 Choke 'on' warning light wire
66 Ashtray illumination
67 RH electric window winder
68 Windscreen wiper – windscreen washer switch
69 Ignition-starter switch
70 Cigar lighter
71 Cigar lighter illumination
72 Sun roof dummy switch
73 Electric clock (R.1312)
74 LH window winder switch
75 RH window winder switch
76 Front harness – rear harness junction block
85 LH window winder junction
86 RH window winder junction
87 Luggage compartment light
88 Fuel tank
89 Heated rear screen
90 Handbrake
91 Reversing lights wire junction
92 Rear lights wiring junction
93 LH rear light
94 Licence plate light
95 RH rear light

List of harnesses

A Front harness
B Rear harness
C Combination lighting switch harness
D Direction indicator switch harness
E Alternator wiring R.1302-R.1312
F Licence plate light wiring
G Cigar lighter wiring
H Hazard warning light system harness

I Fuses harness
J Fuses harness
K LH window winder harness
L RH window winder harness
M Window winder relay harness
P Negative lead
Q Positive lead

Wire identification

Each wire is identified by a number followed by a letter(s) indicating the wire and sleeve colours and finally a figure indicating the diameter.

Wire and sleeve colours

Beige	White	Blue	Clear	Grey	Yellow
Be	Bc	B	C	G	J

Black	Salmon	Pink	Green	Maroon
N	S	R	V	M

Wire diameters

No.	1	2	3	4	5	6
mm	9/10	12/10	16/10	20/10	25/10	30/10
Gauge	19	16	14	12	10	9

Example

No.	Wire colour	Sleeve colour	Diameter
10	Bc	B	1

This is a No. 10 white wire, with a blue sleeve, 9/10 mm diameter (19 gauge)

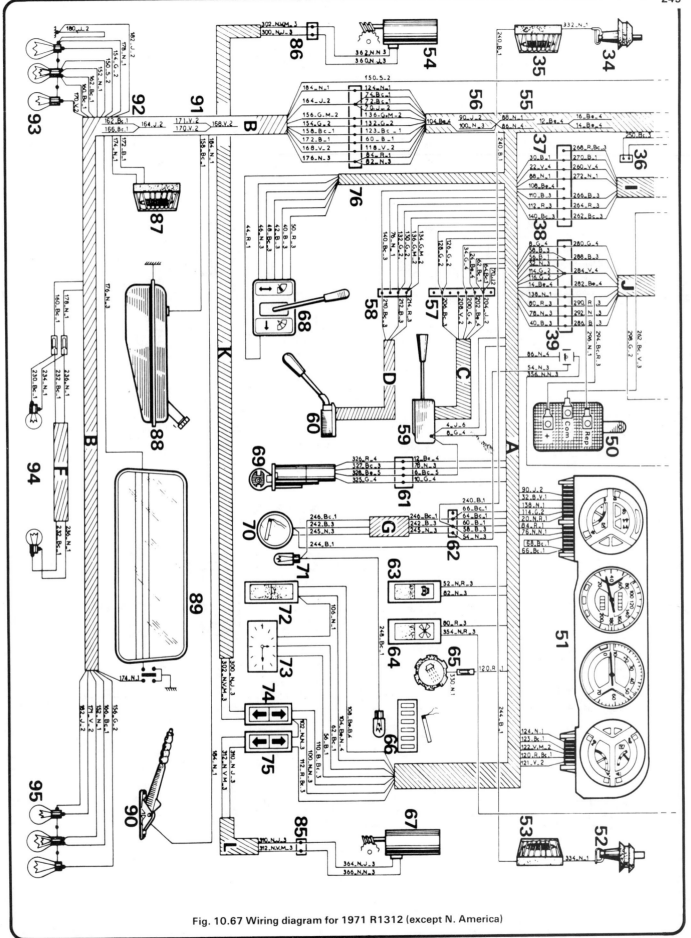

Fig. 10.67 Wiring diagram for 1971 R1312 (except N. America)

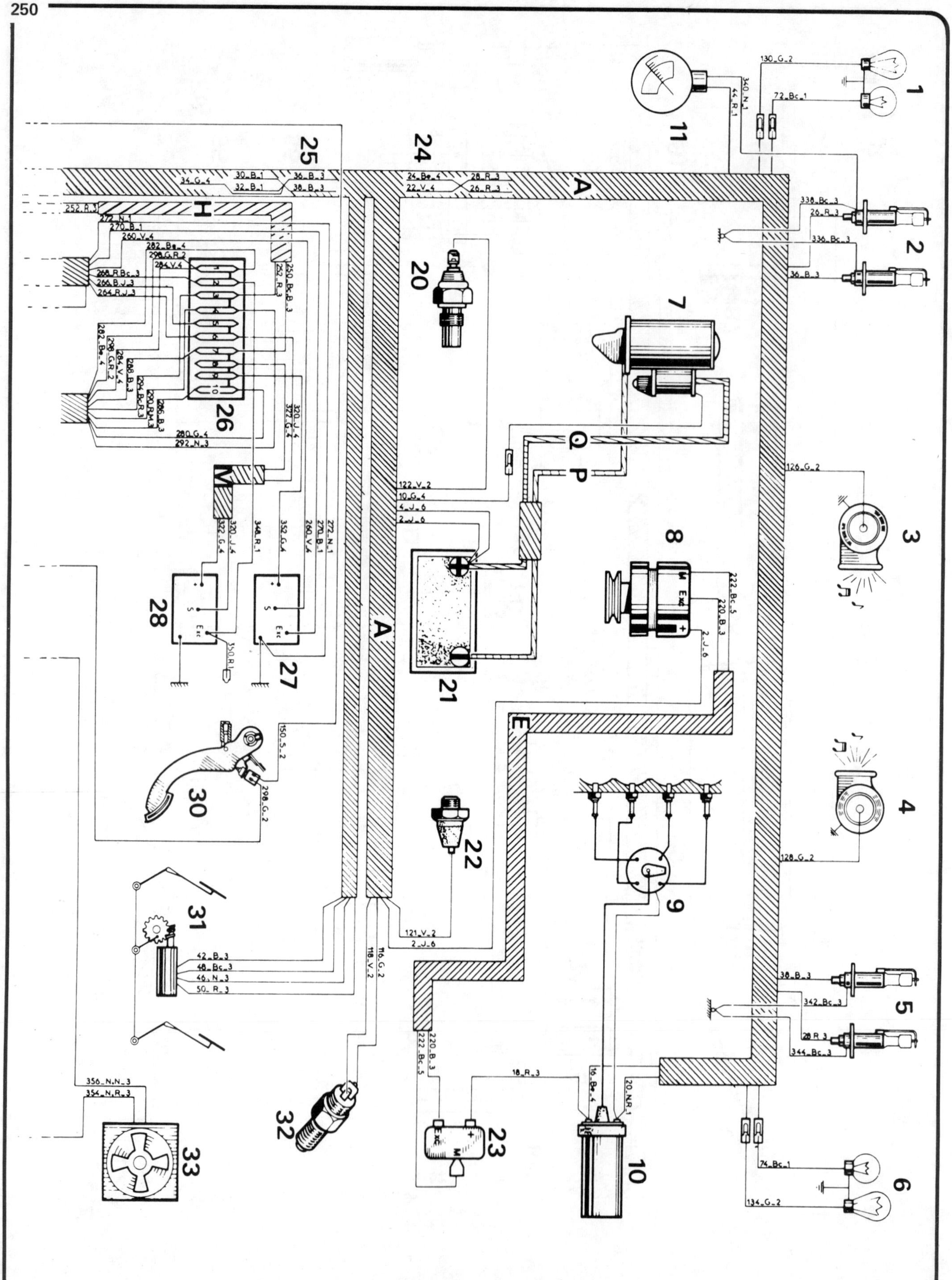

1

130.G.2

44.R.1

340.N.1

72.Bc.1

11

25

24

A

34.G.4   30.B.1   36.B.3
32.B.1   38.B.3

24.Bc.4   28.R.3
22.V.4   26.R.3

252.R.V

272.N.1
270.B.1
260.V.4
282.Bc.4
298.GR.2
264.V.4
268.R.Bc.3
266.B.J.3
264.R.J.3

282.Bc.4
284.V.4
280.B.J.3
270.R.J.3
286.B.3
296.B.J.3
280.G.4
292.N.3

250.B.B.3
252.R.J

H

338.Bc.3
26.R.3

336.Bc.3

36.B.3

2

20

7

126.G.2

3

320.J.4
322.G.4

Q
P

122.V.2
10.G.4
4.J.6
2.J.6

M

320.J.4
348.R.1
352.G.4
260.V.4
272.N.1
270.B.1

8

222.Bc.5
220.B.3
2.J.6

28

S
Exc

S
Exc

27

350.R.1

21

E

128.G.2

4

30

150.S.2

208.G.2

22

9

38.B.3
342.Bc.3

5

28.R.3
344.Bc.3

31

42.B.3
48.Bc.3
46.N.3
50.R.3

121.V.2
2.J.6

118.V.2
116.G.2

32

220.B.3
222.Bc.5

18.R.3

16.Bc.4
20.NR.1

23

10

74.Bc.1

6

134.G.2

356.N.N.3
354.N.R.3

33

Fig. 10.67 Wiring diagram for 1971 R1312 (except N. America) (continued)

Key to wiring diagrams Figs. 10.68 and 10.69

1 LH front direction indicator and sidelight
2 LH headlights
3 LH horn
4 RH horn
5 RH headlights
6 RH front direction indicator and sidelight
7 Starter
8 Alternator
9 Distributor
10 Ignition coil
11 Electric windscreen washers
13 Cooling fan motor relay
14 Cooling fan
15 Mosta temperature switch
16 Junction
20 Water temperature switch
21 Battery
22 Oil pressure sender switch
23 Regulator
24 Junction on dipped beam wires
25 Junction on main beam wires
26 Fuses
27 Dipped beams relay
28 Electric window winder relay
29 Sunroof relay
30 Brake switch
31 Windscreen wiper
32 Reversing lights switch
33 Heater-ventilator
34 LH interior light earth (ground)
35 LH interior light
36 Hazard warning lights system connection
37 Junction block between front harness – fuses harness
38 Junction block between front harness – fuses harness
39 Earthing (grounding) point
43 LH Front brake
44 RH front brake
45 Windscreen wiper time switch
46 Sunroof thermal cut-out
47 Junction block between the injection system wiring
50 Flasher unit
51 Instrument panel
52 RH interior light earth (ground)
53 RH interior light
54 LH electric window winder
55 Junction on + wires after ignition switch
56 Earth (ground) wires junction
57 Junction block between front harness – comb. lighting switch harness
58 Junction block between front harness – direction indicator switch harness
59 Combination lighting switch

60 Direction indicator switch
61 Junction block between front harness – ignition switch wiring
62 Junction block between front harness – cigar lighter wiring
63 Heated rear screen switch
64 Heating – ventilating motor switch
66 Ashtray illumination
67 RH electric window winder
68 Windscreen wiper – windscreen washer switch
69 Ignition starter switch
70 Cigar lighter
71 Cigar lighter illumination
72 Sunroof switch
73 Clock
74 LH window winder switch
75 RH window winder switch
76 Junction block between front harness and rear harness
77 Brake warning light wire junction
78 LH rear brake
79 Sunroof
80 RH rear brake
85 RH window winder wire junction
86 LH window winder wire junction
87 Luggage compartment light
88 Fuel tank
89 Heated rear screen
90 Handbrake
91 Reversing lamps wire junction
92 Rear lights wire junction
93 LH rear light
94 Licence plate light
95 RH rear light
100 Injection system
101 Cold start injector
102 No. 4 cylinder injector
103 No. 3 cylinder injector
104 No. 2 cylinder injector
105 No. 1 cylinder injector
106 Triggering contacts
108 Air temperature sensor
109 Push-on terminal and socket on cold start injector feed wire
110 Pressure sensor
111 Throttle switch
112 Temperature time switch
113 Water temperature sender
114 Control box
115 Main relay
116 Fuel pump relay
117 Wire junction
118 Wire junction
119 Fuel pump

List of harnesses

A Front harness
B Rear harness
C Combination lighting switch harness
D Direction indicator switch harness
E Alternator wiring
F Licence plate light wiring
G Cigar lighter wiring

H Hazard warning light system harness
I Fuses wiring
J Fuses wiring
K LH window winder harness
L RH window winder harness
M Window winder relay harness
R Injection harness

S Injection harness
T Injection harness
U Injection harness
V Sunroof relay harness
X Sunroof harness
P Negative lead
Q Positive lead

Wire identification

Each wire is identified by a number followed by letters indicating the wire and sleeve colours, if fitted, and a number indicating the diameter.

Wire and sleeve colours

Beige	White	Blue	Clear	Grey	Yellow	Black	Pink	Red	Green	Maroon
Be	Bc	B	C	G	J	N	S	R	V	M

Example

No.	Wire colour	Sleeve colour	Diameter
10	Bc	B	1

This is a No. 10 white wire with a blue sleeve, 9/10 mm diameter (19 gauge). On the electronic injection wiring, each wire is identified by a single number, which is stamped on the wire.

Wire diameters

No.	1	2	3	4	5	6
mm	9/10	12/10	16/10	20/10	25/10	30/10
Gauge	19	16	14	12	10	9

252

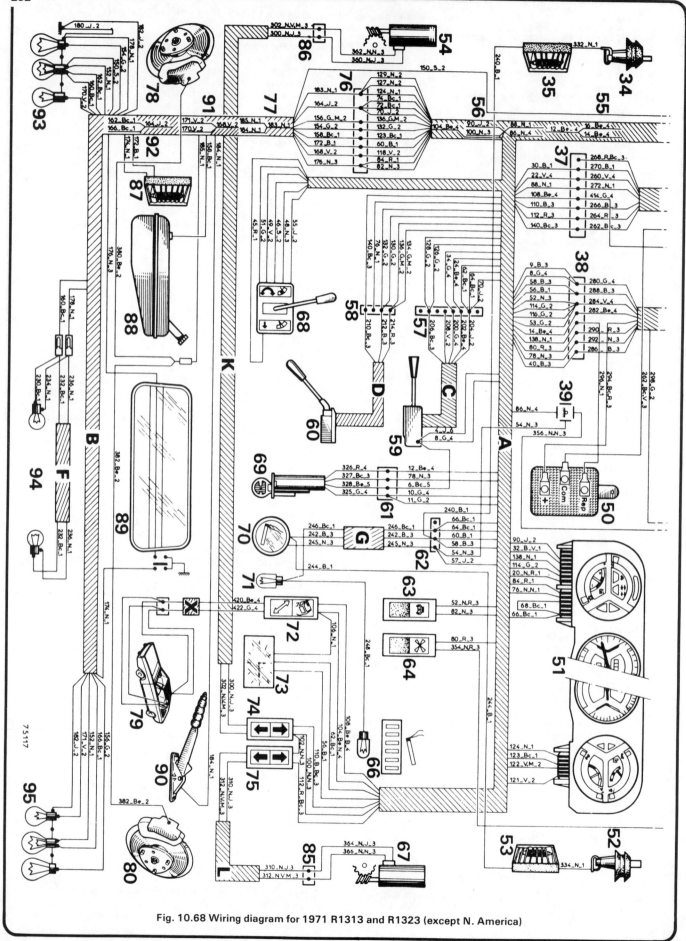

Fig. 10.68 Wiring diagram for 1971 R1313 and R1323 (except N. America)

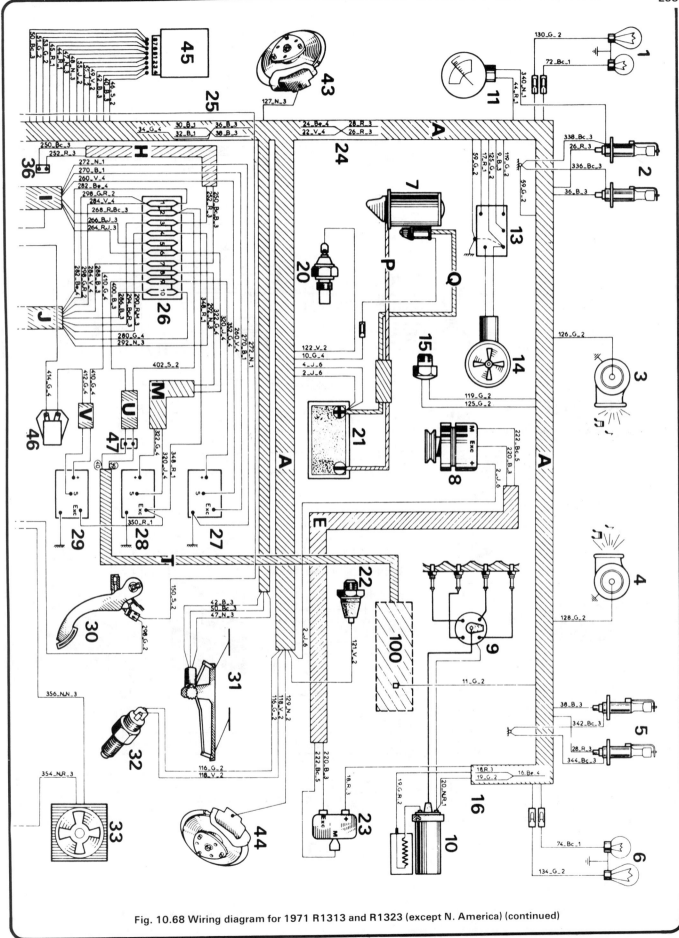

Fig. 10.68 Wiring diagram for 1971 R1313 and R1323 (except N. America) (continued)

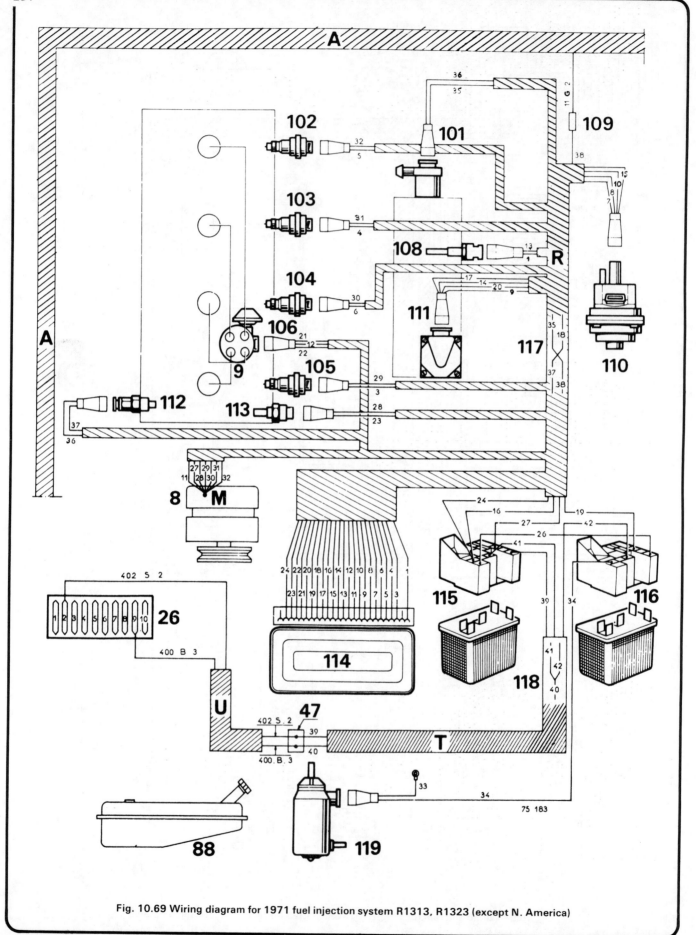

Fig. 10.69 Wiring diagram for 1971 fuel injection system R1313, R1323 (except N. America)

Key to wiring diagrams Figs. 10.70, 10.71 and 10.72

1   LH front sidelight and direction indicator
2   LH headlights
3   LH horn
4   RH horn
5   RH headlights
6   RH front sidelight and direction indicator
7   Starter
8   Alternator
9   Distributor
10   Ignition coil
11   Electric window winder
12   Earth wires junction
20   Temperature switch
21   Battery
22   Oil pressure switch
23   Regulator
24   Dipped beam wire junction
25   Main beam wire junction
26   Fuses
27   Dipped beams relay
28   Electric window winder relay
30   Brake switch
31   Windscreen wiper
32   Reversing lights switch
33   Heating and ventilating fan
34   LH interior light earth
35   LH interior light
36   Wire junction hazard warning light system
37   Junction block front harness – fuses harness
38   Junction block front harness – fuses harness
39   Earth terminal
40   Electric windscreen washer pedal
41   Wire junction windscreen wiper
42   Wire junction windscreen wiper
50   Flasher unit
51   Instrument panel
52   RH interior light earth switch
53   RH interior light

54   LH electric window winder
55   Junction on + wires after ignition switch
56   Earth wires junction
57   Junction block front harness – combination lighting switch
58   Junction front harness – direction indicators switch
59   Combination lighting switch
60   Directions indicators switch
61   Junction block front harness – ignition switch wiring
62   Junction block front harness – cigar lighter wiring
63   Rear screen demister screen
64   Heating-ventilating fan switch
65   Choke On warning light wire
66   Ashtray illumination
67   RH electric window winder
68   Windscreen wiper-windscreen washer switch
69   Ignition-starter switch
70   Cigar lighter
71   Cigar lighter illumination
72   Sunroof dummy switch
73   Electric clock
74   LH window winder switch
75   RH window winder switch
76   Junction block front harness-rear harness
85   Junction LH window winder
86   Junction RH window winder
87   Luggage compartment light
88   Fuel tank
89   Rear screen demister
90   Handbrake
91   Wire junction reversing lights
92   Wire junction Rear lights
93   LH rear light
94   Licence plate light
95   RH rear light

List of harnesses

A   Front
B   Rear
C   Combination lighting switch
D   Direction indicators switch
E   Alternator wiring
F   Licence plate light
G   Cigar lighter
H   Hazard warning lights system
I   Fuses
J   Fuses

K   LH window winder
L   RH window winder
M   Window winder relay
T   Fuel injection
U   Fuel injection
V   Sunroof relay
X   Sunroof
P   Negative lead
Q   Positive lead

Wire identification

Each wire is identified by a number followed by a letter(s) indicating wire colour, a figure indicating diameter and a number referring to the unit to which it is connected.

Wire colours

Beige	White	Blue	Clear	Grey	Yellow	Black	Salmon	Red	Green	Maroon
Be	Bc	B	C	G	J	N	S	R	V	M

Wire diameters							Example: R.1300 (110. B3. 37)			
No.	1	2	3	4	5	6	No.	Wire colour	Diameter	Unit
mm	9/10	12/10	16/10	20/10	25/10	30/10	110	B	3	37

This is a No. 110 blue wire, 16/10 mm diameter, connected to unit 37.

256

Fig. 10.70 Wiring diagram for R1300 to 1976 (except N. America)

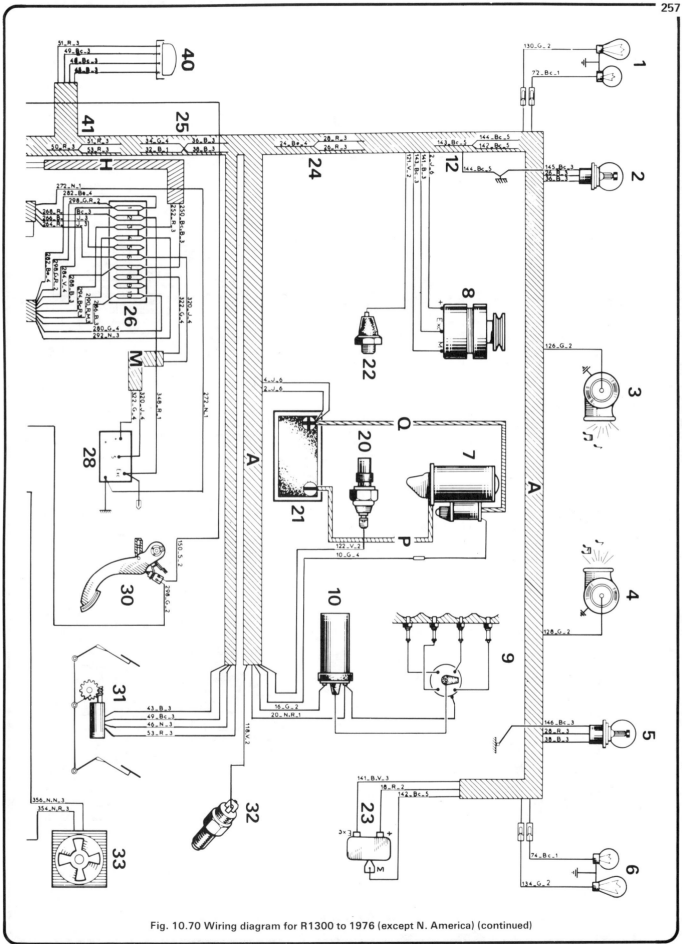

257

Fig. 10.70 Wiring diagram for R1300 to 1976 (except N. America) (continued)

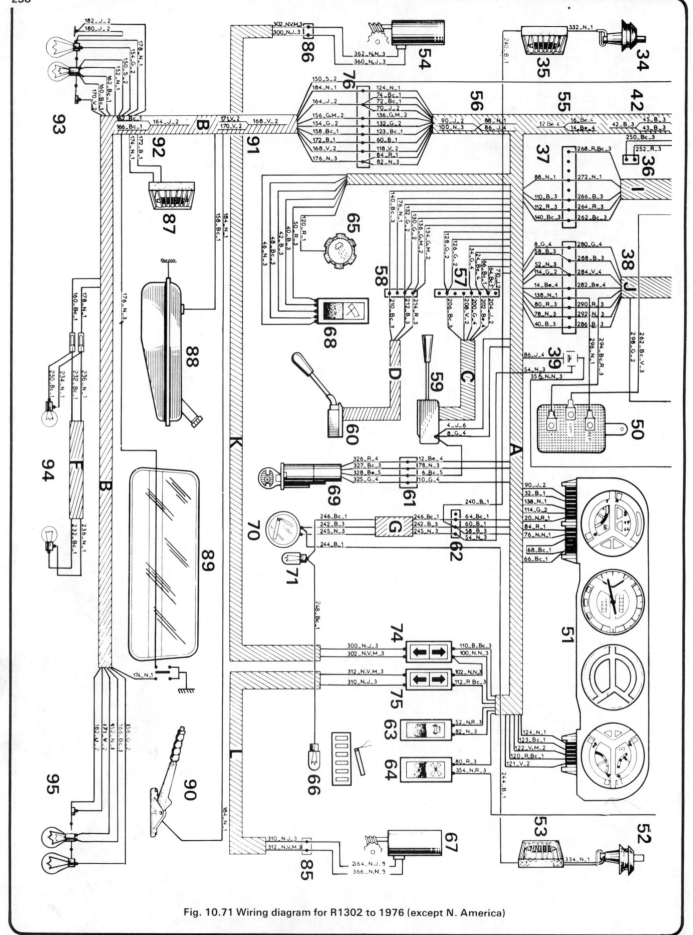

Fig. 10.71 Wiring diagram for R1302 to 1976 (except N. America)

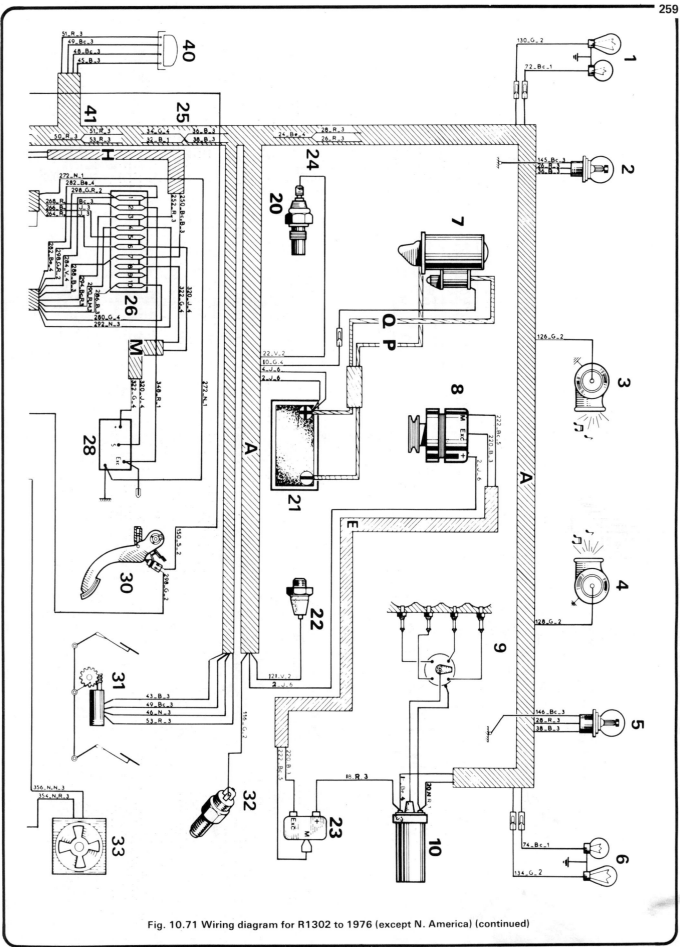

Fig. 10.71 Wiring diagram for R1302 to 1976 (except N. America) (continued)

Fig. 10.72 Wiring diagram for R1312 and R1322 to 1976 (except N. America)

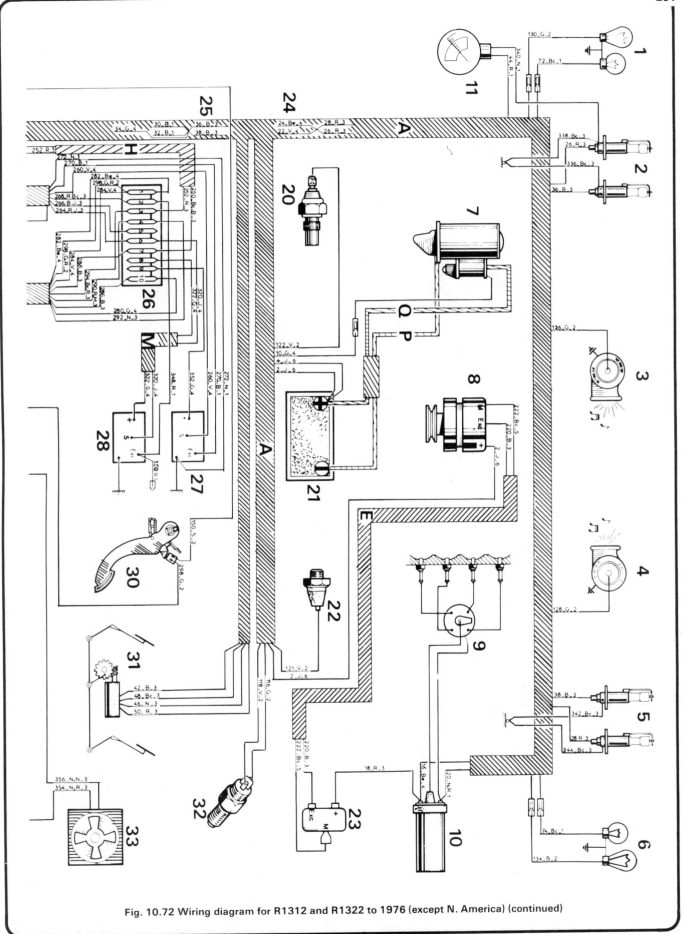

Fig. 10.72 Wiring diagram for R1312 and R1322 to 1976 (except N. America) (continued)

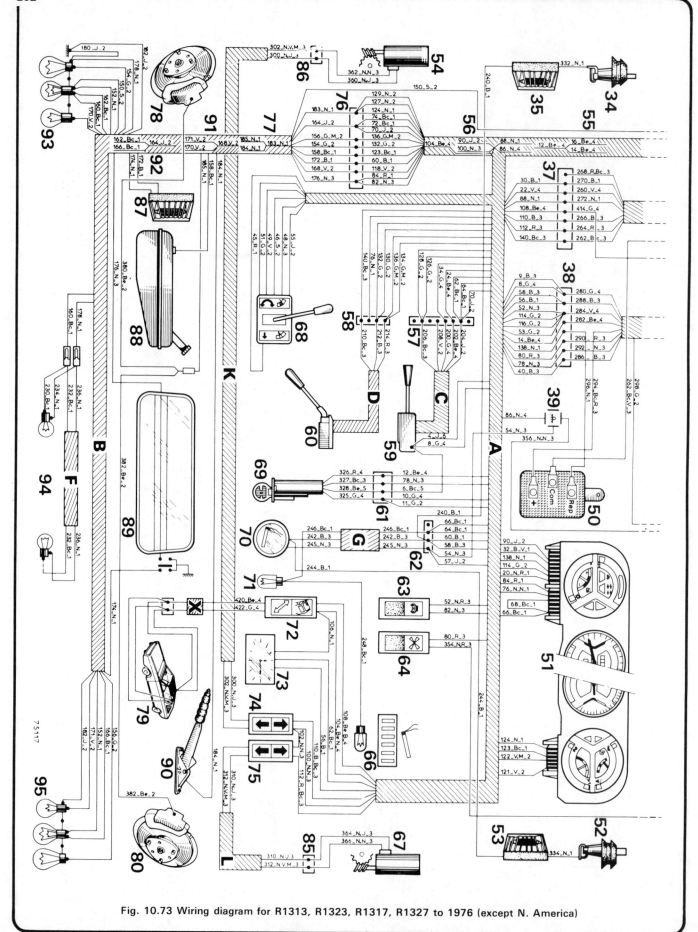

Fig. 10.73 Wiring diagram for R1313, R1323, R1317, R1327 to 1976 (except N. America)

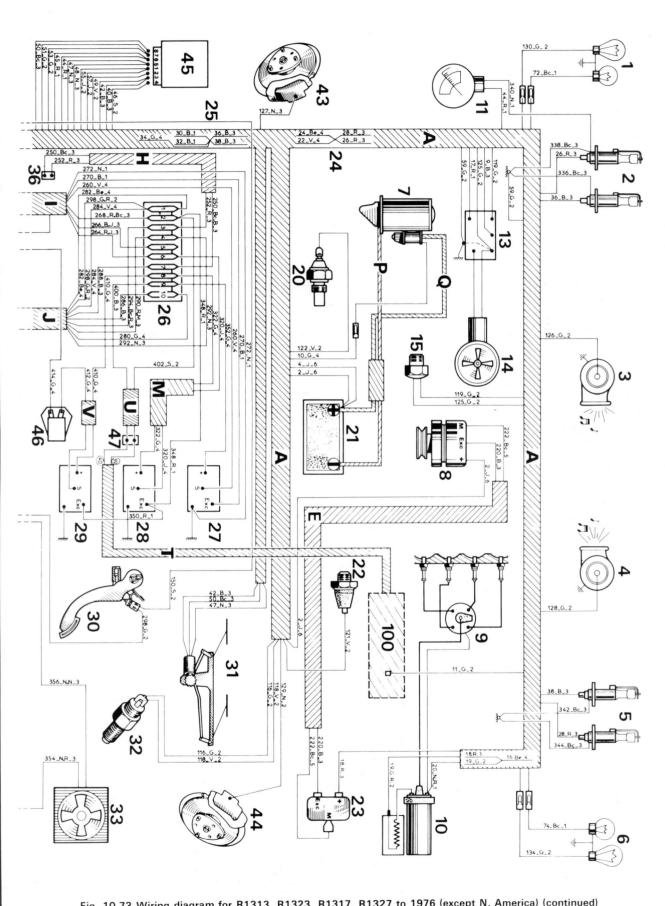

Fig. 10.73 Wiring diagram for R1313, R1323, R1317, R1327 to 1976 (except N. America) (continued)

Key to wiring diagram Fig. 10.73

1 LH front direction indicator and sidelight
2 LH headlights
3 LH horn
4 RH horn
5 RH headlights
6 RH front direction indicator and sidelights
7 Starter
8 Alternator
9 Distributor
10 Ignition coil
11 Electric windscreen washers
13 Cooling fan motor relay
14 Cooling fan
15 Coolant temperature switch
16 Junction
20 Coolant temperature switch
21 Battery
22 Oil pressure switch
23 Regulator
24 Junction dipped beam wires
25 Junction main beam wires
26 Fuses
27 Dipped beams relay
28 Electric window winder relay
29 Sunroof relay
30 Brake switch
31 Windscreen wiper
32 Reversing lamps switch
33 Heating-ventilating fan motor
34 LH interior light earth
35 LH interior light
36 Hazard warning lights system connection
37 Junction block front harness to fuses harness
38 Junction block front harness to fuses harness
39 Earth point
43 LH front brake
44 RH front brake
45 Windscreen wiper time switch
46 Sunroof cut-out
47 Junction block fuel injection wires
50 Flasher unit
51 Instrument panel
52 RH interior light earth

53 RH interior light
54 LH electric window winder
55 Junction + wires after ignition switch
56 Earth wires junction
57 Junction block front harness to comb. lighting switch harness
58 Junction block front harness to direction indicator switch harness
59 Combination lighting switch
60 Direction indicators switch
61 Junction block front harness to ignition switch wiring
62 Junction block front harness to cigar lighter wiring
63 Rear screen demister switch
64 Heating-ventilating motor switch
66 Ashtray illumination
67 RH electric window winder
68 Windscreen wiper-windscreen washer switch
69 Ignition starter switch
70 Cigar lighter
71 Cigar lighter illumination
72 Sunroof switch
73 Clock
74 LH window winder switch
75 RH window winder switch
76 Junction block front harness to rear harness
77 Brake warning light wire junction
78 LH rear brake
79 Sunroof
80 RH rear brake
85 Wire junction RH window winder
86 Wire junction LH window winder
87 Luggage compartment light
88 Fuel tank
89 Rear screen demister
90 Handbrake
91 Wire junction reversing lamps
92 Wire junction rear lights
93 LH rear light
94 Licence plate light
95 RH rear light
100 Injection system

List of harnesses

A Front
B Rear
C Combination lighting switch
D Direction indicator switch
E Alternator
F Licence plate light
G Cigar lighter
H Hazard warning light system
I Fuses
J Fuses

K LH window winder
L RH window winder
M Window winder relay
T Fuel injection
U Fuel injection
V Sunroof relay
X Sunroof
P Negative lead
Q Positive lead

Wire identification

Each wire is identified by a number followed by a letter(s) indicating wire colour, a number indicating diameter and a number referring to the unit to which it is connected.

Wire colours

Beige	White	Blue	Clear	Grey	Yellow	Black	Pink	Red	Green	Maroon	Violet	Orange
Be	Bc	B	C	G	J	N	S	R	V	M	Vi	Or

Wire diameters

No.	1	2	3	4	5	6	7	8	9
mm	7/10	9/10	10/10	12/10	16/10	20/10	25/10	30/10	45/10

Example (110 B 3. 37)

No.	Wire colour	Diameter	Unit
110	B	3	37

This is a No. 110 blue wire 10/10 mm diameter connected to unit 37

Key to wiring diagram Fig. 10.74

1 LH front direction indicator and sidelight
2 LH dipped beam headlight
3 LH main beam headlight
4 LH horn
5 RH horn
6 RH main beam headlight
7 LH dipped beam headlight
8 RH front direction indicator and sidelight
9 Electric windscreen washer pump
10 Ignition coil
11 Wire junction – optional air conditioner
12 Distributor
21 Oil pressure switch
22 Coolant temperature sensor
23 Coolant temperature switch
25 Starter
26 Alternator
27 LH headlight earth
29 Alternator earth on body
30 Regulator
33 LH front brake
35 Reversing lights switch
39 Battery
42 Wire junction – air conditioning magnetic clutch
44 RH front brake
45 Wire junction – brake pad wear indicator
46 Hearing – ventilating fan motor
47 Junction block – window winder harnesses
52 Earth
54 Earth junction – window winder harnesses
55 Heating-ventilating fan motor
58 Brake fluid level indicator (Nivocode)
60 Windscreen wiper plate
61 Junction block – front harness to windscreen motor
67 Earth junction plate
74 Instrument panel
75 Connector 1 on instrument panel
76 Connector 2 on instrument panel
77 Connector 3 on instrument panel
78 Connector 4 on instrument panel
81 Hazard warning lights switch
82 Junction block – front harness to Hazard warning lights switch
83 Junction block – front harness to time switch relay
84 Time switch relay
85 Rear screen demister switch
86 Junction block – front harness to rear screen demister switch
87 Time switch relay earth
90 Heating-ventilating motor rheostat
91 LH window winder switch
92 Junction block – LH window winder switch
93 RH window winder switch
94 Junction block – RH window winder switch wiring
95 Junction block – automatic transmission selector

96 Air conditioner blower casing
97 Wire junction – air conditioning wiring
98 Wire junction – starter to automatic transmission
99 Heater rheostat illumination
100 Wire junction – heater rheostat illumination
101 Wire junction – sunroof
105 LH door pillar switch
106 Accessories plate
107 Accessories plate feed
108 Junction block – front harness to accessories plate
109 Junction block – front harness to accessories plate
110 Junction block – front harness to accessories plate
111 Junction block – front harness to accessories plate
112 Junction block – front harness to accessories plate
113 Junction block – front harness to accessories plate
117 Stoplights switch
119 Junction block – front harness to ignition – starter switch wiring
120 Ignition-starter switch
124 Glove compartment illumination
127 RH door pillar switch
130 Junction block – front harness to lighting switch harness
131 Lighting switch
132 Junction block – front harness to windscreen wiper switch
133 Windscreen wiper switch
137 Junction block – front harness to cigar lighter wiring
139 Cigar lighter
141 Wire junction – cigar lighter illumination
142 Radio wire junction
145 Wire junction – LH door window winder motor
146 LH window winder motor
151 LH window winder motor
152 Wire junction – RH in interior light
153 Wire junction – RH door pillar switch
154 Junction block – LH interior light
155 Junction block – front harness to direction indicators harness
156 Direction indicators switch
161 Junction block – front harness to rear harness
162 Handbrake
163 Junction block – front harness to rear harness
169 Wire junction – RH door window winder motor
170 RH window winder motor
177 RH interior light
183 Junction block – LH rear light assembly harness
185 Wire junction – Fuel gauge
191 Luggage compartment light
193 Rear screen demister switch
194 Fuel gauge
198 Junction block– RH rear light assembly harness
201 LH rear light assembly
202 Licence plate light
203 RH rear light assembly
204 Earth

List of harnesses

A Engine front
B Rear
C Interior lights – door switches
D LH interior light
E Cigar lighter
F LH window winder
G RH window winder
H Lighting switch
J RH interior light
K Positive and negative starter leads
M Direction indicators

Wire identification

Each wire is identified by a number followed by a letter(s) indicating wire colour, a number indicating diameter and a number referring to the unit to which it is concerned.

Wire and sleeve colours

Beige	White	Blue	Clear	Grey	Yellow	Black	Pink	Red	Green	Maroon	Violet	Orange
Be	Bc	B	C	G	J	N	S	R	V	M	Vi	Or

Wire diameter

No.	1	2	3	4	5	6	7	8	9
mm	7/10	9/10	10/10	12/10	16/10	20/10	25/10	30/10	45/10

Example (10.B9.82)

No.	Wire colour	Diameter	Unit
10	B	9	82

This is a No.10 Blue wire 45/10 mm diameter connected to unit 82

266

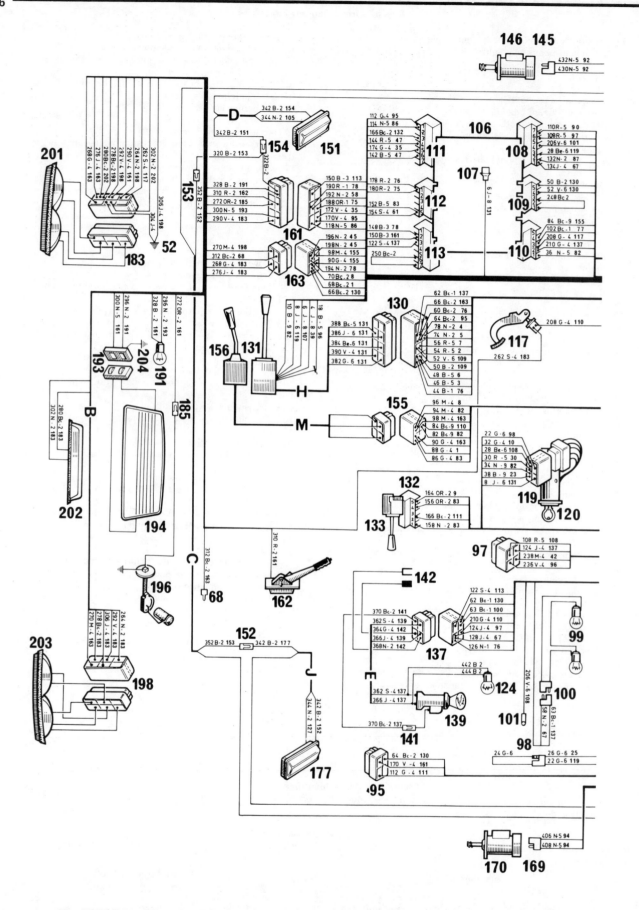

Fig. 10.74 Wiring diagram for R1300, R1317, R1327, R1318, R1328 from 1976 (except N. America)

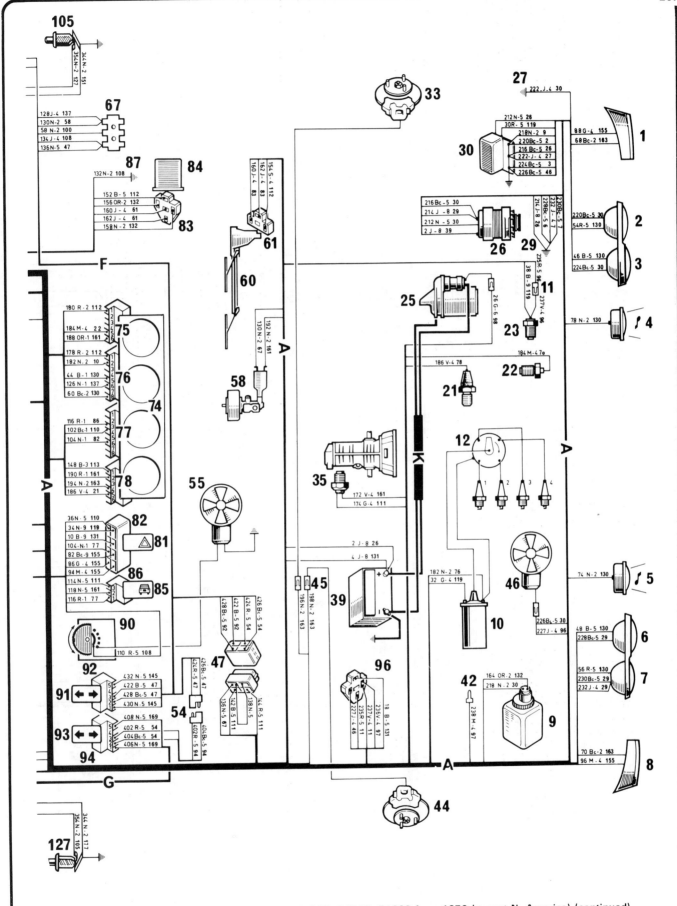

Fig. 10.74 Wiring diagram for R1300, R1317, R1327, R1318, R1328 from 1976 (except N. America) (continued)

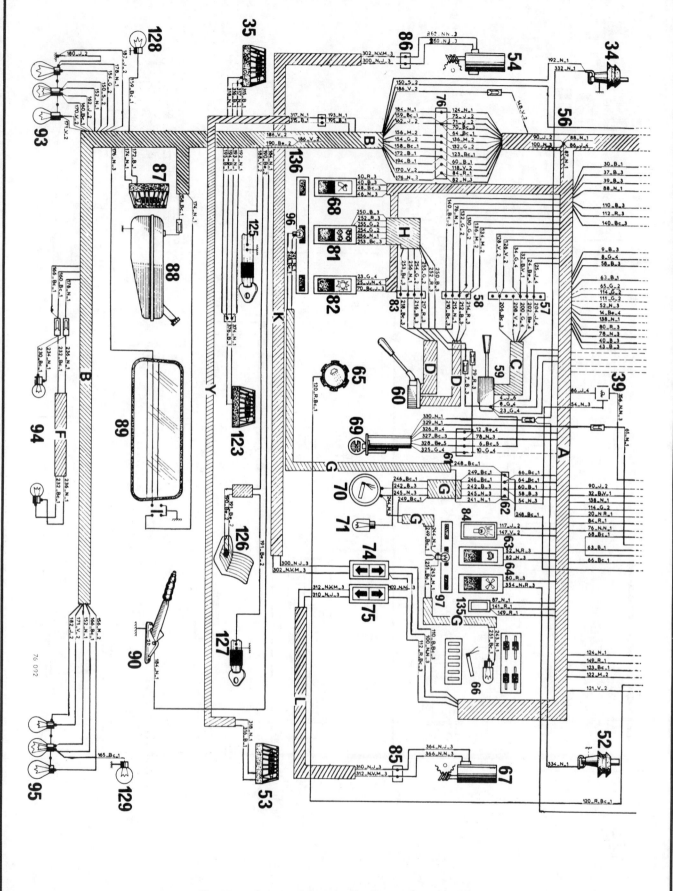

Fig. 10.75 Wiring diagram for 1973 R1304 (N. America)

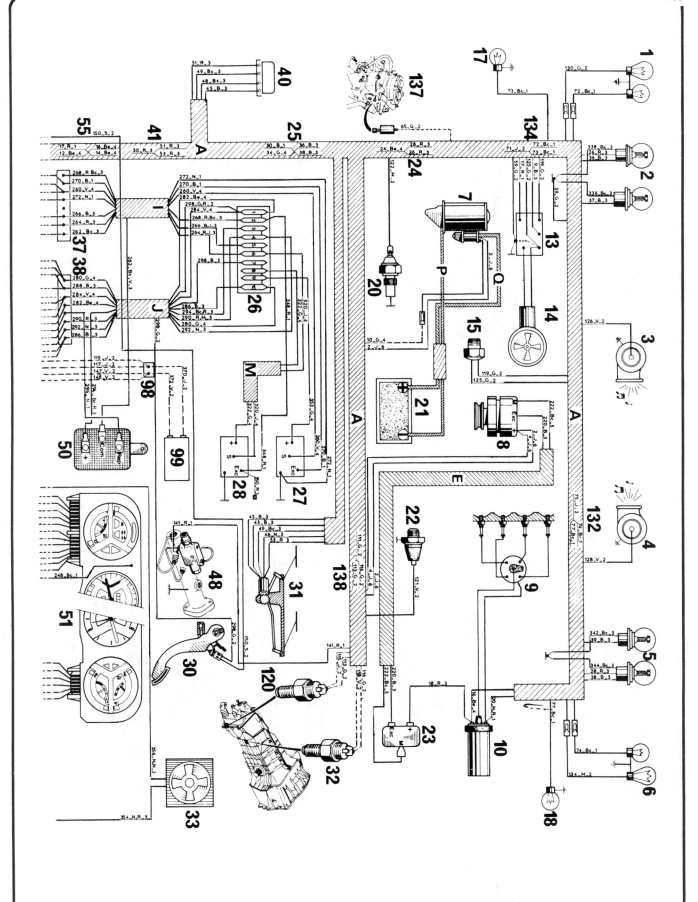

Fig. 10.75 Wiring diagram for 1973 R1304 (N. America) (continued)

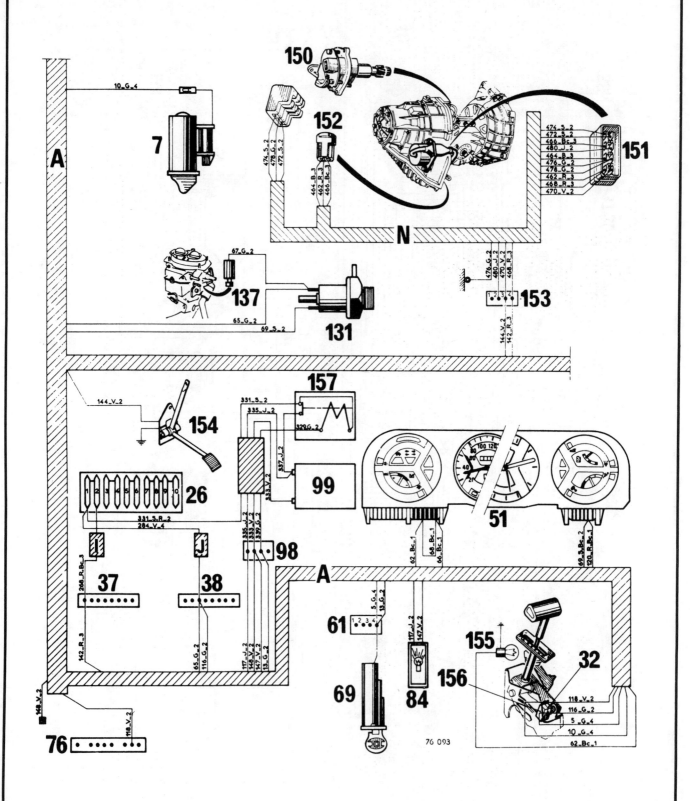

Fig. 10.76 Wiring diagram for 1973 R1304 automatic transmission (N. America)

Key for wiring diagrams Fig. 10.75, 10.76 and 10.77

1 LH front directional signal and sidelight
2 LH horn headlights
3 LH horn
4 RH horn
5 RH headlights
6 RH front directional signal and headlight
7 Starter
8 Alternator
9 Distributor
10 Ignition coil
13 Cooling fan motor relay
14 Cooling fan motor
15 Mosta temperature switch
17 LH illuminated catseye reflector
18 RH illuminated catseye reflector
19 Wire junction ignition coil to regulator
20 Water temperature switch
21 Battery
22 Oil pressure switch
23 Regulator
24 Wire junction-headlight dipped beams
25 Wire junction-headlight main beams
26 Fuses
27 Headlights relay
28 Electric window winder relay
30 Stoplight switch
31 Windshield wiper
32 Back-up lamps switch
33 Heating – ventilating fan motor
34 LH interior light ground
35 LH door pillar switch
37 Junction block between front harness – fuses wiring
38 Junction block between front harness – fuses wiring
39 Ground
40 Windshield washer pedal
41 Junction for windshield wiper wires
43 LH front brake
44 RH front brake
47 Junction block between injection wires
48 Brake pressure drop warning light switch
49 Accelerator pedal (solenoid flap valve switch)
50 Flasher unit
51 Instrument panel
52 RH interior light ground
53 RH door pillar switch
54 LH electric window winder
55 Junction on '+' wires after ignition switch
56 Junction on ground wires
57 Junction block between front harness – combination lighting switch
58 Junction block between front harness – directional signal switch
59 Combination lighting switch
60 Directional signal switch

61 Junction block between front harness – ignition switch wiring
62 Junction block between front harness – cigar lighter wiring
63 Rear screen heater switch
64 Heating – ventilating switch
65 Choke 'on' warning light switch
66 Ashtray and heater controls illumination
67 RH electric window winder
68 Windshield wiper switch
69 Ignition – starter switch
70 Cigar lighter
71 Cigar lighter illumination
72 Sunroof dummy switch
73 Clock
74 LH window winder switch
75 RH window winder switch
76 Junction block between front harness – rear harness
77 Wire junction – brake warning light
78 LH rear brake
80 RH rear brake
81 Hazard warning lights system switch
82 Headlights switch
83 Junction block
84 Safety belts 'not fastened' warning light
85 Wire junction RH window winder
86 Wire junction LH window winder
87 Trunk illumination
88 Fuel tank
89 Heated rear screen
90 Parking brake 'on' warning light switch
93 LH rear light assembly
94 Licence plate light
95 RH rear light assembly
96 Light for LH switches
97 Light for RH switches
98 Wire junction between front harness – buzzer
99 Buzzer
120 Neutral switch
121 3rd-4th speed switch
123 Rear seat illumination
125 Driver's safety belt switch
126 Passenger's seat switch
127 Passenger's safety belt switch
128 LH illuminated catseye reflector
129 RH illuminated catseye reflector
130 Water temperature switch
131 Solenoid flap valve
132 Wire junction – RH sidelights
133 Junction for solenoid flap valve groundwire
134 Wire junction – LH sidelights
135 Brake pressure drop warning light switch
136 Junction for safety belt ground wires
137 Idling speed damper
138 Wire junction – back-up lamps and neutral switch

Automatic transmission

150 Governor
151 Computer unit
152 Sealed multiple plug
153 Junction block
154 Kick-down switch
155 Selector illumination
156 Safety switch for starter solenoid
157 Buzzer relay

Electronic injection

100 Injection system
101 Cold start injector
102 No. 4 cylinder injector
103 No. 3 cylinder injector
104 No. 2 cylinder injector
105 No. 1 cylinder injector
106 Triggering contacts
108 Air temperature sensor
109 Plug & socket on cold start injector feed wire
110 Pressure sensor
111 Throttle butterfly switch
112 Temperature time switch
113 Water temperature sensor
114 Computer unit
115 Main relay
116 Fuel pump relay
117 Wire junction
118 Wire junction
119 Fuel pump

List of harnesses

A Front harness
B Rear harness
C Combination lighting switch harness
D Directional signal switch harness
E Alternator harness
F Licence plate light
G Cigar lighter wiring
H Hazard warning lights system wiring
I Fuses wiring
J Fuses wiring
K LH window winder wiring
L RH window winder wiring
M Window winder relay harness
N Automatic transmission
R Injection harness
T Injection harness
U Injection harness
Y Interior light wiring
P Negative lead
Q Positive lead

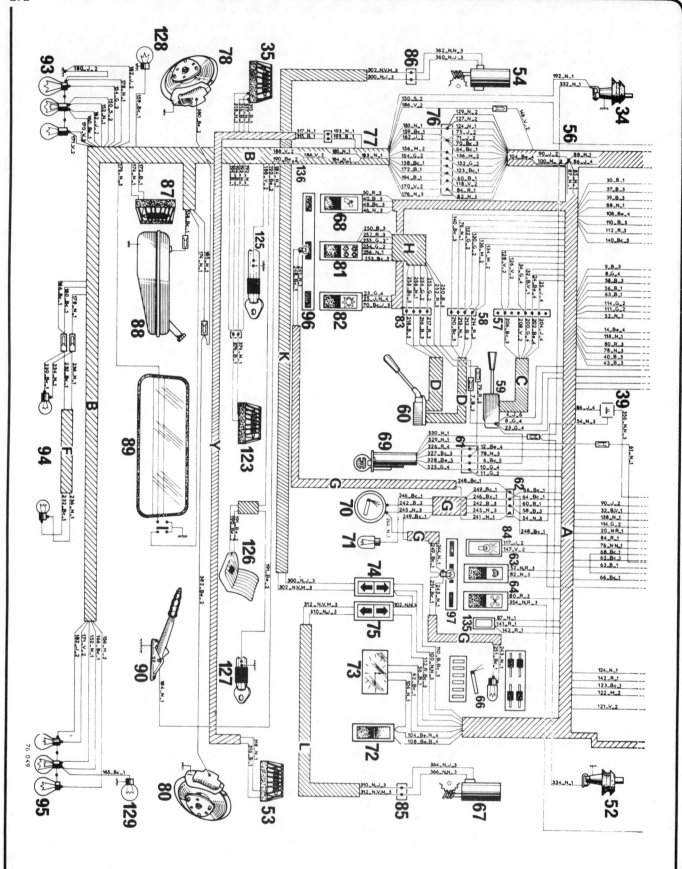

Fig. 10.77 Wiring diagram for 1973 R1313 (N. America)

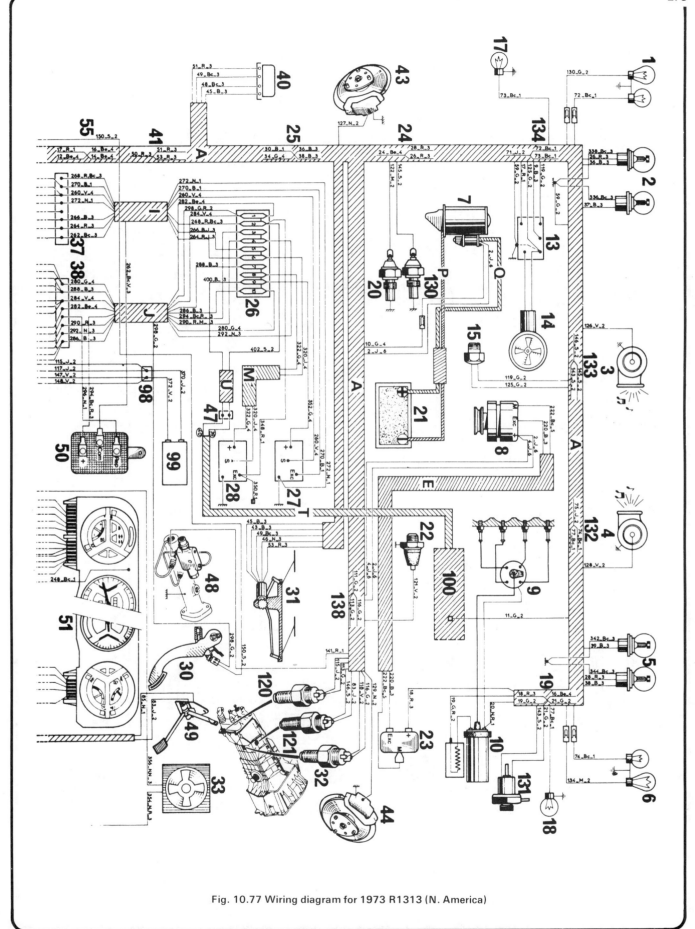

Fig. 10.77 Wiring diagram for 1973 R1313 (N. America)

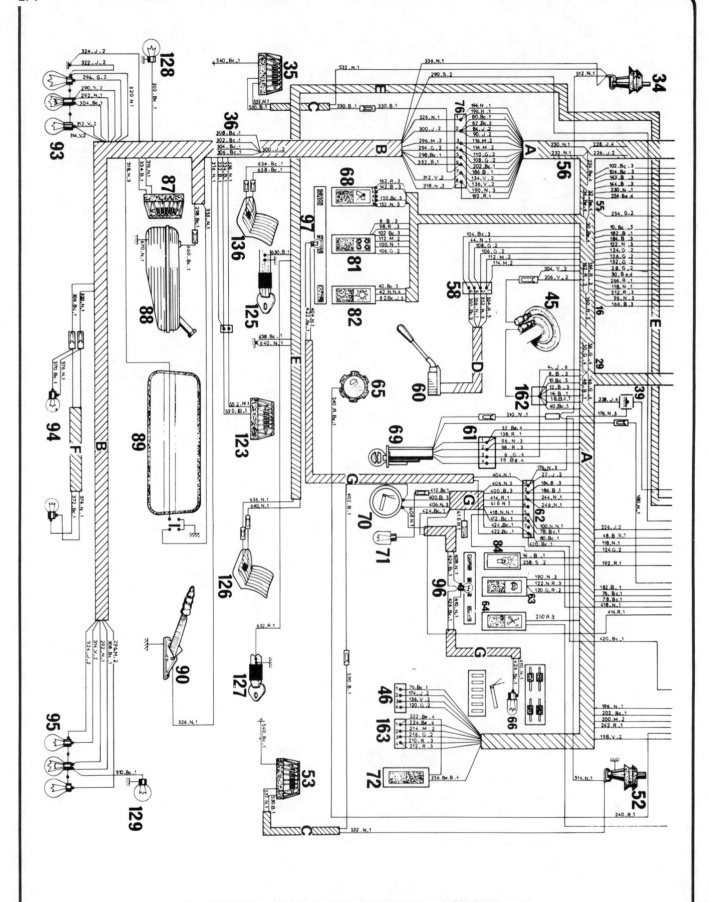

Fig. 10.78 Wiring diagram for 1974 R1204, R1314, R1324 (California)

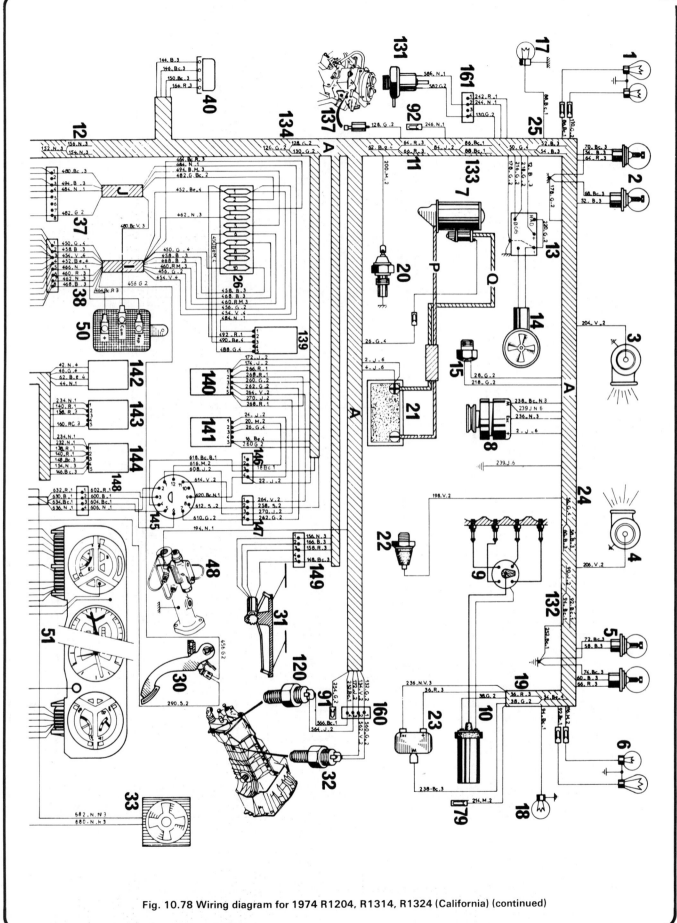

Fig. 10.78 Wiring diagram for 1974 R1204, R1314, R1324 (California) (continued)

276

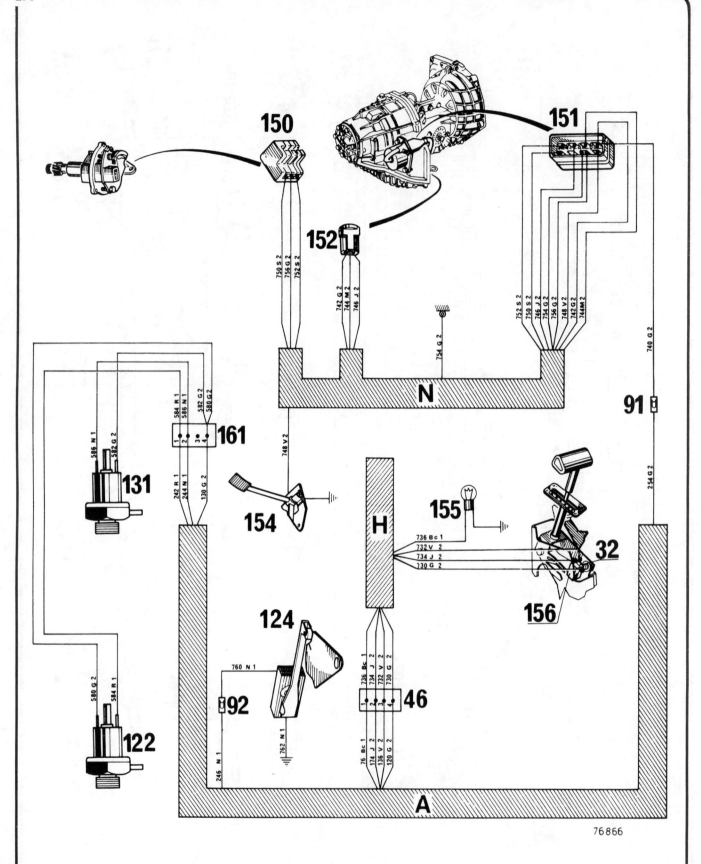

Fig. 10.79 Wiring diagram for 1974 R1304, R1314, R1324 automatic transmission (N. America)

76866

Key to wiring diagrams Figs. 10.78, 10.79 and 10.80

1 LH front directional signal and sidelight
2 LH headlights
3 RH horn
5 RH headlights
6 RH front directional signal and sidelight
7 Starter
8 Alternator
9 Distributor
10 Ignition coil
11 Wires junction – RH and LH headlights 'dipped beam'
12 Wires junction – windshield wiper park (by relay)
13 Cooling fan motor relay
14 Cooling fan motor
15 Temperature switch on radiator
16 Wires junction – windshield wiper 'fast speed' (by relay)
17 LH front illuminated catseye reflector
18 RH front illuminated catseye reflector
19 Wires junction ignition coil to regulator
20 Water temperature switch
21 Battery
22 Oil pressure switch
23 Regulator
24 Wires junction – RH headlights 'main beam'
25 Wires junction – LH headlights 'main beam'
26 Fuse box
29 Headlights main beam relay
30 Stoplight switch on brake pedal
31 Windscreen wiper
32 Back-up lamps switch
33 Heating-ventilating fan motor
34 LH door pillar switch
35 LH interior light
36 Wires junction – rear light assemblies
37 Junction block front harness to fuse wiring
38 Junction block front harness to fuses wiring
39 Ground
40 Windshield washer pedal
43 LH front brake (R.1313-R.1323)
44 RH front brake (R.1313-R1323)
45 Horns switch in steering wheel
46 Junction block – front harness to selector harness (auto-transmission)
47 Junction block – injection relays harness R.1313-R.1323)
48 Brake pressure drop warning light
49 Accelerator pedal – light throttle (P.L.) switch (R.1313-R.1323 US)
50 Flasher unit
51 Instrument panel
52 RH door pillar switch
53 RH interior light
55 Junction on '+' wires after ignition switch
56 Junction on ground wires
58 Junction block – front harness to directional signal wiring
60 Combination 'main-dipped beam' and directional signal switch
61 Junction block – front harness to 'ignition starter' switch harness
62 Junction block – front harness to cigar lighter wiring
63 Heated rear screen switch
64 Heating-ventilating switch
65 Choke 'on' warning light switch
66 Ashtray and heater controls illumination
68 Windshield wiper switches
69 Ignition starter switch
70 Cigar lighter

71 Cigar lighter illumination
72 Sunroof dummy switch
73 Clock (R.1313-R.1323)
76 Junction block – front harness to rear harness
79 Plug and socket junction – front harness to air conditioning compressor wire
81 Hazard warning lights system switch
82 Lighting switch
84 Safety belts 'not fastened' warning light
87 Trunk illumination
88 Fuel tank gauge unit
89 Heated rear screen
90 Parking brake 'on' warning light switch
91 Plug and socket junction – front harness to automatic transmission harness
92 Plug and socket for cam switch on throttle butterfly control (auto-transmission)
93 LH rear light assembly
94 Licence plate light
95 RH rear light assembly
96 Light for RH switches
97 Light for LH switches
99 5th speed switch (R.1313-R.1323 US)
100 Injection system (R.1313-R.1323)
109 Plug and socket junction – cold start injector wire (R.1313-R.1323)
120 Neutral switch
121 3rd-4th speed switch (R.1313-R.1323 US)
122 Solenoid flap valve for distributor vacuum control (auto-transmission & R.1313-R.1323)
123 Rear seat illumination
125 Driver's safety belt switch
126 Passenger's seat switch
127 Passenger's safety belt switch
128 LH rear illuminated catseye reflector
129 RH rear illuminated catseye reflector
130 Water temperature switch (R.1313-R.1323)
131 Solenoid flap valve for exhaust gas recycling control (California)
132 Wires junction for RH sidelights
133 Wires junction for LH sidelights
134 Wires junction – solenoid flap valve to idling speed damper
136 Driver's seat switch
137 Idling speed damper
138 Wires junction – 3rd-4th speed switch – water temperature switch & distributor vacuum solenoid flap valve (R.1313-R.1323)
139 Relay '+' after switch
140 Starting authorisation relay
141 Starting relay
142 Headlights relay
143 Windshield wiper fast speed relay
144 Windshield wiper 'park' relay
145 Safety belts 'in use' detector
146 Junction block – front harness to safety belts 'in use' detector
147 Junction block – front harness to safety belts 'in use' detector
148 Junction block – front harness to safety belts 'in use' detector
149 Junction block – front harness to windshield wiper motor wiring
160 Junction block – front harness to transmission case switches wiring
161 Junction block for exhaust gas recycling solenoid flap valves and distributor vacuum capsule (auto-transmission)
162 '+' Junction plates after switch
163 Junction block – front harness to air conditioning system wiring

Automatic transmission

122 Solenoid flap for distributor vacuum control
124 Cam switch on throttle butterfly control
131 Solenoid flap valve for exhaust gas recycling control

150 Governor
151 Computer

152 Sealed multiple plug and socket
154 Kick-down switch

155 Selector illumination
156 Neutral switch

Electronic injection

100 Injection system
101 Cold start injector
102 No. 4 cylinder injector
103 No. 3 cylinder injector
104 No. 2 cylinder injector

105 No. 1 cylinder injector
106 Triggering contacts
108 Air temperature sensor
109 Plug and socket on cold start injector feed wire

110 Pressure sensor
111 Throttle butterfly switch
112 Temperature time switch
113 Water temperature sensor
114 Computer unit

115 Main relay
116 Fuel pump relay
117 Wire junction
118 Wire junction
119 Fuel pump

List of harnesses

A   Front harness
B   Rear harness
C   Interior light wiring
D   Directional signal and headlight main – dipped beam changeover switch harness

E   Safety belts harness
F   Licence plate light wiring
G   Cigar lighter wiring
H   Gear selector wiring (auto-transmission)

I   Fuses wiring
J   Fuses wiring
N   Automatic transmission
P   Negative lead

Q   Positive lead
R   Injection harness
T   Injection harness
U   Injection harness

278

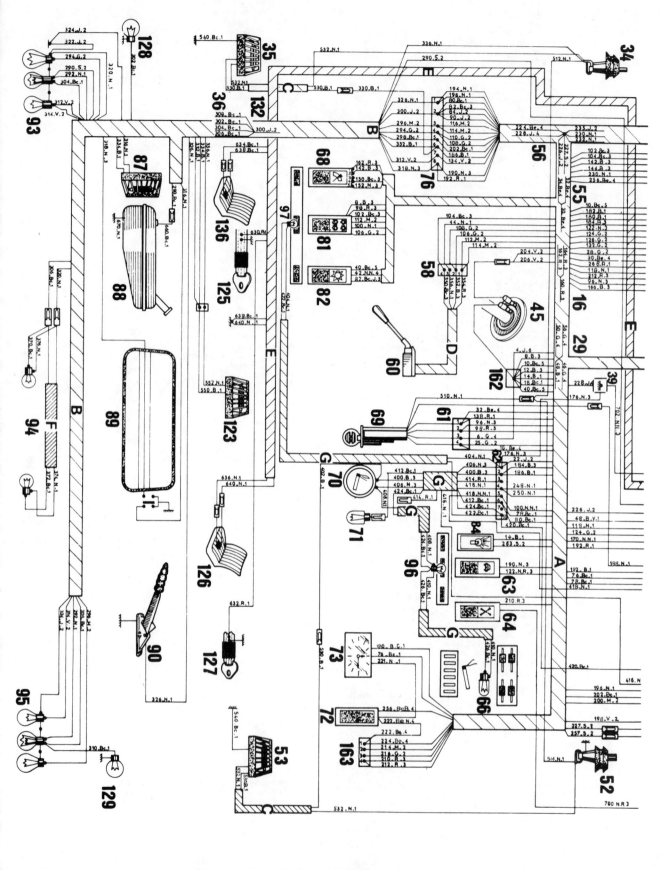

Fig. 10.80 Wiring diagram for 1974 R1313 (N. America)

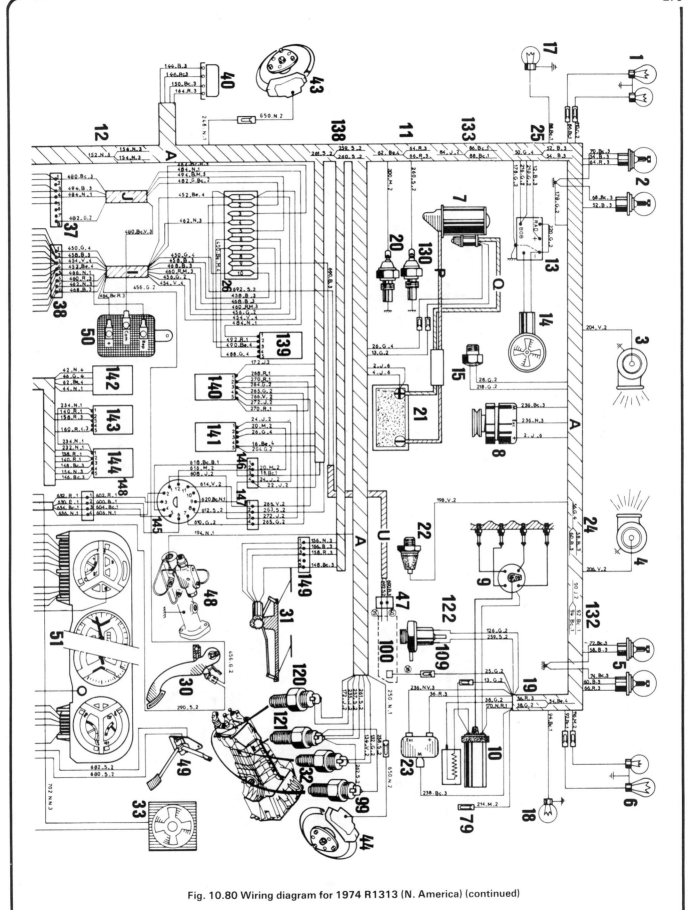

Fig. 10.80 Wiring diagram for 1974 R1313 (N. America) (continued)

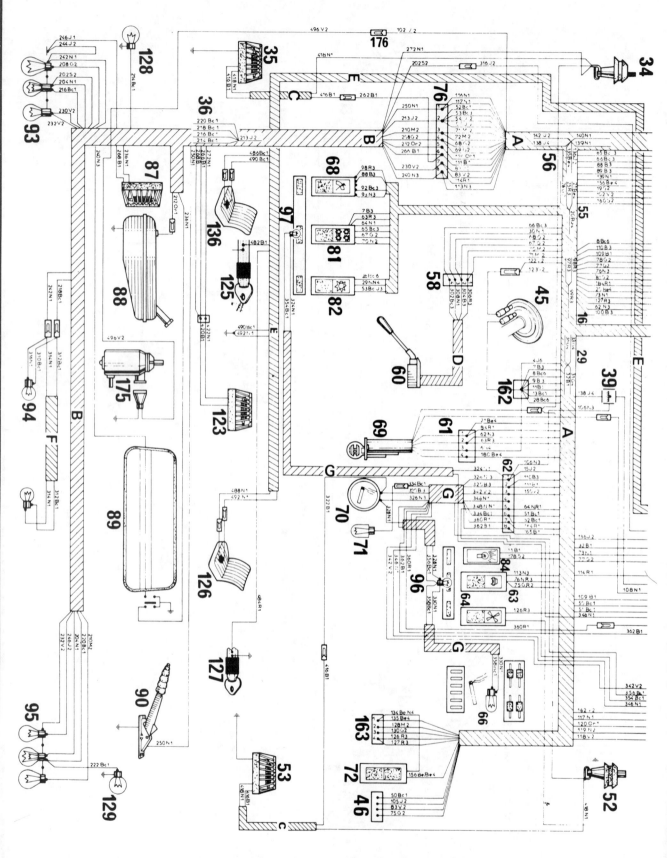

Fig. 10.81 Wiring diagram for 1975 R1308 (N. America)

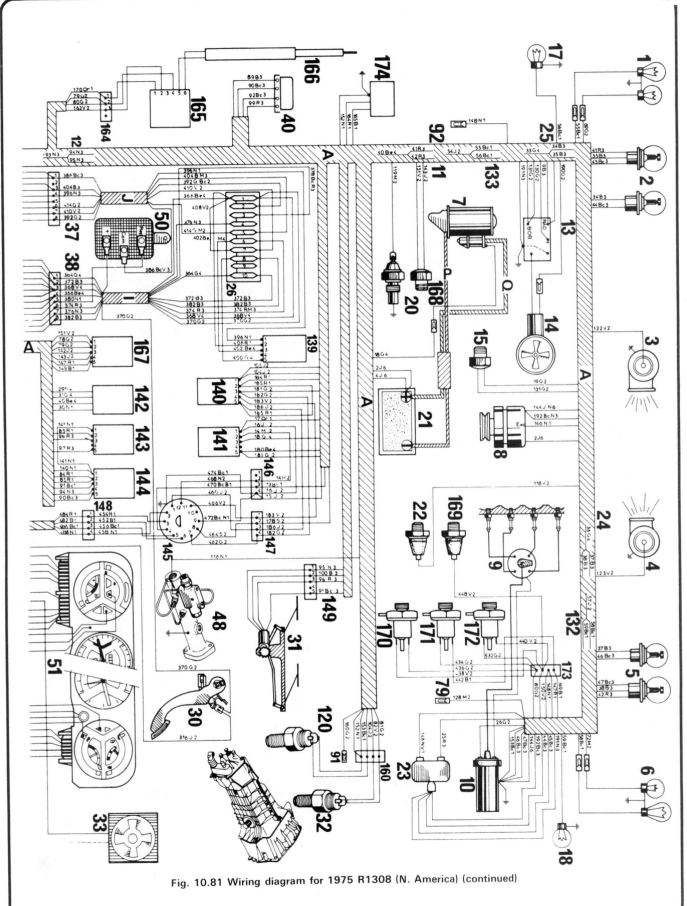

Fig. 10.81 Wiring diagram for 1975 R1308 (N. America) (continued)

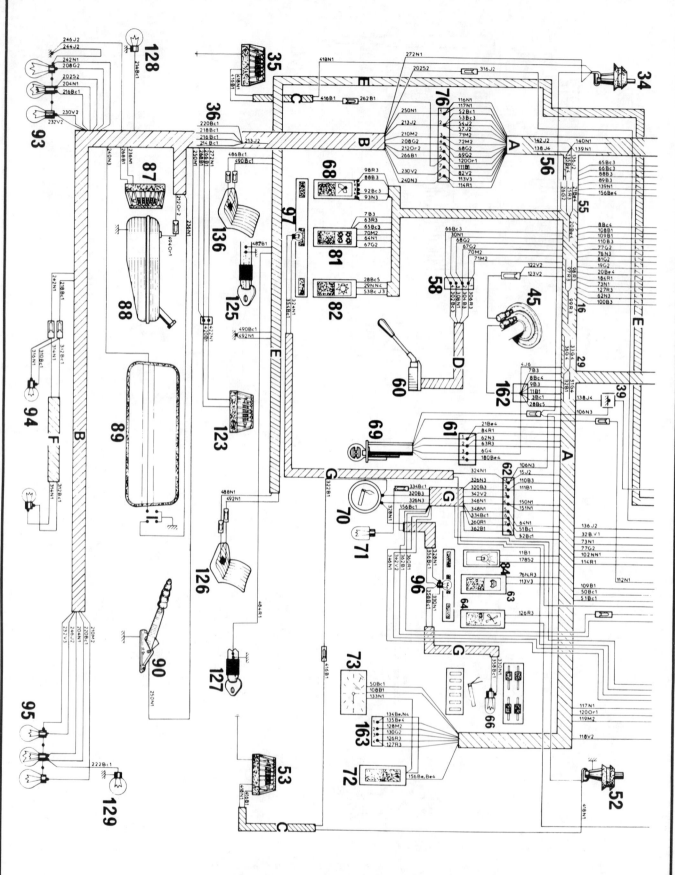

Fig. 10.82 Wiring diagram for 1975 R1316 (N. America)

283

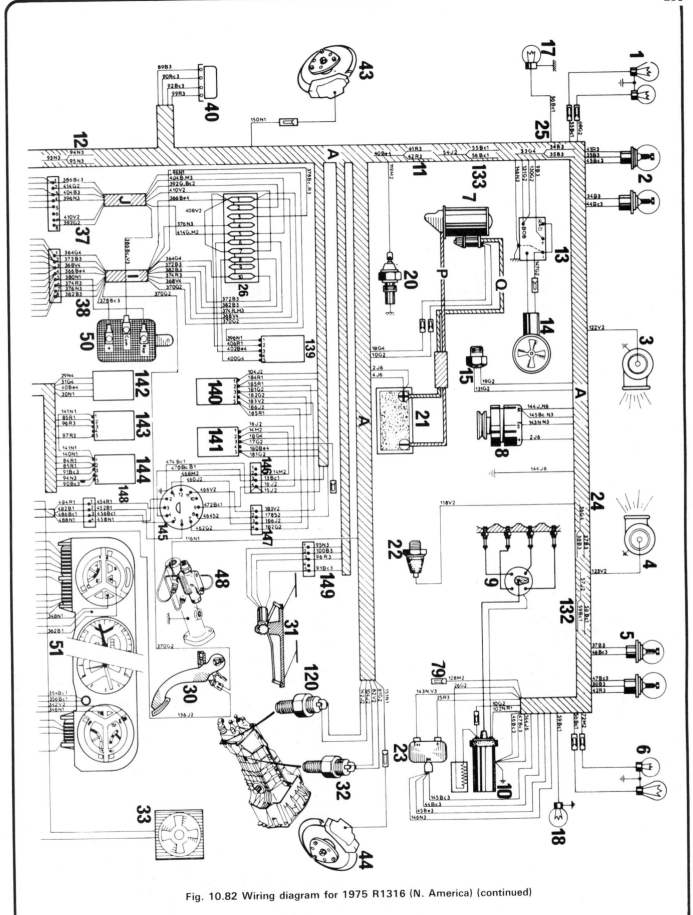

Fig. 10.82 Wiring diagram for 1975 R1316 (N. America) (continued)

284

Key to wiring diagram Figs. 10.81, 10.82 and 10.83

1 LH front directional signal and sidelight
2 LH headlights
3 LH horn
4 RH horn
5 RH headlights
6 RH front directional signal and sidelight
7 Starter
8 Alternator
9 Distributor
10 Ignition coil
11 Wires junction – RH and LH headlights 'dipped beam'
12 Wires junction – windshield wiper park (by relay)
13 Cooling fan motor relay
14 Cooling fan motor
15 Temperature switch on radiator
16 Wires junction – windshield wiper 'fast speed' (by relay)
17 LH front illuminated catseye reflector
18 RH front illuminated catseye reflector
20 Coolant temperature switch
21 Battery
22 Oil pressure switch
23 Regulator
24 Wires junction – RH headlights 'main beam'
25 Wires junction – LH headlights 'main beam'
26 Fuse-box
29 Headlights main beam relay
30 Stoplight switch on brake pedal
31 Windshield wiper
32 Back-up lamps switch
33 Heating-ventilating fan motor
34 LH door pillar switch
35 LH interior light
36 Wires junction – rear light assemblies
37 Junction block front harness to fuses wiring
39 Ground
40 Windshield washer pedal
43 LH front brake (R.1313 – R.1323)
44 RH front brake (R.1313 – R.1323)
45 Horns switch in steering wheel
46 Junction block – front harness to selector harness (auto-transmission)
47 Junction block – injection relays harness (R.1313 – R. 1323)
48 Brake pressure drop warning light
50 Flasher unit
51 Instrument panel
52 RH door pillar switch
53 RH interior light
55 Junction on '+' wires after ignition switch
56 Junction on ground wires
58 Junction block – front harness to directional signal wiring
60 Combination 'main-dipped beam' and directional signal switch
61 Junction block – front harness to 'ignition-starter' switch harness
62 Junction block – front harness to cigar lighter wiring
63 Heater rear screen switch
64 Heating-ventilating switch
66 Ashtray and heater controls illumination
68 Windshield wiper switch
69 Ignition starter switch
70 Cigar lighter
71 Cigar lighter illumination
72 Sunroof dummy switch
73 Clock (R.1313 – R.1323)
76 Junction block – front harness to rear harness
79 Push-on spade terminal and socket – front harness to air conditioning compressor wire

81 Hazard warning lights system switch
82 Lighting switch
84 Safety belts 'not fastened' warning light
87 Trunk illumination
88 Fuel tank gauge unit
89 Heated rear screen
90 Parking brake 'on' warning light switch
91 Push-on spade terminal and socket – front harness to automatic transmission harness
92 Push-on spade terminal and socket for cam switch on throttle – butterfly control (auto-tranmsission)
93 LH rear light assembly
94 Licence plate light
95 RH rear light assembly
96 Light for RH switches
97 Light for LH switches
100 Injection system (R.1313 – R1323)
109 Push-on spade terminal and socket junction – cold start injector wire (R.1313 – R.1323)
120 Neutral switch
122 Solenoid flap valve for distributor vacuum control (auto-transmission & R.1313 – R.1323)
123 Rear seat illumination
125 Driver's safety belt switch
126 Passenger's seat switch
127 Passenger's safety belt switch
128 LH rear illuminated catseye reflector
129 RH rear illuminated catseye reflector
132 Wires junction for RH sidelights
133 Wires junction for LH sidelights
136 Driver's seat switch
139 Relay '+' after switch
140 Starting authorisation relay
141 Starting relay
142 Headlights relay
143 Windshield wiper fast speed relay
144 Windshield wiper 'park' relay
145 Safety belts 'in use' detector
146 Junction block – front harness to safety belts 'in use' detector
147 Junction block – front harness to safety belts 'in use' detector
148 Junction block – front harness to safety belts 'in use' detector
149 Junction block – front harness to windshield wiper motor wiring
160 Junction block – front harness to transmission case switches wiring
161 Junction block for exhaust gas recycling solenoid flap valve and distributor vacuum capsule (auto-transmission)
162 Junction plate '+' after switch
163 Junction block – front harness to air conditioning system wiring
164 Junction block – front harness to temperature sensor wiring (R.1308)
165 Temperature switch (R.1308)
166 Temperature sensor (R.1308)
167 Solenoid flap valve relay (R.1308)
168 Coolant temperature switch for anti-pollution system (R.1308)
169 Oil temperature switch (R.1308)
170 Branching valve (R.1308)
171 Advance vacuum capsule (R.1308)
172 Anti-detonation solenoid flap valve (R.1308)
173 Junction block – front harness to solenoid flap valves wiring (R.1308)
174 Maintenance indicator (R.1308)
175 Electric fuel pump
176 Push-on spade terminal and socket – fuel pump feed wire

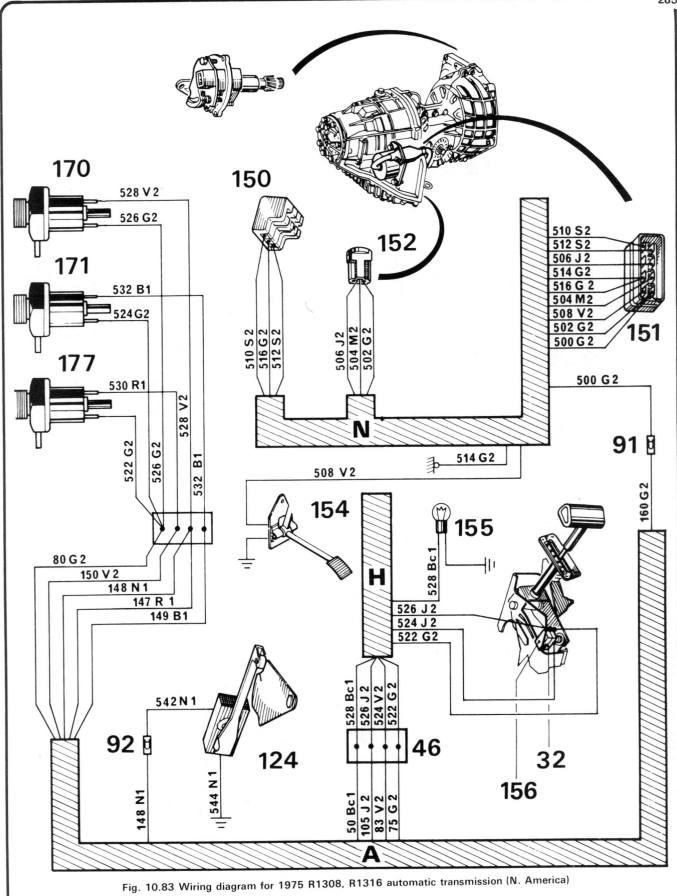

285

170
528 V 2
526 G2

171
532 B1
524 G2

177
530 R1

150

152

510 S 2
512 S 2
506 J 2
514 G2
516 G 2
504 M2
508 V 2
502 G2
500 G2

151

510 S 2
516 G 2
512 S 2

506 J 2
504 M 2
502 G 2

522 G 2
526 G 2
528 V 2
532 B 1

500 G 2

514 G 2

508 V 2

91

160 G 2

N

154

155

528 Bc 1

H

526 J 2
524 J 2
522 G 2

80 G 2
150 V 2
148 N 1
147 R 1
149 B 1

542 N 1

92

148 N 1

544 N 1

124

528 Bc 1
526 J 2
524 V 2
522 G 2

46

50 Bc1
105 J 2
83 V 2
75 G 2

32

156

A

Fig. 10.83 Wiring diagram for 1975 R1308, R1316 automatic transmission (N. America)

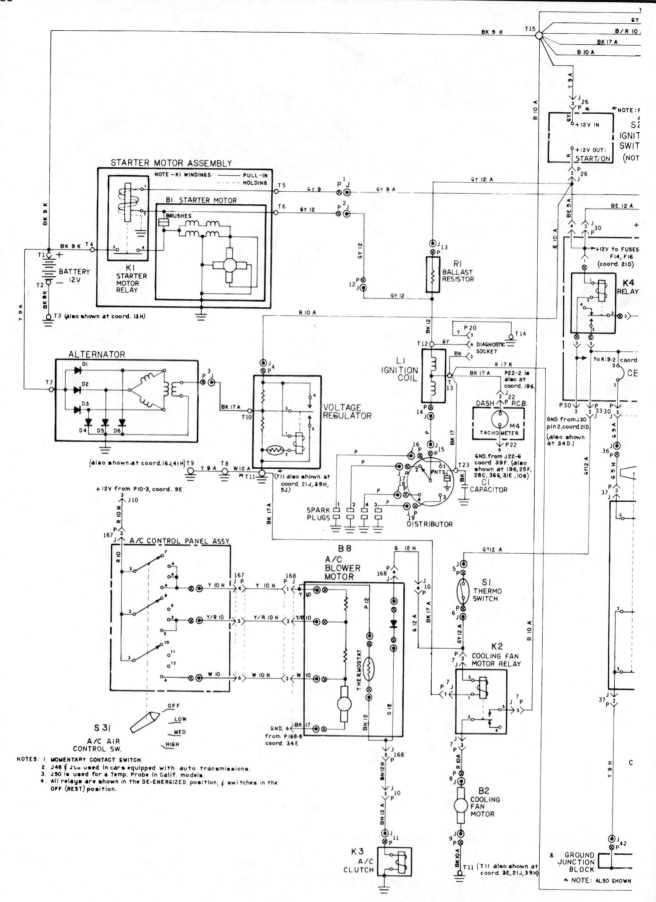

Fig. 10.84 Wiring diagram for 1978 R1317, R1327 Gordini (N. America), 1977 version differs in detail only

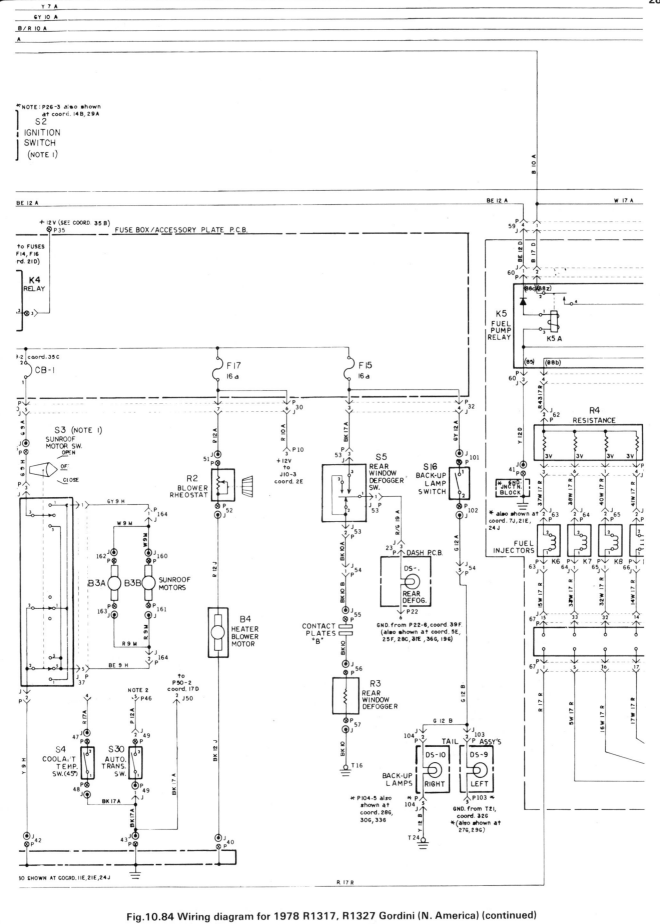

Fig.10.84 Wiring diagram for 1978 R1317, R1327 Gordini (N. America) (continued)

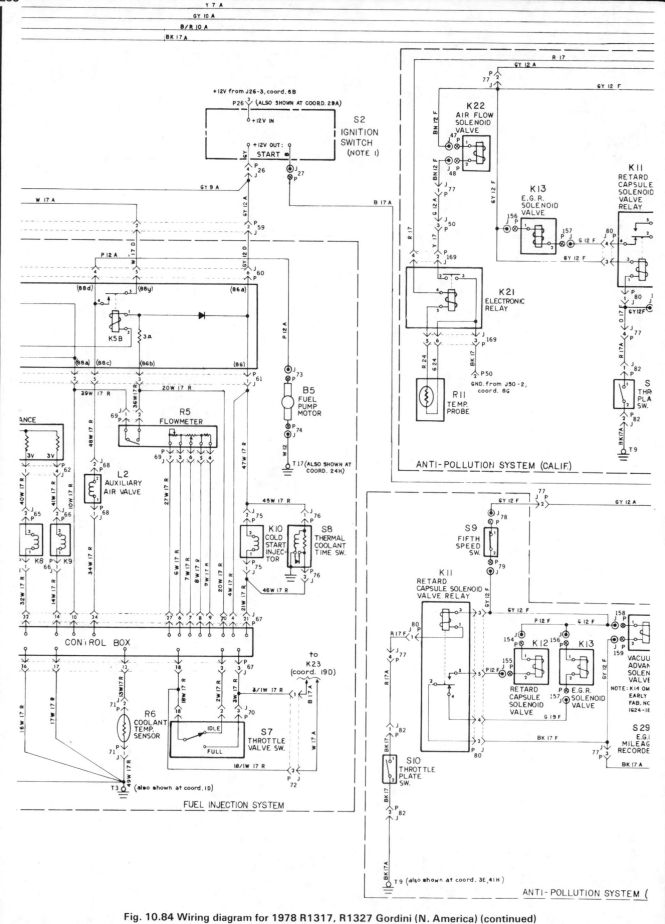

Fig. 10.84 Wiring diagram for 1978 R1317, R1327 Gordini (N. America) (continued)

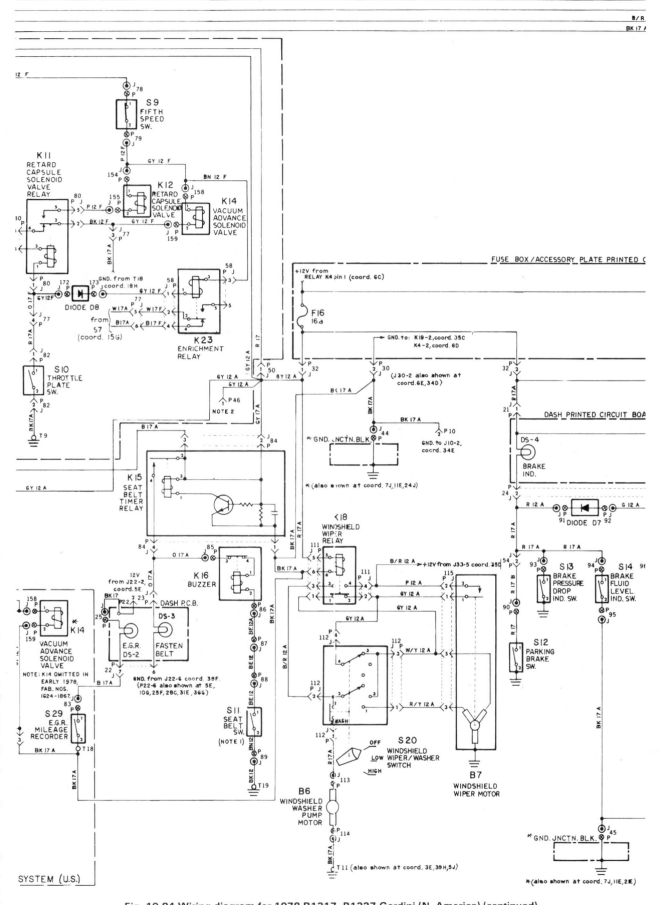

Fig. 10.84 Wiring diagram for 1978 R1317, R1327 Gordini (N. America) (continued)

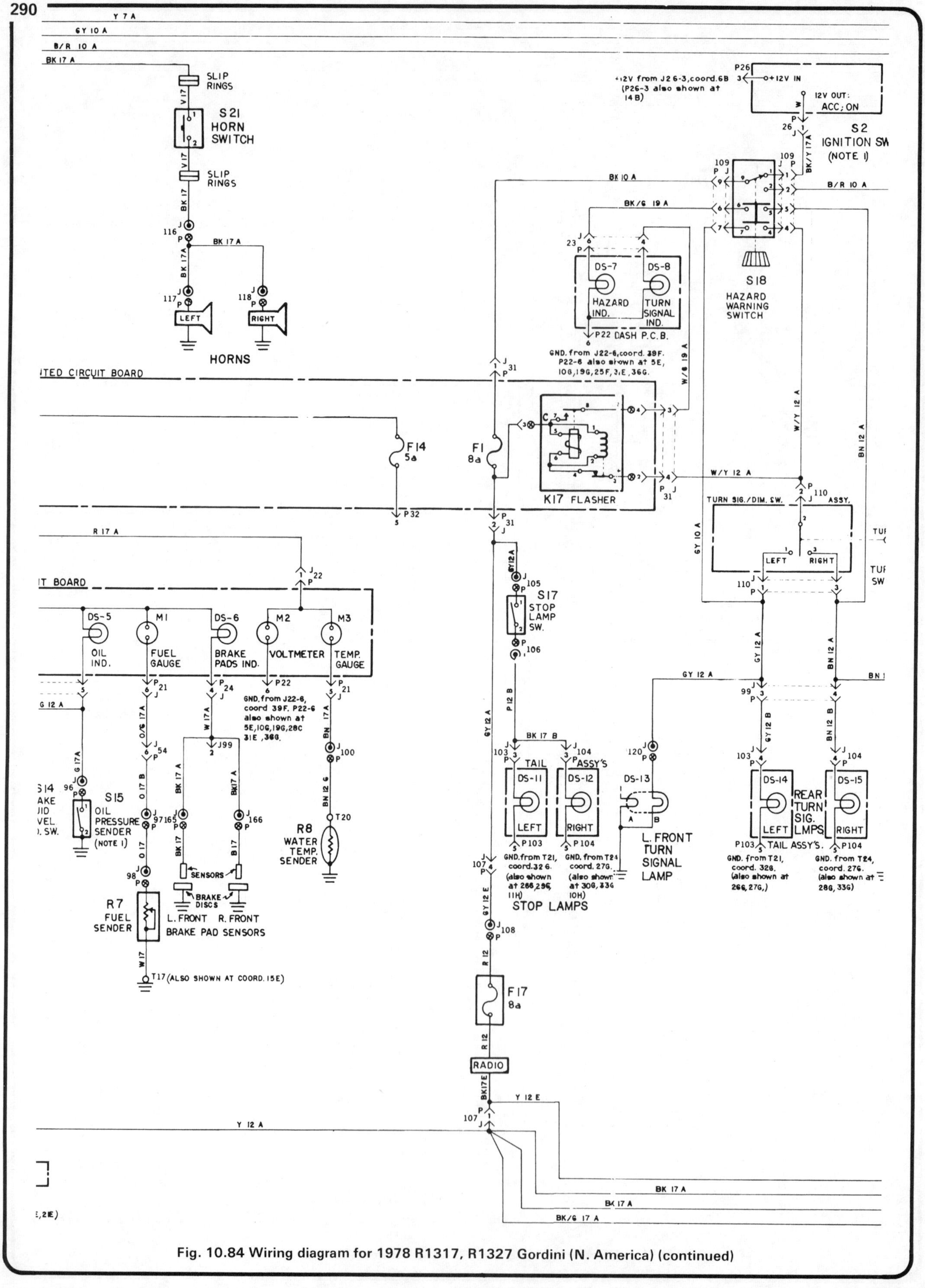

Y 7 A

GY 10 A

B/R 10 A

BK 17 A

SLIP RINGS

V 17

S 21
HORN SWITCH

SLIP RINGS

BK 17

116 J P

BK 17 A

BK 17 A

117 J P

118 J P

LEFT

RIGHT

HORNS

TED CIRCUIT BOARD

F14 5a

F1 8a

J 31 P

+12V from J26-3, coord.6B
(P26-3 also shown at 14B)

P26 3

o +12V IN

12V OUT: ACC; ON

S2 IGNITION SW (NOTE 1)

26 P

BK/Y 17 A

109 P J

109 P J

B/R 10 A

BK 10 A

BK/G 19 A

23 J 6 P 4

DS-7 HAZARD IND.

DS-8 TURN SIGNAL IND.

P22 DASH P.C.B.

GND. from J22-6, coord. 39F.
P22-6 also shown at 5E,
10G,19G,25E,3.E,36G.

S18 HAZARD WARNING SWITCH

W/B 19 A

K17 FLASHER

W/Y 12 A

W/Y 12 A

P 31

J P 31

J 22 P

R 17 A

IT BOARD

DS-5
OIL IND.

M1
FUEL GAUGE

DS-6
BRAKE PADS IND.

M2
VOLTMETER

M3
TEMP. GAUGE

P 21 J

O/G 17A J 24

W 17A 2

P 21 J

GND. from J22-6,
coord 39F. P22-6 also
shown at
5E,10G,19G,28C
31E ,36G.

G 12 A

G 17A

S14
AKE
JID
VEL
. SW.

96 J P

S15
OIL PRESSURE SENDER
(NOTE 1)

O 17 B J 54

O 17

BK 17 A J

97 165

BK 17

B17A J

166

B 17

BN 17 A J 100

BN 12 G

R8
WATER TEMP. SENDER

T20

98 J P

W 17

R7
FUEL SENDER

SENSORS

BRAKE DISCS

L. FRONT   R. FRONT
BRAKE PAD SENSORS

T17 (ALSO SHOWN AT COORD. 15E)

GY 12A

J 105 P

S17
STOP LAMP SW.

J P 106

P12 B

GY 12 A

BK 17 B

J 103 P

TAIL

J 104 P

ASSY'S

DS-11
LEFT

DS-12
RIGHT

P 103

P 104

GND. from T21,
coord. 32 6.
(also shown
at 286,296,
11H)

GND. from T24
coord. 27G.
(also shown
at 30G,33G,
10H)

J 107 P

GY 12 E

STOP LAMPS

J 108 P

R 12

F 17
8a

R 12

RADIO

BK17 E

107 P J

Y 12 A

120 J P

DS-13
A   B

L. FRONT
TURN
SIGNAL
LAMP

GY 12 A

TURN SIG./DIM. SW.

110 J P

LEFT   RIGHT

110 J P

GY 10 A

ASSY,

TUR

TUR
SW

BN 12 A

GY 12 A

GY 12 B

99 J P

BN 12 A

BN I

J 103 P

DS-14
LEFT

J 104 P

REAR TURN SIG. LMPS

DS-15
RIGHT

P 103   TAIL ASSY'S.

P 104

GND. from T21,
coord. 328.
(also shown at
286,27G,)

GND. from T24,
coord. 27G.
(also shown at
286,33G)

Y 12 E

BK 17 A

BK 17 A

BK/G 17 A

2E)

Fig. 10.84 Wiring diagram for 1978 R1317, R1327 Gordini (N. America) (continued)

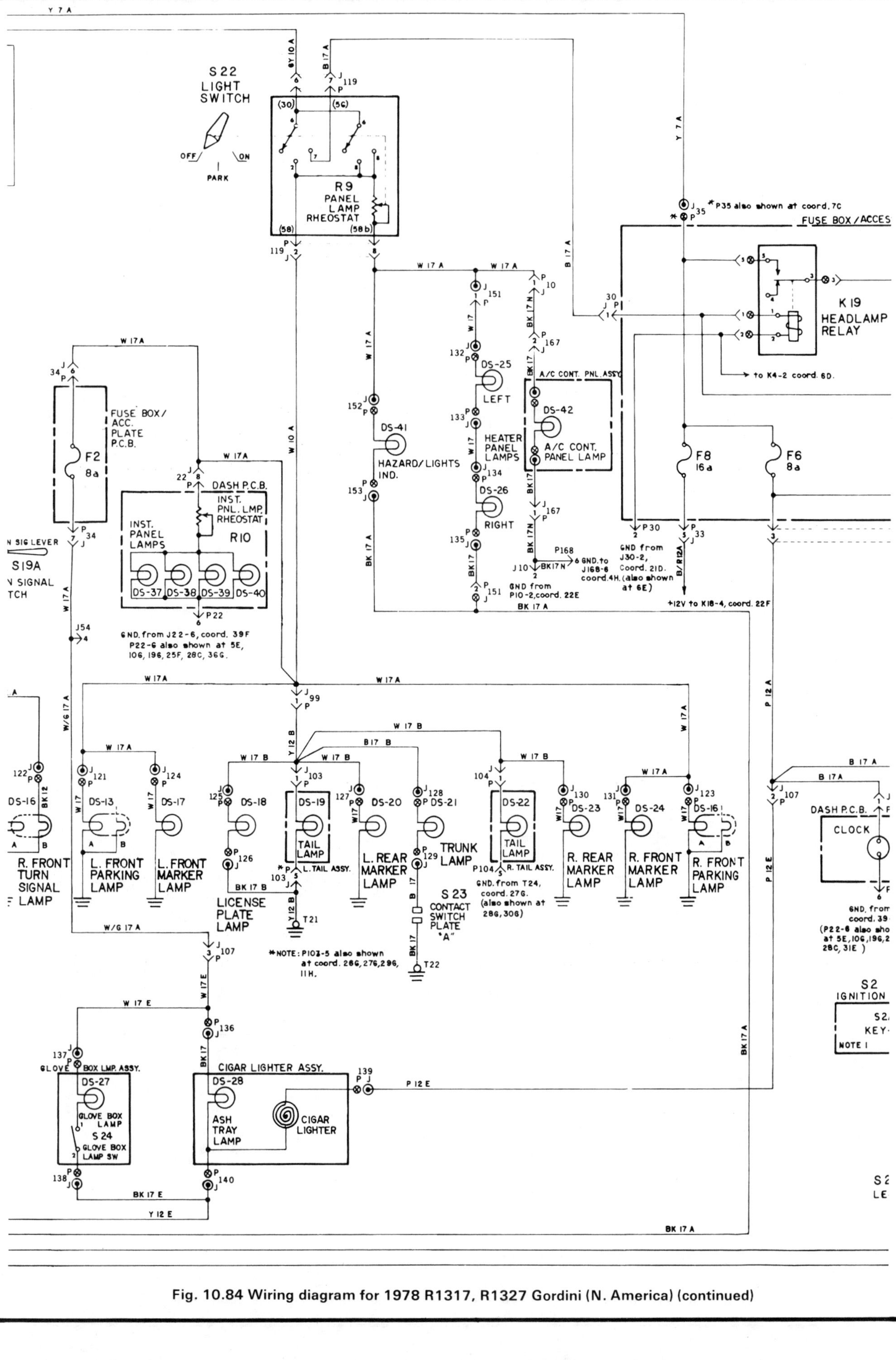

Fig. 10.84 Wiring diagram for 1978 R1317, R1327 Gordini (N. America) (continued)

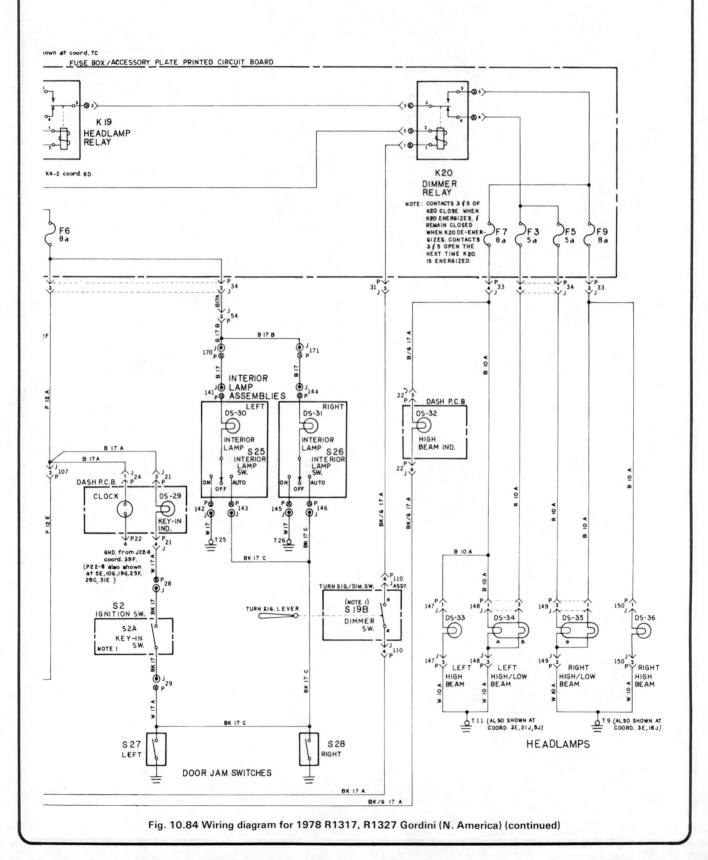

Fig. 10.84 Wiring diagram for 1978 R1317, R1327 Gordini (N. America) (continued)

Key to Wiring Diagram Fig. 10.84

Component	Symbol	Grid
Accessory plate/fuse box P.C.B.		8C, 23D, 36C
A/C control panel assembly		2G, 34C
Alternator		2D
Auxiliary air valve	L2	13E
Battery		1C
Brake pad sensors		25G
Capacitor	C1	5E
Cigar lighter		32H
Circuit breaker	CB-1	7D
Clock		36F
Control box (Fuel Injection)		13G
Dash P.C.B.		19G, 25E, 28C, 29H, 36F, 39F
Diagnostic socket	P20	5D
Diodes	DI thru D6	1E
	D7	23F
	D8	18D
Distributor		5E
E.G.R. mileage recorder	S29	19H
Flasher	K17	28D
Flowmeter	R5	14E
Fuel gauge	M1	25E
Fuel pump	B5	15E
Fuel sender	R7	25G
Fuse box/accessory plate P.C.B.	F1 thru F16	8C, 24D, 36C, 30D
Fuse, radio	F17	27H
Fuel gauge	M1	25E
Tachometer	M4	5E
Temperature gauge	M3	26E
Voltmeter	M2	25E
Ground junction block		7J, 11E, 21E, 24J
Horns, left & right		25C
Ignition coil	L1	5D
Lamps:		
A/C control panel	DS-42	34D
Ash tray	DS-28	31H
Back-up, left	DS-9	11H
Back-up, right	DS-10	10H
Brake indicator	DS-4	23E
Brake pad indicator	DS-6	25E
E.G.R. indicator	DS-2	19G
Fasten belt indicator	DS-3	19G
Glove box	DS-27	31H
Hazard indicator	DS-7	28C
Headlamp, left high beam	DS-33	39H
Headlamp, left high/low beam	DS-34	40H
Headlamp, right high beam	DS-36	41H
Headlamp, right high/low beam	DS-35	40H
Heater panel, left	DS-25	33C
Heater panel, right	DS-26	33D
High beam indicator	DS-32	39F
Instrument panel	D6-36 thru 40	31E
Interior, left	DS-30	37F
Interior, right	DS-31	38F
Key-in	DS-29	36F
License plate	DS-18	32F
Marker, left front	DS-17	31F
Marker, right front	DS-24	34F
Marker, left rear	DS-20	32F
Marker, right rear	DS-23	34F
Oil pressure warning indicator	DS-5	24E
Parking, left front	DS-13A	31F
Parking, right front	DS-16A	35F
Rear window defogger indicator	DS-1	10F
Stop, left	DS-11	27F
Stop, right	DS-12	28F
Tail, left	DS-19	27F
Tail, right	DS-22	33F
Trunk	DS-21	33F
Turn signal indicator	DS-8	28C
Turn signal, left front	DS-13B	28F
Turn signal, left rear	DS-14	29F
Turn signal, right front	DS-16B	30F
Turn signal, right rear	DS-15	30F
Motors:		
A/C blower	B8	4G
Cooling fan	B2	5H
Fuel pump	B5	15E
Heater blower	B4	9G
Starter	B1	2C

Component	Symbol	Grid
Sunroof	B3A, B3B	8F
Windshield washer pump	B6	21H
Windshield wiper	B7	22G
Radio		27H
Rear window defogger	R3	10G
Regulator		4E
Relays:		
Air flow solenoid valve	K22	17B
Buzzer	K16	20F
Clutch A/C	K3	4J
Cooking fan motor	K2	5G
Cold start injector	K10	14F
Dimmer	K20	39C
E.G.R. solenoid valve	K13	17C, 8G
Electronic	K21	16D
Enrichment	K23	20D
Flasher	K17	28D
Fuel injector cyl. 1	K6	12F
Fuel injector cyl. 2	K7	12F
Fuel injector cyl. 3	K8	12F
Fuel injector cyl. 4	K9	12F
Fuel pump	K5	12D
Headlamp	K19	35C
Relay	K4	6C
Retard capsule solenoid valve	K12	17G, 19C
Retard capsule solenoid valve relay	K11	16G, 18D
Seat belt timer	K15	20F
Starter motor	K1	2C
Vacuum advance solenoid valve	K14	18G, 20C
Windshield wiper	K18	21F
Resistors:		
Ballast	R1	5C
Blower rheostat	R2	9E
Coolant temperature sensor	R6	13H
Flowmeter	R5	14E
Fuel sender	R7	25G
Inst. panel lamp rheostat	R10	29G
Panel lamp rheostat	R9	32B
Rear window defogger	R3	10G
Resistance	R4	12E
Temperature probe	R11	16E
Water temperature sender	R8	26G
Spark plugs		4F
Switches:		
A/C air control	S31	2G
Auto transmission	S30	8H
Back-up lamp	S16	27E
Brake fluid level indicator	S14	24F
Brake pad sensor, left		25C
Brake pad sensor, right		25G
Brake pressure drop indicator	S13	23F
Coolant temperature (45°C)	S4	7H
Dimmer	S19B	38G
Door jam, left	S27	36J
Door jam, right	S28	38J
E.G.R. mileage recorder	S29	19H
Fifth speed	S9	17F
Glove box lamp	S24	30H
Hazard warning	S18	29B
Horn	S21	25B
Ignition	S2	6B, 14B, 29A, 36H
Interior lamp, left	S25	37F
Interior lamp, right	S26	38F
Key-in	S2A	36H
Light	S22	32B
Light throttle	S10	16H, 18D
Oil pressure sender	S15	24F
Parking brake	S12	23G
Rear window defogger	S5	10E
Seat belt	S11	20H
Stop lamp	S17	27E
Sunroof motor	S3	7F
Thermal coolant time	S8	15F
Thermoswitch	S1	5F
Throttle plate	S10	16H, 18E
Trunk lamp	S23	33F
Turn signal	S19A	29D
Windshield wiper/washer	S20	21G
Tachometer	M4	5E
Temperature gauge	M3	26E
Turn signal dimmer switch assembly	S19	38G, 29D
Voltage regulator		4E
Water temperature sender	R8	26G

Lug terminals

Lug	Grid	Car location
T1	1C	Under hood; positive terminal of battery
T2	1C	Under hood; negative terminal of battery
T3	1D, 13H	Gnd. Under hood, left rear side of engine block; below water pump
T4	1C	+12v. Under hood, left side of engine on starter motor relay
T5	3C	+12v. Under hood, left side of engine on starter motor relay
T6	3C	+12v. Under hood, left side of engine on starter motor relay
T7	1D	+12v. Under hood, left rear of engine block on alternator
T8	3E	Gnd. Under hood, left rear of engine block on alternator
T9	3E, 16J, 41H	Gnd. Under hood, right rear side of engine; on ignition coil bracket
T10	3E	+12v. Under hood; left front; on regulator
T11	3E, 5J, 21J, 39H	Gnd. under hood, left front; on regulator
T12	5D	+12v. under hood, right rear, near neg. battery terminal; on ignition coil
T13	5D	Under hood, near neg. battery terminal; on ignition coil
T14	6D	Gnd. Under hood, left of alternator, mounted on diagnostic socket bracket

Lug	Grid	Car location
T15	6A	+12v. Inside car, left side of steering column below Turn signal SW. Remove steering column cover plate
T16	9H	Gnd. Inside right side of rear window
T17	15E, 24H	Gnd. Under rear of car, on front side of fuel tank
T18	18H	Gnd. Under hood, left rear; left of brake fluid reservoir
T19	20H	Gnd, Rear of driver seat on right bracket; on floor
T20	26F	Under hood, below alternator; on water temperature sender
T21	32G	Gnd. Rear of car, behind left tail lamp assembly
T22	33G	Gnd. Inside rear window, left side; near contact plates, (refer to location of J56 disconnect)
T23	5E	+12v. Under hood; on distributor
T24	10J	Gnd. Rear of car, behind right tail lamp assembly
T25	37G	Gnd. Inside car, approx. 1ft. from left interior lamp; going toward the rear of the car
T26	37G	Gnd. Inside car, approx. 1ft. from right interior lamp; going toward the rear of the car

Chapter 11 Suspension and steering

Contents

Fault diagnosis 31
Front anti-roll bar – removal and refitting 4
Front hub bearings – renewal 10
Front shock absorber/coil spring – renewal, testing and refitting . 3
Front suspension arm balljoint – renewal 8
Front suspension arm flexible bushes – renewal 7
Front suspension lower arm – removal and refitting 6
Front suspension upper arm radius rod –
removal and refitting 5
General description 1
Maintenance and inspection 2
Power steering gear – removal and refitting 25
Power steering pump – removal, refitting and bleeding 24
Power steering pump drivebelt – removal,
refitting and adjustment 23
Rear anti-roll bar – removal and refitting 14
Rear axle beam – removal and refitting 17

Rear hub bearings (disc brakes) – renewal and adjustment 12
Rear hub bearings (drum brakes) – renewal and adjustment 11
Rear shock absorber and coil spring –
removal, testing and refitting 13
Rear suspension lower trailing link – removal and refitting 15
Rear suspension upper wishbone arm – removal and refitting 16
Roadwheels and tyres 30
Steering angles and front wheel alignment 29
Steering column – removal and refitting 27
Steering column bushes – renewal in car 28
Steering gear – overhaul 26
Steering gear (manual) – removal and refitting 21
Steering rack bellows – renewal 19
Steering shaft flexible coupling – removal and refitting 22
Steering track rod end balljoints – renewal 18
Steering wheel – removal and refitting 20
Stub axle carrier – removal and refitting 9

Specifications

Front suspension

Type	Independent with upper and lower arms, coil spring and telescopic shock absorber. Anti-roll bar
Camber	*1.0° to 2.0° (non adjustable)
Castor	3.0° to 5.0°
King pin inclination variation between sides	1°
Toe-out	1.0 to 4.0 mm (0.039 to 0.16 in)
*Before October 1973	0° 30' to 2° 30'

All suspension and steering angles to be set with vehicle loaded to obtain specified ride height – see text.

Rear suspension

Type	Beam axle location by trailing links and upper arm. Coil springs, telescopic shock absorbers and anti-roll bar
Camber angle	0° to 0° 30' non-adjustable
Toe-out	0 to 1.5 mm non-adjustable

Steering

Type	Rack and pinion with universally-jointed shaft. Power assisted option
Turning circle	10.25 m (33 ft 6 in)
Ratio	20 : 1
Number of turns, lock-to-lock	3.5

Roadwheels and tyres

Roadwheel type	Pressed steel or cast alloy
Size	4.50 x 13 or 5.50 x 13 depending upon model
Tyre type	Radial ply
Size	145 SR 13, 155 SR 13, 165 SR 13, 165 HR 13

Pressure*	Front	Rear
Except 165 HR 13	1.8 bar (26 lbf/in²)	1.9 bar (27 lbf/in²)
165 HR 13	1.9 bar (27 lbf/in²)	2.0 bar (29 lbf/in²)

*For continuous high speed operation, increase these pressures by 0.14 bar (2.0 lbf/in²)

Torque wrench settings

	Nm	lbf ft
Front suspension		
Shock absorber top mounting	15	11
Shock absorber lower mounting pivot pin	80	59
Shock absorber lower mounting locknut	60	44
Suspension arm balljoint taper pin nuts	50	37
Axle nut	160	118
Upper arm pivot pin nut	100	74
Lower arm pivot pin nuts	110	81
Rear suspension		
Trailing link pivot bolts	30	22
Upper arm clamp bolts	15	11
Upper arm pinch-bolt	30	22
Upper arm inboard pivot bolt	110	81
Shock absorber upper mounting	15	11
Shock absorber lower mounting	30	22
Steering		
Tie-rod end balljoint nuts	35	26
Steering wheel nut	45	33
Universal joint bolts	35	26
Flexible coupling bolts	15	11
Tie-rod to rack end fitting bolts	35	26
Rack end fitting locknuts	40	29
Roadwheel nuts	70	51

1 General description

Front suspension

The front suspension consists of upper and lower suspension arms, the out-board ends of which are connected through balljoints to the stub axle carriers.

Attached to the upper arms are coil springs and telescopic shock absorbers.

An anti-roll bar is connected to the suspension upper arms as also are radius rods which control the castor angle.

Rear suspension

The rear suspension consists of a beam axle which is located by trailing links at the out-board ends and a wishbone type arm at the centre.

Coil springs and hydraulic telescopic shock absorbers are located between the axle and the bodyframe.

An anti-roll bar is connected to the trailing links.

Steering

The steering system is of rack-and-pinion type having a steering column which incorporates a universal joint and flexible coupling. Power steering is optionally available.

2 Maintenance and inspection

1 At the intervals specified in 'Routine Maintenance', check the wheel alignment as described in Section 29.

2 Due to the use of flexible bushes and mountings in the suspension

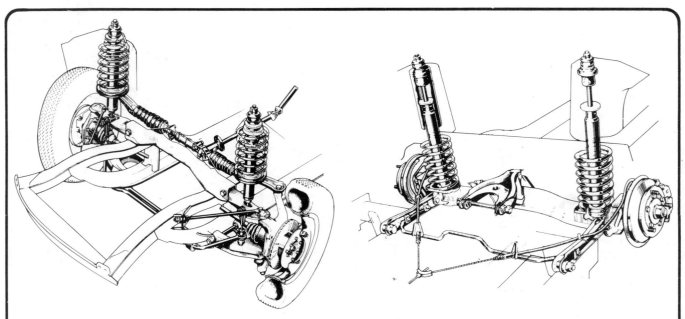

Fig. 11.1 Front suspension and steering (Sec 1)   Fig. 11.2 Rear suspension (Sec 1)

system, maintenance is virtually eliminated except for occasionally checking the torque wrench settings of all the system nuts and bolts.
3   Inspection of the suspension and steering system must be regularly carried out to check all the following likely faults.
4   Inspect the steering rack housing gaiters for splits. If evident renew at once. Provided the split has only just occurred, wiping away some of the old lubricant and replenishing it will probably suffice. If the split has gone unnoticed for a long time then the steering gear will have to be completely stripped and thoroughly cleaned to remove dirt and grit which will have entered.
5   With the help of an assistant, one person should move the steering wheel in both directions a few degrees while the other one checks for movement in the balljoints at the ends of the track rods. Any lost motion before the roadwheels start to move or movement of the balljoint socket in relation to the steering arm, will indicate wear in the balljoints and it must be renewed.
6   Jack up each wheel in turn and grip the top and bottom of the tyre and try and rock it. Any movement will probably be due to wear in the suspension arm flexible pivot bushes or balljoints. Renew as required.
7   On rear hubs, provided the bearing preload has been correctly adjusted the roadwheel should spin noiselessly and smoothly. If these conditions cannot be achieved even after correct adjustment, then the bearings must be worn and they should be renewed.
8   Finally, push down each corner of the car to test the efficiency of the shock absorbers. If the car bounces two or three times before attaining its normal ride height, suspect that the shock absorber has lost its damping efficiency.
9   On cars equipped with power-assisted steering, regularly check the connecting hoses for leaks or deterioration.

10 Check the pump fluid level at weekly intervals. If cold, the fluid level should be at the MIN mark. If hot (after several miles driving) the level should be at the MAX mark, (no higher) on the combined reservoir cap/dipstick.
11 Use only Dexron type fluid for topping up or a complete refill.
12 At specified intervals, check the belt tension as described in Section 23.

3   Front shock absorber/coil spring – removal, testing and refitting

1   The front shock absorber can be removed separately or together with the coil spring.

Removal as a separate unit
2   Place a temporary strut between the shock absorber mounting pin and the suspension lower arm inboard pivot pin.
3   Open the bonnet and prise out the blanking plug from the top of the spring turret on the wing valance.
4   A special tool (SUS 505, SUS 600) will be required to pass through the hole in the wing valance and engage with the tool baseplate. The nut at the top of the tool strut is then tightened to compress the spring. If the special tool cannot be borrowed a suitable substitute can be made up using a length of studding, nuts and a U-shaped baseplate or claws.
5   Check that the spring lower coil is free from its seat on the shock absorber.

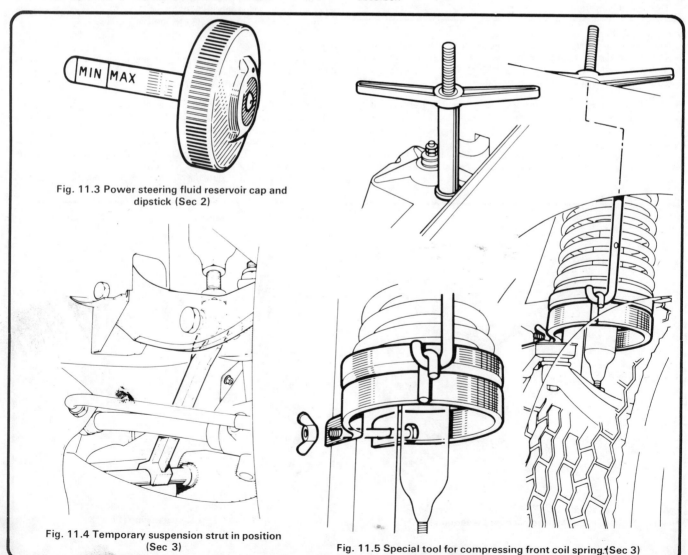

Fig. 11.3 Power steering fluid reservoir cap and dipstick (Sec 2)

Fig. 11.4 Temporary suspension strut in position (Sec 3)

Fig. 11.5 Special tool for compressing front coil spring (Sec 3)

3.6 Front shock absorber top mounting

4.3 Anti-roll bar insulator and clamp

6   Disconnect the shock absorber top mounting (photo).
7   Disconnect the shock absorber lower mounting and remove it from the car.

Removal with coil spring
8   Raise the front of the car and remove the roadwheel.
9   Compress the coil springs using a suitable spring compressor. These are readily available from most motor accessory stores and have hooked ends for engaging over the spring coils.
10 Check that the spring is free from its seat in the shock absorber and the underside of its wing valance turret.
11 Disconnect the shock absorber top and bottom mountings and lift it away together with the compressed spring.
12 Slide the spring and compressor from the shock absorber. If the spring is to be changed, slowly release the compressor aand transfer it to the new spring, compressing it to approximately the same length as the original spring.

Testing
13 Grip the bottom mounting of the shock absorber in a vice. Hold the flats of the nut not the threads.
14 With the shock absorber held vertically, fully extend and contract the unit several times. The movement should be slow, smooth and stiff. If there is any lack of resistance or jerky motion, then the shock absorber requires renewal.
15 Due to the fact that new shock absorbers are usually stored flat, before fitting a new unit, apply the same pumping action as just described, but in this case it will be to prime the shock absorber.

Refitting
16 This is a reversal of removal but observe the following points:

   (a) Screw the shock absorber bottom mounting fully home before tighening the locknut to specified torque
   (b) Make sure that the upper mounting components are replaced in their original sequence
   (c) Do not release the spring compressor until the shock absorber has been securely connected to its top and bottom mountings

---

4   Front anti-roll bar – removal and refitting

1   Remove the undertray.
2   Disconnect the end links from the bar.
3   Unbolt and remove the flexible mounting clamps (photo).
4   Withdraw the bar from the car.

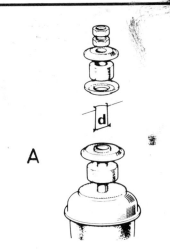
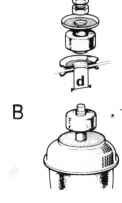

d = Hole diameter

A   For vehicles with removable cups and fixing hole
    d = 16.5 mm (21/32") diameter

B   For vehicles with welded cups and fixing hole
    d = 18 mm (23/32") diameter

Fig. 11.6 Typical front shock absorber top mountings (Sec 3)

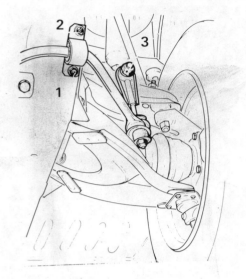

Fig. 11.7 Front anti-roll bar end attachment (Sec 4)

1   Nut   2   Clamp   3   Link nut

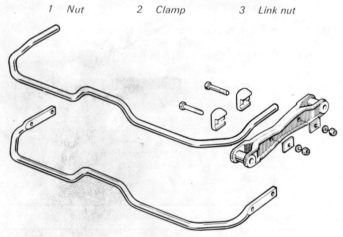

Fig. 11.8 Front anti-roll bar components (alternative types shown)
(Sec 4)

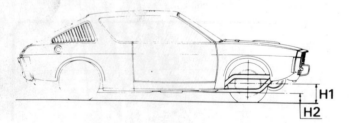

Fig. 11.9 Front suspension height setting diagram (Sec 4)

H1   Hub centre to floor
H2   Underside of lower chassis member to floor
H1-H2 = 80.0 mm (3.2 in)

Fig. 11.10 Special front suspension balljoint splitter tool (Sec 5)

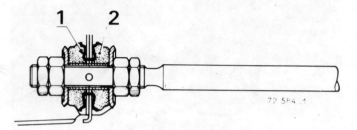

Fig. 11.11 Radius rod front end mounting (Sec 6)

1   Cup   2   Flexible cushion

5   Renew the rubber insulators and cushions as necessary.
6   Refitting is a reversal of removal, but do not fully tighten the nuts
until the car has been loaded to give a dimension H1 minus H2 of 80.0
mm (3.2 in) where H1 is hub centre to floor and H2 is bottom face of
bodyframe lower side member and floor.

5   Front suspension upper arm and radius rod – removal and refitting

1   Raise the front of the car and take off the roadwheel.
2   Release the locknut at the shock absorber bottom mounting.
3   Disconnect the radius rod from the suspension upper arm. Do not
disconnect the threaded end of the radius rod.
4   Remove the bottom mounting pin from the shock absorber.
5   Disconnect the suspension arm balljoint from the stub axle carrier.
Without the special tool (T.Av 47 6) this can be very difficult owing to
lack of room in which to fit a conventional balljoint splitter. The best
alternative will be to drive in forked wedges after the taper pin nut has
been unscrewed to within a few threads. If the balljoint has been
renewed then the easiest way is to unscrew the balljoint fixing nuts
and bolts.
6   Remove the suspension arm pivot pin from the inboard end of the
arm.
7   Lift the suspension arm and disconnect it by unscrewing the shock
absorber bottom mounting.
8   Refitting is a reversal of removal, but do not fully tighten nuts and
bolts until the car has been loaded to provide dimensions as given in
the Figure.
9   If the radius rod has to be removed for any reason, measure the
lengths of the exposed threads before unscrewing the nuts and
locknuts. If this is done then the castor setting will be restored
approximately to its original setting. Even so, have your dealer check
the castor angle on completion of the work.

6   Front suspension lower arm – removal and refitting

1   Raise the front of the car and remove the roadwheel.
2   Using a suitable balljoint splitter tool, disconnect the balljoint
which connects the lower arm to the stub axle carrier.
3   Unscrew the nut and withdraw the pivot pin from the inboard end
of the lower arm. Remove the suspension arm.
4   Refitting is a reversal of removal, but smear grease on the pivot
pin before inserting and do not tighten the nuts and bolts fully until the
car has been loaded to give a ride height as shown in the Figure.

7   Front suspension arm flexible bushes – renewal

Upper arm
1   With the arm removed from the car as previously described, press
out the old bush. If a press or wide enough opening vice is not
available, the bush can be drawn out using a bolt, nut, washers and
distance pieces.
2   Fit the new bush so that it is centralised with 6.0 mm (0.24 in)
overlap at each end.

Lower arm

3   Renew the bushes in the lower arm in a similar way to that described for the upper arm.

4   The bushes must be pressed in to give a 'between bush' dimension as shown in the Figures.

8   Front suspension arm balljoint – renewal

1   If wear has occured in the balljoints or if the rubber dust excluder is split then the balljoint must be renewed.

Upper arm balljoint

2   Raise the front of the car and remove the roadwheel.

3   Place a spacer strut or blocks between the underside of the upper arm and the pivot pin of the lower arm.

4   Unscrew the nut from the balljoint taper pins and using forked wedges, separate the balljoint from the eye of the stub axle carrier.

5   Unbolt the (castor) radius rod from the suspension arm.

6   Center punch the heads of the balljoint retaining rivets and drill them out taking care not to damage the suspension arm.

7   Remove the old balljoint and fit the new one using the nuts and bolts supplied. Make sure that the heads of the bolts are on the dust excluder side.

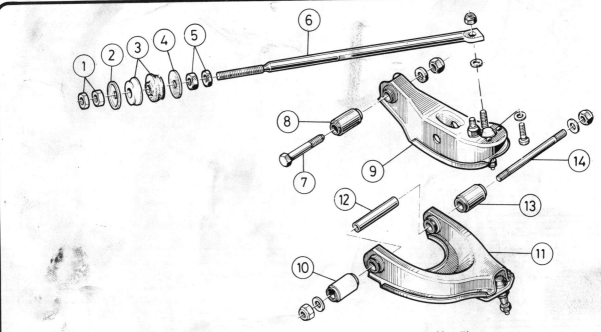

Fig. 11.12 Front suspension arm components (Sec 7)

1 Nuts	5 Nuts	9 Upper arm	12 Spacer tube
2 Cup	6 Radius rod	10 Flexible bush	13 Flexible bush
3 Flexible cushions	7 Pivot bolt	11 Lower arm	14 Pivot pin
4 Washer	8 Flexible bush		

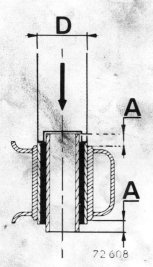

Fig. 11.13 Suspension upper arm bush fitting diagrams (Sec 7)

A   6.0 mm (0.24 in)
D   Tube for fitting bush 26.0 mm (1.02 in)

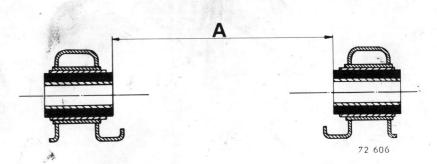

Fig. 11.14 Suspension lower arm bush fitting diagram (Sec 7)

A   151.0 mm (5.94 in)

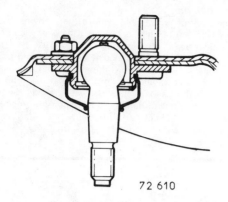

72 610

Fig. 11.15 Sectional view of suspension upper arm balljoint (Sec 8)

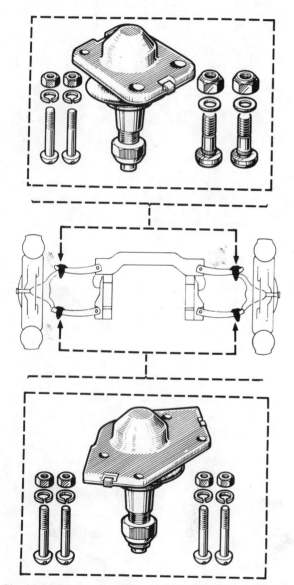

Fig. 11.16 Front suspension arm balljoint repair kits (Sec 8)

8   Reconnect the radius rod to the suspension arm and the balljoint to the stub axle carrier.
9   Tighten the nuts and bolts to the specified torque.
10   Remove the spacer strut and refit the roadwheel then lower the car to the ground.

11   It is recommended that the steering angles are checked as described in Section 29.

Lower arm balljoint
12   The operations are very similar to those described for the upper arm balljoint except that the arm must be removed from the car as described in Section 6.

9   Stub axle carrier – removal and refitting

1   Raise the front of the car and remove the roadwheel. Secure the car on axle stands.
2   Remove the hub/disc assembly as described in Chapter 9.
3   Use an extractor to disconnect the steering track rod end balljoint, and the suspension upper and lower arm balljoints.
4   This will allow the stub axle carrier to be withdrawn. Do not pull the driveshafts as this may separate the inboard couplings.
5   Refit the hub/disc assembly as described in Chapter 9.
6   Fit the whole assembly to the vehicle sliding it over the driveshaft and fitting the balljoints to their correct locations.
7   If the driveshaft and hub/disc assembly interior are perfectly clean, no difficulty should be experienced during this operation. Tapping the shaft lightly through the hub, with the lead hammer, will enable the axle nut to draw on the hub when sufficient thread is showing.
8   If greater difficulty is experienced Renault tool T, Av 236 should be used.
9   Tighten the axle nut and balljoints to their specified torque.
10   When tightening the axle nut, use a lever placed between two roadwheel studs to stop the hub/disc from rotating, but protect the threads of the studs from damage.
11   It will now be necessary to check the geometry of the front axle assembly (see Section 29).

10   Front hub bearings – renewal

1   With the stub axle carrier and hub/disc removed as described in the preceding Section, a press or bearing extractor will be required to renew the bearings.

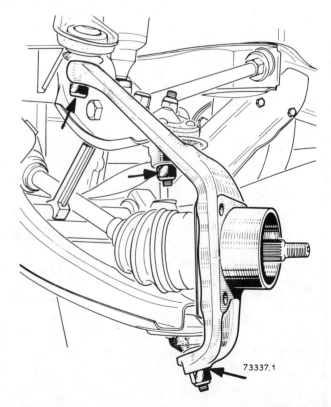

73337.1

Fig. 11.17 Stub axle carrier disconnection points (Sec 9)

Outer bearing on hub

2   Using a claw type bearing extractor, draw the bearing from the hub taking care not to damage the seal. A new seal is recommended in any case.
3   Check the stub axle for signs of wear or damage and renew if necessary. Before reassembly check that all components are quite clean and that new parts are cleaned of their protective coating.
4   Lubricate all items with wheel bearing grease prior to assembly.
5   Press in a new bearing so that the sealed face of the bearing will face outwards. This is carried out using a piece of 35 mm (1.375 in) tubing.

Inner bearing in stub axle carrier

6   Remove the bearing closure plate.
7   Press out the inner bearing using a piece of 80 mm (3.125 in) tube.
8   Inspect the stub axle for wear or damage and renew if necessary. Ensure that all components to be used in the assembly are clean and lubricated with wheel bearing grease prior to assembly.
9   Press the new bearing into position ensuring that the sealed end will face towards the closure plate.
10 Use a piece of 68 mm (2.69 in) tube to press the bearing home.
11 Smear wheel bearing grease into the cavity of the stub axle.
12 Insert the distance sleeve and press the hub/disc into the stub axle carrier.
13 Apply a strip of sealant and fit the inner bearing closure plate.
Note: *Some later models are equipped with a different design of front hub bearing assembly incorporating a new stub axle carrier, bearings (with lip type front seal), bearing closure plate, bearing thrust washer (incorporating deflector, bearing spacer and driveshaft deflector). The methods employed to change these bearings is the same as previously described. Component parts are not interchangeable between the older and later designs.*

---

11 Rear hub bearings (drum brakes) – renewal and adjustment

---

1   Remove the brake drum as described in Chapter 9, Section 10. The hub inner bearing will remain on the stub axle. The outer bearing race will be displaced during withdrawal of the brake drum.

11.8 Rear hub/drum grease seal

2   The bearings must be renewed as a set (inner and outer).
3   Draw the inner bearing race from the stub axle.
4   Prise the grease seal out of the hub and then drive the bearing outer tracks from the hub. Wipe the grease from the hub interior.
5   Press the new tracks into the hub.
6   Renew the grease seal deflector if necessary, pulling the new one into position using the axle nut and a suitable distance piece.
7   Use the same method to draw the new inner bearing onto the stub axle.
8   Fit a new grease seal to the hub and apply grease to its lips (photo).
9   Partly fill the hub with wheel bearing grease and work some into the bearing rollers.
10 Fit the hub/drum to the stub axle.

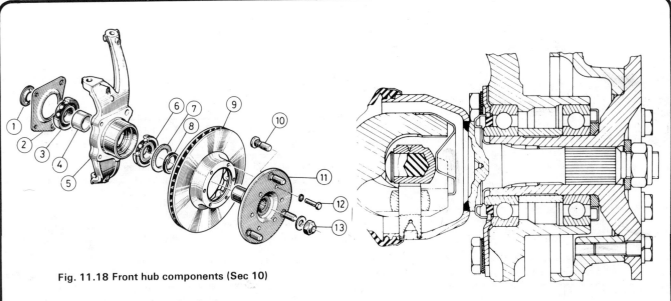

Fig. 11.18 Front hub components (Sec 10)

1   Seal
2   Bearing closure plate
3   Inner bearing
4   Spacer
5   Stub axle carrier
6   Outer bearing
7   Spacer
8   Seal
9   Brake disc
10 Roadwheel stud
11 Hub
12 Hub to disc connecting bolt
13 Axle nut

Fig. 11.19 Sectional view of front hub (Sec 10)

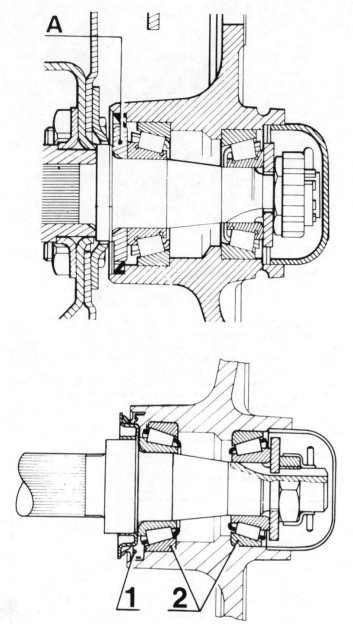

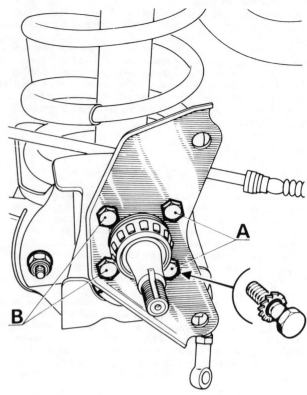

Fig. 11.21 Rear hub caliper bracket bolts (Sec 12)

A   Remove first   B   Remove second

backplate or caliper bracket bolts will first have to be removed as the bolt heads will obstruct the fitting of an extractor.
6   If a new thrust washer is to be fitted to the stub axle, it is recommended that it is first heated to make it easier to tap into position using a piece of tubing.
7   Fit the new bearing tracks into the hub then a new grease seal. Apply grease to the seal lips.
8   Partly fill the space between the bearing tracks with wheel bearing grease.
9   Slide the hub/disc onto the stub axle, fit the outer bearing race, thrust washer nut, nut lock and then adjust as described in Chapter 9, Section 8.

Fig. 11.20 Sectional view of alternative types of rear hub (Sec 11)

A   Thrust washer   2   Bearing outer tracks
1   Grease seal

11 Adjust the bearings as described in Chapter 9, Section 8.
12 Half fill the grease cap with grease and tap it squarely into position.

12 Rear hub bearings (disc brakes) – renewal and adjustment

1   Remove the hub/disc as described in Chapter 9, Section 8. The inner bearing will remain on the stub axle while the outer bearing will be displaced as the hub/disc is withdrawn.
2   The bearings must be renewed as a set (inner and outer).
3   Prise the grease seal from the hub and then drive out the bearing tracks. Wipe the grease from the hub interior.
4   Withdraw the bearing from the stub axle using a suitable claw type extractor.
5   If the thrust washer must be removed from the stub axle, draw it off in a similar way to that used for removal of the bearing, but the

13 Rear shock absorber and coil spring – removal, testing and refitting

1   Disconnect the shock absorber top mounting.
2   Raise the rear of the car and support on axle stands. Remove the roadwheel. Support the axle beam on a jack.
3   Disconnect the shock absorber bottom mounting.
4   Compress the shock absorber upwards as far as it will go.
5   Unscrew the bolt from the brake pipe three-way union.
6   Lower the axle beam until the coil spring and shock absorber can be withdrawn.
7   Refitting is a reversal of removal but make sure that the mounting cups and cushions are in their correct sequence.
8   Tighten nuts only to specified torque wrench settings.
9   The coil spring can be removed on its own using the same method, but there is no need to disconnect the shock absorber top mounting.
10 Testing the shock absorber is carried out as described in Section 3 for a front unit.

14 Rear anti-roll bar – removal and refitting

1   Unbolt the ends of the bar from the suspension trailing links and remove the bar.

2 Renew the insulators if they are deformed.
3 Refitting is a reversal of removal.

15 Rear suspension lower trailing link – removal and refitting

1 Raise the car, support securely under the sidemembers and remove the roadwheel.
2 If drum brakes are fitted, remove the drum (Chapter 9) and

disconnect the handbrake cable from the shoe lever and from the brake backplate..
3 Withdraw the handbrake cable through the trailing link.
4 Unbolt the anti-roll bar from the trailing link.
5 Disconnect the trailing link by unscrewing and removing the pivot pins.
6 If the flexible bushes in the link are worn they can only be renewed as a complete link assembly.
7 Refitting is a reversal of removal, but do not tighten the pivot pin

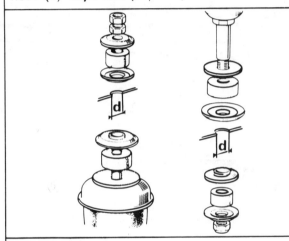

For vehicles with removable cups and fixing hole (d) 16,5 mm (21/32") diameter.

For vehicles with welded cups and fixing hole (d) 18 mm (23/32") diameter.

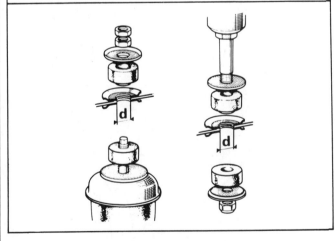

Fig. 11.22 Rear shock absorber mountings (Sec 13)

d = Hole diameter

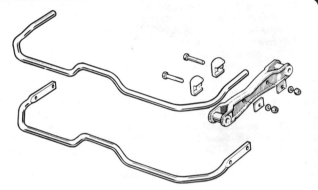

Fig. 11.23 Rear anti-roll bar components (alternative types shown) (Sec 14)

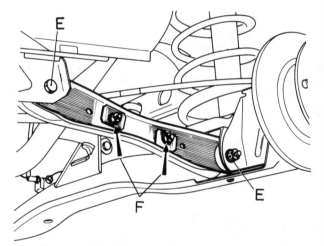

Fig. 11.24 Rear suspension lower trailing link (Sec 15)

E Pivot pins
F Anti-roll bar anchor bolts

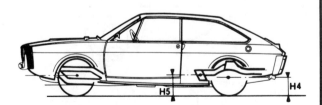

Fig. 11.25 Rear suspension height setting diagram (Sec 15)

H4 Centre of hub to floor
H5 Underside of bodyframe sidemember (ahead of rear roadwheel) to floor
H4-H5 = 65.0 mm (2.6 in)

nuts to their specified torque until the car has been loaded to provide the setting shown in the diagram.

16 Rear suspension upper wishbone arm – removal and refitting

1   Raise the rear end of the car and support it with axle stands placed under the side members.
2   Disconnect the brake pressure regulator control link from the underside of the wishbone.
3   Remove the clamp bolts from the wishbone.
4   Unscrew and remove the nuts from the ends of the pivot rod.
5   Slide the rod out towards the left-hand side of the car passing it through the hole in the sidemember.
6   Remove the wishbone arm.
7   Where necessary, remove the flexible bush and renew it. Tighten the bush fixing bolt to the specified torque.
8   Renewal of the flexible bushes in the wishbone can be carried out on a press or in a vice. A bolt, nut, washers and distance pieces will also serve to remove the old bush and draw the new one into position. The outer projection of each bush must be equal to give a dimension D of 243.0 mm (9.6 in) as shown in the diagram.
9   Refitting is a reversal of removal, but do not tighten the pivot rod nuts until the car has been loaded and set as described in Section 15, paragraph 9.
10 Check the setting of the brake pressure regulator (Chapter 9).

17 Rear axle beam – removal and refitting

1   Raise the rear of the car and support it securely on axle stands placed under the sidemembers of the bodyframe.
2   Disconnect the rear shock absorber bottom mountings and compress each one upwards.
3   On cars with drum rear brakes, remove the drums and disconnect the handbrake cables from the shoe levers. Then withdraw them through the brake backplates all as described in Chapter 9.
4   On cars with disc rear brakes, disconnect the handbrake cables from the calipers.
5   Disconnect the trailing links from the rear axle by removing the pivot pins.
6   Disconnect the brake pipelines from the three-way union and then unscrew the fixing bolt from the union.

7   Pull each side of the axle beam down in turn and withdraw the coil roadspring.
8   Support the axle beam on a jack and then unclamp the wishbone arm from the centre of the axle beam.
9   Refitting is a reversal of removal, but do not tighten the trailing link bolts until the car has been loaded and set as described in Section 15, paragraph 9.
10 Bleed the rear brake circuit.

18 Steering track rod end balljoints – renewal

1   Wear in the balljoint will require renewal of the complete pressed-steel track rod and balljoint assembly as they are fabricated as one unit.
2   Raise the front of the car and remove the roadwheel.

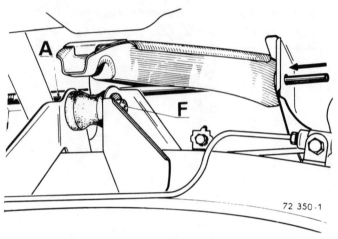

Fig. 11.27 Rear suspension upper wishbone showing clamp flexible bush (F) and pivot pin (A) (Sec 16)

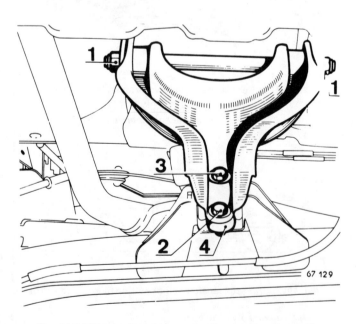

Fig. 11.26 Rear suspension upper wishbone arm (Sec 16)

1	Pivot pin nuts	3	Clamp bolt
2	Clamp bolt	4	Clamp

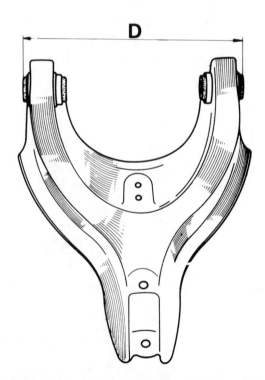

Fig. 11.28 Rear suspension upper wishbone flexible bush setting diagram (Sec 16)

D   243.0 mm (9.6 in)

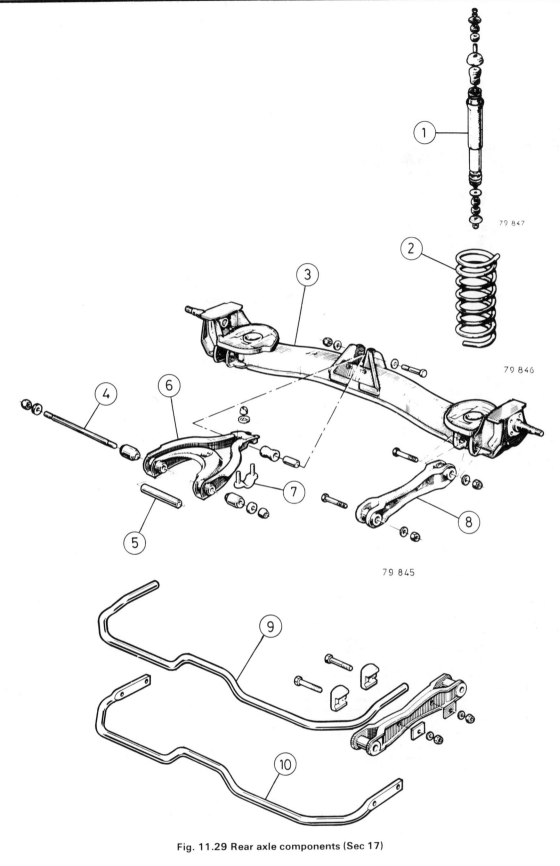

Fig. 11.29 Rear axle components (Sec 17)

1	Shock absorber	4	Pivot pin	7	Clamp	10	Alternative design of
2	Coil spring	5	Spacer tube	8	Trailing link		anti-roll bar
3	Axle beam	6	Wishbone	9	Anti-roll bar		

18.3 Typical balljoint splitter tool

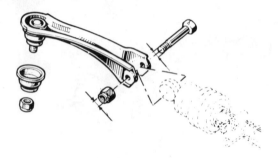

Fig. 11.30 Steering track-rod (Sec 18)

3   Unscrew the balljoint taper pin nut except for a few threads and then fit a balljoint splitter tool to separate the balljoint from the steering arm on the stub axle carrier (photo).
4   Unscrew and remove the connecting bolt from the inboard end of the tie-rod.
5   Refit by reversing the removal operations then refer to Section 29 and check the wheel alignment.
6   If both track rods are removed at the same time make sure that the small boss is towards the front of the car when the rod is installed. This is because the LH and RH rods are not interchangeable.

19 Steering rack bellows − renewal

1   Disconnect the track rod balljoint from the steering arm on the stub axle carrier.
2   Release the locknut on the rack and fitting and counting the number of turns unscrew the end fitting from the rack.
3   Prise back the securing rings and withdraw the bellows.
4   If there has been any loss of lubricant, turn the steering to extend the rack and wipe away the old grease from the rack and apply a liberal coating of fresh molybdenum disulphide type grease to the rack and teeth.
5   Fit the new bellows with retaining rings.
6   Screw the rack end fitting into the rack counting the turns until it takes up its original setting.
7   Reconnect the balljoint to the steering arm.
8   Check the front wheel alignment as described in Section 29.

20 Steering wheel − removal and refitting

1   Prise out the embellisher from the centre of the steering wheel.

2   Set the steering wheel and roadwheels in the straight ahead position.
3   Unscrew the steering wheel fixing nut, but do not completely remove it.
4   Rock the wheel from side to side and pull it towards you. A little gentle thumping under the rim with the hands will usually dislodge the steering wheel, but if it is exceptionally tight on its shaft then a puller will have to be used.
5   Apply a smear of grease to the shaft taper or splines and refit the wheel with the steering still centred. Make sure that the wheel spokes are in the lower segment of the wheel.
6   Tighten the fixing nut to the specified torque.

21 Steering gear (manual) − removal and refitting

1   Open the bonnet and remove the battery and its tray.
2   Unscrew the flexible coupling bolts.
3   Disconnect the track rods from the rack end fittings.
4   Unscrew the four mounting bolts, check very carefully the location of any steering box height setting shims and retain them. On cars which have eccentric cam type adjusters to alter the steering box height, mark their positions precisely.
5   Remove the steering gear from the crossmember.
6   Refitting is a reversal of removal, but if a new steering assembly has been fitted, have your dealer check the steering box height setting in case shims of different type numbers are required. The shim slot is positioned according to the number stamped on it. This has the effect of moving the steering box up or down in relation to the steering arm balljoints. On cam type adjusters, the mounting bolt is released sufficiently to enable the cam to be turned which again will lower or raise the position of the steering box.

22 Steering shaft flexible coupling − removal and refitting

1   Remove the steering gear as described in the preceding Section.
2   Drill out the flexible coupling rivets.
3   Fit the new coupling using the nuts and bolts supplied and making sure that the nuts are on the steering housing side of the coupling.

23 Power steering pump drivebelt − removal, refitting and adjustment

1   To renew a drivebelt, release the pump, adjuster link and mounting bolts, and pivot the pump until the drivebelt can be slipped off the pulley rim.
2   Fit the new belt and prise the pump until the total deflection at the centre of the longest run of the belt under moderate thumb pressure is between 4.5 and 5.5 mm (0.18 and 0.22 in). Tighten the pump adjuster link and mounting bolts. After ten minutes operation, readjust the tension to between 5.5 and 6.5 mm (0.22 and 0.26 in).

24 Power steering pump − removal, refitting and bleeding

1   Remove the pump drivebelt as described in the preceding Section.
2   Remove the pump mounting and adjuster link bolts.
3   Remove the reservoir cap and withdraw the pump sufficiently to be able to tip the fluid out into a container.
4   Disconnect the flexible hoses from the pump.
5   Refitting is a reversal of removal, tension the drivebelt and make sure that the flexible hose which has the connecting clip is pushed at least 25.0 mm (1.0 in) onto the pump pipe stub.
6   Fill the system with clean fluid and bleed as described in the following paragraphs.
7   Fill the pump fluid reservoir with specified fluid.
8   Turn the steering slowly to full lock in both directions. Top up the reservoir.
9   Start the engine and again turn the steering slowly from lock to lock. Top up the reservoir.
10 Switch off the engine and check the fluid level as described in Section 2.

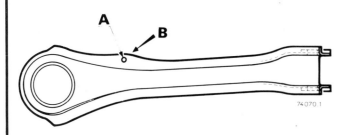

Fig. 11.31 Front facing boss (A) on steering tie-rod (Sec 18)

B   Profile projection

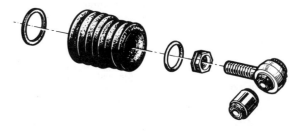

Fig. 11.32 Steering rack bellows components (Sec 19)

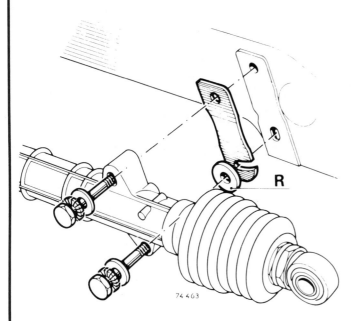

Fig. 11.33 Manual steering gear height setting shim (Sec 21)

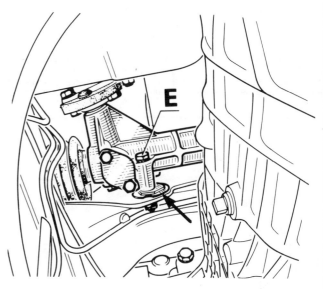

Fig. 11.34 Manual steering gear adjusting cam (Sec 21)

E   Mounting bolt

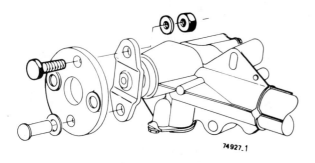

Fig. 11.35 Steering shaft flexible coupling (Sec 22)

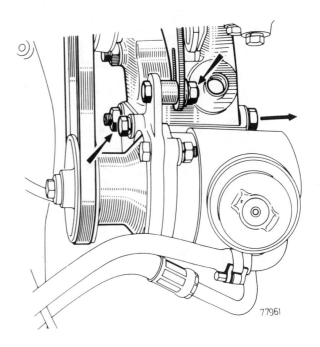

Fig. 11.36 Power steering pump (Sec 24)

25 Power steering gear – removal and refitting

1   Syphon out the fluid from the pump reservoir at the same time turning the steering from lock to lock to empty the hydraulic ram.
2   Remove the pinch-bolts from the universal joints on the steering shaft.
3   Working under the bonnet, remove the battery and its tray.
4   Remove the bolts and disconnect the rack end fittings.
5   Disconnect the reservoir and pump pipelines from the rotary valve housing on the steering gear.
6   Carefully mark the position of the housing on the crossmember before unbolting it.
7   Withdraw the steering gear.
8   Refitting is a reversal of removal, make sure that the pipe connections are correctly made.
9   As the steering gear is pushed into position and the universal joints connected to the steering gear pinion, the steering rack must be centralised (see Section 29) and the steering wheel correctly aligned.
10 Fill and bleed the system as described in Section 24.
11 Have your dealer check the steering gear height setting and other steering angles. The power assisted steering housing is adjusted simply by moving it within the limits of its elongated mounting bolt holes, no shims or eccentric cam adjusters being fitted.

26 Steering gear – overhaul

1   It is not recommended that either the manual or power-operated steering gear is dismantled, but in the event of a fault developing then obtain a new assembly or a factory reconditioned unit which are available from many motor factors on an exchange basis.
2   Apart from the non-availability of some internal spare parts, special tools and gauges are required to perform a satisfactory job.

27 Steering column – removal and refitting

1   Disconnect the battery.
2   Extract the screws and remove the lower shroud from the upper steering column.
3   Remove the steering wheel as described in Section 20.
4   Remove the combination switches from the steering column as described in Chapter 10.
5   Disconnect the clutch cable and brake push rod from the foot pedals. Remove the pedals and the cross shaft as described in Chapter 5.
6   Disconnect the stop lamp switch and the ignition switch wiring plug.

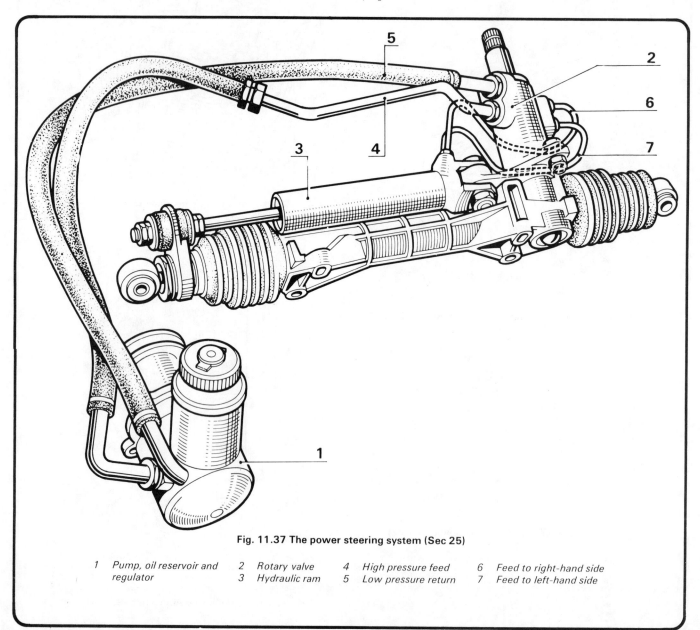

Fig. 11.37 The power steering system (Sec 25)

1 *Pump, oil reservoir and regulator*	2 *Rotary valve*	4 *High pressure feed*	6 *Feed to right-hand side*
	3 *Hydraulic ram*	5 *Low pressure return*	7 *Feed to left-hand side*

7   Unscrew and remove the connecting bolt from the universal joint at the lower end of the steering column shaft.
8   Working within the engine compartment, unscrew and remove the bolts which secure the pedal bracket to the rear bulkhead.
9   Unscrew and remove the column upper bracket bolts from the underside of the facia panel, lower the column/shaft assembly and draw it from the short universally-jointed shaft.
10 Remove the assembly from inside the car.
11 If required, the ignition/steering lock arm can be removed as described in Chapter 4.
12 The steering shaft can be removed by carefully tapping it downwards to eject the bottom bush and then having extracted the circlip from the top of the column, tapping the shaft upwards to eject the top bush. Withdraw the shaft.
13 Refitting is a reversal of removal, but connect the steering shaft to the lower universally-jointed shaft with the steering gear centred (see Section 29).

14 Tighten the column and bracket bolts only finger tight initially so that the universally-jointed shaft can be set correctly and its pivot bolt tightened to the specified torque wrench setting.
15 Check the clutch and brake pedal adjustment (Chapters 5 and 9).

28 Steering column bushes – renewal in car

1   Removal of these bushes with the column withdrawn is described in the preceding Section, but it is possible to renew the bushes without having to remove the column from the car.
2   Disconnect the battery.
3   Remove the steering wheel (Section 20).
4   Remove the steering column switches (Chapter 10).
5   Remove the brake pedal stop-lamp switch.
6   Extract the circlip from the top of the column.
7   Unscrew and remove the pivot bolts from the universal joint.

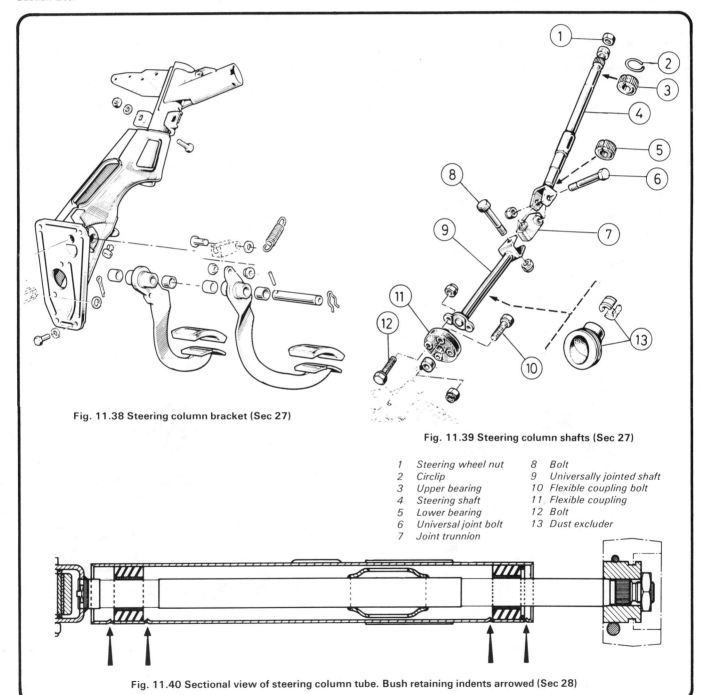

Fig. 11.38 Steering column bracket (Sec 27)

Fig. 11.39 Steering column shafts (Sec 27)

1   Steering wheel nut   8   Bolt
2   Circlip   9   Universally jointed shaft
3   Upper bearing   10   Flexible coupling bolt
4   Steering shaft   11   Flexible coupling
5   Lower bearing   12   Bolt
6   Universal joint bolt 13   Dust excluder
7   Joint trunnion

Fig. 11.40 Sectional view of steering column tube. Bush retaining indents arrowed (Sec 28)

8   Tap the end of the steering shaft down using a plastic faced hammer until the bottom bush is ejected from the column tube. This bush is of the split type.
9   Prise out the top bush using a screwdriver.
10   Apply grease to the new bushes.
11   Grind or file off the outside of the worn split bushes to reduce the overall diameter by about 2.0 mm (0.079 in). This is to enable the original bush to be used as a fitting guide tool.
12   Locate the new split bush on the steering shaft and locate the old bush against it. If the shaft is now tapped upwards, the old bush will push the new one into position between the tube indents. Remove the old bush.
13   Fit the top bush by tapping it into position using a piece of tubing.
14   Fit the top bush circlip.
15   Reconnect the universal joint.
16   Refit the brake pedal stop lamp.
17   Fit the steering column switches and the steering wheel.
18   Reconnect the battery.

29 Steering angles and front wheel alignment

1   Accurate front wheel alignment is essential to provide good steering and roadholding characteristics and to ensure even and slow tyre wear.
2   It is preferable that any checking or adjustment of the steering and suspension angles is carried out by your dealer using special setting equipment, but for information purposes the following details are given:

Wheel alignment consists of four factors:

Camber
3   This is the angle at which the roadwheels are set from the vertical when viewed from the front of the vehicle. Camber is regarded as positive when the roadwheels are tilted outwards at the top. The angle is not adjustable on the models covered by this manual.

Steering axis (kingpin) inclination
4   This is the angle, when viewed from the front of the vehicle, between the vertical and an imaginary line drawn between the upper and lower suspension arm balljoints. The angle is not adjustable.

Castor
5   This is the angle between the steering axis and a vertical line when viewed from each side of the vehicle. Positive castor is indicated when the steering axis is inclined towards the rear of the vehicle at its upper end. Castor is adjustable by varying the length of the radius rods which are connected to the suspension upper arm.

Toe
6   This is the amount by which the distance between the front inside edges of the roadwheel rims differs from that between the inside edges at the rear of the wheel. If the distance between the rims at the front of the wheel is less than that at the rear, then the roadwheels are said to toe-in. If the distance is greater the wheels toe-out.
7   With the arrival of tracking gauges on the retail market it is now possible for the home mechanic to check and adjust the front wheel toe provided the following essential requirements are observed:

(a)   Car on a level floor
(b)   Tyres correctly inflated
(c)   Suspension bushes and steering balljoints unworn
(d)   Hub bearings unworn

8   The steering must be centred. This is achieved when the rivet head on the flexible coupling is aligned with the mark (B) on the steering rack housing and the dimension (C) is 65.0 mm (2.6 in) for cars with manual transmission or 61.0 mm (2.4 in) for those with automatic transmission. This dimension can be checked by pushing a rod of known length under the bellows, but normally the fact that the roadwheels and steering wheel arm are in the straight ahead position will confirm that the rivet head is positioned at its centre point of the steering lock.
9   The car must be loaded so that H1 minus H2 = 128.0 mm (5.04 in) refer to Fig. 11.9.
10   To adjust the toe to conform with Specifications, disconnect the track rods from the track end fittings.
11   Release the locknut (E).
12   To decrease the toe-out unscrew the rack end fittings, to increase the toe-out screw them in. Each half turn of the end fitting will alter the toe by 1.5 mm (0.06 in). Temporarily reconnect the track rods. When

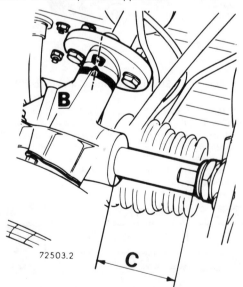

Fig. 11.41 Steering gear centred (Sec 29)

B   Rivet and housing alignment mark
C   65.0 mm (2.6 in) manual transmission
      61.0 mm (2.4 in) automatic transmission

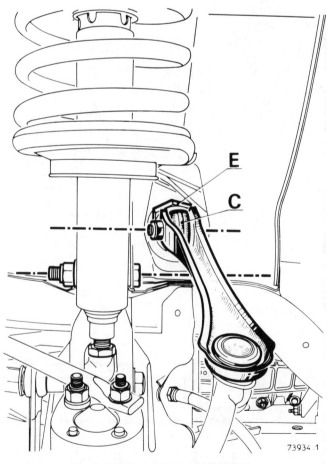

Fig. 11.42 Steering tie-rod (Sec 29)

C   Rack end fitting
E   Rack end fitting locknut

using the tracking gauge to check the toe, push the car forward so that the roadwheel turns through 180° between checking the inside rim measurements at front and rear of the roadwheel.

13 Make sure that both rack end fittings are turned an equal amount. When the toe setting is correct, reconnect the track rods and tighten the locknuts. Do not allow the balljoint to twist while the locknut is being tightened.

30 Roadwheels and tyres

1 The roadwheels may be of pressed steel or cast alloy type according to model.
2 Keep the wheels clean and rust or corrosion free.
3 Always tighten the wheel nuts to the specified torque and keep the threads lightly greased.

4 Whenever a roadwheel is removed, check that the mounting stud holes have not been deformed by overtightening.
5 The tyres fitted as standard are of radial ply construction. Their section varies according to vehicle model (see Specifications).
6 Check the pressure every week. A lower pressure in one tyre may be due to a puncture – check for a nail or flint.
7 Regularly inspect the tread and both sidewalls for deep cuts or other damage.
8 Moving the roadwheels between the front and the rear axles (but not from side to side) does help to even out the tread wear particularly if it is done every 4000 ot 5000 miles (6400 or 8000 km).
9 Renew the tyres when the tread pattern has been reduced to a depth of 1.0 mm (0.039 in).
10 Have the wheels (front wheels certainly) balanced when the tyres are first fitted and it is recommended that they are re-balanced half way through their life to compensate for tread wear.

31 Fault diagnosis – suspension and steering

Symptom	Reason(s)
Front suspension and steering	
Heavy steering	Corroded or seized balljoints
	Incorrect suspension geometry and track
	Power steering unit defective
Lost motion (steering)	Worn flexible coupling bolt holes
	Worn steering column universal joint
	Loose steering wheel
	Worn balljoints
	Worn rack and pinion mechanism
Wheel wobble and vibration	Worn hub bearings
	Loose wheel bolts
	Worn suspension arm bushes
	Driveshafts bent or out of balance
	Driveshaft couplings worn
	Front roadwheels out of balance
	Wear in rack and pinion and balljoints
	Incorrect steering geometry
Poor roadholding and cornering	Shock absorber unserviceable
Sensitive to road camber	Wear in upper or lower suspension arm balljoints
	Wear in hub bearings
Rear suspension	
Wheel wobble and vibration	Shock absorber rubber bushes worn
	Loose shock absorber mounting
	Suspension arm bushes worn
Uneven tyre wear	Rear stub axles twisted or out of alignment
	Rear hubs incorrectly adjusted for endfloat
Poor roadholding and cornering	Shock absorber unserviceable

Chapter 12 Bodywork and underframe

Contents

Bonnet – removal and refitting	9
Bonnet release catch – renewal	10
Centre console – removal and refitting	31
Door – removal, refitting and adjusting	22
Door lock – removal and refitting	21
Door trim panel – removal and refitting	19
Door window winder and glass – removal and refitting	20
Facia panel (to 1976) – removal and refitting	30
Facia panel (1977 on) – removal and refitting	32
Front protective shield – removal and refitting	7
Front seat – removal, refitting and adjusting	28
Front wing – removal and refitting	8
General description	1
Interior rear view mirror (windscreen bonded type)	34
Maintenance – bodywork and underframe	2
Maintenance – upholstery and carpets	3
Major body damage – repair	5
Minor body damage – repair	4

Radiator grille – removal and refitting	6
Rear deflector – removal and refitting	16
Rear protective shield – removal and refitting	18
Rear quarter-light (deflector type) – removal and refitting	24
Rear quarter-light (fixed) – removal and refitting	26
Rear quarter-light (opening type) – removal and refitting	25
Rear quarter-light (wind-down type) – removal and refitting	23
Rear quarter louvre – removal and refitting	17
Rear seat – removal and refitting	29
Safety belts – maintenance, removal and refitting	33
Scuttle grille panel – removal and refitting	11
Sill embellisher – removal and refitting	15
Tailgate – removal and refitting	12
Tailgate counterbalance struts – removal and refitting	13
Tailgate lock – removal and refitting	14
Towing bracket – fitting	35
Windscreen and tailgate glass – removal and refitting	27

Specifications

Body type	Unitary, all steel welded three door Coupe style body
Dimensions, weights	Refer to 'Quick Reference Chart' in Introductory Section of this Manual

1 General description

The bodyshell and underframe is of unitary, all-steel, welded construction.

The model range is limited to a three-door design with a variation to include a sunroof.

The only detachable body panels are the bolt-on type front wings.

Later models have adequate underbody corrosion protection including wax injection of the box sections.

2 Maintenance – bodywork and underframe

1 The general condition of a vehicle's bodywork is the one thing that significantly affects its value. Maintenance is easy but needs to be regular. Neglect, particularly after minor damage, can lead quickly to further deterioration and costly repair bills. It is important also to keep watch on those parts of the vehicle not immediately visible, for instance the underside, inside all the wheel arches and the lower part of the engine compartment.

2 The basic maintenance routine for the bodywork is washing – preferably with a lot of water, from a hose. This will remove all the loose solids which may have stuck to the vehicle. It is important to flush these off in such a way as to prevent grit from scratching the finish. The wheel arches and underframe need washing in the same way to remove any accumulated mud which will retain moisture and tend to encourage rust. Paradoxically enough, the best time to clean the underframe and wheel arches is in wet weather when the mud is thoroughly wet and soft. In very wet weather the underframe is usually cleaned of large accumulations automatically and this is a good time for inspection.

3 Periodically, it is a good idea to have the whole of the underframe of the vehicle steam cleaned, engine compartment included, so that a thorough inspection can be carried out to see what minor repairs and renovations are necessary. Steam cleaning is available at many garages and is necessary for removal of the accumulation of oily grime which sometimes is allowed to become thick in certain areas. If steam cleaning facilities are not available, there are one or two excellent grease solvents available which can be brush applied. The dirt can then be simply hosed off.

4 After washing paintwork, wipe off with a chamois leather to give

2.4 Clearing sill drain hole

an unspotted clear finish. A coat of clear protective wax polish will give added protection against chemical pollutants in the air. If the paintwork sheen has dulled or oxidised, use a cleaner/polisher combination to restore the brilliance of the shine. This requires a little effort, but such dulling is usually caused because regular washing has been neglected. Always check that the door and ventilator opening drain holes and pipes are completely clear so that water can be drained out. Bright work should be treated in the same way as paintwork. Windscreens and windows can be kept clear of the smeary film which often appears, by adding a little ammonia to the water. If they are scratched, a good rub with a proprietary metal polish will often clear them. Never use any form of wax or other body or chromium polish on glass (photo).

3 Maintenance – upholstery and carpets

1   Mats and carpets should be brushed or vacuum cleaned regularly to keep them free of grit. If they are badly stained remove them from the vehicle for scrubbing or sponging and make quite sure they are dry before refitting. Seats and interior trim panels can be kept clean by wiping with a damp cloth. If they do become stained (which can be more apparent on light coloured upholstery) use a little liquid detergent and a soft nail brush to scour the grime out of the grain of the material. Do not forget to keep the headlining clean in the same way as the upholstery. When using liquid cleaners inside the vehicle do not over-wet the surfaces being cleaned. Excessive damp could get into the seams and padded interior causing stains, offensive odours or even rot. If the inside of the vehicle gets wet accidentally it is worthwhile taking some trouble to dry it out properly, particularly where carpets are involved. *Do not leave oil or electric heaters inside the vehicle for this purpose.*

4 Minor body damage – repair

The photographic sequences on pages 318 and 319 illustrate the operations detailed in the following sub-sections.

Repair of minor scratches in bodywork

If the scratch is very superficial, and does not penetrate to the metal of the bodywork, repair is very simple. Lightly rub the area of the scratch with a paintwork renovator, or a very fine cutting paste, to remove loose paint from the scratch and to clear the surrounding bodywork of wax polish. Rinse the area with clean water.

Apply touch-up paint to the scratch using a fine paint brush; continue to apply fine layers of paint until the surface of the paint in the scratch is level with the surrounding paintwork. Allow the new paint at least two weeks to harden; then blend it into the surrounding

paintwork by rubbing the scratch area with a paintwork renovator or a very fine cutting paste. Finally, apply wax polish.

Where the scratch has penetrated right through to the metal of the bodywork, causing the metal to rust, a different repair technique is required. Remove any loose rust from the bottom of the scratch with a penknife, then apply rust inhibiting paint to prevent the formation of rust in the future. Using a rubber or nylon applicator fill the scratch with bodystopper paste. If required, this paste can be mixed with cellulose thinners to provide a very thin paste which is ideal for filling narrow scratches. Before the stopper-paste in the scratch hardens, wrap a piece of smooth cotton rag around the top of a finger. Dip the finger in cellulose thinners and then quickly sweep it across the surface of the stopper-paste in the scratch; this will ensure that the surface of the stopper-paste is slightly hollowed. The scratch can now be painted over as described earlier in this Section.

Repair of dents in bodywork

When deep denting of the vehicle's bodywork has taken place, the first task is to pull the dent out, until the affected bodywork almost attains its original shape. There is little point in trying to restore the original shape completely, as the metal in the damaged area will have stretched on impact and cannot be reshaped fully to its original contour. It is better to bring the level of the dent up to a point which is about $\frac{1}{8}$ in (3 mm) below the level of the surrounding bodywork. In cases where the dent is very shallow anyway, it is not worth trying to pull it out at all. If the underside of the dent is accessible, it can be hammered out gently from behind, using a mallet with a wooden or plastic head. Whilst doing this, hold a suitable block of wood firmly against the outside of the panel to absorb the impact from the hammer blows and thus prevent a large area of the bodywork from being 'belled-out'.

Should the dent be in a section of the bodywork which has a double skin or some other factor making it inaccessible from behind, a different technique is called for. Drill several small holes through the metal inside the area – particularly in the deeper section. Then screw long self-tapping screws into the holes just sufficiently for them to gain a good purchase in the metal. Now the dent can be pulled out by pulling on the protruding heads of the screws with a pair of pliers.

The next stage of the repair is the removal of the paint from the damaged area, and from an inch or so of the surrounding 'sound' bodywork. This is accomplished most easily by using a wire brush or abrasive pad on a power drill, although it can be done just as effectively by hand using sheets of abrasive paper. To complete the preparation for filling, score the surface of the bare metal with a screwdriver or the tang of a file, or alternatively, drill small holes in the affected area. This will provide a really good 'key' for the filler paste.

To complete the repair see the Section on filling and re-spraying.

Repair of rust holes or gashes in bodywork

Remove all paint from the affected area and from an inch or so of the surrounding 'sound' bodywork, using an abrasive pad or a wire brush on a power drill. If these are not available a few sheets of abrasive paper will do the job just as effectively. With the paint removed you will be able to gauge the severity of the corrosion and therefore decide whether to renew the whole panel (if this is possible) or to repair the affected area. New body panels are not as expensive as most people think and it is often quicker and more satisfactory to fit a new panel than to attempt to repair large areas of corrosion.

Remove all fittings from the affected area except those which will act as a guide to the original shape of the damaged bodywork (eg headlamp shells etc). Then, using tin snips or a hacksaw blade, remove all loose metal and any other metal badly affected by corrosion. Hammer the edges of the hole inwards in order to create a slight depression for the filler paste.

Wire brush the affected area to remove the powdery rust from the surface of the remaining metal. Paint the affected area with rust inhibiting paint; if the back of the rusted area is accessible treat this also.

Before filling can take place it will be necessary to block the hole in some way. This can be achieved by the use of zinc gauze or aluminium tape.

Zinc gauze is probably the best material to use for a large hole. Cut a piece to the approximate size and shape of the hole to be filled, then position it in the hole so that its edges are below the level of the surrounding bodywork. It can be retained in position by several blobs of filler paste around its periphery.

Aluminium tape should be used for small or very narrow holes. Pull a piece off the roll and trim it to the approximate size and shape required, then pull off the backing paper (if used) and stick the tape over the hole; it can be overlapped if the thickness of one piece is insufficient. Burnish down the edges of the tape with the handle of a screwdriver or similar, to ensure that the tape is securely attached to the metal underneath.

Bodywork repairs – filling and re-spraying

Before using this Section, see the Sections on dent, deep scratch, rust holes and gash repairs.

Many types of bodyfiller are available, but generally speaking those proprietary kits which contain a tin of filler paste and a tube of resin hardener are best for this type of repair. A wide, flexible plastic or nylon applicator will be found invaluable for imparting a smooth and well contoured finish to the surface of the filler.

Mix up a little filler on a clean piece of card or board – measure the hardener carefully (follow the maker's instructions on the pack) otherwise the filler will set too rapidly or too slowly.

Using the applicator apply the filler paste to the prepared area; draw the applicator across the surface of the filler to achieve the correct contour and to level the filler surface. As soon as a contour that approximates to the correct one is achieved, stop working the paste – if you carry on too long the paste will become sticky and begin to 'pick up' on the applicator. Continue to add thin layers of filler paste at twenty-minute intervals until the level of the filler is just proud of the surrounding bodywork.

Once the filler has hardened, excess can be removed using a metal plane or file. From then on, progressively finer grades of abrasive paper should be used, starting with a 40 grade production paper and finishing with 400 grade wet-and-dry paper. Always wrap the abrasive paper around a flat rubber, cork, or wooden block – otherwise the surface of the filler will not be completely flat. During the smoothing of the filler surface the wet-and-dry paper should be periodically rinsed in water. This will ensure that a very smooth finish is imparted to the filler at the final stage.

At this stage the 'dent' should be surrounded by a ring of bare metal, which in turn should be encircled by the finely 'feathered' edge of the good paintwork. Rinse the repair area with clean water, until all of the dust produced by the rubbing-down operation has gone.

Spray the whole repair area with a light coat of primer – this will show up any imperfections in the surface of the filler. Repair these imperfections with fresh filler paste or bodystopper, and once more smooth the surface with abrasive paper. If bodystopper is used, it can be mixed with cellulose thinners to form a really thin paste which is ideal for filling small holes. Repeat this spray and repair procedure until you are satisfied that the surface of the filler, and the feathered edge of the paintwork are perfect. Clean the repair area with clean water and allow to dry fully.

The repair area is now ready for final spraying. Paint spraying must be carried out in a warm, dry, windless and dust free atmosphere. This condition can be created artificially if you have access to a large indoor working area, but if you are forced to work in the open, you will have to pick your day very carefully. If you are working indoors, dousing the floor in the work area with water will help to settle the dust which would otherwise be in the atmosphere. If the repair area is confined to one body panel, mask off the surrounding panels; this will help to minimise the effects of a slight mis-match in paint colours. Bodywork fittings (eg chrome strips, door handles etc) will also need to be masked off. Use genuine masking tape and several thicknesses of newspaper for the masking operations.

Before commencing to spray, agitate the aerosol can thoroughly, then spray a test area (an old tin, or similar) until the technique is mastered. Cover the repair area with a thick coat of primer; the thickness should be built up using several thin layers of paint rather than one thick one. Using 400 grade wet-and-dry paper, rub down the surface of the primer until it is really smooth. While doing this, the work area should be thoroughly doused with water, and the wet-and-dry paper periodically rinsed in water. Allow to dry before spraying on more paint.

Spray on the top coat, again building up the thickness by using several thin layers of paint. Start spraying in the centre of the repair area and then, using a circular motion, work outwards until the whole repair area and about 2 inches of the surrounding original paintwork is covered. Remove all masking material 10 to 15 minutes after spraying on the final coat of paint.

Allow the new paint at least two weeks to harden, then, using a paintwork renovator or a very fine cutting paste, blend the edges of the paint into the existing paintwork. Finally, apply wax polish.

5 Major body damage – repair

The principle of construction of these vehicles is such that great care must be taken when making cuts, or when renewing major members, in order to preserve the basic safety characteristics of the structure. In addition, the heating of certain areas is not advisable.

In view of the specialised knowledge necessary for this work, and of the alignment jigs and special tools frequently required, the owner is advised to consult a specialist body repairer.

6 Radiator grille – removal and refitting

1 The type of grille and headlamp trim panels will depend upon the model and date of production.
2 Extract the two screws from the top of the grille. Pull the grille out at the top and pull it upwards out of its locating peg holes (photo).
3 Extract the headlamp trim panel screws and remove the panels.
4 On earlier models, the headlamp trim panels will have to be released before the grille can be withdrawn.
5 Refitting is a reversal of removal.

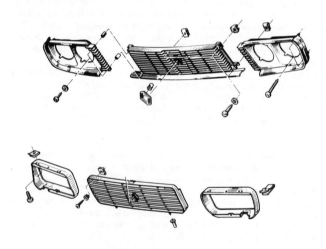

Fig. 12.1 Radiator grilles (Sec 6)

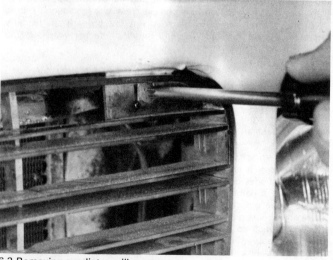

6.2 Removing a radiator grille screw

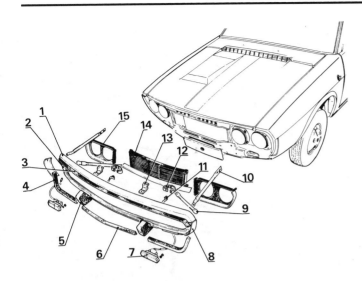

Fig. 12.2 Early type front protective grille (Sec 7)

1 Top band	9 Lower tie-bars
2 Bottom band	10 Upper tie-bars
3 Shield strip (top)	11 Overrider tie-rods
4 Shield strip (side)	12 Lower brackets
5 Overriders	13 Upper brackets
6 Shield strip (bottom)	14 Radiator grille
7 Parking lamps	15 Headlamp embellishers
8 Outer embellishers	

7 Front protective shield – removal and refitting

Early models

1   Disconnect the leads from the front parking lamps.
2   Remove the headlamp trim panels and the radiator grille as described in the preceding Section.
3   Remove the overriders.
4   Remove the overrider tie rods.
5   Remove the upper brackets and tie-bar mountings.
6   Remove the protective shield assembly.

Later models

7   Remove the radiator grille and the headlamp trim panels.
8   Remove the outboard headlamps (see Chapter 10), to provide better access to the shield mountings.
9   Remove the upper and lower fixing bolts at each end of the main section.
10   Remove the bracket bolts.
11   Identify the parking/flasher lamp leads and disconnect them.
12   Refitting of both types is a reversal of removal.

8 Front wing – removal and refitting

1   Remove the protective shield and headlamp trim panels as described in Section 7.
2   Remove the bolts from the door pillar, body sill, wing inner panel and the front end panel and undertray.
3   Remove the wing. The joint sealing mastic may require cutting with a sharp knife to release it. Scrape away the mastic.
4   Before refitting the new wing, apply a thick bead of mastic to clean joint faces.

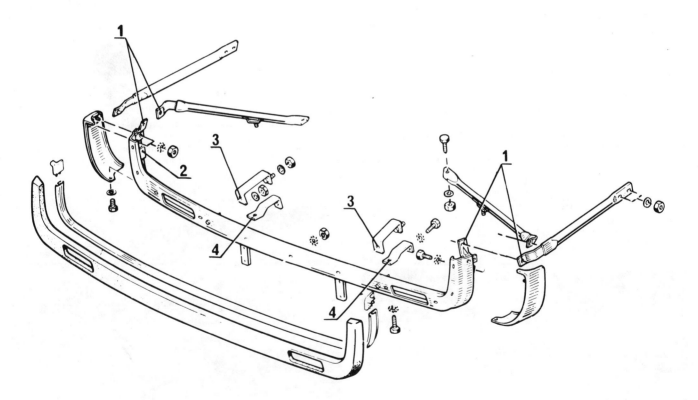

Fig. 12.3 Later type front protective grille (Sec 7)

1 Upper fixings	2 End fixings	3 Brackets	4 Brackets

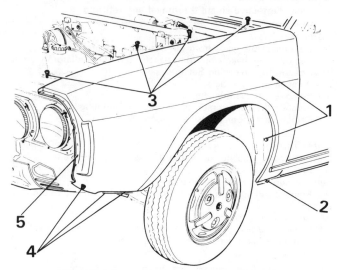

Fig. 12.4 Front wing removal points (Sec 8)

1   *Body pillar screw*   4   *Undertray screw*
2   *Body sill screw*   5   *Front end panel screw*
3   *Wing inner panel*

5   Refitting is a reversal of removal.
6   Coat the underside of the wing with suitable protective compound. Spray the top surface to match the body colour.

---

9   Bonnet – removal and refitting

1   The bonnet may be removed after disconnecting the hinges in one of the two following ways.
2   Either drive out the hinge roll pins or mark the position of the hinge on the panel cross-rail and unbolt the hinges (photos).
3   The help of an assistant will be required to lift the bonnet from the car.
4   Refit by reversing the removal operation. Adjust the hinge position if necessary to give correct alignment within the body aperture.

---

10   Bonnet release cable – renewal

1   Should the bonnet release cable break, it is still possible to open

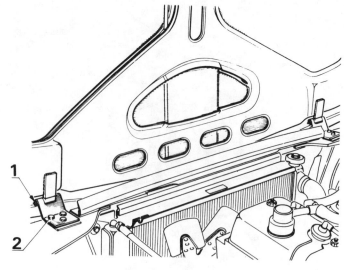

Fig. 12.5 Bonnet hinge (Sec 9)

1   *Roll pin*   2   *Hinge bolt*

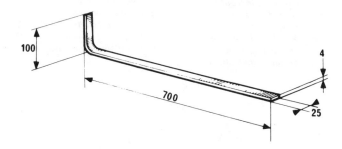

Fig. 12.6 Bonnet releasing tool (Sec 10)

Dimensions in mm

the bonnet using a lever made up to the dimensions shown in the diagram.
2   Remove the right-hand front roadwheel and pass the tool through the aperture under the front wing through which the steering tie-rod emerges.

9.2A Bonnet hinge. Pivot roll pin arrowed

9.2B Bonnet hinge nuts

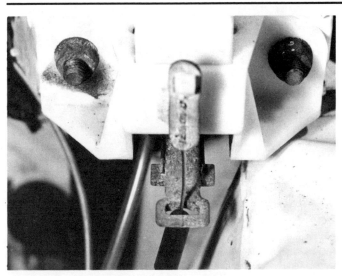

10.5 Bonnet release cable and catch

3   Press the lever on the nearest bonnet catch upwards to open one side of the bonnet.
4   Prise the released side of the bonnet open carefully to be able to insert the tool and move the lever on the second bonnet catch.
5   To renew the cable, disconnect the cable end fittings and then pull the cable sleeves into the vehicle interior (photo).

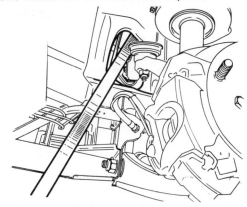

Fig. 12.7 Passing tool into engine compartment (Sec 10)

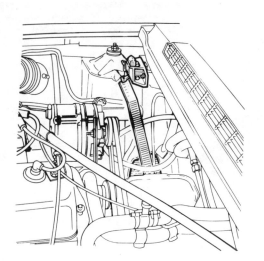

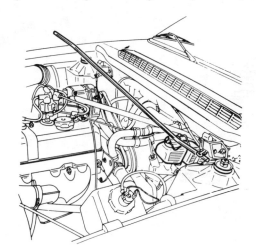

Fig. 12.8 Releasing bonnet catches (Sec 10)

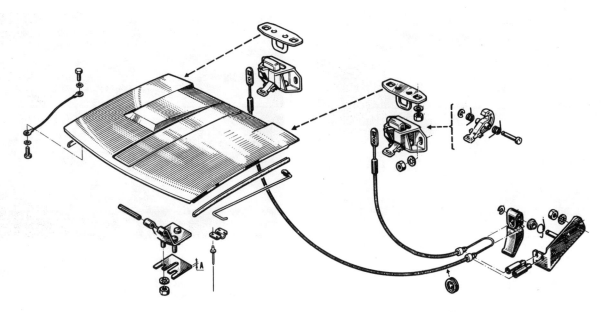

Fig. 12.9 Bonnet and release components (Sec 10)

This sequence of photographs deals with the repair of the dent and paintwork damage shown in this photo. The procedure will be similar for the repair of a hole. It should be noted that the procedures given here are simplified – more explicit instructions will be found in the text

In the case of a dent the first job – after removing surrounding trim – is to hammer out the dent where access is possible. This will minimise filling. Here, the large dent having been hammered out, the damaged area is being made slightly concave

Now all paint must be removed from the damaged area, by rubbing with coarse abrasive paper. Alternatively, a wire brush or abrasive pad can be used in a power drill. Where the repair area meets good paintwork, the edge of the paintwork should be 'feathered', using a finer grade of abrasive paper

In the case of a hole caused by rusting, all damaged sheet-metal should be cut away before proceeding to this stage. Here, the damaged area is being treated with rust remover and inhibitor before being filled

Mix the body filler according to its manufacturer's instructions. In the case of corrosion damage, it will be necessary to block off any large holes before filling – this can be done with zinc gauze or aluminium tape. Make sure the area is absolutely clean before...

...applying the filler. Filler should be applied with a flexible applicator, as shown, for best results; the wooden spatula being used for confined areas. Apply thin layers of filler at 20-minute intervals, until the surface of the filler is slightly proud of the surrounding bodywork

Initial shaping can be done with a Surform plane or Dreadnought file. Then, using progressively finer grades of wet-and-dry paper, wrapped around a sanding block, and copious amounts of clean water, rub down the filler until really smooth and flat. Again, feather the edges of adjoining paintwork

The whole repair area can now be sprayed or brush-painted with primer. If spraying, ensure adjoining areas are protected from over-spray. Note that at least one inch of the surrounding sound paintwork should be coated with primer. Primer has a 'thick' consistency, so will fill small imperfections

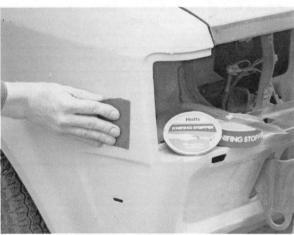

Again, using plenty of water, rub down the primer with a fine grade of wet-and-dry paper (400 grade is probably best) until it is really smooth and well blended into the surrounding paintwork. Any remaining imperfections can now be filled by carefully applied knifing stopper paste

When the stopper has hardened, rub down the repair area again before applying the final coat of primer. Before rubbing down this last coat of primer, ensure the repair area is blemish-free – use more stopper if necessary. To ensure that the surface of the primer is really smooth use some finishing compound

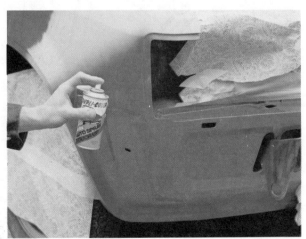

The top coat can now be applied. When working out of doors, pick a dry, warm and wind-free day. Ensure surrounding areas are protected from over-spray. Agitate the aerosol thoroughly, then spray the centre of the repair area, working outwards with a circular motion. Apply the paint as several thin coats

After a period of about two weeks, which the paint needs to harden fully, the surface of the repaired area can be 'cut' with a mild cutting compound prior to wax polishing. When carrying out bodywork repairs, remember that the quality of the finished job is proportional to the time and effort expended

11.2 Washer tubes under scuttle

12.5A Tailgate lock

12.5B Tailgate lock striker

6   Unbolt the release lever.
7   Fitting the new cable is a reversal of removal.

11 Scuttle grille panel – removal and refitting

1   This panel may need to be removed for access to the windscreen wiper motor and linkage (see Chapter 10).
2   Extract the cross-head fixing screws and lift the grille until the windscreen washer tubes can be disconnected (photo).
3   Refitting is a reversal of removal, but make sure that the rubber seals are in good condition.

12 Tailgate – removal and refitting

1   Open the tailgate fully and have an assistant support it while the support struts are unbolted. Fold up the legs.

2   Pull back the weatherseal to expose the hinge bolts.
3   Mark the position of the hinge plates on the body shell. Then unscrew the bolts and lift the tailgate away.
4   Refit by reversing the removal operation, check the tailgate alignment within the body shell.
5   Check the operation of the tailgate latch. If adjustment is required, use shims under the striker (photos).

13 Tailgate counterbalance struts – removal and refitting

1   Raise the rear parcels shelf to clear the pegs.
2   Remove the fixed trim from the rear parcels shelf to give access to the screws.
3   Have an assistant support the tailgate and then disconnect the strut from it.
4   Refitting is a reversal of removal.

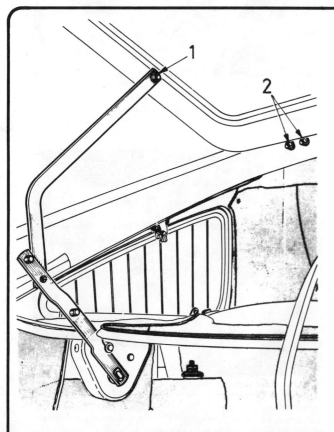

Fig. 12.10 Tailgate strut nuts (1) and hinge nuts (2) (Sec 12)

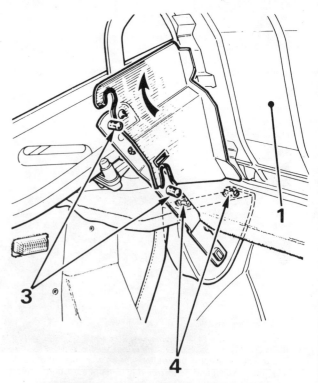

Fig. 12.11 Tailgate counterbalance (Sec 13)

1   Rear parcels shelf   4   Screws
3   Pegs

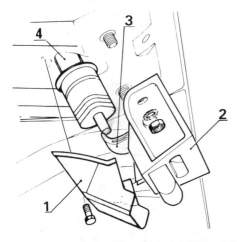

Fig. 12.12 Tailgate lock (early models) (Sec 14)

1	Cover	3	Locking hook
2	Housing	4	Barrel

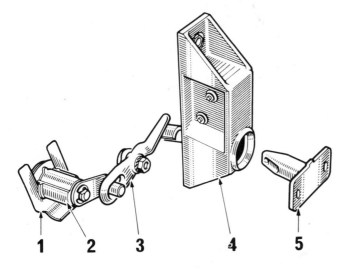

Fig. 12.14 Tailgate lock dismantled (later models) (Sec 14)

1	Forked clip	4	Lock
2	Button	5	Striker plate
3	Operating lever		

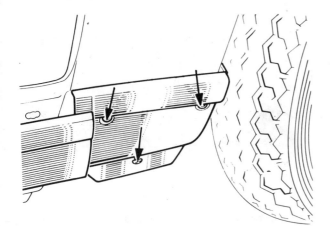

Fig. 12.16 Sill front embellisher. Torx screws (arrowed) (Sec 15)

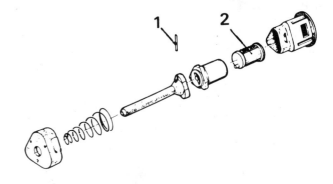

Fig. 12.13 Tailgate lock barrel dismantled (Sec 14)

1	Roll pin	2 Barrel

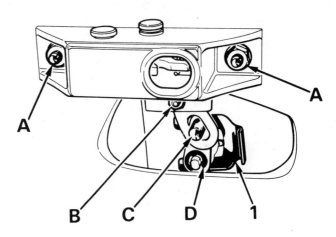

Fig. 12.15 Tailgate lock fixing (later models) (Sec 14)

A	Nut	D	E clip
B	Nut	1	Forked clip
C	Operating pin		

14 Tailgate lock – removal and refitting

Early models
1   Open the tailgate, remove the cover and the housing.
2   Remove the spring by releasing the clip and driving out the pin.
3   The push-button/barrel assembly must be withdrawn from outside, but before this can be done, the retaining lugs will have to be depressed. A piece of close fitting tubing with a chamfer on its internal rim will serve to do this.
4   The lock barrel can be dismantled if the rollpin is driven out.

Later models
5   Remove the nuts (A) and withdraw the lock.
6   Remove the nuts (B).
7   Slide out the clip (1).
8   Remove the turn button.
9   The lock barrel can be dismantled if the E-clip (D) is extracted from the operating pin (C).
10 Reassembly and refitting are reversals of dismantling and removal.

15 Sill embellisher – removal and refitting

1   The front section is retained by Torx screws.
2   The main section is secured by clips.

16 Rear deflector – removal and refitting

1   This is retained to the tailgate by nuts. These are accessible using a box spanner or socket inserted through the holes on the inner face of the tailgate.

17 Rear quarter louvre – removal and refitting

1   Unscrew the internal fixing screw.
2   Slide the louvre rearwards to release it from its locating pegs.

18 Rear protective shield – removal and refitting

1   Unscrew the mounting bolts from the luggage compartment floor.
2   Working through the holes in the rear panel remove the upper mounting nuts.
3   Withdraw the protective shield far enough to be able to disconnect the lamp wires.
4   The shield can be dismantled by removing the fixing screws, the brackets and the top embellisher strip.
5   Reassembly and refitting are reversals of removal and dismantling,

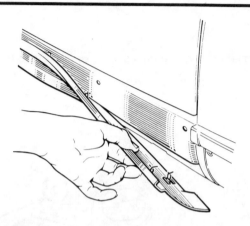

Fig. 12.17 Sill main embellisher (Sec 15)

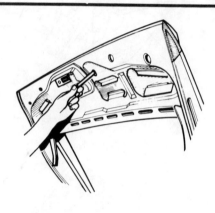

Fig. 12.18 Unscrewing rear deflector nut (Sec 16)

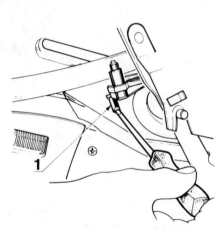

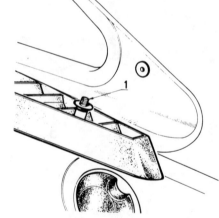

Fig. 12.19 Rear quarter louvre screw (1) (Sec 17)

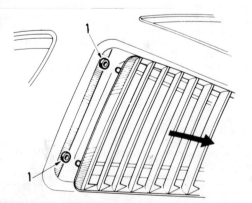

Fig. 12.20 Removal direction for rear quarter louvre (Sec 17)

1   Locating pegs

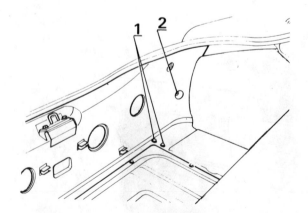

Fig. 12.21 Rear protective shield screws (Sec 18)

1   Lower   2   Upper

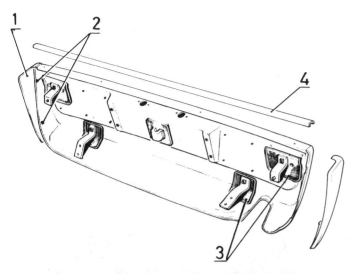

Fig. 12.22 Rear view of protective shield (Sec 18)

| 1 | Side embellisher | 3 | Mounting brackets |
| 2 | Fixing screws | 4 | Top embellisher |

but make sure that the rubber insulators are located between the shield and the mounting brackets.

19 Door trim panel – removal and refitting

1   Prise back the plastic cover from the upper end of the armrest/door pull (photo).
2   Extract the three screws which hold the assembly to the door (photo).
3   Drive out the roll pin and remove the remote control handle (photo).
4   On appropriate models, prise out the embellisher from the window regulator handle, unscrew the retaining nut and pull off the handle.
5   Insert the fingers or a wide blade between the bottom edge of the trim panel and the door and unclip the panel using a sharp jerking pull (photo).
6   Carefully peel away the waterproof sheet.
7   Refit by reversing the removal operations.

20 Door window winder and glass – removal and refitting

1   Remove the door trim panel as described in the preceding Section.

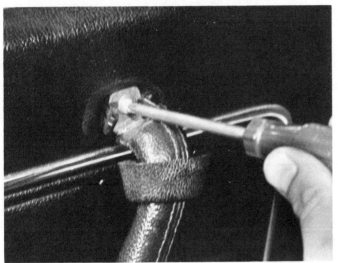

19.1 Door armrest screw

19.2 Door armrest screw

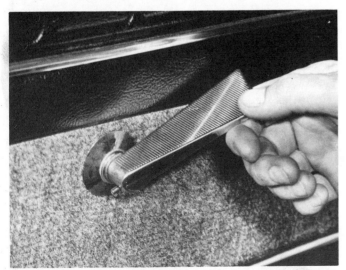

19.3 Remote control handle and roll pin

19.5 Door trim panel clip

Hand-operated window regulator

2   Temporarily refit the regulator handle and wind the window nearly to the closed position.

3   Remove the handle and unscrew the regulator fixing bolts.

4   Manoeuvre the regulator within the door cavity until the counter-balance arms can be slid out of the channel at the bottom of the window glass (photo).

5   Support the glass and withdraw the regulator through the large opening in the door interior panel.

6   To remove the glass, disconnect the door quarter-light dividing channel at its top end. Remove the door glass weatherseals.

7   Remove the four screws shown.

8   Tilt the dividing channel forwards and pull the main glass panel upwards tilting its upper edge downwards towards the rear of the car to remove it.

9   If the glass bottom channel is removed, it must be refitted in accordance with the diagram.

10   To remove the door quarter-light, pull the frame upwards out of the door.

11   The glass can be detached from the quarter-light frame by extracting the two strut screws and prising the frame apart.

Electric window regulator

12   The operations are similar to those just described for the mechan-

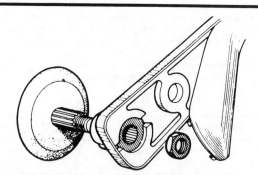

Fig. 12.23 Window regulator handle (Sec 19)

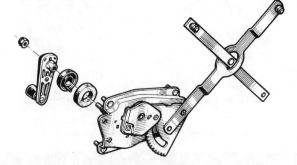

Fig. 12.24 Mechanical type window regulator (Sec 20)

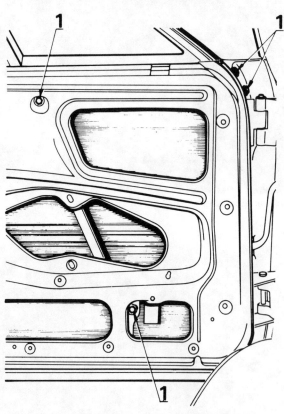

Fig. 12.25 Door glass removal points (Sec 20)

1   *Channel frame screws*

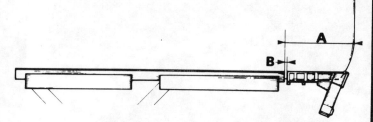

Fig. 12.26 Glass channel and positioning diagram (Sec 20)

$A = 120 \, mm \, (4\frac{3}{4} \, in)$ $B = 5 \, mm \, (\frac{3}{16} \, in)$

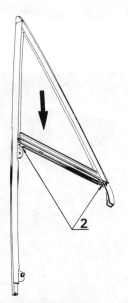

Fig. 12.27 Fixed quarter light and frame (Sec 20)

2   *Screws*

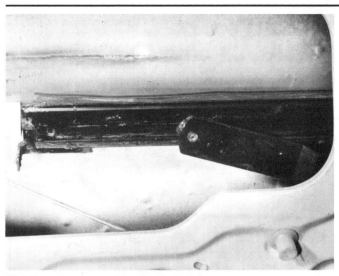
20.4 Door glass lower channel and winder arm

ical regulator except that before commencing operations, operate the window control until the glass top edge is 20.0 mm (0.79 in) from the tip of the quarter-light divider channel. Disconnect the battery and once the trim panel has been removed, disconnect the leads from the winder motor (photo).

13 Refitting is a reversal of removal, but adjust the position of the divider channel by loosening the bolt at its bottom end until the main glass slides up and down smoothly without judder. Refer also to Chapter 10, Section 30.

21 Door lock – removal and refitting

1   Raise the window to its fullest extent.
2   Remove the trim panel as described in Section 19.
3   Unbolt the remote control lever housing (photo).
4   Working at the edge of the door, extract the three lock securing screws (Torx type) (photo).
5   Remove the lock rod retaining clip.
6   Reach within the door cavity and free the door lock push-button.
7   Withdraw the lock assembly through the aperture in the door cavity (photo).
8   Refitting is a reversal of removal.

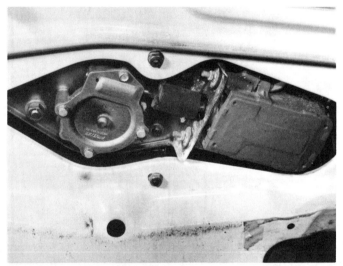
20.12 Door glass electric motor and gear

21.3 Door lock remote control spindle housing

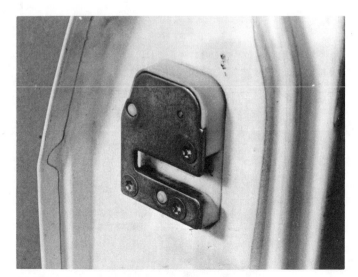
21.4 Door lock at edge

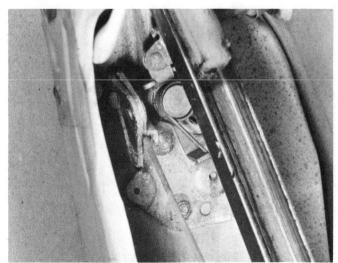
21.7 Door lock viewed from door interior

22 Door – removal, refitting and adjusting

1   Open the door to its fullest extent and support its lower edge on jacks or blocks with a pad of rag as as insulator.
2   The door may be removed in one of two ways. Either extract the circlip and tap out the hinge pins or remove the hinge retaining nuts

from the inside of the body pillar. If the latter method is used then access to the nuts is obtained by removing the interior side trim panels.
3   On cars with electric windows, withdraw the door only after disconnecting the wiring and feeding it through the hole in the pillar.
4   Refitting is a reversal of removal, but if the hinges were unbolted then tighten them only finger tight until the door alignment has been

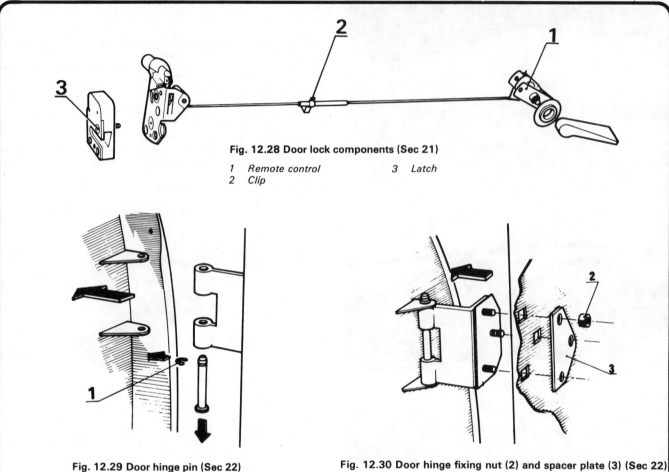

Fig. 12.28 Door lock components (Sec 21)

1   Remote control   3   Latch
2   Clip

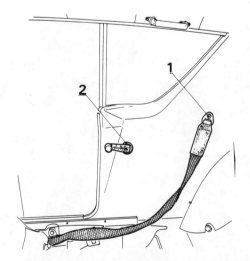

Fig. 12.29 Door hinge pin (Sec 22)

1   Circlip

Fig. 12.30 Door hinge fixing nut (2) and spacer plate (3) (Sec 22)

Fig. 12.31 Quarter trim panel (Sec 23)

1   Belt anchorage
2   Window regulator handle

22.5 Door lock striker

checked. Where necessary use spacer plates between hinge and pillar.

5   Finally, adjust the position of the lock striker to give smooth positive closure of the door. Torx type screws are used on the striker (photo).

23 Rear quarter-light (wind down type) – removal and refitting

1   Disconnect the seat belt anchorage.
2   Remove the window regulator handle as described for the front door in Section 19.
3   Remove the rear seat as described in Section 29.
4   Pull the trim panel from its fixing clips.

5   Remove the sill embellisher, door seal and rubbing strip.
6   Temporarily refit the regulator handle and wind up the window.
7   Remove the regulator fixing nuts, also the two screws which hold the vertical channel.
8   Manoeuvre the regulator lifting arm to free it from the channel at the bottom of the glass.
9   Support the glass and then withdraw the channel and the regulator assembly through the door aperture.
10 To remove the glass, prise out the external weatherseal and then withdraw the weatherseal in three stages by tilting as shown in the diagrams.
11 Refitting is a reversal of removal, but adjust the position of the window channel by means of the bottom fixing screw to enable the glass to slide up and down smoothly.

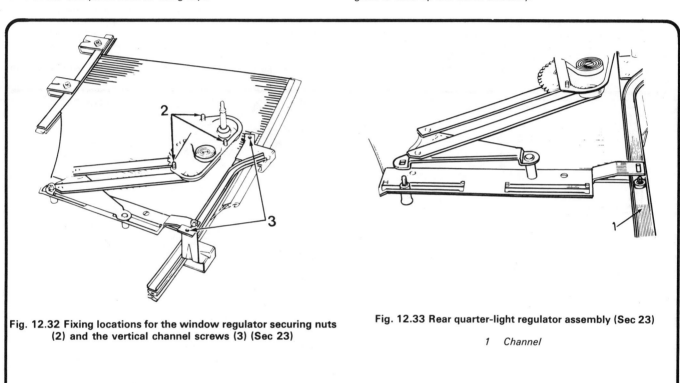

Fig. 12.32 Fixing locations for the window regulator securing nuts (2) and the vertical channel screws (3) (Sec 23)

Fig. 12.33 Rear quarter-light regulator assembly (Sec 23)

1   Channel

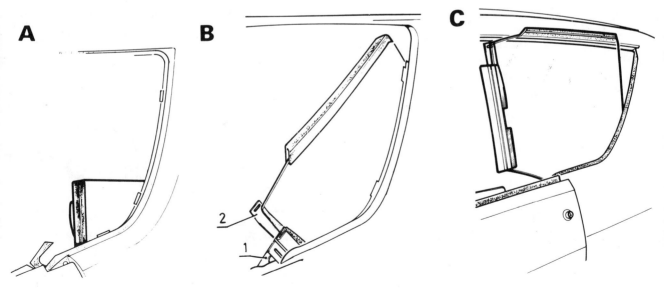

Fig. 12.34 Rear quarter-light glass removal in stages A, B and C (Sec 23)

1   Moulded seal   2   Window base end

24 Rear quarter-light (deflector type) – removal and refitting

1   This type of window was fitted to pre 1976 models.
2   Remove the grab handle.
3   Extract the two screws from the window bottom bracket.
4   Extract the lock securing screw.
5   Have an assistant remove the window from outside the car.
6   If a new glass is being fitted then the brackets must be carefully tapped into position in accordance with the diagram.
7   To refit the window, engage the top bracket. Use a strip of metal as a slide to engage the bottom bracket by pushing the glass so that it slips over the weatherstrip.
8   Refit the lock.

25 Rear quarter-light (opening type) – removal and refitting

1   This type of window was fitted to 1976 Renault 15 models.
2   The window may be removed by extracting the two screws which hold the lock to the parcel lining and then tilting the glass out beyond its normal travel until the two hinges are free of the pillar.
3   Refitting is a reversal of removal.

26 Rear quarter-light (fixed) – removal and refitting

1   Before this glass can be removed, the louvre must be withdrawn as described in Section 17.
2   Remove the glass in a similar way to that described for the windscreen in the next Section.

27 Windscreen and tailgate glass – removal and refitting

1   Removal of either the windscreen or rear window will be required for one of two reasons; the glass shattering or cracking or deterioration of the rubber surround causing water leaks into the interior of the vehicle. Remove the wiper arms.
2   Where the glass has shattered, the easiest way to remove the

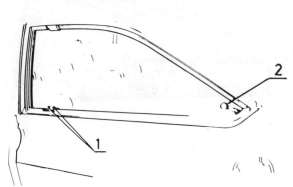

Fig. 12.35 Deflector type window (Sec 24)

1   *Bottom bracket screws*   2   *Lock screw*

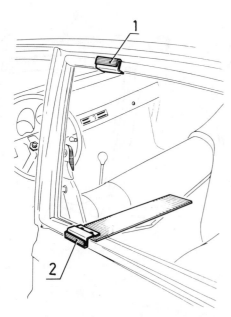

Fig. 12.37 Deflector type window brackets (Sec 24)

1   *Top bracket*   2   *Bottom bracket with tool*

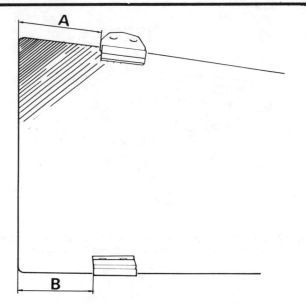

Fig. 12.36 Deflector type bracket fixing diagram (Sec 24)

A   *125.0 mm (4.9 in)*   B   *120.0 mm (4.7 in)*

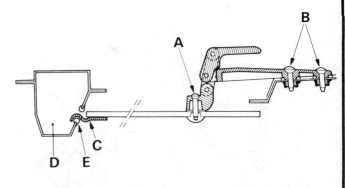

Fig. 12.38 Opening type quarter-light details (Sec 25)

A   *Lock-to-glass screw*   D   *Pillar*
B   *Lock-to-panel screws*   E   *Hinge pivot*
C   *Hinge*

screen is to stick a sheet of self-adhesive paper or plastic sheeting to each side and push it from the inside outwards. Seal the air intake grille on the scuttle and air ducts and radio speaker slots in the facia panel to prevent glass crystals from falling into them during the removal operation. Protect the surface of the bonnet with a blanket to prevent scratching.

3   Where the glass is to be removed intact or just cracked (laminated type) or to renew the rubber weatherseal, make up two pads of cloth and with the aid of an assistant press the two top corners of the screen from the inside outwards and at the same time pulling the rubber surround from the upper corners. Remove the rubber surround as soon as the screen is withdrawn and clean the edges of both the glass and the body screen frame.

4   Commence refitting by positioning the rubber surround round the edge of the windscreen glass. Place the assembly flat down on a bench or table.

5   Lay a length of string or thin cord in the channel in the inner side of the rubber surround.

6   The string should be about 3 mm (0.125 in) diameter and the ends should overlap at the bottom edge by 100 mm (4 in) and leave a few inches to grip with the hands.

7   Place a bead of sealing mastic in the lower two corners of the screen frame.

8   Locate the lower edge of the screen surround in the body frame so that the two ends of the string hang inside the car, then pull both ends of the string while an assistant presses the glass and surround into position as the operation progresses.

9   The string will finally emerge from the top centre of the rubber surround and the screen and rubber surround lip should be in correct engagement with the screen frame.

10 Using either a sealing mastic gun or tube, insert the nozzle between the rubber surround lip and the outer surface of the screen frame and insert a thin even bead of sealer. Press the rubber surround hard to spread the sealer and to ensure correct location. Wipe away any excess sealer with a paraffin moistened cloth.

11 The embellisher should be located round the seal before it is fitted. You will need to improvise here and fabricate a suitable tool to insert the embellisher strips. The official Renault tool for the job is No 438. When the strips are fitted, locate the corner piece to complete.

---

28 Front seat – removal, refitting and adjusting

1   Raise the locking lever.

2   Push the seat fully forward on its runners and unscrew the seat rear mounting bolts. These are of Torx type.

3   Now push the seat fully back and unscrew the front bolts (photo).

4   Using a screwdriver, release the tensioner clip.

5   Remove the seat from the car.

6   The reclining seat back can be adjusted in the following way if it fails to operate correctly. Remove the trim panel from the back of the seat back. Unlock the locknut and turn the threaded cable adjuster as necessary.

28.3 Front seat screw

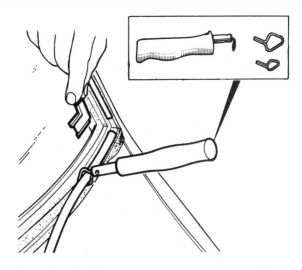

Fig. 12.39 Windscreen trim fitting tool (Sec 27)

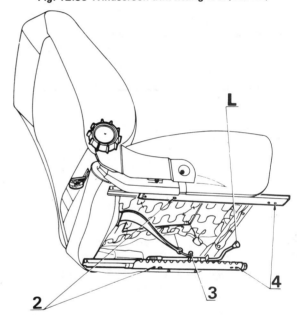

Fig. 12.40 Front seat (Sec 28)

L	Locking lever	3	Tensioner clip
2	Slide rear bolts	4	Slide front bolts

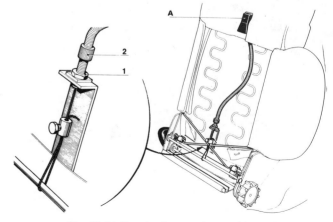

Fig. 12.41 Seat back control cable (Sec 28)

A   Control lever   1   Locknut   2   Cable adjuster

7   Refitting the seat is a reversal of removal.
8   If it is necessary to remove the slides from the floor after the seat has been removed, these two are retained by Torx type screws.

29 Rear seat – removal and refitting

1   Pull the front edge of the seat cushion upwards to disengage its lip and then pull the cushion out from under the base of the seat back.
2   To remove the seat back, release the retaining tabs at its base and lift upwards to disengage the hook at the upper edge.
3   Refitting is a reversal of removal.

30 Facia panel (to 1976) – removal and refitting

1   Prise off the trim panel from the top of the facia using a screwdriver to release it from its clips.
2   Extract the four screws (now exposed) which hold the cowl. Pull the cowl from the angle bracket and disengage the clips.
3   Remove the facia top fixings.
4   Working at the base of the facia panel, remove the fixing screws.
5   Refitting is a reversal of removal.

31 Centre console – removal and refitting

1   If the car is fitted with automatic transmission, unclip the embellisher, open the slot in it and slip it off the speed selector control

lever. Take out the selector indicator plate. Extract the two screws which hold one side of the bristle type dust excluder. On manual cars, release the gearchange lever gaiter (Chapter 6).
2   Extract the two screws from the upper casing.
3   Extract the six screws from each side of the gearchange lever.
4   Extract the four screws from the forward end of the console.
5   Refitting is a reversal of removal.

32 Facia panel (1977 on) – removal and refitting

1   Remove the centre console as described in the preceding Section, also the instrument panel as described in Chapter 10.
2   Remove the two heater control panel fixing screws.
3   Extract the screw which holds the facia to the windscreen frame lining.
4   Release the bracket at each end of the facia panel (photo).
5   Lift the facia panel to disengage its mounting hooks, tilt it slightly to clear the steering wheel and withdraw it.
6   Refitting is a reversal of removal.

33 Safety belts – maintenance, removal and refitting

1   Inspect the condition of the belts regularly for signs of fraying, particularly around the anchorages.
2   To clean the belts, use detergent and warm water, nothing else.
3   Static or inertia reel type belts may be fitted according to year of production and model.

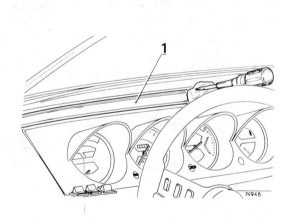

Fig. 12.42 Prising off early type facia panel trim (1) (Sec 30)

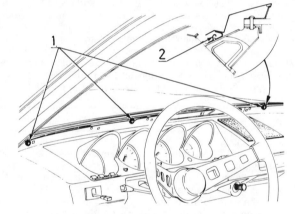

Fig. 12.43 Cowl assembly fixing (Sec 30)

1   Screws   2   Angle bracket retainer

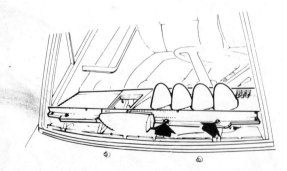

Fig. 12.44 Facia panel upper fixing screws (arrowed) (Sec 30)

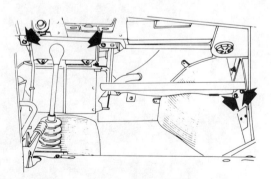

Fig. 12.45 Facia lower fixing screws (arrowed) (Sec 30)

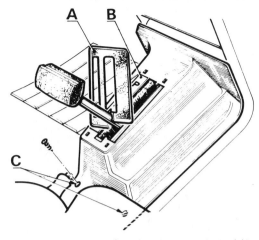

Fig. 12.46 Centre console (automatic transmission) (Sec 31)

A Embellisher   C Screws
B Indicator plate

Fig. 12.47 Centre console screw locations (Sec 31)

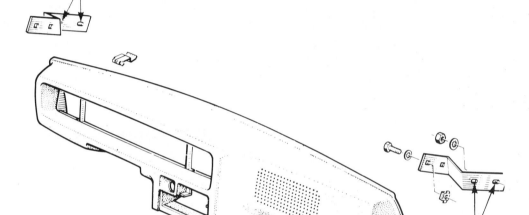

Fig. 12.48 Later type facia panel and brackets. Bracket screw holes (arrowed) (Sec 32)

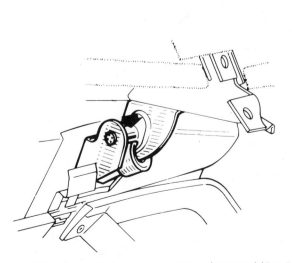

Fig. 12.49 Later type facia lower mountings (arrowed) (Sec 32)

32.4 Facia support brackets

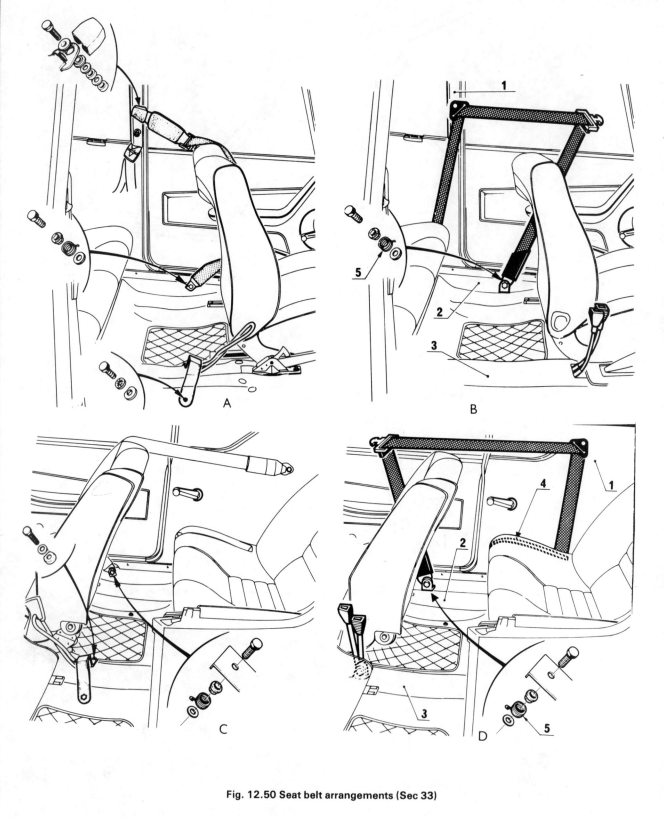

Fig. 12.50 Seat belt arrangements (Sec 33)

A   Saloon – earlier models
B   Saloon – later models
1   Centre pillar
2   Side member
3   Floor centre section
5   Return spring

C   Coupe – earlier models
D   Coupe – later models
1   Rear quarter lining
2   Side member
3   Floor centre section
4   Belt stowage
5   Return spring

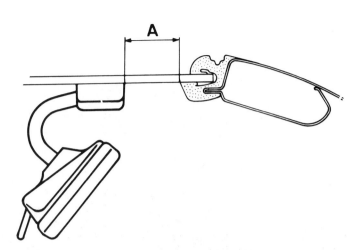

Fig. 12.51 Interior rear view mirror positioning diagram (Sec 34)

A   44.0 mm (1.73 in)

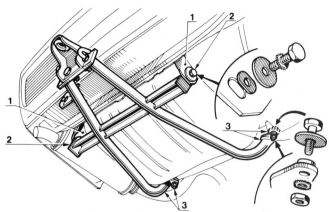

Fig. 12.52 Typical (Renault) towing bracket (Sec 35)

1   *Rear lash-down hook*   3   *Side member bolts*
2   *Bolt*

4   If the belts have been removed, make sure that the anchor components are refitted in their original sequence.
5   On inertia reel belt systems, make sure that the tension spring used to swivel the belt mounting lug is given one complete turn to preload it.
6   Rear seat belts can be fitted to the anchorage points located on the rear inner wing panels and the rear floor panel.

34 Interior rear view mirror (windscreen bonded type)

1   On some models, the mirror is bonded to the windscreen. In the event of a new screen being fitted, the mirror will have to be fixed to the glass using a special glass bonding adhesive.

2   The mirror base must be positioned in the centre of the screen at a distance of 44.0 mm (1.73 in) from the edge of the rubber weatherseal.

35 Towing bracket – fitting

1   Towing brackets are available for all models, the following description covers the official Renault kit.
2   Offer up the towing bracket to align with the two rear lash-down hooks.
3   Screw in the fixing bolts with washers correctly positioned.
4   Attach the front bolts to the holes in the side members. These holes on some models may need opening out to 10.5 mm (0.41 in) diameter.
5   Check that the front bolt does not foul the exhaust pipe. If it does, release the exhaust pipe clamp and adjust the setting of pipe and silencer slightly.
6   Fit the towing ball and then tighten all nuts and bolts securely.
7   Details for connecting the wiring harness are given in Chapter 10, Section 39.

Conversion factors

Length (distance)

Inches (in)	X	25.4	= Millimetres (mm)	X 0.0394	= Inches (in)
Feet (ft)	X	0.305	= Metres (m)	X 3.281	= Feet (ft)
Miles	X	1.609	= Kilometres (km)	X 0.621	= Miles

Volume (capacity)

Cubic inches (cu in; in^3)	X	16.387	= Cubic centimetres (cc; cm^3)	X 0.061	= Cubic inches (cu in; in^3)
Imperial pints (Imp pt)	X	0.568	= Litres (l)	X 1.76	= Imperial pints (Imp pt)
Imperial quarts (Imp qt)	X	1.137	= Litres (l)	X 0.88	= Imperial quarts (Imp qt)
Imperial quarts (Imp qt)	X	1.201	= US quarts (US qt)	X 0.833	= Imperial quarts (Imp qt)
US quarts (US qt)	X	0.946	= Litres (l)	X 1.057	= US quarts (US qt)
Imperial gallons (Imp gal)	X	4.546	= Litres (l)	X 0.22	= Imperial gallons (Imp gal)
Imperial gallons (Imp gal)	X	1.201	= US gallons (US gal)	X 0.833	= Imperial gallons (Imp gal)
US gallons (US gal)	X	3.785	= Litres (l)	X 0.264	= US gallons (US gal)

Mass (weight)

Ounces (oz)	X	28.35	= Grams (g)	X 0.035	= Ounces (oz)
Pounds (lb)	X	0.454	= Kilograms (kg)	X 2.205	= Pounds (lb)

Force

Ounces-force (ozf; oz)	X	0.278	= Newtons (N)	X 3.6	= Ounces-force (ozf; oz)
Pounds-force (lbf; lb)	X	4.448	= Newtons (N)	X 0.225	= Pounds-force (lbf; lb)
Newtons (N)	X	0.1	= Kilograms-force (kgf; kg)	X 9.81	= Newtons (N)

Pressure

Pounds-force per square inch (psi; lbf/in^2; lb/in^2)	X	0.070	= Kilograms-force per square centimetre (kgf/cm^2; kg/cm^2)	X 14.223	= Pounds-force per square inch (psi; lbf/in^2; lb/in^2)
Pounds-force per square inch (psi; lbf/in^2; lb/in^2)	X	0.068	= Atmospheres (atm)	X 14.696	= Pounds-force per square inch (psi; lbf/in^2; lb/in^2)
Pounds-force per square inch (psi; lbf/in^2; lb/in^2)	X	0.069	= Bars	X 14.5	= Pounds-force per square inch (psi; lbf/in^2; lb/in^2)
Pounds-force per square inch (psi; lbf/in^2; lb/in^2)	X	6.895	= Kilopascals (kPa)	X 0.145	= Pounds-force per square inch (psi; lbf/in^2; lb/in^2)
Kilopascals (kPa)	X	0.01	= Kilograms-force per square centimetre (kgf/cm^2; kg/cm^2)	X 98.1	= Kilopascals (kPa)

Torque (moment of force)

Pounds-force inches (lbf in; lb in)	X	1.152	= Kilograms-force centimetre (kgf cm; kg cm)	X 0.868	= Pounds-force inches (lbf in; lb in)
Pounds-force inches (lbf in; lb in)	X	0.113	= Newton metres (Nm)	X 8.85	= Pounds-force inches (lbf in; lb in)
Pounds-force inches (lbf in; lb in)	X	0.083	= Pounds-force feet (lbf ft; lb ft)	X 12	= Pounds-force inches (lbf in; lb in)
Pounds-force feet (lbf ft; lb ft)	X	0.138	= Kilograms-force metres (kgf m; kg m)	X 7.233	= Pounds-force feet (lbf ft; lb ft)
Pounds-force feet (lbf ft; lb ft)	X	1.356	= Newton metres (Nm)	X 0.738	= Pounds-force feet (lbf ft; lb ft)
Newton metres (Nm)	X	0.102	= Kilograms-force metres (kgf m; kg m)	X 9.804	= Newton metres (Nm)

Power

Horsepower (hp)	X	745.7	= Watts (W)	X 0.0013	= Horsepower (hp)

Velocity (speed)

Miles per hour (miles/hr; mph)	X	1.609	= Kilometres per hour (km/hr; kph)	X 0.621	= Miles per hour (miles/hr; mph)

Fuel consumption*

Miles per gallon, Imperial (mpg)	X	0.354	= Kilometres per litre (km/l)	X 2.825	= Miles per gallon, Imperial (mpg)
Miles per gallon, US (mpg)	X	0.425	= Kilometres per litre (km/l)	X 2.352	= Miles per gallon, US (mpg)

Temperature

Degrees Fahrenheit = (°C x 1.8) + 32

Degrees Celsius (Degrees Centigrade; °C) = (°F - 32) x 0.56

*It is common practice to convert from miles per gallon (mpg) to litres/100 kilometres (l/100km), where mpg (Imperial) x l/100 km = 282 and mpg (US) x l/100 km = 235

Index

A

About this manual – 2
Accelerator cable
   renewal and adjustment – 115
Acknowledgements – 2
Air cleaner
   removal and refitting – 92
Air cleaner assembly and ancillary components
   servicing – 91
Air conditioning system – 83
Air injection system
   description and maintenance – 113
Alternator
   brush
      renewal – 221
   description, maintenance and testing – 219
   diode carrier
      renewal – 223
   overhaul – 222
   removal and refitting – 221
Automatic transmission – 179 *et seq*
Automatic transmission
   description – 179
   driveplate
      removal and refitting – 184
   electronic computer
      removal and refitting – 183
   fault diagnosis – 188
   fluid
      checking, draining and refilling – 181
   governor
      removal, refitting and adjusting – 182
   kickdown switch
      adjusting – 183
      testing – 182
   oil cooler
      fitting – 184
   removal and refitting – 183
   specifications – 179
   speed selector control
      removal, refitting and adjusting – 181
   torque wrench settings – 179
Auxiliary driving lamps – 243

B

Battery
   maintenance and precautions – 218
   removal and refitting – 218
Bleeding the brakes – 212
Bleeding the power steering – 306
Bodywork and underframe – 312 *et seq*
Bodywork and underframe
   centre console
      removal and refitting – 330
   description – 312
   front protective shield
      removal and refitting – 315
   front wing
      removal and refitting – 315
   interior rear view mirror (windscreen bonded type) – 333
   maintenance – 312, 313
   rear deflector
      removal and refitting – 322
   rear protective shield
      removal and refitting – 322
   rear quarter light (deflector type)
      removal and refitting – 328
   rear quarter light (fixed)
      removal and refitting – 328
   rear quarter light (opening type)
      removal and refitting – 328
   rear quarter light (wind-down type)
      removal and refitting – 327
   rear quarter louvre
      removal and refitting – 322
   repair
      major damage – 314
      minor damage – 413
   scuttle grille panel
      removal and refitting – 320
   sill embellisher
      removal and refitting – 321
Bodywork repair sequence (colour) – 318, 319
Bonnet
   release cable
      renewal – 316
   removal and refitting – 316

Braking system – 196 *et seq*
Braking system
  bleeding the hydraulic system – 212
  caliper mounting bracket
    removal and refitting – 202
  description and maintenance – 197
  discs
    removal and refitting – 204
  drum
    renovation and renewal – 209
  fault diagnosis – 216
  front disc caliper
    removal, overhaul and refitting – 200
  front disc pads
    inspection and renewal – 197
  handbrake cable
    adjustment – 215
  handbrake cables
    renewal – 215
  handbrake control lever
    removal and refitting – 215
  hydraulic pipes and hoses – 213
  master cylinder
    overhaul – 209
    removal and refitting – 209
  pedal
    removal and refitting – 216
  pressure drop indicator
    description, removal and refitting – 211
  pressure limiting valve
    removal, refitting and adjustment – 210
  rear disc caliper
    mechanical overhaul – 202
    removal, seal renewal and refitting – 201
  rear disc pads (Gordini)
    inspection and renewal – 199
  rear drum brakes
    adjustment – 205
  rear shoe linings
    checking for wear – 205
  rear wheel cylinder
    removal, overhaul and refitting – 209
  Servo (Master Vac) unit
    description and testing – 213
    removal and refitting – 214
    servicing – 214
  shoes
    renewal (Bendix self-adjusting) – 207
    renewal (Girling self-adjusting) – 208
    renewal (manual adjusters) – 207
  specifications – 196
  switches – 216
  torque wrench settings – 197
Bulbs – 231, 234

C

Catalytic converter – 115
Capacities, general – 6
Carburettor
  description – 96
  idle speed and mixture
    adjustment – 96
  modification for North American automatic transmission
  vehicles (Weber 32) – 103
  overhaul
    general – 98
    Solex 32/32 SEIEMA – 99
    Weber 32 DARA – 102
    Weber 32 DIR – 100
  removal and refitting – 98
  specifications – 85
Carpets
  maintenance – 313
Clutch – 137 *et seq*

Clutch
  adjustment – 137
  cable
    renewal – 139
  description – 137
  fault diagnosis – 142
  pedal
    removal and refitting – 141
  release bearing
    renewal – 140
  release fork and shaft
    removal and refitting – 140
  removal, inspection and refitting – 139
  specifications – 137
  torque wrench settings – 137
Coil (ignition) – 133
Condenser – 133
Connecting rod/piston/liner assemblies (1289 cc – type 810 engine)
  removal and refitting – 34
Connecting rod/piston/liner assemblies (1565 cc, 1605 cc, 1647 cc – type 807, 821, 843, 844 engines)
  removal and refitting (engine in car) – 53
Contact breaker points
  renewal and adjustment – 123
Conversion factors – 334
Cooling heating and air conditioning systems – 71 *et seq*
Cooling system
  coolant mixtures – 74
  coolant pump
    removal and refitting (807, 821, 841, 843, 844 engines) – 77
    removal and refitting (810 engine) – 77
  coolant temperature and electric fan switches – 77
  description and maintenance – 71
  draining, refilling and bleeding – 73
  fault diagnosis – 84
  specifications – 71
Crankcase ventilation system
  1289 cc (type 810) engine – 45
  1565 cc, 1605 cc, 1647 cc (type 807, 821, 843, 844)
  engines – 62
Cylinder head
  1289 cc (type 810) engine
    dismantling, decarbonisation and reassembly – 44
    removal and refitting (engine in car) – 32
  1565 cc, 1605 cc, 1647 cc (type 807, 821, 843, 844) engines
    dismantling, decarbonisation and reassembly – 60
    removal and refitting (engine in car) – 50

D

Dimensions, general – 6
Direction indicator, hazard warning unit – 231
Distributor
  contact breaker points – 123
  overhaul – 130
  removal and refitting – 129
  variations on North American vehicles – 130
Door
  lock
    removal and refitting – 325
  removal, refitting and adjusting – 326
  trim panel
    removal and refitting – 323
  window winder and glass
    removal and refitting – 323
Drivebelt
  removal, refitting and tensioning – 76
Driveshafts – 189 *et seq*
Driveshafts
  coupling
    bellows renewal (Bendix ball type) – 194
    bellows renewal (type GE 86) – 191
    overhaul (type GI62) – 192
  description and maintenance – 189

fault diagnosis – 195
removal and refitting – 190
specifications – 189
torque wrench settings – 189
Dwell angle
checking and adjusting – 126

E

Electrical system – 217 *et seq*
Electrical system
description – 218
fault diagnosis – 17, 244
specifications – 217
wiring diagrams – 246 to 293
Emission control systems
description – 113
fault diagnosis – 120
Engine – 21 *et seq*
Engine (general)
description – 27
fault diagnosis – 18, 70
oil and filter – 32
operations possible with engine in car – 32
removal methods – 32
specifications – 21
torque wrench settings – 27
Engine (1289 cc type 810)
ancillaries removal – 39
dismantling
complete (engine removed) – 40
general – 39
examination, renovation and dismantling of major assemblies – 40
reassembly – 45
removal and refitting
leaving automatic transmission in car – 38
leaving manual transmission in car – 35
with automatic transmission – 39
with manual transmission – 36
separation from and reconnection to
automatic transmission – 39
manual transmission – 38
start-up after overhaul – 50
Engine (1565 cc, 1605 cc, 1647 cc – type 807, 821, 843, 844)
ancillaries removal – 39, 57
dismantling
complete (engine removed) – 57
general – 39, 57
examination, renovation and dismantling of
major assemblies – 58
reassembly – 62
removal and refitting – 56
start-up after overhaul – 50, 69
Exhaust gas recirculation system
description and maintenance – 114
maintenance indicator – 115
Exhaust system – 116

F

Facia panel
removal and refitting
to 1976 – 330
1977 on – 330
Fault diagnosis – 17 *et seq*
Fault diagnosis
automatic transmission – 188
braking system – 216
clutch – 142
cooling system – 84
driveshafts – 195
electrical system – 17, 244
emission control system – 120
engine – 18, 70

fuel system – 120
ignition system – 136
manual transmission – 178
steering – 311
suspension – 311
Firing order – 121
Front wheel alignment – 310
Fuel emission control systems – 85 *et seq*
Fuel evaporative control system – 113
Fuel injection system
accelerator cable switch
adjustment – 108
auxiliary air control valve
description, removal and refitting – 111
control box
removal and refitting – 111
description and precautions – 104
fault diagnosis – 120
fuel filter
renewal – 110
fuel injector
removal and refitting – 110
fuel injector hoses
renewal – 111
fuel pump
removal and refitting – 110
idle speed and mixture
adjustment – 107
pressure regulator
adjustment – 110
removal and refitting – 111
throttle switch
adjustment – 108
Fuel pump (carburettor system)
description and cleaning – 92
overhaul – 94
removal and refitting – 92
testing – 94
Fuel system
description and maintenance – 91
fault diagnosis – 120
specifications – 85
Fuel tank (carburettor system)
level transmitter
removal and refitting – 94
removal, cleaning, repair and refitting – 95
Fuses and relays – 230

G

Glossary – 7

H

Head lamp
beam alignment – 233
bulb
renewal – 231
removal and refitting – 233
Heater
dismantling and reassembly – 81
removal and refitting – 79
Heating and ventilation systems – 78
Horns – 237
Hub bearings
front
renewal – 300
rear
renewal and adjustment (disc brakes) – 302
renewal and adjustment (drum brakes) – 301

I

Ignition system – 121 *et seq*

Ignition system
  coil and condenser – 133
  description – 123
  diagnostic socket and TDC pick-up
      removal and refitting – 132
  dwell angle – 126
      fault diagnosis – 136
  specifications – 121
  switch/steering column lock
      removal and refitting – 134
  timing – 126
  transistorized
      checking – 134
Instrument panel
  removal and refitting
      from March 1976 – 235
      to March 1975 – 234
Instruments
  removal and refitting – 235
Introduction to the Renault 15 and 17 – 2

J

Jacking – 11

L

Lamp bulbs
  renewal
      exterior – 234
      headlamp – 231
      interior – 234
Lubricants and fluids – 13
Lubrication system
  1289 cc (type 810) engine – 45
  1565 cc, 1605 cc, 1647 cc (type 807, 821, 841, 843, 844
  engine) – 61

M

Maintenance, routine – 15
Manifolds – 116
Manual transmission – 143 *et seq*
Manual transmission
  description – 144
  dismantling
      type 352 – 151
      type 395 – 162
  dismantling, examination and reassembly
      type 365 – 177
  examination and renovation
      type 352 – 153
      type 395 – 166
  fault diagnosis – 178
  gearchange linkage
      removal, refitting and adjusting – 147
  lubrication – 147
  reassembly
      type 352 – 154
      type 395 – 166
  removal and refitting – 149
  specifications – 143
  torque wrench settings – 144

O

Oil filter – 32
Oil pump
  removal and refitting (engine in car)
      1298 cc (type 810) engine – 34
      1565 cc, 1605 cc, 1647 cc, (type 807, 821, 841, 843, 844)
      engines – 53

R

Radiator
  removal and refitting – 75
Radiator grille
  removal and refitting – 314
Radio
  fitting – 240
  interference suppression – 242
Roadwheels *see* **Wheels**
Routine maintenance – 15

S

Safety belts
  maintenance, removal and refitting – 330
Safety first! – 14
Seat
  front
      removal, refitting and adjusting – 329
  rear
      removal and refitting – 330
Seat belt warning system – 240
Spare parts
  buying – 8
  to carry in car – 18
Spark plug conditions (colour) – 131
Spark plugs and HT leads – 133
Speedometer cable
  renewal – 235
Starter motor
  description – 224
  overhaul
      Ducellier – 225
      Paris/Rhone – 228
  removal and refitting – 224
  testing in car – 224
Steering
  angles and front wheel alignment – 310
  column
      removal and refitting – 308
  column bushes
      renewal in car – 309
  description – 295
  fault diagnosis – 311
  gear (manual)
      overhaul – 308
      removal and refitting – 306
  maintenance and inspection – 295
  rack bellows
      renewal – 306
  shaft flexible coupling
      removal and refitting – 306
  specifications – 294
  torque wrench settings – 295
  track rod end balljoints
      renewal – 304
  wheel
      removal and refitting – 306
Steering (power)
  fault diagnosis – 311
  gear
      overhaul – 308
      removal and refitting – 308
  pump
      removal, refitting and bleeding – 306
      pump drivebelt
      removal, refitting and adjustment – 306
Sump pan
  removal and refitting (engine in car)
      1289 cc (type 810) engine – 34
      1565 cc, 1605 cc, 1647 cc (type 807, 821, 841, 843, 844)
      engines – 52
Suspension and steering – 294 *et seq*

Suspension (front)
  anti-roll bar
    removal and refitting – 297
  arm balljoint
    renewal – 299
  arm flexible bushes
    renewal – 298
  description – 295
  fault diagnosis – 311
  lower arm
    removal and refitting – 298
  maintenance and inspection – 295
  shock absorber/coil spring
    removal, testing and refitting – 296
  specifications – 294
  stub axle carrier
    removal and refitting – 300
  torque wrench settings – 295
  upper arm and radius rod
    removal and refitting – 298
Suspension (rear)
  anti-roll bar
    removal and refitting – 302
  axle beam
    removal and refitting – 304
  description – 295
  fault diagnosis – 311
  lower trailing link
    removal and refitting – 303
  maintenance and inspection – 295
  shock absorber and coil spring
    removal, testing and refitting – 302
  specifications – 294
  torque wrench settings – 295
  upper wishbone arm
    removal and refitting – 304
Switch
  removal and refitting
    courtesy lamp – 231
    rocker – 231
    steering column – 231

T

Tailgate
  counterbalance struts
    removal and refitting – 320
  glass
    removal and refitting – 328
  heated window – 240
  lock
    removal and refitting – 321
  removal and refitting – 320
Thermostat
  removal, testing and refitting – 74
Timing cover oil seal (1565 cc, 1605 cc, 1647 cc – type 807, 821, 843, 844 engines)
  removal – 56

Timing (ignition)
  general – 126
  specifications – 121
Tools
  general – 9
  to carry in car – 18
Towing – 11
Towing bracket
  fitting – 333
  wiring harness
    fitting – 243
Transmission (automatic) *see Automatic transmission*
Transmission (manual) *see Manual transmission*
Tyres
  general – 311
  pressures – 294
  specifications – 294

U

Upholstery
  maintenance – 313
Use of English – 7

V

Valve clearances
  adjustment
    1298 cc (type 810) engine – 49
    1565 cc, 1605 cc, 1647 cc (type 807, 821, 841, 843, 844) engines – 69
Vehicle identification numbers – 8
Voltage regulator – 223

W

Weights (kerb) – 6
Wheels
  general – 311
  specifications – 294
Window winder (electric)
  dismantling and reassembly – 237
Windscreen glass
  removal and refitting – 328
Windscreen washer – 240
Windscreen wiper
  blades and arms
    removal and refitting – 238
  motor
    overhaul – 239
  motor and linkage
    removal and refitting – 238
Wiring diagrams – 246 to 293
Working facilities – 10

Printed by
Haynes Publishing Group
Sparkford Yeovil Somerset
England